The State of the Poor

OVERSTONE

Printed in England by Antony Rowe Ltd, Chippenham

The State of the Poor

Volume 2

FREDERIC MORTON EDEN

THOEMMES PRESS

This edition published in 2001 by

THOEMMES PRESS
11 Great George Street, Bristol BS1 5RR, United Kingdom

http://www.thoemmes.com

The State of the Poor
3 volumes : ISBN 1 85506 262 3

Reprinted from the 1797 edition

PUBLISHER'S NOTE

The publisher has gone to great lengths to ensure the quality of this reprint but
points out that some imperfections in the original book may be apparent.
This book is printed on acid-free paper, sewn, and cased in a durable buckram cloth.

● Overstone is an imprint of Thoemmes Press.

THE

STATE OF THE POOR:

OR,

AN HISTORY

OF THE

LABOURING CLASSES IN ENGLAND,

FROM THE CONQUEST TO THE PRESENT PERIOD;

In which are particularly confidered,

THEIR DOMESTIC ECONOMY,

WITH RESPECT TO

DIET, DRESS, FUEL, AND HABITATION;

And the various Plans which, from time to time, have been propofed, and adopted, for the
RELIEF of the POOR:

TOGETHER WITH

PAROCHIAL REPORTS

Relative to the Adminiftration of Work-houfes, and Houfes of Induftry; the
State of Friendly Societies; and other Public Inftitutions; in feveral
Agricultural, Commercial, and Manufacturing, Diftricts.

WITH A LARGE APPENDIX;

CONTAINING

A COMPARATIVE AND CHRONOLOGICAL TABLE OF THE PRICES OF LABOUR, OF PROVISIONS,
AND OF OTHER COMMODITIES; AN ACCOUNT OF THE POOR IN SCOTLAND; AND MANY
ORIGINAL DOCUMENTS ON SUBJECTS OF NATIONAL IMPORTANCE.

BY SIR FREDERIC MORTON EDEN, BART.

IN THREE VOLUMES.

VOL II.

LONDON:

PRINTED BY J DAVIS,

For B & J WHITE, Fleet-ftreet; G G. & J. ROBINSON, Paternofter-row; T PAYNE, Mew's gate;
R. FAULDER, New Bond-ftreet; T. EGERTON, Whitehall; J. DEBRETT, Piccadilly;
and D. BREMNER, Strand.

1797.

Contents of the Second Volume.

Parochial Reports ;—ENGLAND.

C O N T E N T S.

C O N T E N T S.

PAROCHIAL REPORTS.

BEDFORDSHIRE.

DUNSTABLE.

THIS parish is supposed to contain about 340 acres of land, and about 1000 inhabitants, who are, chiefly, of the Established Church. There is one small congregation of Quakers, and one of Anabaptists. The number of houses that pay the window-tax is 115: the number exempted, 78. The number of inns, or ale-houses, is 18. The parishioners are employed in agriculture, manufactures, inn-keeping, horse-keeping, &c. One farm consists of 100 acres: the others are small.

The parish is, principally, in pasture. Wheat, barley, and beans, are cultivated, in that part, which is open field. The rent of land is about £3. an acre. The land-tax is at 3s. in the pound; and produces £247. 18s. There are no commons, or waste lands. Farmers chiefly rent their own tithes. The common wages of labour, in husbandry, are, 1s. a day, without board; 20d. a day, has lately been given, on account of the dearness of provifions. In the ftraw work, which is the ftaple manufacture of the place, a woman can earn from 6s. to 12 s. a week; children, from 2 s. to 4 s. a week. This bufinefs has given employment, for the laft 20 years, to every woman, who wifhed to work: and, for 10 years back, ftraw work has fold well, particularly in the fpring. Earnings in this line, have, for the laft four years, been exceedingly great, which, in fome meafure, perhaps, accounts for the Poor's Rates not having rifen during that period. The ftraw is chiefly manufactured into hats, bafkets, &c. A few women in the town make lace. A manufacture of whiting employs about 10 hands. The principal fupport of the inhabitants, feems to be the great turnpike road, which paffes through the town, and which accounts for the number of inns and ale-houfes.

The following were the prices of provifions at Dunftable, in September 1795: beef 4½d. the pound; mutton 5d.; veal 6d.; bacon 9 d.; butter 1 s.; milk 1¼ d. the quart, (but little fold); potatoes 2 s. the bufhel; bread 1s. 8d. the half-peck loaf; coals 1 s. 10 d. the bufhel.

Very large charities belong to this parifh, which are applied, towards clothing, educating, apprenticing out children; maintaining impotent and aged women; diftributing bread to the poor, &c. No fatisfactory account of the money, thus annually expended, could be obtained. From various information, however, it feems clear, that in confequence of thefe donations, poor people from the neighbouring parifhes endeavour, by every means in their power, to obtain fettlements here, and are often fuccefsful. I have generally found, that donations in money and other charities, eafe more the Rates of neighbouring parifhes, than thofe of the place in which they are, actually, diftributed.

Moft of the Poor in Dunftable receive a parifh allowance: the weekly penfions to 18 families, at prefent, amounts to £.1. 12s. 6d.: ten perfons are in a poor-houfe, where they are farmed, at 3 s. 6d. each, a-week. The poor in the workhoufe have been farmed many years: the farmer finds victuals, and cloaths, &c. and has their earnings: thofe who can work, are employed in the ftraw manufacture. The mafter of the poor-houfe does not obferve any conftant rotation of diet. No militia families are, at prefent, chargeable to the parifh.

Of four Friendly Societies in the town, only one has taken the benefit of the late Act of Parliament.

Table of Baptisms, Burials, Marriages, and Poor's Rates at Dunstable.

Years.	Baptisms.		Burials.		Marriages.	Net Rates.			Expenditure on the Poor.			Rate in the pound.	
1680	—		—		2								
1685	48		—		6								
1690	54		—		5								
1691	42		—		5								
1692	27		—		4								
1693	39		—		—								
1694	38		—		—								
1695	36		—		—								
1696	34		—		—								
1697	27		—		—								
1698	35		47		3								
1699	34		21		7								
1700	22		36		—								
1720	30		28		5								
1740	26		37		6								
1760	—		—		10								
	Males.	Females.	Males.	Females.									
1773					—	215	12	0	203	4	7½	3	0
1774					—	269	8	10	267	6	6	4	0
1775	11	10	16	12	7	310	19	7	252	19	4	4	0
1776	20	19	2	8	5	200	0	10¼	241	18	10	3	0
1777	18	11	7	10	5	259	6	7	240	10	11½	4	0
1778	18	17	17	17	5	311	9	10	263	17	2	4	6
1779	20	18	21	20	11	351	6	10½	358	8	5	5	0
1780	11	21	18	19	13	206	2	2¼	196	7	5½	3	0
1781	14	18	13	14	8	324	4	2	336	12	11½	4	6
1782	15	12	9	15	5	292	15	9	242	6	0½	4	0
1783	20	18	14	12	8	293	13	4	268	13	2½	4	0
1784	10	7	8	16	8	365	4	5	387	5	10	5	0
1785	22	9	9	10	9	322	19	8	301	7	3	4	6
1786	12	15	13	18	3	364	2	8	315	11	0	5	0
1787	16	9	15	19	5	328	5	3	377	3	0½	4	6
1788	11	15	14	10	8	326	6	2½	304	3	0½	4	6
1789	11	12	10	10	10	329	4	1¼	299	9	7½	4	6
1790	17	20	9	11	9	288	15	6	311	11	9¼	4	0
1791	13	15	10	16	15	327	5	3	317	18	9	4	6
1792	21	17	16	9	4	293	14	6	277	19	8	4	0
1793	15	11	18	12	7	291	12	0	313	3	5	4	0
1794	15	16	10	10	5	293	11	10	344	14	5	4	0
1795	—	—	—	—	—	298	12	7	277	19	10¼	4	0

The

The rates, at an average, are affeffed upon three-fourths of the real rental. About £. 10. or £. 11. are annually paid, out of the rates, towards the county ftock. Removals of vagrants, &c. coft about 7s. a-week, this town being a gieat thoroughfare. The Veftry clerk is allowed 3 guineas a year, and about 2 s. 6 d. a month is fpent in Veftry meetings.

September, 1795.

HOUGHTON REGIS.

BY a la'e fuivey, the parifh of Houghton Regis was found to contain 4340 acres, exclufive of about 100 acres of common, fituated at 4 miles diftance from the reft of the parifh. 47 houfes pay the commutation tax ; the number exempted could not be afcertained. The occupations of the inhabitants aie, agriculture, ftraw work, and a little lace-making. The prices of provifions, and the wages of labour, are neaily the fame here as at Dunftable. There are 6 alehoufes in the parifh. The average rent of land is about 14 s. an acie. The land-tax, (which is, here, ufually paid by the landlord,) amounts to £. 434 9s. od. which is about 2s. 8d. in the pound. Farms are fiom £.30 to £:150 a-year. Wheat, barley, oats, beans, and fome turnips, and clover, are cultivated. There are 50 or 60 acies of common in the parifh, befides the 100 acres above mentioned. The parifh is, nearly, all open field : but an application is intended to be made to Parliament, next feffions, for an inclofure bill. Harveft work here is entirely peiformed by men : labourers wives and daughters, do veiy little more, than drefs victuals for the family. A few poor women glean, make ftiaw work, and lace. Tithes are taken in kind; they let foi £ 800 a-year. One friendly Society meets in this parifh. There are here 2 fmall Calvinift meeting-houfes ; the congregations partly belong to this parifh.

The Poor are principally maintained by a parifh allowance at home. £. 12. 6s. od. a-month is paid among 32 out-penfioners, who have, moftly, families : 5 other families receive occafional relief. Some money is likewife paid to the families of militia men, but the amount could not be coirectly afcertained. There is alfo a poor-houfe, in which, at prefent, 4 poor people are fupported. The poor in the houfe were farmed till about
a month

a month ago : the contractor, for maintaining them, usually received 2 s. a head, weekly, in summer; and 2s. 6d. in winter : last year his allowance was raised to 3s in summer, and 3s. 6d. in winter. About £.16 a year is paid out of the rates towards the county stock. Assessments are made as nearly on the full rental as possible. A Subscription, amounting to £.50, was distributed among the poor, last winter and spring.

Table of Baptisms, Burials, Marriages, and Poor's Rates.

Years	Baptisms			Burials			Net Assessment	Total Expenditure	Rate in the pound
	Males	Fem.	Total	Males.	Fem	Total			
1768	13	7	20	12	8	20			
1769	9	14	23	11	10	21			
1770	8	9	17	8	8	16	£. s. d.	£. s d	s. d.
1771	9	11	20	9	15	24	188 14 0	181 5 11	1 6
1772	10	5	15	5	12	17	189 1 0	176 0 0	1 6
1773	12	10	22	10	14	24	189 9 9	196 8 10¾	1 6
1774	7	7	14	10	10	20	189 8 9	209 10 9	1 6
1775	7	10	17	5	14	19	253 12 0	262 18 10	2 0
1776	6	11	17	3	9	12	253 4 3	237 8 1	2 0
1777	12	19	31	6	13	19	220 14 4	241 6 9	1 9
1778	8	10	18	7	10	17	254 16 9	241 9 7½	2 0
1779	16	10	26	9	2	11	256 9 4	210 8 10½	2 0
1780	8	13	21	14	13	27	192 11 3	265 18 4	1 6
1781	10	6	16	12	9	21	319 18 9	327 17 1¼	2 6
1782	9	15	24	4	7	11	323 11 11	322 7 7	2 6
1783	9	8	17	10	11	21	258 12 6	238 5 0.	2 0
1784	2	5	7	10	7	17	227 17 9	267 13 8¼	1 9
1785	8	4	12	5	8	13	228 0 10	232 3 5	1 9
1786	10	10	20	11	3	14	261 11 0	260 11 11	2 0
1787	9	4	13	11	5	16	296 5 11	326 7 3¾	2 3
1788	8	8	16	5	10	15	263 9 0	260 11 3	2 0
1789	6	8	14	8	8	16	307 8 4	261 0 9¼	2 3
1790	5	13	18	4	6	10	246 15 2	205 3 0	1 9
1791	10	4	14	9	4	13	288 10 6	253 4 0	2 0
1792	8	7	15	5	7	12	281 10 10	264 19 0	2 0
1793	5	9	14	5	7	12	245 1 9	236 3 0	1 9
1794	4	6	10	4	10	14	334 6 6	309 19 8	2 3
1795, the year, including the collection, ends at Easter,							373 8 9	423 10 4	2 6

September, 1795.

HUMBERSHOE.

THE hamlet of Humberſhoe is ſituated in the town of Maikyate ſtieet, in the pariſh of Studham.   It contains about 120 acres, and 170 inha-, bitants, wheieof a few are Anabaptiſts : 15 houſes pay the commutation tax; and 19 are exempted; in the lattei is included an empty houſe, which would be chargeable if inhabited.   The town of Maikyate-ſtieet, lies in 2 counties, and 3 paiiſhes : it is ſituated on one of the gieat noith ioads ; and chiefly depends upon travelleis for ſuppoit.   This place is a ſingular inſtance of the great inequality of the poor's rates in neighbouiing pariſhes.   In Humbeiſhoe, (which is on one ſide of the ſtieet,) they are at 9s. in the pound : but in the 2 hamlets on the oppoſite ſide, they aie not more than 2s. 6d. or 3s. in the pound.   The reaſon aſſigned is, that the hamlet of Humberſhoe has very little land, and a number of iuinous houſes. The inhabitants are, principally, innkeepers, common tradeſmen, and ſhop-keepers : there is, likewiſe, one farmei, a few ſtraw woikers, and the reſt are, moſtly, agiicultural labourers.

The prices of proviſions are ; beef 4¼ and 5d. the pound ; mutton 6d. ; lamb 6¼ or 7d. ; veal 7d. ; butter 11¼ ; bread 2s. the half peck loaf; coals 22d. and 2s. the buſhel ; potatoes, of which very few are ſold, are 1s. 6d. the buſhel ; milk 2d. the quart, but very little is ſold.

The wages of common labour are 7s. a week all the year, without board.   In hay harveſt, men receive 9s. a week; in corn harveſt 40s. a month, and diet.   The wages for ſtraw work vary from 2s. 6d. to 12s. a week according to the demand, for the manufacture.   The chief article manufactured is ſtraw hats.

The rent of land is about 15s. an acre.   The land-tax is £.31. 1s. 0d. and is collected at 2s. 3¼d. in the pound, on the net rental.   There is one farm of £.84 a year : the reſt of the hamlet is let in ſmall parcels.   A compoſition of from 3s to 4s. an acre is taken in lieu of tithes.   There aie neither commons, or open fields in this hamlet.

There are no friendly Societies in this neighbourhood.   The number of alehouſes in the hamlet is 4.

The poor are maintained at home : the following is a liſt of thoſe who receive parochial aſſiſtance.

Age

	Age.	Weekly Allowance.
		s. d.
A labourer; lame; - -	60	- 1 6
A labourer; - - - about 70 ⎫		
His wife; - - - about 70 ⎬		- 4 0
3 children; orphans; from 8 to 12 years of age;		- 9 0
A decayed gentleman; - -	75	- 3 0
A baſtard; - - -	7	- 1 0
A baſtard; - - -	7	- 1 0
A tailor's widow; bedridden; -	85	- 4 0
A militia-man's family; - - -	-	- 3 0

£ 1 6 6

Beſides the above-mentioned perſons, ſeveral poor people have their houſe-rents paid by the pariſh : the ſum, annually diſburſed, for this purpoſe, amounts to £ 6. 16s. Occaſional relief is alſo given to the indigent. The aſſeſſments are at full rental. Out of the Rates about 30s. a year, are paid towards the county ſtock; and between £ 3. and £ 4. to conſtables. The veſtry-clerk is allowed one guinea a year.

Years	Net Sum collected by Rate.			Total Diſburſements.			Rate in the Pound.
	£	s	d	£	s.	d.	
1777	90	13	1¾	91	4	5	
1778	89	0	8¾	86	11	3¾	
1779	46	13	6½	40	2	2¾	
1780	41	14	0¾	45	6	10	
1781	49	0	4	50	0	3	
1782	48	4	4½	36	19	6½	
1783	53	16	7½	66	8	10	
1784 ⎫ 1785 ⎭	[1]72	10	5	[1]85	5	5	
							s. d.
1786	69	9	2	102	11	9½	
1787	37	2	4	31	4	0½	3 0
1788	64	4	4	67	16	9	4 6
1789	99	3	3	100	4	1¾	7 6
1790	112	3	2	91	7	6½	9 0
1791	78	10	4	153	2	1¼	6 0
1792	74	17	0	73	0	0¾	6 0
1793	77	2	8	68	10	6	6 0
1794	108	7	0	115	0	0½	9 0
1795	111	14	1½	111	12	8½	9 6

September, 1795.

[1] Whether theſe ſums are for 1784, or 1785, or for both years, the book does not determine.

LEIGHTON BUZZARD.

OF the extent and population of the townſhip of Leighton Buzzard, no ſatisfactory account could be obtained : the regiſters afford no clue towards aſcertaining the number of inhabitants, as, of five hamlets, belonging to the pariſh of Leighton Buzzard, four bury, and one chriſtens here. The following extracts, taken indifferently, rather indicate a decline in the population :

Years	Baptiſms.	Years.	Baptiſms	Years.	Baptiſms.
1732	71	1760	61	1770	63
1733	66	1761	41	1771	62
1734	76	1762	59	1772	54
	213		161		179

There are 31 ale-houſes : 198 houſes pay the window-tax : the number exempted, could not be made out. The occupations of the inhabitants are, agriculture, ſhop-keeping, lace-making, &c. Common labourers earn from 6s. to 7s. a week, beſides their breakfaſt ; in harveſt, they receive two guineas a month, and board : Lace-makers, generally, are paid from 8d. to 10d. a day : a few can earn from 1s. to 1s. 3d. The prices of proviſions are : beef, 5d. the pound ; mutton, 5d. to 6d. ; veal, 6d. ; bacon, 9d to 10d. ; butter, 11d. ; potatoes, 8d. the peck ; milk, 2d. the quart. The uſual price of the half-peck loaf of wheaten bread was 1s. 6d. : it lately ſold for 2s. 6d.

The operation of Rates, and of other taxes, prevents farmers from being very communicative, reſpecting the rent of land. It is ſaid, however, that open fields do not let for more than 10s an acre ; while encloſed meadow produces 30s. About 300 acres of common belong to the pariſh, and hamlets ; on which the Poor obtain turf. Farms are from £ 50. to £ 250. a year. Beans, wheat, oats, and barley, are the principal articles of cultivation. The greateſt part of the pariſh conſiſts of open field. Corn tithe is taken in kind ; and hay, in compoſition, at about 4s. an acre. The amount of the land tax is £ 415 14s and is generally paid by the landlord. Aſſeſſments are ſaid to be, on the net rental : this

may,

may, fometimes, happen to new tenants, but perfons who occupy theii own eftates, are ufually rated, upon an old affeffment.

In this town, are 3 friendly Societies, containing, altogether, about 100 members. There is here one Quaker, and one Anabaptift congregation. Very few Poor are to be found among the Quakers ; the reafon of which feems to be, (as a Quaker obferved,) " that as foon as a member becomes idle, drunken, or otherwife depraved, he is expelled from the Society."

The Poor are paitly maintained in a work houfe, and paitly at home : 19 peifons are at prefent in the houfe ; fome of them are old people and children unable to woik. The boys are fent out to work for the farmeis : and a little lace is made by the women, in the houfe. The whole earnings are about 50s. a month. 44 out-penfioners receive at piefent £ 4. a week. 4 militia families receive 9s. 4d. a week, from the parifh, which is reimburfed by the county treafurer.

Years.	Net Affeffments.			Total Expenditure			Rate in the Pound.	
	£.	s.	d.	£.	s.	d.	s.	d.
1782	509	9	3½	503	1	3¼	3	6
1783	512	11	2	474	10	3¼	3	6
1784	658	13	2	629	14	11¾	4	6
1785	513	9	7½	493	4	6¼	3	6
1786	678	7	6	562	16	1¼	4	6
1787	453	10	3½	494	6	3	3	0
1788	458	7	8	490	5	4	3	0
1789	693	9	7½	676	8	8	4	6
1790	544	9	8	556	8	1	3	6
1791	700	18	11	6/1	0	3	5	0
1792	549	11	6	570	12	11	4	0
1793	626	4	9	633	4	3¼	4	0
1794	711	6	0	781	11	10	5	0
1795	629	4	3	640	7	5	4	0

The following are the Particulars of the Expenditure in 1782
and 1792.

		£.	s.	d.			£.	s.	d.
1782	Poor	427	6	3	1792	Poor	521	6	3
	Militia	42	1	4		Removal of va-			
	Conftables, or-					grants	8	19	0
	ders, &c.	29	14	2		Towards land-tax	0	4	0
	Lofs of bills	3	19	6½		Doctor's bill	20	0	0
						Purchafing houfe	12	16	2
		£. 503	1	3½		Lofs of bills	7	7	6
							£. 570	12	11

In this town there is an alms-houfe, for 8 poor women, who have
each an apartment, clothes, fuel, and 2s. 6d a week. Donations,
amounting to about £ 22. are yearly diftributed in bread to poor parifhioners. The work-houfe is in an excellent fituation, but, at prefent,
does not appear to be very cleanly.

Table of Diet in the Work-houfe.

	Breakfaft.	Dinner	Supper.
Sunday.	Bread, cheefe, and beer ; or milk pottage.	Beef, bread, pudding, fauce, and broth.	Bread, cheefe, and beer.
Monday	Bread and broth.	Cold meat.	Ditto.
Tuefday	Same as Sunday	Same as Sunday.	Ditto.
Wednefday	Same as Monday.	Same as Monday	Ditto
Thurfday	Same as Sunday.	Same as Sunday.	Ditto
Friday	Same as Monday	Same as Monday	Ditto
Saturday.	Bread, cheefe, and beer.	Suet dumplings, or milk, or water-pottage	Ditto.

September, 1795.

BERKS.

B E R K S.

R E A D I N G.

THE extent of the parish of St. Mary, Reading, is estimated at 900 acres. 240 houses pay the commutation tax; the number exempted could not be learnt. The inhabitants are tradesmen, farmers, agricultural labourers, and manufacturers, but principally, the latter Sail-cloth, sacking or sack-cloth, gauze, ribbon, and pins, are made here. The weavers of sacking can earn 16s. a week; of gauze, from 15s. to 30s. a week; of sail-cloth, 18s. a week; spinners of hemp are paid about 3s. a week. Sail-cloth is the only manufacture that is brisk at present. The war, although injurious to other manufactures, affords full employment to this. Common labourers earn 9s. a week.

The prices of provisions are: beef, 4 d. to 7 d. the pound; mutton, 6d.; veal, from 5d to 7d.; lamb, from 6½d. to 7d.; butter, from 11d. to 1s. 0½d.; bacon, 8½d. to 10d.; milk, 2½d. the quart; wheaten bread, the quartern loaf, 11½d.; coals, 56s. the chaldron.

Farms in this parish are from £ 200. to £ 300. a year. Wheat is the principal produce: but every other common grain, and root, is here cultivated. The rent of land is from 30s. to 40s. an acre. The land-tax is £ 656. 17s. which is about 2s. in the pound. There are no commons or waste lands in this parish. The number of inns or ale-houses is 17: the whole number in Reading, which consists of 3 parishes, is 62.

One third of the inhabitants of Reading is supposed to dissent from the Established Church. The various persuasions are, Quakers, Independents, Anabaptists, and Methodists: they have each one house of worship in Reading.

The Poor of this parish are chiefly maintained in a work-house, which was erected, about 20 years ago, at the expence of £ 1400; about £ 650. of which has been paid off. The building seems a comfortable and convenient lodging for the Poor, but is not always sufficiently aired. The

lodging

lodging rooms contain 2, 3, and 4 beds a-piece : the beds are of flocks, and feathers. In winter about 80 or 90 persons are generally in the house. The number, at present, does not exceed 70, most of whom are children, and old people. They are chiefly employed in spinning hemp : 2 looms for weaving sail-cloth were lately erected in the house. Some of the Poor are sent out to work for the farmers. No regular account is kept of their annual earnings, which are from £ 70 to £ 80 A few years back £ 160. were laid out in repairing some houses belonging to the parish, which now produce £ 13. 8s. a year. About £ 350 a year are paid to out-pensioners : 1s. or 1s. 6d is the usual weekly allowance to each. If their necessities require more, they are, usually, taken into the work house.

Table of Diet in the Work-house.

	Breakfast	Dinner	Supper
Sunday.	Bread, cheese, and beer.	Meat, pudding, vegetables, and bread.	Bread, cheese, and beer
Monday.	Bread and broth.	Bread and cheese.	Ditto
Tuesday.	Milk pottage.	Bread and broth.	Ditto.
Wednesday	Milk pottage.	Cold meat.	Ditto.
Thursday.	Bread and cheese.	Same as Sunday	Ditto.
Friday.	Bread and broth.	Cold meat.	Ditto.
Saturday.	Milk pottage.	Bread and cheese.	Ditto.

Old people are allowed tea, bread and butter, for breakfast.

Years	Males	Fem	Total	Males	Fem	Total.	MARRIAGES.
	BAPTISMS.			**BURIALS.**			
1680	—	—	45	—	—	49	17
1685	—	—	63	—	—	53	20
1690	—	—	59	—	—	47	21
1691	—	—	68	—	—	73	16
1692	35	30	65	32	27	59	13
1693	26	25	51	27	35	62	16
1694	27	19	46	38	39	77	20
1695	27	21	48	30	25	55	22
1696	24	21	45	34	30	64	20
1697	22	30	52	44	31	75	16
1698	18	25	43	36	36	72	18

1699

Years	BAPTISMS Males	Fem	Total	BURIALS. Males	Fem	Total	MARRIAGES.	Poor's Rate. £.	s.	d.	Net Expenditure £.	s.	d.
1699	24	23	47	31	33	64	18						
1700	31	29	60	33	29	62	26						
1720	32	31	63	43	35	78	14						
1740	29	25	54	39	40	79	26						
1760	23	32	55	34	33	67	18						
1775	40	32	72	43	42	85	28						
1776	42	39	81	31	33	64	20						
1777	36	32	68	29	40	69	30						
1778	33	37	70	38	42	80	27						
1779	44	40	84	47	60	107	27	845	15	7	1049	9	4
1780	43	38	81	56	59	115	40	835	15	7	901	1	11
1781	47	32	79	42	32	74	15	942	6	3	894	4	8½
1782	40	31	71	29	36	65	27	947	18	5	1014	6	9¼
1783	41	36	77	55	40	95	30	1060	10	9½	1167	2	4½
1784	33	41	74	34	42	76	18	1191	10	0½	1168	9	5
1785	37	39	76	41	49	90	20	1123	5	1¾	1146	14	11
1786	38	41	79	41	30	71	26	979	0	11½	1034	0	10½
1787	39	43	82	36	47	83	23	1015	16	5½	808	16	7¼
1788	35	36	71	65	55	110	32	1030	15	0¾	816	18	0¾
1789	40	37	77	36	42	78	32	1100	4	9	1152	17	8¼
1790	36	45	81	33	39	72	18	1079	7	4½	1081	1	1¾
1791	36	45	81	45	49	94	27	1323	15	3	1288	18	1¾
1792	40	51	91	38	47	85	32	1028	6	6¼	1004	19	2
1793	48	38	86	43	50	93	26	970	6	11¾	898	7	8
1794	20	39	59	47	48	95	17	1062	13	4¼	1192	2	5½
1795	———— year ending in May—							1226	9	10¼	1012	19	6¼

£ 1226. 9s. 10¼d. the Rate laſt year, amounted to 3s. 6d. in the pound on houſes, and 5s. 2d. on land; the ſums marked under the column of net expenditure in the years 1787, 1788, and 1793, were the net expenditure on the Poor.

The following minutes, reſpecting births and burials, were obligingly furniſhed by Mr. Sturges, the preſent incumbent.

From

From 1764 to 1770, 212 males, and 220 females were born, of which 22 were baftards; and 244 males, and 263 females were buried From 1771 to 1791, 65 baftards were born.

The amount of each year's Poor's Rate is accurately fet down in the above Table, but the laft column does not correctly denote the exact expenditure on the Poor, except in the year 1787, 1788, and 1793: in fome years, the intereft of money borrowed by the parifh is included; in others, the charge of falaries is omitted

This parifh has, at prefent, a ftanding overfeer. It is, generally, 1 think obferved, that ftanding overfeers keep down the rates more than officers, annually elected The annual falary paid the overfeer is £ 30. a year ; the veftry clerk, £ 10. ; the governor of the work-houfe, £ 31. 10s. and board ; and the furgeon, who attends the Poor, £ 18. 18s

Donations amounting to about £ 100. a year, are diftributed among the Poor. 12 perfons belonging to this parifh are in different alms-houfes, and receive from 7d. to 21d. a week

Many of the labouring clafs of the community, here, poffefs very little œconomy, or forefight. It is not uncommon for a healthy young fellow, who has ample means of fupporting himfelf, and family, by his own induftry, to requeft his parifh to pay the midwife for his firft child. It very rarely happens, that a labourer fupports himfelf, wife, and 2 children, without applying for parochial aid : weavers, who can earn 18s. a week, do not hefitate foliciting relief, if a temporary ftagnation of bufinefs curtails their common receipts, and reduces them to thofe difficulties, which a little parfimony might have obviated. Tea is generally ufed here, twice a-day, by the Poor : the other part of their diet is, principally, the beft wheaten bread ; and, occafionally, a little bacon : it is feldom fufficiently boiled, and is thought to give them the fallow complexion which is much obfervable here. In point of expence, their general diet as much exceeds, as, in point of nutrition, it falls fhort of, the north country fare, of milk, potatoes, barley bread and hafty-pudding.

In Reading are three friendly Societies, who have all complied with the late Act of Parliament. The Rates, in the two other parifhes of this town, are, generally, fomewhat lower than they are in St. Mary's.

July, 1795.

S T R E A T-

STREATLEY.

Expences and Earnings of a Labourer's Family in the Parish of Streatley.

THE man is 50 years of age; has a wife and feven children, three of whom are out at fervice: the ages of the four youngeft, at home, are as follows; five, feven, twelve, fourteen. The two oldeft, who are boys, drive the plough, for fome neighbouring farmers. The two youngeft do not work. The wife earns about 1s. 6d a week, throughout the year. The man in winter earns 8s. a week; and, at prefent, 12s. a week. For about ten days in the wheat harveft he receives 3s. a day. So that, altogether, the earnings of the family, confifting of fix perfons, amount, annually, to about £46. The following are their expences:

	£		
8 half-peck loaves a week, or 410 in the year, at 1s. 9d. each	36	8	0
2 lb. of cheefe a week, at 7d. the lb. yearly - -	3	0	8
2 lb. of butter a week, at 9d. the lb. yearly -	3	18	0
2 lb. of fugar a week, at 9d. the lb. yearly - -	3	18	0
2 oz. of tea a week, at 3s. the lb. yearly - -	0	19	6
½ lb. of oatmeal a week, at 3d. the lb. yearly - -	0	6	6
½ lb. of bacon a week, at 3d. the lb. yearly - -	3	5	0
2d. in milk every week, yearly - - -	0	8	8
Candle, foap, falt, ftarch, blue, &c. yearly about -	2	7	4
Houfe rent - - - - - -	2	5	0
Fuel is chiefly beech-wood collected in the woods: what is bought cofts about - - - -	1	0	0
Shoes - - - - -	1	10	0
Shirts and fhifts - - - -	2	10	0
Other clothes - - - -	2	2	0

	£		
Total Annual Expences	63	18	8
Total Annual Earnings	46	0	0
Deficiency	17	18	8

The

The earnings appear to be very high, but the expences are enormous: it is however neceſſary to obſerve, that the articles conſumed, weekly, in the family, are marked at the preſent prices, which, in ſome inſtances are a third, and upwards, higher than they were a year ago. The houſe-rent is paid by the pariſh, and ſeveral well-diſpoſed perſons furniſh the man with old clothes, and ſometimes with ſhirts: in caſe of ſickneſs, he receives parochial relief. Beſides this, the pariſh has lately adópted the plan of allowing 1s 6d. a week to poor perſons, for every child, that is not old enough to work. This labourer has, in conſequence, received one week's pay for his two younger children: his yearly receipt on this account will amount to £ 7. 16s. This mode of relief is to be continued as long as the preſent high price of proviſions keeps up. The great conſumption of bread in this family is very ſtriking: their principal diet is tea, ſugar, bread, cheeſe, and butter: they eat bacon boiled, generally, once a week. The Poor here ſeldom taſte fleſh meat. That very cheap, and nutritive root the potatoe, is very little cultivated, or uſed here.

During the laſt 7 years, the Poor's Rates were 3s. in the pound, except in one year, when they were 3s. 6d. This year, including the expence of raiſing men for the navy, it is expected they will amount to 6s. or 7s. in the pound.

Streatley is ſituated on the banks of the river Thames, which works an excellent mill, and is wholly a farming pariſh, about four ſquare miles in extent; farms are from £ 100 to £ 300. a year. Wheat, barley, and oats, are the principal articles of cultivation. Very few cows are kept in proportion to the ſize of the farms. The rent of land is about 16s an acre. There are ſeveral acres of good common. Labourers in general, have their houſe-rents paid by the pariſh. The Thames during the winter ſeaſon frequently overflows its banks, and continues in that ſtate for ſome time, whereby the Poor in the lower part of the pariſh are often much diſtreſſed. There are no friendly Societies in the pariſh.

In the neighbouring pariſh of Pangburn, which is wholly agricultural, the rates are 3s. 6d. in the pound. The Poor are moſtly farmed in this part of the country.   *July*, 1795.

                                                                    WAL-

WALLINGFORD.

THE parish of St. Mary, Wallingford, contains about 30 acres of land. The number of houses, charged to the commutation tax, is 112 : the number exempted, could not be ascertained. The inhabitants are chiefly petty tradesmen.

The prices of provisions are: beef, 5½d. the pound ; mutton, 6d. ; veal, 5d ; lamb, 6¼d. ; bacon, 10d. ; bread, 21½d. the half-peck loaf; butter, 1s. ; new milk, (of which but little is sold,) 2d. the quart ; eggs, ½d. each ; coals, £3. 7s. 6d. the chaldron.

The wages of common labourers are, from 8s. to 7s. the week : the farmers do not appear to be much inclined to raise wages, but, usually, allow their labourers provisions, at less, than the selling price, during a dear season.

In the neighbouring parishes, farms are large ; from £200. to £300. a year; and in the adjoining parish of Cholsey is a farm of £800. a year, in which there is a barn supposed to be the largest in England : it is 101 yards in length, and 18 in width, and was the repository for the Abbot of Reading's tithes, who resided here in the summer. The chief articles of cultivation are turnips, clover, barley, wheat, and oats. The crops, between this place and Oxford, are very luxuriant. In the neighbourhood of Wallingford, tithes are, mostly, compounded for. The land-tax raised annually by the town of Wallingford is £296. 7s. 10d. which is about 22½d. in the pound.

The number of inns or alehouses is 16.

In Wallingford are 4 Dissenting congregations; viz. 1 of Lady Huntingdon's chapels, 1 of John Wesley's, 1 Anabaptist, and 1 Quaker meeting-house.

The contractor, who farms the Poor, receives £300. a year, for which he undertakes to supply all the Poor belonging to the parish, with victuals, and clothes. The parish pays doctor's, and attorney's bills, &c. The Poor are not employed in any manufacture ; but such as can do a little work, are allowed to go out of the poor-house, wherein they are maintained by the contractor.

The introduction of a woollen or linen manufacture, would, perhaps, be ferviceable to this part of the country. A mixture of agriculture and manufactures, more efpecially, when the latter are fcattered through a country, feems to be the moft effectual method of keeping the Poor in conftant employment. Country manufacturers efcape the immorality and diffipation, too much connected with large towns; and have this further advantage, that, in the occafional ftagnation, to which all manufactures are fubject, or upon an unufual demand for agricultural labour, they can vary their occupation; a mode of life, which, (notwithftanding the many national advantages pointed out by the advocates for the divifion of labour,) feems to be, not more conducive to the health, than congenial to the natural difpofition of mankind *.

The following is the ufual weekly rotation of diet in the poor-houfe:

	BREAKFAST.	DINNER.	SUPPER.
Sunday,	Milk pottage, or broth.	Butcher's meat, bread, and vegetables.	Bread and cheefe.
Monday,	Do.	Cold meat.	Do
Tuefday,	Do.	Same as Sunday.	Do
Wednefday,	Do	Same as Monday.	Do.
Thurfday,	Do.	Same as Sunday.	Do.
Friday,	Do.	Same as Monday.	Do.
Saturday,	Do.	Same as Sunday.	Do.

There are no friendly Societies, at prefent, in Wallingford. There were two, which were not inftituted upon a good plan. Their funds de-

---

* This place owes much to the late Sir William Blackftone, who formed many plans for its benefit, and improvement. To his activity the town is indebted for two new turnpike roads; the one opening a communication by means of a new bridge over the Thames at Shillingford, between Oxford and Reading; the other leading to Wantage through the vale of White Horfe in Berkfhire. The advantages derived from hence to the town of Wallingford may be eftimated from the gradual increafe of its malt trade between the years 1749 and 1779, of which an account (comprehending the number of net bufhels of malt made in Wallingford) is here fubjoined.

Average of 5 years ending	Midfummer	1754	49,172 Bufhels of Malt.
Do.	of do.	1759	58,676
Do.	of do.	1764	97,370
Do.	of do.	1769	101,086
Do.	of do.	1774	113,135
Do.	of do.	1779	107,254

See *Preface to Sir Wm. Blackftone's Reports;* p. xxi.

cayed.

cayed fo faft, that they found it advifeable to break up their clubs, and divide what money remained, among the members.

The parifh of St. Leonard in this town has no poor houfe : the Poor are relieved at home. The following is a lift of regular penfioners.

		Weekly allowance.	
		s.	*d.*
An old foldier aged 70; and his wife ;	- -	3	0
A foldier's family of 3 children ;	- -	7	6
A labourer's widow ; aged 65 ;	- -	2	0
A labourer's widow ; aged 35 ;	- -	1	0
A widow, and 3 children ;	- - -	6	0
A widow, and 3 children ;	- - -	2	0
A bafket-maker ; aged 50;	- - -	1	0
An orphan boy ;	- - - -	1	6
An unmarried woman ; fick ; aged 25 ;	- -	2	6
A boy ; aged 11 ;	- - -	1	6
A boy ; aged 10;	- - -	1	6
A baftard ;	- - - - -	1	6

Laft month, the cafual payments amounted to £2. 5s. 6d. The beft wheaten bread has been immemorially ufed by every defcription of people. Perfons, here, remember wheat, in 1761, being at £7. a load. (A load is 5 quarters ; 8 bufhels to the quarter ; each bufhel of 9 gallons.) In 1740 wheat was £20. a load, and, about 1756, it fold at £24. a load.

About 140 acres of land belong to St. Leonard's. About 30 acres of common are annexed to the whole town.

Between £9. and £10. is annually paid from the Poor's Rate of St. Leonard's, towards the county ftock ; and about £6. from St. Mary's.

The regifter of St. Mary's has, all along, been kept in fuch a loofe, incorrect manner, that very little information could be picked out of it : the following years are, I believe, pretty correct. Accounts could not be procured of Poor's Rates, prior to 1790. From report, however, it feems, that the Rates were 4s. in the pound in 1779, 6s. in the pound in 1780, and have not been lower fince that period. For a few years, during which the farming of the Poor was difcontinued, the Rates were 11s. and 12s. in the pound. It is also said, that in 1750 the disbursements for the Poor, in the parish of St. Mary, amounted to £80.—a sum, which was then thought high.

Baptisms, Burials, and Poor's Rates, in the Parish of St. Mary, Wallingford.

Years	BAPTISMS			BURIALS.			Poor's Rates.			Net Expenditure.			Rate in the pound.
	Males	Fem	Total	Males	Fem	Total	£.	s.	d.	£	s	d.	s.
1720	14	10	24	5	7	12							
1740	9	9	18	9	10	19							
1760	17	8	25	—	—	—							
1775	11	6	17	4	7	11							
1776 } 1777 }	20	23	43	{ 7 { 10	4 6	11 16							
1778	11	15	26	—	—	—							
1779	10	7	17	—	—	—							
1791	—	—	—	—	—	—	465	9	6	492	5	1½	10
1792	10	17	27	12	10	22	418	3	3	421	11	8½	9
1793	—	—	—	—	—	—	469	7	0	510	3	1	10
1794	—	—	—	—	—	—	435	9	9	499	11	0¼	9
1795	—	—	—	—	—	—	343	1	3	348	18	0½	7

Under the management of the parish these years. }
Farmed }

Baptisms, Burials, Marriages, and Poor's Rates in the Parish of St. Leonard, Wallingford.

Years	BAPTISMS			BURIALS			Marriages	Poor's Rate.			Net Expenditure			Rate in the pound	
	Males	Fem	Total	Males.	Fem	Total.		£.	s	d.	£	s	d.	s.	d.
1699	—	—	—	—	—	—	—	6	0	9	5	16	3	—	—
1712	—	—	—	—	—	—	—	12	15	6	8	12	1	—	—
1714	—	—	—	—	—	—	—	9	6	2	8	17	2	—	—
1716	—	—	—	—	—	—	—	10	16	11	9	17	2	—	—
1717	—	—	—	—	—	—	—	11	5	2	11	2	9	—	—
1718	—	—	—	—	—	—	—	6	3	9	6	13	0	—	—
1720	7	5	12	1	2	3	2	16	0	7½	16	7	9	—	—
1740	2	5	7	3	3	6	6	—	—	—	—	—	—	—	—
1760	2	4	6	6	5	11	0	—	—	—	—	—	—	—	—
1767	—	—	—	—	—	—	—	56	11	9	56	1	10	2	0
1768	—	—	—	—	—	—	—	42	12	0	39	12	0	2	0
1769	—	—	—	—	—	—	—	66	3	9	53	14	3½	3	0
1770	—	—	—	—	—	—	—	73	5	0½	71	17	0	3	0

Years

Years.	Baptisms			Burials			Marriages	Poor's Rate			Net Expenditure			Rate in the pound.	
	Males	Fem	Total	Males	Fem	Total.		£.	s.	d.	£	s.	d.	s.	d.
1771	—	—	—	—	—	—	—	45	6	3	38	2	7	2	6
1772	—	—	—	—	—	—	—	33	16	9	40	9	8	2	0
1773	—	—	—	—	—	—	—	67	17	6	74	2	5½	3	0
1774	—	—	—	—	—	—	—	80	16	0	67	10	8	3	6
1775	8	5	13	6	7	13	5	82	18	6	85	0	11	3	6
1776	12	9	21	12	6	18	1	72	9	0	76	5	8	3	0
1777	10	8	18	6	5	11	1	94	13	0	95	18	8¾	4	0
1778	10	6	16	7	4	11	1	95	10	6	90	13	8⅕	4	0
1779	5	9	14	8	10	18	2	93	18	6	121	13	6½	4	0
1780	7	7	14	8	5	13	4	160	17	6	181	11	10	7	0
1781	6	14	20	7	10	17	1	174	0	5	160	15	9	7	6
1782	7	7	14	8	5	13	1	154	13	0	177	8	6¼	6	0
1783	7	9	16	6	7	13	2	156	4	6	178	9	8½	6	0
1784	9	6	15	10	9	19	5	168	14	6	161	17	1	6	0
1785	6	8	14	7	5	12	2	141	13	9	137	11	11	5	6
1786	9	4	13	14	3	17	7	153	14	6	173	17	8	6	0
1787	12	11	23	6	7	13	4	153	14	6	172	1	4	6	0
1788	9	6	15	5	5	10	4	153	19	0	150	3	5½	6	0
1789	7	7	14	7	5	12	4	154	7	0	151	8	4	6	0
1790	7	7	14	1	5	6	4	157	19	6	151	3	6	6	0
1791	8	3	11	8	4	12	8	185	5	0	229	11	8	7	0
1792	11	4	15	7	10	17	3	162	2	0	163	3	11	6	0
1793	9	11	20	8	4	12	1	110	3	0	118	8	10	4	0
1794	4	10	14	2	9	11	7	139	8	6	150	6	8½	5	0
1795	—	—	—	—	—	—	—	142	16	6	132	4	2	5	0

July, 1795.

NEW WINDSOR.

THE parish of New Windsor, from the very uncertain information obtained respecting its extent, appears to contain somewhat more than 5100 acres. Its population, from the number of houses, and the average of births, and burials, may be estimated at near 3000 inhabitants. About 470 houses
pay

pay the houfe or window-tax : between 60 and 70 are exempted. The number of inns or alehoufes is 27.

Table of Baptifms, Burials, and Marriages.

Years.	Baptifms.	Burials.	Marriages.
1680	38	62	3
1700	57	46	
1775	84	77	
1776	78	69	
1777	86	72	
1778	101	85	
1779	80	74	
1780	75	76	
1781	95	66	
1782	94	74	
1783	106	79	
1784	92	106	
1785	91	70	26
1786	77	97	21
1787	95	94	25
1788	105	80	29
1789	94	94	14
1790	107	118	13
1791	82	97	28
1792	98	97	22
1793	85	96	24
1794	82	77	30

The parifh, exclufive of buildings, confifts, principally, of parks, gardens, pleafure grounds, &c.; concerning which, the information was fo contradictory, that its authenticity could not be relied on. Tithes are compounded for. The amount of the land-tax is £976. 10s. 0d. to which the King contributes £120. which fum is called by the parifhioners, Debenta Money. There are no commons, or wafte lands. The prices of provifions are : beef, 6d. to 8d. the pound; mutton, 6d. to 7d.; veal, 7d.; bacon,10d.; falt butter, 10d.; frefh butter, 14d.; new milk, 3d. the quart; at the King's farm old milk is fold for ½d. the quart.

Common

Common labourers receive 9s. a week, and beer; in hay harveft, 10s. a week, and beer; in corn harveft, 2s. a day, and dinner. Thefe wages, are higher, by a fhilling a week, than they were laft year.

There is one fmall Methodift congregation in this parifh. There are three friendly Societies; in each of which the number of members is limited to 81. Their rules have been confirmed by the Magiftrates, according to the provifions of a late Act of Parliament.

The Poor are either relieved at home, or in a poor-houfe, which is a very convenient building, and feems to be kept tolerably clean. Feather beds are ufed: there are 6 or 7 in each room: 2 perfons fleep in a bed. 96 paupers, chiefly old people, and children, are, at prefent, in the houfe. The latter are inftructed in reading, till they are 7 years of age; and are, then, put to a free-fchool, where they are clothed and educated till they are 14 years of age; when the boys are bound apprentices till they are 21 years old, with an apprentice fee of £10. arifing from the intereft of donations bequeathed for that purpofe. In the poor-houfe, linen and ftockings are manufactured for the ufe of the houfe. For all other work (which confifts in picking hair, wool, &c. for other manufactures,) the Poor are allowed 2d. in every 1s. they earn for the houfe. Their annual earnings do not exceed £20. or £25 a-year. 75 regular out-penfioners receive, at prefent, £81. 11s. 10d. a month. About £100. are, annually, paid to cafual Poor. The parifh books were not acceffible; but in the returns made to Parliament in 1786, the Poor's Rate in 1783 is ftated at £1114. 15s. 11d.; in 1784, at £1099. 4s. 6d.; in 1785, at £892. 17s. 3d. and the expenditure for the Poor in 1776, at £721. 9s. 0d. From the information of the overfeer it appears, that the Rates have not varied much during the laft 20 years; that in 1794, (at 2s. 6d. in the pound on a low valued rental,) they produced £1190.; and this year (at 2s. in the pound) £952. In addition to thefe fums, the King pays £100. a year, Poor's Rate, for his poffeffions in the parifh; and £20. a-year, towards repairing the church.

Table of Diet in the Poor-houfe.

	BREAKFAST.	DINNER.	SUPPER
Sunday,	Bread and broth.	Mutton and vegetables.	Bread and cheefe for adults. Bread and butter for children.
Monday,	— Do. —	Cold meat.	—— Do
Tuefday,	— Do. —	Beaf and vegetables.	—— Do.
Wednefday,	— Do. —	Same as Monday.	—— Do.
Thurfday,	— Do. —	Same as Tuefday.	—— Do.
Friday,	— Do. —	Same as Monday.	—— Do
Saturday,	— Do. —	Bread and cheefe.	—— Do.

At dinner and fupper, a pint of fmall beer is allowed to a grown perfon; and a lefs quantity to children. Women, who can procure themfelves tea and fugar, have bread and butter, at breakfaft, inftead of broth.
About £300. (whereof £100. were given by his Majefty) were collected
laft winter, and fpring, in voluntary contributions, for the Poor. Bread
was bought, and fold to them at reduced prices: about £.150 of the money ftill remain in the hands of the parifh officers, and will be applied towards the relief of the Poor next winter.

The houfes within the limits of the Caftle, do not belong to this
parifh *.   *September*, 1795.

B U C K S.

B U C K I N G H A M.

THE parifh of Buckingham confifts of the borough of Buckingham
and 5 hamlets; it contains, by eftimation, 3800 acres, and about 2000
inhabitants, whofe occupations are, principally, agriculture and lace-making. The number of houfes, that pay the window tax, is 230; about
180 are exempted.

Labourers chiefly work by the piece; earnings are irregular, from 1s.
to 1s. 6d. a day. Women, on an average, earn 8d. or 9d. a day, by lace-
making. The parifh fupports feveral roundfmen, particularly during winter. Farms are from £60. to £300. a year. Wheat, barley, and beans,
and oats, in an inconfiderable degree, are the principal articles of cultivation. There are no commons. A great part of the parifh is in pafture:
one hamlet confifts of open field; the others are all old inclofure. Every
farmer rents his tithes of the Marquis of Buckingham.

The prices of provifions are: beef, 4½d. and 5d. the pound; mutton, 5d;

* In Domefday Book-(i 62 d) the Caftle of Windfor is faid to be part of the manor of
Clivore, (i e Cleivar,) and to have been held by Earl Harold, before the Conqueft.

veal, 5d.; bacon, 9d. and 10d.; butter, 9d; milk, 1d. the quart, (small meafure); potatoes, 6d. and 8d. the peck; coals, 2s. the cwt. There are 26 inns, or ale-houfes, in Buckingham.

Table of Baptifms, Burials, Marriages, and Poor's Rates.

Years	BAPTISMS			BURIALS			Marriages	Total Receipts			Total Difburfements.			Rate in the Pound.	
	Males	Fem	Total	Males	Fem	Total									
1680	—	—	68	—	—	—	—									
1740	30	13	43	10	29	39	35								
1760	30	30	60	18	23	46	—		£.	s.	d.				
1774	—	—	—	—	—	—	—	£ s. d.	904	19	10				
1775	44	37	81	21	18	39	—	839	4	8	837	3	1		
1776	41	36	77	15	29	44	—	570	17	9	507	4	7		
1777	40	32	72	29	27	56	—	917	18	10	858	14	0		
1778	32	36	68	20	31	51	—	922	7	9	869	13	10		
1779	34	36	70	38	46	84	—	1054	11	2	1002	6	5		
1780	33	26	59	32	25	57	24	1070	0	11	1093	10	5		
1781	39	40	79	34	33	67	21	918	19	0	951	5	9		
1782	19	38	57	42	37	79	18	970	0	0	850	0	0	Poor farmed this year:
1783	27	27	54	20	37	57	18	935	0	0	850	0	0	— Do.
1784	39	40	79	34	36	70	18	1243	5	9	1250	15	10		
1785	36	25	61	30	33	63	20	1049	9	1¾	1044	16	7		
1786	28	39	67	18	29	47	22	1144	14	10	1172	4	7		
1787	41	27	68	13	29	42	19	1105	13	6	1078	9	0		
1788	27	34	61	22	20	42	27	1124	6	1	1100	1	7		
1789	27	46	73	19	23	42	16	1111	10	8	1096	5	2		
1790	39	36	75	12	28	40	17	1124	10	3	1120	4	6		
1791	37	36	73	13	19	32	30	1127	19	10	1137	16	1		
1792	40	34	73	19	27	46	21	1200	13	0	1223	6	0		
1793	46	43	89	15	33	48	21	1218	6	7	1185	6	9	s.	d.
1794	35	35	70	14	18	32	14	1150	19	0	1241	9	0	5	9
1795	—	—	—	—	—	—	—	1410	0	0	1557	0	0	7	0

The above account of the Rates is extracted from the Treasurer's books, which do not specify the net sums annually raised by assessments. The column of total receipts includes compositions for bastardy, forfeitures to the Poor, and money reimbursed by the county treasurer on account of relief to the families of militia men. The sums under the head of total re-

E receipts,

ceipts, in the years 1794, and 1795, are, nearly, the fums affelled. In the
difburfements are included about £10. annually paid to conftables. Near
£300. a year are expended on the families of militia men: the greater
part however of this fum is repaid by the county.

The nominal rental of the borough and 5 hamlets, upon which the
affellments are made, is £3996. 12s. 6d.; and, it is faid, the real rental is
about £5000. The land-tax is £613. 0s. 6d. which is near 2s. 6d. in
the pound, on the real rental.

In Buckingham are, one Prefbyterian chapel, one Quaker meeting-
houfe, one Methodift chapel, and one congregation of the followers of
Dr. Prieftley.

The Poor are maintained, at home, or in the work-houfe; in which
there are, at prefent, 14 Paupers, confifting of women, children, and old
men, fome of whom are infane. Till within the laft two months, the
Poor, in this houfe, were let to a Contractor, who farmed them at various fums; from 2s. to 3s. each weekly. He ufually received fuch perfons, as the parifh chofe to fend. The laft month's expences of the
work-houfe were £11. 17s. 5d. The earnings of the houfe, (chiefly
from lace-making,) amount to about 15s. a month. The prefent mafter of the work-houfe has a falary of 7s. 6d. a-week. No regular bill of
fare has been obferved; but, fince the parifh has taken the work-houfe
into their own hands, the inmates have been allowed meat once a-day.
The houfe is very fmall, and new furniture is much wanted. 104 regular out-penfioners receive, in the whole, £7. 11s. 0d. every week. There
are likewife 2 hofpitals in the parifh, one for 6, the other for 8 poor widows; who are there provided with neceffaries, and receive each, 17s in
money, every year. About £24 in donations, are annually diftributed
to the Poor; and in a large houfe, belonging to the parifh, 24 poor
families are allowed to live rent free. A friendly Society exifted here a
few years ago; but, in confequence of difputes among the members,
it broke up, and none other has been eftablifhed fince its diffolution.
Buckingham is a place of very little trade, and the inhabitants, in general,
feem poor.   *September*, 1795.

MAIDS

MAIDS MORTON.

THIS parifh contains, by eftimation, 900 acres; 69 families; and about 310 inhabitants. 19 houfes pay the window tax; 43 are exempted. There is one ale-houfe in the parifh.

The occupations of the parifhioneis are, agriculture, and lace-working. The prices of provifions are much the fame, as at Buckingham. The wages, of laboureis, are fiom 1s to 1s. 2d. a day, with beer; but woik is, chiefly, done here by the piece, and a man's eainings, in this way, amount to 15d. or 18d. a day. Here, are feveial roundfmen in winter,.who receive 6d. a day from their employeis; and from 6d. to 9d. from the parifh, accoiding to the wants of theii families.

Farms are, fiom £17. to £90 a year. Wheat, barley, and beans, are the chief articles of cultivation. Theie are about 30 acres of old enclofuie: the ieft of the parifh is open field. Tithes aie taken in compofition. The rent of land is from 18s. to 20s. an acre: the land-tax is levied at about 2s. in the pound: in fome inftances it is paid by the landlord; in others by the tenant. Theie aie from 60 to 70 acies of common in the parifh.

Methodifin prevails much here: feveral of the inhabitants are of that peifuafion.

Years	BAPTISMS.		BURIALS.		Maiiages.
	Males	Fem	Males.	Fem.	
1775	4	2	3	0	4
1776	3	0	3	1	2
1777	3	2	0	2	2
1778	3	2	2	4	2
1779	4	2	4	7	4
1780	5	1	3	1	1
1781	3	4	3	6	3
1782	2	4	2	6	2
1783	8	7	2	3	2
1784	5	4	3	5	1
1785	2	3	2	2	3

E 2

Years.	Baptisms. Males.	Fem.	Burials. Males.	Fem.	Marriages.	Poor's Rate Net Assessment. £. s. d.	Total Expenditure. £. s. d.	Rate in the Pound. s. d.
1786	8	2	6	4	0			
1787	2	1	4	5	1	138 5 4¾	135 1 0	3 3
1788	2	6	2	5	6	148 14 10½	144 10 4¼	3 6
1789	6	4	6	2	3	192 16 0	201 6 9½	4 6
1790	8	3	4	2	5	117 12 10½	130 8 8¼	2 9
1791	2	1	8	7	2	— — —	— — —	— —
1792	1	6	4	0	4	149 15 5¼	154 11 9	3 6
1793	8	2	4	2	3	128 8 4½	139 15 11	3 0
1794	6	2	5	5	5	129 16 4	150 2 8¾	3 0
1795	—	—	—	—	—	160 10 3¾	154 9 4	3 9

The affeffments are faid to be upon the net rental   The Poor of the parifh have an allowance at home.   At prefent, 14 Poor people, (feveral of whom have families,) receive £1. 17s. 6d weekly.   Occafional relief is given to others   Exclufive of the Rate mentioned in the book, the inhabitants were lately rated at £25. to buy bread for the ufe of the Poor.   Laft winter, about £30. were raifed, by voluntary fubfcriptions, for the fame purpofe.   An annual donation of about £4. is likewife diftributed amongft indigent parifhioners.   There are no friendly Societies in the parifh.

September, 1795.

STONY STRATFORD.

THE town of Stony Stratford is a confiderable through-fare : it confifts of a long ftreet, each fide of which is in a different parifh.   The parifh, on the fouth-fide of the town, contains 30 acres of land.   The land-tax, amounts to £123. 1s. and is about 3s. 7d. in the pound.   The population could not be afcertained ; but has varied very little for many years.   The inhabitants are common tradefmen, inn-keepers, and lacemakers : the latter confift entirely of women : they earn from 6d to 1s. a day.   Day-labourers receive from 1s. to 1s. 4d.   There are 12 alehoufes in the parifh : the number of houfes paying window-tax is 120 : the number exempted could not be afcertained.   There is an Anabaptift

5   chapel

chapel here. The following are the Poor's Rates, in the southern parish, for a few years:

Years.	Net Affeffments.			Total Expenditure.			Rate in the Pound.	
	£.	s.	d.	£.	s.	d.		
1787	210	9	0	221	19	4		
1788	178	12	0	191	13	1		
1789	212	2	0	202	10	11	s.	d.
1790	183	14	0	172	3	1	5	2
1791	266	15	3	302	17	4	7	6
1792	166	8	0	207	13	10	4	10
1793	196	5	6	204	8	7	5	6
1794	195	10	0	218	13	9	5	6
1795	230	15	3	263	14	6½	6	6

The Rates are faid to be affeffed on the net rental.

The Poor, of this and the other parish in Stony Stratford are maintained in a work-houfe. The rent is £ 16. a-year, two-thirds of which are paid by this parish. There are now 11 perfons, (10 of which belong to this parish,) in the houfe. No regular courfe of diet is obferved, but meat is allowed 3 days in the week. 18 regular penfioners receive, in weekly allowances, £ 1. 11s.; and a few others have occafional relief.

There are two friendly Societies in Stony Stratford, one of which meets in this parish. *September*, 1795.

WINSLOW.

THIS parish contains about 1400 acres, and 1100 inhabitants: 101 houfes pay the window-tax, and, (it is fuppofed,) about 110 are exempted. The occupations are fhop-keeping, inn-keeping, farming, lace-making, and day-labour. Labourers earn from 6 s. to 7 s. a week, befides breakfaft; in hay time, 7 s. a week, and board; and during the corn harveft, 2 guineas a month and board. Lace-makers earn, from 8 d. to 9 d. a day, on an average. There feems to be here a great want of employment: moft labourers are, (as it is termed,) *on the Rounds*; that is, they go to work from one houfe to another *round* the parish. In winter, fometimes, 40 perfons are on the rounds. They are wholly paid by the

the parifh, unlefs the houfeholders choofe to employ them; and, from thefe circumftances, labourers often become very lazy, and imperious. Children, about ten years old, are put on the rounds; and receive from the parifh, from 1s. 6d to 3s. a week.

The prices of provifions are: beef, 4 d to 5 d. the pound; mutton, 5¼d.; veal, 5¼d.; bacon, 9¼d.; butter, 11d; potatoes, 8d. the peck; pit coal, 2s 3d the bufhel; fea-coal, 2s. the bufhel; a loaf of wheaten bread, weighing 8¼lb 1s. 6d.; this is the ufual price; however, it was lately as high as 2s 3d : very little milk is fold here.

Farms are from £ 60. to £ 400 a year. About 200 acres are arable land, and cultivated with wheat, beans, and oats : the remainder of the parifh is grafs-land. There are no commons. In 1744 a hamlet belonging to the parifh, containing about 400 acres, was enclofed; and in 1766 the other part of the parifh was enclofed. Upon the enclofure of the open fields, land was given in lieu of tithe. The rife of the Rates is chiefly afcribed to the enclofure of common fields; which, it is faid has leffened the number of farms, and, from the converfion of arable into pafture, has much reduced the demand for labourers. An old man of the parifh fays, that, before the enclofures took place, land did not let for 10s. an acre, and that, when he was young, the name of roundfman was unknown in the parifh. It muft however be confidered, that, now a great part of the labour done in the parifh, is paid for, out of the Poor's Rate, in money given to roundfmen. The rent of land is from a guinea to £ 2. 15s. an acre. The land-tax, (now at 7s. 6d. in the pound,) produces £ 233. 17s.

There is a fmall congregation of Methodifts at Winflow. It is a market town : the number of inns or ale-houfes is, at prefent, 14; but, it is thought that, when licences are renewed, feveral will be fuppreffed. There are no friendly Societies in the parifh.

The Poor are maintained, partly, at a work-houfe, and, partly, at their own houfes. 16 Paupers are at prefent in the work-houfe, under the care of a Contractor, who farms them at 3 s. a week each, and is likewife allowed their earnings : he received only 2s. a week before the late dearnefs of provifions took place. The people in the houfe are old women and children, and one man. Lace-making is their chief employment. Their diet is not regulated by any particular bill of fare.

The

The following is a List of Indigent Persons who receive regular weekly Pensions from the Parish.

No of Persons		Ages	Weekly Pensions s. d.
1	A groom's widow ; a lace-maker ; -	48	1 0
1	A single woman ; - -	35	1 0
1	A labourer's widow ; - - -	57	2 0
5	A saddler's wife, and four children : her husband deserted her ; - - -	37	4 6
1	A whitesmith's widow ; - -	57	1 0
11	Eleven bastards, (at 1s. 6d. weekly each.) -	—	16 6
1	A labourer's widow ; - -	57	1 6
2	A labourer's widow and daughter ; the former	70	3 0
1	A tanner, paralytic ; - -	60	5 0
1	A baker's widow, lame ; - - -	60	2 6
1	A labourer's widow ; - - -	65	1 6
1	A labourer's widow ; - -	75	2 6
1	A single woman, sick ; - -	30	0 6
1	A labourer's widow ; - -	60	2 0
2	A butcher and his wife ; the former aged -	70	5 0
1	A labourer's widow ; - - -	80	2 6
1	A butcher's widow ; - -	58	2 0
1	A widow ; - - -	80	1 6
6	A labourer's widow, and 5 children ; -	40	6 0
1	A bricklayer's widow ; - -	56	1 6
1	An orphan boy ; - - - -	—	1 6
1	A labourer's widow ; - - -	70	2 0
1	A labourer's widow ; - - -	55	1 6
1	A gardener's widow ; - -	80	1 6
1	A single woman ; - - -	70	1 6
2	A shoemaker, and his wife ; the former -	60	3 0
2	A labourer's widow, and son ; the former -	70	2 6
1	A labourer's widow ; - - -	70	2 0
1	A woman at Buckingham ; - -	—	1 6
1	A blacksmith ; - - -	65	1 6
1	A woman, bed-ridden ; - -	70	3 0
1	An orphan ; - - - -	20	1 0
55			£. 4 5 6

Besides

Besides these weekly pensioners, many receive occasional relief, whose names are not inserted in the regular list. During the late dear season, the Poor of the parish went in a body to the Justices to complain of their want of bread. The Magistrates sent orders to the parish-officers to raise the earnings of labourers, to certain weekly sums, according to the number of their children; a circumstance that should invariably be attended to in appoitioning parochial relief. These sums were from 7s. to 19s.; and were to be reduced, proportionably with the price of bread.

Table of Baptisms, Burials, Marriages, and Poor's Rate.

Years	Baptisms Males	Baptisms Fem	Total of Baptisms	Burials Males	Burials Fem	Total of Burials	Marriages		Net money raised by Assessments £.	s.	d.	Total Expenditure £.	s.	d.	Rate in the Pound s.	d.
1680	6	6	12	10	12	22										
1685	8	14	22	4	10	14	1									
1690	21	27	48	12	12	24	2									
1691	11	5	16	5	8	13	3									
1692	22	16	38	12	12	24	1									
1693	13	15	28	12	7	19	1									
1694	13	11	24	11	14	25	5									
1695	27	18	45	9	10	19	9									
1696	17	16	33	17	14	31	7									
1697	—	—	38	—	—	26	9									
1698	—	—	29	—	—	34	4									
1699	—	—	42	—	—	30	4									
1700	—	—	40	—	—	43	4	1772	388	0	0	387	9	7½	3	0
1720	10	12	22	24	21	45	1	1773	311	0	9¾	303	0	11¾	2	4
1740	16	15	31	—	—	—	—	1774	304	8	0	282	0	0	2	4
1775	22	18	40	17	17	34	5		436	15	11	418	5	11	3	4
1776	15	10	25	11	7	18	7		432	1	0	455	11	4	3	4
1777	20	21	41	7	11	18	4		389	13	7½	365	6	3½	3	0
1778	14	13	27	7	11	18	7		395	15	8¾	371	1	11¼	3	0
1779	23	11	34	16	15	31	2		396	0	0	417	7	11	3	0
1780	19	13	32	20	12	32	3		387	15	0	437	19	11½	3	0
1781	15	20	35	8	16	24	5		463	1	3¾	511	8	6½	3	4
1782	14	14	28	11	11	22	4		433	0	8	488	13	2	3	4
1783	17	14	31	5	8	13	3		576	2	9¾	606	7	10	4	4
1784	11	16	27	26	15	41	7		Accounts wanting			—	—	—	—	—
1785	17	15	32	7	11	18	4		531	12	3	587	16	3	4	0
1786	16	14	30	16	15	31	9		574	0	0	629	7	9½	4	4
1787	19	24	43	12	12	24	9		574	1	2	602	4	5	4	4
1788	18	16	34	13	12	25	3		533	15	6	558	14	6	4	0
1789	20	21	41	17	11	28	11		533	16	6	579	16	3½	4	0
1790	18	26	44	12	16	28	16		533	0	5	551	5	2	4	0
1791	17	15	32	7	11	18	7		484	9	7½	498	3	8½	3	8
1792	19	19	38	11	13	24	6		752	7	5¼	781	5	0¾	5	8
1793	15	16	31	14	11	25	6		531	17	10	555	15	6¾	4	0
1794	18	29	47	9	16	25	4		664	12	11	694	13	6	5	0
1795	—	—	—	—	—	—	—		795	14	3	801	16	1¼	6	0

It

It is faid that houfes aie affeffed at two-thirds of their real rent ; and lands at their full value. Out of the Rates about £ 10. a-year are paid to conftables, &c. ; and about £ 11. annually, to the county ftock. Near £ 40. are now, yearly, paid to the families of militia men : about half the fum is re-paid to the parifh by the county treafurer. *September,* 1795.

CHESHIRE.

CHESTER.

THE city of Chefter includes 9 parifhes : its extent is à fquare of about 2¼ miles.

In a lately-publifhed hiftory of Manchefter, it is faid, that Chefter contains 3428 families ; 6697 males, and 8016 females ; in all 14,713 fouls. Mr. Bedward, the treafurer of the city, eftimates the population at 17,000.

The following number of houfes pays the commutation tax ;

In the paiifh of St. John	311
St. Ofwald	320
St. Peter	137
St. Bridget	78
St. Olave	20
St. Michael	78
St. Mary	143
St. Martin	39
Trinity	220
Total	1346

The number of exempted houfes could not be afcertained, but, from the above lift of families, and of taxed houfes, it is fair to prefume, that it is about 2000.

Chefter is not remarkable for it's activity in trade or manufacture. The people are, chiefly, fmall tradefmen, farmers, and labourers. Many families of independent fortune refide here. About 30 or 40 people carry on a cotton work; about 100 are needle makers. Two iron founderies employ a few hands.

The prices of provifions are: beef, mutton, veal, and pork, 4d. to 5d. the pound; butter, 15d. to 16d. for 24oz.; new milk, 2d. the quart; old milk, 1d. the quart; potatoes, 2s for 90lb.; wheat, 14s. to 15s. for 38 quarts; barley, 6s 6d; oats, 4s. to 4s. 6d. the fame quantity.

Labourers receive in winter, from 1s. 4d. to 1s. 6d. the day; in fummer, 1s. 6d to 2s and beer. In harveft wages vary much, according to the demand; from 2s. 6d. the day to 4s. with 2 quarts of ale. The number of public-houfes in Chefter is 135.

The rent of land, near the city, is from £ 1. 10s. to £ 4. an acre. The average rent may be reckoned at £ 1. 18s. The farms are fmall, from £ 30. to £ 100 a-year; hay, and pafture are, principally attended to. In the neighbouring parifhes, farms have, of late years, been much confolidated.

The land-tax is collected in the different wards, and not in the parifhes: it varies from 8d. to 2s. 6d. in the pound. Tithes are, partly, taken in kind; but, principally, compounded for. In the neighbouring parifhes, they are, generally, taken in kind.

There are no commons in the Chefter parifhes; nor any modern inclofures, except near the river Dee, where many thoufand acres of fand, (a part of which belongs to thefe parifhes,) have, within a few years, been brought into cultivation. The improvement arifing from embanking, and inclofing, is here very vifible: tracts, once the moft fterile, and unproductive, are now covered with abundant vegetation.

No fatisfactory information could be obtained relative to friendly Societies, of which there are about 3 or 4 in Chefter. They confift of 70 to 100 members each, and have all had their rules confirmed by the Magiftrates. Their number, of late years, has much decreafed.

Several friendly Societies broke up, in confequence of lofing their funds; partly by the failure of a Bank, and partly by an unfuccefsful Canal near this town, in which thoufands of pounds have been funk: Thefe accidents alfo difheartened others.

The

The different parifhes in the city were, in fome refpects, incorporated by an Act of Parliament paffed in 1761 * : Every parifh, however, fupports its own Poor. There is a general Poor houfe in Chefter, to which every parifh can fend it's Poor, upon paying a certain fum annually, for the maintenance of each Pauper. The original intention was to have eftablifhed a houfe of induftry ; a plan, which has, at different times, been carried into execution, continued for a few years, and then dropped. For the laft 2 or 3 years, very little work has been done in the houfe. The Poor-houfe is fituated near the river : the lodging-rooms, and other apartments are large, and well aired. There are 15 or 16 beds in a room : they are of chaff or ftraw ; but are much infefted with bugs. There are no fmall apartments for married people. The Poor in the houfe at prefent, are chiefly aged perfons and children. Old women fpin flax, and pick oakum. The children, at ten years of age are fent out apprentices to Manchefter and other places. About 11 deaths occur, annually, in the houfe.

The affeffments in the different parifhes vary much. The Rates laft year, were upon an average 2s in the pound. The following table exhibits the prefent number of Poor, in the poor-houfe ; weekly out-penfioners; the total of their weekly allowances ; and the amount of the rates laft year.

Parifhes	No of Poor in the Poor-houfe	No of Weekly Penfioners	Total Weekly Allowances			Poor's Rate in 1794.		
			£.	s.	d.	£.	s.	d.
St. Ofwald	33	44	4	3	0	697	9	3¼
St. John	16	49	4	2	6	586	12	3¾
St. Mary	20	40	3	17	6	449	19	7½
Trinity	15	38	3	5	6	292	5	5
St. Michael	1	8	1	0	6	129	0	9¼
St. Bridget	2	15	1	7	9	153	5	1
St. Peter	9	19	1	6	9	196	0	6
St. Martin	1	8	0	11	0	84	4	10
St. Olave	11	6	0	8	6	92	6	4
Total	108	227	20	3	0	2681	4	2¼

The Poor's Rates of this year will, it is fuppofed, exceed £ 3000. Many poor people receive occafional affiftance from the parifh officers.

* 2 G 3 c 45

Expences

Expences of the In and Out Poor of the several Parishes in the City of Chester, from th first day of May, 1759, to the first day of May, 1760, &c. &c.

Each Year ending 1st May.	St. Oswald.			John.			Mary.			Trinity.			Michael.			Bridget.		
	£.	s.	d.	£.	s.	d.	£.	s.	d.	£.	s.	d.	£.	s.	d.	£.	s.	d.
1760	200	13	9¾	348	14	7	148	11	0	168	8	6½	52	16	10	118	17	7
1761	123	3	0¾	262	6	10¼	125	7	1	108	1	2¾	25	17	8¾	70	4	5
1762	131	13	5	315	13	0¾	201	5	7¾	106	5	5	33	15	6¼	67	2	9
1763	139	7	9	240	10	4	179	10	3¼	93	9	6¾	73	4	0¼	78	11	1
1764	119	5	6	192	2	7½	149	4	4	88	7	0½	62	4	9½	80	10	0
1765	231	16	8¾	218	0	2½	222	12	11	107	18	8½	75	12	0	84	5	6
1766	203	2	11¾	261	2	10	212	19	10¾	116	11	9¾	61	17	4½	80	0	4
1767	208	14	0	329	7	5	221	16	0¼	114	15	2¼	53	3	9	95	18	2
1768	194	15	9½	321	17	7	257	16	0	149	8	0	65	16	7¼	93	17	0
1769	208	9	3¾	331	9	2¾	274	15	9¼	181	10	4¾	83	1	1½	114	7	11
1770	238	9	1½	259	17	3¾	283	17	3¼	157	5	10¾	85	7	4¼	134	14	3
1771	180	2	0¼	202	9	10½	216	3	10¾	75	19	0¼	78	2	2	95	17	4
1772	231	4	1	246	4	4½	221	14	9	84	18	3½	65	15	5¾	94	14	11
1773	227	15	1¼	263	14	11¼	243	9	9	70	6	10½	53	7	6	73	4	0
1774	247	16	1¼	288	14	9	294	5	7	118	11	2	78	4	11½	101	6	11
1775	271	14	7	298	18	6¼	223	7	1¼	137	17	9½	49	0	9¾	76	5	7
1776	208	5	2	294	13	6½	238	18	10½	121	5	1¾	52	10	9	87	4	9
1777	251	0	8¼	297	9	8¾	227	11	0½	84	10	5	53	14	2	69	4	9
1778	271	15	3	348	4	5¼	315	3	8¼	130	11	7½	96	17	0	82	15	2
1779	338	1	9	404	4	3¾	375	7	6	137	15	3¼	121	15	8½	86	16	0
1780	340	7	3¾	390	16	9	333	1	1½	161	9	2½	95	15	3	91	11	5
1781	408	6	6½	367	0	2½	282	16	1¼	190	2	1½	104	3	8½	90	4	6
1782	397	13	6	378	12	10	358	14	11¼	235	14	0	132	2	6	79	0	6
1783	397	2	8	516	17	7	465	9	6½	346	17	9	124	17	3½	120	7	10
1784	334	3	3	365	13	2	407	6	0½	281	16	7½	68	10	11	41	18	6
1785	423	8	10	474	9	4½	378	13	10½	233	8	8	91	18	5	142	12	10
1786	438	6	8	557	11	2½	487	12	3½	265	14	8	124	14	6½	116	18	5
1787	429	0	6	500	19	7½	520	1	11	231	2	9	75	6	8½	137	9	5
1788	602	5	0	733	10	4½	673	16	3¼	262	2	8½	146	15	6½	236	19	6
1789	607	17	0	564	5	7	592	14	1	241	1	1½	119	8	4	168	11	1½
1790	623	8	9	583	17	10	454	10	6½	191	14	4	153	9	0	155	8	3
1791	526	17	4½	422	8	8	380	18	7½	153	1	5	124	19	7	123	9	10½
1792	490	18	2	470	4	11½	409	0	9	210	9	9	116	14	10	110	5	11½
1793	457	11	3½	429	11	1	369	4	5¾	208	7	5½	88	10	8½	103	1	8½
1794	546	10	5½	521	9	5	374	12	6½	247	2	1½	126	0	11¼	142	12	5
1795	637	9	11½	544	3	8½	508	8	6¾	320	4	0	144	4	3	154	2	6

pences of the In and Out Poor of the several Parishes in the City of Chester, from the first day of May, 1759, to the first day of May, 1760, &c. &c.

Year ending May.	Peter.			Martin.			Olave.			John's Hospital.			Abbey Court			ANNUAL EXPENCE.		
	£.	s.	d.	£.	s.	d.	£.	s.	d.	£.	s.	d.	£.	s.	d.	£.	s.	d.
60	88	13	2	122	11	5¼	0	2	6½	0	0	0	42	13	6½	1292	3	1
61	63	4	0¼	77	19	6¾	1	5	3	0	0	0	21	13	11	879	6	4
62	70	14	2½	71	2	5¼	8	10	4	0	0	0	23	6	10	1029	9	8
63	60	8	11½	53	16	4¼	17	1	9	1	15	8½	18	9	10	956	11	8¾
64	52	18	3¼	39	11	3	14	2	9	0	0	0	6	3	8½	804	10	3¼
65	57	7	2	52	3	2½	12	19	7½	5	10	1	6	5	8¼	1074	11	10¾
66	46	5	7½	62	10	6¼	40	16	4½	2	4	2	6	7	7½	1093	19	7¼
67	29	11	5¾	72	7	7½	29	14	1¼	5	19	8¾	5	14	8¾	1167	2	3
68	58	12	6½	70	6	10	22	8	7¼	7	11	0	6	3	1½	1248	13	1
69	70	12	1¼	84	8	2½	52	9	3¾	0	15	0¼	6	10	2¼	1407	19	7¼
70	87	15	10¼	84	19	9¾	55	14	4¼	0	9	4½	20	10	2¾	1409	0	10
71	47	19	1¾	56	3	0½	50	14	1¼	4	4	10½	24	12	2¼	1032	7	8¼
72	54	13	5¼	33	3	4	69	9	9¼	5	10	7	22	2	4¾	1129	11	5¾
73	49	0	0	35	7	3	56	8	7	3	8	5½	19	7	3¾	1095	9	10
74	70	8	9	30	13	4	70	7	5	0	0	0	0	0	0	1300	8	11¾
75	42	6	3¼	26	17	5½	56	6	6¾	0	1	10¼	0	0	0	1182	16	7¼
76	33	1	3¼	38	8	4½	55	1	0	0	0	0	0	0	0	1129	8	10¾
77	45	6	3	24	7	10	44	4	5	0	0	0	0	0	0	1097	9	3½
78	70	3	11¾	42	19	5¾	48	11	4½	0	0	0	0	0	0	1407	2	0
79	114	16	0	37	14	9½	47	12	11	0	0	0	0	0	0	1664	4	3½
80	96	0	6¼	35	3	5¾	49	2	5¾	0	0	0	0	0	0	1593	7	7¼
81	88	16	6½	31	0	2½	21	7	4½	0	18	3½	0	0	0	1584	15	8
82	107	16	4	28	18	4½	37	4	1	2	3	4½	0	0	0	1758	0	5¼
83	93	11	4	56	6	11	69	11	3	3	19	6	0	0	0	2195	1	8
84	80	12	0	55	19	10	64	5	8	6	13	9	0	0	0	1706	19	9
85	165	15	2	90	14	11½	98	11	5	7	10	0	0	0	0	2107	3	6½
86	183	5	3	101	5	7	78	13	4	8	18	3	0	0	0	2363	0	2½
87	191	12	10½	104	10	7	43	2	2½	8	2	8	0	0	0	2301	9	3½
88	253	3	9½	106	3	0¾	56	8	11	11	11	3	0	0	0	3082	16	5½
89	229	11	5	92	1	4½	49	2	7	14	12	0¾	0	0	0	2679	4	8¼
90	154	11	6	77	11	11	22	12	10	17	2	6	0	0	0	2434	7	5½
91	136	17	10	58	17	11	15	2	0	16	13	3	0	0	0	1959	6	6½
92	156	7	11	47	15	9	21	16	1	13	11	9	0	0	0	2047	5	11
93	145	12	0½	56	7	8	18	14	5¼	14	13	2¼	0	0	0	1891	14	0¾
94	157	0	1	61	19	9½	38	14	7½	15	11	3	0	0	0	2231	13	7¾
95	205	1	10	74	1	3½	70	1	9	14	18	0	0	0	0	2672	15	9¼

(Years 77–83:) A manufacture was carried on in the Poor-house these years.

(Years 89–92:) A manufacture in the Poor-house these years.

The voluntary contributions laſt year for the relief of the Poor, amounted to £ 491. 17s. 1. ; of which £ 156. 11s 8d. remain to be diſtributed upon a future occaſion. 8000 perſons, nearly half the population of Cheſter, applied laſt winter for relief.

The following Items of Sums paid out of the Rates, for different Charges, reſpect the Poor-houſe.

Houſe-rent	£ 90	0	0
Doctor's ſalary	18	0	0
Chaplain's ditto	18	0	0
Treaſurer's ditto	5	5	0
Clerk's ditto	60	0	0
Beadle's ditto	10	0	0
	£ 201	5	0

Beſides the above ſalaries, 10s. a week, and victuals, are paid to a tailor.

Weekly Bill of Fare in the Poor-houſe at Cheſter.

	Breakfaſt	Dinner	Supper
Sunday,	Broth and bread.	Beef, potatoes, &c.	Bread, and butter.
Monday,	Milk, gruel, and bread.	Butter, milk, and potatoes.	Milk, gruel, and bread.
Tueſday,	As Sunday.	As Sunday.	As Sunday.
Wedneſday,	As Monday.	As Monday.	As Monday.
Thurſday,	As Sunday.	As Sunday.	As Sunday.
Friday,	Milk, gruel, &c.	Beef, ſoup, and potatoes.	Milk, gruel, and bread.
Saturday,	Ditto, ditto.	Oatmeal haſty-pudding.	Ditto, ditto, ditto.

1 lb. of bread a day is allowed to grown perſons ; 6 oz. of beef, on meat days, and 1 pint of beer ; children receive a proportionable quantity. Butter-milk is ſerved on potatoe and haſty-pudding days.

Of Diſſenters from the Eſtabliſhed Church, there are at Cheſter, one congregation of Preſbyterians, one of Independents, one of Anabaptiſts, one of Antinomians, one Catholic chapel, and a meeting-houſe belonging to a ſect called the New Jeruſalem.

St. John's Hoſpital and Abbey Court are extraparochial. Only one perſon, from St. John's Hoſpital, is at preſent in the work-houſe ; none
from

from Abbey Court; neither are any of their out-poor paid at the houfe. The Corporation connives at their fupporting their Poor feparately, and difpenfes with their paying their quota of houfe-rent. Neither are the out-poor of St. John's Hofpital paid at the houfe, fo that an account of their number could not be obtained. The people of this town find great difadvantage from the parifhes not having been completely united, when the Act of Parliament, above alluded to, was paffed. Removals and expen-five appeals are continually taking place between the parifhes. They alfo find the great number of annual guardians to be very inconvenient: when one fet of guardians had eftablifhed a manufacture, &c. perhaps at a great expence, their fucceffors often viewed it in a different light, and wholly difcountenanced the plans their predeceffors had adopted: fo that, although a manufacture of cotton, linen, woollen, &c. has often been fet on foot, it never continued more than 6 or 7 years at a time.

The Poor, here, have generally a diflike to come into the work-houfe.

Regular weekly out-poor of the feveral parifhes,
   coft laft year,   -   £ 904   0   2
Meat, drink, wafhing, and clothes, for the poor-
   houfe,   -   -   -   -   989   19   7½

The expence of houfe-poor, in the above articles, was about 3s. 11d. weekly for each perfon.

November, 1795.

HIGH WALTON.

THE townfhip of High Walton, in the parifh of Runcorn, contains about 300 acres, and 110 inhabitants, chiefly farmers and labourers, all of the Eftablifhed Church. 15 houfes pay the window-tax; and 7 are exempted.

The prices of provifions are: wheat, 14s. 6d. for 70 lb. weight; barley, 6s. for 36 quarts; oats, 4s. 3d. for 36 quarts; butchers' meat,

o   4½d.

4½d. to 5d. the pound; butter, 11d.; old milk, 3 pints for 1d.; butter-milk, 2 quarts for 1d.

The wages of common labourers are 8s. a-week, throughout the year, without victuals: a few have 9s.

The rent of land is from 20s. to 35s. an acre. Farms are chiefly of £ 20. and £ 30 a-year: one is as high as £ 130. Land is principally managed with a view to the dairy. The land-tax is £ 23 16s. and amounts to about 1s. 2d in the pound. This tax is, here, ufually paid by the tenant. Tithes are taken in kind. There are no commons: about 16 acres were enclofed 23 years ago. There are no friendly Societies in the townfhip.

The Poor have a weekly allowance at home. 2 guineas a-year are paid to the work-houfe at Kindeıton. This ferves as a check on the Poor, be-caufe, if any are refractory, they are threatened with being fent thither. This ftep, however, has as yet been found unneceffary.

		Weekly Allowance
The following are the Weekly Poor;		s. d.
A labourer's widow; aged 55;	- -	2 0
A labourer's widow; aged 45;	- -	2 6
A family deferted by their father;	-	2 0
A poor woman;	- - -	0 6
		7 0

5 houfe-rents are paid; and feveral perfons have occafional relief. The Poor do not all live in the townfhip.

Years.	Net Rates.	Total Expenditure.	Rate in the Pound.
	£. s. d.	£. s. d.	
1772	8 3 10½	8 5 5	
1773	8 3 10	11 17 7½	
			s. d.
1774	29 18 4½	24 13 6	
1775	21 17 10½	18 2 10	1 6
1776	16 5 3	14 16 9½	1 0
1777	32 11 4	34 10 8½	2 0
1778	40 14 2	58 9 1	2 6

4

Years.

Years.	Net Rates.			Total Expenditure.			Rate in the Pound.	
	£.	s.	d.	£.	s.	d.	s.	d.
1779	56	19	10	58	14	7½	3	6
1780	48	17	0	48	19	3½	3	0
1781	73	5	6	68	6	1½	4	6
1782	65	3	0	59	19	1	4	0
1783	57	0	1	53	1	4	3	6
1784	48	17	0	60	2	9	3	0
1785	57	3	7¾	51	8	11	3	6
1786	49	3	0	62	16	14	—	—
1787	46	12	3	47	9	9	2	9
1788	42	7	6	43	5	7	2	6
1789	46	12	3	38	4	4	2	9
1790	42	7	6	35	16	1	2	6
1791	63	11	3	57	19	4	3	6
1792	33	18	0	33	14	10	2	0
1793	25	8	6	20	7	7	1	6
1794	50	17	0	37	10	0	3	0
1795	42	7	6	33	3	4½	2	6

As affeffments are made upon an old valuation, property is rated much below the prefent rental. This townfhip, which is about 2½ miles from Warrington, is much more burthened with Poor, than Mickle Traffoid, which is about 5 miles from Chefter on the Warrington road. No fatiffactory reafon can be affigned for this difference, unlefs, perhaps, the proximity of the former to a manufacturing country, be confidered a fufficient one.   *November*, 1795.

MICKLE TRAFFORD.

THE townfhip of Mickle Trafford is fituated in the parifh of Plimpfton in the county of Chefter. Its extent is neal a fquaie mile, or 640 acies; its population about 200 inhabitants, (all of the eftablifhed Church,) who are either farmers, or agricultural labourers. 24 houfes pay the window-tax; 16 are exempted. The price of piovifions is much the fame as in Chefter. Wages of labourers, aie from 1s. 6d to 2s. a day, with beer. Farms are from

VOL. II.   G   £16.

£16. to £200. a year; chiefly from £50. to £60. a year. The dairy is the main object attended to by farmers. The average rent is about 25s. an acre. Tithes are taken in kind. There are about 12 acres of common in the township. There is no friendly Society here; and only 2 ale-houses.

This township claims a share of Kinderton work-house, but sends no Poor thither. It pays 2 guineas a year house-rent to the governor of the house, and agrees to pay 1s. a week, for each Pauper that may be sent thither. 13 poor families are chargeable at present, and receive weekly allowances from 1s. to 3s. each, at home. Several house-rents are also paid. From the year 1778, to 1783, the township was connected with the house of industry at Chester: during those years, the rates were higher than usual, which the people here ascribe to the misconduct or mismanagement of the clerk of the Chester work house, in making unreasonable charges on this township; upon the whole, the connection was found to be disadvantageous, and was, therefore, soon discontinued. The assessments, at present, are upon about two thirds and a little more, of the real rental.

Years.	Net Rates.			Total Expenditure			Rate in the Pound.	
	£.	s.	d.	£.	s.	d.	s.	d.
1730	17	2	7½	17	16	1	—	—
1758	45	13	0	56	10	3	1	0
1776	45	13	0	45	6	1½	1	0
1777	22	16	6	22	14	1	0	6
1778	91	6	0	103	16	11½	2	0
1779	Accounts in this and 3 following years not settled.							
1783	102	14	3	89	0	8	2	3
1784	45	13	0	44	9	9	1	0
1785	51	7	1½	48	16	1½	—	—
1786	68	5	9	68	4	7	1	6
1787	79	13	4½	85	6	0	1	9
1788	68	5	9	66	15	1½	1	6
1789	47	8	5	46	12	6	1	0
1790	56	18	1½	64	17	3½	1	3
1791	79	13	4½	81	13	4	1	9
1792	68	4	9	68	0	7	1	6
1793	60	13	11	73	7	10	—	—
1794	68	5	9	68	3	1½	1	6
1795	68	5	9	83	5	4½	1	6

CORN-

CORNWALL.

GWENNAP.

THE parish of Gwennap is situated in the hundred of Kirrian; and is from 7 to 8 or 9 miles south-west of Truro: its extent is nearly 4 square miles; and the number of inhabitants about 4000, all of the established Church. They are, mostly, engaged in mining. The principal copper mines in Cornwall are in this neighbourhood. In the parish of Gwennap the most considerable are, the Consolidated Mines, the United Mines, Poldice, Huel Unity, Huel Jewell, and Irefavan. The mining business is a lottery in which there are more blanks than prizes : the prizes, however, are sometimes very high : the Huel Virgin in Gwennap was, perhaps, the greatest ever known. In the first fortnight's working, it yielded copper which sold for £5700.; in the next three weeks, and 2 days, as much copper as sold for £9600. To raise the first mentioned quantity, the adventurers expended not more than £100.; to raise the second, a trifle more, in proportion to the quantity. This mine has continued to be worked, with great profits to the land-owner, and adventurers, for more than 30 years. The number of people employed in the mines of Cornwall cannot easily be ascertained. Including the streamers, who are a distinct body from the miners, the number of men, women, and children, employed in raising the ore, washing, stamping, and carrying it, is supposed to amount to 16,000 persons ; of whom at least 12,000 are capable of bearing arms. These men are better paid than most labourers in England [1]. Ordinary wages are about 40s. a month.

There are 8 inns or ale-houses in the parish ; and 3 friendly Societies, containing, altogether, about 400 members.

The prices of provisions, at present, are : wheat, 11s. the bushel; barley, 4s. 6d ; butcher's meat, 5½d. the pound.

Farms are small : the principal articles of cultivation are, wheat, barley,

[1] General View of the County of Cornwall, drawn up for the consideration of the Board of Agriculture   20—22

oats,

oats, and potatoes. Towards the weftern part the of county, the laft article is much attended to; and about Penzance two crops of potatoes in a year are not uncommon. An inftance is mentioned, in the work above cited[1], of one Cornifh acre, (which is equal to one acie, and one eighth, ftatute meafure,) producing 900 Winchefter bufhels in one year. Tithes are ufually rented by the tenant. One half of the parifh is wafte land.

Years	Poor's Rates		
	£.	s.	d.
1776	503	1	4
1783	718	18	0
1784	511	2	4
1785	512	2	4
1786	623	15	$1\frac{1}{2}$
1787	491	2	6
1788	578	15	$9\frac{3}{4}$
1789	693	9	$11\frac{1}{2}$
1790	798	10	8
1791	769	1	0
1792	640	18	$3\frac{1}{4}$
1793	614	18	$3\frac{1}{2}$
1794	722	13	8
1795	704	8	$11\frac{1}{4}$

Thefe 4 yeais are taken from the Returns to Parliament The fiift fum denotes the net expences of the Poor in 1776; the fubfequent fums, are the Poois Rates of each year

The Poor are chiefly relieved in their own houfes: 40, however, are maintained in a work-houfe, in which there is no fort of manufactory. Their weekly allowance is 2s. 3d. each. The Poor's Rates in this parifh are much eafed by the lord's dues being taxed, as the mines are very profitable to the land-owners.   *March*, 1796.

KENWYN.

THIS parifh lies a little to the northward of Truro : its extent is 5 miles in length, and 3 miles in breadth. It contains about 3000 inhabitants, who are all of the eftablifhed Church with the exception of a few Baptifts, and

[1] p. 38.

Inde-

Independents. Owing to opening of new tin and copper-mines, the population has of late years much increased. The inhabitants are chiefly miners. The number of inns or ale-houses in the parish is 18 : there are 4 friendly Societies, containing altogether about 300 members. The price of provisions, wages of labourers, size of farms, and other circumstances relating to the parishioners, and the parish, are much the same, as stated in the preceding report. About one third of the parish is waste land. The Poor are relieved at their own houses.

Years	Poor's Rates			
	£.	s.	d.	
1776	678	5	4	
1783	847	17	8	These years are taken from the Returns to Parliament The sum under the year 1776 is the net expence of the Poor
1784	553	9	3	
1785	651	16	6	

Years	£.	s.	d.	Rate in the Pound	
				s.	d.
1789	511	13	3	10	6
1790	698	9	3	15	0
1791	790	1	9	17	0
1792	574	18	9	12	0
1793	538	8	0	11	0
1794	718	6	11½	15	0
1795	628	19	1½	12	6

March, 1796.

CUMBERLAND.

AINSTABLE.

THIS parish is nearly a square of 8 miles: it contains about 5120 acres, whereof 3480 are common, and produce good pasturage for sheep and black cattle : the number of sheep amounts to 1200. Farms are small, and principally occupied by proprietors. About 400 acres have been

been enclofed in the common fields, within the laft 50 years. The average rent of land is about 18s an acre; but it is obfervable, that here and in moft parts of Cumberland, an extenfive common right is attached to moft arable lands, which, unlefs this circumftance is taken into confideration, are eftimated much above their intrinfic value. On the ftrong lands good wheat is produced; and on the light and fandy parts of the parifh, barley, rye, peafe, clover, turnips, oats, and potatoes, are cultivated: the two laft articles form the principal part of the diet of a Cumberland labourer. The wages of labour are much the fame, here, as in the neighbouring parifhes of Kirkofwald and Hefket. This parifh contains 98 families, of which 5 are Prefbyterians; and 434 inhabitants, moft of whom, with the exception of a few ruftic artifans, are employed in agriculture: 50 houfes, (2 of which have about 6 windows,) pay the commutation tax; 48 are exempted.

No book of parifh accounts could be met with: the expence however of maintaining the Poor is much higher than formerly. The prefent annual expenditure is about £65. 18s. a year, which amounts to 10½d. in the pound on the full rental Two removals into this parifh, (neither of which were contefted,) took place within the laft 20 years. The Poor are now farmed, with the exception of lunatics, for £49. a year.

The following is a lift of the Paupers maintained by the Contractor:

M. Y. a mafon's widow, aged 73.

A. F. a labourer's widow, aged 80.

R H. a weaver's widow.

M. I. a widow, aged 80.

T. S. a blackfmith's wife, aged 78; rather infane at times; occafionally chargeable.

M. B. a taylor's widow, aged 82.

M. N. receives 10s. annually from this parifh, and 10s. from Cumahitton. The two parifhes, in order to avoid a conteft, agreed to join in maintaining her.

The following are lunatics:

F. G. aged 38; fhe has been 18 years under the parifh care: her weekly maintenance cofts 4s. 6d.

I H. aged 30; fhe cofts the parifh 2s. a week.

The intereft of £50. is, likewife, annually diftributed among poor perfons who do not receive parochial aid.　　　　　*December*, 1794.

　　　　　　　　　　　　　　　　　B R O M-

BROMFIELD.

THIS parifh is remarkable for lying in two of the five wards, into which the county of Cumberland is divided. It is nearly, if not quite, ten miles in length from Eaft to Weft ; lying in a line parallel to the Solway Frith, fiom which it is fepaiated by the parifh of Abbey Holme ; excepting at Allonby, its weftern extremity, where the Fiith-is one of its boundaiies. Its bieadth nowhere exceeds three or four miles ; and in fome paits it is not moie than two. The whole parifh contains twelve villages, or townfhips, the church being nearly centrical.

The foil, fituation, and ciicumftances of this paiifh are favourable to agiicultuie. The cultivated land lets in geneial, one acre with another, for £1. an acie : which, confidering that it is moie than three hundred miles from the metropolis, near no flourifhing fea-poit, or laige town, and has no mines, no great works, or manufactories in it, feems to be a fufficient proof of its being well adapted to farming. Land fo ciicumftanced feldom lets at an higher piice, even within twenty or thirty miles of London. Theie are no very confiderable eftates in the parifh ; not more than two, oi three, that are woith £300. a year. Formerly, the owners of the land in this paiifh weie in general the occupants; but this is no longer the cafe. One half of it at leaft is fuppofed to be now held by farmers, whofe farms, for the moft pait, aie not large, very few exceeding £100. a year: moft commonly they aie about half that fum.

The piice of labour is certainly not low in this parifh. Day-labouieis eain from 1s. to 2s a day, according to their merits, and the kind of labour they are employed in ; thofe two fums being the minimum and the maximum of the piice of labour by the day. The wages of men-fervants employed in hufbandry, who aie hired from half-year to half-yeai, aie from 9 to 12 guineas a year ; whilft women, who here do a large poition of the woik of the farm, with difficulty get half as much. It is not eafy to account foi fo ftiiking an inequality ; and ftill lefs eafy to juftify it.

It is remaikable, that in this paiifh, exclufive of Allonby, the numbei of inhabitants has vaiied but little foi the laft hundied yeais.

In 1700 the Baptifms weie	32.	Mariiages	16.	Buiials	28
In 1750	—	28.	—	14.	- -	24.
In 1790	—	22.	- -	16.	—	18.

4

But,

But, it is to be obferved, as accounting pretty fully for the apparent decreafe in the foregoing lift in the later periods, that, in 1743, a Chapel of Eafe
was built at Allonby ; and that in 1776, the inhabitants of that diftrict
ceafed to make their entries in the parifh regifter kept at Bromfield.

According to an actual enumeration[1], made at the defire of the perfon
to whom the author is indebted for the account of this parifh, the prefent
ftate of its population is as follows ; viz :

		Men	Women.	Children	In all.
Dundraw	-	24	23	12	59
Kelfick	-	14	17	8	39
Moor Row	-	16	17	10	43
Whey Rigg	-	17	16	9	42
Blencogo	-	53	72	59	184
Bromfield	-	17	22	24	63
Scales	-	21	23	21	65
Crookdake	-	48	54	35	137
Langrigg	-	50	57	59	166
Mealrigg	-	18	24	23	65
Weft Newton		48	52	93	193

	Men	Women	Children	In all
Total	326	377	353	1056

Allonby, including men, women, and children   320

                                                        1376

So that, with fundry odd houfes, and fome fmall hamlets, the inhabitants whereof are not herein enumerated, the whole population of this
parifh may be fairly eftimated at upwards of 1400.

That the people might more conveniently levy and gather their ceffes
and taxes, many of thefe townfhips were long ago confolidated into little
diftinct bodies or corporations, here called Quarters. Of thefe there are
five in the parifh ; whofe hiftory, as to the Poor's Rates, here follows :

About thirty years ago, the Quarter of Allonby and Weft-Newton
paid to the Poor £16. per ann. : twenty years ago, they paid £30 : at prefent, viz. in 1793, when this furvey was made, on an average, they pay
£60. per ann.   This is an aftonifhing increafe; and not eafily accounted
for.   The Quarter of Langrigg, &c. twenty-five years ago, paid £10. ;
fifteen years ago, £20. ; at prefent, £34.   Bromfield Quarter, twenty

[1] Since inferted in the Hiftory of Cumberland, ii 318. but the totals are there, inaccurately
fet down.

years ago, paid £34.; at present, £60. Twenty years ago Dundraw and Kelsick also paid £34.; but at present £55. Blencogo twenty years ago paid £8: twelve years ago, this Quarter had no Paupers: at present its Poor cess is £22.

A district less liable to extrinsic, or adventitious influence, than this parish could not easily be named : yet, even here, it appears, that within the last twenty years, the Poor's Rates have nearly doubled; this is the more extraordinary, as there are no manufactories in the parish ; and indeed hardly any other inhabitants in it besides a working peasantry. Much of the period herein specified has been blessed with peace : neither have the people there been visited with any uncommon calamities; nor even with very hard times. Taking both men and women into the account, the present Rates here impose a tax of six shillings and sixpence per poll : and if rated by the actual rent of the land, probably, about ninepence in the pound : in Blencogo, only, it seems not to exceed sixpence in the pound. All perhaps that is necessary to add, is, that the expences of litigations, and removals, are not included in this estimate : and that there are no Box Clubs, or Friendly Societies in the parish ; and above all, no benefactions, or regular annual charities bequeathed to the Poor, a circumstance which, it has been observed in other districts, always has a considerable influence on the Poor's Rates.   *October,* 1793.

CALDBECK.

THE parish of Caldbeck contains, by estimation, 12,800 acres, of which about 8500 are common. Of 1780 inhabitants, 156 are, mostly, masters of families belonging to different trades ; 54 are miners ; and the rest are employed in agriculture. They are all of the Established Church, except about 25 Quaker families. Hesket-newmarket, in this parish, is a small, but ancient, market-town. The average rent of land is about 15s. an acre : the land-tax is collected by the purvey at the rate of about $3\frac{1}{4}$d. in the pound on the full rental. Tithes are paid in kind ; about 400 acres are tithe-free, having formerly belonged to Holm-Cultram Abbey,

which, being of the Ciftertian oider, claimed an exemption fiom tithe, under the council of Lateran.

The wages in harveft are 1s. a day, with victuals: in other agricultural
employments, men, and women, are paid between Maitinmas and Candlemas, 10d a day, with victuals; and, the reft of the year, 1s. a day,
with victuals.

Years	Poor's Rate, total collection			Net Expenditure on the Poor.		
	£.	s.	d.	£.	s.	d.
1775	87	0	0			
1776	69	12	0			
1777	69	12	0			
1778	104	8	0			
1779	139	4	0			
1780	139	4	0			
1781	139	4	0			
1782	130	10	0			
1783	104	8	0			
1784	130	10	0			
1785	130	10	0			
1786	174	0	0			
1787	208	16	0	202	1	2
1788	208	16	0	176	2	6
1789	139	4	0	78	6	8
1790	121	16	0	99	17	2
1791	129	4	0	121	11	11
1792	165	6	0	138	16	4
1793	208	16	0	183	17	0
1794	208	16	0	196	5	0

Total Poor's Rate in 20 years 20) 2808 16 0

Yearly average £140 8 9½ = 8¾d. in the pound on the full rental.
Two contefted removals, which took place, a few years ago, will not
foon be forgotten by the parifhioners.

	£.	s.	d.
The attorney's bill for attendance, &c. was -	44	8	2
Expences of witneffes, horfe-hire, journeys, &c.	34	15	0
Total expence of the two removals - -	79	3	2
Another contefted removal coft the parifh -	4	13	0
Another - - - - -	1	9	0

From Jan. 1755 to Jan. 1775 the Baptisms were 567—Burials 398—Marriages 153
From Jan. 1775 to Jan. 1795 Baptisms -   750—Burials 463—Marriages 156

There is one friendly Society in this parish, instituted in 1784; the number of members is 130. Their stock at present amounts to £220: they meet once a month, pay 6d. into the box, and spend 2d. While the stock does not exceed £150 a sick member is allowed 4s. a week; and when it is above £150.—5s. a week; and if £200.—6s. a week. If the disorder does not wholly prevent working, the allowance is to be proportionably reduced. Members aged 70 years, and upwards, are allowed 4s. a week, without any obligation to work. The rules have been confirmed by the Justices.

The following weekly pensions are allowed to the Poor:

		Weekly Allowance	
		s.	d.
1	To H. aged 42 ; a widow, with a small family ;	3	0
2	M. S. a single woman, aged 60; lame ;	2	6
3	W. B. between 70 and 80 years of age ; a clogger; lame ;	1	6
4	J. H. aged 76 ; a collier; old age, and poverty threw him on the parish ;	1	0
5	A single woman, aged 65; old and infirm	2	0
6	R. a carpenter's widow, aged 55 ;	0	9
7	E. S. aged 82 ;	1	0
8	J. H formerly a carpenter, aged 75 ; old and poor ;	1	0
9	A labourer's widow, with a family ; aged 45 ;	1	0
10	An unmarried woman, aged 60 ;	1	0
11	A small farmer's widow, aged 34; rather idle ;	1	6
12	A. B. formerly a farmer ; with a family ;	2	0
13	T. a widow, aged 60 ;	1	6
14	J. J.	2	0
15	S. and family ; he is a collier, about 30 years old ;	1	6
16	J S.	1	0
17	A carpenter's widow ;	1	6
18	A. S aged 40 ; a tailor, with a family ;	2	0
19	M. aged 50; indolent and lame ;	1	6
20	S. aged 60; lame ;	1	6

Weekly Allowance.

			s	d.
21 P. a paper-maker's widow ; aged 60 ;	—	—	1	0
22 H. aged 45 ; a labourer's widow, with a family ;	—	1	6
23 S. and wife ; each about 70 years of age; he makes fieves;	2	6
24 S. a collier's widow, aged 65 ;	—	—	—	1	0
25 T. a tailor, and family ;	—	—	1	0
26 A baftard child ;	—	—	—	0	6
27 Do.	—	—	—	—	1	0
28 Do.	—	—	—	—	—	2	6
29 Do.	—	—	—	—	1	6
30 Do.	—	—	—	—	1	0
31 Do.	—	—	—	—	1	6
32 Do.	—	—	—	—	1	6
33 Do.	—	—	—	1	6

As feveral of the above Paupers live in diftant parts of the parifh, no very fatisfactory account, refpecting them, could be obtained.

The intereft of a donation of £50. is applied towards binding out poor children apprentices.   *December*, 1794.

CARLISLE.

A FEW years ago a work-houfe was erected in Carlifle, at the following expence :

	£.	s.	d.
Purchafe of ground - - - -	90	0	0
Intereft - - - -	6	18	9
Yaid different contractors for building, &c.	737	0	0
Furniture, and other expences, eftimated at	166	1	3

Total expence, £.1000 0 0

The work-houfe properly belongs to the 4 quarters of St. Mary's within the walls of Carlifle, but Poor are likewife admitted from feveral parifhes, and townfhips in the country, by which, it is fuppofed, the proprietors are con-

fiderable

fiderable gainers. The conditions are, For each parifh fending Poor, to pay £4. a year houfe-rent, for lefs than 10 paupers ; £5. a year for lefs than 15; and for 15 and upwards, £6. a year. No lunatics, or perfons with infectious diforders, are admitted. At prefent 13 parifhes and townfhips are under agreement, to fend their Poor to the work-houfe: the number fent, however, is very different, at different periods of the year: at prefent, only 20 are there, 5 of whom are under 12 years of age Befides thefe, there are in the houfe 18 Poor belonging to the city, of whom 2 are under 12 years of age. The whole number, including the mafter and his wife, is 40. The proprietors of the houfe are entitled to all earnings : very little work, however, is done in the houfe: few will come hither, that can work Thofe in the houfe, able to do any thing, either fpin, or are fent out to various employments, chiefly in the cotton manufactory. The following is the amount of earnings, for one year, from Auguft, 1793:

					£.	s.	d.
Earnings in Auguft 1793,	-	-	-	-	2	13	4
September,	-	-	-	-	2	4	1
October,	-	-	-	-	1	12	8
November,	-	-	-	-	1	9	1
December,	-	-	-	-	1	3	5
January 1794,	-	-	-	-	1	19	0
February,	-	-	-	-	1	16	10
March,	-	-	-	-	1	11	7
April,	-	-	-	-	1	8	1
May,	-	-	-	-	1	13	3
June,	-	-	-	-	1	13	8
July,	-	-	-	-	1	4	4
					£20	9	4
20 Paupers from country parifhes, each at 2s. 2d. a week; annually					113	13	4
13 country parifh rents at £4.	-	-	-		52	0	0
Total annual receipts,			£		186	2	8

The following is a copy of the Rules of the work-houfe :

1, That the feveral perfons, upon their admiffion, fhall deliver to the mafter, the houfehold furniture, linen, and clothes which they may be poffeffed of; that they may be clothed, if neceffary, and have

their

their proper apartments affigned them by the mafter, who is to take care that the males and females have feparate apartments, except only fuch as are married.

2, That they fhall be employed, (unlefs prevented by want of health,) every day during their refidence in the work-houfe, except Sundays, Chriftmas day, and Good Friday, for fo many hours as the day-light in the different feafons of the year will admit; being allowed to reft half an hour at breakfaft, an hour at dinner, and an hour at fupper: the intervals to be noticed by the mafter, in fuch mode, as he fhall think proper.

3, That the mafter fhall adapt the various employments to each perfon, in fuch manner, as fhall be beft fuited to his or her ability; having regard to age, and fex: and fhall be attentive, that they are employed conftantly during the hours of work; and if any one be found remifs, or negligent, in performing what is required, to the beft of his or her power and ability, or fhall wafte, or damage the goods committed to his or her care, or fhall break the windows, or deface the walls, the mafter fhall punifh fuch perfon in fuch manner, as to him fhall feem juft, and beft adapted to the nature of the offence: and fhall enter in a book, to be kept by him, for the infpection of the committee, the name of every perfon, who fhall be fo punifhed; expreffing the punifhment inflicted, and the nature of the offence.

4, That the mafter fhall be particularly careful to prevent among the people committed to his charge, all profane curfing, or fwearing; all indecent behaviour, or expreffions, affaults, quarrels, or abufive words: and to encourage them to natural kindnefs, and good offices; that they may live together in chriftian charity. All offenders, in any of thefe cafes, to be punifhed by the mafter; provided always, and it is the intent and meaning of thefe regulations, that no punifhment fhall be inflicted upon any of the Poor, exceeding that of confinement, or alteration in diet; unlefs particularly ordered by the committee.

5, That all the beds be made by the healthy who lie in them, by turns, as foon as they rife: thofe of the fick, by perfons appointed for that purpofe, before the hour of nine in the morning; the rooms and paffages to be fwept before ten; and wafhed once a week, at leaft.

6, That

6, That no perfons fhall be allowed to fmoke in their bed-rooms, or to burn a candle there, but at the difcretion of the mafter.

7, That no one fhall abfent himfelf from the work-houfe, without leave from the mafter, or miftrefs ; and any perfon having admiffion (i. e. I fuppofe permiffion) fiom the mafter or miftiefs, and not returning at the appointed time, in an orderly manner, fhall be reftrained from going out thence for one month.

8, That all who are able fhall follow the mafter, or whom he fhall appoint, to church, every Sunday in decent order ; and after divine fervice fhall to return, on pain of forfeiting their next meal.

9, That the children be wafhed and cleaned every morning ; and a proper perfon appointed to inftruct them in the performance of fuch work as may be thought moft beneficial ; and they fhall not be permitted to play till they have finifhed their tafks.

10, That a committee of three fhall vifit the houfe once a week, inquire into the management of the mafter and miftrefs, and hear the complaints and grievances of the Poor, who are hereby requefted to take notice, that, for every frivolous, or unjuft complaint, made by the Poor, of or againft the mafter, or miftrefs, they will be moft feverely punifhed.

11, That thofe regulations fhall be read over to the Poor once a week, who fhall be affembled for the purpofe ; and their names called over, that none may pretend ignorance.

Graces before and after meat are appointed to be faid by the mafter at each meal. There are alfo forms of prayer to be read regulaily, by the mafter, before breakfaft, and after fupper.

The work-houfe is two ftories high in front, and three backwards ; and can accommodate about 40 perfons. The front is 72 feet in length, by about 24 in breadth. On the ground-floor, are the work-room, about 40 feet by 12, the back-kitchen, the lodging-room for lame Paupers, the coal-cellar, beer-cellar, and dungeon for the confinement of the refractory : on the firft floor, which is entered from the ftreet, on one fide are the kitchen, larder, mafter's, and committee-room ; on the other, the dining-hall, about 36 feet long ; behind which are 5 lodging-rooms, each about 8 feet by 10: on the upper ftory 13 lodging-rooms are difpofed

on

on each fide of a long paffage, at the extremity of which are, the men's hofpital, the women's hofpital, and the lying-in room. Behind the houfe is a yard, 30 feet by 20.

The mafter is allowed a yearly falary of £15. together with meat, drink, wafhing, and lodging, for himfelf, and family.

Table of Diet in the Work-houfe.

Sunday.
- Breakfaft.—Hafty-pudding, and milk, or beer.
- Dinner.—Broth, beef, and bread, with beer.
- Supper.—Bread, and broth.

Monday.
- Breakfaft.—Hafty-pudding, and milk, or beer.
- Dinner —Potatoes, mixed with a little milk, and butter; broth, bread, and beer.
- Supper.—Hafty-pudding, or boiled milk and bread.

Tuefday.
- Breakfaft.—Hafty-pudding, and milk, or beer.
- Dinner.—Boiled milk and bread.
- Hafty-pudding, and milk, or beer.

Wednefday; fimilar to Sunday.

Thurfday; fimilar to Monday.

Friday.
- Breakfaft.—Hafty-pudding, and milk, or beer.
- Dinner.—2 flices of boiled beef, and foup.
- Supper.—Bread, and broth.

Saturday.
- Breakfaft.—Hafty-pudding, and milk, or beer.
- Dinner.—Boiled milk and bread.
- Supper.—Bread, cheefe, and beer.

On Chriftmas-day the Paupers are allowed roaft mutton, plum-pudding, beft cheefe, and ale.

	£.	s.	d.
The ftanding officer's falary, formerly £15. is this year advanced to	20	0	0
The clerk's falary, for keeping the books - -	5	4	0
Average annual expences of removals, law &c. about -	14	0	0
Ditto of furgery, midwifery, &c. about - - -	7	0	0
Ditto of repairs in work houfe, and other cafual expences, about	10	0	0
	£ 56	4	0
To which may be added the falary of the mafter of the work-houfe	15	0	0
	£ 71	4	0

Years.	Annual Collection. £. s. d.	Years.	Births.	Burials.	Marriages.
1774 to Aug. 1775	260 0 0	1774	94	58	27
1775 — 1776	260 0 0	1775	84	94	28
1776 — 1777	357 10 0	1776	84	65	44
1777 — 1778	325 0 0	1777	105	82	36
1778 — 1779	325 0 0	1778	82	85	52
1779 — 1780	357 10 0	1779	89	131	42
1780 — 1781	422 10 0	1780	119	146	20
1781 — 1782	399 14 3	1781	113	123	39
1782 — 1783	360 0 0	1782	120	129	52
1783 — 1784	360 0 0	1783	123	109	34
1784 — 1785	396 0 0	1784	129	97	43
1785 — 1786	432 0 0	1785	128	130	69
1786 — 1787	432 0 0	1786	124	131	48
1787 — 1788	432 0 0	1787	134	123	39
1788 — 1789	396 0 0	1788	129	112	52
1789 — 1790	216 0 0	1789	103	141	45
1790 — 1791	114 0 0	1790	104	145	54
1791 — 1792	114 0 0	1791	111	205	46
1792 — 1793	180 0 0	1792	146	131	63
1793 — 1794	216 0 0	1793	116	145	70
		1794	132	163	42

20) 6355 4 3

Average of 20 years £ 317 15 2½   21) 2369 21) 2545 21) 945

Average of 21 years   112¾   121⅐   45⅗

It is fuppofed this year's collection will amount to £ 288., which fum is collected at the rate of 1s. 2d. in the pound, on the full rental. The work-houfe was finifhed in 1786; and the above-mentioned expences of building, &c. amounting to £1000., were paid out of the Rates of 3 or 4 years about that period; fince which the inftitution has pioduced a very confiderable faving to the parifh; principally, by difcouraging applications to the parifh: for, although it is certain, that in the woik-houfe the Pooi are far better provided with the important neceffaries of food, clothing, habitation, and fuel, than they could be, by their moft induftiious exeitions at home, this mode of receiving parochial relief is univerfally dif-liked : many diftreffed families prefer the chance of ftarving among friends and neighbours, in their own native village, to the moitifying alternative of being well fed, well lodged, and well clothed in a Poor-houfe, the motley receptacle of idiots, and vagrants.

Exclufive of the Poor in the houfe, 32 Paupers, including 4 baftaids, receive parochial affiftance.

St. Mary's Quarter contains 367 houfes, that pay the window-tax, of which number 170 are ftated to have above 6 windows; it is eftimated that not above 10 feparate houfes are exempted. It is however to be obferved, that a great proportion of the houfes are double tenements. The inhabitants aie gentry, tradefmen, and manufacturers ; what proportion one clafs bears to another, it is not eafy to determine.

The land-tax is collected by the puivey, at the iate of $1\frac{1}{2}$d. in the pound, on the full rental.

In Cailifle are 6 Friendly Societies ; 5 of men, and 1 of women. One of the former is wholly compofed of men employed in the cotton ftamperies. The dates of their eftablifhment, and number of members in each, are, as follows :

	Dates of Eftablifhment.	No. of Members.	
1	1772	240	Men.
2	1778	140	Men (Stampeis).
3	1781	170	Men.
4	1781	150	Men.
5	1781	135	Women.
6	1782	145	Men.

The members of each Society are not felected from any particular parifh. In the Society marked number 2, a fick member is allowed 6s. a week : and when incapacitated by old age, from working, the fame allowance, weekly, for life. The fund of this Society, confifting, at prefent, of £240. it is expected, will be foon fufficient to enable it to augment it's weekly allowance to 8s. A copy of the Rules of the Female Friendly Society in Carlifle could not be procured ; but, the following is a fhort Abftract of the Rules of a very fimilar Female club, eftablifhed at Wigton in this county.

I   Healthy

Healthy women under 43 years of age are admitted, on paying 1s. 9d. entrance-money, 7d. box-money, and 1d. towards providing a doctor. A member of 3 years standing is allowed, in case of sickness, 5s. a week for the first 10 weeks; and 3s. a-week, afterwards; but no sickness, or lameness, in the time of pregnancy, entitles a member to relief from the Society; but if they are the consequence of pregnancy, such member is entitled to the allowance, to commence one month after her lying-in. £ 5. are allowed towards the funeral expences of a member, and £ 2. towards the funeral expences of a husband; but a member cannot receive the last allowance more than once in her life. Widows are allowed £ 2. on the death of a child; and unmarried members £ 2. on the death of a father, brother, &c. Members disclosing the secrets of the Society, upbraiding one another, refusing to be silent, after due notice, &c. are liable to a fine; the framers of these Rules, which are very minute, seem to have entertained strong ideas of the loquacity of the sex. The following Rule seems well calculated to punish dissoluteness of manners, among the female part of the labouring class. If any single or unmarried woman, having had a child, before she entered this Society, shall commit the same crime, when in the Society, she shall be excluded; or, if any married woman shall have a child in the absence of her husband, she also shall be excluded, provided she cannot satisfy the Society in six months. Members of 20 years standing are allowed 2s. a week for life, while the fund consists of £ 100. and upwards. For managing the concerns, and keeping the keys of the strong box of this Society, two stewardesses are taken by rotation, and continue six months in office; two collectors, who are chosen by the stewardesses, collect fines, &c.: a beadle, and warden, (both females,) are likewise taken by rotation; the former is the message bearer, and the latter inspects the public affairs of the Society, to see that the officers discharge their duty, and attends the door, on club nights. A committee, of six women, is taken by rotation, from the roll, every six months, whose business is to determine all controversies, to accept members, with the concurrence of the stewardesses, and to give their assent to the lending or disposing of money, or other things, belonging to this Society. The club meets once a month at an ale-house in Wigton, the landlady of which is bound under the penalty of 2s. 6d. to find them good ale.

In the Society marked No. 1, the business is managed by a committee

of

of 12 members: it has likewife it's ftewards, treafurers, warden, and clerk. No perfon can be admitted a member, who is above 31 years of age. Sick members, who cannot work, are allowed 5s. a week: the fick, who can work a little, are allowed a weekly fum, not exceeding 5s. at the difcretion of the committee. Members 70 years old, are allowed 4s. a week during life. £ 5. are paid towards the funeral of a member. The members meet monthly, fpend 2d. and pay 6d. each, to the box.

In another Society, fick members are allowed from 6s. to 8s. a week, according to the funds of the Society. From 1 guinea to £ 5. is allowed for the funeral of a member. The members meet monthly, fpend 2d. and pay 6d. each, into the box.

Caldewgate Quarter contains about 1200 acres of inclofed land, and about 400 acres of common. The rent of land varies from £ 1. to £ 5. an acre. Tithes are taken in kind: the compofition for tithe pigs, is 3s. a litter, or 7s 6d. annually, for each fow. The inhabitants are, with the exception of a few farmers, tradefmen, manufacturers, and inn-keepers. 136 houfes, whereof 18 have about 6 windows, pay the commutation tax: it is fuppofed, that not more than 20 are exempted. There are, however, a great number of double tenements occupied by poor families.

Wages are extremely various. In this Quarter, there are two ftamperies, which employ about 55 men in the manufacture, as many boys, 30 women, and about 30 common labourers: there are, alfo, 2 breweries, and 2 cotton manufactories. Journeymen ftampers, when in full employment, can earn a guinea a week in fummer, and 15s. in winter: however, they each pay 2s a week to an affiftant boy. Apprentices receive 5s. a week, during their firft 5 years; and 7s. a week, during the remaining 2 years of their fervice. Labourers in the ftamperies earn 7s. and 7s. 6d. a week. Women receive from 3s. to 12s. a week. A good weaver, with conftant work, can earn 12s. or 15s. a week; but, in general, 8s. or 9s. a week, feem to be their ufual earnings. It fhould be obferved, that, of late, manufacturers have not been able to get full employment.

The diet of thefe people is very different from that in the furrounding country parifhes: tea is fubftituted for hafty pudding; and butcher's meat for butter, milk, and potatoes.

This Quarter agrees with the proprietors of St. Mary's work-houfe, for the

the maintainance of their Poor: at prefent only 2 perfons, belonging to Caldewgate, are in the houfe. 30 paupers, 6 of whom have families, receive parochial relief at their own homes: among them are included 11 baftards, for fome of which the Quarter receives 1s. 6d. weekly, from the reputed fathers.

The following are the annual collections for the Poor, &c. No accounts befoie 1785 could be obtained.

Years.	£.	s.	d.		s.	d.
1785	224	0	0	collected at 1	4	in the pound on the full rental.
1786	280	0	0	—— 1	8	
1787	168	0	0	—— 1	0	
1788	168	0	0	—— 1	0	
1789	112	0	0	—— 0	8	
1790	168	0	0	—— 1	0	
1791	226	0	0	—— 1	4	
1792	120	0	0	—— 0	8	
1793	120	0	0	—— 0	8	
1794	213	10	0	—— 1	2	

10)1799 10 0

Aver. of 10 yrs. 179 19 0

The annual average expence of officers, meetings, journeys, orders, &c. is eftimated at	- - -	£ 8	0 0
Ditto of attorney's bills	- - -	10	0 0
Book-keeper's falary	- - - -	1 4	0
		£19	4 0

Caldewgate Quarter, containing feveral large manufactories, is liable to a great influx of ftrangers, fo that removals often take place: generally not lefs than 5 perfons are annually removed from, and about 1 or 2 received into the Quarter, under orders of removal. Contefts enfue on thefe occafions; one Pauper often produces two or three litigations. The inhabitants pique themfelves on their courage and refolution, in defending parochial privileges, and would rather fpend £20. in getting rid of a Pauper, than maintain him at half that expence. No certificates are granted.

A dona-

A donation of 40s. is annually diftributed in equal proportions, among 20 poor widows ; and another donation of 2 guineas each, to 10 poor people of the Quarter, who do not receive parochial aid, is annually given at Candlemas. 137 families, who were eftimated to amount to one third of the population of the Quarter, partook of the contributions lately raifed for the relief of the neceffitous.

Cumerfdale Quarter contains about 2000 acres : the average rent of land is about 15s. an acre. 21 houfes, whereof one has above 6 windows, pay the commutation tax : 20 are exempted. The inhabitants are chiefly farmers. The land-tax is collected, by the purvey, at the rate of 1½d in the pound. Tithes are paid in kind. About 800 acres were enclofed 27 years ago.

No regular accounts are preferved refpecting the Poor's Rate. The total collection, laft year, amounted to £62. 6s. 4½d. which is about 9¾d. in the pound. The Rates are faid to have increafed within the laft few years. This Quarter, as well as Caldewgate, pays £4. yearly to the work-houfe ; but has no Poor there at prefent. The following perfons receive a parifh allowance at home.

		s.	d.
1 A weaver's widow, with 3 children; - -		1	6
2 A widow aged 75 ; lame ; - -		1	6
3 R. L. aged 50 ; unmaried ; fick ; - -		1	6
4 M. C. a fingle woman, aged 60 ; was a farmer's fervant ;		1	0
5 A foldier's widow, and 3 children ; - -		2	0
6 A labourer's widow, aged 75 ; - -		1	7
7 A baftard ; - - - -		1	0
8 A baftard ; - - - -		1	6
9 A baftard ; - - - -		1	6
10 A baftard ; - - - -		1	6

Some houfe-rents are likewife paid ; and a few other perfons receive occafional relief. Removals are not very frequent ; about 2 occur every 3 years.

In Rickergate Quarter, 80 houfes pay the window-tax, of which 21 are ftated to have above 6 windows. Its extent is about 480 acres. The rent of land is fiom £1. to £5. an acre. The land-tax is collected by the purvey at the rate of about ¼d. in the pound. Tithes are payable in kind ; but a compofition of 2s. in the pound is often taken for hay. The inhabitants are, chiefly, tradefmen, inn-keepers, and manufacturers.

No accounts, previous to 1784, refpecting the Poor, are preferved. The following fums fhew the annual parochial affeffments collected for the ufe of the Poor, and other purpofes.

	£.	s.	d.		
From July 1784 to July 1785	97	10	0		
From July 1785 to July 1786	97	10	0		
From July 1786 to July 1787	108	9	0	A valuation took place this year,
From July 1787 to July 1788	99	18	0	and the Rate was collected at 1s. 6d in the pound
From July 1788 to July 1789	99	18	0	1 s. 6d.
From July 1789 to July 1790	83	5	0	1	3
From July 1790 to July 1791	66	12	0	1	0
From July 1791 to July 1792	116	11	0	1	9
From July 1792 to July 1793	133	4	0	2	0
From July 1793 to July 1794	149	17	0	2	3

10)1052 14 0

Average of 10 years 105 5 4¼ $\frac{2}{10}$

The annual expence of meetings and other cafualties amounts
to about   -   -   -   -   - £2 0 0
The ftanding officer's falary about   -   -   - 5 0 0

Within the laft 3 years, there have been 4 removals from, and 3 removals into, this Quarter; which, with fome conteft, that arofe in confequence, coft the Quarter upwards of £40.

Rickergate Quarter pays £4. a year to the proprietors of the Poor-houfe, for the liberty of fending their Poor thither; but at prefent, all the neceffitous, (who are comprifed in the following lift,) receive an allowance at home.

Weekly Allowance

	s.	d.
1 A foldier's wife, aged 45 ; - - - -	2	0
2 A nailer's wife, aged 70 ; - - - -	1	6
3 A boy, 12 years old ; parents dead ; - - -	1	0
4 H. H. a lame man, and almoft blind ; - -	1	9
5 An unmarried woman ; } fifters ; between 60 and 70 years		
6 Ditto ; } of age ; - -	2	0

7 An

Weekly Allowance.

		s.	d.
7 An infirm old man, aged 85;	}		
8 His daughter, aged 45;	}	2	0
9 A bricklayer's widow, aged 65;		1	0
10 W. P. a nailer, and family;		3	0
11 A boy, 10 years old, whose parents are dead, receives in cloaths, &c.		1	6
12 A labourer's widow, aged 76;		1	0
13 A soldier's widow, aged 71;		1	0
14 An Irishman;		1	0
15 B. R. and 5 children; (husband pressed into the Navy) in cloaths, &c.		7	0
16 J. A. formerly a soldier; now a taylor, with a family;		4	0
17 A soldier's wife, and 1 child;		2	0
18 A soldier's wife, and 1 child;		2	0
19 A militia man's wife;		1	0
20 Ditto;		3	0
21 Ditto;		3	0
22 A militia serjeant;		2	0
23 A militia serjeant;		2	0
24 A bastard;		1	0
25 Ditto;		2	0
26 Ditto;		1	6
27 Ditto;		1	6
28 Ditto;		2	0

It has been a general rule in Cumberland, for many years past, not to grant certificates. This Quarter, however, granted one about 2 years ago to a nailer: he lives at Wigton, where he can make a shift to support himself and family, but, if removed into this parish, would certainly become chargeable.

		Houses.	Families.	Inhabitants.
In 1763 }	the city and suburbs	{ ——	1059	4158
1780 }	of Carlisle contained	{ 891	1605	6299
1787	- - -	{ 3864 Males } { 4813 Females }		Total 8677

Part of the parish of St. Cuthbert is included in this enumeration.

February, 1795.

CASTLE-

CASTLE-CARROCK.

THE parish of Castle-carrock contains, by estimation, 750 acres of cultivated land, 600 acres of low common, and 1500 acres of mountainous
common. The number of inhabitants is 232 ; whereof 15 are artificers,
or manufacturers of the common necessaries and implements in husbandry ; 20 lime-workers ; and the rest agricultural labourers. No house in
the parish has more than 6 windows : 31 pay the commutation tax ;
11 are exempted.

The greatest part of this parish remains in dales, or doles, as they are
called ; which are slips of cultivated land belonging to different proprietors, separated from each other by ridges of grass-land : about 100 acres
may have been enclosed within the last 50 years. The land-tax is here
collected by the purvey, and amounts to about 5d. in the pound on the
full and fair rental. Tithes are paid in kind : last year tithe wool sold
for 8s. 6d. the stone of 16lb. The rent of land is, on an average, 18s.
an acre. Men, in harvest, receive 1s. and women 10d. a day, with victuals. Threshers, hedgers, &c. are paid, from 8d to 10d. a day ; weed-
ers, 6d. a day ; wool-spinners earn 4d. a-day, and victuals. Labourers,
at the lime-kilns, receive 7s. 6d. a-week, without victuals.

A Table of Baptisms and Burials.

Years.	Baptisms.	Burials.	Years.	Baptisms.	Burials.
1774	10	4	1784	7	4
1775	3	2	1785	12	2
1776	15	2	1786	8	5
1777	8	4	1787	11	4
1778	3	3	1788	6	6
1779	11	2	1789	11	2
1780	7	7	1790	10	2
1781	10	3	1791	6	2
1782	3	2	1792	7	3
1783	6	3	1793	7	2
			20) 161		63
			Yearly average	8 $\frac{1}{20}$	3 $\frac{1}{7}$ nearly.

The inhabitants are chiefly of the Eftablifhed Church.

This parifh, formerly, joined with a neighbouring parifh in the maintenance of the Poor ; for which they paid £ 4. annually ; and is a week with each Pauper At prefent, the Poor are relieved at home: the following are the regular penfioners in the parifh of Caftle-carrock.

J G. aged 30 ; was incapacitated from working by a kick from a horfe : he is allowed 2s. a week.

J D. aged 70 ; gained his fettlement here by fervice : old age, and poverty, threw him on the parifh: his weekly allowance is 1s 6d.

J. H aged 65 ; was once a fmall farmer ; but being now very poor, receives occafional relief, which amounts to about 15s in the courfe of the year.

A child, 8 years old, whofe parents are dead, cofts the parifh 1s. a week.

A male baftard, of the fame age, cofts the parifh 1s. a week.

No perfon works for the parifh ; nor is there any other charitable fund to refort to, but the Poor's Rates.

A Friendly Society was eftablifhed in the year 1780. The number of members is 29. Their Rules have undergone confiderable alteration, and are now before the Magiftrates for confirmation.

No certificates can be remembered ; and only three removals are known to have taken place during the laft 20 years. None were contefted. A removal was contefted about 22 years ago, and is faid to have been very expenfive, but the law charges cannot now be afcertained.

No regular accounts are preferved refpecting the expenditure of money in parochial charges. The annual collections for the ufe of the Poor, and other parifh expences, appear to have varied during the laft 20 years from £ 20. to £ 34. In 1793, however, only £ 20. 10s. 6d. were collected. From the beft information obtainable relative to thefe matters, £ 26. may be ftated as the annual average amount of parochial affeffments. This fum amounts to about 10¼d. in the pound on the full, and fair rental.

There is a fmall fchool in this parifh, but it is not fufficient to maintain the teacher ; he has a fmall property of his own.

December, 1794.

CROG-

CROGLIN.

OF 7000 acres, the eftimated extent of the parifh of Croglin, 890 only are cultivated; the remainder, amounting to 6110 acres, is fell, or mountainous common. The number of houfes paying the commutation tax is 26; none have more than 6 windows: 15 are exempted. Of 163 inhabitants, (84 males, and 79 females,) 2 are blackfmiths, 2 fhoe-makers, 4 joiners, 1 taylor, 2 lime-burners; and the reft agricultural labourers They are diftributed into 2 villages, and a few fcattered cottages. From 1672 to 1691, the number of baptifms was 106; of burials, 140:—from 1772 to 1791, of baptifms, 133; of burials, 104. Tenements let from £ 3. to £ 45. a year. The whole rental of the parifh is £ 672. The average rent of open fields is 9s. 6d. the acre; of inclofures 15 or 16s. The land-tax may be eftimated at, nearly, 4½d. in the fair rental. About 100 acres of common field have been enclofed within the laft 50 years; but a great part of the arable land ftill remains in narrow crooked dales, or ranes, as they are called. Scanty crops of oats, and barley, are the principal produce. Labourers in harveft earn 1s. a day, with victuals; women, 10d; hedgers, from 8d. to 10d. a day, with victuals; and lime-burners, during 2 months, in the fummer, 1s. 6d a day, without victuals.

The parifh book, previous to 1779, is unintelligible; fince that period the total difburfements for the Poor and other purpofes, have alone been entered. The following years only could be made out:

Years.	Total Difburfements		
	£.	s.	d.
1779	16	5	7½
1780	13	7	7½
1782	17	2	1
1784	14	12	1
1785	19	8	6¼
1786	11	12	3
1787	14	5	9½
1788	9	0	0½
1789	6	8	4
1790	5	17	0¾
1791	2	11	8
1792 and 1793	2	12	4½
12)	133	3	6
Average of 12 years	£ 11	1	11½

K 2

The

The average amount of the Poor's Rate, (collected by the purvey,) amounts to about 3¾d in the pound on the fair rental. The parish formerly joined with others in keeping a poor-house; but has lately allowed it's Poor relief at home. At present, there is not a single Pauper in the parish. A donation of £ 20. was bequeathed last year, the interest of which is directed to be annually distributed, at Christmas, among the Poor of the village of Croglin. This well-intended gift, will, probably, soon create Poor enough to receive it. There have been 2 removals, (one from, the other into the parish,) within the last 14 years. Above 40 years ago there was a removal, which is said to have been very expensive. There is one Friendly Society, of only 5 members, which means to break up very speedily.

December, 1794.

CUMREW.

THIS parish contains, by estimation, 800 acres of cultivated land, and 1200 acres of fell, or mountainous common. The land is cultivated in the old Cumberland manner: the grass ridges in the fields are from 20 to 40 feet wide, and some of them 1000 feet in length: grazing cattle often injure the crops. Great flocks of sheep are kept on the common in summer, and brought into the low grounds in winter. The stock of the parish consists of 1000 sheep, 100 horses, and 260 head of black cattle, of the Cumberland breed. There are no manufactories, great roads, or rivers in the parish. The average rent of land is 14s. an acre. Oatmeal is paid in lieu of tithe-hay and corn. Sheep, wool, &c. are tithed in kind. 184 acres of common have been enclosed within the last 50 years.

Of 146 inhabitants, 7 are common artificers: the rest are employed in agriculture. 27 houses, (only one of which has above 6 windows,) pay the commutation tax; 7 are exempted. The inhabitants are chiefly of the established Church.

3

Table

Table of Poor's Rates, Baptiſms, Burials, and Marriages.

	Total Aſſeſſment	Expend on Poor	Years	Bapt	Bur	Mar
Aſſeſſments from June 1773 to June 1774 were	£14 6 7½	£11 8 9	1774	10	4	2
June 1774 to June 1775 —	15 10 7	12 17 4	1775	2	2	4
June 1775 to June 1776 —	15 8 8	12 9 4	1776	8	1	1
June 1776 to June 1777 —	19 11 6	13 15 6	1777	9	3	2
June 1777 to June 1778 —	16 3 4	12 11 0	1778	9	5	1
June 1778 to June 1779 —	15 12 1	No accounts	1779	5	5	2
June 1779 to 8th July 1780 —	16 14 2	12 15 2	1780	4	8	0
8th July 1780 to 17th July 1781 }	No accounts of theſe years		1781	4	4	1
17th July 1781 to 5th July 1782 }	preſerved.		1782	7	10	0
5th July 1782 to 7th July 1783 —	12 19 5½	6 0 1½	1783	2	3	3
7th July 1783 to 18th June 1784 —	12 0 6	8 17 6	1784	7	0	1
18th June 1784 to 10th June 1785 —	14 0 6	10 7 5	1785	5	2	1
10th June 1785 to 2d June 1786 —	16 8 4	11 11 0	1786	5	8	4
2d June 1786 to 25th May 1787 —	9 0 7	5 10 1	1787	7	4	5
25th May 1787 to 19th Aug 1788 —	13 3 8½	7 12 5	1788	6	3	3
19th Aug. 1788 to 12th June 1789 —	9 7 1	5 16 2	1789	5	3	0
			1790	8	2	3
	14) 200 7 1½	13) 131 11 9½	1791	5	2	0
			1792	8	5	0
Average of 14 years Aſſeſſment	£14 6 2½	£10 2 5¼	1793	1	3	3
Average of 13 years Expenditure on Poor	10 2 5¼					
			20)	117	77	36
Average of Baptiſms, Burials, and Marriages for 20 years	-	-	-	5¾	3¾	1¾

The average amount of parochial aſſeſſment is levied at the rate of about 4d in the pound on the full rental.

The Poor have a pariſh allowance at home. From the following deſcription of their ages, maintenance, &c. it appears that the annual expenditure of the pariſh, on the Poor, amounts to about £14. a year.

1. E E. 80 years of age; gained a ſettlement by marrying a Pauper belonging to this pariſh about 6 years ago: ſhe was born lame, but occaſionally follows agricultural employment. She receives an allowance of 1s. every week.

2. E. D. 72 years of age, a labourer's widow; obtained her ſettlement here by marriage. She has been chargeable 5 or 6 years, and receives a weekly allowance of 1s.

3. A. D. a labourer, receives occaſional relief from the pariſh, to the annual amount of about 10s. He belongs to a Friendly Society, from which he receives 4s. a week. He has been long ſick, and has a ſmall family of children to maintain.

4. A baſ-

4 A baftard child, 2 years old, coft the parifh 2s. a week.

5. A baftard child, between 5 and 6 years of age, cofts the parifh 1s. 6d. a week

In this parifh there is one Friendly Society, which was inftituted in 1780. The number of members is, at prefent, between 60 and 70. Their Rules are now receiving confiderable alteration, in order to be fubmitted to the Magiftrates at the Quarter Seffions, for confirmation, in conformity to a late Act of Parliament.

Only two removals can be recollected to have taken place within the laft 20 years, neither of them were contefted.

The following are the ufual wages in this parifh:

To men, in harveft, with victuals, 1s. a day.

To women, in harveft, with victuals, 10d. a day.

To threfhers, and hedgers, with victuals } 8d. a day.
and } 10d. a day.

To labourers, at the lime-kilns, without } victuals, about 2 months in the fummer } 1s. 6d a day.

December, 1794.

CUMWHITTON.

THE parifh of Cumwhitton contains about 7 fquare miles, of which the greateft part is common : the inclofed land is divided into fmall farms, which are from £ 5. to £ 50. a-year, and, principally, occupied by the owners. The number of families is 86, who are all of the eftablifhed Church ; except one Quaker, and one Roman Catholic family. No houfe in this parifh has above 6 windows : 50 pay the commutation tax ; the number exempted is 41, of which 5 are uninhabited. The inhabitants are, wholly, employed in agriculture The average rent is about 18s. an acre ; right of common included. The land-tax is collected by the old fettled purvey, and, as nearly as can be calculated from the rent of land, amounts to 3½d. in the pound. This parifh pays tithe wool, and lamb in kind ; and a modus of oatmeal, in lieu of tithe-corn and hay. The Dean and
Chapter

Chapter of Carlisle, who are appropriators of this benefice, leafe out their tithes, and even furplice fees; and pay their curate, Mr. Edmund Wills, (who is a great nephew of Bifhop Gibfon,) ten pounds a year.

There are no Friendly Societies in the parish.

Years	Affeffments £. s. d.			Net Expenditure on the Poor			Baptifms	Burials
1773	27	5	9	The overfeer's account of				
1774	39	4	1¼	Difburfements for the Poor are			15	8
1775	37	4	0	loft, except for a few years back;			2	6
1776	37	5	11	and, even then, only the fum total			7	7
1777	37	6	1½	the parifh books			4	8
1778	41	3	1¼				5	8
1779	28	17	7	— — —			8	4
1780	31	13	7½	— — —			8	9
1781	34	16	7	— — —			6	6
1782	39	16	2½	— — —			9	6
1783	32	10	5½	— — —			13	5
1784	53	17	0	of which £ 32. 19s. were expended			12	6
1785	29	8	11½	in repairing the parifh church.			8	2
1786	28	15	10	— — —			10	5
1787	32	11	10½	— — —			11	3
1788	25	13	5½				12	6
1789	28	0	10	£.	s.	d.	9	7
1790	40	18	5	31	15	4	16	7
1791	25	1	9¼	21	16	5½	12	6
1792	40	0	6	36	16	0	13	6
1793	33	3	7	29	14	7	9	9
1794	nearly -			30	0	0	12	4
1795	will be nearly			35	0	0	12	9
21)	722	15	8½				—	—
Average	34	8	4	Average			9⅗	6¼

The average of marriages, during the above period, was 4 annually.

As there is no Pound Rate in this parifh, the above fums are collected by the old purvey; but allowing £ 34. 8s. 4d. to be the average fum collected annually, it will amount to about 4d. in the pound on the full rental. The affeffment includes money raifed for the relief of the Poor, and other purpofes: it receives an annual augmentation of an uncertain fum

fum from the farmer of the tithes, which varies from £3. to £3. 10s.; and which is included in each year's ftatement.

The Poor receive a parifh allowance at home : their ages, fex, maintenance, and other (it is hoped not uninterefting) particulars, are minuted in the following table ; in which it was thought unneceffary to particularize their names.

J L. aged 80, and his wife, aged 82, have had parochial aid above 20 years. They were formerly engaged in agriculture, and obtained a fettlement here, by renting a tenement of £10. a year. A hurt, which the hufband got by a fall, incapacitated him from working, and threw him on the parifh: his wife, occafionally, fpins a little lint, and earns about 3 farthings a day, befides doing her other neceffary houfehold work. They receive, at prefent, 2s regularly, every week, and about £1 6s annually, for houfe-rent, for digging and carting peats and turves for fuel, &c

M D aged 80, and her fon J aged 45, were formerly employed in agriculture The caufes of the mother's having recourfe to the parifh, were old age, and natural infirmities, which, although induftrious, fhe could not provide againft: that of the fon, was a lamenefs which could never be accounted for He earns a little money, by making bafkets, bee hives, &c. The weekly pay allowed them is 1s 6d. They obtained their fettlements by birth

M D 55 years of age, an agricultural labourer, was likewife, from a perfonal misfortune, obliged to apply to the parifh. Her prefent allowance, befides rent, fuel, &c is 1s. a week.

M R 100 years of age, befides houfe-rent, fuel, &c receives 9d a week, from the parifh Her fon allows her 3d a week more She is the widow of a very noted beggar, who would never follow any other occupation ; and of whom fome very laughable anecdotes are related. She obtained her fettlement by birth.

J N and his wife, between 80 and 90 years of age, formerly rented a fmall farm, which gave them a fettlement, but took no care to provide againft old age, and it's natural attendants They receive from the parifh about £4 annually, in various neceffaries

M. N. 70 years of age, was an agricultural fervant. Sicknefs obliged her

to

to folicit parochial relief: her fettlement was difputed, but, at laft, the two contending parifhes compromifed the matter, by agreeing to bear an equal fhare in her maintenance, and each allows her 5s. a year; which, added to her earnings from fpinning, &c. fuffice to maintain her.

A. S. 60 years of age, a farmer's widow, receives a weekly allowance of 1s : fhe refided in another parifh, but, upon becoming burthenfome, was removed thither.

Befides thefe regular penfioners, other indigent parifhioners receive occafional relief, in houfe-rent, fuel, &c. No work is done on account of the parifh; nor are there any other charities here, or annual donations for the Poor.

It cannot be remembered, that a certificate was ever granted to a parifhioner; or that any certificated perfon ever fettled here. Only 2 removals from the parifh, and 1 into it, have occurred within the laft 20 years. None of them were contefted.

	s.	d.
The expence of an uncontefted removal was; to the Juftice	4	6
For paper - - - - -	0	1½
Overfeer's allowance - - -	1	6
	6	1½

Wages by the day are: threfhing, hedging, ditching, digging turves, and peat, 8d; reaping, from 10d. to 1s.; mowing, from 1s. to 1s 3d. Women, by the day, earn, fometimes, 6d., but, moftly, 4d., for weeding corn, hoeing turnips, &c.; in harveft, 10d.; in hay making, 6d.; and by fpinning wool, from 4d. to 6d.

Skim-milk, which is very generally ufed, is fold, 3 pints for ½d.: the prices of other provifions are fluctuating.

The ufual food of labourers is: For breakfaft, hafty-pudding, made with oatmeal and water, which is eat with milk, and fometimes with a little butter:—for dinner, the diet is more variable; potatoes form the moft ufual difh, and are eat with a little butter or bacon; and are fucceeded by milk and barley bread.—butcher's meat boiled, and a flour pudding, are ufually the dinner on a Sunday; and fometimes on a week day; more efpecially during harveft:—the common fupper is milk, boiled with oatmeal, which is eat with barley bread.

The following is a ftatement of the expence of the ufual daily fare of a labourer.

		s.	d.
Breakfaft; hafty-pudding and milk	- -	0	1
Dinner; potatoes ¼d. butter, or bacon ½d. milk and bread ½d.	0	1¼
Supper; boiled milk, and bread	- - -	0	0¾
		0	3

This fum, however, is more, than any poor perfon expends in a day's provifions.

The following is a ftatement of the earnings and expences of a tailor in this parifh; he is 30 years of age, has a wife and 3 daughters whofe ages are 5 years,—2 years,—2 months :

	£.	s.	d.
The man earns 8d. a day, and victuals for 50 weeks in the year, 2 weeks being allowed for indifpofition, &c.	10	0	0
He has an apprentice who earns him 2s a week	5	0	0
Wife fpins lint, reaps a little in harveft, &c. and earns yearly about	3	0	0
Total earnings	£ 18	0	0

EXPENCES.

	£.	s.	d.
Houfe rent, 16s.—fuel, peat and turf, 10s.—befides the man's labour - - -	1	6	0
Barley, 18 bufhels, at 5s.—£ 4. 10s. : oat-meal, 26 ftone, at 2s 4d.—£ 3. 8d. : butter, 50lb. at 8d.—£ 1 13s. 4d.	9	4	0
Milk, 180 quarts, 15s; treacle, 5s.: malt and hops, 5s.	1	5	0
He gets potatoes planted in the neighbouring fields, for the turf and peat afhes, and a little reaping in harveft; they coft him about 8d. a bufhel,—30 bufhels	1	0	0
Cheefe, 4s.; tea and fugar, 10s.; candles, foap, falt, &c. £ 1.	1	14	0
Midwife, 5s. once in 2 years, 2s. 6d.; no other expences are incurred at a lying-in, it being the cuftom in this place for every neighbour to make a fmall prefent, on thefe occafions - - -	0	2	6
He feeds a pig, and fells part of the pork; balance of expence about - - -	1	0	0
Clogs and fhoes, 10s.; other cloathing, &c. £ 1. 18s. 6d.	2	8	6
	£ 18	0	0

This man has a careful wife, who could fupport herfelf and family with her hufband's earnings, viz. 4s. a week.

The following is a ftatement of the earnings and expences of a woman, aged 61, and is an inftance of Cumberland economy among many others that might be pointed out.

	£.	s.	d.
She fpins wool for her neighbours about 15 weeks a year, and earns 4d. a day and victuals, - - -	1	10	0
The remaining 37 weeks, fhe fpins lint at home for a manufacturer, and earns 13½d. a week - - -	2	1	7½
Total earnings,	£3	11	7½
Intereft of £10. - - -	0	10	0
Total income,	£4	1	7½

EXPENCES.

	£.	s.	d.
Houfe-rent, 10s.—fuel (peat and turf), 7s. - -	0	17	0
Barley, 2½ bufhels at 5s. - - - -	0	12	6
Oatmeal, 6 ftone at 2s. 4d. - - -	0	14	0
Butter, 8 lb. at 8d.—5s. 4d.—Milk, 220 quarts, 5s. 6½d.	0	10	10½
She gets 3 pecks of potatoes planted for her: her turf afhes produce about 9 bufhels: balance of expence about	0	2	0
Tea, not ufed: fugar and treacle - - -	0	4	0
Salt, candle, foap, &c. &c. - - -	0	4	0
Clogs, (one pair in 2 years,) 1s. 6d: fhoes one pair in 7 years, 6d. - - - - -	0	2	0
Butcher's meat, 1s. 6d.: wheaten bread, 1s. - -	0	2	6
Shifts, 2s. 9d.; other cloaths, &c. 10s. - -	0	12	9
Total expences,	£4	1	7½

This woman's earnings are fmall; but fhe makes her expences correfpond. She feems perfectly happy, content and cheerful; and always takes care to avoid debt. Her father rented a fmall farm of only £8. a year; and as he was very lame, fhe was obliged to do the greateft part of the work. On his death fhe difpofed of the ftock, &c. and after difchaiging all his debts and funeral expences, a furplus of £10. remained, which fhe placed in the hands of her landlord; the intereft of which pays her

rent.

ient. When she was able to reap in harvest, she earned a little more money; yet, notwithstanding her present scanty income, she has no thoughts of applying to the parish: She receives no assistance whatever from her friends. Her common diet is hasty-pudding, milk, butter, and potatoes. She was brought up in a most frugal manner, and feels no inconvenience from being obliged to live so abstemiously. She never had a tea-pot in her house, at any period of her life.

The common expence of clogs, for a year, in this country (supposing no shoes to be worn) is 4s. 4d. for a man that works out of doors; and about 3s 8d for a man within doors; for a woman 3s. 6d.; and for a boy, about 12 years old, 3s. &c

April, 1796.

G I L C R U X.

THIS parish contains about 1200 acres, of which 100 are common. 24 houses pay the commutation tax, of which number 10 are stated to have 7 windows; 12 are exempted. There are 207 inhabitants, of whom, 11 are colliers, 2 shoe-makers, 1 a carpenter, 2 blacksmiths, 1 a clogger, 1 a tailor, 3 publicans; and the rest farmers, and agricultural labourers. The inhabitants are all of the established religion. The rent of land is from 6s. to to 21s. an acre: the average is about 14s. The land-tax is at the rate of 3¾d. in the pound; and amounts to £10. 4s 10½d. Tithes are paid in kind, with the exception of hay, for which a small modus is paid. About 400 acres, of common-field, have been enclosed, within the last 50 years. The wages of labourers are, in harvest, 10d. 1s. and 14d. a day, with victuals; at other times of the year, 10d. a day, with victuals.

The parish rents part of a poor-house at Cockermouth for £2. a year. This is intended as a check on the class of indigent persons, that fall within the description of " Sturdy Beggars." No Pauper, undeservedly necessitous, has ever been sent thither. The following is a list of those who receive parochial aid:

J. H. aged 36; formerly a sailor; now insane; receives from the parish £8. 15s. a year; and £1. 10s. annually, from a sailors' club at Whitehaven.

L. M.

L. M aged 66, unmarried; has been chargeable above 30 years; re-eeives £4. a year.

J. W. aged 70; unmairied, receives about £3. 18s. a year.

A baftard cofts the parifh 1s. 6d. weekly; and cloaths.

Another baftard cofts the parifh 1s. weekly; and cloaths.

Of 3 removals, (namely 2 into, and 1 from the parifh;) which have taken place within the laft 20 years, 1 was contefted a few years ago. The attorney's bill on that occafion amounted to £14.

The Poor's Rate is collected by the purvey: the only difburfements from it are for the Poor, removals, and journeys of overfeers.

Years	Poor's Rate. £. s. d.			Years.	Baptifms.	Burials.
1775	35	12	6	1775	3	1
1776	16	2	5½	1776	4	7
1777	16	3	9½	1777	6	4
1778	31	18	2	1778	6	3
1779	27	13	3½	1779	2	1
1780	33	7	4	1780	4	1
1781	no account			1781	4	2
1782	29	8	9¾	1782	4	3
1783	27	7	10½	1783	10	8
1784	29	14	10	1784	5	4
1785	24	13	3	1785	4	6
1786	27	16	9	1786	4	4
1787	30	5	9½	1787	5	2
1788	26	13	10	1788	2	1
1789	27	8	1	1789	6	3
1790	35	17	1½	1790	6	8
1791	44	15	9½	1791	2	2
1792	49	3	6½	1792	7	2
1793	36	12	9½	1793	9	4
1794	46	1	11½	1793	5	4

19) 596 17 11¾   20) 98   20) 70

Aver. of 19 yrs. 31 8 3¾   Aver. of 20 yrs. 4 9/10   3½

The average is about 9¾d. on the full rental.

January, 1795.

H A R.

HARRINGTON.

THIS parifh is fituated on the coaft, a little to the fouthward of Workington: of 1600 acres, (it's eftimated extent,) 700 acres, of common, were enclofed about 20 years ago. The number of inhabitants is 1412 : whereof 252 are failors; 268 colliers; about 500 are engaged in various occupations relative to commerce, and manufacture ; and the reft are farmers, and agricultural labourers : they are chiefly of the eftablifhed church   101 houfes pay the commutation, or window-tax ; 6 of which have above 6 windows : 163 are exempted. The whole number of houfes is 264 ; of families 307. Land lets from 5s. to 25s. an acre : the average price may be ftated at 13s. or 14s. The land-tax annually raifed in this parifh is £.13. 6s. 10½d. which is about 2½d. in the pound on the full rental. Labourers, here, are principally employed in the collieries ; and work by the piece : they earn from 1s. 3d. to 2s. 6d a day

No account, refpecting the Poor's Rate, goes farther back than 1779. The following table exhibits the annual collection for the Poor, and other purpofes, from that period ; and, in a few of the fubfequent years, the net fums annually expended on the Poor :

Years.	Total collected. £. s. d.	Net Expend. on the Poor. £. s. d.	Baptifms.	Burials.
1774	— — —	— — —	30	11
1775	— — —	— — —	37	19
1776	— — —	— — —	38	30
1777	— — —	— — —	36	34
1778	— — —	— — —	34	11
1779	68 16 3	— — —	21	13
1780	82 11 6	— — —	37	18
1781	82 11 6	— — —	24	32
1782	96 6 9	— — —	37	10
1783	55 1 0	— — —	37	8
1784	96 6 9	— — —	42	28
1785	110 2 0	— — —	37	21
1786	96 6 9	— — —	30	12
1787	81 9 0	69 16 1	30	27
1788	82 14 0	64 16 2	38	25
1789	96 7 11	84 9 3	24	20
1790	110 2 0	101 14 5	31	25
1791	123 17 3	115 18 3	26	22
1792	166 7 0	160 19 0	45	34
1793	111 7 4	104 5 10	37	23
1794	153 2 8	145 10 2	39	25
	16) 1613 9 8	21) 710	21) 448

Aver. of 16 yrs. 100 16 10¼   Aver. of 21 yrs. 33⅘   21⅓

This average is at the rate of 1s. 4d. in the pound on the full rental.

This

This year the parifh began to maintain the Poor in Workington poor-houfe; for which £10. a year are paid for rent; and 2s. 2d. a week for every Pauper, fent thither, lunatics excepted. The Poor have fuch a diflike to this mode of provifion, that it is expected this new fyftem will lower the Rates very confiderably.

The following is the lift of the Poor.

2 children, orphans; one 5, the other 9 years old: their father was a footman

N. T. a failor's widow, aged 40, fick; has 3 children, 3, 6, and 10 years old.

M. T. a farmer's widow, aged 60; has her houfe-rent paid by the parifh.

L. L. a widow, aged 65; and her daughter, aged 40, deferted by her hufband; receives annually 30s. for houfe-rent.

J. J. a baker, lame, aged 60; his wife nearly of the fame age: laft year they were allowed 5s. a week from the parifh; but now prefer receiving 30s. annually for houfe-rent, to going to Workington poor-houfe.

E. P. a failor's widow, with 4 children, aged 35; received 3s. a week laft year: the parifh now only pays her houfe-rent.

R. H aged 55, a failor's widow, receives 34s. annually, for houfe-rent: laft year fhe received a weekly penfion.

J. G. a baker, afflicted with the rheumatifm; he and his wife, aged 48, received, laft year, 2s. a week: at prefent, their only allowance is 30s. annually, for houfe-rent.

J. H a widow, aged 64; paralytic; receives 21s. a year for houfe-rent.

J. J. 42 years of age; has had 6 baftards; has 26s. yearly, for houfe-rent; laft year, fhe had 2s. a week.

T. a butcher's widow, aged 70; had 2s. a week laft year; receives now 30s. for houfe-rent.

J. S. aged 60; a miner: laft year he received 1s. 6d. a week; but now, rather than go to the poor-houfe, he declines receiving any thing from the parifh.

M. G. a failor's widow, aged 68; has a weekly allowance of 1s. 6d.

J. T. aged 28; a militia man's wife, is allowed 2s. a week.

J. P. aged 42; a miner's widow, with 2 children; had laft year 2s. a week; at prefent receives 30s. annually, for houfe-rent.

M. B.

M. B. A labourer's widow, aged 65; receives 6d. a week.
A baftard child, 6 years old.

There is a Friendly Society in this parifh, confifting of colliers: their number is about 160: they have no printed rules. Mr. Curwen contributes liberally towards raifing their funds; but if any of the members work 12 days for another mafter, they are excluded from receiving any benefit. Six removals from this parifh have taken place fince 1786: none were contefted; although preparations were made for that purpofe: the expences of 4 of thefe removals were £9. 4s. 8d.— £1. 9s. 2d —£1. 0s. 6d. —£11. 2s. 0d. *January*, 1795.

H E S K E T

THE form of the parifh of Hefket is very irregular: it contains about 19,200 acres, (whereof the greater part is common,) and is divided into four quarters, namely, Hefket, Plumpton, Stonfield, and Petrill-Crooks; there are feven villages in the parifh, called Hefket, Low Hefket, Aketyate, Nunclofe, Armathwaite, Old Town, and Cawthwaite. 260 families occupy lands; 70 families are cottagers: the number of inhabitants, who with the exception of a few mechanics, and innkeepers, are employed in agriculture, is 1150. They are, moftly, of the eftablifhed Church. Many cottages have been pulled down within the prefent century; and the following table of births, burials, and marriages, exhibits a declining population. 160 houfes, (11 of which have 6 windows,) pay the commutation tax: 70 are exempted.

Births from 1682 to 1702—761 ⎫ decreafe, 196.
1770 to 1790—565 ⎭
Burials from 1682 to 1702—591 ⎫ decreafe, 215
1770 to 1790—376 ⎭
Marriages from 1672 to 1691—160 ⎫ decreafe, 2.
1770 to 1790—158 ⎭

The chief articles of cultivation are wheat, oats, barley, turnips, peafe, and clover; fome potatoes are alfo grown. Rye, of late years, has not been much attended to in Cumberland, being efteemed a great impoverifher of the land The common courfes of crops, are, 1 fallow, 2 wheat,
3 barley,

3 barley, or oats; 4 oats, or peafe; or, 1 turnips, 2 barley, 3 clover one year, 4 oats. Good grafs land lets at 30s. and 40s. an acre: it is ufed, chiefly, for dairying, and for the occafional grazing of droves, that pafs through the parifh. Farms are fiom £10. to £100. a year; the land-tax is collected by the puivey at the iate of about 2½d. in the pound on the full rental. No more than 200 acres have been enclofed, within the laft 50 years; a large portion, however, of the parifh appears to have had it's hedges planted a little before that peiiod.

In harveft, men receive from 10d. to 14d. a day, with diet: women, from 10d. to 1s. with diet. A haymaker gets from 8d. to 1s. a day, with diet. In wintei, till Candlemas, the wages of agricultural labour, are 8d. a day, with victuals; and, after Candlemas, 10d. a day, with victuals. Mowing grafs, is 2s. 6d. an acre. Ditching, from 4d. to 9d. a rood. A headman's yearly wages are from £10. to £14. A next fervant from £8. to £10. a year: a boy of 12 years of age, 25s; a dairy-maid from £4. to £5.; other women fervants from £3. to £3. 10s.

The Poor's Rate was collected by the purvey, till about four years ago, when a valuation and pound-rate took place. The fum annually expended on the Poor could not be made out; but the fums below are the annual collections for the ufe of the Poor and other purpofes.

Years.	Total collected.			Years.	Total collected.		
	£.	s.	d.		£.	s.	d.
1774	157	10	0	1784	210	0	0
1775	105	0	0	1785	157	10	0
1776	140	0	0	1786	157	10	0
1777	105	0	0	1787	210	0	0
1778	122	10	0	1788	157	10	0
1779	157	10	0	1789	157	10	0
1780	157	10	0	1790	205	11	1½
1781	262	10	0	1791	202	15	0
1782	210	0	0	1792	256	1	9½
1783	210	0	0	1793	228	8	3½
				1794	229	17	10½

10) 1627 10 0

Average of 10 years £.162 15 0

11) 2172 14 1

Aveiage of 11 years £ 197 10 4½

Average of 10 years, from 1774 to 1783 inclusive, £162 15 0
Average of 11 years, from 1784 to 1794 inclusive, 197 10 4½

2) 360 5 4½

Average of 21 years, from 1774 to 1794 inclusive, £180 2 8¼

This average is collected at the rate of 6½d. in the pound on the full rental.

This parish has made an agreement with the parish of St. Mary, Carlisle, in consequence of which, the latter receives all descriptions of Poor from Hesket into a work-house in Carlisle; for which Hesket pays £4. annually for house rent; and 2s. 6d. a week, with every Pauper sent to Carlisle. Occasional relief is, however, given to a number of poor people at home: a parish meeting is held every month, to which the necessitous apply, and are relieved at the discretion of the overseers; if they refuse what is offered them, they are sent to the work-house—an alternative, which they always wish, and, generally, contrive, to avoid. The following is a list of the Poor, who, at present, receive occasional parochial aid, at their own homes.

1 C. L. aged 75; a widow; her late husband was an idle, unsteady fellow.
2 E. S. a farmer's widow; aged 75; old age brought her on the parish.
3 M G. a soldier's widow, aged 65.
4 G. A. formerly rented a small farm; his age is about 80.
5 His wife, nearly of the same age.
6 J. C. a blacksmith, aged 25; he is not very industrious.
7 H's wife, as idle as her husband: they have 3 children.
8 J. T. aged 80; was a small farmer.
9 J. H. aged 70; a blacksmith.
10 A B. a labourer's widow, aged 80.
11 M R a labourer's widow, aged 75.
12 J B. a small farmer's widow, aged 70.
13 The wife of J S. aged 30; insane.
14 S T. aged 35, deserted by her husband, a groom; has 5 children.
15 S. E. a widow, with three children, aged 55.
16 M R. a small farmer's widow, aged 67.

17 S.

17 S. a blind beggar, and his wife.

18 M. N a mafon's widow, aged 30; has 2 children.

19 S K. a labourer's widow, aged 75.

20 S. B. deferted by her hufband, a tailor; fince which fhe has had 2 baftards.

21 R. H. aged 76; was a weaver, but is now blind.

22 C. a widow, aged 55; deaf.

23 G. S. aged 75; was a maltfter, and farmer.

24 J. G. aged 45; is a broom-maker, and has a fmall family.

The number of Paupers in the work-houfe at Carlifle is very fluctuating: at prefent, there are in it 12, belonging to this parifh.

No accounts are preferved refpecting removals or certificates. An old man, however, who had ferved the office of overfeer 14 years, fays, that as near as he can guefs, taking one year with another, about 5 removals happen every 3 years; 3 into, and 2 from, the parifh. 6 or 7 contefts took place, during his continuance in office.

The intereft of a donation of £50. is annually diftributed to the indigent, who do not receive parochial relief.

There is one Friendly Society in Hefket, confifting of 140 members.

January, 1795.

KIRKOSWALD.

THE parifh of Kirkofwald contains by eftimation 12,800 acres; of which the greater part is mountainous common. The parifh confifts of two parts; Kirkofwald, and Staffold divifion. In the former there are 654 inhabitants, confifting of the families of 8 tailors, 3 weavers, 16 common labourers, 1 cooper, 3 mafons, 5 fhoe-makers, 1 officer of excife, 2 joiners, 1 furgeon, 5 blackfmiths, 1 butcher, 2 inn-keepers, 4 carpenters, 3 paper-makers, 1 rope-maker, 1 grocer, 3 millers, 1 dyer, 1 fuller, 10 miners, 1 fchool-mafter, and 1 gardener; all of which are of the Church of England, except one Prefbyterian, and one Quaker family.—In Staffold, there are 283 inhabitants: the families are; 1 mill-wright, 2 fhoe-makers,

6 com-

6 common-labourers, 1 blackfmith, 1 gardener, 1 mafon, and 1 weaver, all of the Church of England, except 6 Prefbyterians. The total population of the paiifh is 937.

In Kirkofwald divifion 56 houfes pay the commutation tax, of which 8 have above 6 windows; and 78 are exempted. In Staffold divifion, 41 houfes, (4 of which have above 6 windows,) pay the commutation tax; and 20 are exempted.

Tenements are from £ 30. to £ 150. a year: the cultivated parts of the parifh are very productive; fallowing, liming, and dunging being much attended to. The clay lands produce good crops of wheat, barley, and oats: in the lighter foil, turnips have been intioduced with fuccefs: clover and grafs feeds are, likewife, fometimes fown. Some lands let as high as 45s. an acre: the average, however, of the whole parifh cannot be ftated at more than 14s. or 15s. There are about 6,000 fheep, (chiefly fhort Scots,) in the parifh. The average weight of fleeces is 7 to the ftone of 16lb. It is obferved, that the higheft grounds, and coarfeft herbage, produce the heavieft fheep, and worft wool. Few cattle are bred for fale. The eftates of the principal proprietors are tithe-free: others pay in kind. The land-tax is collected by the purvey, at the rate of about 2¼d. in the pound, in Kirkofwald divifion, and, in Staffold divifion, at 2¾d. in the pound, on the full rental. There have been very few enclofures made within the laft 50 years.

In harveft men receive 1s. and 1s. 2d. a day, and victuals; women 10d. and 1s. a day, and victuals. Threfhers, ditchers, &c. earn from 4s. to 5s. a week, and victuals. The general employment of the female part of a labourer's family, not only here, but in moft parts of Cumberland, is fpinning lint, or flax; when they are not otherwife engaged. All the coarfer fort of linen ufed by the inhabitants, is chiefly manufactured at home, and is thought to be more durable than that made by a profeffional manufacturer. The wages of fpinners are, however, very inconfiderable: a woman muft labour hard at her wheel, 10 or 11 hours in the day, to earn 4d. Whether the poverty of women engaged in this manufacture, is afcribable to low wages, I fhall not, here, attempt to inveftigate; but the fact certainly is, that in the north of England, where fpinning is much attended to, many more women, than men, are neceffitated to folicit parochial affiftance.

6   Befides

Befides the linen manufacture for houfhold ufe, there is a fmall manufactory of paper in the parifh.

There are two Friendly Societies: one, inftituted in 1758, confifts of 68 members; the other was eftablifhed in 1783, and has 84 members. Their regulations are very fimilar, and are foon to be fubmitted to the magiftrates for confirmation.

Each divifion feparately maintain it's own Poor: and does not join with the other, except in repairing the church In Staffold divifion are the folfollowing Paupers:

H. B. a fmall farmer's widow, aged 70 : fhe receives 1s. 6d. a week.

T. L. aged 70 ; once a farmer, now afflicted with the rheumatifm : his weekly allowance is 2s.

E. T. a farmer's widow, with a fmall family, aged 60 : has 2s. a week from the parifh.

A baftaid child, 2 years old, cofts the parifh 1s. 6d. a week.

A baftard child, 4 years old, cofts the parifh 1s. 3d. a week.

Befides thefe, 6 or 7 poor families have their houfe-1ents, which amount to from 12s to 20s. yearly, difcharged by the divifion.

The following are the Poor in Kirkofwald divifion.

J. R. aged 73 ; formerly a fmall farmer ; mere poverty and old age brought him on the parifh : his weekly allowance is 2s.

H. H. aged 48, a paper-maker's widow, with 4 children : fhe receives 2s. 6d. weekly.

A. S. aged 42, a labourer's widow ; an induftrious woman, with a fmall family ; the parifh allows her 2s. 6d. a week.

M. T. a widow, aged 70, receives 2s. a week.

A baftard child, 8 years old, cofts the parifh 1s. a week.

J. H. a widow, 45 years old, has a family, and receives 3s 6d. a week. Her hufband was a fhoe-maker.

M. I. a mafon's widow, aged 94, thrown on the parifh, through poverty and mere old age : her weekly allowance is 3. 6d.

M. W. a dyer's widow, aged 42, receives 1s. 6d. a week.

J. B. aged 36, deferted by her hufband, who left her with 2 children : fhe is allowed 2s. a week.

A baftard child, cofts the parifh 1s. a week.

M. D.

.M. D. aged 78 ; is a miller's widow, and receives a weekly allowance of 1s. 6d.

C. T. aged 83, a weaver's widow ; and her infirm daughter, aged 36, 1eceive weekly 2s.

W. N. aged 84 ; was a hufbandman ; old age and poverty brought him on the parifh : he receives 1s. 6d. a week.

J. A. a fmall farmer's widow, aged 80 ; receives 2s. a week.

A baftard child, cofts the parifh 1s. a week.

Another, 1s. 6d. a week.

Another, 1s. 6d. a week.

Another, 1s. 6d. a week.

Another, 2s. a week.

Befides thefe regular penfioners, others receive occafional relief.

About 5 years ago, a ftranger, with a certificate, fettled in Kirkofwald divifion. Three ceitificates are known to have been granted from it ; but not within the laft 20 years. Within that period 4 removals have occurred ; 2 from, and 2 into this part of the parifh : none were contefted. One perfon was, likewife, removed from Staffold a few years ago, without occafioning litigation ; and another peifon, within the laft 20 years, was received into it, under an order of removal : this was contefted, and coft the parifh between £ 12. and £ 13.

Years.	Difburfements in Kirkofwald Divifion			Collections by Chuich-wardens for the whole parifh			Collections by Ovei-feers for the whole parifh			Baptifms	Burials	Mairiages.
	£.	s.	d.	£.	s.	d.	£.	s.	d.			
1774	45	7	4	14	14	9	7	12	8	15	6	4
1775	42	11	4¼	8	2	10½	7	13	4	15	11	3
1776	44	13	6	2	17	8½	6	13	2½	17	18	9
1777	46	1	10	2	12	1½	8	10	7½	22	14	5
1778	42	7	2	2	12	6	3	15	10	16	10	4
1779	68	16	8½	2	13	1½	4	15	2½	20	9	5
1780	70	4	3	2	12	6	6	17	1½	19	10	9
1781	81	9	0	5	6	0	3	16	0	21	9	4
1782	100	10	2	3	12	6	6	12	5	18	15	7
1783	102	13	4	2	12	0	7	11	4	20	16	6
1784	107	18	6	1	15	2	8	9	5¼	13	13	2

Years.	Disbursements in Kirkoswald Division			Collections by Churchwardens for the whole parish			Collections by Overseers for the whole parish			Baptisms.	Burials	Marriages
	£.	s.	d.	£.	s.	d.	£.	s.	d.			
1785	97	18	2	No accounts.			7	11	4	15	11	7
1786	83	1	5½	2	13	1½	7	11	7	19	14	7
1787	62	1	5	2	13	3½	5	13	9	19	11	2
1788	82	14	11	2	13	3¾	4	4	0½	15	9	10
1789	No accounts.			18	2	1	5	16	6½	17	14	1
1790	89	6	10	2	13	3¾	7	11	8	17	18	4
1791	140	5	2	2	13	3¾	9	9	7	16	15	4
1792	No accounts.			No accounts.			No accounts.			15	18	5
1793	93	1	8¾	2	13	9½	7	3	7	25	19	7
1794	122	12	4	5	5	7½	8	18	9¾			
									20)	354	260	105

Average of 20 years - 17¾ 13 5½

The average of the Poor's Rate for 19 years is £ 80. 3s. 11d. which is about 9¾d. in the pound on the full rental. The Poor's Rate, till within the last 3 or 4 years, was collected by the purvey: a sort of valuation was then made, and, in consequence, a pound-rate has been introduced; but, as is the case in most other parishes where a pound-rate is used, it is here so much disguised, that without various explanations, (which are rarely given without great reluctance,) it becomes very difficult to ascertain what proportion parochial taxes bear to the rental of the parish.

In Staffold division, the accounts have not been regularly preserved; but from the best information that could be obtained, the Poor's Rate, during the last 20 years, has varied from £ 3. to £ 36. 18s. The annual average may be stated at £ 16. or £ 17. which is about 4d. in the pound on the full rental. *December*, 1794.

NENT HEAD.

THE following is a statement of the earnings and expences of a miner, who lives at Nent Head, on Alston Moor in this county.

He is 45 years of age; has a wife, and 7 children, 2 of which are boys, and 5 girls: the eldest girl is 18 years old; the youngest 1 year old.

EARN-

EARNINGS.

	£.	s.	d.
He earns on an average, yearly - - -	26	0	0
His wife and children, occasionally, wash ore, and earn yearly about	18	0	0
Total - £	44	0	0

YEARLY EXPENCES.

	£.	s.	d.
House-rent - - - - -	3	0	0
Fuel (peat) - - - - -	1	0	0
Barley bread - - - -	5	10	0
Milk - - - - -	1	16	0
Butcher's meat - - - -	10	0	0
Potatoes - - - - -	4	0	0
Oatmeal - - - - -	4	0	0
Cheese - - - - -	1	0	0
Tea and sugar - - - -	3	10	0
Butter - - - - -	3	0	0
Soap, candles, and groceries - - -	2	0	0
Cloathing, and other incidental expences - -	5	4	0
Total - £	44	0	0

This man had 3 other children which died: he says, the total expence of his wife's 10 lying-ins amounted to near £ 20.

The following are the earnings and expenditure of another miner's family of the same place.

The man is 39 years old; has a wife and 4 boys, and 4 girls, living: he has lost 2 children: the eldest is 18; his youngest 1½ year old.

EARNINGS.

	£.	s.	d.
The man earns every year about - - -	30	0	0
The oldest boy works in the mines, and earns yearly, about	18	0	0
The rest of the family earn - - - -	0	0	0
Total - £	48	0	0

EXPEN-

EXPENCES.

	£	s.	d.
House-rent - - - - -	3	0	0
Peat for fuel cofts nothing but labour to dig it - -	0	0	0
Bread, (barley and rye) - - - -	10	0	0
Oatmeal - - - - -	5	0	0
Butcher's meat, (chiefly beef) - - -	8	0	0
Potatoes - . - - - -	4	0	0
Butter - - - - -	5	0	0
Milk - - - - - -	0	10	0
Tea and fugar - - - -	3	10	0
Wheat flour - - - - -	0	10	0
Cheefe - - - - -	0	16	0
Cloaths, groceries, &c. - - - -	7	14	0
Total -	£48	0	0

The parifh of Alfton, in which Nent Head is fituated, is very extenfive, and is moftly common. In it are 46 ale-houfes : the miners are much given to drinking, but become more fober, when married : they live chiefly on crowdie, barley, rye, and butcher's meat. Poor's Rates are 2s. 10d. in the pound, and amount annually to about £900 : 2 years fince, the Rates were at 2s. 6d. ; and 8 or 10 years ago, at 1s. 6d. The land is all in grafs. *March*, 1796.

SEBERGHAM.

THIS parifh contains by eftimation 2420 acres of old cultivated land ; and by admeafurement 2576 of common, which was divided about 28 years ago. About 80 of the inhabitants are employed in the coal-pits, 13 are bleachers, 2 blackfmiths, 7 joiners, 3 weavers, 2 fhoe-makers, and 4 publicans. They are all of the eftablifhed Church. 80 houfes pay the commutation tax ; 9 are ftated to have above 6 windows : and 148 are excepted.

The average rent of land is 14s. an acre : the land-tax is collected by the purvey', at the rate of about 2¼d. in the pound. Tithes are paid for by composition; which is regulated by an Act of Parliament, relative to this parish, that passed a few years ago: the clergyman receives annually the price of a certain number of bushels of wheat; the value whereof is fixed at certain periods by two persons, one appointed by each party.

Labourers in harvest have 1s. a day and victuals, men and women; in other works of husbandry, between Martinmas and Candlemas 10d. a day; and 1s. a day and victuals the rest of the year.

In this parish there are no Friendly Societies or charities.

The Poor of this parish were farmed for some years back; but upon the Contractor's not allowing them sufficient victuals, the Justices refused their acquiescence; and a parish allowance is now given to each Pauper at home. The following is a description of the persons that receive parochial aid.

G. E aged 80; a weaver: he receives 1s. 6d. a week.

A. B. aged 70; a maltster's widow, lame; she receives 1s. 6d. weekly.

A. M. aged 46; lame in her hands, has had 7 bastards, and receives at present for two of them, 2s. 6d. a week.

A. W. aged 66; a miner's widow, receives 1s. a week.

———; a bastard child, 1s. 6d.

M. P. aged 74; a carpenter's widow, receives 1s a week.

J. S. aged 70; a miner, sickly; receives 1s. 6d. weekly
2 bastards; twins; cost 3s. a week.

S. B. a labourer, (whose child is an idiot,) receives weekly 1s.

A G aged 50; lame; receives weekly 2s. 6d.

M. D aged 70; receives 2s. 9d a week.

S. G. deranged in her mind, receives weekly 2s.

B. R. aged 83; a widow, has 1s. 6d. a week.

' The *purvey* originally was a composition in money for the king's *purveyance*, or providing for his houshold when he went on a progress into different parts of the kingdom. In some places it was paid in cattle or other provisions in kind: hence in Lancashire they have a manner of laying assessments still called *on-lay*. Against king James's return out of Scotland through the county of Cumberland in September 1617, the Justices of the Peace were ordered to compound for the king's purveyance at the rate of £108 or thereabouts: which sum being laid on the whole county, became afterwards a standard for regulating other assessments; and when the sum of £108 was raised, it was called one purvey, and so on In the year 1665, for the greater ease and convenience, the purvey was fixed at the precise sum of £100. So that now where the sum of £100 is raised, it is called one purvey; where £200. two purveys; and so on Thirty-seven purveys and a half are raised for the land-tax, when it is 4s. in the pound.—*Nicolson and Burn's History of Westmoreland and Cumberland.* i. 13.

A. F.

A. F. aged 68; a widow, receives weekly 1s.

J. T. and family; he is rather foolish, and his wife is idle; they receive 2s. a week.

J. R. aged 70; was a farmer, he receives 1s. a week.

— C. aged 70; blind, receives 1s. 3d. a week.

— and —, 2 bastard children, cost weekly 3s.

A. B. a widow, (with a young child,) receives 6d. weekly.

J. B. and his daughter, an idiot, now big with a bastard child, receive 1s. 6d. a week.

Exclusive of the above regular pensions, some house-rents are paid, but not more than 10s. each.

The Poor's Rates are collected by the purvey, and are wholly expended on the Poor, except in the article of removals and overseers' journies.

Years.	Assessments.			Baptisms.	Burials.	Marriages.
	£.	s.	d.			
1775	76	10	0	27	12	2
1776	63	5	0	18	21	5
1777	71	8	0	27	21	4
1778	76	10	0	34	8	5
1779	97	0	0	22	18	0
1780	97	0	0	26	12	7
1781	112	4	0	25	21	5
1782	111	12	0	19	20	10
1783	111	0	0	28	21	7
1784	112	4	0	25	15	8
1785	112	4	0	25	9	3
1786	147	18	0	30	13	10
1787	129	18	11	30	16	8
1788	149	12	1	23	18	7
1789	130	14	4	25	15	9
1790	112	6	4	30	12	5
1791	95	14	0	23	20	2
1792	76	17	0	20	15	5
1793	76	17	0	20	8	1
1794	82	8	8	24	13	4
	20) 2043	3	4	20) 501	20) 308	20) 107

Average of 20 yrs. 102 3 2 $25\frac{1}{20}$ $15\frac{1}{3}$ $5\frac{1}{3}$

Within the last 10 or 12 years there have been only 2 contested removals, which cost the parish about £10. each.   *December*, 1794.

        WAR-

WARWICK.

THE parifh of Warwick is fituated on the river Eden, about 6 miles from Carlifle : it confifts of 600 acres of common, and 1126 acres of cultivated land. The number of inhabitants, at prefent, is 347. The population has received a confiderable increafe within the laft 18 months, in confequence of a manufactory, for fpinning cottcn, having been erected in the neighbourhood : 42 families are employed folely in agriculture ; 10 in manufactures ; 10 in both agriculture and manufactures ; and 1 in trade and agriculture. 28 houfes pay the commutation tax, only 2 of which are ftated to have above 6 windows ; 35 houfes are exempted, a few of which are cottages, that have been built within the laft 20 years. Eftates in this parifh are about £20 a year, and chiefly occupied by proprietors : the average rent of land is 19s. or 20s an acre. Good wheat is grown near the river ; and in other parts of the parifh, turnips, potatoes, rye, barley, oats, and clover, and other grafs feeds, are cultivated. Tithe is, moftly, paid in kind. There is a fmall common in the middle of the parifh : almoft the whole of the cultivated land has been enclofed within the laft 50 years. It formerly, although divided, lay in long flips, or narrow dales, feparated from each other by ranes, or narrow ridges of land, which are left unplowed. In this manner, a great deal, and, perhaps, the whole of the cultivated lands in Cumberland, was anciently difpofed. The land-tax is collected by the purvey, and, as nearly as can be afcertained, amounts to 3d. in the pound on the full and fair rental. The wages of labourers are much the fame as in the neighbouring parifh of Wetheral.

The Poor, who are regular penfioners, are enumerated in the following lift.

A. S. aged 50 ; a little infane ; was formerly employed in needle-work ; has been chargeable fome years : the parifh allows 4s. weekly, for her maintenance.

M. B. a widow, aged 45 ; has received parochial aid, about 10 years : her allowance is £2. a year, which added to her earnings by fpinning, and working for farmers, is fufficient to maintain her, and her children.

M. B. a widow, aged 40 years ; has been chargeable 5 years : fhe receives 3s. a week. Her hufband was a weaver, but in confequence of bad health, was obliged to apply for affiftance from the parifh,

parifh, which, fince his death, has been continued to his widow, and children.

M. W. aged 60; a widow, with a fmall family; has received parochial aid 20 years; her prefent allowance is £2 a year; her own endeavours were not fufficient for their fupport: her hufband rented a fmall farm in the parifh.

A few other indigent parifhioners receive occafional relief. There are no parifh books previous to the year 1789.

Affeffments for the Poor and other purpofes from 16 June	Total Affeffments.			Expend on the Poor.		
	£.	s	d.	£.	s	d.
1789 to 1 May 1790 were	62	1	7	14	6	6
From 1 May 1 90 to 18 May 1791	49	19	4	36	1	3
From 18 May 1791 to 17 May 1792	41	9	0	25	6	2
From 17 May 1792 to 9 May 1793	38	5	2	25	12	6
From 9 May 1793 to 5 May 1794	48	12	4½	30	1	7½

No certificate has been granted by this parifh, or any certificated perfons received into it within the recollection of any of the parifhioners: only one Pauper came into it by a removal, which was not contefted.

January, 1795.

WETHERAL.

THE parifh of Wetheral, by a late admeafurement, was found to contain 7556 acres of cultivated land; and by eftimation 2500 acres of common. Of 1413 inhabitants, 116 are employed in manufacturing cotton; 55 are artificers, for making implements of hufbandry, houfhold furniture, &c.; and the reft follow the various occupations of agriculture. There are 6 petty grocers fhops in the parifh: 172 houfes, of which 6 only have above 6 windows, pay the commutation tax; 129 are exempted. There has been very little variation in thefe matters during the laft 20 years.

The rent of land varies from 5s. to 50s. an acre: the average is about 14s. The land-tax is collected, by the purvey, at the rate of about 2d. in the pound on the full rental. Tithe is payable in kind in near five fixths of the parifh, for all produce; except for hay, of which the tithe is payable in kind, in about one third of the parifh.

The

The following is a statement of the tithes paid by a farm of 100 acres; rent £80. a year.

Acres.		Gross Produce £.	Value of the Tithe £.	s.	d.
10 — Turnips,	- - - -	25	0	0	0
10 — Barley,	- - - -	50	5	0	0
10 — Oats,	- - - -	28	2	16	0
10 — Pease,	- - - -	25	2	10	0
10 — Oats,	- - - -	20	2	0	0
15 — Meadow, &c in hay,	- - -	30	3	0	0
7 — Depastured with sheep,	- -	14	1	8	0
28 — Depastured with horses, and black cattle		35	0	0	0
100		£227	£16	14	0

The above statement is sometimes below the amount, but, in bad seasons, considerably, above it. About 3000 acres have been enclosed within the last 50 years

Labourers in husbandry, affistant masons, &c. receive, in summer, from 16d. to 18d. a day, without victuals; and about 13d. a day, without diet, throughout the year. Women, in harvest, earn 1s. a day, and their dinner; and in weeding corn, &c. 10d. a day without, and 6d. with, victuals.

In this parish are two Friendly Societies, whose rules are very similar.

The Poor of this parish have been farmed for several years back; about a month ago, however, a house was hired by the parishioners, and has been converted into a work-house, wherein the under-mentioned Paupers are lodged, and maintained.

R. A. aged 40; has been supported, 4 years, by the parish: he was formerly a labourer in husbandry, and was reduced by blindness, to apply for parochial affistance.

R. A. aged 88; has been 6 years under the care of the parish: he was formerly a small farmer, and became a Pauper, from old age and its attendant misfortunes.

J. B. aged 40 years; was born lame, and has been chargeable these last three years: he was once a labourer in husbandry, and can still do a little work.

M. G. aged 52; has been 6 years on the parish: she became a little

6   insane,

infane, in confequence, (it is fuppofed,) of her hufband, who was a blackfmith, having deferted her.

E. P. aged 42; a fpinfter, was always rather idiotifh; has had two baftard children; and has been chargeable above 12 years.

M. H. aged 40; is a lunatic, and is kept in a private houfe, for 4s. a week: her hufband, a labourer, is not chargeable to the parifh.

S. and her 4 children have had a parifh allowance feveral years. Since the erection of the work-houfe, they have not received any thing; but are expected to enter it very foon.

12 Children from 3 to 14 years of age; one is a baftard; the others belong to parents, who are utterly incapable of fupporting them.

No out-penfions are granted, except on account of young baftard children. The rent of the work-houfe is £8. The mafter's falary is £17. a year; and he, and his wife, are allowed their victuals; but the parifh is to receive their earnings.

The women have been employed in fpinning wool, for cloathing, and bed cloaths for the work-houfe. No plan is, yet, fixed on for the future employment of the Poor; but fpinning of wool is moftly talked of, and will, probably, be adopted.

The following has been the monthly expence of the work-houfe:

Auguſt 1794				*September* 1794.				*October* 1794.			
	£	s	d.		£.	s.	d.		£.	s.	d.
Butcher's meat,	1	0	6	Butcher's meat,	1	7	6	Butcher's meat,	-	1	7	9
Groceries,	-	0	3 6¼	Doctor's bill,	0	6	10½	Bread corn,	-	2	6	10
Bread corn,	-	1	17 8	Bread corn,	2	1	4	Milk and butter,	-	0	14	4¼
Potatoes,	-	0	9 1	Milk and butter,	0	17	8½	Groceries,	-	0	2	10½
Milk and butter,	0	14	6	Groceries,	0	3	10¼	Potatoes,	-	-	0	1	0
	£4	5	3¼	Onions,	-	0	1	3	Coals for the winter, 97 Winchefter bufhels,	}	2	11	6
				Potatoes,	-	0	6	4½				
					£5	4	10¾			£7	4	3¾

Table of Diet in the Work-houfe.

	Breakfaft.	Dinner.	Supper.
Sunday,	Hafty-pudding or boiled milk.	Meat and broth:—Each perfon has half a pound of meat; befides which, the mafter divides 4 or 5 pounds, as he thinks proper.	Broth and milk.
Monday,	The fame as Sunday.	Potatoes, generally ftewed, or hafhed, with the broken meat of Sunday.	Boiled milk.

Tuefday,

	Breakfaſt.	Dinnei.	Supper.
Tuefday,	The fame as Sunday.	Potatoes, and buttei	Milk, and barley, boiled.
Wednefday,	The fame as Sunday	The fame as Sunday.	The fame as Sunday.
Thurfday,	The fame as Monday.	The fame as Monday.	The fame as Monday.
Friday,	The fame as Sunday	5lb beef ſtewed with potatoes.	Boiled milk.
Saturday,	The fame as Sunday	The fame as Sunday.	The fame as Sunday.

The earlieſt preſerved account of paiiſh expenditures commences in 1779, but from the confuſed manner in which the diſburſements were entered, the firſt year's account could not be made out.

	Total Collection			Expence for the Pooi		
	£.	s.	d.	£.	s.	d.
The Aſſeſſments fiom 14th June 1780 to 17th July 1781　were	151	19	10	143	7	9
from 17th July 1781 to 19th July 1782　—	108	15	3	95	12	0
fiom 19th July 1782 to 13th July 1783　—	117	17	0¾	112	18	8¾
from 13th July 1783 to 28th June 1784　—	162	2	0	131	11	1
from 28th June 1784 to 22d June 1785　—	145	2	1½	123	2	8¼
from 22d June 1785 to 23d June 1786　—	175	16	4	162	10	11
from 23d June 1786 to 15th June 1787　—	171	8	2½	156	11	0½
from 15th June 1787 to 8th Sept. 1788　—	275	5	4	222	3	8
from 8th Sept. 1788 to 3d Aug. 1789　—	176	6	3½	143	12	6½
from 3d Aug. 1789 to 2d Aug 1790　—	142	15	0¼	111	17	6¼
from 2d Aug. 1790 to 17th Dec. 1791　—	203	0	7	191	19	9
fiom 17th Dec. 1791 to 19th Sept. 1792　—	107	19	3¼	95	8	8¼
from 19th Sept 1792 to 8th Feb. 1794　—	198	9	9	187	14	9
Yearly average of 13 years and 8 months -	£157	2	5	£138	2	6¼

This aveiage amounts to about 6½d. in the pound on the full and fair rental.

Fiom the right hand column are excluded all parochial charges, except what aϲtually ariſe from the maintenance, cloathing, houſe-rent, fuel, medical aid, &c. for the Poor.

No perſon can recolleϲt that a certificate was ever granted by the pariſh ; or that a certificated perſon ever came into it. Within the laſt 10 years, 5 removals from the pariſh have taken place; three were conteſted ; and, within the fame time, four Paupers have been received by the pariſh, under orders of removal. No records remain relative to tranfaϲtions of this nature, ecedent to that period.

The

The following is a ftatement of the earnings and expences of a labourer's family in this parifh :

The man is 44 years old, has a wife and 3 children ; a boy 10 years old ; 2 girls of 8 and 6 years. The man about 30 weeks in the year gets his victuals at home, and earns 9s. a week ; the remaining part of the year, he earns 5s. a week, and his victuals.—Annual earnings

	£.	s.	d.
and his victuals.—Annual earnings	19	0	0
Wife fpins lint occafionally, by which fhe earns yearly about	1	0	0
She earns in harveft about	1	5	0
The children earn nothing	0	0	0
Total earnings	£ 21	5	0

EXPENCES.

	£.	s.	d.
Houfe-rent £ 1. 11s. ; fuel, (coal,) £ 1. 16s. ; the wife's father carts the coals a little below the common price	3	6	0
Barley meal, 60 ftone at 1s. 8d.	5	0	0
Milk, 1040 quarts, at ½d. £ 2. 13s. 4d. : potatoes, 20 Winchefter bufhels, £ 1. 5s.	3	8	4
Butter, 40lb. at 8d.—£ 1. 6s. 8d. : oatmeal, 40 ftone, at 2s. 4d.—£ 2. 6s. 9d.	3	13	5
Tea, fugar, and groceries, £ 2. : clogs, 18s.	2	18	0
Cloathing, and other expences	2	19	3
Total expences	£ 21	5	0

Since the dearnefs of provifions took place, this family have ufed very little flour; and have reduced their other articles of confumption : they feed a pig annually, part of which they fell ; perhaps a balance of 20s. ought to have been added to the expences on that account.

In the above account, the prefent wages and prices of provifions are given, but the earnings are ftated at more than this man really made laft year : he was fick and unable to work near a quarter of a year laft winter ; but as he belonged to a club, from which he received 6s. a week, during the firft 6 weeks, and 4s. a week afterwards during his illnefs, his family made a fhift to fupport him and themfelves with his club-money. Potatoes and falt formed the greateft part of their meals. In fact, the labourers" families, in this county, generally reduce their expences to a level with their earnings ; and potatoes, which are a cheap food, are therefore ufed more or lefs as neceffity requires.

The contraft is very great between the above account, and the following ftatement of the earnings and expences of a manufacturer and his family, in the fame parifh.

This family confifts of a man aged 50, his wife, and 4 boys, 16 : 14 : 10: and 4 years old ; and 2 girls, 12 and 6 years old.

EARNINGS.

				£.	s.	d.
The man weaves callicoe, and earns about 7s. a week	-	18	4	0
Oldeft boy	ditto	ditto	8s. a week	-	20	16	0
Second	ditto	ditto	5s. a week	-	13	0	0
His wife, a girl, and boy, by winding cotton, earn 2s. 6d. a week - - - - -				6	10	0

Total earnings   -   £ 58 10 0

EXPENCES.

£. s. d.

Fuel, £ 2. 10s.—Rent, £ 1. 19s.   -   -   -   4 9 0

Oatmeal, 70 ftone at 2s. 4d.—£ 8. 3s. 4d. : barley, 45 Winchefter bufhels at 5s. —£ 11. 5s. : potatoes, 56 bufhels at 1s.—£ 2. 16s.   -   -   -   22 4 4

Butter, 50lb. at 8d.—£ 1. 13s. 4d. : tea and fugar, £ 2.   -   3 13 4

Butcher's meat, £ 8. 10s.: cheefe, £ 1.: candles, £ 2.   -   11 10 0

Soap, and other groceries, £ 2. 10s.: clogs, £ 1. 10s.: fhaes, £ 1.   -   -   -   -   -   5 0 0

Milk in fummer, 2s. a week : beer, in winter, 2s. a week   5 4 0

Cloaths, and other expences   -   -   -   -   6 9 4

Total expences   -   £ 58 10 0

This family is very improvident ; their earnings are great, yet they bear every mark of abject poverty ; and get into debt. It is fuppofed, if their earnings were doubled, that they would not fave any thing.

The

The following is the ftatement of the earnings and expences of another family, which confifts of a man 38 years of age, his wife, and 3 boys, whofe ages are 7 : 5 : and 2.

EARNINGS.	£.	s.	d.
He is a callicoe-weaver, and earns about £ 21. a year -	21	0	0
His wife has begun to weave, and earns about £ 8. befides taking care of her family - - - -	8	0	0
Total earnings - £	29	0	0

EXPENCES.	£.	s.	d.
Rent, £ 1. 10s.: fuel, £ 1. 15s. - - -	3	5	0
Barley, 2s. 6d. a week—£ 6. 10s: oatmeal, 50 ftone at 2s. 6d.—£ 5. 16s. 8d. : 1560 quarts of milk at ½d. £ 3. 5s.: 52lb. of butter at 8d.—£ 1. 14s. 8d. - -	17	6	4
Butcher's meat, £ 3. 10s.: potatoes, 30 bufhels, £ 1. 10s. -	5	0	0
Candles, £ 1.: foap, and other groceries, 10s. - -	1	10	0
Clogs, 13s: fhoes, 5s.: cloaths, 15s. - -	1	13	0
Other expences - - - - -	0	5	8
Total expences - £	29	0	0

This man and his wife have not been able to get any new cloaths for themfelves, thefe feveral years back ; they had been fortunately well provided with this neceffary article, previous to their marriage. *April*, 1796.

WORKINGTON.

THE parifh of Workington is fituated near the mouth of the river Derwent. It's length is about 4 miles and a half; it's breadth about 2 miles; fo that it's extent may be computed at 9 fquare miles. Workington contains between 11 and 1200 houfes; and above 6000 inhabitants; of whom about 600 are employed in the collieries contiguous to the town, owing to the coal trade, which is chiefly carried on from this port to Ireland. The population and commerce of Workington have, of late years, confiderably increafed.

creafed   There are now above 150 veffels, (on an aveiage about 130 tons each,) belonging to this port.

Theie are here, ioperies, fail-cloth, and cordage manufactories; and, near the town, an extenfive iron foundeiy, which employs a confideiable number of hands   It contains 2 blaft furnaces for melting oie; a flitting and rolling mill; feveial fuinaces for cafting, and a mill foi boiing cannon, &c. The oie is brought fiom Furnefs; and the iron-ftone dug near Harington.

Meat is, generally, dearer here than in moft paits of Cumbeiland: cod, duiing the feafon is plentiful, and often fells for $\frac{1}{2}$d the pound: herrings are not unfrequently brought from the Ifle of Man.

The Poor of this parifh are, chiefly, fupported in a large and commodious work-houfe, which can take in 150 perfons.   It is placed a little out of the town, in an open healthy fituation   The coft of the building, (which was firft inhabited by the Poor on the 28th of October 1793,) amounted to £1400. and was advanced by Mr. Curwen, the principal proprietor in this parifh, under an order of veftry.   For the liquidation of this fum the townfhip agreed to pay annually out of the Poor's Rate 8 per cent. whereof $4\frac{1}{2}$ per cent. is yearly applied to difcharge the current intereft, and $3\frac{1}{2}$ per cent. towaids paying off the principal: the inftalments carry compound intereft; but feveral yeais muft elapfe before the whole fum can be paid off.   The beneficial confequences refulting to the townfhip fiom this mode of providing for the Poor, will beft appear from the following ftatement extracted from the books belonging to the work-houfe:

For 8 years, preceding the inftitution, the fums collected
    for the maintenance of the Poor in this townfhip
    amounted to   -   -   -   £ 5197 13 $11\frac{3}{4}$

The annual average of which is   £ 649 14 $2\frac{3}{4}$
The fums collected in the 2 following
    years were   -   -   -   -   794   7 $4\frac{3}{4}$
The annual average of the 2 years   £ 397   3 $8\frac{1}{4}$
                 ———————

        Annual faving   £ 252 10 $6\frac{1}{2}$

Upon referring to the returns made to parliament in the year 1786, I
                                   find

find the expences for the Poor in 1776, and the Poor's Rates in 1783, 1784, and 1785, were as follows ;

Years.	£.	s.	d.
1776	174	4	10
1783	341	1	5
1784	410	2	4
1785	410	1	8

The Poor's Rate is collected at about 6d. in the pound on the fair rental. Every possible attention is paid to the Poor; and such as have need of parochial assistance are comfortably and amply provided for in the workhouse. I need, however, hardly repeat an observation I have made, that a work-house with all it's comforts, is not attractive: and, perhaps, the circumstance of it's not being so, is the principal cause of it's being highly beneficial.

I have been chiefly induced to notice this parish, from having been, obligingly, favoured with accounts of several Friendly Societies in the town and neighbourhood, of which a short account is here inserted. I think the reduction of the Poor's Rate is, in some degree, ascribable to the operation of these excellent institutions, as well as to the establishment of a work-house.

The Sisterly Society, at Workington, was instituted in the year 1793, under the patronage of Mrs. Curwen; and is governed by the Lady Patroness, whose office is perpetual. She is assisted by a committee of 12 members, 2 stewardesses, and a secretary, all elected annually at the anniversary meetings. There are likewise monthly meetings, at which the subscriptions are paid; delinquents fined, or reprimanded; and all other business, relative to the concerns of the Society, regularly transacted. The Society now consists of 225 members. In it's infancy, the entrance-money was 2s. 6d.: since January 1796 it has been 5s.

	£.	s.	d.
Sums collected since the commencement of the Society to Jan. 1796 - - -	300	3	9
Mr. Curwen's donation of £50.: a legacy from a lady, £20.: other donations, £5. 5s. - -	75	5	0
	£375	8	9
Disbursed in the above period - ‹, -	111	18	6
	£263	10	3
Interest, received for sums, remaining in the hands of the Lady Patroness - - -	19	18	6
Total amount of the present fund,	£283	8	9

The Coal-miners' Society, at Workington, was instituted on the 1st Jan. 1792, under the patronage of Mr. Curwen, who for every £10. collected by the Society, advances £3. :—and as a foundation, he advanced at the commencement, - - - - - £10 10 0

The collections since that period, together with Mr.
Curwen's proportion, amount to - - - 366 3 9

£376 13 9

Each member contributes 1s. a week; but by common consent, the weekly quota may be augmented. The mode of distribution to members, who are incapacitated from following their respective employments, is as follows: 5s. a week, for the first 13 weeks; 3s. a week for the next 13 weeks; 2s. 6d. a week for the next 13 weeks; and if the claimant still continues ill, 2s. a week while he is unable to work. The class of people, of whom this Society is composed, is extremely liable to various casualties.

The disbursements, since the institution of the Society, 　　£. s. d.
amount to - - - - - 375 18 4

Fund remaining on 1st Jan. 1796, 　　15 5

It seems, therefore, highly necessary for the Society, either to increase their weekly subscription, or to reduce the weekly allowance.

The Friendly Society, at Workington, which is, likewise, under the patronage of Mr. Curwen, commenced in October 1783; and is governed

by

by a prefident, a committee of 10 members, two ftewards, and a fecretary, who are all elected annually.

	£.	s.	d.
Donations to the Society by J. C. Curwen Efq. -	21	0	0
Mrs. Curwen - -	10	10	0
Anthony Bacon Efq. -	4	4	0
Thomas Harrifon Efq. -	2	2	0
	£ 37	16	0
13 years fubfcription of the members -	383	11	8
Intereft on the feveral fums unapplied - -	83	16	0
	£505	3	8
Difburfements between Oct. 1783 and 1ft Jan. 1796	358	3	4
Prefent fund, (carrying 5 per cent. intereft) £147	0	4	

The relief allowable to proper objects, previous to the 1ft Jan. 1796, was 5s. a week for 26 weeks, and afterwards 3s. a week during the incapacity of a member. The allowance is now, 7s. 6d. a week for the firft 13 weeks; 5s. 6d. a week for next 13 weeks; and 3s. 6d. a week afterwards. On the death of an indigent member, £2. 2s. are allowed towards his funeral.

The Honourable Society, at Workington, was inftituted in March 1792: it's number of members is now 100. The Society is governed by a prefident, 2 ftewards, one clerk, and 2 wardens, elected quarterly.

	£.	s.	d.
The amount of the collections fiom March 1792 to 1ft Jan. 1796 - - - - -	160	7	11
Difburfements during that period - -	59	4	2
Prefent fund - £101	3	9	

Each member of this Society, of 18 months ftanding, claiming relief, is allowed 7s. 6d. a week, for 12 months, during his incapacity to work; and 4s. a week afterwards, during the continuance of his illnefs. All fuperannuated members receive 4s. a week.

The Coalminers' Society at Harrington, (which I have flightly mentioned in
3

in the account of that parifh,) commenced in January 1793. It is under the patronage of Mr. Curwen, who contributes £3. for every £10. colle&ed in the Society.

	£.	s.	d.
His donation at the commencement - - -	10	10	0
Sums colle&ed, (including Mr. Curwen's proportion,)			
between Jan. 1793, and 1ft Jan. 1796 - -	132	4	3
	£142	14	3
Difburfements during the above period - -	125	0	7
Prefent fund - £17	17	13	8

The monthly contribution of each member is 6d. To a fick member, 6s. a week are allowed during the firft 12 weeks; and 2s. a week afterwards, during the continuance of his illnefs. On the death of a member, £5. are paid to the widow, or other furviving reprefentatives.

The Coalminers' Society at Ewanrigg, in the neighbourhood of Workington, is under the patronage of Mr. Curwen, who for every £10. colle&ed in the Society, contributes £3. It commenced in January 1795.

	£	s.	d.
The colle&ions within the year ending Jan. 1796	22	4	6
Mr. Curwen's donation and contribution -	17	3	2
Total -	£39	7	2
Difburfements during the year — —	8	0	0
Fund on 1ft Jan. 1796	£31	7	2

March, 1796.

CUMBERLAND.

THE following is a ftatement of the ufual annual expenditure and receipts of an agricultural labourer in the county of Cumberland: his family confifts of himfelf, a wife, and 5 children. The age of the parents is about 33, and that of the children from half a year to 9 years.

January.

	£.	s.	d.
January.—5 ftone of oatmeal, at 1s. 11d. - -	-	9	7
1 bufhel of potatoes (i. e. 3 Winchefter bufhels)	-	2	8
2 lb. of butter, at 8d. - -	-	1	4
62 quarts of milk, at ½d. - -	-	2	7
4 lb. of treacle, at 4d. - -	-	1	4
2 pecks of barley, (i. e. 3 Winchefter pecks)	-	5	3
Salt, - - - -	-	0	2
Candles, - - -	-	0	4
Soap, &c. - - - -	-	0	6
Houfe-rent, - - -	-	2	6
Fuel, - - - -	-	1	6
Cloaths, repairs in furniture, &c. -	-	5	0
	£1	12	9
February.—Similar to January - - -	£1	12	9
March.—The fame - - - - -	£1	12	9
April.—The fame - - - -	£1	12	9
May.—1½ ftone of oatmeal at 2s. - -	-	3	0
3 pecks of potatoes, at 10d. - -	-	2	6
2 lb. of butter, at 7d. - -	-	1	2
155 quarts of milk, at 2d. - -	-	6	5
3 pecks of barley, at 11d. - - -	-	8	3
Salt, foap, &c. - - -	-	0	9
3 lb. of bacon, at 6½d. - - -	-	1	7½
Houfe-rent - - -	-	2	6
Fuel - - - -	-	1	0
Cloaths, repairs of furniture, &c. - -	-	5	0
	£1	12	2½
June.—Nearly fimilar to May - - -	£1	12	2½
July.—1½ ftone of oatmeal, at 2s. - -	-	3	0
1 peck (i. e. 3 Winchefter pecks) of potatoes	-	1	0
3 lb. of butter at 6d. - -	-	1	6

	£.	s.	d.
Brought over -		5	6
July.—155 quarts of milk, at 2d. - -		6	5
3 pecks of barley, at 11d. - - -		8	3
Salt, foap, &c. - - - -		0	9
4 lb. of beef or mutton, at 3d. - - -		1	0
Houfe-rent - - - - -		2	6
Fuel - - - - -		1	0
Cloaths, repairs of furniture, &c. - -		5	6
	£1	10	5

Auguſt.—Nearly fimilar to July - - - £1 10 5

September.—Nearly fimilar to Auguſt; except that more potatoes, and, peihaps, a little lefs milk in this
month are confumed; and that bacon is ufed
inftead of mutton. The monthly expence may
be ftated at - - - £1 8 0

October.—Nearly fimilar to September - - £1 8 0

November.—The expences of this month may be ftated at £1 10 0

December.—4 ftone of oatmeal, at 1s. 10d. - -	7	4
1 bufhel of potatoes - - - -	2	8
3 lb. of butter at 8d. - - -	2	0
62 quarts of milk, at ½d. - - -	2	7
4 lb. of treacle, at 4d. - - - -	1	4
1½ peck of barley - - - -	3	9
1½ ftone of flour, at 2s. - - -	3	0
8 lb. of mutton at 3½d. - - -	2	4
Salt, candles, foap, &c. - - - -	1	8
Houfe-rent - - - -	2	6
Fuel - - - - -	2	0
Cloaths, repairs of furniture, &c. - -	5	0
	£1 16 2

EXPEN-

EXPENCES.			Work days.				RECEIPTS.		
	£.	s.	d.		s.	d.		£.	s.	d.
January,	1	12	9	25 at	1	0	amount to	1	5	0
February,	1	12	9	24 —	1	0	————	1	4	0
March, -	1	12	9	26 —	1	3	————	1	12	6
April, -	1	12	9	26 —	1	4	————	1	14	8
May, -	1	12	2½	26 —	1	4	————	1	14	8
June, -	1	12	2½	26 —	1	4	————	1	14	8
July, -	1	10	5	26 —	1	6	————	1	19	0
Auguft, -	1	10	5	26 —	1	6	————	1	19	0
September,	1	8	0	26 —	1	4	————	1	14	8
October,	1	8	0	26 —	1	2	————	1	10	4
November,	1	10	0	26 —	1	0	————	1	6	0
December,	1	16	2	24 —	1	0	————	1	4	0

$£$18 18 5 $£$18 18 6

The above, it is to be obferved, is a general ftatement of a labourer's earnings and expences in the country, where fuel is to be procured, at a confiderable lefs expence, than in towns; becaufe, in the former fituation, the wife and children can, often, collect wood fufficient; or, perhaps, turf or peat is within a fmall diftance. Potatoes are, alfo, ftated at fomewhat lower than they are ufually fold in the markets, not becaufe they are to be bought cheaper in the country, but becaufe labourers are often permitted to fet a few on the farm where they work. In the article of cloathing, great economy is ufed in this part of the world: the parents often make the few they poffeffed when they married, (clogs, fhirts, fhifts, &c. excepted,) laft them till their children are able to earn their own maintenance, and in fummer the children go without many articles of drefs. In fuch a family as the one above defcribed, it requires the moft rigid parfimony, to fpare any thing, towards putting a child to fchool.

January, 1795.

P 2   DERBY-

DERBYSHIRE.

CHESTERFIELD.

THE townſhip of Cheſterfield contains by eſtimation 500 acres The rent of land, not built on, is from £ 3. to £ 4. 10s. an acre. The land-tax annually raiſed is £ 208. 1s.

In 1783 the number of houſes was 777: inhabitants 3,335.
>   1788   —   815:   —   3,626.
>   1791   . —   866:   —   3,987.

In Cheſterfield there are 370 houſes, that pay the houſe or window tax; and 496 that are exempted. The number of inns or ale-houſes is 52: of Friendly Societies 10; only one of which has had it's rules confirmed by the Magiſtrates. Each Society, on an average, confiſts of 80 members.

The members of the Society at the Nag's Head pay monthly 1s each to the box, and 2d. for expences. Perſons who have been regiſtered members for 2 years, are allowed weekly, in caſe of ſickneſs, 8s a week, during one year; and if they continue ill a longer time, 5s a week, during the remainder of their illneſs. From £ 2 to £ 5 are allowed towards the funeral of a member, to be paid to his widow, repreſentative, or friend. A member, on the death of his wife, receives from each brother member 6d. The Society is governed by a preſident, and 1ſt and 2d ſtewards, who are choſen by election, and ſucceed each other by rotation. They continue in their reſpective offices a year. On the preſident's removal the ſenior ſteward ſucceeds him, and a junior ſteward is elected

The Society at the Old Angel is governed by a maſter, 2 wardens, and 12 aſſiſtants, elected by the whole body. The maſter continues in office a year: the eldeſt warden ſucceeds him; the younger warden, the elder; and a new warden is choſen out of the whole body: the maſter and wardens nominate the 12 aſſiſtants, who continue in office a year. No perſon is admitted, who belongs to two clubs, or to one, when the allowance

I   is

is above 4s. a week : and members are forbidden to enter into clubs whofe
pay is above 4s. a week, under pain of exclufion. At the monthly meetings, 6d. is paid by each member to the box, and 2d. fpent: fick members receive 4s. weekly. Perfons entering the army, navy, merchants' or
Faft India Company's fervice, are excluded.

The allowance for funerals is according to the deceafed member's ftanding, fiom £1. to £3.

No great manufacture is carried on at Chefterfield ; but three or four
iron founderies in the neighbourhood, employ many hands from this
place. About 50 perfons are likewife employed in the potteries ; neai the
fame number in ftocking-making ; and about 40 in a fmall carpet manufactory. The other inhabitants are fhop-keepers, tradefmen, inn-keepers,
a few mechanics, farmers, and agricultural labourers. Chefterfield is fituated in a farming country ; it is a market town, and toleiably well fupplied with grain, and other provifions; of which the ufual prices are :
flour, 2s. to 2s. 6d. the ftone ; oatmeal, 2d. the lb. ; mutton, 4½d. ; veal,
4d. ; beef, 4½d ; bacon, 7½d. ; butter, 10d. for 16 ounces; potatoes, 10d.
the peck ; eggs, ½d. each ; wheat, 26s. to 28s. the load, of 3 Winchefter
bufhels ; malt, 39s. 6d. for 6 Winchefter bufhcls. A little oat bread is
ufed here, but the chief confumption is wheaten bread.

Common laboureis earn 9s. and 10s. a week : men, woiking at the
founderies, receive about 14s. a week ; ftocking-weavers, from 1s 6d. to
2s 6d. the day ; mafons, joiners, &c. about 2s. 6d. a day.

Some years back the inhabitants were chiefly Diffenters : at the prefent
not more than one fifth of them, it is fuppofed, diffent fiom the eftablifhed Church : there are in Chefterfield, 1 Calvinift, 1 Piefbyterian, 1 Methodift, and 1 Quaker place of worfhip.

The Pooi aie paitly maintained at home, and paitly in a woik-houfe.
The number at prefent in the woik houfe is 28 ; of which 12 aie children, 8 men, and 8 women : 25 receive weekly penfions fiom the pariih,
which amounted a week or two ago, to £1 15s. 2d : 10 Paupeis receive
occafional relief ; and 6 houfe-rents are paid. To give fome idea of the
ufual weekly allowance, and other ciicumftances relative to the Poor of
this parifh, I fubjoin a lift of the out-poor in Chefterfield, piinted verbatim, fiom a lift of the chuich-wardens and oveifeeis, that was taken in
September

September 1781, and is the only one that could be met with. It would have been more satisfactory, had it minuted the occupations, as well as the ages, and places of abode, of the individuals therein mentioned.

A List of the Out-Poor.

	per week	
	s	d
Andrew Ann, widow, aged 61 years, lives in Holywell street	1	0
Bateman Sarah, widow, and 2 children, Cucknal	1	6
Beeston William, 63, Salter-gate	1	6
Cade Elizabeth, sick, 76, Shambles	1	0
Catledge Samuel, son, sick, 7, Holywell-street	1	6
Chauntry Elizabeth, widow, 85, Lordsmill-street	1	6
Crowder, Mary, child, Sheffield	1	0
Dale Widow, Retford	0	9
Denbigh John, his family, Melton Mowbray, Leicestershire	1	6
Dickenson's —— wife, and 2 children, Beckingham	1	6
Dolphin Sarah, 68, Gluman-gate	1	0
Elliot Martha, widow, 46, 3 children, Margaret 9, Richard 5, Sarah 3, Lordsmill street	2	0
Fidler Anne, deaf and dumb, Lordsmill-street	1	0
Gosling Anne, widow, 52, St Mary's-gate	1	0
Heald Elizabeth, widow, 85, Gluman-gate	1	0
Heald Isabel, widow, 65, Hollis-lane	1	0
Heywood's ——, 2 children, Pentridge	1	6
Higgins Mary, 41, Gluman-gate	1	0
Lee Sarah, her bastard child, 2, Newbold	1	0
Lenthal Paul, sick, 67, Holywell-street	1	0
Lowe Alice, widow, 69, Gluman-gate	1	0
Marsh Mary, widow, 70, Holywell-street	1	0
Naylor Rebecca, and 2 children, Sarah 4, Elizabeth 1, Rawmarsh, Yorkshire	1	6
Nuttal Henry, lame, 66, Salter-gate	1	0
Parker Elizabeth, widow, 76, Durant Green	1	0
Parker Tabitha, her bastard child, 1, Beetwell-street	1	6
Pymn Dorothy, widow, 76, Salter-gate	1	0
Ratcliffe, Ann, widow, 83, Tapton	1	0

Shenthall

	s.	d.
Shenthall Daniel, lame, 29, his wife, 29, and 3 children, Sarah 7, Anne 3, Thomas 5 months, New-fquare - - -	3	0
Sherwin Ellen, her baftard child, Gluman-gate - -	1	0
Smedley Martha, blind, 23, Holywell-ftreet - - -	1	0
Smith Martha, her baftard child, 6, Holymoor-fide - -	1	0
Spencer Anne, widow, blind, 80, Chaddefdon - -	1	0
Stocks Ann, her baftard child, 1, White Cote - - -	1	0
Taylor Thomas, fick, and his wife, Stony Houghton - -	2	0
Tomlinfon —— child, 6, Weft-barrs - - -	1	0
Tomlinfon Margaret, hufband run away, 62, Weft-barrs -	1	0
Watts Lydia, widow, 68, Salter-gate - - - -	1	6
Webfter Jofeph, for lodging - - - -	0	8
Whyatt Martha, 43, Salter gate - - -	1	0
Whyatt Mary, 46, Salter-gate - - - -	1	0
Wragg ——, baftard child, Darley - - -	1	0
Wright Arthur, lame, Clay-lane - - - -	1	0

RENT PAID.

		£.	s.	d.
Bolton John, Chefterfield - -	per ann.	1	10	0
Denbigh Elizabeth, Ditto - - - -		1	19	0
Mafon Godfrey, Brampton Moor - - - -		2	10	0
Ratcliffe Widow, Chefterfield - - - -		1	10	0
Shentall Daniel, Ditto - - - - -		1	14	0
Spencer Ann, Chaddefdon - - - -		1	0	0
Spencer Widow, Chefterfield - - - -		1	10	0
Wragg Mary, Derby - - - -		1	10	0

A Lift of the Paupers in the Work-houfe.

Blake Elizabeth, aged 73 years
Bingham Thomas, baftard child, 3
Catledge Samuel, 3
Downs Martha, 36, ⎫
—— William her fon, 4 ⎬
—— Mary her daughter, 1 ⎭
Denbigh Samuel, 66

Elliott

Elliott Elizabeth, 59
Elliott John, baftard child, 3
Higginbotham Mary, baftard child, 4
Hopkinfon Mary, 26, and 2 baftard children, ⎫
————— James, 6   ⎬
————— Henry, 2   ⎭
Inman Samuel, 67   ⎫
———— Sarah his daughter, 4   ⎬
Lee Ann, 36
Nailor Sarah, 24   ⎫
.—— Benjamin, her baftard fon, 18 months ⎬
Newbold Jemima, 16, infirm
North Hannah, 82
Perkin Martha, 47
Slater George, 70
———— Thomas, 72
Stanley Samuel, 3
———— Sarah, 5
Storer Samuel, 88
Townend George, 6
Watton Anne, 48   ⎫
———— William, her fon, 7   ⎬
Wright David, 71
York Mary, 58.

The following table exhibits the baptifms, burials, and annual difburfements from the Poor's Rates, for various purpofes.

Years.	Baptifms	Burials.	Marriages.	Total Difburfements.		
				£.	s.	d.
1700	72	82	38			
1774	82	60	Year ending at Eafter	334	12	7¾
1775	76	68	— —	321	10	7
1776	88	123	— —	333	9	6
1777	93	85	— —	328	6	7
1778	87	78	— —	347	4	6
1779	107	100	— —	332	17	6

Years.

Years	Baptisms.	Burials.			Total Disbursements.		
					£.	s.	d.
1780	102	76	Year ending at Easter		409	9	3
1781	110	115	—	—	469	10	4½
1782	144	77	—	—	449	2	4½
1783	115	84	—	—	567	2	4½
1784	137	82	—	—	531	17	5½
1785	147	93	—	—	500	6	0
1786	142	92	—	—	653	5	4
1787	147	99	—	—	546	18	1
1788	151	130	—	—	676	5	8
1789	143	95	—	—	711	19	0
1790	133	129	—	—	575	15	9¾
1791	161	79	—	—	596	15	7½
1792	170	132	—	—	567	15	7
1793	160	96	—	—	588	1	0
1794	156	129	—	—	586	18	2½
1795	—	—	—	—	680	8	3½

The last year's assessments were raised at 2s. in the pound on the net rental.

The accounts are so indistinct, that the annual expenditure on the Poor could not be made out. Since the year 1786, the constables' charges have been defrayed from the Poor's Rate: last year £108 7s. 3d. were paid on that account; and the year before £44. 12s. The sums paid them, in former years, are not entered. The attorney's bill, paid last year from the Rate, amounted to £36. 12s. 10d.: this charge usually amounts to about £30. a year. 10 guineas a year, are paid to a doctor for the Poor. The master of the work-house is allowed an annual salary of £10.; together with his victuals. The bell-man, and beadle, likewise, receive from the Poor's Rate, cloaths and wages, amounting, altogether, to about £20. a year.

This township has considerable pecuniary aid from various charities, of which the following are the principal: —A donation of £10. a year was given in aid of the Poor's Rate. There is an hospital for 5 poor widows; 2 of whom receive an allowance of 1s. and 3 of 2s. a week: In another hospital, 6 poor widows receive each 1s. a week; together with a two-penny loaf, every Sunday. The fum of £40. is annually diftiibuted to poor houfe-keepers, in fums of £1. Six poor widows ieceive each £10. a year: 8 poor boys, who aie not chargeable to the town, aie apprenticed, from a donation of £40. a year. The coiporation, from a donation at their difpofal, gives away 50 or 60 ftone of beef, among the Pooi, at Chiiftmas. There is a free-fchool for the education of 20 poor boys; and in addition to thefe charities, feveial fmall bequefts aie annually diftributed among the Poor, in articles of food, and cloathing. The coiporation are the truftees for many of the above donations; and it is much to be defired, that they would annually favour the Public with an account of their receipts and difburfements.

The work-houfe is built in a good fituation: it is kept clean, and is fufficiently fpacious. Theie are 8 or moie beds in each room. Each bed is filled with chaff, and has 2 fheets, a blanket, and coverlid. The inmates, when fick, are removed into a fmall adjoining building; in which, likewife, are lodged lunatics, and perfons labouring under infectious diforders. There is a large work-room for Paupers to work in. Mr. Howard, when he infpected this houfe, fuggefted fome alterations for rendering the rooms airy, which accordingly took place. That indefatigable man, in the purfuit of his philanthiopic views, vifited moft of the work-houfes in the kingdom.

The Poor in the houfe are employed in fpinning lint, and wool; principally for houfehold confumption. The men are fometimes fent out to work in the neighbourhood. No regular account of eainings is kept; but the mafter of the work-houfe thinks, they amount to about £30. a year, on an average.

Certificates are rarely granted by this parifh: about 3 or 4 removals occur every year. The parifh maintains 10 baftards, that are chargeable; and is reimburfed by the fathers, for maintaining 7 others.

The following is the weekly rotation of Diet in the work-houfe.

	Breakfaſt	Dinner	Supper
Sunday,	Milk pottage.	Bread, beef, broth, and potatoes.	Broth and bread
Monday,	Ditto.	Puddings, fauce, and beei.	Pint of beei, and bread
Tuefday,	Ditto.	Bread, cheefe, and beer	Bread and beer.
Wednefday,	Ditto.	As Sunday.	As Sunday.
Thurfday,	Ditto.	As Monday	As Monday.
Fiiday,	Ditto.	As Sunday.	As Sunday.
Saturday,	Ditto.	As Tuefday.	As Tuefday.

The

The proportion of food is 1 ſtone of beef to 30 perſons. 3 oz. of cheeſe to each adult perſon. Wheaten bread is uſed, and is apparently very good: there is no butter in the ſauce; it is compoſed of water, vinegar and treacle. *May*, 1795.

DERBY.

IN the pariſh of St. Alkmund, Derby, 181 houſes pay the houſe or window-tax; 63 are exempted. The land-tax amounts to £158.

The following were the Poor's Rates for a few years back, on the net rental.

	s.	d.	
Year ending Eaſter 1788	1	10½	on land.
——	1	3	on houſes.
1789	2	3	on land.
——	1	6	on houſes.
1790	1	10½	on land.
——	1	3	on houſes.
1791	1	6	on land.
——	1	0	on houſes.
1792	1	6	on land.
——	1	0	on houſes.
1793	1	6	on land.
——	1	0	on houſes.
1794	2	3	on land.
——	1	6	on houſes.
1795	2	3	on land.
——	1	6	on houſes.

More money is raiſed from the land than from the houſes towards the Poor's Rates. An additional rate was made this year to provide men for the Navy.

The work-houſe ſeems in every reſpect the beſt in Derby: it is airy, clean, and well provided with good bedding, (of feather beds,) and other neceſſary furniture.

Weekly

Weekly bill of faie.

	Breakfaft.	Dinnei.	Suppei.
Sunday,	Milk pottage.	Butcher's meat, &c	Biead and brotli.
Monda},	Ditto	Milk pottage and bread.	Milk pottage.
Tuefday,	Ditto	As Sunday.	As Sunday
Wednefday,	Ditto	As Monday.	As Monda}
Thurfday,	Ditto	As Sunday.	As Sunday.
Friday,	Ditto.	Biead, cheefe, and beei	As Monda}
Saturday,	Ditto.	Suet pudding	As Monday

On meat days each perfon ieceives about 8 oz. of meat, and, on Friday, from 2 to 3 oz. of cheefe, ½ lb. of bread, and 1 pint of beer. Thofe, who do not eat their allowance at dinner, may receive it afterwards. Women, when they wafh, and other perfons, during feveie labour, have an additional allowance of victuals.

The number of perfons now in the woik-houfe is 36; of whom 6 aie under 7 years of age; 8 between 7 and 12, who do a little work, and the reft chiefly middle-aged women. Thofe who can work, are moftly employed in the filk, and cotton mills; and, altogether, earn about 16s. a week: they are allowed 2d. in the fhilling for themfelves.

The following is a lift of Out-penfioners

		Age.	Weekly Allowance.
			s.	d.
1	A carpenter, lame; - - -	70	2	0
2	A ftocking-weaver's widow; - -	70	1	6
3	A filk-manufacturer's wife; with a fick fon;	70	2	6
4	A foldier's wife; - - - -	58	1	0
5	A ftocking-weaver's widow, infirm; -	60	1	6
6	A widow, with a fick daughter; -	62	2	0
7	2 children; - - - -	—	2	0
8	A carpenter's widow; - - -	60	0	6
9	A labourer's widow; - -	58	1	3
10	A foldier's widow; - - -	60	1	6
11	A labourer's widow, with 2 children; -	56	1	6

Carried over - 17 3

	Age.	Weekly Allowance.
		s. d.
Brought over - -		17 3
12 A widow; lame; - - -	50	1 0
13 A hatter; lame; - - -	56	1 6
14 A fawyer's widow, with a child; -	45	1 6
15 A fawyer's widow; - -	78	1 6
16 A maltfter's widow; paralytic; -	62	1 0
17 A ftocking-weaver's wife; lame; -	54	1 6
18 A farmer, and his wife, each about; -	80	4 0
19 A ftocking weaver's widow, and 1 child; -	55	1 0
20 A woman, who paid £50. to the parifh on con- } dition of receiving a weekly allowance of 4s. }	50	4 0
21 A ftocking-weaver; - - -	80	1 6
22 A labourer, and family; - -	55	1 0
23 A labourer's widow; - - -	60	1 0
24 A labourer's widow; - - -	70	1 0
25 A foldier's child; - - - —		1 3
26 A foldier's wife, and 2 children; -	50	2 0
27 12 baftards, coft weekly - - - —		15 6
28 17 receive cafual relief, amounting, weekly, to about		14 0

Total of weekly allowances - £ 3 11 6

10 militia men's wives, belonging to other parifhes, receive
weekly - - - - - £ 1 10 0

The population of the parifh of All-Saints, Derby, was accurately taken
in 1789, when the number of houfes was found to be 532; and of inhabitants, 2675. 300 houfes pay the houfe or window-tax; 232 are exempted.

The following table fhews the annual difburfements from the Poor's
Rate, fince the year 1773. In 1709, the Rate amounted to £115.
16s 1d.

Years.

Years.	Annual Disbursements.			Rate in the Pound.	
	£.	s.	d.	s.	d.
Ending in May 1773	787	6	8½	2	6
1774	811	2	9¼	2	6
1775	843	7	1¼	2	6
1776	846	17	5	2	6
1777	788	16	1¼	2	1
1778	892	9	8	2	6
1779	866	18	7¼	2	6
1780	899	5	10¾	2	6
1781	836	2	8	2	1
1782	831	5	9	2	0
1783	813	18	0¼	2	0
1784	721	2	6	1	10
1785	706	19	9½	1	10
1786	731	11	2½	1	10
1787	631	9	2½	1	10
1788	674	5	6¾	1	10
1789	783	11	11	1	10
1790	692	4	1	1	10
1791	756	3	5½	1	10
1792	289	7	6½ for the first half year: the other half year was not inserted in the book		
1793	614	13	1	1	9
1794	898	5	10	2	1

Ending in May 1795.—The accounts of this year are not made up, but the Rate is the same as that ending in May 1794.

The following are the particulars of sums received in the year ending in May 1794:

	£.	s.	d.
Receipts on account of bastardy - -	139	12	2
By cash reimbursed for relieving Paupers belonging to other parishes - - - -	30	3	6
Carried over - £	169	15	8

	£.	s.	d.
Brought over -	169	15	8
By cafh, from county treafurer, for money advanced			
to corporals, drummers, &c. - -	96	6	6
Reimburfements, for money paid to militia men -	100	8	3
By 5 affeffments - - - -	740	13	9
By balance from the late overfeer - -	30	0	0

£ 1137 4   2

Deduct deficiencies, from poor perfons
not paying the Rate   - £ 94 17   6½
Other deductions   -   -   144   0   9½

£ 238 18   4   £ 238 18   4

Total expenditure   -   £ 898   5   10

The earnings of the Poor, which amount annually to about £ 145. are not noticed in the account ending in 1794; but each week's earnings are accounted for by the mafter, and deducted from his weekly bill of expences. In other years the earnings were received by the overfeer, and accounted for in the general receipts.

The following articles are included in each year's expenditure:

	£.	s.	d.
Standing officer's falary - - - -	15	0	0
Surgeon's falary - - - -	15	0	0
Salary of the mafter of the poor-houfe - -	10	0	0
Expences at veftry meetings, &c. about - -	2	10	0

Total   -   £ 42 10   0

The number of Poor, at prefent, in the work-houfe, is 53, of whom 9 are under 8 years of age; 15 from 8 to 14, who work at the filk, or cotton mills, and earn each, from 1s. to 2s. 6d. a week: the others are, moftly, old and infirm. They work 12 hours in the day, exclufive of meal times. Thofe who work, are paid 2¼d. in the fhilling, out of their earnings. The earnings, during the laft 3 weeks, were as follows:

4   Firft

	£. s. d.		£. s. d		£. s. d
Firſt week's earnings	2 3 9	Second week's earnings	3 4 0½	Third week's earnings	3 2 9
Allowance to Poor	0 4 10½	Allowance to Poor	0 7 8	Allowance to Poor	0 8 0
Net earnings to the		Net earnings to the		Net earnings to the	
Houſe - £ 1 18 10½		Houſe - £ 2 16 4½		Houſe - £ 2 14 9	

56 out-penſioners, (among whom are 22 widows, and 14 baſtaids,) receive £4. 15s. 3d. weekly. The wives of 22 militia men receive weekly, £3. 8s. 3d. ; which ſum, it is expected, will be 1eimburſed by other pariſhes.

The following is one week's expenditure in the Houſe :

	£	s.	d.
103lb. of beef, at 3½d. - - -	1	10	0½
6 buſhels of wheat - - -	2	14	0
Grinding wheat - - -	0	2	0
3 ſtone of flour - - -	0	7	9
Oatmeal and ſalt - - -	0	3	6
Potatoes - - - -	0	3	6
Barm - - - -	0	1	6
Veal, for the maſter's table - -	0	0	10
58lb. of beef, at 3½d. - - -	0	15	5½
Baking - - - -	0	2	1
Groceries - - - -	0	4	6
Milk - - - - -	0	7	6
Treacle - - - -	0	0	4
Total of one week -	£ 6	13	0

Table of Diet in the Work-houſe.

	Breakfaſt.	Dinner	Supper
Sunday,	Milk pottage	Beef, veal, or mutton, with bread, pota-toes, &c. and broth.	Beer, and bread.
Monday,	Ditto.	Bread, cold meat, and broth.	Ditto.
Tueſday,	Ditto.	As Sunday.	Ditto.
Wedneſday,	Ditto	As Monday.	Ditto.
Thurſday;	Ditto.	As Sunday.	Ditto.
Friday,	Ditto.	As Monday.	Ditto.
Saturday,	Ditto.	Suet dumplins.	Ditto.

The

The mafter allows about 3lb. of butcher's meat, weekly; and at fupper, daily, a pint of fmall beer, to each adult; and proportionably, to children. About 2 certificates are granted annually; and about 4 removals from this parifh occur every year.

The fmall parifh of St. Michael, Derby, confifts wholly of buildings: it contains 640 inhabitants: 65 houfes pay the window-tax; and about 63 are exempted   The land-tax raifed here amounts to £45.

In the following fums, (which are the annual difburfements from the Poor's Rate,) are included money paid to church-wardens, highways, &c. which, upon an average, amounts, annually, to £12.

Years.	Total Difburfements.			Rate in the pound on the net rent.	
	£.	s.	d.	s.	d.
1774	129	6	$4\frac{1}{2}$	1	6
1775	92	10	$7\frac{1}{4}$	1	0
1776	98	5	8	1	0
1777	110	16	$8\frac{1}{2}$	1	0
1778	115	13	$6\frac{1}{2}$	1	0
1779	169	7	$6\frac{1}{2}$	1	6
1780	163	7	5	2	0
1781	131	7	$1\frac{1}{2}$	1	6
1782	141	16	11	1	6
1783	122	6	$5\frac{1}{2}$	1	6
1784	113	3	1	1	6
1785	125	2	$11\frac{1}{2}$	1	6
1786	156	12	$7\frac{1}{2}$	1	6
1787	194	4	$0\frac{3}{4}$	2	0
1788	151	0	5	2	0
1789	178	6	$2\frac{1}{2}$	2	0
1790	162	13	$1\frac{1}{2}$	2	0
1791	196	11	$8\frac{1}{2}$	2	0
1792	191	17	9	2	0
1793	230	13	$0\frac{1}{2}$	2	6
1794	238	10	4	2	6
1795	Accounts not fettled.				

There

There is no poor-houfe in this parifh; but the neceffitous are relieved at their own homes. At prefent, 28 Paupers, who have, moftly, families, receive altogether, weekly, £2. 19s. 2d.; befides which, about 12s. a week are difburfed in cafual payments; exclufive of the charge of maintaining the wives of foldiers, and militia men, which could not be afcertained.

There is a houfe in this parifh, which was given, for 8 poor men, and 4 women, who likewife receive, each, 2s. 6d. a week.

About 2 perfons are removed, annually, from this parifh. There have been no certificates granted during the laft 3 years: before that period, about 1 certificate was granted annually.

In the parifh of St. Peter's, Derby, 209 houfes pay the houfe or window tax; and 126 are exempted. The land-tax amounts to £121. 5s. 2d

The following is the fulleft account that could be obtained of parochial income and expenditure:

Years.	Collections.			Difburfements.			Rate in the pound on net rent.			
							on land.		on houfes	
	£.	s.	d.	£.	s.	d.	s.	d.	s.	d.
1780	—	—	—	606	5	11¾	2	6	1	3
1781	—	—	—	551	4	6½	2	6	1	3
1782	697	18	11½	643	0	10½	2	6	1	3
1783	663	3	9	613	16	10½	2	6	1	3
1784	755	11	11	697	18	6½	2	9	1	4½
1785	651	5	1½	598	9	0½	2	6	1	3
1786	824	14	7	777	11	5	3	6	1	9
1787	740	19	2	687	19	6¼	3	0	1	6
1788	684	3	3¾	632	18	9½	2	6	1	3
1789	731	11	10¾	673	12	10¾	3	0	1	6
1790	No account could be obtained relative						3	0	1	6
1791	to the collection or expenditure in						2	9	1	4½
1792	1790 and fubfequent years.						2	9	1	4½
1793	—	—	—	—	—	—	2	9	1	4½
1794	—	—	—	—	—	—	3	0	1	6

The rental of land in this parifh is to the rental of houfes as £17. 16s. is to £60. 16s. which is 1 to 3½. About £160. are annually added

to

to the Poor's Rate, from rents of houfes and land belonging to the parifh.

The Poor are, partly, maintained in a work-houfe, the mafter of which is allowed, for his fuperintendence, and for collecting the affeffments, a falary of £20. a year. A furgeon receives 10 guineas a year. The number of inmates, at prefent, is 39, of which 15 are under 12 years of age. Thofe who are able to work, either knit or fpin, for the ufe of the houfe; or are employed in the neighbouring filk or cotton mills; and receive 2d. in a fhilling for themfelves. Their earnings in 4 weeks were as follows:

	£.	s.	d.
	1	0	7
	1	2	2
	1	3	6
	1	2	6
	£4	8	9

Deduct 2d. in the 1s. or one fixth - 0 14 9½

The earnings of the parifh amount to - £3 13 11½

The work-houfe is fmall, but the rooms are neat and well aired: the beds are filled with feathers.

The following is a Table of the Diet.

	Breakfaft.	Dinner.	Supper.
Sunday,	Milk pottage	Beef, broth, bread, potatoes, &c.	Bread and broth.
Monday,	Ditto	Baked puddings with fuet.	Bread and beer.
Tuefday,	Ditto.	As on Sunday.	As on Sunday.
Wednefday,	Ditto	Ditto.	Ditto.
Thurfday,	Ditto.	Milk pottage.	Bread and beer.
Friday,	Ditto	As on Sunday.	As on Sunday.
Saturday,	Ditto.	{ Dumplins and treacle fauce, in fummer. Peafe pottage, in winter. Sometimes bread, cheefe, and beer. }	As on Monday.

The bread ufed here is wheaten, and leavened: other work-houfes in the town ufe the fame fort. On meat days, about 30 lb. of meat, (bones included,) are divided among 40 perfons.

The weekly bills of the work-houfe, (including groceries and baking,) were, lately, as follows:

R 2

25 April

	£.	s.	d.
25 April 1795.—4 bushels of wheat, at 8s. 9d. -	1	15	0
128 lb. of beef at 3½d. - -	1	17	4
Oatmeal - - -	0	2	0
Butter and eggs - - -	0	3	2
Veal, 7 lb. at 3d. - -	0	1	9
Milk - - - -	0	8	0
Potatoes - - -	0	5	0
Washing - - -	0	1	4
Barm, (or yeast) - - -	0	0	8
Other articles - - -	0	0	2
	£4	14	5
2d May 1795.—Wheat - - -	£1	16	0
130 lb. of beef at 3½d. - -	1	17	11
Oatmeal - - -	0	1	5
Milk - - - - -	0	8	0
Butter - - -	0	3	0
Potatoes - - - -	0	5	5½
Washing - - -	0	1	4
Barm - - -	0	1	2
Other articles - - -	0	0	3½
	£4	14	7
7th May 1795.—Wheat - - -	1	16	0
112 lb. of beef at 3½d. - -	1	12	8
Butter and eggs - - -	0	3	0
Oatmeal - - -	0	2	10
28 lb. of veal at 3½d. - -	0	8	2
Milk - - -	0	8	0
Potatoes - - - -	0	5	5½
Oil - - - -	0	0	7
Barm - - - -	0	0	8
Washing - - -	0	1	4
Other articles - - -	0	0	3
	£4	18	11½

The

The following is a lift of the out-penfioners belonging to the parifh.

	Age	Weekly Allowance.	
		s.	d.
An unmarried woman ; fubject to fits ;	58	1	0
A widow, and 3 children ;	40	3	0
A bricklayer's widow ;	70	1	0
A foldier's widow ;	70	1	0
A ftocking-weaver, and his wife ; both infirm ; each about	66	1	0
A ftocking-weaver's widow, and 1 child ;	40	1	0
A widow ;	75	1	0
A ftocking-weaver, and 2 children ;	70	1	0
A foldier's wife, and 2 children ;	—	1	0
A joiner's wife, lame ; with three children ;	30	1	0
A labourer's widow ; with 2 children ;	40	1	0
An orphan, under 7 years of age ;	—	1	0
A blind man ;	30	1	0
A foldier's child ;	—	1	0
A ftocking-weaver, and his wife ;	70	1	0
A filk-twiner's widow ;	65	1	0
A labourer's widow ;	60	1	0
2 lame children ;	—	2	0
A lame man, and his wife ; each about	70	1	0
An infirm woman ;	25	1	0
A widow, and 3 children ;	50	1	0
A blind woman ;	—	1	0
A butcher's widow ; with 3 children ;	45	2	6
A labourer's widow ; with 2 children ;	22	3	0
A feaman's wife, and one child ;	23	1	0
A labourer's widow ; fick ;	60	1	0
A foldier's wife ; and 4 children ;	28	4	0
A bricklayer's widow ; and 3 children ;	38	2	0
A woman, deferted by her hufband ; with 1 child ;	—	1	0
An innkeeper's widow ;	74	1	6
A fhoemaker's widow ;	80	1	6
The family of a diforderly perfon who has abfconded ;	—	1	6

Carried over - £2 4 0

Weekly Allowance.

	£.	s.	d.
Brought over - -	2	4	0
To thefe may be added 9 baftards - -	0	15	0
The wives of 3 militia men, belonging to the parifh -	0	10	6
The wives of 5 ditto, belonging to other parifhes, reimburfed	0	12	0
Three houfe rents are alfo paid; they amount annually to	6	19	11

The cafual payments amount, weekly, to 6s. In the work-houfe there are about 5 or 6 deaths, upon an average, every year. About 3 certificates are granted annually. The perfons fent out of the parifh under orders of removal, are, chiefly, pregnant girls. It is faid that not more than 5 appeals on removals have taken place within the laft 10 years : about 5 paupers are removed every 2 years. Thefe circumftances, although they often materially affect parochial expenditure, are feldom recorded in the books, and are, generally, only obtainable from hearfay information.

The extent of the parifh of St. Werburgh, Derby, is about 700 acres. The population, in 1789, was found to be 1935 inhabitants. 228 houfes pay the houfe or window-tax; 170 are exempted.

An old parifh book contains accounts of the Difburfements for the Poor, from the year 1687. The following table was formed from that and other documents ; but a book was unfortunately miffing, that contained the accounts of 16 years, between 1769 and 1786. The net expences of the Poor in 1776, and the Rates in 1783, 1784, and 1785, are fupplied from the returns made to Parliament.

Years.		£.	s.	d.
1687	In the difburfements of this and moft	72	5	2
1688	of the 14 following years are included	58	4	0
1689	affeffments for church-wardens, high-	82	0	5
1690	ways, &c. - - -	79	18	$9\frac{1}{2}$
1691	— — —	62	3	10
1692	— — —	67	15	11
1693	— — —	67	4	0
1694	— — —	98	17	$7\frac{3}{4}$
1695	— — —	80	11	9
1696	— — —	84	2	$0\frac{1}{2}$
1697	— — —	98	13	$1\frac{1}{2}$

Years.				£.	s.	d.		
1700	—	—	—	86	16	0		
1701	—	—	—	109	19	4		
1704	—	—	—	70	4	8		
1705	—	—	—	88	17	0		

Years.		£.	s.	d.	£.	s.	d.	Rate in the Pound on the nominal rental
								s.	d.
1708	Weekly pay to 34 Paupers	62	18	7					
	Cafual payments -	9	0	6					
	Houfe rents -	9	8	0				s.	d.
	Church-wardens bills	27	5	7—	108	12	8	2	0
1768	Difburfements for the Poor				237	17	4	2	0
1769	Ditto - - -				287	6	$10\frac{3}{4}$	2	6
1776	Ditto - - -				222	0	0	0	0
1783	Poor's Rates - -				340	8	2	0	0
1784	Ditto - - -				344	16	1	0	0
1785	Ditto - - -				344	18	9	0	0
1786	Difburfements for the Poor				607	11	1	4	0
1787	— — —				670	12	9	5	0
1788	— — —				511	13	$7\frac{1}{4}$	4	0
1789	— — —				515	0	7	4	0
1790	— — —				466	17	6	3	6
1791	Ditto — — —				397	12	9	3	6
1792	— — —				265	18	3	2	0
1793	— — —				277	13	$6\frac{1}{2}$	2	0
1794	— — —				425	3	10	3	0
1795	— — —				462	15	$5\frac{1}{2}$	3	6

The Rates in Derby fall very unequally on different perfons; fome pay as much for a net rental of £10. as others do for £20. The nominal rental is higher than the real rental in the following proportion: a 1s. affeff-ment is levied at the rate of 6d. in the pound on houfes, and 9d. in the pound on land; fo that the nominal Rate for 1795, 3s. 6d. in the pound, is in fact 4s. $4\frac{1}{2}$d. in the pound.

In the work-houfe are 24 paupers, of various defcriptions. 52 out-pen-fioners, of whom 17 are baftards, 18 widows, 3 militia men's wives, who ferving for the parifh, and 6 foldiers wives, receive weekly, at prefent, £4. 2s. The families of 16 militia men belonging to other parifhes, are likewife paid here.

The

The work-houfe is fimilar to others in Derby, except in the article of bedding. The beds are filled with chaff; a blanket often fupplies the place of a coverlid.

The following is the ufual weekly rotation of Diet in the Work-houfe.

	Breakfaſt.	Dinner.	Supper
Sunday,	Milk pottage	Butcher's meat, &c. &c.	Bread, and broth.
Monday,	Ditto	Snet puddings	Milk pottage.
Tuefday,	Ditto.	As Sunday	As Sunday.
Wednefday,	As Monday	As Monday	As Monday.
Thurfday,	As Sunday	As Sunday	As Sunday
Friday,	Ditto.	Bread and cheefe.	Bread, cheefe, and beer.
Saturday,	Ditto	Dumplins.	Boiled beer and bread.

Various donations, doles, &c. amounting to about £ 17. are annually diftributed to fuch Poor as do not receive parochial affiftance.

The following table comprehends the baptifms and burials in the parifhes of All Saints, St. Michael, and St. Werburgh, Derby.

	ALL SAINTS.		ST. MICHAEL.		ST. WERBURGH.	
Years	Baptifms	Burials.	Baptifms.	Burials.	Baptifms.	Burials.
1774	87	64	—	—	—	—
1775	85	90	25	32	87	52
1776	98	73	20	13	64	64
1777	92	60	17	9	89	46
1778	74	72	17	26	86	75
1779	72	86	16	28	72	60
1780	83	83	16	15	71	75
1781	78	75	20	20	68	79
1782	76	88	26	28	81	82
1783	86	55	24	12	79	46
1784	85	91	26	18	66	51
1785	92	101	19	16	90	48
1786	107	66	20	20	60	74
1787	102	79	28	27	79	71
1788	92	105	15	32	73	76
1789	85	66	25	20	80	61
1790	111	72	23	20	78	51
1791	105	82	19	33	75	59
1792	76	71	20	11	68	59
1793	69	83	20	22	58	81
1794	87 Regifter not completed		23	25	66	64

The

The town of Derby confifts of the 5 parifhes, above enumerated; the Poor's Rates have rifen a little, during the laft 2 or 3 years, in confequence of the ftagnation of bufinefs, occafioned, perhaps, in fome degree, by the war; the high price of provifions; and the increafed number of chargeable perfons from foldiers' and militia men's families. There are 8 Friendly Societies in Derby; and 101 ale-houfes, or inns. So that it appears, from reckoning up the houfes in the different parifhes, that, nearly, every 16th houfe is an ale-houfe.

Number of houfes in All Saints   532

St. Alkmund   244

St. Michael   128

St. Peter   335

St. Werburgh   398

Ale-houfes   101) 1637 (16;

The rent of land, in the Derby parifhes, is fiom £ 2. 10s. to £ 4. 10s.; the average may be ftated at about £ 3. the acre. There are feveral canals cutting in the neighbourhood, in which common labourers earn from 2s. to 2s. 6d. a day. Children, from 7 to 12 years of age, earn from 1s. to 2s. 6d a week, in the filk and cotton mills. Stocking-weavers earn, according to their ability, and induftry, from 6s. to 20s. a week. In the paper and china manufacture, men earn from 10s. to 21s. a week.

The prefent prices of provifions, (16th May,) are: beef, fiom 4d. to 6d. the pound; mutton, 5d; veal, 4d; bacon, 8d; butter, 9½d. to 10d.; potatoes, 1s. the peck; milk, 2d. the quart; flour, fiom 2s 4d. to 2s. 9d. the ftone; oatmeal, 1s. 6d. for 8lb; wheat, 9s to 9s 4d. the bufhel; barley, 45s. the quarter; malt, 7s. 3d. the bufhel.

The twifting of filk is the ancient and piincipal manufacture in this town. There are 12 mills; of which 11 are now at work, and give employment to about 1000 people, who are chiefly women and children. About 100 perfons are employed in ftocking-weaving. Both filk and worfted ftockings are made here. A few years ago three cotton mills were erected, for carding, roving, and fpinning cotton; and employ about 500 hands, including children. 50 perfons work in a paper-mill; and about 60 in a porcelain manufactory. The reft of the inhabitants are gentlemen, tradefmen, fhop-keepers, inn-keepers, a few farmers, and labourers.

Brown wheaten bread is univerfally preferred here for common ufe, and thofe who can afford it, often eat butcher's meat.

Theie are 3 Diffenting meeting-houfes, all of different denominations. The number of fcholais, who attend the various Sunday fchools, eftablifh-ed in Deiby, amounts to 440.

Laft winter £.480. weie collected, and diftributed in bread, to the Poor.

May, 1795.

WIRKSWORTH.

THE townfhip of Wirkfworth compiehends about 2200 acres. The number of houfes, including 36 ale-houfes, is 607 ; which contain, by eftimation, 620 families, and 2800 inhabitants. 152 houfes pay the window-tax, and 455 are exempted. Many well-informed people in the parifh are of opinion that the population has rather decreafed within the laft 20 years : it was, however, not thought worth while to examine the regifters in order to determine this point, as there are a number of chapel-ries adjoining to the parifh, whofe baptifms and burials are inferted, pro-mifcuoufly, in the regifter of Wirkfwoith. The inhabitants are, chiefly, of the eftablifhed Church   There are 4 Sunday fchools in the parifh, which inftruct about 60 fcholars

There are feveral confiderable lead-mines in this townfhip ; in which a third part of the inhabitants is employed   About 220 perfons work in a cotton manufactory. Several wool-combers refide heie. Poor women and children pick cotton, and fpin worfted. A common labourer earns fiom 1s 4d. to 1s. 8d a day   Miners aie paid about 10s a week. The wages in that employment aie extremely iriegular   Women can eain fiom 5½d. to 6d a day, in fpinning worfted ; and from 3s. to 5s. a week, in fpinning cotton   Childien from 8 to 14 yeais of age earn from 1s to 5s. a week   Overfeers in the cotton works receive 12s. a week. The mining bufinefs is veiy dull at prefent, and does not afford much employment.

The prices of piovifions are : flour, 2s. 2d. to 2s. 9d. the ftone ; oat-meal, 2s. 4d. the ftone ; potatoes, 10d the peck ; butter, 9d. for 16 oz. ;

milk,

milk, from 1½d. to 2d. the quart; beef, 4d. to 5d. the lb.; mutton, 5d.; veal, 4d.; bacon, 7d to 8d.; eggs, 3 for 2d.

The rent of land is from £1 1s. to £3. The average is about £2. The land is moftly in grafs; tithe is compounded for at 3s an acre, a compofition which is thought very low. The land-tax amounts to £160. Here are 8 Friendly Societies; the average number of members in each is about 85.

The parifh accounts have been kept in a very carelefs manner: the following table, which was not without confiderable difficulty extracted from the books fcattered in different parts of the townfhip, exhibits the annual amount of difburfements for 20 years. From an account in the hands of a private perfon, accidentally met with, were obtained the affeffments and difburfements in 1689. The former amounted to £126. 9s. 5d.; the latter to £125 15s. 1½d

| Years. | Total Difburfements. |||
	£.	s.	d.
Ending in May 1775	480	13	10
1776	No accounts.		
1777	384	4	10
1778	434	6	6
1779	567	8	9½
1780	623	14	3¼
1781	703	6	2½
1782	712	9	5
1783	686	9	9
1784	719	12	6½
1785	661	3	4
1786	699	6	0
1787	616	11	8
1788	582	3	4¾
1789	554	10	9
1790	589	14	5½
1791	666	14	6
1792	735	9	0
1793	657	9	8½
1794	829	16	4½
1795	794	13	2

S 2

The

The returns made to Parliament in 1786 ftate the expences for the Poor in 1776 at £ 493. 13s. 5d. ; and the affeffments in 1783, at £ 650. 16s. ; in 1784, at £ 647. 9s. 11d. ; and in 1785, at £ 565. 19s.

The laft year's difburfements were collected at about 2s. 3d. in the pound for houfes, and 3s. 7d. in the pound for land on the net rental.

Since the year 1781, the conftables' bills, amounting annually to between £ 30. and £ 40. have been paid out of the Poor's Rate: The expences of veftry meetings rarely exceed £ 3. a year. The falary of the mafter of the work-houfe, who, alfo, collects the affeffments, is £ 16. 16s. a year, together with board for himfelf, and his wife. The furgeon's falary is £ 14. a year. The work-houfe is an old building, not originally intended for the purpofe, to which it is now applied. It is not in a good fituation ; but is, as far as it's conftruction will permit, kept clean, and airy.

The following is the weekly rotation of Diet.

	Breakfaft	Dinner.	Supper
Sunday,	Bread, and broth.	Bread, broth, butcher's meat, potatoes, &c.	Milk pottage, and bread.
Monday,	Milk pottage	Baked puddings, and treacle fauce.	Ditto.
Tuefday,	Ditto	Bread and milk.	Ditto.
Wednefday,	As Sunday.	As Sunday.	As Sunday.
Thurfday,	As Tuefday	As Tuefday.	As Tuefday.
Friday,	As Sunday.	As Sunday.	As Sunday.
Saturday,	As Tuefday	As Tuefday.	As Tuefday.

On meat days the proportion of meat is about 20lb. for 30 perfons.

The children are kept very clean ; and are inftructed in their catechifm, in reading, &c. There are 3 lunatics at prefent in the houfe. Few of the inmates are able to work; thofe, who are, fpin lint, tow, &c. for the ufe of the houfe: they are allowed 1d. for every 7d. of fpinning. The rooms are of various fizes, and contain from 2 to 7 beds each. The beds and pillows are filled with chaff. Each bed has 2 fheets, 1 blanket, and 1 coverlid.

The deaths in the work-houfe were in 1792,—6; in 1793,—5; in 1794,—7.

The expences of the laft month, (April,) were as follows :

	£.	s.	d.
Flour and baking - - - -	1	5	7
Oatmeal - - - -	3	14	2
Carried over -	£ 4	19	9

	£	s.	d.
Brought over -	4	19	9
Milk - - - - - - -	2	2	0
Grocery - - - - - -	1	7	7½
Sundries - - - - - -	1	2	2
Mercery - - - - -	0	3	9½
Butcher's meat, (veal,) - - - -	0	3	10
Oatmeal - - - - - -	1	1	3
Cooperage - - - - -	0	1	2
Shoes - - - - - -	0	7	11
	£ 11	9	6

Pigs belonging to the work-houfe were killed this month; and therefore the confumption of butcher's meat appears in the above account very inconfiderable.

The Poor in the work-houfe at prefent amount to 28; of which 12 are under 7 years of age; 1 of 25; 3 of 34; 3 of 44; 2 of 64; 4 of 74; and 3 of 83.

The following lift of the regular weekly penfioners exhibits their ages, occupation, and weekly allowance; befides which the parifh pays 10 houfe-rents, amounting to £ 11. 9s. annually.

	Age	Weekly Allowance	
		s.	d.
A miner's widow, infane; - -	55	1	0
A miller; infirm; - - - -	55	1	6
A blind man; - - - -	20	1	0
A farmer's widow, lame; - - -	70	1	0
A miner's widow; - - - -	68	0	6
A labourer; - - - - -	80	1	0
A miner; - - - - -	76	1	6
A rag-gatherer; - - - -	74	1	0
A fhoe-maker, and 3 children; - -	28	0	6
A woman, with 2 children, deferted by her hufband;	35	1	0
A widow; - - - - -	66	1	0
A wool-comber's widow, and 4 children; - -	38	2	0
A miner's widow; - - - -	70	1	6
Carried over -		14	6

	Age.	Weekly Allowance
		s.	d.
Brought over -		14	6
A miner's widow, and fon ; he is infane ;	70	1	6
A miner's widow, and 5 children ;	40	4	0
A widow ;	70	1	0
A widow ;	74	1	0
A joiner, infirm ;	74	1	0
A miner's widow, infirm ;	60	1	6
A labourer's widow ;	80	1	0
A miner's widow ;	80	1	6
A miner's widow, and a child ;	30	1	0
A tailor's wife, deferted by her hufband ;	50	0	6
A miner's widow :	70	1	0
A baftard ;	—	0	6
A fick man ;	26	0	9
A wool-comber, infirm ;	60	1	6
A miner's widow ;	40	0	9
A miner's widow ;	40	1	6
A fhoemaker, afthmatic ;	74	1	6
A miner, blind ;	50	3	0
A miner's widow, and 3 children ;	32	4	0
A miner's widow ;	80	1	0
A widow ;	76	0	9
A miner and wife ;	74	2	6
A fpinfter, infirm ;	58	1	6
A labourer's widow ;	80	1	6
A miner's widow ;	60	1	0
A miner's widow, infirm ;	60	2	0
A rag-gatherer, lame :	76	1	6
A wool-comber, and large family ;	28	0	6
A miner's widow, infane ;	60	0	6
A farmer, infirm ;	73	1	6
A carrier ;	76	1	6
A fpinfter, lame ;	60	1	6
A miner's widow ;	74	1	0
Carried over -		£3 1	3

	Age.	Weekly Allowance.
		£. s. d.
Brought over -		3 1 3
A blind man ;	28	0 2 0
A butcher's widow ;	76	0 1 0
A tanner, reduced by poverty ;	80	0 2 0
A miner, infirm ;	76	0 0 6
A cotton-fpinner and family ;	50	0 0 9
A child, whofe father abfconded ;	3	0 1 3
A widow ;	76	0 1 0
A mafon's widow ;	50	0 2 0
A miner's widow ;	50	0 0 6
A labourer ;	80	0 1 0
A woman, whofe hufband deferted her ;	70	0 0 6
A wool-comber, and his wife ;	80	0 2 6
A widow ;	70	0 1 6
A labourer ;	—	0 1 0
Ditto ;	—	0 1 0
A hofier's widow, and 2 children ;	40	0 1 0
A cotton manufacturer, lame ;	25	0 1 0
A fadler's widow, and 6 children ;	—	0 4 0
		£ 4 5 9
9 foldiers' wives, and 6 children ;		0 15 0
A militia man's wife ;		0 1 6
19 baftards ;		1 5 4
6 ditto, for which the fathers reimburfe the money ;		0 9 1
		£ 6 16 8
43 poor people receive cafual relief: their laft month's allowances were		£ 6 2 5½
Coals, books, warrants, &c.		1 5 0
		£ 7 7 5½

The fubfcriptions for the Poor laft winter amounted to £60. which were laid out in purchafing coals, beef, and potatoes. The Poor in the work-

work-houfe have oat-bread, but no beer or cheefe is allowed, except at Chriftmas: a foit of gruel, called water pottage, confifting of a fmall proportion of oatmeal, and a fmall onion boiled with water, was eaten with bread, twice, and fometimes thrice, a day, by many poor people, in this neighbourhood: it was much ufed during the late hard feafon: the value of fuch a mefs for each adult perfon was about 1¼d.

Several fmall donations, amounting to £45 10s. are annually diftributed among the Poor, who do not receive any parochial affiftance.

Here is alfo an hofpital, containing apartments for 4 poor widows, who have an allowance of 5s. 6d. a month, each; and twice in the year, each of them receives a donation of 16s. 6d.   *May*, 1795.

D E V O N.

CLYST ST. GEORGE.

THE parifh of Clyft St. George is one mile and three quarters in length, and, nearly, the fame in breadth. The number of inhabitants is about 150. 18 houfes pay the commutation tax: one is a double tenement: about 28 cottages are exempted. The men are wholly employed in agriculture; the women make lace, and fpin. All the inhabitants are of the Church of England.

Farms, in general, in this neighbourhood are from £200. a year, down to £50. One farmer, however, rents an eftate of £400. a year. The ufual tenure is a leafe for 14 years. The principal articles of cultivation are wheat, barley, oats, turnips, and, lately, potatoes have been much attended to. This parifh contains many orchards. There are no commons or wafte lands: the whole parifh has been many years inclofed. A marfh, however, adjoining the river Ex, on which this parifh is fituated, is ftill capable of improvement. In the adjacent parifhes, are many valuable, though fmall, commons: the proprietors of which, as well as the public, would probably receive great benefit from a general enclofure bill. Tithes

I   are

are compounded for at 2s. 6d. in the pound on the actual rent. 40s. an acre, feem about the average rent; but the landlord pays all Poor's rates, taxes, and repairs, which were altogether computed at 5s. in the pound, before the prefent fcarcity. The land-tax is about 2s. in the pound on the net rental.

The prices of provifions are greatly increafed within the laft two years: the Poor cannot now purchafe meat at lefs than $4\frac{1}{2}$d. or 5d. the pound. Wheat, at prefent, fells for 12s the bufhel, Winchefter meafure; butter at 13d the pound; common cheefe at 4d. the pound.

Agricultural labourers, in general, receive 1s. a day, and liquor; a few farmers give 14d. a day, and liquor: during the corn harveft, meat is added

There is only one public-houfe, and no Friendly Society in the parifh; but a few of the inhabitants are members of Friendly Societies eftablifhed in the neighbourhood: moft of them have had their rules confirmed by the Magiftrates The grand inducement to enter into thefe Societies, feems to be in a great meafure taken away by a late Act, " to prevent the removal of poor perfons, until they fhall become actually " chargeable' "

No labourer can, at prefent, maintain himfelf, wife, and two children, on his earnings: they have all relief from the parifh, either in money, or in corn at a reduced price Before the prefent war, wheaten bread, and cheefe, and, about twice a week, meat, were their ufual food: it is now bailey bread, and no meat: they have, however, of late, made great ufe of potatoes. Their common earnings are 6s. a week, and liquor. An induftrious healthy man, however, can earn 8s. a week, by tafk work, on an average, throughout the year. Labourers' children, here, are often bound out apprentices, at 8 years of age, to the farmers by the parifh; a labourer, prior to the prefent fcarcity, if his wife was healthy, could maintain two young children on his 6s. a week, and liquor, without any parochial relief. A very few years ago, labourers thought themfelves difgraced by receiving aid from the parifh; but this fenfe of fhame is now totally extinguifhed.

The Poor are, in general, maintained by weekly penfions from the parifh: fome receive occafional relief. The following table exhibits the grofs fums, annually raifed by the Poor's Rate, and the net fums annually

' 35 Geo 3 c 101.

expended on the Poor: in the latter of which is included the maintenance of the families of militia men The county Rates, which on an average amount to £7 a year, are to be deducted from the fum expended on the Poor.

Years	Baptisms			Burials			Marriages	Amount of Rates collected	Annual Expenditure on the Poor		
	Males	Fem	Total	Males	Fem	Total					
1680	2	2	4	2	4	6	8				
1685	9	3	12	3	0	3	9				
1690	3	6	9	1	1	2	4				
1691	2	3	5	0	3	3	5				
1692	4	4	8	6	6	12	4				
1693	6	6	12	1	2	3	3				
1694	3	1	4	7	3	10	1				
1695	4	4	8	2	2	4	2				
1696	5	3	8	2	3	5	3	There are no accounts of Poor's			
1697	3	2	5	6	3	9	3	Rates prior to 1720. The parish			
1698	4	4	8	1	3	4	3	is rated, upon a nominal rental of			
1699	5	2	7	1	1	2	2	£860: it's real rental is £1200, or £1300.			
1700	2	1	3	3	6	9	7	£.	£.	s.	d.
1720	3	1	4	2	4	6	2	70	48	7	8
1740	0	1	1	5	1	6	2	52	38	6	8
1760	2	3	5	3	2	5	4	76	58	10	11
1775	5	5	10	3	2	5	2	94	64	18	4
1776	6	5	11	1	2	3	1	80	57	17	6
1777	7	3	10	5	5	10	3	74	48	5	2
1778	10	6	16	3	3	6	1	64	53	14	5
1779	2	4	6	4	1	5	1	111	81	11	6
1780	5	5	10	2	4	6	4	126	87	13	5
1781	0	8	8	2	3	5	2	146	106	9	11
1782	3	3	6	2	1	3	2	116	81	12	8
1783	3	8	11	2	2	4	1	104	72	11	2
1784	6	2	8	4	0	4	0	92	69	19	8
1785	2	9	11	1	3	4	2	90	64	0	7
1786	8	4	12	4	3	7	1	90	64	14	5
1787	3	2	5	2	1	3	3	76	56	6	3
1788	3	1	4	1	5	6	3	96	65	3	4
1789	2	2	4	5	2	7	6	112	82	2	3

Years.

Years	BAPTISMS			BURIALS			Marriages	Amount of Rates collected	Annual Expenditure on the Poor.		
	Males	Fem	Total	Males	Fem	Total					
1790	8	5	13	5	3	8	3	128	89	0	1
1791	0	7	7	0	5	5	1	130	95	19	11
1792	3	8	11	3	0	3	1	117	85	13	3
1793	3	3	6	1	2	3	2	115	80	14	7
1794	3	6	9	1	2	3	0	156	116	17	6
1795	5	5	10	6	3	9	2	132	93	17	5

*February,*1796.

SOUTH TAWTON.

THE parish of South Tawton contains about 5000 acres : the number of inhabitants is 2500 : they are chiefly employed in the various branches of the serge manufacture, which is here carried on to a confiderable extent. Nine tenths of the women in the parish, (all of the poorest class,) are spinners, and are regularly supplied by the serge-makers with constant employment. Their number may be estimated at 600 or 700.

73 houses pay the window tax : about 200 are exempted. The wages of agricultural labourers are 1s. 2d. a day : spinners cannot earn above 6d. or 7d. a day : a common labourer earns about £18. 5s. a year ; and his wife, about £9. 2s. 6d.

The prices of provisions are : butcher's meat, upon an average, 4d. the pound ; wheat, from 10s. to 11s. the bushel ; barley, from 4s 6d. to 5s. a bushel ; milk, ½d. the quart ; potatoes, 5d. the peck. The number of ale-houses is 4.

Farms, in this parish, are small : the usual tenure is for a term of years, at rack rent. The principal articles of cultivation are turnips, potatoes, wheat, barley, and oats. Tithes are compounded for. The commons and waste lands amount to about 1000 acres. An intelligent parish officer states the rental of the parish at £3500. a year ; but a gentleman, who has farmed his own estate upwards of 40 years, and is well acquainted with the nature and extent of the parish, thinks that the rental does not exceed £3000. a year.

T 2

There

There are two Friendly Societies in this parish, (one for males, and the other for females,) both of which have had their rules confirmed by the Magistrates. The Poor are chiefly maintained by a parish allowance at home : a few reside in a small work-house The clergyman distributes the money that is collected at church, every month among the most deserving of the necessitous. The usual diet of labourers is milk and potatoes; barley, or wheaten bread; and, occasionally, a little bacon.

Table of Baptisms, Burials, and Marriages.

Years	BAPTISMS			BURIALS.			Marriages.
	Males	Females.	Total.	Males	Females.	Total.	
1780	35	20	55	10	15	25	9
1781	18	24	42	10	18	28	8
1782	27	31	58	24	31	55	12
1783	26	18	44	17	19	36	13
1784	33	25	58	9	19	28	12
1785	31	26	57	9	16	25	8
1786	27	27	54	24	18	42	19
1787	38	24	62	12	16	28	wanting.
1788	30	18	48	14	13	27	12
1789	35	30	65	19	14	33	15
1790	22	33	55	6	14	20	10
1791	26	29	55	11	14	25	8
1792	25	22	47	14	12	26	8
1793	21	25	46	20	20	40	14
1794	33	30	63	8	12	20	11
1795	22	21	43	17	18	35	26

According to the returns made to Parliament,   £.   s.   d.
The net expences of the Poor in 1776 were 339 15 4
The Poor's Rates in   -   - 1783 — 549 2 0
1784 — 576 3 4
1785 — 575 17 2

Since that period, the Poor's Rates have, upon an average, amounted to about £800. a year.   January, 1796.

TIVER-

TIVERTON.

THE parifh of Tiverton is a very irregular oblong: it's greateft length is above 9 miles, and greateft breadth about 8. The number of inhabitants is 7096. They are diftributed through the different quarters of the parifh according to the following table:

	Farm-houfes	Cottages	Total No of houfes	Men	Women	Children	Total.
In the town of Tiverton,	—	—	1074	1279	1895	2169	5343
In Pitt quarter, without the town,	63	37	105	186	194	325	705
In Tidcombe quarter,	30	29	59	95	96	144	335
In Clare quarter,	52	5	57	96	98	143	337
In Prior's quarter,	44	18	62	120	104	152	376
			1357	1776	2387	2933	7096

The number of baptifms, marriages, and burials, recorded in the parifh regifter of St. Peter's church, Tiverton, in the following periods, of fix years each:

					Baptifms.	Marriages.	Burials.
From 1	January	1560 to	1	January 1566	484	137	327
1	March	1581 to	1	March 1587	704	170	549
1	March	1601 to	1	March 1607	789	239	484
1	March	1620 to	1	March 1626	1226	315	808
1	March	1640 to	1	March 1646	1272	270	1411
1	March	1660 to	1	March 1666	914	221	906
1	March	1680 to	1	March 1686	1101	322	1060
1	March	1700 to	1	March 1706	1116	331	1175
1	March	1720 to	1	March 1726	1070	284	1175
1	March	1740 to	1	March 1746	895	340	1472
1	January	1760 to	1	January 1766	891	292	915
1	January	1780 to	1	Januaiy 1786	1144	367	1038
25	March	1784 to	25	March 1790	1216	321	960

Probable State of the Population of Tiverton parifh, at different periods; eftimated from the average of burials every 6 years, at the
rate of one perfon in 43½ dying, yearly.

Years.				Perfons.
1565	—	about	—	2545
1585	—	—	—	4154
1605	—	—	—	3683
1625	—	—	—	6032
1645	—	—	—	8228
1665	—	—	—	6742
1685	—	—	—	7859
1705	—	—	—	8693
1725	—	—	—	8698
1745	—	—	—	7946
1765	—	—	—	6808
1785	—	—	—	7699
1790	—	—	—	7134

The average of fix years is taken for every period calculated from the
lifts of burials only, at the rate of one perfon out of 43½ dying every year:
this proportion nearly agrees with the number of inhabitants in 1790, which
was found, by tale, to amount to 7096.

From this account it appears, that the population was more flourifhing in
the beginning of this century, than at prefent. A manufacture of ferges
was eftablifhed here foon after the Revolution; but was much injured towards the clofe of the laft reign, by the introduction of Norwich ftuffs,
and other woollens, into the foreign markets: and in 1770 there were
1800 perfons lefs in the parifh, than there were 40 years before. Within
a few years, however, feveral new branches of manufacture have been
eftablifhed in Tiverton, and the Poor now find conftant employment, in
weaving white ferges, coatings, beavers, &c. There are, at prefent, 1000
looms in Tiverton, of which nearly 700 are daily at work; about 200
combers are conftantly employed. The returns of trade are eftimated at
about £150,000 a year.

                                                           The

The public charities in Tiverton are exceedingly numerous. Above 90 donations, (fome of which are very confiderable,) have been given to this town fince the commencement of the reign of Queen Elizabeth. The purpofes to which thefe charities are applied, are extremely various. Alms-houfes are fupported; fchools endowed; fcholars fent yearly to the univerfities; fums of money lent annually to poor manufacturers and hufbandmen; old and infirm perfons provided with a comfortable maintenance; cloaths and provifions occafionally diftributed among the Poor; and many charitable inftitutions are kept up, through the zeal of both deceafed, and living benefactors: notwithftanding which, the Poor's Rates have been regularly progreffive, and, in the year 1790, amounted to the fum of £ 3204 2s. 3d.

The numerous Poor of Tiverton are, principally, maintained and employed in an hofpital, erected in 1704, in purfuance of an act paffed in the year 1698. In the year 1740 a large woollen manufacture was fet up in the houfe, for the employment of the Poor there, by a voluntary fubfcription of £1020: it was, however, found to be fo very difadvantageous, and fo many loffes were fuftained by wafte, and keeping manufactured goods on hand without an opportunity of fale, that, in the following year, the materials were fold, and the manufacture given up.

The buildings are erected upon a good plan, and the extenfive workfhops in the hofpital fquare feem well calculated for the employment of the Poor. The houfe can accommodate 300 perfons befides the mafter's family. The Poor are regularly fupplied with vegetables, from a large garden adjoining. The parifh concerns were managed by the governors and guardians of the parifh under the act of 1698, until the year 1769, when the hofpital act was laid afide; and the government of the Poor has fince that period been conducted under the general Poor laws.

There is one congregation of Methodifts, and a Calvinift's chapel in Tiverton.

Sunday fchools were introduced in 1785: in 1790 there were 9 in the town, and the number of fcholars was 240.

The

The following table exhibits the weekly rotation of diet appointed, 7th March 1782, for the Poor in the hofpital.

Days.	Meals	Men.	Women	Working Children	Children
SUNDAY,	Breakfaft,	Bread, 6 oz / Cheefe, 2 oz	5 oz / 2 oz	4 oz / 2 oz	3 oz / 1 oz and half
	Dinner,	Peafe, 1 quart / Beer, 1 pint	1 quart / 1 pint	1 pint and half / Half pint	1 pint / ¼ pint
	Supper,	Bread, 6 oz / Milk, 1 pint & half	5 oz / 1 pint and half	4 oz / 1 pint and half	3 oz / 1 pint
MONDAY,	Breakfaft,	Bread, 6 oz / Broth, 1 quart	5 oz / 1 quart	5 oz / 1 pint and half	4 oz / 1 pint
	Dinner,	Cheefe, 1 oz / Pudding, 1 pound	1 oz / 1 pound	1 oz / 12 oz	1 oz / 8 oz
	Supper,	Bread, 6 oz / Milk, 1 pint & half	5 oz / 1 pint and half	4 oz / 1 pint and half	3 oz / 1 pint
TUESDAY,	Breakfaft,	Bread, 6 oz / Broth, 1 quart / Cheefe, 1 oz	5 oz / 1 quart / 1 oz	5 oz / 1 pint and half / 1 oz	4 oz / 1 pint / 1 oz
	Dinner,	Bread, 8 oz / Cheefe, 3 oz / Beer, 1 pint	6 oz / 2 oz / 1 pint	4 oz / 2 oz / 1 pint	3 oz / 1 oz / ¼ pint
	Supper,	Bread, 5 oz / Cheefe, 2 oz	4 oz / 2 oz.	4 oz / 2 oz.	3 oz / 1 oz.
WEDNESDAY,	Breakfaft,	Bread, 6 oz / Broth, 1 quart / Cheefe, 1 oz	5 oz / 1 quart / 1 oz	5 oz / 1 pint and half / 1 oz	½ oz / 1 pint / 1 oz
	Dinner,	Bread, 4 oz / Flefh, 6 oz / Bowl of vegetables	3 oz / 6 oz. / Bowl of vegetables	3 oz / 5 oz. / Bowl of vegetables	2 oz / 4 oz. / Bowl of vegetables
	Supper,	Beer, 1 pint / Bread, 6 oz / Milk, 1 pint & half	1 pint / 5 oz / 1 pint and half	1 pint / 4 oz / 1 pint and half	Quarter pint / 3 oz / 1 pint
THURSDAY,	Breakfaft,	Bread, 6 oz / Broth, 1 quart / Cheefe, 1 oz	5 oz / 1 quart / 1 oz	5 oz / 1 pint and half / 1 oz	4 oz / 1 pint / 1 oz
	Dinner,	Peafe, 1 quart / Beer, 1 pint	1 quart / 1 pint	1 pint and half / Half pint	1 pint / Quarter pint
	Supper,	Bread, 6 oz / Milk, 1 pint & half	5 oz / 1 pint and half	4 oz / 1 pint and half	3 oz / 1 pint
FRIDAY,	Breakfaft,	Bread, 6 oz / Broth, 1 quart / Cheefe, 1 oz	5 oz / 1 quart / 1 oz	5 oz / 1 pint and half / 1 oz	4 oz / 1 pint / 1 oz
	Dinner,	Bread, 4 oz / Flefh, 6 oz / Bowl of vegetables	3 oz / 6 oz. / Bowl of vegetables	3 oz / 5 oz. / Bowl of vegetables	2 oz / 4 oz. / Bowl of vegetables
	Supper,	Bread, 5 oz / Cheefe, 2 oz.	4 oz / 2 oz.	4 oz / 2 oz.	3 oz / 1 oz.
SATURDAY,	Breakfaft,	Bread, 6 oz / Broth, 1 quart / Cheefe, 1 oz	5 oz / 1 quart / 1 oz	5 oz / 1 pint and half / 1 oz	½ oz / 1 pint / 1 oz
	Dinner,	Pudding, 1 pound	1 pound	12 oz	8 oz
	Supper,	Bread, 6 oz / Milk, 1 pint & half	5 oz / 1 pint and half	4 oz / 1 pint and half	3 oz / 1 pint.

An Account of the feveral Taxes, and Rates, collected in Tiverton, at diffe-rent periods fince the year 1612.

Years	Subfidy or Land Tax £ s d	Poor's Rates £ s. d.	Church Rates £ s d.	Liberty Rates £ s. d	Total Rates £ s d.
1612	— — —	120 0 0	— — —	— — —	120 0 0
1656	— — —	472 18 4	— — —	— — —	472 18 4
1680	— — —	499 18 9	— — —	— — —	499 18 9

Years.

Years.	Subsidy or Land Tax.	Poor's Rates	Church Rates.	Liberty Rates[1].	Total Rates
	£. s. d.	£. s d.	£. s d.	£ s d.	£. s. d
1685	713 14 0	604 11 8	— — —	— — —	604 11 8
1686	— — —	510 5 1½	— — —	— — —	510 5 1½
1688	— — —	402 10 0	— — —	— — —	402 10 0
1689	921 4 9	— — —	— — —	— — —	— — —
1690	1662 1 6½	— — —	— — —	— — —	— — —
1692	— — —	763 2 8	— — —	— — —	763 2 8
1696	— — —	952 13 1½	— — —	— — —	952 13 1½
1697	— — —	1189 2 8	— — —	— — —	1189 2 8
1698	1484 10 5	820 12 6	— — —	— — —	820 12 6
1699	— — —	1130 7 2	— — —	— — —	1130 7 2
1700	— — —	734 3 10½	— — —	— — —	734 3 10½
1710	2238 18 10	960 4 2	— — —	— — —	960 4 2
1720	1679 4 1½	946 4 11½	— — —	— — —	946 4 11½
1730	1119 9 5	1213 9 10	— — —	— — —	1213 9 10
1740	2238 18 10	1173 1 3	— — —	— — —	1173 1 3
1750	1679 4 1½	1215 8 4½	— — —	— — —	1215 8 4½
1760	2238 18 10	1190 8 8	— — —	— — —	1190 8 8
1765	2238 18 10	1528 6 8	— — —	— — —	1528 6 8
1766	2238 18 10	1535 4 6	— — —	— — —	1535 4 6
1767	1679 4 1½	1539 5 5	— — —	— — —	1539 5 5
1768	1679 4 1½	1532 14 2	— — —	— — —	1532 14 2
1769	1679 4 1½	1360 17 10	173 1 6	191 8 1½	1725 7 5½
1770	1679 4 1½	1446 2 6½	171 9 0	— — —	1617 11 6½
1771	2238 18 10	1663 0 4	409 13 8½	— — —	2072 14 0½
1772	1679 4 1½	2099 17 9	171 14 6	91 3 0	2362 15 3
1773	1679 4 1½	2547 11 9	171 7 0	— — —	2718 18 9
1774	1679 4 1½	2537 17 0	85 10 0	— — —	2623 7 0
1775	1679 4 1½	2518 13 10	127 4 1½	— — —	2645 17 11½
1776	2238 18 10	2502 19 4	504 11 0	178 13 8	3186 4 0
1777	2238 18 10	2110 15 0	207 6 5½	— — —	2318 1 5½
1778	2238 18 10	2275 10 10	493 3 6	175 1 8	2943 16 0
1779	2238 18 10	2284 2 10	496 2 0	525 19 0	3306 3 10
1780	2238 18 10	2274 6 10	451 9 1	— — —	2725 15 11
1781	2238 18 10	2144 18 6	197 11 0½	— — —	2342 9 6½
1782	2238 18 10	2183 11 11	471 4 3	504 10 3	3159 6 5
1783	2238 18 10	2347 1 5	335 2 0	— — —	2682 3 5
1784	2238 18 10	2370 1 11	335 2 0	321 17 9	3027 1 8
1785	2238 18 10	2737 6 0	335 2 0	257 11 0	3329 19 0
1786	2238 18 10	3068 10 2	160 1 8	170 4 11	3398 16 9
1787	2238 18 10	2718 16 11	319 15 10	169 10 6	3208 3 3
1788	2238 18 10	3394 9 2	200 0 0	— — —	3594 9 2
1789	2238 18 10	3140 17 5	159 8 4	169 14 0	3469 19 9
1790	2238 18 10	3204 2 3	159 6 0	170 6 2	3533 14 5

The above tables, as well as many other particulars relative to Tiverton, were extracted from Dunsford's Historical Memoirs of Tiverton, published in 1790. *January*, 1796.

[1] A rate to provide for the expences of Tiverton liberty exclusively, instead of the county rate, to which the inhabitants of the borough are not assessed.

DORSETSHIRE.

BLANDFORD.

THE extent of this parish is estimated at 12 furlongs by 8; or 960 acres. The population was accurately taken in April 1773, and found to amount to 927 males, and 1164 females. The number of inhabitants is thought to have increased, since that period. A few of them are Roman Catholics, a few are Methodists; and the Presbyterians have a small chapel in Blandford. As this parish furnished 3 men to the Navy, the number of houses, chargeable to the window-tax, may be estimated at 204 : not more than 30 are exempted. There are 20 inns or ale-houses in the parish. The inhabitants consist of inn-keepers, shop-keepers, common mechanics, a few farmers, and labourers ; the women, and children, are, chiefly, employed in making thread and wire buttons for shirts, &c. Farms are from £40. to £150. a year. Wheat and barley are the principal articles of cultivation. Turnips and oats are also produced. The average rent of land is estimated at about £1. 10s. an acre. The land-tax is collected at nearly 1s 4d. in the pound. There are about 100 acres of common. Tithes have, generally, been compounded for ; but the farmers are apprehensive of being soon called upon to pay them in kind.

The prices of provisions are : beef, 5½d. the pound ; mutton, 5½d ; bacon, 10d. ; pickled pork, 9d. ; butter, 11d. ; bread, 11½d. the quartern loaf ; potatoes, 6d. the peck ; milk, 1d. the pint in winter, and ½d. in summer. Common labourers are paid 1s the day, without victuals ; and in some instances, since the late scarcity, 1s. 4d. the day. In harvest 1s. 6d is the usual daily pay of an agricultural labourer.

There is one Friendly Society here, consisting of 60 members, whose rules have not been confirmed, according to the provisions of a late act of parliament.

The Poor of this parish are mostly relieved in the work-house, which is in a good situation, and is tolerably neat, and convenient : there are 22 beds,

beds, (of feathers, flocks, and chaff,) in 3 lodging-rooms. Since Eaſter laſt, the Poor in the work-houſe have been under the direction of the pariſh officers, but previous to that period they were generally farmed for 2s 6d. a head, weekly. There is no regular maſter, or miſtreſs, at preſent, but 2 paupers have the care of the work-houſe, during the abſence of the over-ſeers. There are at preſent in the houſe 36 perſons, of whom 13 are children, 6 men, and the reſt, moſtly, old women. Thoſe, who are able to work, and are not engaged in the buſineſs of the houſe, are employed in button making.

108 regular penſioners, (moſt of whom have families,) receive £9 in weekly allowances from the pariſh : ſeveral others have occaſional relief.

Table of Diet in the Work-houſe.

	Breakfaſt.				Dinner.	Supper.
Sunday,	Broth made with flour, onions, water, &c.				Meat and vegetables	Bread and cheeſe
Monday,	Ditto.	—	—	—	Bread and cheeſe.	Ditto.
Tueſday,	Ditto.	—	—	—	Ditto.	Ditto.
Wedneſday,	Ditto.	—	—	—	As Sunday	Ditto.
Thurſday,	Ditto	—	—	—	Bread and cheeſe.	Ditto
Friday,	Ditto	—	—	—	Ditto	Ditto.
Saturday,	Ditto.	—	—	—	Ditto.	Ditto

Each grown perſon is allowed on Sundays, and Wedneſdays, $\frac{3}{4}$ lb. of bread, and on other days of the week 1 lb.; they likewiſe receive 2 pints of beer daily; the weekly allowance of cheeſe is $1\frac{1}{2}$ lb., or $\frac{1}{2}$ lb. of cheeſe, and $\frac{1}{4}$ lb. of butter. Children have a ſmaller allowance.

The rapid riſe of the Poor's Rates, in this pariſh, is generally attributed to the high price of proviſions; the ſmallneſs of wages, and the prevailing ſpirit, among the gentlemen of landed property in this neighbourhood, of conſolidating ſmall farms; and the conſequent depopulation of villages : the effects of which, it is ſaid, oblige ſmall induſtrious farmers to turn la-bourers, or ſervants; who, ſeeing no opening towards advancement, become regardleſs of futurity, ſpend their little wages as they receive them, without reſerving a proviſion for old age; and, if incapacitated from working, by a ſickneſs that laſts a very ſhort time, inevitably fall on the pariſh. Many of theſe notions, I think, are falſe; but the prevailing opinions of a coun-try, even when erroneous, are worth noticing. The political architect, who diſdains to make uſe of the cement of cuſtom and prejudice, will rear but tottering fabricks; he will diſpleaſe thoſe, on whom he intends to confer a favour, if they are not prepared to receive it; as overbearing hoſts, who,

U 2   through

through mere good nature, furfeit their unwilling guefts, while they mean to be kind, create difguft.

It is faid, that there are now only 2 farms in the village of Durwefton, about 3 miles from hence, which contained about 30 fmall farms 20 years ago : and, what is more fingular, the town of Abbey Milton, which in the ancient times of abbatial grandeur was the central market of the county, is now converted into a fifh-pond. The proprietor, the Earl of Dorchef-ter, pulled down the houfes as the tenants died off, and removed the church to a diftant fpot, wheie he erected very fubftantial cottages for fuch of the inhabitants as could not procure a more convenient habitation.

There are feveral charities and donations belonging to this parifh : they are under the direction of the corporation, and are faid to be wretchedly managed. In one alms-houfe, 10 poor people receive, each, 2s. 6d. a week, and cloaths ; and in another, 6 poor perfons receive 1s. 6d. a week, to-gether with cloathing, and fuel.

The following is a ftatement of the domeftic economy of a labourer's fa-mily. The man is 52 years of age ; his eldeft daughter is 18 ; another daughter 8 ; and 2 fons 6 and 3 years of age. His eldeft daughter has re-fided with him, and managed the family concerns, fince the death of her mother, which happened about 2 months ago. The other children earn nothing. His houfe-rent is paid by the parifh, and, during the illnefs of his wife, he received a few fhillings in occafional relief. He was allowed, a fhort time fince, 4s. a week for a fick child ; but upon it's death, the allow-ance was withdrawn. The ufual breakfaft of the family is tea, or bread and cheefe ; their dinner, and fupper, bread and cheefe, or potatoes fometimes mafhed with fat taken from broth, and fometimes with falt alone. Bullock's cheek is generally bought every week to make broth. Treacle is ufed to fweaten tea, inftead of fugar. Very little milk or beer is ufed. For cloath-ing, both for himfelf and family, the man is principally indebted to the charity of his neighbours.

	Weeks.	£.	s.	d.
He earned laft year from Harveft to the 7th March 1795,				
6s. a week - - - -	22½	6	15	0
From 7th March till Harveft, 7s. a week -	25½	8	18	6
About 4 weeks in Harveft, 1s. 6d. a day, or 9s. a week	4	1	16	0
	52	£17	9	6

Table

Table of Baptisms, Burials, Marriages, and Poor's Rates.

Years	Baptisms			Burials			No of Poor buried	Marriages	Poor's Rate			Net Expenditure on the Poor			Rate in the pound	
	Mal	Fem	Total	Mal	Fem	Total			£	s	d	£	s	d	s	d
1746	20	30	50	14	26	40	—	23	227	16	4	239	12	8	1	4
1747	26	25	51	20	37	57	—	21	227	4	2	223	6	7		
1748	21	22	43	33	37	70	—	25	196	15	10	210	18	8		
1749	27	32	59	17	21	38	—	29	196	7	6	194	14	9		
1750	23	25	48	25	32	57	—	21	253	5	8	286	12	7		
1751	20	16	36	17	11	28	—	17	233	19	0	236	2	6		
1752	27	32	59	22	24	46	—	8	232	12	0	227	18	8		
1753	22	24	46	50	46	96	—	24	232	1	0	245	3	7		
1754	36	18	54	22	40	62	—	—	275	11	7	264	1	5		
1755	21	24	45	32	34	66	—	—	235	4	0	223	8	11		
1760	21	28	49	33	13	46	—	—	276	5	4	276	2	4		
1770	19	27	46	21	26	47	—	—	253	17	0	326	19	8		
1775	31	16	47	29	31	60	—	8	443	16	8	376	13	5		
1776	27	20	47	29	35	64	—	21	357	13	4	383	6	10		
1777	30	37	67	17	20	37	—	16	315	16	4	295	12	3		
1778	34	22	56	31	27	58	—	22	359	18	8	353	2	2	1	4
1779	18	28	46	25	30	55	—	16	358	14	8	395	19	9	1	4
1780	28	32	60	38	23	61	—	21	456	6	8	456	13	2	1	8
1781	31	25	56	25	38	63	—	24	561	0	0	587	2	3	2	0
1782	50	34	64	29	19	48	—	20	563	6	0	503	0	1	2	0
1783	45	34	79	27	38	65	—	19	517	3	8	682	0	11		
1784	27	51	78	23	18	41	16	11	573	8	0	602	10	4	2	0
1785	34	19	53	22	23	45	16	16	578	6	0	627	5	0	2	0
1786	26	35	61	24	40	64	24	16	828	0	10	750	19	11		
1787	32	36	68	25	24	49	12	15	880	13	0	847	0	2	3	0
1788	27	35	62	22	14	36	10	15	677	14	4	712	1	6	2	4
1789	25	24	49	27	24	51	10	10	771	17	4	784	13	1	2	8
1790	31	24	55	11	34	45	16	17	961	16	8	848	3	2	3	4
1791	38	45	83	28	36	64	18	24	769	1	4	911	8	4	2	7
1792	38	28	66	17	21	38	13	18	850	4	0	771	0	0	3	0
1793	43	34	77	33	38	71	18	20	758	5	4	814	17	5	2	6
1794	37	26	63	22	21	43	10	25	1032	10	8	1178	4	4	3	8
1795	—	—	—	—	—	—	—	—	945	13	4	1020	18	8	3	4

The Rate in the laſt column denotes the aſſeſſment on houſes: land is
rated one-third higher. The aſſeſſments are nearly at full rental. The
County

County Rates, paid out of the Poor's Rates, and included in the above expenditure, amount to about £ 10. a year.

At Wimborn, a fmall market town between Southampton and Blandford, the Rates laft year, at 3s. in the pound, amounted to £ 900. This
year it is expected they will exceed £ 1200. The parifh of Wimborn
contains a confiderable quantity of arable land, and a large common.
Farms are from £ 100. to £ 1000. a year. The wages of labour are rather
higher than at Blandford.

October, 1795.

D U R W E S T O N.

THE extent of this parifh is eftimated at 800 acres. The number of
inhabitants is nearly 300 : they confift of 2 farmers, 2 inn-keepers, a
few button-makers, common mechanics, and agricultural labourers.   10
houfes pay the window tax ; about 50 are exempted.

Provifions are rather cheaper than at Blandford : wages here, till very
lately, were 6s. a week : they are now 8s. and 9s. : much work is done
by the piece, in which cafe the labourer generally earns the greateft
wages. The farmers fay, that, upon the whole, their men earn 9s. or 10s.
a week, all the year round. The average rent of land is 10s. an acre.
The land-tax is ufually paid by the landlord. It is collected at about 2d
in the pound, and produces £ 54. 11s. 4d. A compofition is paid in lieu
of tithe. Wheat, barley, oats, turnips, and apples, are the chief articles
of cultivation. There are fome uncultivated downs in this parifh, but no
commons. The number of ale-houfes is 2.

Years.	Poor's Rates.			Net Expenditure on the Poor		
	£.	s.	d.	£.	s.	d
1774	37	14	6	35	17	2
1775	44	0	3	45	4	6
1776	50	6	0	44	17	3
1777	44	0	3	45	7	6
1778	50	6	0	43	19	1
1779	39	16	5	38	13	9

Years.

Years.	Poor's Rates.			Net Expenditure on the Poor.		
	£.	s.	d.	£.	s.	d.
1780	52	7	11	54	13	11
1781	50	6	0	46	0	3
1782	58	13	8	58	14	5
1783	75	9	0	76	5	8
1784	71	5	2	69	15	11
1785	100	12	0	93	16	8
1786	100	12	0	101	18	1
1787	104	15	10	98	1	0
1788	100	12	0	88	2	4
1789	92	4	4	94	2	4
1790	92	4	4	81	19	1
1791	115	5	5	113	16	5
1792	115	5	5	95	13	5
1793	94	6	3	103	4	7
1794	134	2	8	141	14	10
1795	147	5	10	131	6	0

It is expected that the Poor's Rates will increafe, very confiderably, this year. From the net expenditure, about £ 10 a year are paid towards the county ftock. The overfeer, (who is one of the above-mentioned farmers,) could give no account what the Rate was in the pound, but believed the rental of the parifh amounted to about £ 500. a year, according to which the rental of laft year was 5s. 10d. in the pound. The other farmer, who is an old man, fays, that about 50 years ago the parifh only paid 6d. a week to a poor woman, who could fcarcely be prevailed on to accept it. The reafons affigned for the increafe in the Rates, are, the dearnefs of provifions; the confolidation of 40 farms into 2; and the introduction of a great number of labourers, from different parts of the kingdom, in confequence of the alterations which Mr. Portman, the principal proprietor, is making on his eftate: feveral of thefe labourers have acquired a fettlement in the parifh

The Poor are maintained by a parifh allowance. 19 regular penfioners, (including 2 militia men's families,) receive 40s. a week. Very poor people, in general, have their rents paid by the parifh; and a few have occafional relief in money. There are no Friendly Societies in the parifh.

October, 1795.
DUR.

DURHAM.

ST. MARGARET'S.

THE chapelry of St Margaret, in Durham, confifts of the townfhips
of Framwelgate and Croffgate: it is near 3 miles in length, and contains
1500 inhabitants; all of the eftablifhed Church, with the exception of a
few Roman Catholics, and Independents. About 200 houfes pay the window-tax, and 100 are exempted. The parifhioners are chiefly employed
in the woollen manufactures; viz. in making moreens, ftuffs, and carpet-
ing. Butcher's meat is on an average 4½d. a lb.; wheat, in September
1795, was at the enormous price of 12s. a bufhel Labourers in the manufactories earn 1s. 6d. a day; and in agriculture 1s. 4d. a day. There
are 7 ale-houfes in the townfhip of Framwelgate, and 6 in Croffgate. A
Friendly Society is eftablifhed here, into which no perfon is admitted, who
is difaffected to the eftablifhed Church or State; they meet every fixth
week, fpend 3d. in beer, and pay 1s. each into the box: when a member
is fick, he receives for 20 weeks, (if his illnefs fhould continue fo long,)
6s. a week; and after that time, the allowance is at the option of the Society: £ 8. are paid to the wife or neareft relation of a member at his
death, and £ 2. are allowed to defray the funeral expences of each member's wife.

Rent of land is from 10s. to 40s. an acre: near the town, land is let
in fmall parcels; but in the country, the farms are from £ 40. to £ 200. a
year. Tithes are partly paid in kind, and partly by compofition; but for
the greateft part of the chapelry a modus is taken. There are near 1000
acres of common in Framwelgate townfhip: about 200 acres were inclofed, in the year 1771, in Croffgate. The Poor in the townfhip of
Framwelgate are contracted for, at £ 210. a year, exclufive of the poor-
houfe: they are vifited twice a week, by 2 of the principal inhabitants,
who make an entry of their obfervations in a book, which is kept for
that purpofe. The Poor of the townfhip of Croffgate are contracted for
at 2s. 2d. each a week, in the work-houfe. The out-poor are allowed
weekly fums according to their feveral exigencies.

The

The following is the Bill of Fare in the Work-house.

	Breakfaft.	Dinner.	Suppe
In Summer, every day,	Bread and milk.	Meat and broth, with roots Since the late enoimous price of wheat, no bread has been ufed.	Bread and milk, or hafty-pudding and tieacle.
In Winter, ditto.	Hafty-pudding made of oatmeal, and eaten with milk or treacle.	Ditto.	Ditto.

Table of Baptifms, Burials, and Marriages.

Years.	BAPTISMS.			BURIALS.			MARRIAGES.
	Males.	Females.	Total.	Males.	Females.	Total	
1680	20	15	35	33	36	69	12
1685	19	18	37	22	17	39	20
1690	17	27	44	22	18	40	15
1691	23	18	41	14	9	23	10
1692	21	27	48	13	18	31	17
1693	15	24	39	15	18	33	14
1694	18	14	32	16	14	30	12
1695	23	31	54	40	33	73	12
1696	12	27	39	24	23	47	22
1697	24	24	48	16	24	40	12
1698	16	20	36	21	29	50	11
1699	28	23	51	24	26	50	19
1700	29	17	46	44	26	70	12
1720	21	22	43	27	23	50	12
1740	20	25	45	41	47	88	10
1760	16	15	31	27	19	46	13
1775	21	20	41	29	31	60	16
1776	15	22	37	27	27	54	18
1777	32	18	50	15	21	36	24
1778	26	25	51	31	27	58	16
1779	23	24	47	26	37	63	17
1780	25	28	53	17	24	41	21
1781	22	28	50	22	21	43	25
1782	28	33	61	42	42	84	22

Years.	BAPTISMS.			BURIALS.			MARRIAGES.
	Males.	Females.	Total	Males.	Females.	Total	
1783	19	21	40	39	31	70	18
1784	32	24	56	22	34	56	24
1785	30	33	63	33	29	62	19
1786	26	28	54	36	55	91	21
1787	36	26	62	29	36	65	18
1788	37	22	59	30	37	67	13
1789	24	27	51	24	40	64	17
1790	30	28	58	28	35	63	18
1791	26	28	54	15	28	43	20
1792	31	29	60	52	46	98	29
1793	39	36	75	28	26	54	19
1794	38	26	64	33	33	66	25
1795 to 19 Nov.	29	19	48	43	31	74	15

The Poor's Rates in Framwelgate were about £ 100. a year, 20 years
ago; but in 1795 they amounted to £ 210.—In Croffgate, the Poor were
maintained till the year 1795 at 1s. 8d. a week each; but now coft
2s. 2d. each.

November, 1795.

ST. NICHOLAS.

THE inhabitants of this parifh, are principally employed in various manufactures, but chiefly in the woollen trade.   The prices of provifions are
very high, and the wages of labour are fo low as to bear no proportion
to them.   The number of ale-houfes is 22.   Here are 5 Societies called Life
Clubs; which allow £ 8. to the nearest relative of a deceafed member, but
the ftewards deduct £ 3. for the expences of the funeral.   The inhabitants
are moftly of the eftablifhed Church; there are however feveral Methodifts, and a few Papifts: there is 1 Prefbyterian meeting-houfe, and 1
Quakers'

Quakers' meeting-houfe in this parifh. This parifh has a co-extenfive right, with the other parifhes of the city of Durham, to pafturage on the extenfive commons or wafte lands of Framwelgate Moor and Brathfide Moor. There are not 20 acres of enclofed land in the parifh.

The Poor of this parifh are partly maintained in a work-houfe, and partly relieved at home. Theie was fo general a reluctance in this city to communicate any information refpecting the Poor, that this account is neceffarily very imperfect. From the returns made to Parliament in 1786, I find that the expences for the Poor, in 1776, amounted to £246. 5s. ; and the Poor's Rates, in 1783, to £455. 3s. ; in 1784, to £456. 19s. 4d. ; and in 1785, to £442. 2s. I fhould imagine that fince that period they have confiderably increafed ; as the Poor here appear to be very numerous, and very neceffitous.

Table of Diet in the Work-houfe.

	Breakfaft.	Dinner.	Supper.
Sunday,	Hafty pudding and milk.	Boiled beef, bread, and broth.	Cold milk and bread, or boiled.
Monday,	Ditto	Broth and bread,	Ditto.
Tuefday,	Ditto.	Suet pudding or dumplin.	Ditto.
Wednefday,	Ditto.	Frumenty and bread.	Ditto.
Thurfday,	Ditto.	Boiled beef, bread, and broth.	Ditto.
Friday,	Ditto.	Broth and bread.	Ditto.
Saturday,	Ditto.	Milk boiled with wheaten bread.	Ditto.

Table of Baptifms, Burials, and Marriages

Years.	Baptifms.	Burials.	Marriages.
1760	36	43	10
1775	49	25	13
1776	49	42	12
1777	50	27	8
1778	54	32	9
1779	44	31	12
1780	51	26	12
1781	45	26	10
1782	43	34	11

X 2

Years.

Years.	Baptifms.	Burials.	Marriages
1783	52	23	13
1784	59	22	14
1785	57	30	12
1786	45	39	9
1787	57	26	14
1788	58	38	15
1789	58	27	11
1790	62	19	14
1791	63	26	14
1792	46	34	13
1793	56	36	19
1794	52	34	22

The following are the earnings and expences of a man who is an hoftler at one of the inns in this city. He is 45 years of age ; has 6 children, all boys ; the eldeft is 10 years, and the youngeft 9 months old.

EARNINGS.

	£.	s.	d.
The man earns 9s. a week, (befides being allowed his diet;) yearly - - - - -	23	8	0
His wife earns 2d. a week by fpinning, yearly - -	0	8	8
Total earnings -	£ 23	16	8

EXPENCES.

	£.	s.	d.
Barley meal, 3s. 4d. a week, yearly - - -	8	13	4
Milk, 1s. 2d. a week, yearly - - -	3	0	8
Potatoes, 8d a week, yeaily - - - -	1	14	8
Oatmeal, 10d. a week, yearly - - -	2	3	4
Tea and fugar, 1s. a week, yearly - - -	2	12	0
Soap, blue, &c. 3d. a week, yearly - - -	0	13	0
Butcher's meat, 10d. a week, yearly - - -	2	3	4
Salt, 1d. a week, yearly - - - -	0	4	4
Carried over -	£ 21	4	8

			£		
Brought over	-	-	21	4	8
House rent, yearly - -	-	-	1	0	0
Fuel, yearly - - -	-	-	1	6	0
Lying-in costs annually, about -	-	-	0	8	0
Cloaths, and other expences, yearly about	-	-	2	10	0
Total expences	-	£	26	8	8

No butter or beer is used by this family: they occasionally receive a few old cloaths from their neighbours; but do not afk relief of the parish.

March, 1796.

HOLY ISLAND.

THE parish of Holy Island, in the county palatine of Durham, contains 4 chapelries, viz. Keyloe, Lowick, Ancroft, and Tweedmouth; all of which, as well as the parish itself, are perpetual curacies, under the patronage of the Dean and Chapter of Durham. The chapelries are not included in the following account. Two small townships with a few single dwelling-houses belong to the Mother Church, on the neighbouring coast; and are distinguished below, by the term *continental*.

Holy Island is 7 miles in circumference, consists of 1023 acres, and contains 330 inhabitants. The extent of the continental part cannot be easily ascertained; but is not very extensive: it, probably, does not amount to more than 3000 acres. It is all enclosed, and in a state of cultivation. Three years ago, it contained 361 inhabitants.

The number of houses in Holy Island paying the commutation tax is 51. Two, three, and even four families reside under the same roof; but only one pays the window-tax: no houses are exempted. On the continental part 11 houses pay the window-tax: 39 are exempted.

The principal employment of the inhabitants of the island, is fishing for haddocks, ling, cod, and codling, in the summer; and for lobsters, in the winter.

winter.   Agriculture is the chief occupation on the continental part.
There are no manufactories in the parifh.

The average prices of provifions are: butcher's meat, 4d. the pound;
haddocks, 1s. the fcore; and all white fifh very reafonable; wheat, 5s. the
Winchefter bufhel; flour; 2s the ftone of 14 lb.; oatmeal, 2s. the peck, or
16 quarts; butter, 8d. the pound of 18½ oz. The high prices of laft year are
not noticed.

There are at prefent 13 fifhing-boats, called Cobbles, kept at Holy Ifland;
7 of which are employed in the white fifhery in fummer.   They are all
engaged in lobfter fifhing in winter; it commences on the firft of December.   Four men go in a boat to fifh for haddocks, cod, &c.; and three
in a boat to fifh for lobfters.   Some agricultural labourers, and mechanics,
follow lobftering in the winter.   The feafon for taking lobfters continues
till the firft of June, and was a few years ago a very lucrative branch of
bufinefs; but, during the two laft years, December has been the only fuccefsful month: the fifhermen have, therefore, been obliged to return to
white fifhing very early in the fpring.   A company of fifhmongers in
London has contracted for all the lobfters taken at this place; and, I believe,
all along the coaft.   Prior to this year, 7s. were the price of a fcore of full-fized
lobfters, which now coft 8s.   Agricultural labourers earn 1s. 4d. a day;
mafons, 2s.; and joiners, 1s. 8d.

The farms on the ifland are fmall: the principal articles of cultivation are,
fmall oats, barley, turnips, and potatoes   On the continental part, the
farms in general are large: there is one at 800, and another at 600 guineas
a year.   The rent of land is £2. an acre for about 40 acres of old enclofure adjoining to the town of Holy Ifland.   On the continental part
three fourths of the land are in a ftate of tillage, and produce good crops of
oats, barley, turnips, and potatoes.   A fingle farm of 800 acres, tithe-free,
lets at a guinea an acre; fome land lets at £1. 13s.; and fome at 10s. an
acre; but the greateft part averages at £1. 10s.   The rental of land in
Holy Ifland amounts to about £450.; and the total rental of the ifland,
(including houfe-rent, kelp, tithe of fifh, and harbour dues,) amounted laft
year to £667. 12s; and the land-taxto £34.; £15. of which are paid by
the cuftom-houfe officers ftationed here.   The rental of land in the continental part of the parifh, amounts to £235. 5s., and the land-tax to
£64. 1s. 5d., of which two cuftom-houfe officers pay £10.   The proprietors

prietors of land, and meffuages in the ifland, are divided into two claffes; the one denominated *Freeholders*; and the other *Stallengers*. The latter are, in the ftrict fenfe of the term, as much freeholders as the former, and have a right to vote at the county election. About 40 acres only were enclofed prior to the divifion of the common, which took place three years ago; when land was fet-off in lieu of all tithes, which entirely belong to the Crown, not excepting even the Eafter offerings. The leffee of the Crown has lately re-let the property of the Crown, (the tithe of fifh excepted,) and his own lands, under one leafe for the term of 13 years for £430. annual rent; in confequence of which it is expected that the total rental of the ifland will next year amount to above £800. The common at Holy Ifland, previous to the divifion, was a ftinted one; and a freeholder had a right to put 30 fheep, 4 black cattle, and 3 horfes upon it: a ftallenger had only a right of common for a horfe and a cow. Of the firft clafs of land-holders there were 26; of the fecond 31. Since the divifion, the property in Holy Ifland has gotten into fewer hands. The manerial rights, as well as the tithes, belong to the Crown; to which a fixteenth, for giving up proprietors' right of foil, was awarded on the divifion. The ware, or fea-weed, whether burnt into kelp, or ufed as manure, is the fole property of the Crown. 506 acres of unimproveable land, which were awarded to the Crown, are burrowed with rabbits.

On the continental part there are 2 inns or ale-houfes; in the ifland, 5; befides which, many other lodgings are let to bathers, during the feafon; or rather, families receive bathers to board. The general weekly charge for each perfon, both in private, and in public-houfes, before laft fummer, was 10s. 6d. exclufive of tea and fugar: 12s. were demanded laft fummer.

There are feveral perfons on the continental part, and a few on the ifland, Diffenters; of the Prefbyterian perfuafion. Their meeting-houfe ftands in the chapelry of Lowick. Sir Carnaby Haggerfton laft year built a chapel for celebrating mafs, near his own manfion, which ftands in the chapelry of Ancroft.

There is no houfe of induftry in the parifh of Holy Ifland. On the divifion of the common in the years 1792, and 1793, a fmall piece of ground was awarded, for the purpofe of a poor-houfe being erected;

but

but there is no probability of one being foon built. Paupers in geneial have a weekly allowance paid quarteily ; fome receive 1s. a week; fome 1s. 6d. ; and fome 2s.

Table of the Baptifms, Burials, and Marriages.

Years	Baptisms.			Burials.			Marriages.
	Males.	Females	Total	Males.	Females.	Total	
1680	11	6	17	8	6	14	11
1685	10	10	20	14	11	25	15
1690	8	6	14	10	4	14	15
1691	8	7	15	11	8	19	15
1692	15	6	21	10	6	16	14
1693	10	6	16				7
1694	6	5	11		Regifter torn.		10
1695	9	10	19				3
1696	14	9	23	7	11	18	12
1697	5	10	15	3	3	6	13
1698	8	8	16	6	5	11	9
1699	6	6	12	6	4	10	8
1700	4	4	8	5	3	8	3
1720	11	14	25	12	8	20	5
1740	9	10	19	7	3	10	2
1760	3	7	10	2	2	4	5
1775	5	2	7	4	4	8	2
1776	5	4	9	5	6	11	3
1777	6	4	10	5	2	7	6
1778	6	2	8	4	10	14	3
1779	3	2	5	5	3	8	1
1780	4	6	10	2	3	5	3
1781	4	2	6	3	6	9	3
1782	2	5	7	7	1	8	2
1783	4	5	9	3	4	7	2
1784	4	3	7	4	2	6	7
1785	4	4	8	5	4	9	2
1786	4	4	8	2	1	3	3
1787	2	3	5	2	2	4	2

Years.

Years.	BAPTISMS.			BURIALS			MARRIAGES.
	Males.	Females.	Total.	Males.	Females	Total	
1788	6	1	7	0	6	6	0
1789	2	2	4	1	0	1	0
1790	5	4	9	4	5	9	1
1791	4	4	8	4	3	7	1
1792	1	3	4	7	6	13	3
1793	7	4	11	1	4	5	1
1794	2	4	6	4	4	8	0
1795	5	2	7	1	6	7	2

N. B. Under the year 1759, are 15 burials entered in the regifter ; and in the year 1761, there are 16.—Marriages cannot be correctly numbered by the regifter in parifhes on the borders; as the parties very frequently go into Scotland to be married. *January,* 1796.

MONKWEARMOUTH.

THE parifh of Monkwearmouth is between 4 and 5 miles in length from eaft to weft, and near 2 miles in breadth from north to fouth. It is bounded by the parifh of Weftington on the weft, Bolden and Whitburn on the north, the River Wear on the fouth, and the German Ocean on the eaft. It contains 5 townfhips, or conftableries, viz. Monkwearmouth, Monkwearmouth Shore, Fulwell, Southwick, and Hylton. There are between 1200 and 1300 families in the parifh, confifting of above 5000 perfons, a great many of whom are crowded in fmall tenements, containing only 2 or 3 rooms each. Moft of the inhabitants refide in the two firft-mentioned townfhips, which form a part of the port of Sunderland. 274 houfes pay the window-tax ; the number exempted is not eafy to be afcertained, but is very numerous ; and, from the population, I fhould imagine, that the number of tenements not chargeable is double the number of houfes affeffed. The religious perfuafions in this parifh are very various; there are Proteftants, Catholics, Methodifts, and other Diffenters of various denominations. The Catholics are the leaft numerous.

VOL II   Y   The

The inhabitants are occupied in agriculture, and in the various branches of business connected with the coal trade, and the extensive commerce carried on from Sunderland, to the Baltic, Holland, and France. Many ships are built on the shore of the river Wear; in the last war, frigates, and even ships of the line, were constructed here, and there is now building at Southwick, a ship of 1200 tons burthen. There are 10 ship-carpenters' yards in this parish. Much window glass is made here : there are likewise 2 potteries, several iron works, and free-stone and lime-stone quarries in abundance in the parish. Lime, to a large amount yearly, is sent in small vessels to various parts of Yorkshire, and Scotland.

The prices of provisions are, in general, higher here than in Durham market, on account of the great stock required, at the port of Sunderland, for victualling ships, &c. Cod, ling, haddocks, herrings, and other fish, are in great abundance, here, at various seasons. Agricultural labourers receive from 14d. to 16d. the day, and at present rather more. A good servant in husbandry is allowed, besides his board, from 12 to 14 or 15 guineas a year. Wages have been much increased, since the war.

Farms, in general, do not exceed 100 acres. The principal articles of cultivation are wheat, oats, barley, potatoes, turnips, and clover. There is much pasture, and meadow in the parish. The western part, being out of the reach of manure, is poor. The rent of land is from 10s. to £4. an acre : the whole rental could not easily be ascertained. The land-tax of this parish is £64. 18s. 3d. Tithes are chiefly in lay-hands, and are, usually, let to the tenant. There have been no commons in the parish for several years. The living is a curacy, in the gift of Sir Hedworth Williamson, Bart. and worth rather more than £100. a year.

The Poor, in many of the townships, are in a miserable condition ; nor has any judicious plan yet been adopted for administering relief to them in a beneficial manner. In the northern townships the Rates have risen to an enormous height, particularly since the commencement of the war. Part, however, of their rise, may, without imputing any thing to mismanagement, be fairly ascribed to the great increase in trade, population, buildings ; and, I hope I may add, without being considered paradoxical, that the influx of wealth, which this parish has experienced within the last 40 years, has produced a more than proportionable addition of Poor.

In the townſhips of Fulwell and Hylton [1], the Poor's Rates are more moderate than in the adjoining townſhips. Southwick partakes both of huſbandry, trade, and manufactures ; and the Rates are there, as might be expected, higher than in Hylton and Fulwell.

Years	Bapt	Burials	Mar	Poor's Rate in Monkwearmouth £. s. d	Poor's Rate in Monkwearmouth Shore £. s. d.	
1775	—	—	—	— — —	370 4 0	Net Expenditure of 1775:
1776	—	—	—	82 15 0	— — —	the ſums in ſubſequent years
1782	—	—	—	103 13 3	— — —	denote the Poor's Rate.—
1783	—	—	—	104 10 6	452 4 3	The years 1776, 1783, 1784,
1784	—	—	—	107 17 11	440 0 3	and 1785, were taken from
1785	—	—	—	118 9 6	450 18 9	the returns made to Parlia-
1787	—	—	—	— — —	383 12 0	ment in 1786.
1791	102	146	52	— — —	— — —	
1792	128	165	49	141 4 4	481 3 10	
1793	145	155	60	— — —	676 8 6	
1794	136	186	47	152 14 5½	686 5 0	

The church-books of this pariſh, which extended very far back, were, in 1790, unfortunately deſtroyed by a fire burſting out at midnight in the miniſter's houſe, which adjoins to the church.

The aſtoniſhing iron bridge now conſtructing under the auſpices of Rowland Burdon, Eſq. over the river Wear, has one of it's ſtone piers erected on the Monkwearmouth ſhore ; and there is very little doubt but this great work will prove of ineſtimable utility to the county.

	Feet	Inches
Span of the arch	236	0
Height from low water	100	5
Width	32	0

January, 1796.

[1] Hylton Caſtle, which about 50 years ago was highly improved and embelliſhed, by John Hylton, Eſq but is now neglected and uninhabited, is the principal manſion in this pariſh.

SOUTH

SOUTH SHIELDS.

THE chapelry of St. Hildo, South Shields, is fituated in the parifh of Jarrow, at the north-eaft extremity of the county of Durham, and extends about a mile and a half along the fouth fide of the river Tyne, and about 2 miles from north to fouth. The town was formerly celebrated for it's falt-works; having once contained 200 large iron pans for boiling fea-water. This trade began to decline about the year 1755, in confequence of having loft the London market; and there are now only 6 or 8 pans, which are principally ufed to fupply the town, and the fhips belonging to the port.

The Dean and Chapter of Durham are lords of the manor, and proprietors of the whole town, except about 3 acres of glebe, the parfonage, and 2 other houfes, and 1 of the Prefbyterian meeting-houfes. The town is ill paved, and very dirty: the houfes are ill built; a circumftance, which, in an opulent fea port, is afcribed to the leafehold tenure under the church; and it is fuppofed to be owing to the fame caufe, (although the expofed fituation of the country may have its effect,) that the land around Shields fcarcely exhibits a fingle tree [1].

The number of families that pay the window-tax is 550: the number of houfes exempted could not poffibly be afcertained; fome idea, however, of their proportion may be formed from the fubjoined table of births and burials. It is fuppofed that the population amounts to 15,000 fouls: this conjecture is corroborated by the parifh-clerk's lift of families, from which he receives a yearly offering: it enumerates 2500 families; befides which many poor families are omitted. From the average of births, and burials,

[1] The natural fituation of the town is far from unpleafant, but has been much deformed by immenfe mountains of cinders and afhes, (from the falt-pans,) having been laid near to it: and fince the falt trade has declined, other hills continue to be formed in the fame diforder, by the gravel of the Thames, which is brought as ballaft in the colliers, and thrown out in unfeemly heaps near the town. Within thefe 2 years a melancholy accident happened: the cinder hills above-mentioned were fet on fire by a falt proprietor imprudently laying hot cinders upon them; 3 people who lived in houfes built upon them were fuffocated in their beds, others much injured, feveral houfes demolifhed, and the hills ftill continue to burn, and to emit a fulphurous fmell.

during

during the laft 7 years, it would feem, that the above account of the population is much exaggerated. The people may be divided into three claffes ;
Durham, Yorkfhire, and Scotch men : the laft clafs is very numerous : two
ninths of the whole population are Proteftant' Diffenters, and have 3 meeting-houfes: there are likewife, in Shields, 1 Quaker's, 2 Roman Catholic
families, and a great many Methodifts.

The inhabitants are chiefly engaged in the various occupations and
trades relative to commerce. The number of fhips belonging to North
and South Shields, which are the port of Newcaftle, exceeds 500 : they
average 200 tons and upwards by regifter. No river in England, except
the Thames, can exhibit an equal quantity of fhipping. That the
trade from this port is one of the principal nurferies of feamen, is evident from the Act paffed laft year for procuring a fupply of men for the
Navy, from the different parts of the kingdom ². The number of men
directed to be levied were as follows :

				Men.
By the port of London	-	-	-	5704
Liverpool	-	-	-	1711
Newcaftle	-	-	-	1240
Hull	-	-	-	731
Whitehaven	-	-	-	700
Sunderland	-	-	-	669
Briftol	-	-	-	666
Whitby	-	-	-	573
Yarmouth	-	-	-	506 &c.

The whole number to be raifed by the ports of England is 17,948.

There is a place near the church in South Shields called the Mill-dam,
formed by nature, to afford a moft excellent dock :—the water already
flows into the dam, which, with a little deepening, might be made fufficiently capacious to contain 300 fhips. In winter time, the navigation of
the Tyne is much obftructed by the number of veffels which are laid up,
and a confiderable expence is incurred from the wear and tear of cables,
&c. which would in a great meafure be faved by the conftruction of a
dock. The Dean and Chapter of Durham can forward this, or any great
and laudable undertaking, that may be fuggefted for the benefit of South
Shields : there is a great public fpirit in the inhabitants for improvement,

---

' In another account with which I am favoured, the number of Diffenters is ftated at one-
tenth.

² 25 Geo 3. c 9

and

and could the tenure be changed or commuted, (a meafure which feems to be practicable, even without diminifhing the revenues of the church,) this port would very foon rival Liverpool and Briftol.

There are 162 public-houfes in South Shields, but only one church, which was confiderably enlarged in 1786 : the expence whereof amounted to £2600. and was defrayed by the fale of the new pews, without any tax on the inhabitants. The Dean and Chapter of Durham are the patrons of this chapelry. The tithes are let by them to a perfon, who re-lets them to the tenants of each eftate.

The farms are fmall : the principal articles of cultivation are, wheat, barley, oats, turnips, beans, and potatoes. There are no commons, except a few acres along the coaft, which are called the Bent.

The only manufactories in South Shields are four glafs-houfes; two for making crown; and two for making bottle glafs. There are very few agricultural labourers in the chapelry; they earn, each, about 2s. a day; carpenters, 3s. 6d.; glafs-men, from 2s. 6d. to 3s. 6d.

The prices of provifions are: beef, 5d. the pound; mutton, 4½d.; veal and lamb, 4d.

There are four Friendly Societies, which allow from £10. to £15. a year for life to the neareft relative of a deceafed member : there are like-wife fix called Life Clubs, which pay a fingle benefaction of about £7. to the neareft relation of a deceafed member.

The Poor are contracted for by a refpectable perfon, at 2s. 6d. weekly, for provifions and cloaths, for each Pauper that is maintained in the Poor-houfe, or Houfe of Induftry, as it is called. The number of inmates at prefent is 73. The weekly out-penfions at prefent amount to about £20. The expenditure for the Poor this year will, it is thought, exceed £2000.

Table of Diet in the Poor-houfe.

	Breakfaft.	Dinner.	Supper.
Sunday,	Hafty-pudding.	Beef, &c.	Broth and bread.
Monday,	Ditto.	Peafe foup.	Boiled milk.
Tuefday,	Ditto.	Barley boiled in milk.	Bread and milk.
Wednefday,	Ditto.	Beef, &c.	Broth and bread.
Thurfday,	Ditto.	Peafe foup.	Boiled milk.
Friday,	Ditto.	Suet dumplins.	Cold milk.
Saturday,	Ditto.	Barley boiled in milk.	Bread and milk.

In 1793, 7 males, and 5 females, died in the houfe; and in 1794, 2 males, and 4 females.

Table

Table of Baptisms, Burials, Marriages, and Poor's Rates.

Years	BAPTISMS			BURIALS.			MARRIAGES.
	Ma	Fem	Tot	Mal	Fem	Tot	
1680	51	65	116	44	32	76	13
1685	46	45	91	34	25	-59	20
1690	70	50	120	50	30	80	14
1691	64	48	112	45	56	101	19
1692	63	45	108	55	35	90	21
1693	58	46	104	40	29	69	13
1694	55	59	114	31	44	75	14
1695	60	60	120	72	49	121	22
1696	58	66	124	74	37	111	16
1697	53	51	104	46	38	84	21
1698	60	48	108	61	57	118	16
1699	52	51	103	65	66	131	12
1700	63	48	111	69	68	137	28
1720	59	57	116	44	35	79	14
1740	61	72	133	70	67	137	44
1760	83	83	166	29	24	51	28
1775	118	120	238	71	92	163	24
1776	123	97	220	109	113	222	52
1777	137	112	249	88	101	189	59
1778	127	127	254	134	123	257	53
1779	115	123	238	106	129	235	37
1780	127	124	251	63	97	160	39
1781	126	126	252	120	134	254	39
1782	106	107	213	85	106	191	60
1783	131	130	261	157	157	314	66
1784	137	122	259	112	109	221	59
1785	132	129	261	147	147	294	55
1786	125	105	230	148	166	314	63
1787	123	152	275	105	119	224	42
1788	121	155	276	145	148	293	47
1789	117	111	228	167	181	348	51
1790	139	165	304	139	130	269	45
1791	130	143	273	136	133	269	52
1792	149	154	303	164	199	363	49
1793	158	175	333	186	213	399	47
1794	151	155	306	209	227	436	58
1795							53

36)7074   36)6934   37)1365

1961¼   192⅜   37 nearly.

Poor's Rates.			Net Expend.			Rate in the Pound.
£.	s.	d.	£.	s	d.	
329	0	0	378	11	10½	
367	10	0	357	5	6	
383	15	0	376	4	8	
390	17	10	383	19	6	
428	1	4	426	2	9	
628	17	11	597	2	8	
648	11	6½	577	5	7½	
711	7	7	598	7	5	
356	18	9	309	2	7	
734	1	2	691	13	8	
774	3	8	774	3	8	
898	14	2	889	3	10½	
1240	4	2½	1224	17	9	d.
1116	18	0				6 Paid a month.
1127	16	0				6 Do.
—						0 Do.
1130	3	0				6 Do.
1351	6	0				7½ Do.
1281	2	0				7 Do.
1795	5	6				8 Do.
1985	18	0				11 Do.

The Rate is laid upon only ¼ of the rental.

	Baptisms	Burials.	Marriages.
The yearly average from 1690 to 1700 inclusive was -	111½	101 6/11	17 9/11
From 1775 to 1784 inclusive -	243½	220 6/10	48 1/10
From 1785 to 1794 inclusive -	278 9/10	320 9/10	50 9/10

October, 1795.

STAN-

STANHOPE.

STANHOPE in extent is about 17 miles by 6 : its population is eftimated at 3600 inhabitants, and is fuppofed not to have varied much for
fome years back.   There are 520 houfes which pay the window tax ; the
number exempted could not be afcertained.   Farming and mining, but
more efpecially the latter, are the principal occupations.   The inhabitants
are chiefly of the Church of England ; but there is one congregation of
Methodifts, and one of Prefbyterians.   The prices of provifions are as follows:—Wheat, 13s. ; barley, 6s. ; and oats, 4s. a bufhel : beef, 5s. the ftone;
mutton, 4d. to 4½d. the lb. ; butter, 11d. for 21 oz. ; new milk, ½d. the
pint ; old milk, ½d. the quart, wine meafure : potatoes, 9d. the peck ; they
were 6d. a peck at Michaelmas.   The wages of common labourers are from
7s. to 9s. a week, without board : mafons, 14s. a week ; when they work
by the piece, they can earn from 16s. to 20s a week.   Miners alfo work
by the piece, and their earnings are very fluctuating ; from £5. or £6. to
£50. or £60. a year ; the average is about £25.   In this parifh there are 20
ale-houfes   Here are two Friendly Societies, confifting together of about
80 members ; the orders of each have been confirmed.   The rent of land is
very various ; in fome inftances from £3. 10s. to £4. an acre ; in others,
7s 6d : the average of good land is 45s. ; of the lefs valuable, 15s.   Farms
let from £5. to £300 a year, but chiefly from £15. to £30   The tenure
is various in this parifh ; being cuftomary, copyhold, and freehold. Wheat,
barley, oats, and fome turnips, are cultivated ; but the principal part of
the enclofed land is in pafture.   Tithes are chiefly taken by compofition.
Land-tax is collected at about 3½d. in the pound : it is thought that about
three fourths of this parifh are mountainous common.   The Poor have
been farmed for many years : about 15 years ago they were farmed for
£250. ; but the expence has gradually increafed fince that period : the
year before laft, the expence was £495. and laft year £494. ; and the Contractor fays, that he fhall lofe £100. by his laft bargain, and will not take
the Poor this year under £700. 22 poor people are at prefent in the
houfe, and 100 families receive weekly relief out of it : thefe out-poor,
                                                                          the

the Contractor fays, will coft him £450. for the year ending at May-day next. The Poor-houfe was built about 15 years ago; it is, like moft others in the hands of contractors, in a dirty ftate. The following bill of fare is among the rules of the houfe; but at prefent it is not regularly obferved, on account of the dearnefs of provifions:

	Breakfaft	Dinner	Supper.
Sunday,	Hafty-pudding, &c	Boiled meat, pudding, broth, &c	Broth, bread, and milk.
Monday,	Ditto.	Ditto	Ditto.
Tuefday,	Ditto	Flour pudding and milk.	Bread and milk.
Wednefday,	Ditto	As Sunday.	As Sunday.
Thurfday,	Ditto.	As Tuefday.	As Tuefday.
Friday,	Ditto	As Sunday.	As Sunday.
Saturday,	Ditto	Potatoes and butter.	Bread and milk

N. B. Inftead of boiled meat, the Poor have, now, hafhed meat with potatoes, twice a week.

This parifh is divided into 4 quarters, and each quarter's account is fettled every 3 months; fo that, to get at one full year's Rate, the 16 fums, gathered from the different parts of the book, muft be thrown into one aggregate fum; which was done to obtain the Rates of fome of the following years:

	Amount of the Rates.			Rate in the Pound.	
	£	s.	d.	s.	d.
1766	388	9	8	1	0
1770	—	—	—	0	8½
1771	—	—	—	0	10
1780	—	—	—	1	1
1786	—	—	—	0	9
1791	581	15	8	1	2
1796	826	16	10	1	4

Out of thefe fums, about £100. are paid annually into the county ftock, and 6 guineas to the veftry clerk.

The mining bufinefs is faid to be rather unproductive to thofe employed therein, at prefent, there not being fo much metal got as formerly; and the wages for getting a certain quantity of ore are not more now, than many years ago; on which account feveral perfons have lately gone to work at the coal mines near Newcaftle, Sunderland, &c. Many miners keep a cow, which makes land let fo high. They ufe much oatmeal made into crowdie; and milk, and barley bread. The women fpin jerfey, and can

earn

earn 3d. or 4d. a day ; many of them manufacture their own woollen and linen apparel. The lead miners are generally lefs profligate than thofe who work in the coal mines, are better cloathed and moftly better informed.

Statement of a Miner's annual Earnings and Expences.

The man aged 44 years; his wife 42; his eldeft fon 16; a daughter 12 ; one boy 6, and another 4 years old.

	£.	s	d.
The man earns on an average about £ 25. a year - -	25	0	0
Oldeft boy earns - - - - -	7	0	0
Total - £ 32	32	0	0

The other children earn nothing; the wife takes care of the houfe, and fpins lint.

EXPENCES.

	£	s	d.
Barley bread - - - - -	7	10	0
Wheat and rye - - - - -	2	10	0
Oatmeal - - - - -	5	4	0
Butcher's meat - - - - -	2	10	0
Milk - - - - -	1	10	0
Potatoes - - - - -	1	8	0
Butter - - - - -	2	10	0
Tea and fugar - - - - -	2	0	0
Groceries - - - - -	1	10	0
Houfe-rent - - - - -	1	10	0
Fuel - - - - -	1	12	0
Cloathing, &c. &c. - - - - -	5	0	0
Total - £ 34	34	14	0

This family receive nothing from the parifh, fo that the expences muft be near £ 3. over-rated.

Statement of a Mafon's annual Earnings and Expences.

	£.	s.	d.
The mafon is 40 years of age; has a wife and 4 children, whofe ages are 12, 10, 4, and 2: he earns yearly about	28	0	0

EXPEN-

EXPENCES.

	£.	s.	d.
House-rent - - - - - -	2	0	0
Fuel - - - - - -	2	0	0
Barley bread and flour - - - -	6	10	0
Oatmeal - - - - - -	3	0	0
Milk - - - - - -	1	10	0
Butter - - - - - -	1	10	0
Cheese - - - - - -	0	10	0
Butcher's meat - - - - -	3	0	0
Tea and sugar - - - - -	2	0	0
Potatoes - - - - -	2	0	0
Cloaths, &c. - - - - -	4	0	0
Total -	£ 28	0	0

March, 1796.

SUNDERLAND.

THIS parish contains 130 acres: in 1794 the population was estimated at about 13,000 inhabitants, and they are supposed to be now much increased: the parishioners, &c. are shop-keepers, inn-keepers, ship-wrights, &c. ; but the principal employment of the labourers is in coal-heaving, (that is, putting coals out of the keels into the ships): keel-men, sailors, &c. Here are no manufactories. The inhabitants are of the Church of England, Presbyterians, Quakers, and Methodists; the Presbyterians have 4 chapels. Butcher's meat is from 5d. to 6d. the lb ; wheat, 12s. a bushel; oats, from 3s. to 3s. 6d. ; barley, 5s ; potatoes, 10d. the peck ; new milk, 1½d. the quart. Sailors, in time of war, earn from £ 40. to £ 100. a year ; and in time of peace, generally about £ 25 a year, and board, while on a voyage : keel-men, at all times from about £ 30. to £ 50. a year : coal-heavers, on the river, in time of war, from £ 30. to £ 50. a year ; and in time of peace, 10s. a week : common labourers, in the

Z 2   county

county adjoining, earn 9s a week. In this parish there are 187 ale-houses. There are 24 Friendly Societies: the average number of members in each, is supposed to be 50 to 60: most of them have had their rules confirmed by the Magistrates ; of these 4 or 5 are women's clubs. The landtax, paid annually in this parish, amounts to £ 120. 13s. About ⅔ of this parish is a common. The Poor are supported partly in a poor-house and partly at their own houses. 176 persons are at present in the poorhouse: there have been 29 deaths, and 12 births in the house since 1st May 1795. 36 of those now in the house are children, under 12 years of age ; about ⅔ of them are bastards : these children are employed in a pin manufactory, and altogether earn from about £ 30. to £ 40. a year ; the boys are generally bound apprentices to the sea service : the remainder of the people in this house are chiefly old women and prostitutes ; few old men are found here, being mostly employed as scavengers in the streets ; in picking oakum, &c. The house is in a very good situation : there are 4 or 5 beds in each apartment ; the beds have wooden bottoms, and are filled with chaff ; each bed has 2 blankets, 1 sheet, and 1 rug. A fever prevails now in the house, and has done so for some time back.

The following is the Bill of Fare.

	Breakfast	Dinner	Supper.
Sunday,	Hasty-pudding and milk.	Beef and bread.	Bread and broth.
Monday,	Ditto.	Old milk and bread.	Water gruel and bread.
Tuesday,	Ditto.	Pease-soup and bread.	Boiled milk and bread
Wednesday,	D.tto.	Rice milk and bread.	Boiled milk, or gruel, and bread.
Thursday,	Ditto.	As Sunday.	As Sunday
Friday,	Ditto.	As Monday.	As Monday.
Saturday	Ditto.	Barley-milk and bread.	Boiled milk, or gruel, and bread.

The bread is made of wheat and rye ; 6 oz. are allowed to each person at dinner and supper, on meat days; and on other days of the week ½lb. at each of their meals: ½lb. of meat is served to each person on Sundays and Thursdays. The victuals in the house cost about £ 26. or £ 27. a week. There are at present 279 poor families supported at their own houses, who receive about £ 17. a week ; also 43 militia men's families, and the families of 225 impressed men, who, at 1s. each, receive about £ 30. a week. About 4 years ago, an Act of Parliament was obtained to oblige the shipping

ping of this port to contribute towards the Poor's Rate according to the tonnage, which raifed laft year £ 829: 4 years ago it was found that 931 perfons were chargeable, and that 702 of thefe were from the fhipping.

Table of Baptifms, Burials, Marriages, &c.

Years.	Baptifms.	Burials.	Marriages	Amount of the Rates.			Rate in the Pound.	
				£.	s.	d.		
1755	293	353	—	—	—	—		
1762	—	—	—	522	18	6		
1763	—	—	—	738	15	9		
1764	—	—	—	758	1	9		
1765	259	412	—	—	—	—		
1768	—	—	—	1230	12	$1\frac{1}{2}$		
1769	—	—	—	882	7	9		
1770	—	—	—	905	12	6		
1775	326	563	—	—	—	—		
1776	—	—	141	1334	11	$10\frac{1}{2}$		
1777	—	—	—	1306	10	$1\frac{1}{2}$		
1778	—	—	—	1505	2	$4\frac{1}{2}$		
1779	—	—	—	2137	0	$4\frac{1}{2}$		
1780	—	—	—	1521	13	$10\frac{1}{2}$		
1781	—	—	—	1522	15	9		
1782	—	—	—	1659	16	6		
1783	—	—	—	1415	11	6		
1784	—	—	—	1367	8	3		
1785	335	581	—	1485	19	3		
1786	—	—	138	2104	9	3		
1787	—	—	—	1794	0	0		
1788	—	—	—	1685	14	0		
1789	—	—	—	1591	10	0		
1790	—	—	—	1985	13	3		
1791	—	—	—	1708	3	0		
1792	—	—	—	1887	13	$1\frac{1}{2}$		
1793	—	—	—	3298	5	7	s.	d.
1794	—	—	—	3770	4	0	3	4 } On the net
1795	321	466	126	4700	0	0	5	0 } rental.

Ending at Eafter.

The

The money raifed by the fhipping is included in the above accounts. The number of men raifed laft year for the Navy, by this port, was 669.

An old man, who is a fhepherd on the common for this town, brought up 10 children by his own labour, without receiving any affiftance from the parifh, or any one; to fome of his boys he gave a decent education : he has only 4 children living: his earnings were generally 5s. or 6s. a week, and he was chiefly employed in hufbandry.

A man, who lives a little diftance from Sunderland, and is employed in the coal mines, gives this account of his earnings and expenditure. He is 45 years old, his wife is 40; he has 3 children, (all girls,) whofe ages are 14, 6, and 2.

	£.	s.	d.
He, after deducting houfe-rent and fuel, (which is allowed to the mafter every fortnight,) earns about 23s in the fortnight; which amount in the year to - -	29	18	0
Befides his regular wages he had given him laft year -	5	5	0
Total - £	35	3	0

EXPENCES.

	£.	s.	d.
His family has bread meal, confifting of wheat, rye, and barley, allowed them at 1s. 6d. a ftone by the owner of the coal-mines; at the rate of half a ftone a week for each perfon, amounts annually to - - -	9	15	0
Butcher's meat, 2s. a week - - - -	5	4	0
Milk, 1s. a week - - - - - - -	2	12	0
Oatmeal, 10d. a week - - - -	2	3	4
Tea, 2d. do. - - - - - -	0	8	8
Sugar, 1s. do. - - - - -	2	12	0
Salt and pepper, 2½d. do. - - - -	0	10	10
Potatoes, 3½d. do. - - - -	0	15	2
Barley to boil with milk, 1¼d. do. - - -	0	5	5
Soap, 4½d. do. - - - - -	0	19	6
Toward the maintenance of a baftard child of his wife before her marriage, at 6d. a week - - -	1	6	0
Wear and tear of work-geer, at 2s. a fortnight - -	2	12	0
Cloaths and cafual expences - - - -	5	19	1
Total - £	35	3	0

This

This man has been fometimes fick himfelf; had a boy died, and a former wife; but has hitherto fupported his family without any relief from the parifh. No butter or beer is ufed in his houfe at prefent[1].

March, 1796.

TANFIELD.

THE parochial chapelry of Tanfield is fituated in the parifh of Chefter-le-ftreet: it is near ten miles in circumference; and contains about 2000 inhabitants, all of the Church of England, who are moftly employed in the coal mines, and coal works. The wages of labourers in hufbandry are from 1s. 4d. to 1s. 6d. a day; and in the mines, and coal works, from 2s. to 3s. The farms are fmall: grafs, wheat, and oats, are the principal articles of produce; to which may be added potatoes, which have of late years been much attended to, and now form the chief diet of labourers' families The cheapnefs of fuel feems the caufe, why this very ufeful vegetable is much more generally ufed in the north, than in the fouthern parts of the kingdom. Beef and mutton are from 4d. to 6d. the pound. Land lets from 10s. to 50s. the acre. The commons and wafte lands amount to about 1500 acres. No part has been inclofed, although every part is very improveable, and every fpecies of produce might be raifed, with the certainty of a good market at Newcaftle, which is only fix miles diftant. Here, as in other coal countries, the furface of the earth is neglected for the infide; it may, however, be doubted, whether the mines about Tanfield, have, of late years, been profitable to their owners. The colliery rents have confiderably decreafed, and many of the collieries in the neighbourhood have been fhut up. The great length and expence of coal roads, (feveral of the mines being fix or feven miles diftant from the Tyne,) are heavy drawbacks; and, with many other circumftances, (which it is unneceffary here to detail,) have given the collieries on the river below Newcaftle-bridge a decided advantage.

There are two paper-manufactories in Tanfield, that employ about ten men each. The number of ale-houfes in the chapelry is fixteen. 130 houfes pay the window tax: 270 are exempted.

[1] For other particulars relative to Sunderland, fee p. 162.

Of

Of the Poor, about 20 are received into, and maintained in the work-houfe: other diftreffed families, which are very numerous, are relieved at home.

Table of Diet in Tanfield Work-houfe.

	Breakfaft.	Dinner.	Supper
Sunday,	Hafty-pudding, with milk or beer.	Butcher's meat, with peafe pudding, or other vegetables.	Broth, and bread.
Monday,	Ditto.	Peafe foup, and bread	Milk boiled with oatmeal.
Tuefday,	Ditto	Boiled barley, and milk.	Milk, and bread.
Wednefday,	Ditto	The fame as Sunday	Broth, and bread.
Thurfday,	Ditto	The fame as Monday.	Milk boiled with oatmeal
Friday,	Ditto	Suet pudding, and dumplins.	Milk and bread.
Saturday,	Ditto	Boiled barley, and milk.	Broth, and bread.

Table of Baptifms, Burials, and Marriages, Rental, and Poor's Rates.

Years	Baptisms		Burials.		Marriages.	Affeffed Rental	Affeffed Poor's Rate.			Rate in the pound on the affeffed rental.	
	Males.	Fem.	Males.	Fem.		£.	£.	s.	d.	s.	d.
1760	47	49	31	34	27						
1775	48	42	33	39	20						
1776	60	33	30	33	16						
1777	46	35	31	31	21						
1778	48	47	38	32	25						
1779	40	57	29	24	30	6377	345	9	0	1	1
1780	41	61	31	38	17	6575	328	15	0	1	0
1781	40	57	34	43	28	6468	323	8	0	1	0
1782	52	32	33	22	14	5658	282	18	0	1	0
1783	42	49	36	48	19	5824	291	4	0	1	0
1784	47	47	43	41	16	5842	292	2	0	1	0
1785	42	42	26	32	16	5723	281	3	0	1	0
1786	44	53	27	34	24	5609	490	16	0	1	9
1787	54	47	39	39	16	5351	468	5	0	1	9
1788	43	36	39	43	19	5337	400	5	0	1	6
1789	41	37	30	23	18	5324	465	17	0	1	9
1790	42	42	32	23	17	5368	536	10	0	2	0
1791	35	37	38	49	20	5452	545	4	0	2	0
1792	32	44	22	28	13	5674	567	8	0	2	0
1793	31	34	35	46	17	5660	566	0	0	2	0
1794	37	46	30	25	13	5680	568	0	0	2	0
1795	31	40	36	35	20	5845	584	10	0	2	0

The

The colliery rents in 1795 amounted to £1380
The rent of lands - - - 4465

Total - £5845

In fome of the firft mentioned years, 1779, &c. the colliery rents were £2000. a year. *January*, 1796.

E S S E X.

COLCHESTER.

THE parifh of All Saints contains, by admeafurement, 256 acres, 2 roods, 12 perches : the number of inhabitants could not be learned ; but the whole population of Colchefter is eftimated at about 8000 fouls The number of houfes paying the window tax, is 58 ; of which 6 are double tenements : the number of houfes exempted could not be afceitained. The inhabitants are chiefly engaged in trade and manufactures. Land, un-built on, lets at £1. 2s an acre, upon an average. The land-tax amounts to £163. and is about 4s. 2d. in the pound on the net rental. A pecu-niary compofition, which is very variable, is paid, in lieu of tithes. There are 2 public-houfes in the parifh : in the 16 parifhes of Colchefter there are 75 inns or ale-houfes. There are no commons, or wafte lands, in the parifh.

The prices of provifions are : beef, 5½d. the pound ; mutton, 5½d. ; veal, 5½d. ; poik, 6d. and 6½d. ; bacon, 9d ; butter, 10d. ; wheat, 80s. the quaitei ; barley, from 28s. to 41s. ; malt, from 44s. to 49s. ; flour, the ftone, fiom 2s 11d. to 3s 2d.

The principal manufacture heie is the coarfe woollen called baize ; the greateft pait of which is expoited to Spain The trade is in a declining ftate, owing, it is fuppofed, to the war between Spain and France. About 100 looms aie employed in the filk manufacture ; and theie are likewife, in this paiifh, a few wool-card makers. Weavers earn from 8s. to 9s. a week ; woolcombeis, fiom 10s. to 12s. ; fpinners, from 4d to 6d. a day ; children, 8 or 9 years old, earn by fpinning, from 2d. to 3d. a day ; card-makers, 2s. a day ; women weavers, from 5s. to 5s. 6d. a week. Agri-cultuial labouiers receive, during harveft, fiom 1s. 8d. to 2s a day ; common laboureis, 1s. 6d. a day.

VOL. II.　　　　　A a　　　　　Befides

Besides 16 churches in the town of Colchester, there are 1 Quaker, 1 Presbyterian, 1 Dissenting, 1 Anabaptist, and 1 of John Wesley's chapels. The number of Dissenters, of different denominations, is supposed to amount to 1500.

There are 18 Friendly Societies, consisting each of from 20 to 40 members. They pay 1s. monthly into the box. Sick persons receive from 8s. to 10s. a week; and aged members, 6s. a week. I believe all the Societies have complied with the late Act of Parliament.

The parishes in Colchester were formerly incorporated for the purpose of supporting their Poor; but by some means or other, about 50 years ago, they were disunited, and now each parish manages its own Poor. The Rates are very different in different quarters of the town: they are the highest in St. Mary Magdalen, and the lowest in All-Saints parish. For this no satisfactory reason can be assigned: the common one given is, that parishes, whose Rates are high, have little land, few rich people, a great number of poor cottages, and few good houses. The nominal Rate in this town is said to be upon the rack rent, whenever it can be discovered, except on small houses of from 30s. to 50s a year, when it is upon half rental. Various manœuvres, however, are used to conceal the real rent; and, upon the whole, I should imagine it exceeds the nominal rental in the proportion of about 7 to 5.

The Poor in this parish have a weekly allowance, and generally have cottages found them by the parish. A surgeon has 8 guineas annually for attending the Poor. The following is a list of regular out pensioners:

		Age	Weekly Allowance.	
			s.	d.
1 M. C. an unmarried woman; rather disordered in her understanding;	- - -	76	3	6
2 M. M. a tailor; lame;	- - -	62	2	6
3 — W. a blacksmith's widow;	- -	80	5	0
4 A person who attends her;	- - -	—	2	6
5 — W. and 3 children; her husband is in the army;	45	3	6
6 — H. a widow;	- - - -	68	2	6
7 V. — a widow;	- - - -	70	5	0
8 S. a labourer's widow, with 4 children;	- -	45	2	0
9 B. a soldier's widow, with 2 children;	- -	30	2	0
10 S. a farmer; lame;	- -	65	2	6
11 E. I. an unmarried woman; with sore eyes;	-	60	2	0
12 — E. a cutler's widow;	- -	50	2	3

13 An

			Age.	Weekly Allowance
13 An orphan girl;	-	-	-	-	10	1s. 6d.
14 An orphan girl; her underſtanding is a little deranged;	-	-	-	-	-	18	1	6
14 A baſtard;	-	-	-	-	-	—	1	6

Table of Baptiſms, Burials, Marriages, and Poor's Rates.

Years	Baptiſms			Burials			Marriages	Poor's Rate			Net Expenditure on the Poor.			Rate in the pound on nominal rental
	Males	Fem	Total	Males	Fem	Total		£.	s.	d.	£.	s.	d.	
1680	3	7	10	12	11	23	77							
1685	7	5	12	7	6	13	10							
1690	3	11	14	10	7	17	11							
1691	2	6	8	7	10	17	17							
1692	6	2	8	2	0	2	27							
1693	6	5	11	10	7	17	25							
1694	1	3	4	11	15	26	8							
1695	3	6	9	12	13	25	15							
1696	10	13	23	11	11	22	19							
1697	7	8	15	7	8	15	15							
1698	3	9	12	7	6	13	21							
1699	7	5	12	9	6	15	27							
1700	3	7	10	5	5	10	32							
1720	7	11	18	15	6	21	22							
1740	14	9	23	13	7	20	11							
1746	—	—	—	—	—	—	—	51	8	7	51	9	9	
1747	—	—	—	—	—	—	—	49	8	0	56	5	11	
1748	—	—	—	—	—	—	—	81	10	7	76	12	0	
														s. d.
1760	12	13	25	4	6	10	19							
1775	28	20	48	2	4	6	27	156	4	6	166	3	8	5 6
1776	11	24	35	2	8	10	17	162	12	9	191	3	10	6 0
1777	22	27	49	6	5	11	21	165	3	6	198	0	9¼	6 0
1778	13	25	38	7	6	13	18	165	0	0	186	4	4	6 0
1779	23	29	52	4	7	11	15	167	4	10	162	10	4¼	6 0
1780	21	18	39	10	4	14	15	180	16	9	188	6	1½	7 0
1781	15	14	29	6	4	10	13	184	18	6	220	5	0	7 0
1782	17	19	36	10	6	16	18	180	5	0	171	12	3½	7 0
1783	15	18	33	5	4	9	17	164	12	5	169	2	5	6 0
1784	26	29	55	8	9	17	23	162	9	0	174	10	0¼	6 0
1785	27	22	49	7	8	15	18	184	12	0	180	14	3	7 0
1786	18	36	54	4	3	7	16	190	19	6	194	12	10	7 0
1787	23	26	49	5	5	10	24	161	15	6	167	12	1½	6 0
1788	34	23	57	1	3	4	11	164	2	0	168	0	8¼	6 0
1789	22	33	55	6	4	10	32	139	5	6	171	14	6	5 0
1790	20	24	44	1	4	5	19	152	17	3	165	10	6	5 0
1791	21	25	46	5	8	13	30	137	8	0	168	9	11¼	5 6
1792	22	25	47	7	4	11	18	138	6	9	138	6	9	5 0
1793	26	25	51	8	6	14	20	139	11	0	123	1	11	5 0
1794	15	16	31	4	6	10	23	139	8	6	160	14	10	5 0
1795	18	14	32	5	4	9	3	140	12	6	136	10	6	5 0

The

The baptifms are only brought down to the 15th of June 1795, and the burials to the 12th of June 1795. It is to be obferved, that as the paiifh-church of St. Botolph is in ruins, it's marriages and baptifms are entered in the books of All Saints; but burials of the parifh of St. Botolph are folemnized in the church-yard of St. Botolph. From hence it may be inferred, that no very accurate eftimate of the population of All Saints can be formed from the regifters, as they have not regularly diftinguifhed the perfons belonging to each parifh. It fhould likewife be obferved, that, previous to the Marriage Act, feveral marriages were celebrated in All Saints church, although neither of the parties belonged to the parifh.

The parifh of St. Mary Magdalen contains about 50 acres of land; and about 250 inhabitants, who are chiefly employed in making baize. 15 houfes pay the commutation tax; 30 feparate houfes are exempted. The population of this parifh has continued much the fame for feveral years back. The prices of provifions, and wages of labour, are much the fame as in All Saints parifh: the inhabitants of both parifhes belong to the Friendly Societies before-mentioned. The land-tax, amounting to £31. 16s. is at the rate of about 5s. 6d. or 6s. in the pound on nearly the net rental. Land lets at about £1. an acre. Tithes are taken, chiefly, in compofition. There are a great many gardens in the parifh; the reft is grafs land.

The Poor are maintained at home, and receive weekly allowances from the parifh. That their maintenance is extremely burthenfome, the following account will demonftrate. No Rate-book prior to 1790, or account-book prior to 1781, could be procured.

Years.			Poor's Rate.				Net Expenditure on Poor.			Rate on the nominal rental. [1]	
			£.	s.	d.		£.	s.	d.	s.	d.
1781	-	-	65	0	6	-	123	6	1½		
1782	-	-	83	9	8	-	155	9	11½		
1783	-	-	128	5	1	-	117	15	8¼	- 27	0
1784	-	-	65	8	6	-	66	17	8		
1785	-	-	65	0	7	-	65	10	8½		

[1] The nominal is nearly the full rental.

Years.

Years.	Poor's Rate.			Net Expenditure on Poor.			Rate on the nominal rental.	
	£.	s.	d.	£.	s.	d	s.	d.
1786 - -	61	15	10½	- 68	11	10¼		
1787 - -	65	18	0	- 63	4	6½		
1788 - -	65	11	9	- 76	8	5½	s.	d.
1789} 1790} - -	184	17	0¹	- 78	11	11	- 19	0
1791 - -	83	9	6	- 97	19	10¾	- 17	0
1792 - -	44	10	0²	- 49	7	7	- 19	0
1793 - -	77	0	2	- 73	0	10	- 19	0
1794 - -	30	18	0²	- 37	18	11½	- 17	0
1795 Ending in May	60	18	0	- 50	11	1½	- 16	0

In the parish of St. James the Rates are as follows:

Years.	Poor's Rate.			Net Expenditure on Poor.			Rate on the nominal rental.	
	£.	s.	d.	£.	s.	d,	s.	d.
1789 - -	465	13	0	- 455	9	5½		
1790 - -	412	18	6	- 502	19	2		
1791 - -	561	1	6	- 567	7	0	s.	d.
1792 - -	505	10	2	- 473	12	1½	- 11	6
1793 - -	476	2	0	- 481	13	3¾	- 10	6
1794 - -	469	4	6	- 467	7	6½	- 10	6
1795 - -	439	13	0	- 538	13	5½	- 9	6

There are 9 ale-houses in the parish of St. James. The land-tax is £ 230. 10s. which is about 4s. 2d. in the pound. 69 houses pay the commutation tax: about 100, it is supposed, are exempted. The extent of the parish is 170 acres, whereof the greatest part is garden ground. Rent is, upon an average, £ 2 10s. an acre. Population is thought to be rather declining. There are only 3 Paupers in the parish work-house: at present

¹ There is here some confusion in the book. £ 184. 17s. are probably 2 years collection The disbursements in 1789 could not be made out.

² These accounts appear to be inaccurate: a 17s. rate must have produced more than £ 30 and a 19s. rate more than £ 44.

50

50 families receive an allowance at home, which amounts, weekly, to £ 8. 10s. Several poor perfons have their houfe-rent paid by the parifh ; and others receive occafional relief   About £ 1400 were collected laft winter, and diftributed among the Poor in different parts of Colchefter.

July, 1795.

GLOUCESTERSHIRE.

BRISTOL.

THE extent of the city of Briftol, and it's liberties, is about 3 miles from eaft to weft ; and 2½ miles from north to fouth. Of the population, the accounts are very various. One of the Briftol Guides ftates the number of houfes, in 1757, at 13,000, and of inhabitants at 90,000 ; and in 1794 at 100,000, including the Hot-wells and Clifton. In another fimilar publication, the number of houfes, in 1793, is eftimated at 16,000 ; and of inhabitants at 88,500, including the Hot-wells and Clifton   The great increafe of population, which has taken place within the prefent century, has been chiefly confined to the out-parifhes. Almoft half of what is properly called the City has been deftroyed to make room for the Exchange, the Market, the Bridge, Clare-ftreet, Union-ftreet, &c. ; and although many houfes have lately been built, yet many more have been pulled down : the new buildings are on a larger fcale and take up more ground, but they are not fo well inhabited as the old ones : many of them have been turned into mere offices for brokers, infurers, attornies, &c. or warehoufes for tradefmen, who have in a great meafure deferted their houfes in town, and retired with their families to the neighbouring villages   It is owing to thefe circumftances that the number of births and burials within the city is leffened ; and that the conclufion, they afford, is, that the popu-

lation

lation of Briftol has declined within the laft 20 years. The number of marriages, however, has confiderably increafed ; and it fhould be further remarked, that, in the following enumeration, the baptifms and burials of Diffenters, of whom there are many very numerous fects at Briftol, are not inferted The numbers were extracted with great fidelity from the parifh regifters, by a clergyman of the Church of England.

In all the parifhes the numbers of *Baptifms, Burials, Marriages,* were, in 12 years, from 1689 to 1700,   7864   7920   2414

in 12 years, from 1729 to 1740,   17343   18123   5435

in 12 years, from 1769 to 1780,   14321   14843   6409

An actual enumeration was made in the parifh of St. Philip and St Jacob, in 1781, when the number of houfes was found to be 1594, (of which 65 were either warehoufes, or uninhabited,); of males, 4435 ; of females, 5415 ; total number of inhabitants, 9850 Notwithftanding the prefent war has taken off many of the parifhioners ; the marriages have increafed almoft a feventh, and the baptifms more than a feventh, fince the year 1780.

The number of marriages for 15 years previous to 1780 was - 1504

Ditto   -   -   for 15 years to the end of 1795 - - 1711

Increafe of marriages in 15 years - 207

The number of baptifms for 15 years previous to 1780 was - 3939

Ditto   -   -   for 15 years to the end of 1795 - - 4620

Increafe of baptifms in 15 years - 681

Briftol is not more a commercial than a manufacturing town : independent of the various trades immediately connected with fhipping concerns, there are feveral important manufactures carried on here. Glafs-making is the principal. There are near 20 glafs-houfes in and near the city, for making bottle, crown, or flint-glafs ; feveral works for lead, in every ftage of it's manufacture ; brafs-wire, and brafs-works ; feveral iron and copper founderies ; potteries ; two large floor-cloth manufactories ; &c.

       The

The prices of provisions are: beef, from $4\frac{1}{2}$d. to 5d. a pound; mutton, 5d. to 6d; veal, 6d.; bacon, from 9d. to 10d.; butter, from 11d. to 1s; potatoes, 6d. a peck; bread, 4lb. for 1s.; wheat, 12s. a bushel; barley, 4s. 2d. a bushel; oats, from 3s. to 3s. 6d. a bushel; coals, cost about $3\frac{1}{2}$d. the bushel: they are chiefly brought from the extensive mines at Kingswood, about 2 miles from the city; the colliers of which speak a jargon that is peculiar to them, and perfectly unintelligible to a stranger.

The wages of labourers in the different manufactures vary from 7s. to 35s. a week: common labourers earn 1s. 6d. a day, throughout the year, without victuals: from 10s. to 15s. appear to be the common earnings in a week: children are employed in the cotton-manufacture, and earn from 1s. 6d. to 3s. a week.

The number of ale-houses in the city of Bristol is 354. The land-tax amounts to £ 7391. 10s. 8d. and is paid by the tenants. The rent of land in the neighbourhood of the city, is from £ 3. to £ 5. an acre.

The Poor of Bristol are managed by a corporation called "The Corporation of the Poor," and are partly supported in a work-house called St. Peter's Hospital, and partly at home by a parish allowance. The number at present in the work-house, is 287; viz. 61 men, 190 women, 19 boys, and 17 girls: there are also 63 poor persons of different descriptions in an hospital, or pest-house belonging to the work-house: total, 350. In 1794 there were in the work-house 70 men, 198 women, 25 boys, and 31 girls, and 66 in the pest-house: total, 390. The persons in the work-house are mostly old people and children, insane, lame, blind, &c. The only work at present is picking oakum, by which very little is earned [1]. A few years ago a manufactory for spinning wool was set up, but after 3 years experiment, it appeared they had lost £ 600. by it, and it was therefore wholly discontinued. The master says that the house was not built with a view

[1] In a pamphlet published in 1681, entitled, "Some Proposals for the Employment of the Poor, by T Firmin," the author says, that the city of Bristol contracted with one Mr King and others, for the employment of 500 of their poor people, in the way of spinning, and that for the first year he was obliged to pay them $2\frac{1}{4}$d for 1600 yards of yarn If we suppose that each spinner spun 800 yards of coarse yarn every day, (which is a moderate day's work,) the weekly earnings of each would be $7\frac{1}{4}$d; and the weekly earnings of 500 spinners would have amounted to £ 1 12s 6d; so that at this rate, the expence, in 1681, of employing such, (or, perhaps, all) of the Poor of Bristol, that were able to work, was £ 812. 10s.

to its préfent úfe, and is, therefore, not one of the moft convenient. There are 12 or 15 beds, principally of flocks, in each apartment: it is probably owing to this circumftance, and the number of old and difeafed perfons, that the houfe is infefted with vermin, particularly bugs: to a vifitor, theie appears, upon the whole, to be a want of cleanlinefs.

Bill of Fare.

	Breakfaſt.	Dinner	Supper.
Sunday,	Water-gruel.	Soup made of bullock's head.	Bread and cheefe.
Monday,	Ditto.	Peafe-foup.	Ditto.
Tuefday,	Ditto.	Meat and potatoes,	Ditto.
Wednefday,	Broth	Bread and cheefe.	Ditto.
Thurfday,	Water-gruel.	As Tuefday.	Ditto.
Friday,	Broth.	Peafe-foup.	Ditto
Saturday,	Gruel.	Bread and cheefe.	Ditto.

1lb. of meat, and the fame quantity of bread, are allowed to each perfon, on meat days. On Sundays, Wednefdays, and Saturdays, 6 oz. of cheefe are allowed for the 2 meals; and on other days, 3 oz.: the Poor eat their victuals in their lodging rooms.

The following account of the receipts and difburfements of the Corporation for the Poor, in the year ending in 1787, is copied *verbatim*, from the printed ftatement of St. Peter's hofpital. I have added a few other years, for the infoimation of fuch perfons as may wifh to inveftigate more fully the domeftic economy of a large city work-houfe.

Account of Difburfements ending the 31ſt of March 1787.

	£.	s.	d.
To balance of laft year's account, due to John Innall	25	9	2

	C.	qrs.	lb.		£.	s.	d.			
To beef and mutton,	333	1	0	at different prices	426	11	6			
To cheefe	85	2	0	at ditto	123	8	7			
To bacon					0	3	6			
To flour, 300 facks					468	15	0			

		£.	s.	d.			
To gruts, 130 bufhels, at different prices		43	0	0			
To peafe, 147¼ ditto, at ditto		47	1	6			
					90	1	6

			£.	s.	d.		s.	d.
Carried over			1109	0	1	25	9	2

	£.	s.	d.	£.	s.	d.
Brought over,	1109	0	1	25	9	2
To falt, 34 cwt. - - -	19	11	0			
To butter - - - - -	9	0	0			
To garden-ftuff, bought of fundries - -	16	3	11½			
To rice, 14 cwt. o qrs. 12 lb. at different prices -	18	16	5			

$\overline{}$ 1172 11 5½

To malt, 823 bufhels, at ditto - -	209	10	6
To hops, 2 cwt. 3 qrs. 9 lb. at ditto - -	11	17	9
To balm - - - -	7	3	6
To wine, brandy, and ale for the fick - -	2	19	7½
To milk - - - - -	20	16	2½

	£.	s.	d.
To grocery - -	10	16	9
To ftarch and blues - -	1	3	6

12 0 3

To vinegar - - - - 2 14 10

$\overline{}$ 267 2 8

CLOATHING, VIZ.

To William Till Adams, for fhoes - -	17	12	11
To leather, bought of Thomas Salmon -	13	10	0
To hemp and wax, bought of fundries - -	0	7	1
To breeches, paid for 16 pair of leather -	4	0	0
To linen bought of William Baylis - -	41	0	0
To haberdafhery bought of John Howarth -	5	6	0
To hofiery bought of fundries - -	12	11	6
To kerfeys and ferges bought of John Bryant - - -	10	3	0
To druggets, 2 pieces, bought of Richard Pearfon - - -	8	8	9

18 11 9

To linfeys and ferges, bought of fundries	3	17	10
To linfey, paid John Player for 1 piece	2	0	3
To paid —— Hunt for 2 great coats -	2	4	0
To paid —— Viner for hats - -	1	4	0

9 6 1

122 5 4

FURNITURE, VIZ.

| To earthen-ware, bafkets, befoms, brufhes, &c. bought of fundries - - - - | 8 | 6 | 6 |
| To a mahogany writing-defk bought of Tho. Shapland | 3 | 13 | 6 |

2   Carried over, £12 0 0—1587 8 7½

	£.	s.	d.	£.	s.	d.
Brought over,	12	0	0—1587	8	7¼

	£.	s.	d.			
To tin-ware and oil bought of George Williams - - -	3	10	0			
To lamp-lighting, paid Edward Stone -	0	15	0			
				4	5	0
To braziery, paid William Wafbrough -			-	0	9	0
To thrumbs and cards, paid fundries -			-	2	2	3
					18 16	3

REPAIRS, VIZ.

To John Huifh, for tyler's work -	14	3	6			
To —— Clifford, for white-liming -	1	2	6			
To hair for tyler's ufe - -	0	6	8			
				15	12	8
To Auftin and Lewis, for bricks and lime - -				6	7	6
To Sarah Lewis, for glazing - -				9	1	0
To James Perry, for hooper's work - -				10	4	0
To Jofeph Panting, for carpenter's work	39	13	6			
To ditto, for coffins of different fizes -	27	3	0			
To Edward Stock, for ditto do. -	10	15	0			
				77	11	6
To James Begg, for mafon's work -	16	14	0			
To Daniel Hague, for ditto - -	5	14	6			
				22	8	6
To John Broom, for ironmongery - -				5	15	0
To Benjamin Hill, plumber - - -				0	8	5
To —— Durnell, for fweeping chimnies - -				0	12	8
To Sufannah White, pump-maker - -				0	14	0
To Thomas Hancock, wheel-wright - -				2	0	0
To Aaron Auftin, for mending the clock - -				0	6	6
To Walter Swayne, for a new furnace, &c. - -				4	2	0
					155	3 9
To candles, 22 dozen, bought of Thomas Shapland				8	8	0
To foap, 8 cwt. bought of ditto - -				26	8	0
To lees - - - -				5	13	9
					40	9 9
To coal, 1525 horfe-loads, bought of Mary Lear -			-	82	12	0
To James Norton, for ftationary - £4 16 0						
To indentures, &c. - - 2 12 0						
				7	8	0

Carried over, £7 8 0—1884 10 4¼

To

	£.	s.	d.	£.	s.	d.
Brought over,	7	8	0—1884	10	4½

To Cocking and Rudhall, for printing   £. s. d.
  and advertising   -   -   26 17 6
To Samuel Bonner, for ditto   do.   12 3 0
To William Pine, for ditto   do. - 9 14 0
To William Routh, for ditto   do. - 8 1 6

			56 16 0			
				64	4	0

To Sir John Hugh Smith Bart. for 1 year's interest
  of £1000. - - - -   -   -   50 0 0
To Poor, and land-tax for the lodge - £1 16 9
To the Chamber of Bristol, for chief rent   3 8 0
To the Dean and Chapter, for ditto - 0 8 4

		5 13 1	

To Richard Hill, assignee to the estate of Mr. Mills,
  for 3 years rent of the lodge, at £10. *per annum* - 30 0 0

			35 13 1

SALARIES AND WAGES, viz.

To the Rev Thos Broughton, chaplain,
  1 year's salary - - - - £40 0 0
To John Brown, apothecary, for 1 year's
  attendance and medicines - - 120 0 0
To John Innal, master £50 0 0
To ditto during the va-
  cancy of a mation,
  for extra service - 10 10 0

		60 10 0	

To Anne Turner, matron, for 9 months
  and 3 weeks salary, at £30. *per ann.*   24 4 6

			244 14 6

To Edward Allen, clerk, 52 weeks at 16s. £41 12 0
To James Brown, officer, 52 ditto at 8s.   20 16 0
To John Baxter, ditto, 52 ditto at 12s.   31 4 0
To William Collier, ditto, 52 ditto at 7s.   18 4 0
To M. Paradise, baker, } 46 ditto at 2s. 6d.   5 15 0
  deceased   -   }
To — Hulbert, ditto, deceased, 6 do. at 9s. 2 14 0
To Francis Hobbs, brewer, 52 ditto at 1s. 2 12 0

		122 17 0	

To Hester Clayton, knitter,-6 ditto at 2s. 0 12 0
To   ditto   ditto, 46 ditto at 3s. 6 18 0

		7 10 0	

Carried over, £. 375 1 6—2034 7 5½

	£.	s.	d.	£.	s.	d.
Brought over,	375	1	6—	2034	7	5½

To Mary Trapp's executors, 1 month's   £. s. d.
salaıy - - - -   2 6 0
To Anne Dagge, midwife, 1 yeaı's ditto   6 0 0
To nuıfes, wafhers, baıbeıs, coblers,
gate-keepeıs, &c. - -   26 14 5
                             35 0 5
                                        410 1 11

To fending home 199 Irifh vagrants - -   97 10 0
To taking up and removing vagrants to
their parifhes - - -   91 3 8
To Ofborne and Seager, folicitors, for
drawing paffes and oıders, attendance,
and taking affidavits - -   106 0 0
                             197 3 8

To Walter Wiltfhire for conveying paffengers to
London - - - -   9 10 0
                                       304 3 8

To burials, 285 - - : -   28 9 8
To extra reliefs paid by the mafter - -   694 3 6
To paid with 25 apprentices, put out to different
trades- - - - -   26 6 0
To fundry incidental expences paid by the mafter
and matron - - -   36 19 6½
To farmeı John Hopkins, 1 year's difburfements on
Shirehampton eftate - -   35 15 6
To a depofit to Bath hofpital - - -   3 0 0
To William Witherell for hauling oakum and cord
wood - - -   6 8 0
To Daniel Burgefs, for convicting Sufannah Mil-
ledge, alias Miller, of a felony -   16 11 0
To fundry churchwaıdens for the rent of their alms-
houfes - - - -   40 0 6
                                       887 13 8½

*To paid by the feveral churchwardens, from the 31ſt
of March 1786, to the 29th of September following, viz.*

To 1072 Poor on pay bill - -   £2561 17 9

7   Carıied over,   £ 2561 17 9   £ 3636 6 9

	£.	s.	d.		£.	s.	d.
Brought over,	2561	17	9		3636	6	9
To 1115 casual reliefs - -	1157	17	6				
To 10 burials - - -	3	15	0				
				3723 10 3			

To paid by the several churchwardens, from the 29th of September 1786, to the 25th of March 1787, viz.

	£.	s.	d.				
To 1048 Poor on pay bill - - £	2330	16	0				
To 1074 casual reliefs - -	1012	18	0				
To 11 burials - - -	4	2	6				
				3347 16 6			
					7071	6	9
					10707	13	6

	£.	s.	d.				
To balance to the 31st of March 1787, in the treasurer's hands - - -	3230	10	11				
To ditto in the master's hands - -	58	6	4				
To ditto in the matron's hands - - -	2	16	10½				
				3291 14 1½			
				£ 13999 7 7½			

Cr.   *viz.*

	£.	s.	d.		£.	s.	d.
By balance of last year's account in the treasurer's hands - - - - -	2580	10	8				
By ditto in the late matron's hands - -	1	3	10				
				2581 14 6			
By cash received for fines of sundry guardians -	19	18	6				
By ditto received for repayments of sundry persons	15	17	4				
By ditto received for the maintenance of ditto -	108	17	8				
By ditto received for spinning - - -	0	11	10				
By ditto received for oakum - - -	22	3	0				
By ditto received for burials - -	1	0	6				
				168 8 10			
By amount of several small receipts - - -				249	4	3½	
By the year's assessment on the inhabitants - -				11000	0	0	
				£ 13999 7 7½			

The

The affeffments on the feveral parifhes were as follows:

		£.	s.	d.			£.	s.	d.
All Saints	—	249	14	0	St. Michael	—	544	10	0
St. Auguftine	—	1201	4	0	St. Nicholas	—	1037	6	0
Caftle-Precincts	—	595	2	0	St. Peter	—	457	12	0
Chrift-Church	—	597	6	0	St. Philip and Jacob	—	523	12	0
St. Ewen	—	133	2	0	St. Stephen	—	1113	4	0
St. James	—	1699	10	0	Temple	—	491	14	0
St. John Baptift	—	368	10	0	St. Thomas	—	646	16	0
St. Leonard	—	231	0	0	St. Weiburgh	—	249	14	0
St. Mary-Port	—	282	14	0					
St. Mary-Redcliff	—	577	10	0			£ 11000	0	0

Medium Number of the Family in each Month in the Houfe.

1786—	April	324 perfons.		October	294 perfons.
	May	313 ditto		November	300 ditto
	June	300 ditto		December	305 ditto
	July	296 ditto	1787—	January	305 ditto
	Auguft	296 ditto		February	313 ditto
	September	297 ditto		March	334 ditto

Receipts and Expences of the Corporation of the Poor, from the 31ft of March 1787, to 31ft of March 1788.

DISBURSEMENTS.

PROVISIONS.

		Cwt.	qrs.	lb.			£.	s.	d.
Beef and mutton,	-	334	2	13	´	-	451	14	0
Cheefe,	- -	86	0	23	-	-	129	19	0
Flour, 313 facks	-	-	-	-	-	520	10	0
Gruts, 130 bufhels, £38. 7s. 6d.; peafe, 156 bufhels, £42. 16s.					81	3	6
Salt, butter, garden ftuff, and rice	-	-	-	60	18	10
Malt, 938 bufhels	-	-	-	-	225	18	8
Hops, barm, wine, brandy, milk, and groceries	-	-	51	10	2

Carried over £ 1521 14 2

	£.	s.	d.
Brought over -	1521	14	2

;CLOATHING.

Shoes, breeches, linen, haberdafhery, flannel, hofiery, kerfeys, and
   boys' cloaths, worfted, hats, and fundries   -   -   170 14 4

FURNITURE.

Tin-wares, lamp-oil, brufhes, bafkets, earthen-ware, &c.   -   16 13 8

REPAIRS, &c.

Tiler's work, paint, &c. £10. 11s.; mafon, £32. 1s.; glazier,
  £4. 15s. 6d.; hooper, £3. 13s. ; cord, wood, and faggots,
  £45. 9s.; carpenter, £77. 4s. ; ironmonger, £13. 16s. 6d.;
  lime, chimney-fweeper, pump-maker, and wheel-wright,
  £9. 1s.   -   -   -   -   -   196 11 0
Candles, foap, and lees   -   -   -   27 4 0
Coals, 1655 horfe-loads   -   -   -   89 12 11
Stationary, ftamps, indentures, &c.   -   -   -   6 15 2
Printing and advertifing   -   -   -   7 17 6
One year's intereft on bond for £1000   -   -   50 0 0
Poor and land-tax, chief-rent, ground-rent, and renewal of leafe,
  and rent of the lodge   -   -   -   -   51 16 4

SALARIES AND WAGES.

Chaplain's falary, £40.; apothecary's, £120.; mafter, £50.;
  matron, £30.   -   -   -   -   240 0 0
Clerk, parifh officers, baker, brewer, nurfes, and knitter   -   177 16 0
Midwife, barbers, wafhers, coblers, gate-keepers, &c.   -   31 16 4
Sending home 249 Irifh vagrants   -   -   -   121 13 0
Removing other vagrants   -   -   -   160 6 1
Burials, 310   -   -   -   -   31 0 2
Extra reliefs paid by the mafter   -   -   -   1024 3 5
Putting out 70 apprentices, £73 3s 10d.; incidents, £30. 10s. 1½d.
  Charges on Shirehampton eftate, £35 17s. 8d.; Bath hof-
  pital, £10. 4s. 3d. ; rent of alms-houfes, £40. 0s. 6d.; to
  poor houfe-keepers, £5. 8s. 10d.   -   -   195 5 2½

Carried over -   £4120 19 3½

	£.	s.	d.
Brought over -	4120	19	3½

OUT POOR.

	£.	s.	d.
Paid by church wardens to 1062 Poor { from 31 March 1787 / to 29 Sept. 1787 } on the pay bill	2505	3	6
1253 Cafual reliefs, £1102. 2s.; and 10 burials, £3. 15s. -	1105	17	0
1037 Poor on pay bill, from 29 Sept. 1787 to 25 March 1788	2295	8	9
1207 Cafual reliefs, £1096. 16s.; and 8 burials, £3. - -	1099	16	0
Bond paid off - - - - - -	1000	0	0
Balance to 31ft of March 1788, in the Treafurer's hands, } — — — £ 2686 2 2 Ditto in the Mafter's hands - - 48 16 10 }	2734	19	0
	£ 14862	3	6¼

RECEIPTS.

	£.	s.	d.
By balance of laft year's account in the Treafurer's hands -	3230	10	11
Ditto ditto in the Mafter's hands -	58	6	4
Ditto ditto in the Matron's hands -	2	16	10½
Sundry fmall receipts - - - -	435	17	7¼
By dividend in the 5 per cent. annuities - - -	5	18	10
One year's rent of Shirehampton eftate - -	110	0	0
Of Tho. Shapland for 7 cwt. 3 qrs. 14 lb. of tallow - -	15	7	3
By the year's affeffment on the inhabitants - -	11000	0	0
By balance due to Anne Turner, matron - -	3	15	8½
	£ 14862	3	6¼¹

The affeffments on the feveral parifhes were as follows :

	£.	s.	d.			£.	s	d
All-Saints	—	249	14	0	St. Michael	—	544	10	0
St. Auguftine	—	1261	4	0	St. Nicholas	—	1037	6	0
Caftle-Precinct	—	595	2	0	St. Peter	—	457	12	0
Chrift-Church	—	597	6	0	St. Philip and Jacob	—	523	12	0
St. Ewen	—	133	2	0	St. Stephen	—	1113	4	0
St. James	—	1699	10	0	Temple	—	491	14	0
St. John Baptift	—	368	10	0	St. Thomas	—	646	16	0
St. Leonard	—	231	0	0	St. Weiburgh	—	249	14	0
St. Mary-Port	—	282	14	0					
St. Mary-Redcliff	—	577	10	0			£ 11000	0	0

¹ There feems a miftake of 10s. in this account : the various items of receipt, altogether, amount to £ 14862. 13s. 6¼d.

Medium Number of the Family in each Month in the House.

1787—April	345 Perfons.		October	297 Perfons.
May	321		November	309
June	307		December	314
July	307		1788—January	321
Auguft	292		February	327
September	287		March	327

An Account of Receipts and Expences of the Corporation of the Poor, from 31ft of March 1789, to 31ft of March 1790.

DISBURSEMENTS.

	£	s.	d

Balance due to John Innall   11   10   7

PROVISIONS.

C. qrs. lb.

				£	s.	d
Beef, mutton, &c.	367 3 21	-	-	534	4	9
Cheefe	93 1 13	-	-	99	2	11
Flour, 328 facks	-	-	-	642	12	0

Gruts, 120 bufhels, £35. 10s.; peafe, 208 bufhels, £58. 3s. 10¼d.   93   13   10¼

Salt, butter, and garden-ftuff   -   -   -   55   5   2¼

Malt, 1012 bufhels, £237 —Hops, barm, wine, brandy, gin, ale, butter, fifh, milk, and groceries, £73. 18s. 3¼d.   -   310   18   3¼

CLOATHING.

Shoes, leather, linen-drapery, woollen-drapery, hofiery, &c.   -   241   4   2

FURNITURE, &c.

Brufhes, faggots, poldavy, cord wood, earthen-ware, glafs, fand, &c.   -   -   43   19   0¼

REPAIRS, &c.

White-liming, £15. 9s. 6d.; mafon and glazier, £21. 12s.; carpenter, £113. 17s.; ironmonger, £19. 18s. 6d.; foap, candles, and lees, £24. 18s. 6d.; coals, £101. 8s. 2d.; ftationary, and printing, £13. 6d.; junk, £31. 5s.; rent for lodge, and various fmall taxes, £17. 8d.   -   358   9   7

Carried over — £2431   0   7

	£.	s.	d.
Brought over —	2431	0	7

SALARIES AND WAGES.

	£.	s.	d.
Chaplain, £40.; apothecary, £141.; mafter, £50.; matron, £30.; cleik, officers, baker, brewer, and nurfes, £184. 9s.; barbers, coblers, gate-keepers, &c. £32. 15s. 9d. -	478	4	9
Sending home 231 Irifh vagiants - -	119	1	2
Removing other vagrants - - -	119	15	2
Burials 228, and wool, £40. 4s. 3d.; extra reliefs, £507. 17s. 6d.; putting out 16 apprentices, £16. 6s. 6d.; incidents, £48. 15s. 4d.; Shirehampton eftate, £25. 2s. 3d.; rent of alms-houfes, £40. 6d. - -- -	238	16	4

OUT POOR.

	£.	s.	d.		£.	s.	d.
1033 poor on the pay bill	from 31 Maich 1789	2519	1	0			
1353 cafual reliefs	to 29 Sept. 1789	1535	19	6			
1000 pooi on the pay bill	from 29 Sept. 1789	2284	3	0			
1383 cafual reliefs	to 31 March 1790	1387	0	0			
					7726	3	6
Balance in mafter's, matron's, and treafurer's hands -					1041	5	0½
				£	12553	16	4½

RECEIPTS.

	£.	s.	d.
Balance in tieafurer's and matron's hands laft year -	1735	18	2¼
Sundiy fmall receipts - - -	817	18	2
One year's affeffment on the inhabitants -	10000	0	0
	£ 12553	16	4½

The affeffments on the feveral parifhes weie as follows :

		£.	s.	d.			£.	s.	d.
All-Saints	—	226	0	0	St. Michael	—	502	0	0
St. Auguftine	—	1398	0	0	St. Nicholas	—	924	0	0
Caftle Precinct	—	370	0	0	St. Peter	—	336	0	0
Chiift-Chuich	—	324	0	0	St Philip and Jacob	—	394	0	0
St. Ewen	—	86	0	0	St Stephen	—	976	0	0
St. James	—	1922	0	0	Temple	—	524	0	0
St. John Baptift	—	284	0	0	St Thomas	—	480	0	0
St. Leonard	—	178	0	0	St. Weiburgh	—	160	0	0
St Mary-Poit	—	166	0	0					
St. Mary-Redcliff	—	750	0	0		£	10000	0	0

Medium Number of the Family in the Houfe, each month in the year.

1789—Apiil	328 Perfons.		October	330 Perfons.
May	320		November	346
June	323		Decembei	362
July	332		1790—January	370
Auguft	332		Februaiy	369
September	329		Maich	358.

Receipts and Expences of the Corporation of the Poor, from the 31ft of March 1791, *to the* 31ft *of March* 1792.

DISBURSEMENTS.

	£.	s.	d.
To balance due to the Tieafurei laft year -	460	0	0

PROVISIONS.

	£.	s.	d.
Beef and mutton, 405 *cwt* 1*qr* 8*lb*. - - - - -	575	13	0
Ox heads and meat, bought by the matron - -	47	15	5
Cheefe, 107 *cwt* 1*qr*. 1*lb*. - - - -	182	6	0
Flour, 320 facks - - - - -	603	10	0
Giuts, 130 bufhels, £ 37. 2s. 6d ; peafe, 208 bufhels, £ 57. 12s.; peafe and beans, 14s. 4¼d. - - -	95	8	10½
Salt, butter, and garden-ftuff - - - -	61	8	1½
Malt, 920 bufhels - - - - -	253	6	6
Hops, barm, wine, gin, butter, milk, and groceries - -	158	4	10½

Carried over - £ 2437 12 9½

	£.	s.	d.
Brought over -	2437	12	9½

CLOATHING, &C.

Shoes, leather, linen and woollen draperies, haberdafhery, hofiery, breeches, and inftructing fpinneis - - **200 11 3**

FURNITURE, &c.

Mill-puff, thrumbs, brufhes, wares, bafkets, mops, tin-wares, biooms, earthen ware, glaffes, and fundries - - **28 15 4**

Laid, bottles, ftraw, fkins, lint and tow for furgeon's and apothecary's ufes, and drugs - - - - **45 18 4**

REPAIRS, &C.

Mafon's work, £ 7. 1s.; glazier's, £ 8. 7s.; fmith's, £ 3. 14s.; biazier's, £ 22. 11d; plumber's, £ 9. 18s.; carpenter's, £ 97. 5s.; coffins, £ 69. 8s.; hooper's, £ 4. 18s. pump-maker's, £ 21. 12s. 6d. - - - - **244 4 5**

Soap, candles, and lees - - - **21 8 9**

Piinting and advertifing - - - - **12 2 0**

Stationary, ftamps, and indentuies - - - **10 3 8**

Coal - - - - - - **98 7 0**

Junk, 254 cwt. 3 qrs. 24 lb. - - - - **103 8 6**

Rent of Oldfield lodge, land-tax, church-rate, chief-rent, poor-tax, &c. - - - - **17 18 2**

Poftages, 8s. 6d.; lamp-oil, £ 2. 2s. 10d. - - - **2 11 4**

SALARIES AND WAGES.

Chaplain's falary, £ 40.; apothecary's, £ 60.; mafter's, £ 50.; matron's, £ 30. - - - - **180 0 0**

Cleik, parifh officers, baker, brewer, nuifes, and white-limers, **157 8 0**

Midwife's falary, £ 6.; nurfes, barbers, coblers, gate-keepers, £ 28. 16s. - - - **34 16 0**

Sending home 303 Irifh vagiants - - - **166 5 4**

Removals, paffes, and carriage of fundry perfons - - **32 18 1**

Solicitors for diawing paffes, orders, and taking affidavits - **81 2 0**

John Innall, gratuity for attendance at the woollen-manufactory **·10 10 0**

309 burials, and wool - - - - **47 10 8**

Carried over - **£ 3933 11 7½**

	£.	s.	d.
Brought over -	3933	11	7½
Extra reliefs paid by the master - - -	911	6	6
Putting out 18 apprentices - - -	18	17	0
Incidental expences, £ 19. 12s. 11d.; and rent for alms-			
houfes, £ 40. 6d. - - - -	59	13	5

OUT POOR.

	£.	s.	d.
995 Poor on pay bill, from 31ſt March 1791, to 29th Sept. 1791	2507	4	0
1418 Cafual reliefs, from ditto to ditto	1418	4	3
1001 Poor on pay-bill, from 29th Sept. 1791, to 31ſt March 1792	2334	9	0
1377 Cafual reliefs, from ditto to ditto	1247	17	0
Balance in maſter's hands, £ 203. 11d.; mation's ditto, 2d. -	203	1	1
Balance in the treafurer's hands - - -	455	15	1
	£ 13028	18	10

RECEIPTS.

	£.	s.	d.
By balance of laſt year's accounts in the maſter's hands -	149	1	0
Ditto ditto in the mation's - -	0	12	8
Sundry fmall receipts - - - -	686	18	5
By rent of land and houfes at Shirehampton and Hungroad -	156	0	0
By fale of old metal, 960 bufhels of grains, fuet, greafe, and			
old lead - - - -	36	6	9
By the year's affeffment on the inhabitants - -	12000	0	0
	£ 13028	18	10

The Affeffments on the feveral Parifhes were as follows:

Parish	£.	s.	d.	Parish	£.	s.	d.
All Saints	271	4	0	St. Michael	602	8	0
St. Auguſtine	1677	12	0	St. Nicholas	1108	16	0
Caſtle Precinct	444	0	0	·St. Peter	403	4	0
Chriſt-church	388	16	0	St. Philip and Jacob	472	16	0
St. Ewen	103	4	0	St. Stephen	1171	4	0
St. James	2306	8	0	Temple	628	16	0
St. John Baptiſt	340	16	0	St. Thomas	576	0	0
St. Leonard	213	12	0	St. Werburgh	192	0	0
St. Mary Port	199	4	0				
St. Mary Redcliff	900	0	0		£ 12000	0	0

Medium

Medium Number of the Family in the House, each Month in the Year.

1791—April	373 Perfons.	October	362 Perfons.
May	358	November	364
June	351	December	364
July	353	1792—January	373
Auguft	344	February	384
September	349	March	380

Receipts and Expences of the Corporation of the Poor, from the 31ft of March 1792, to the 31ft of March 1793.

DISBURSEMENTS.

PROVISIONS.

	£.	s.	d.
Beef and mutton, 398 *cwt.* 1 *qr.* 23 *lb.* – – –	577	14	6
Meat and ox-heads, bought by the matron – –	43	12	10½
Cheefe, 107 *cwt.* 0 *qr.* 22 *lb.* – – – –	176	2	6
Floui, 310 facks – – – – –	574	0	0
Gruts, 140 bufhels, £ 46. 16s.; peafe, 208 bufhels, £ 62. 8s.; peafe and beans, paid for by the matron, 13s. 1d. –	109	17	1
Salt, 30 *cwt.* butter, and garden ftuff – – –	59	9	1
Malt, 928 bufhels – – – –	266	19	4
Hops, 3*cwt.* 1*qr.* 18*lb.*, £ 18. 17s. 8d.; wine, brandy, ale, gin, butter, fifh, &c.; milk, and groceries – –	70	0	11

CLOATHING.

Shoes, leather, linen-drapery, woollen-drapery, haberdafhery, breeches, hofiery, buckles, and for tafk-work to fpinners	278	6	2

FURNITURE, &c.

Rugs, brown and tin ware, cutlery, brufhes, cord-wood, brooms, laid, bottles, fkins, &c. for the furgeon's and apothecary's ufe; glaffes, &c. – – – –	81	1	11½

REPAIRS, &c.

Mafon's work, tiles, &c. £ 54. 18s. 6d.; glazier, £ 9. 11s. 6d.; fmith, £ 5. 16s. 6d.; brazier, £ 6. 3s.; hoopei, £ 7. 10s.; plumber, £ 7. 12s.; carpenter, and for coffins, £ 91. 15s. 6d.	183	7	0

Carried over - £ 2420 11 5

	£.	s.	d.
Brought over　-　£	2420	11	5
Soap, candles, and lees　-　-　-　-	36	7	0
Printing and advertifing　-　-　-　-	10	15	0
Stationary, ftamps, indentures, &c.　-　-　-	7	11	10
Laths, hair, and painting　-　-　-　-	4	15	0
Junk, 84 *cwt.* 2 *qrs.* 23 *lb.*　-　-　-　-	32	16	6
Coals　-　-　-　-　-	124	3	6
One year's rent of Oldfield lodge, poor-tax, land-tax, church-rate, chief-rent, 2 years fee-farm-rent of St. Peter's hofpital, and poftages　-　-　-　-	24	17	7

SALARIES AND WAGES.

	£.	s.	d.
Chaplain's falary, £ 40.; apothecary's, £ 60.; mafter's, £ 50.; matron's, £ 30.　-　-　-　-　-	180	0	0
Clerk, parifh officers, baker, brewer, nurfes, white-limers　-	145	12	0
Midwife, nurfes, wafhers, barbers, coblers, and gate-keepers　-	33	6	0
Sending home 164 Irifh vagrants　-　-　-	99	19	7
Removing and paffing other vagrants, and carriage of them　-	27	10	5
Solicitors for drawing paffes, orders, and taking affidavits　-	51	7	6
Burials, 256; and wool　-　-　-　-	39	16	10
Extra reliefs paid by the mafter　-　-	466	6	6
Putting out 13 apprentices, £ 13. 13s.; incidents, £ 30. 8s. 9d.; rent of alms-houfes, £ 40. 6d　-　-	84	2	3
Paid treafurer intereft of money on advance, £ 37. 10s. 11d.; 52 returns of price of coin, £ 13.　-　-	87	10	11

OUT POOR.

	£.	s.	d.
1010 Poor on pay-bill, from 31ft March 1792, to 29th Sept. 1792	2572	1	6
1318 Cafual reliefs, from　ditto　to　ditto	1388	15	6
953 Poor on pay bill, from 29th Sept. 1792, to 25th March 1793	2260	13	0
1295 Cafual reliefs, from　ditto　to　ditto	1180	19	0
Balance in the mafter's hands, £ 47. 4s. 11d.; ditto in matron's, £ 1. 13s. 1d.; ditto in the treafurer's hands, £ 2257. 10s. 1d.	2306	8	1
	£ 13549	6	11

RECEIPTS.

RECEIPTS.

	£.	s.	d.
By balance of laft year's account in the treafurer's hands	455	15	1
Ditto ditto in the mafter's hands	203	0	11
Ditto ditto in the matron's hands	0	0	2
Sundry fmall receipts	677	0	9
By a year's rent of 2 houfes, &c. at Shirehampton	69	10	0
Rent of land at ditto	144	0	0
One year's affeffment on the inhabitants	12000	0	0

£ 13549 6 11

The Affeffments on the feveral Parifhes were as follows:

	£.	s.	d.		£.	s.	d.
All Saints	271	4	0	St. Michael	602	8	0
St. Auguftine	1677	12	0	St. Nicholas	1108	16	0
Caftle Precincts	444	0	0	St. Peter	403	4	0
Chrift-church	388	16	0	St. Philip and Jacob	472	16	0
St. Ewen	103	4	0	St. Stephen	1171	4	0
St. James	2306	8	0	Temple	628	16	0
St. John Baptift	340	16	0	St. Thomas	576	0	0
St. Leonard	213	12	0	St. Werburgh	192	0	0
St. Mary-Port	199	4	0				
St. Mary Redcliff	900	0	0		£ 12000	0	0

Medium Number of the Family in each Month in the Houfe.

1792—April	369 Perfons.		October	330 Perfons
May	352		November	352
June	329		December	369
July	323		1793—January	370
Auguft	322		February	375
September	329		March	378

Poor's Rates in the City of BRISTOL.

Year ending in	£.	s.	d.		£.	s.	d.
1743	3500	0	0	1770	8691	16	6
1744	3500	0	0	1771	8270	11	3
1745	3500	0	0	1772	8500	0	0
1746	4500	0	0	1773	10000	0	0
1747	4500	0	0	1774	11500	0	0
1748	4500	0	0	1775	11500	0	0
1749	5000	0	0	1776	11500	0	0
1750	5000	0	0	1777	10000	0	0
1751	4500	0	0	1778	9000	0	0
1752	4500	0	0	1779	11000	0	0
1753	4500	0	0	1780	11000	0	0
1754	4500	0	0	1781	12000	0	0
1755	4500	0	0	1782	12600	0	0
1756	4500	0	0	1783	14000	0	0
1757	4500	0	0	1784	14000	0	0
1758	4500	0	0	1785	14000	0	0
1759	4800	0	0	1786	12000	0	0
1760	6412	6	2	1787	11000	0	0
1761	5628	1	8	1788	11000	0	0
1762	5542	0	0	1789	10000	0	0
1763	6081	14	0	1790	10000	0	0
1764	5828	13	8½	1791	10000	0	0
1765	6442	7	9½	1792	12000	0	0
1766	6732	7	3½	1793	12000	0	0
1767	7523	0	9½	1794	13000	0	0
1768	7881	14	6½	1795	13000	0	0
1769	10394	13	8 Ending in March	1796	13000	0	0

The mafter of the work-houfe fays 1010 poor perfons are at prefent on the out-pay bill, but does not know what they receive, either by the week, or month.

The

The above accounts are taken from a book in the Council-houfe. It is to be obferved, that the above collections only relate to the parifhes within what is called the city and liberties of Briftol; and as this fpace has been built on many years, and the number of inhabitants, from various circumftances, above enumerated, much reduced, it is evident that the increafe of the Rates is not owing to an augmented population, but muft be explained from other caufes.

The Quakers maintain their own Poor; in fome counties they are af-fifted by having eftates and money left them for this purpofe, but no-where fufficient without an additional voluntary fubfcription: this is gene-rally made once a month, in country places, and the allowances are from 2s to 10s. *per* week. In Briftol this Society confifts of more than 200 families: their Poor confift of about 5 men, and 14 women, moftly aged and decayed tradefmen or their widows; and 25 children, moftly orphans: they have an eftate or two left to fupport their Poor, and give a fee with the children when fit to be put out apprentice. In 1700 a large houfe was built and furnifhed at an expence of near £ 1600. in New-ftreet, where their Poor refide, and are employed in different manufactories; the expence, on an average of 20 years, has been about £ 250. *per annum*, and the average number fupported, about 40 perfons The children are taught reading, writing, and arithmetic; and on this plan are all their Poor in Britain and Ireland fupported, with fome fmall local variations, according to their number.

Few cities poffefs fuch a number of public charities as Briftol; there are in it 30 alms-houfes, or hofpitals, in which about 83 men and 230 women refide, who have, in general, as much allowed them as is nearly fufficient for their fupport. There are alfo feveral charity fchools, in which about 960 children are educated, and moft of them are cloathed and main-tained The donations to the Poor of Briftol, in money, are very confi-derable, but their annual amount could not be afcertained.

D d 2   The

The following are the earnings and expences of a labourer about 50 years of age. He has been about 2 months out of regular employment, but ufually woiks at an inn, as horfe-keeper, porter, &c He has a wife and 2 children; one 9 months, and the other 5 years old.

			£.	s	d.
He receives 9s a week regular wages all the year, but no victuals; annually - - - -			23	8	0
His wife, fometimes, earns a fhilling by wafhing; fuppofe annually - - - - -			1	0	0
Total income -	£	24	8	0

In the above account his earnings are ftated as if he had been in conftant employment, but he fays he has not earned 1s. a day for the laft 2 months. Laft fummer he loft 2 children by the fmall-pox; and the fummer before, he was fick for feveral months; yet, notwithftanding thefe diftreffes, he never had recourfe to the parifh, but has been obliged to pawn his beft cloaths, and fell fome articles of furniture to raife a little money: he has not yet been able to redeem his cloaths.

His Expences were as follows:

	s.	d.
Bread, cofts at prefent 4s. 6d. a week; meat, about 6d. a week on an average - - -	5	2
Butter, ½lb. 5½d.; cheefe, ½lb. 3d; tea, 3d.; no fugar -	0	11½
Potatoes, 2 pecks, 1s; milk, ½d. a day (for the child), 3½d.	1	3½
Beer (about 3 pints), 6d.; candles, foap, &c. about 5d. -	0	11
Onions, falt, &c. about 3d - - - -	0	3
Houfe-rent, 1s. 2d; fuel, about 1s. - - -	2	2
Weekly expences -	10	9
	52	
Total expences of a year - £ 27 19 0		

This perfon appeared to be an honeft induftrious man, whofe intention was not to deceive; yet, as he never received any parochial aid, his

expences

expences muft have been ftated rather too high, as they exceed his earnings by £ 3. 11s. He fays, that he and his wife have laid out but little money in cloaths, fince they were married; as they were tolerably equipped on fetting out in life ; but they are now in very great want of this neceffary article, which they have no means of obtaining by their own labour.

The out-parifhes of St. Philip and Jacob, and the out-parifh of St. George, which are fuppofed to be about 10 miles in circumference, and to contain about 16,000 inhabitants, are united with refpect to the maintenance of their Poor. The following table exhibits the amount of their Rates and Expenditure for a few years back:

Years.		Poor's Rate.				Rate uncollected.				Expenditure.		
		£.	s.	d.		£.	s.	d.		£.	s.	d.
1765	-	1178	6	0	-	22	14	0	-	1313	14	2
1766	-	1176	12	6	-	33	0	0	-	1366	2	0
1772	-	1421	16	0	-	25	15	11	-	1680	15	11
1773	-	1828	8	3	-	37	0	3	-	1988	7	10
1774	-	2126	12	0	-	36	3	8	-	2213	9	9
1775	-	2121	15	3	-	65	8	10	-	2229	17	0
1776	-	2312	13	9	-	18	13	10	-	2421	10	10
1777	-	2316	3	1	-	104	10	11	-	2430	11	8
1778	-	2569	0	0	-	160	0	0	-	2646	15	0
1779	-	2019	0	0	-	—	—	—	-	2193	13	9
1783	-	1359	13	0	} Taken from the returns				-	—	—	—
1784	-	1191	8	6	} made to Parliament				-	—	—	—
1785	-	1221	18	0	} in 1786.				-	—	—	—
1790	-	1614	11	10	-	23	1	8	-	1790	10	0
1791	-	1643	16	0	-	64	5	0	-	1786	14	8
1792	-	2141	4	0	-	—	—	—	-	—	—	—

The accounts for the laft 3 years are not fettled, but I am informed that the Rate laft year was 3s. 3d. in the pound on the rack rent, and produced £ 2500.; and that £ 3000. will not be more than fufficient to defray the expenditure of the prefent year.

The

The Poor of thefe parifhes are partly relieved at home, and partly maintained in a work-houfe; in which there are, at prefent, 85 perfons; viz. 16 children, (who are chiefly employed in heading pins,) and 69 old people, who cannot work. The earnings of the children are very trifling. 20 parifh children, (chiefly baftards,) are out at nurfe, at 2s. a week, each. The number of out-poor is about 200: they receive weekly, about £ 30. It is fingular, that here it is thought moft beneficial to the parifhes to maintain the Poor at home, and that the Poor are defirous of getting into the work-houfe　The houfe is pleafantly fituated, and appears to be clean and comfortable: there are 2 or 3 beds, (of flocks, and feathers,) in each room.

The following is the bill of fare:

	Breakfaft.			Dinner.			Supper
Sunday,	Milk pottage.	—		Bread and cheefe.	—		Bread, and cheefe, or butter.
Monday,	Ditto.	—	—	Rice milk.	—	—	Ditto
Tuefday,	Ditto	—	—	Peafe foup.	—	—	Ditto
Wednefday,	Ditto	—	—	Pickled beef, and vegetables.			Ditto.
Thurfday,	Ditto	—	—	Bread, and cheefe.	—		Ditto
Friday,	Ditto	—	—	Peafe foup	—	—	Ditto.
Saturday,	Ditto	—	—	Pickled beef, and vegetables.			Ditto.

3 pints of beer are allowed to each perfon on meat days, and 1 quart on other days. The daily allowance of bread is 1 lb. and of cheefe 9 oz. are given out every week. Once a month 12 lb. of butter are diftributed; and, at particular feafons, better fare is provided, more efpecially for the fick.

The land-tax in thefe parifhes amounts to £568. and is collected at 6d. in the pound.

The number of ale-houfes a few years ago was 150: it is now reduced to 80.

October, 1795.

R O D-

RODMARTON

THE parifh of Rodmarton is fituated about 6 miles to the weft of Cirencefter : it contains 3200 acres of land, of which 150 are meadow and pafture, 250 down land, 60 wood, and the reft arable. About 1628, the inhabitants were numbered by the rector, when they were found to amount to 227, of whom 121 were males, and 106 females. In 1794, the number was 309, (of whom 28 were fervants,); 152 males, and 157 females. There are no Sectarians in this parifh. 9 houfes pay the window tax ; 47 are exempted.

The men are wholly employed in agriculture; the women in fpinning wool ; and the children in carding it. Labourers are paid from 6s. to 9s. a week, except in harveft time, when they receive fomewhat more. They work fiom 6 o'clock in the morning till fix at night in fummer, and in winter during day-light : the ufual diet of labourers is, bread and cheefe, garden ftuff and dumplins for dinner, and tea for breakfaft.

The prices of provifions are : cheefe, on an average, 5d. the pound ; bacon, 7d. and 8d ; bread, 7 lb. for 1s.

There are no ale-houfes or Friendly Societies in the parifh.

The quota paid to the land-tax is £99. 6s. 8d. which in 1792 was at the rate of 16d. in the pound. The farms are all large, the whole parifh being divided into 8, which are held by 6 tenants : the land is chiefly freehold, except a farm of 500 acres, which is a prebendal corps in the church of Salifbury. An allowance of land was made to the rector in lieu of tithes by an act paffed 32 Geo. 3. The commons were all enclofed under the ftatute above-mentioned.

The Poor are relieved at their own homes.

A Table

A Table of Baptisms, Burials, Marriages, Poor's Rates, and Expenditure on the Poor.

Years	Baptisms			Burials			Marriages	Poor's Rates			Net Sum expended on the Poor		
	Males	Fem	Total	Males	Fem.	Total		£.	s.	d.	£.	s.	d.
1680	3	5	8	2	2	4	—	12	9	10	12	10	9½
1685	5	5	10	2	1	3	2	20	17	6	21	2	2½
1690	2	1	3	1	2	3	1	9	12	3	10	10	0
1691	1	1	2	—	3	3	—	9	13	0	11	9	3
1692	5	4	9	2	2	4	2	23	1	6	23	6	0
1693	1	1	2	2	2	4	3	18	9	0	18	5	1
1694	—	4	4	2	2	4	2	18	10	11	18	5	0
1695	3	1	4	4	7	11	2	24	15	6	23	12	1½
1696	1	3	4	1	4	5	—	25	2	0	24	2	11
1697	4	3	7	3	2	5	2	16	11	0	17	1	10
1698	4	2	6	4	2	6	1	19	6	0	18	19	0
1699	2	2	4	1	3	4	4	18	16	0	18	5	0
1700	—	1	1	1	2	3	—	14	10	8½	15	7	7
1720	—	3	3	2	2	4	2	35	2	8	36	6	5½
1740	4	4	8	2	2	4	1	25	19	2	21	18	8
1760	3	3	6	2	2	4	1	32	5	4	32	17	4½
1775	1	5	6	1	1	2	4	58	11	7½	50	0	10¾
1776	9	1	10	1	4	5	1	61	11	6	48	0	7¼
1777	6	6	12	2	4	6	4	63	2	9¾	53	0	2¼
1778	7	4	11	3	3	6	9	72	2	5	67	5	5½
1779	6	7	13	5	5	10	4	87	12	5½	85	4	11½
1780	7	7	14	6	4	10	1	74	17	2	74	5	9
1781	3	6	9	3	4	7	2	73	1	1	64	8	7½
1782	3	6	9	—	4	4	—	71	12	3	65	10	6
1783	6	3	9	7	5	12	4	78	11	5	72	12	2
1784	5	9	14	2	2	4	2	101	16	11	96	16	1½
1785	4	3	7	4	3	7	2	127	14	10½	116	15	8½
1786	4	6	10	8	4	12	1	91	1	2	84	14	6¼
1787	4	9	13	4	2	6	2	78	16	3½	75	16	6½
1788	6	7	13	—	8	8	7	75	9	5	71	0	8½
1789	10	9	19	3	3	6	4	76	18	4½	65	6	5
1790	4	9	13	3	4	7	1	72	11	9	64	14	5
1791	4	6	10	2	3	5	3	72	16	1½	54	19	9
1792	9	4	13	3	2	5	2	88	19	6	84	0	6
1793	1	5	6	4	3	7	3	· 116	19	0½	115	0	4½
1794	3	3	9	2	3	5	—	112	18	8½	110	15	7
1795	5	7	12	5	5	10	1						

37) 313   37) 215   37) 80

Average 8 17/37   Average 5 30/37 Av. 2 6/37   *April,* 1796.

STAPLETON

THE parish of Stapleton is situated about two miles to the north-east of Briftol. The number of its inhabitants, by an enumeration made in December 1795, was found to amount to 1377; they are principally of the established Church: there are, however, a few Quakers and Methodists, and a Baptist meeting-house in the parish. The total number of houses is 254; whereof 84 pay the window tax, and 170 are exempted; so that it appears that the number of inhabitants is very little more than $5\frac{2}{5}$ to a house. They are chiefly colliers, and agricultural labourers: there are likewise several masons, and workers in stone-quarries, in this parish. Day-labourers earn from 8s. to 10s. 6d. a week.

The provisions used here are purchased in the Briftol markets: farms are small, and chiefly pasture; very little corn is cultivated. A large common, containing between 500 and 600 acres, was enclosed in 1783, when half an acre of land was allotted to each of the adjoining cottages, of which there were a considerable number. There is now no waste land in the parish, and labourers find great difficulty in procuring habitations. It may answer to speculators in a great town to build houses, on the chance of receiving lodgers; but, in a small village, few will erect cottages, with a view to procure tenants from the collieries, or the stone quarries. A labourer's children are therefore obliged, when they are old enough to support themselves, and are desirous of becoming housekeepers, to migrate to other parishes. The land lets from £2. to £3. an acre; the land-tax produces £188. 18s. and is nearly 2s. in the pound.

There is no manufacture here, but a few spinning jennies were lately introduced.

Of the Poor, some are relieved at home; and some maintained in the work-house. The following is the usual weekly rotation of diet in the house:

	Breakfaſt.	Dinner.	Supper.
Sunday,	6 oz of bread, 1 oz. of butter, and beer	Boiled beef, potatoes, bread, and ſmall beer.	Bread and cheeſe, and ſmall beer.
Monday,	Broth. — — —	6 oz of bread; 1½ oz. of cheeſe, and beer	Ditto
Tueſday,	Ditto. — —	Boiled beef, potatoes, or car- rots, and beer	Ditto.
Wedneſday,	Ditto. — — —	Same as Monday	Ditto
Thurſday,	Ditto — —	Same as Tueſday.	Ditto
Friday,	Ditto — — —	Milk broth, or rice	Ditto.
Saturday,	Ditto. — — —	Same as Monday	Ditto

The children's allowance of bread, at dinner, is 4 oz. On Whitſun-day, and Chriſtmas-day, the dinner is baked veal, and plum-pudding.

There are in the houſe, at preſent, 3 men, 5 women, and 5 children; laſt year there were 5 men, 7 women, and 8 children. The children are employed in ſpinning flax and hemp; but their earnings are very in-conſiderable. There are at preſent 3 ale-houſes in the pariſh: about 20 years ago, there were 14 or 15; about 7 years ago, only 7, 4 of which were ſuppreſſed ſoon after the king's proclamation on this ſubject was iſſued.

There are two Friendly Societies in the pariſh of Stapleton. One of them was inſtituted on the 9th of May 1792, and conſiſts of 101 mem-bers; its rules exhibit ſo much of the rude ſimplicity of antient times, and are ſo characteriſtic of the manners of Glouceſterſhire ruſtics, that I truſt the reader will be gratified with a few of its regulations in the " honeſt kerſey," though ungrammatical, language of village legiſlators. It is re-markable, that of 46 articles, 15 or 16 relate to eating and drinking. The order of the annual feaſt is ſet down with as much preciſion as the ordi-nances of a royal houſhold.

1, Every member at entrance ſhall pay 2s. 6d. and 1s. 2d. every meet-ing night after, that is to ſay, every four weeks. 1s. ſhall go towards raiſing a fund, and 2d. to be ſpent in drinking and tobacco.

6, No perſon ſhall receive any benefit from the box, until he is free, which ſhall not be, before he has been in the ſociety 12 calendar months: if any perſon or member of this community does receive any pay before he is free, he ſhall be excluded.

7, Every free member being ſick, or lame, ſo as to render him inca-pable

pable of working at his trade or calling, fhall receive 7s. a week of the box ; but if he be able to go to work fooner than a week, he fhall receive 1s. 2d. a day (Sunday excepted) for every day during his illnefs.

8, For the better regulation of the Society, there fhall be a clerk appointed, which fhall act in conjunction with the ftewards in conducting their affairs, and to attend every meeting night, who fhall receive 1d. of each member every quarterly night; and if there be not members enough to raife 5s. it fhall be made good to him from the box.

9, If God is pleafed to take to his mercy any free member of this fociety, there fhall be allowed out of the box £6. to his wife, or to whomfoever he fhall pleafe to leave it, to bury him decent, and in a chriftian-like manner, towards which each member fhall contribute 1s. the next quarterly night following; and the friends of the deceafed fhall acquaint the ftewards of the funeral, who fhall attend at the funeral with 12 of the members, according to their turns, as they are enrolled on the regifter book.

10, If any free member's wife dies, he fhall be allowed out of the fund £3. to bury her, and the fame attendance to be given by the ftewards and members as to a man.   Whofoever refufes fhall forfeit 1s. or be excluded ; towards which every member fhall contribute 6d. the next quarterly night.

11, If it pleafe God to take to him any member of this Society before he be free, there fhall be a contribution of 1s. from each member, and the fame attendance as if he had been free ; whofoever refufeth fhall forfeit 1s. or be excluded.

12, If any member of this Society does any fort of work, while he receives pay of the box, any farther than giving direction to his fervants or workmen, he fhall be immediately excluded.   It is agreed, that if any member or members be drawn to ferve in the militia, that no money fhall be drawn out of the box ; but every member fhall contribute 1s. each to fuch member or members as may be drawn ; and it is farther agreed, that if any member or members fhould meet at the monthly nights, not paying his monthly arrears, fhall fpend 3d. or not be admitted into the club-room.

13, If any member of the Society is proved, after his entrance, to work at the White-Lead Houſe, he ſhall be immediately excluded; leaving his money behind him.

14, If any member of this Society ſhall have occaſion to travel 20 miles, or upwards, he ſhall be allowed 6 months to pay his arrears; but if he then neglects to clear the box, he ſhall be excluded.

15, Since vice and immorality abounds in this age, even to the profanation of the Sabbath, it is agreed, that, if any member of this Society ſhall, on the Sabbath-day, play at peck and toſs, marbles, ſhake in hat, coits, or any other gaming, he ſhall forfeit 2s. 6d. or be excluded; and if any brother member ſees him ſo doing, and gives information thereof to the Society, he ſhall receive 1s. and the other 18d. go to the box.

17, Whereas oftentimes diſputes ariſe in Societies, which cannot be fully determined nor decided by articles, we think it proper, when any diſpute ariſeth in this manner, that there ſhall be a committee of 17 members choſen, that is to ſay, 13 members and the four ſtewards; the members' names ſhall always be thoſe which follow the ſtewards on the regiſter book, who ſhall terminate all diſputes; whoſoever refuſeth, when choſen, ſhall forfeit 1s. or be excluded.

19, If any member ſhall continue ſick or lame, after he has lain on the box 12 months, he ſhall be reduced to half-pay for 12 months more, if he continues ſick or lame ſo long; and, at the end of 12 months, he ſhall be given a ſum of money, according as the above committee ſhall think proper, and then be excluded the Society. Likewiſe, if the fund ſhould be reduced to £10. it ſhall be ſhut up for 6 months, and all payments ſtopped.

22, When any member of this Society dies, one half of the drink allowed by the Society ſhall be carried to the funeral-houſe, and there be diſpoſed of, and the other half ſhall be drank at the houſe where the Society is held; whoſoever preſumes to have more than half, ſhall forfeit 1s. or be excluded. No reflection ſhall be made by any member of this Society on any other member that has had the benefit of the box, on the forfeiture of 2s. 6d. or be excluded: neither ſhall any member raiſe any report on a brother member; if he does, and cannot make his report good, he ſhall forfeit 2s. 6d. or be excluded.

23, If

23, If any member of this Society be imprefled in his Majefty's fervice, he fhall be allowed his fhare of the ftock according to the time he was free; but if he enters into his Majefty's fervice, or on board any merchantman, or if he goes out of the kingdom, he fhall be excluded, leaving his money behind him. No unhealthy man, nor above the age of 41, fhall be admitted into this Society : if any man enters, thinking to defraud this Society, having any private complaint or diforder, he fhall immediately be excluded, leaving his money behind him.

24, When either of the ftewards fhall fetch the money to pay the fick, from the father of the houfe where the Society is held, he fhall be allowed one pint of drink, to be deducted from the next meeting night's drink ; if they have any more, they fhall pay for it themfelves, or forfeit 6d. Whoever refufeth to pay his forfeits, fhall be immediately excluded.

The following Rules refpect the Anniverfary Feaft :

27, There fhall be a feaft held once in a year, which fhall be on Whitmonday, toward which every member fhall pay 1s. 6d. on the meeting night before, or on the morning of the feaft-day before he goes to dinner, on the neglect of which he fhall forfeit 2s. 6d. or be excluded.

28, That the ftewards then acting fhall take care to order the feaft decently, and they fhall be allowed 1s. each for their trouble : likewife in the morning of the feaft day, the ftewards fhall attend at half paft eight of the clock, to provide breakfaft for the members, and to ferve them with drink, on the forfeit of 1s. or be excluded.

29, That the members fhall be allowed no more drink at breakfaft than 2d. *per* member ; whofoever calls for any, unknown to the ftewards, fhall forfeit 1s. or be excluded ; and if the ftewards have any more than each man's 2d. amounts to, they fhall pay it themfelves, or be excluded.

30, That all and every member of this Society fhall attend at the houfe where the Society is held, on the morning of the feaft day, in due time, to walk in proceffion to hear divine fervice, except ficknefs, lamenefs, or being at the diftance of 20 miles, on the forfeiture of 1s. or be excluded.

31, If

31, If any member refuses to follow the procession to hear divine service, hides himself, or stays behind, not keeping his rank when commanded by the stewards, he shall forfeit 1s. for every such offence, or be excluded.

32, If any member behaves himself disorderly going to church or returning from the same, to any member or members of another society, by pushing his stick at them, cursing or guiling at them, or challenging them to fight, or do strike any or either of them, he shall forfeit the sum of 2s. 6d. or be excluded.

33, If any member behaves himself disorderly in the church during divine service, by talking, swearing, or laughing, he shall forfeit 2s 6d. or be excluded; and if any member stays behind drinking, and will not keep his place in following the procession home to the house, but come to dinner drunken, and not in his time to dine with the rest, he shall forfeit 1s. or be excluded.

34, If any member, during the whole day of the feast, shall fight, or challenge to fight, strike, or throw down, wrestle, or challenge to wrestle, or cause any disturbance in the Society, while at dinner, or after dinner, till all the company be dismissed, with any of his brother members, he shall forfeit 2s. 6d. or be immediately excluded.

35, No member, on the feast-day, shall provoke another, by calling him nick-names, or by guiling at him, or casting meat or bones at another, or about the room; neither shall any member feed another by way of fun, and wasting the victuals, to the shame of the company; any such things being done, those that do them shall forfeit 1s. or be excluded.

36, That there shall be allowed no more than 6d. each man, in drink, the first day of the feast; whosoever has more shall pay for it himself, or be excluded.

37, That the stewards take care not to have more drink than each man's 6d. amounts to, otherwise they shall make it good themselves, or forfeit 1s. each, or be excluded; and if any private member fetches any drink unknown to the stewards, they shall forfeit 2s. 6d. or be excluded.

38, That no woman whatsoever shall be suffered to enter the Society-room on a feast day during the time the Society-drink holds; whosoever introduces any woman into the room shall forfeit 1s: neither shall there be any victuals given away on the first day of the feast; whosoever

carries

carries or conveys any victuals out of the club-room on feast days, or hides or pockets any with a defign to carry it away, fhall forfeit 2s. 6d. or be excluded.

39, That no fteward nor private member fhall be allowed to give any victuals away the firft day, but the referve fhall be kept till the next day for as many as pleafe to come to breakfaft; and then the ftewards fhall have liberty to give a flice of bread and meat to any member's wife or child, or to any friend, ufing difcretion, as they think fit; and each member that comes to breakfaft fhall pay 3d. to be fpent in drink; whofoever refufeth fhall forfeit 6d. or be excluded.

The other Friendly Society at Stapleton commenced the 30th of October 1775, and confifts of about 50 members: they meet once a month from fix o'clock till eight in the evening, during the winter half-year; and from feven till nine o'clock in the evening, during the fummer half-year; pay 1s. each to the box, and 2d. to be fpent at the meeting. The age of admiffion is from 21 to 40. A member, of a year's ftanding, is allowed 7s a week, if fick or lame, but with this reftriction, that if in 3 months there appears an impoffibility of his recovery, his allowance fhall be reduced to 4s. a week for life Infirm members unable to work, and perfons 70 years of age, even if they are able to work, are entitled to an allowance of 4s. a week. £3. are paid for the funeral of a free member, and 1s. from each of the members, to his widow, or legatee; or, if he dies inteftate, to his neareft relation. When a member's wife dies, the hufband receives 30s. from the ftock, and 6d. from each member, towards the expences of her funeral. Sick members muft give a week's notice, before they can receive money from the ftock. No perfon can be admitted a member, that works at the White-Lead Houfe[1], mining, or any work under ground. A member that is impreffed into the King's fervice, is allowed the money he has contributed, (in cafe he has not received it on any other account;) but if he voluntarily inlifts himfelf, he is excluded. The Society is governed by 4 ftewards, who are elected at the quarterly meetings; their duty is to vifit the fick and lame twice a week, and to pay them their weekly allowances. All difputes, which cannot be decided by the articles, are referred to a committee of 13 members chofen by a majority of the Society An anniverfary feaft is held on Whit-monday.

[1] This is one of the rules of the other Society

Table

Table of Poor's Rates and Disbursements for the Poor for 20 years.

	Poor's Rates.					Disbursements for the Poor.		
						£.	s.	d.
1776	-	-	⸗	▪	-	307	4	8
1777	-	-	-	-	-	323	18	5
1778	-	-	-	-	-	211	8	10
1779	-	-	-	-	-	210	16	1
1780	-	-	-	-	-	262	8	0½
1781	-	-	-	-	-	236	8	0½
1782	£.	s.	d.	-	-	193	0	4
1783	- 182	1	3	-	-	211	10	1½
1784	- 188	7	2	-	-	248	11	4
1785	- 266	16	3	-	-	399	5	10
1786	-	-	-	-	-	325	19	10
1787	-	-	-	-	-	240	4	0
1788	-	-	-	-	-	281	7	3
1789	-	-	-	-	-	283	9	8

About ⸗
rates in
year, at
the rate.

From the returns made
to Parliament in 1786.

	£.	s.	d.
1790—Weekly disbursements to out-poor	204	0	0
—Work-house, and tradesmen's bills	159	16	2
—Church disbursements - -	43	16	6
—County money for bridges, &c. -	10	8	8

418　1　4

	£.	s.	d.
1791—Weekly disbursements to out-poor	199	18	0
—Work-house and tradesmen's bills	132	14	10¾
—Church disbursements - -	17	9	8½
—County bridge money - -	13	5	8

363　8　3¼

	£.	s.	d.
1792—Weekly disbursements to out-poor	189	1	4½
—Work-house and tradesmen's bills -	167	16	6½
—Church disbursements - -	11	10	3
—County bridge money - -	11	16	8

380　4　10

	£. s. d.	£. s. d.
1793—Weekly difburfements to out-poor	230 0 0	
—Work-houfe and tradefmen's bills -	170 7 8	
—Church difburfements - -	88 1 10½	
—County bridge money - -	9 1 4	
		498 10 10½
1794—Weekly difburfements to out-poor	211 19 11	
—Work-houfe and tradefmen's bills	182 6 5	
—Church difburfements - -	15 15 3	
—County bridge money - -	8 18 2	
		418 19 9
1795—Weekly difburfements to out-poor	275 19 2	
—Work-houfe and tradefmen's bills	180 5 3	
— Church difburfements - -	11 14 3	
—County bridge money - -	12 4 8	
		480 3 4

In 1795 there were 53 baptifms, 38 burials, and 17 marriages.

Laft fummer a collection was made in this parifh of about 10 guineas, which were diftributed among poor families at the rate of 3d. a head every week: as £1. 2s. were paid every week, for about 10 weeks in the months of Auguft, September, and October, it follows, that the number of men, women, and children, relieved weekly, amounted to 88. It is remarkable that during the ten weeks that the Poor were at liberty to apply for relief, not more than 3 or 4 perfons complained of not receiving this allowance. It was at firft propofed to confine the relief to parifhioners; but the contributors very judicioufly and humanely decided, that no diftinction fhould be made between perfons refident in the parifh, and perfons having a legal fettlement there.

April, 1796.

HAMPSHIRE.

GOSPORT.

THE extent of this parish is about 12 or 13 square miles. There were 9 Rates for the relief of the Poor, laft year; each Rate, 6d. in the pound on land, and 4d. on houfes; in the whole, 4s. 6d. in the pound on land, and 3s. on houfes: the fum collected was between £1600. and £1700. Several buildings, which were rated at £200. a year, are now in the hands of Government, and are exempted from the Poor's Rate. In the years ending in 1793 and 1794 there were 10 Rates: this year, however, it is expected that 8 will be fufficient. This reduction of the Rates feems afcribable to the good management of the parifh officers; the parifh however is divided into two parties, which ftrongly oppofe each other in parochial concerns. Few particulars could be learned refpecting the amount of the Poor's Rates in different years. The following extracts are taken from the returns made to Parliament in 1786.

	£.	s.	d.
Expences of the Poor in 1776	837	7	3
Poor's Rate collected in 1783	1133	7	11
Ditto - - 1784	1010	8	4
Ditto - - 1785	1258	17	10

About £30 are annually diftributed to out-penfioners: this article of expenditure was formerly more confiderable than at prefent. The great expence accruing from foldiers' and failors' wives becoming chargeable, is a frequent topic of complaint in this parifh. It fhould however be confidered, that the burthen has not increafed more rapidly than the means of fupporting it; and the influx of Poor into a parifh, intimately connected with Portfmouth, although occafioned by warfare, is more than counterbalanced, by the various branches of induftry, that are called for, by the equipment of fleets and armies:

the

the artificer in the dock-yard, the shop-keeper, and the publican receive too much benefit from military preparation, to have reason to complain that the number of Poor increases ; even the land-holders are compensated by the advance of their rents ; and the farmers by the increased demand, which is thus produced, for the various articles of consumption.

The greater part of the Poor of Gosport is maintained in a work-house. The number in the house at present is 160; in winter, it generally amounts to 200. Their principal employment is picking oakum.

October, 1795.

HAWKLEY—NEWTON-VALENCE.

THE circumference of the parish of Hawkley is about 4 miles : the number of it's inhabitants about 259: they are wholly engaged in agriculture. The rent of land is from 8s. to 20s. an acre, average about 12s. an acre : the land-tax amounts to about 3s. in the pound on the net rental. The tithe is let to the occupiers of the land. There are no commons in Hawkley. The wages of labourers are 1s. 6d. a day. There is no ale-house in the parish : one was put down very lately.

The circumference of the parish of Newton-Valence, is about 10 miles : the number of inhabitants, who are wholly agricultural, is 228. The rent of land is from 5s. to 20s. an acre ; the average about 9s. : the land-tax about 2s. 6d. in the pound on the net rental. The greatest part of the tithe is let to the occupiers ; the rest is taken in kind.

There are two commons in this parish, containing, altogether, about 150 acres. The wages of labourers are 1s. 6d. a day. There is one ale-house in the parish.

There are no Papists, or Protestant Dissenters of any denomination, in Newton-Valence, or Hawkley: nor are there any Friendly Societies in either parish.

The

The following query was sent, amongst others, by the Bishop of Winchester in 1788 :

What number of marriages, births, and burials, may you have at a medium one year with another ?

Answer.—In the last 20 years were registered

In Newton Valence   30 Marriages, which make the { — — — 1½ Marriages.
                    168 Births,   medium for { rather more than 8 Births
                     73 Burials,   one year   { rather less than 4 Burials

In Hawkley   37 Marriages, which make the { nearly — — 2 Marriages.
                    153 Births,   medium for { nearly — — 8 Births.
                    100 Burials,   one year   { — — — 5 Burials.

The parochial system of Newton-Valence, since the heavy advance in the price of provisions took place, has been, to permit each labourer, whether old or young, or with or without a family, to purchase flour at 8s. a bushel ; the extra price is charged to the Poor's Rate. A man with this allowance is supposed to be capable of maintaining a wife and 2 children, and paying his rent from his earnings : when the family exceeds that number, a proportionate allowance is made. The Poor are satisfied with this plan, and think their condition is not affected by the present high price of the necessaries of life. The Poor's Rate is excessively high ; 7s. in the pound on the rack rents ; but the farmers are more benefited by the high price of corn, than injured by the advance in the Poor's Rate.

Table

Table of Baptisms, Burials, Marriages, and Poor's Rates, in the Parish of HAWKLEY.

Years	Baptisms Mal	Fem	Tot	Burials Mal	Fem	Tot	Marriages
1680	—	3	3	1	1	2	—
1685	3	2	5	1	1	2	1
1690	1	1	2	2	—	2	2
1691	3	1	4	—	4	4	—
1692	2	2	4	2	2	4	—
1693	—	—	—	4	2	6	3
1694	2	2	4	1	—	1	4
1695	2	—	2	2	1	3	—
1696	2	3	5	1	—	1	—
1697	1	5	6	1	2	3	—
1698	3	2	5	1	5	6	—
1699	2	—	2	—	2	2	—
1700	1	1	2	2	—	2	—
1720	1	4	5	3	4	7	—
1740	2	4	6	—	—	—	1
1760	4	1	5	1	4	5	3
1775	4	4	8	2	3	5	1
1776	5	3	8	2	3	5	2
1777	2	4	6	5	2	7	1
1778	1	4	5	2	4	6	2
1779	4	5	9	3	2	5	2
1780	4	4	8	4	4	8	—
1781	4	7	11	1	1	2	—
1782	5	5	10	2	—	2	2
1783	7	1	8	2	2	4	3
1784	4	5	9	1	2	3	1
1785	—	1	1	7	3	10	—
1786	3	5	8	3	3	9	4
1787	4	4	8	1	—	1	1
1788	4	5	9	2	3	5	1
1789	4	6	10	2	4	6	4
1790	6	1	7	—	1	1	—
1791	1	2	3	2	—	2	—
1792	5	7	12	2	2	4	1
1793	4	2	6	3	4	7	1
1794	5	2	7	1	—	1	2
1795	5	5	10	4	4	8	2

Poor's Rates.

Years	£	s.	d.
1750	35	15	8
1751	22	7	0
1752	23	1	11
1753	30	4	6
1754	34	12	10
1755	46	19	4
1756	44	8	2
1757	38	16	11
1758	53	1	8
1759	44	0	0
1760	33	12	11
1761	34	18	5
1762	36	0	1
1763	42	7	1
1764	41	13	7
1765	47	3	8
1766	56	4	0
1767	63	12	7
1768	56	18	1
1769	80	12	2
1770	63	12	11
1771	65	2	1
1772	61	16	0
1773	79	13	10
1774	105	4	0
1775	137	7	11
1776	138	3	2
1777	148	4	5
1778	100	4	5
1779	96	13	2
1780	121	15	10

Poor's Rates.

Years	£	s	d.
1781	103	17	11
1782	133	6	10
1783	142	10	6
1784	172	0	7
1785	193	10	3
1786	177	5	8
1787	156	6	7
1788	185	17	5
1789	140	15	9
1790	159	14	7
1791	140	2	6
1792	133	6	4
1793	166	4	11
1794	219	6	6
1795	325	13	8

Average of 16 years, from 1750 to 1765 inclusive. } 38 1 5¼

Average of 15 years, from 1766 to 1780 inclusive. } 91 14 3½

Average of 15 years, from 1781 to 1795 inclusive. } 170 0 0

Table

Table of Baptisms, Burials, Marriages, and Poor's Rates, in the Parish of
NEWTON-VALENCE.

Years	Baptisms			Burials			Mar	Years	Poor's Rates			Years	Poor's Rates		
	Mal	Fem	Tot	Mal	Fem	Tot			£	s	d		£	s	d
1680	5	1	6	1	—	—	—	—	1726	40	2	7	1761	29	0	0
1685	3	5	8	—	—	—	—	—	1727	20	14	8	1762	39	13	1
1690	3	1	4	—	—	—	—	3	1728	21	4	6	1763	28	10	0
1691	2	2	4	—	—	—	—	4	1729	17	4	6	1764	57	18	5
1692	2	1	3	—	—	—	—	—	1730	29	18	6	1765	43	17	0
1693	1	1	2	—	—	—	—	—	1731	59	19	11	1766	58	0	8
1694	4	—	4	—	—	—	—	1	1732	29	12	2	1767	57	9	1
1695	3	3	6	—	—	—	—	4	1733	40	7	5	1768	47	8	4
1696	1	—	1	—	—	—	—	—	1734	33	2	6	1769	43	7	3
1697	—	2	2	3	1	4	—	1735	25	6	9	1770	48	18	4
1698	3	1	4	3	1	4	—	1736	28	18	8	1771	67	0	8
1699	—	—	—	3	1	4	—	1737	18	12	1	1772	79	14	4 ¼
1700	2	2	4	—	—	—	1	1738	22	18	0	1773	90	18	11
1720	4	1	5	1	—	1	1	1739	16	14	3	1774	120	13	6
1740	4	3	7	2	1	3	—	1740	21	16	6	1775	92	11	5
1760	—	1	1	1	3	4	1	1741	20	17	6	1776	92	6	0
1775	5	1	6	—	3	3	—	1742	21	7	4	1777	111	18	5
1776	5	8	13	—	—	—	1	1743	24	13	2	1778	80	11	9
1777	5	4	9	—	4	4	2	1744	15	0	8	1779	83	9	5
1778	5	2	7	3	1	4	2	1745	15	11	8	1780	91	19	6
1779	6	4	10	1	1	2	2	1746	13	19	4	1781	79	6	9
1780	6	6	12	3	4	7	2	1747	26	0	3	1782	48	5	3
1781	4	4	8	—	4	4	1	1748	22	11	1	1783	186	1	11
1782	4	9	13	2	2	4	2	1749	21	7	1	1784	191	6	10
1783	3	4	7	1	2	3	3	1750	22	17	8	1785	187	13	0
1784	4	1	5	2	1	3	4	1751	12	9	0	1786	173	6	5
1785	4	5	9	5	1	6	—	1752	16	12	10	1787	173	4	0
1786	3	5	8	—	—	—	1	1753	11	11	2	1788	216	17	10
1787	6	1	7	2	1	3	—	1754	16	6	7	1789	156	12	1
1788	6	3	9	3	2	5	3	1755	20	6	9	1790	190	4	7
1789	5	2	7	3	3	6	3	1756	20	19	8	1791	143	3	5
1790	2	3	5	—	4	4	1	1757	40	10	10	1792	159	0	9
1791	4	6	10	—	3	3	3	1758	40	2	7	1793	190	4	1
1792	2	2	4	—	2	2	—	1759	34	9	9	1794	161	9	7
1793	1	3	4	—	1	1	3	1760	24	7	0	1795	355	4	2
1794	7	2	9	—	—	—	1								
1795	5	—	5	6	1	1	2								

The aver. of 17 yrs from 1726 to 1742 incluf 27 11 7½ 10/17
Ditto of 17 yrs from 1743 to 1759 incluf. 22 1 9 1/7
Ditto of 18 yrs from 1760 to 1777 incluf 65 9 0
Ditto of 18 yrs from 1778 to 1795 incluf 165 3 4½ 10/18

March, 1796.

PETERSFIELD

THIS parish contains 184 houses: it's extent is about 200 acres. The inhabitants, who are mostly of the established Church, are, in general, engaged in commerce. The wages of common labourers were 7s. a week last year, but have this year advanced to 9s. without board. In harvest, men receive 2 guineas and a half a month, and their board. The prices of provisions are: wheat, 10s. the bushel; bread, 11d. the quartern loaf; beef,

beef, 5½d. the pound; mutton, from 5½d to 6d; veal, 8d; bacon, from 10d. to 11½d; butter, 10d.; potatoes, 1s. the bushel; coals, £ 2. 10s. the chaldron; new milk, 1½d. the quart; old milk, 2d. the gallon.

The rent of land is from £ 1. to £ 3.; the land-tax amounts to £ 213. 13s. 5d. and is about 3s. 4d. in the pound. There are 12 inns or ale-houses in this parish; but no Friendly Societies: 2 existed some time ago; but as soon as the stock amounted to a few hundreds, the clubs were dissolved, and the money divided amongst the members.

The Poor are chiefly supported in a work-house, under the superintendance of a standing overseer, who has been in office above 5 years. He does not reside in the house, but attends at meals, provides victuals, and collects the Poor's Rates. To his good management the reduction of the Rates is principally ascribable. He pays every proper attention to the wants of the necessitous, and administers the concerns of the parish with fidelity, and discrimination: notwithstanding this, he is disliked by the Poor, and several attempts have been made to burn his house; the gentlemen, however, stand by him, and approve of his proceedings.

22 persons, (mostly old women and children,) are at present in the work-house: they are, principally, employed in cleansing the streets. Their earnings are very small, and do not exceed £ 5. or £ 6. a year. In the winter 50 or 60 persons are in the house. 9 families, who are out-pensioners, receive 16s. 6d. a week: 3 militia men's families, belonging to the parish, are allowed 9s. 4d. a week. Parish children, when 9 or 10 years old, are either bound out apprentices, or sent out to service for 4 years: in the latter case, the parish pays 1s. a week with each child, and the master finds employment, board, cloaths, and lodging: at the expiration of the 4 years, the child is generally able to acquire a maintenance. 6 children, of this description, are at present chargeable; and cost the parish 6s. a week.

Assessments are said to be made on the rack rental: the following expences are included in the annual disbursements:

Salary of the standing overseer	-	-	-: £ 30 0. 0
Vestry clerk	- - - - -	-	-: 4 0. 0
Doctors' bills, annually amount to about	- :	-	-: 6 10 0
Removals, appeals, &c (upon the average of the last 20 years,) cost annually	:-	5 0 0

The deficiency arising from uncollected Rates is likewise included in the above expenditure It generally amounts to from £ 1. to £ 6. or £ 7. a year. It is expected, that this year the Rate will not exceed 5s. in the pound.

Some years ago a sacking manufacture was established here;- but not having answered the views of the proprietor, it is nearly discontinued.

o   *Table*

Table of Diet in the Work-house.

	Breakfast	Dinner	Supper
Sunday,	Bread and milk.	Pickled pork, pudding, and vegetables.	Bread and cheese
Monday,	Ditto.	Cold meat, &c	Ditto
Tuesday,	Ditto.	Bread and cheese	Ditto.
Wednesday,	Ditto	As Sunday	Ditto
Thursday,	Ditto	Bread and cheese:	Ditto
Friday,	Ditto	As Sunday.	Ditto
Saturday,	Ditto	Bread and cheese	Ditto

Beer is allowed at dinners and suppers. Half a pound of cheese a week is allowed to each grown person: the bread is not weighed. Sometimes instead of pork or bacon, a little coarse beef is bought for the Poor; broth is then used, but not when pork or bacon is boiled.

Table of Baptisms, Burials, Marriages, and Poor's Rates.

Years.	Baptisms			Burials			Marriages	Poor's Rate			Total Expenditure			Rate in the pound
	Males.	Fem	Total	Males	Fem	Total		£	s	d	£	s	d.	
1765	21	19	40	14	25	39	—	197	16	0	183	8	7	
1766	20	22	42	18	11	29	—	242	12	0	285	11	11	
1767	14	21	35	14	12	26	—	329	10	10	338	3	5	
1768	14	14	28	14	9	23	—	317	15	11	300	14	5	
1769	18	21	39	12	10	22	—	309	7	7	282	6	6	
1770	21	18	39	11	6	17	—	268	5	9	290	5	9	
1771	23	24	47	17	15	32	—	185	9	10	182	11	2	
1772	23	19	42	14	14	28	—	257	9	4	257	0	8	
1773	12	15	27	14	18	32	—	358	14	11	352	13	8	
1774	18	24	42	5	14	19	—	325	3	8	389	11	2	
1775	18	18	36	13	15	28	—	415	2	3	447	6	9	
1776	18	17	35	12	13	25	—	275	14	0	259	2	2¾	
1777	23	12	35	13	13	26	—	279	17	0	262	12	8	
1778	24	16	40	16	14	30	—	208	2	3	215	0	4¾	
1779	19	30	49	10	17	27	—	278	13	6	240	17	5½	
1780	16	28	44	27	25	52	—	173	6	10¼	285	12	7	
1781	24	28	52	18	26	44	—	313	14	3	267	14	1½	
1782	22	26	48	25	24	49	—	306	13	2	414	10	9	
1783	26	26	52	23	21	44	—	286	7	7	394	0	11¾	s. d.
1784	27	21	48	15	19	34	6	484	10	11	515	12	0	7 0
1785	19	19	39	13	15	28	10	545	9	4	579	15	6	8 0
1786	23	27	50	13	14	27	8	391	9	0	515	17	0	6 0
1787	11	26	37	21	13	34	7	375	15	4	401	12	1	6 0
1788	17	19	36	16	11	27	13	375	12	9	418	13	7	6 0
1789	18	24	42	8	13	21	6	547	5	1	562	2	3	9 0
1790	20	22	42	13	13	26	9	512	12	10	549	5	2	8 0
1791	19	18	37	11	12	23	12	449	17	3	544	5	7	7 0
1792	23	33	56	18	11	29	10	320	11	7	394	12	3	5 0
1793	20	20	40	16	13	29	6	374	7	1	427	1	4	6 0
1794	24	24	48	17	20	37	10	379	10	2	457	12	9	6 0
1795	—	—	—	—	—	—	—	384	10	0	403	3	2	6 0

October, 1795.

PORTSEA.

THE parifh of Portfea, (commonly called Portfmouth Common,) is eftimated to contain near 15 fquare miles : it nearly encircles the fmall parifh of Portfmouth

Of late years, Portfea has much increafed both in wealth and population. One of the prefent church-wardens took an enumeration of the houfes about two years ago, and found them to amount to about 3050: 100 or more have been built fince that period. 36 men were raifed by this parifh for the Navy, in purfuance of a late Act; the number therefore of houfes paying window-tax, (reckoning 68 houfes to 1 feaman,) will amount to £2448.

Farms in this parifh are from £200. to £300. a year. The rent of land is from £1. to £3. 10s. an acre.

The following account of Poor's Rates and Parochial Expenditure was principally furnifhed by the church-warden :

Years.	Total Expenditure.			Total Receipts.			
	£.	s.	d.	£.	s.	d.	
1776	1327	8	7				
1781	1338	2	10½				
1782	1947	17	3½				
1783	1824	0	10¼	1387	8	9	
1784	2424	13	0½	1858	7	9	From the Returns to Parliament.
1785	—	—	—	1871	18	3	
1794	2819	4	0	2955	14	4	

The Poor of this parifh are, principally, maintained in a work-houfe. At prefent there are 164 Paupers in the houfe: the ufual number in winter is about 300, but has been known to exceed 340. They are chiefly employed in picking oakum. The earnings by this bufinefs in 1782, were £235. 10s. 7d.; in 1783, £166. 10s. 4d.; in 1784, £146. 6s. 7½d. The weekly and out-poor coft in the year, ending in 1794, £279. 3s. 11d.; militia men's families, £66. 19s. 11d. About

£32. a year, are paid from the Rates to watchmen; and £30. annually, to the gaol. The parish officers are frequently re-chosen, and serve for several years; but have no salary from the parish. In general, they belong to the dock-yards, from whence they receive their wages, and are excused from working, in consideration of their serving a parish office.

The work-house stands in a good situation, about 1 mile from the town, and is tolerably well contrived There are from 2 to 6 feather-beds in a room, and iron bed-steads. The house is kept very clean, and the Poor appear to live very comfortably. Those, who use tobacco, are allowed 2 oz. each, a week. The number of deaths in the house last year, was 31. Either meat-broth, or a sort of gruel called flour-broth, made of flour and water, is their common breakfast: the dinner, 3 days in the week, consists of meat; and on the other 4 days, of bread and cheese: the suppers are bread and cheese. Beer is allowed at bread and cheese meals only. Each adult person has 1 lb of bread a day, and 8 oz. of meat on meat days.

There are 6 Friendly Societies in Portsea; the number of members, in each, is from 80 to 180. Only two have taken the benefit of the late Act of Parliament: the expence attending an application to the Justices, is the common reason given why the other Societies have not had their rules confirmed.

In Portsea are 1 Presbyterian, 2 Methodist, and 2 Anabaptist meeting-houses, and 1 Roman Catholic chapel.   *October*, 1795.

PORTSMOUTH.

IN this parish, as in many others, the parish books were not accessible. From the information however of the parish officers, it appears that in the year ending in 1794, the Poor's Rates (at 4s. 3d. in the pound,) amounted to about £2210.; and the total Receipts to £2778. 17s. 4d.; and that in the year ending in 1795, the Rates (at 3s. 6d. in the pound,) produced £1820; and the total Receipts £2789. 18s. Last year £450. were expended on casual Poor. The Rates in Portsmouth have been as high as 4s. 6d. in the pound, but are seldom at full rental.

The parifh of Portfmouth raifed 9 men for the Navy, from whence, (according to the ufual proportion of 68 houfes to a man,) the number of rateable houfes may be eftimated at 612.

The chuich regifteis are very perfect, and commence foon aftei the era of their eftablifhment by Lord Ciomwell.

Years.	Baptifms.	Buiials.			Marriages.
1550	24	—	—	—	—
1551	19	—	—	—	—
1554	—	19	—	—	—
1775	251	256	—	—	77
1776	250	260	—	—	52
1780	338	510	—	—	123
1781	376	443	—	—	182
1785	266	223	—	—	73
1786	310	290	—	—	63
1790	235	297	—	—	104
1794	347	384	{ of which 70 are iegiftered as Poor. }	—	121

At Portfmouth aie, 1 Prefbyteiian, 1 Arminian, and 2 Anabaptift congregations.

The Poor of this parifh are chiefly maintained in a woik-houfe; in which there are at piefent about 170 peifons, who aie employed in picking oakum. The houfe is faid to be neither well contrived, nor well managed. About 40 out-penfioners receive, each, fiom 1s. to 2s. à week. A ftanding overfeer, with a falary, was appointed laft year; and it is to the appointment of a permanent officer that the late reduction of the Rates is principally attiibuted.

The piopoition of out-penfioneis, both in this paiifh, and in Portfea, is very inconfiderable: when peifons become neceffitous, the parifh geneially infifts on their going into the work-houfe; by which means the expenditure is much reduced; not becaufe the Poor are maintained at a cheapei rate in the houfe than they could be at their own homes, but becaufe the appiehenfion of being obliged to intermix with the vaiious defciiptions of indigent people, ufually found in a large Pooi houfe, deteis many fiom

G g 2   making

making applications for relief. The regulation adopted by the parish, of sending such persons to the work-house as are likely to remain chargeable a long time, is a great incitement to industry, and certainly prevents many frivolous claims for parochial assistance : but it seems to bear hard upon the modest Poor, who are the most deserving objects of national charity. The parishes of Portsmouth and Portsea are much at variance ; nor will either receive a Pauper from the other without an order of removal. It is said that Portsmouth, in order to reduce it's Rates, is endeavouring to get incorporated with Portsea : the latter however is determined to oppose this measure. Both parishes complain of having a great number of casual Poor.

The high price of provisions is sensibly felt, among the labouring classes, in this neighbourhood : the quartern loaf of wheaten bread costs 1s. ;, beef, from 6d. to 7d. the pound ; mutton, 6d. ; veal, 8d. ; bacon, 10½d. ; butter, 10d. to 13d. ; potatoes, 5d. the gallon ; milk, 1d. the pint.

Common labourers earn from 8s. to 9s. a week. All employments and occupations in any degree connected with the Navy, are now actively exerted ; more especially in his Majesty's dock-yards, where there is a great demand for labour : shipwrights receive standing wages of 6s. 6d. a week, but work double tides, (that is, perform double the work usually required,) about two months in three, and are then allowed double wages. Besides this, they can earn about 2s. 6d. a week by watching, in their turns, at 1s a night. Watermen, at present, have constant employment ; but in times of peace, this class of men is almost starving : tailors, shoemakers, and other tradesmen, more particularly publicans, are in full business : in short, war is the harvest of Portsmouth ; and peace, which is so ardently wished for in most other parts of England, is dreaded here.

Statement of the Earnings and Expences of a Labourer in the Dock-yard.

He is 35 years of age ; has a wife and 3 children, of 11, 7, and 3 years of age. The children do no work. The wife earns a shilling now and then.

	£.	s.	d.
Her earnings, in the year, may amount to - -	0	15	0
The man earns 15s. a week, during one half of the year -	19	10	0
Carried over - £	20	5	0

	£.	s.	d.
Brought over	20	5	0
And 10s. 6d. a week during the other half of the year	13	13	0
He earns, by extra-jobs, about	3	0	0
	£36	18	0
15s. (one week's earnings) muſt be deducted for ſicknefs, holidays, &c.	0	15	0
Net earnings	£36	3	0

EXPENCES.

	£.	s.	d.
His houſe-rent is £6. 6s. a year; but one room is let for 1s. 3d. a week, which reduces his rent to	3	1	0
Weekly expence of bread for the family, between 9s. and 10s.—on an average, about 9s. 6d.—annually	24	14	0
	£27	15	0
Surplus of earnings	£8	8	0

The man could give no account of his other expences, but ſays they do not exceed his earnings. The ſum however of 8 guineas ſeems very inadequate to provide five perſons with the other articles of food they muſt want; fuel, cloathing, &c. No milk is uſed in this family. They generally breakfaſt on tea, and ſometimes on bread and cheeſe. A joint of meat is provided once a week; but bread, with a little cheeſe, conſtitutes the principal part of their diet.

October, 1795.

SOUTHAMPTON.

THE town of Southampton contains by eſtimation about 4 ſquare miles, one fourth of which is common. The number of inhabitants, from ſome calculations lately made, is ſuppoſed to be near 9000. Here is a mill for twiſting ſilk, which employs a few children; and a carpet manufactory, which works 4 or 5 looms; but there is no other manufacture.

In

In this town there are one Prefbyteiian, and one Anabaptift congie-gation.

The number of houfes paying the window tax could not be obtained; but, as 10 or 12 men were raifed for the Navy, it may be eftimated at near 700.

The prices of provifion are: beef, from 6d. to 8d. the pound; mutton, from 6d. to 7d.; veal, 8d.; bacon, 10½d.; butter, 15½d.; bread, 1s. 11½d. the half-peck loaf; potatoes, 1od. a peck; coals, 37s. a chal-dion.

The wages of biicklayeis, caipenteis, &c. aie fiom 15s. to 16s. a week; and of common labouieis, fiom 1s. 8d. to 2s. a day. The number of ale-houfes is 30.

Here is one Fiiendly Society, which has had it's ordeis confiimed by the Magiftrates. The land-tax is about £250.

The Poor are paitly maintained in a work-houfe, and paitly at their own homes. In the work-houfe there are, at piefent, 120 perfons; of which, 50 aie children, undei the age of 14 years; the others aie moftly old people: in winter, there are fometimes near 150 in the houfe. 18 children and 4 old men from the woik-houfe are employed at the filk mill; and a few make blankets and cloaths foi the ufe of the houfe. The following is the ufual bill of fare:

	Bieakfaft.	Dinnei.	Suppei.
Sunday,	Onion biotli	Beef, and vegetables	Biead, and cheefe; oi biead, and butter.
Monday,	Bread, and butter	Broth, and biead	Ditto
Tuefday,	As Sunday.	Poik, and vegetables	Ditto
Wednefday,	Ditto. —	Biead, and buttei.	Ditto.
Thuifday,	Ditto —	Salt beef, and vegetables	Ditto.
Fiiday,	Ditto —	Bread, and butter	Ditto.
Saturday,	Ditto —	Biead, and cheefe.	Ditto

2 cups of beer a day (near 3 pints,) aie allowed to giown perfons, and a proportionable quantity to children.

The Rates, duiing the yeais ending in 1792 and 1793, were collected at 4s. in the pound on ¾ of the net rental. This has been the aveiage Rate for the laft 18 years.

The fubjoined particulais of the eainings and expendituie of the corporation of Guardians were extracted fiom their annual accounts for the yeais 1792 and 1793; the only ones that have yet been piinted.

Account

Account of the Guardians of the Poor of the Town of Southampton, from Easter 1791, to Easter 1792.

Dr.	£.	s.	d.
To cash received from the Treasurer of the former Guardians - - -	39	13	1½
To ditto by sale of manufactured articles by the house, exclusive of what was worked up, and used for the supply of the house - - -	95	1	6
To ditto received for earnings of the Poor in the house - - -	34	14	3
To ditto composition received for bastard children - - -	35	0	0
To ditto received for people in the house	35	14	3

Rates assessed on the several Parishes.

	£.	s.	d.
All-Saints' - -	836	17	6
Holy-Rood's - -	552	0	2¼
St. Michael's - -	310	0	10¼
St. Mary's - -	312	6	8
St. Lawrence's - -	211	3	11½
St. John's - -	102	4	10
	2324	14	0¼

	£.	s.	d.
Deficient in collection	374	4	2
Taken from the Overseers by the Corporation for a county rate this year	180	0	0
Ditto for high-ways -	88	5	4
Amount assessed on the parishes -	2967	3	6

Cr.	£.	s.	d.
By cash, debts incurred and not discharged by the former Guardians, £150.; of which were on bond to Sollier & Co. exclusive of the quarter's bills for the house	326	4	4
Master, matron, and beadle's salaries -	66	15	6
Surgeon's, and other salaries - -	81	18	6
Clerk's salary - -	27	6	8
Interest of £1700. - -	76	10	0
Insurance from fire - -	3	3	6
To out-paupers and occasional relief -	448	4	1
Removal of paupers - -	72	11	7
To bastard children out of the house -	16	19	6
Groceries, including butter - -	184	12	7
Cheese - - -	82	13	6
Drapery - - -	100	7	8
Cloathing - - -	7	18	6
Materials, chiefly wool, for employing the Poor - -	125	15	7
Town clerk's fees for examination of paupers as to their parishes, and signing rates	20	19	8
Law-processes - -	28	2	7
For marriages of the Poor - -	15	5	0
Burials of ditto - -	11	0	0
Butcher's meat, including salt pork -	117	1	4
Flour - - -	241	7	4
Malt and hops - -	86	0	9
Wine and spirits - -	17	19	3
Leather and shoes ready made -	31	11	10
Coals and wood for firing -	73	17	6
Garden-stuff - -	35	13	4
Live-stock - -	13	0	6
Sundry disbursements for the house -	40	11	8
Repairs done to the house -	20	1	4
Apprenticing poor children -	13	14	0
Rates returned - -	12	6	3
Subscription to the county hospital -	5	5	0
Expence for lunatics -	7	12	0
Balance in the Treasurer's hands -	152	15	10

	£.	s.	d.
Total receipts of the Guardians of the Poor	2564	17	1¼
	2564	17	1¼

* The sum total, upon casting up the different sums, appears to be less than the sum here set down, by 9s. 7¼d.

Accounts

Accounts from Easter 1792, to Easter 1793.

Dr.	£.	s.	d.
Balance of the preceding year -	152	15	10
To cash from the Corporation annually for the maintenance of 6 boys, £.40. a year.	80	0	0
Received for manufactured articles by house, exclusive of what was used in the house	190	3	4
Earnings of Poor in house - -	36	4	11
Composition for bastardy - -	82	19	0
Received for people in the house -	34	10	0
Interest of £50. - -	2	10	0
Fines for Guardian's non-attendance -	3	13	6

Assessments.

	£.	s.	d.			
All Saints' -	920	11	0			
Holy-Rood's -	560	0	1			
St. Michael's -	337	14	11¼		2457	18	5¼
St. Mary's -	336	18	9			
St. Lawrence's -	198	2	4¼			
St. John's -	104	11	3¼			

Deficiency in the collection 147 10 6

The whole amount of assessments this year, including money paid to county rate, &c. was	2826	2	5

Materials for the employment of the Poor.

	£.	s.	d.			
First year 125 15 7				266	17	2
Second year 141 1 7						

Sale of worked materials.

First year £ 95 1 6				285	4	10
Second year 190 3 4						
Gained, besides the cloathing of all the Poor in the house				18	7	8
Earnings of the Poor, employed out of the house, in 2 years				70	19	4
Gained by the work of the Poor in 2 years, exclusive of their cloathing and attending themselves				89	7	0

£ 3040 15 0¼

Cr.	£.	s.	d.
Cash on account of former Guardians -	10	1	6
Salary to master, matron, and beadle -	50	19	0
Surgeon's salary and extra-wages -	52	15	7
Clerk's ditto - - -	20	7	6
Interest of £1700. at 4¼ per cent. per ann.	40	1	0
Insurance from fire - - -	3	0	0
Out Paupers, including occasional reliefs	529	15	6
Removal of Paupers - -	73	17	2
Allowance for bastard children out of the house - - -	40	12	0
Groceries, including butter - -	146	19	3
Cheese - - -	100	17	9
Drapery - - -	70	2	3
For cloathing, ready made - -	9	18	4
Materials for employing the Poor, principally wool - -	141	1	7
Town-clerk's fees for examination of Paupers as to their parishes and signing of the rates	10	19	2
Law processes - - -	45	5	10
Marriages of Poor - -	18	2	0
Burials of ditto - -	15	17	5
Butcher's meat, including salt pork -	208	0	2
Flour for bread - -	197	0	11
Malt and hops - - -	89	11	11
Wine and spirits - -	14	5	8
Leather and shoes ready made -	29	17	1
Lunatics - -	65	2	8
Coals and wood for firing - -	80	17	0
Garden-stuff - -	29	11	1
Live-stock - -	28	15	3
Sundry disbursements for house	56	12	11
Repairs done to the house -	15	16	8
Apprenticing poor children -	12	3	8
Rates returned - -	21	3	0
Expended in levelling the marsh to employ the people out of work	5	11	5
To militia men's families - -	16	7	0
Subscription to county hospital -	5	5	0
Amount of expences in applying to parliament	465	2	1
Printing the accounts of the poor-house, &c.	3	3	0
Debt discharged -	300	0	0
By balance paid over the present Guardians	25	15	9

£ 3040 15 0

October, 1795.

ISLE of WIGHT.

THE Poor belonging to the various parifhes in the Ifle of Wight are chiefly relieved at a Houfe of Induftry fituated near the town of Newport. It was erected under the authority of an Act of Parliament paffed in 1771[1], whereby 80 acres of the foreft of Parkhurft were vefted in the gentlemen of the ifland for the term of 999 years, under the title of the Corporation or Guardians of the Poor of the Ifle of Wight; and, in order that each parifh might contribute it's fair proportion, an account was taken of the amount of their refpective Poor's Rates for the preceding 7 years, and, according to the average, the ratio of their future payments was determined on; fo that thofe parifhes, whofe parochial charges were the heavieft at the time of the valuation, are now burthened with the greateft quota towards the confolidated fund. One pays 2s. in the pound on the rack rent; another, 15d.; and a third, 3s. 3d. in the pound upon two-thirds of the rent. The Corporation was authorized to borrow £12,000. for the purpofe of erecting the Houfe of Induftry; but this fum being found inadequate to complete the defign, a fecond application was made to Parliament, and by an Act paffed in 1776, the Corporation was empowered to borrow an additional fum not exceeding £8000.; and as the provifions of the former Act had been found by experience to be extremely defective, the whole was repealed, and new powers and regulations provided[2].

The members of the Corporation are fuch inhabitants of the ifland as are feifed in fee, or for life, or of leafehold upon lives, in their own or their wives' right, of lands or property rated to the Poor's Rate at £50. a year; heirs apparent to property rated at £100. a year; all rectors and vicars of the ifland; and all occupiers of lands or property rated at £100. whether in one or more parifhes within the ifland. On the laft Thurfday in June, in every year, 24 directors, (of whom 12 are to be fuch as were not directors in the preceding year,) are elected by the Corporation from their own body; proper perfons for acting guardians are likewife nominated in each parifh by the inhabitants affeffed to the Poor's Rate, and lifts tranfmitted to the directors, from which reprefentatives for each

[1] 11 Geo. 3. c. 43. [2] 16 Geo. 3. c. 53. f. 2.

parifh, (accoiding to the proportion they pay towards the Poor's Rate,) are chofen by ballot, to make up the number of 36 acting guardians, who continue in office one year. A clerk and other neceffary officers are like-wife appointed. The directors and guardians are divided into quarteily, monthly, and weekly committees, the laft of which confift of 2 directors and 5 acting guardians. They meet at the houfe every Saturday, to fettle the governor and ftewaids' accounts of the pieceding week, to give directions for the enfuing week, to hear complaints, to giant occafional relief to peifons out of the houfe, and to attend to fuch cafes as iequiie immediate inveftigation. The following are the moft material of the bye-laws enacted by the Corporation for the iegulation and goveinment of the Houfe of Induftiy:

1, That all poor perfons, fingle or married, without families, who aie unable to maintain themfelves, be taken into the houfe, and not fup-ported out of it by any fettled allowance or penfion.

2, That all poor perfons, whofe families are too large to be maintained by their own labour, may offer one or more of their childien to be received into the houfe, at the difcretion of the weekly committee.

4, That poor perfons received into the houfe, for temporary relief only, fhall not be deprived of their houfhold goods, furniture or other pro-perty. But fuch wearing apparel, and other goods, as any pauper may bring into the houfe, fhall be deemed and taken to be the pro-perty of the guardians of the poor, during the time fuch perfon fhall be maintained in the houfe.

6, That a weekly committee may grant to the ufe of any poor labourer's wife, on the birth of a fourth, fifth, or fixth child, the refpective fums of five fhillings, feven fhillings and fixpence, or ten fhillings and fixpence, according as he may then have living, four, five, or fix children, under fourteen years of age; but, that five fhillings thereof be applied, by the overfeer, to the payment of the midwife.

7, That one churchwarden, or overfeer of the poor, of every parifh, be obliged to apply to the weekly committee on every fitting, either in perfon, or by a director, or acting guardian, and to report, (after due enquiry made by himfelf, at the refpective dwellings of the poor,) the number and ages of the family, and other circumftances, including

the

the place of fettlement, as well as the illnefs of all perfons in his parifh, who may afk for, or ftand in need of, relief, under the penalty of any fum, not lefs than forty fhillings, and not exceeding five pounds, as directed by the Act; but that relief may be granted to any pauper, who may be in the fame manner reported by the furgeon, a director, or acting guardian.

8, That in cafe of an application wherein the preceding regulation hath not been adhered to, the committee, if it fee proper, may entruft a director, or acting guardian, or the furgeon, with an order of relief, to be delivered, or not, to the pauper, according as the perfon, thus entrufted, may find the circumftances of the cafe; or the committee may order the furgeon, or parifh-officer, to vifit the faid pauper, and to make a report, as before required, to the next committee, which may then give relief from the time of the firft application.

11, That the weekly committee, on application of an overfeer, may grant monthly relief out of the houfe to the families of men imprefled into the fea-fervice, during their continuance as imprefled men, not exceeding the fum of one fhilling and fixpence a week, for two children under the age of ten years; the fum of two fhillings a week, for three fuch children; and the fum of three fhillings a week, for four fuch; to be paid weekly by the refpective overfeers, who are required to ftop payment on the death or difcharge of any fuch man, and report the ftate of the family to the next weekly committee; and that this proportion of relief be adopted in all fimilar cafes.

12, That when it fhall appear to a weekly committee that labour in hufbandry cannot be obtained at the ufual wages, on account of a general exifting fcarcity of work, the committee may order any reafonable fum, not exceeding one fourth of the real earnings of fuch labourers, employed by its confent, to be paid by overfeers to the different perfons employing them, fo that fuch earnings do not exceed fix fhillings a week for each man, and fo in proportion for others. And when fuch earnings do necefTarily fall fhort of fix fhillings a week, merely on account of the unfeafonablenefs of the weather, (as in deep fnow or hard frofts,) the deficiency may be made up to that fum, for a man who has a family to maintain.

13, That a fum not exceeding ten pounds in any one year, be laid out in purchafing fpinning-wheels, cards, and fuch like implements of work,

H h 2   for

for the ufe of the induftrious poor women and children ; which, after being marked " HOUSE OF INDUSTRY," may be lent or given them, at the difcretion of the weekly committee; and that work in fpinning, knitting, &c. fhall be fupplied from the houfe, by an order from the faid committee, to all perfons of the above defcription, who may not be able to procure any fuch work elfewhere.

20, That every fingle woman, becoming chargeable to this corporation the fecond time, on account of baftardy, fhall be carried before two juftices of the peace, to be dealt with according to law ; and that all fuch women in the houfe, (except thofe, who are employed in the hard work of the houfe, and thofe who have been punifhed as aforefaid,) as well as all other perfons, who, by reafon of their own criminality or mifconduct, are there kept and maintained, fhall be placed in feparate apartments from the other poor, provided for that purpofe ; fhall have their names entered in the black book; fhall be allowed no folid meat on meat-days ; and wear coarfe yellow coats or gowns, or other difgraceful diftinctions, at the difcretion of the weekly committee.

40, That only one fort of flour be ferved into the houfe, and that, from the whole meal dreffed through a 14s. cloth ; and that only one meal of folid meat be ferved weekly ; the other meat-dinner to be compofed of meat cut into very fmall pieces, the bones broken very fmall, and boiled into broth, properly thickened with vegetables, &c.; and that only 150 lbs. of meat be allowed for that dinner ; but that fat pork or bacon (to be bought in the flitch, without the hams) may be boiled, cut into very fmall flices, with peafe, beans, or potatoes ; for one dinner in the week, not exceeding 50 lbs. ; and that the annexed bill of fare [1] be particularly obferved : fubject, however, to fuch alteration,

[1] BILL OF FARE.

	Breakfaft.		Dinner.				Supper.
Sunday,	Bread and butter.		Boiled beef.[2]	—	—	—	Potatoes.
Monday,	Ditto.	—	Peafe, with the beef liquor.		—	—	Bread and butter.
Tuefday,	Ditto.	—	Bread and butter.	—	—	—	Ditto.
Wednefday,	Ditto.	—	Frefh beef foup.		—	—	Potatoes.
Thurfday,	Ditto.	—	Bread and butter ; or baked pudding.		—	—	Bread and butter.
Friday,	Ditto.	—	Potatoes, or green peafe, or beans ; with fat bacon, or pork, not exceeding 50lbs.				Ditto.
Saturday,	Ditto.	—	Rice-milk.	—	—	—,	Ditto.

[2] When the beef cannot be kept fweet a week, the Sunday's and Wednefday's dinners may be exchanged.

N. B.

teration as the feafon of the year, or other circumftances, may render expedient in the opinion of the weekly committee.

45, That the tea for the poor fick people in the houfe, fhall be bought at the fame place, and of the fame perfon, who contracts for fugar; and fhall be received by the governor, and delivered out in like manner as the other ftores.

49, That every perfon, who, being duly qualified, fhall be elected a director, and fhall refufe to act, fhall forfeit the fum of six pounds; and every guardian, refufing to act when elected an acting guardian, fhall forfeit the fum of four pounds; unlefs reafonable caufe fhall be fhewn and allowed by the majority of the directors and acting guardians prefent at the next general quarterly meeting after fuch election.

50, That if there fhall not be prefent two directors and three acting guardians at any weekly committee, each director of that month not being prefent, fhall forfeit twenty shillings; and every fuch acting guardian, ten shillings.

51, That a chairman be chofen, by every committee, to prefide and regulate the proceedings; and every member of any committee, who fhall not appear in the committee-room within half an hour of the time appointed for their meeting, fhall, if a director, forfeit four shillings; if an acting guardian, two shillings; in cafe fuch default fhall delay the proceeding to bufinefs: and no member (under the fame penalty) fhall leave the committee while fitting, without leave of the chairman: and on no account, if there be not a fufficient number of members remaining to conftitute a committee.

Thefe fines are extremely moderate; and can never operate as compulfory penalties on gentlemen of property. They feem, however, in

N B. The fick have frefh meat and broth, with other provifions, according to the furgeon's directions—who is defired to give written orders for the fame.

The courfe of diet has lately been altered; the following Bill of Fare, which is now ufed in the houfe, was, obligingly, communicated to me, with other information, by the governor:

	Breakfaft.	Dinner.	Supper.
Sunday,	Onion broth.	Beef cut fmall; the bones broken, and boiled into foup, and thickened with vegetables: bread.	Potatoes, butter, falt, and beer.
Monday,	Ditto. —	Pork, greens, beer, and bread. —	Bread, butter, and beer.
Tuefday,	Ditto. —	Beef in foup, thickened with rice.	Potatoes, butter, falt, and beer.
Wednefday,	Ditto —	Rice milk, with butter and treacle.	Bread, cheefe, and beer.
Thurfday,	Ditto. —	Pork with greens, or potatoes, beer, and bread.	Potatoes, butter, falt, and beer.
Friday,	Ditto. —	Bread, cheefe, and beer. —	Ditto.
Saturday,	Ditto. —	Pork and peafe: no bread. —	Ditto.

7

the

the prefent ftate of the inftitution to be very unneceffary. The directors and guardians are very regular in their attendance on committee days, &c.; and only one inftance occurs in the annexed accounts of a fine having been paid by either a guardian or director, during the laft 3 years.

59, That every quarterly committee of accounts fhall examine into all the accounts of the preceding quarter, and fhall prepare them for publication, and after they have thoroughly examined them, they fhall fet their hands to the fame: and the feparate articles of the incidental expences, paid by the governor, fhall be entered in the quarterly account-book, in the fame manner as the bills, &c.; and no bills or falaries of officers fhall be paid by the treafurer, till a printed order be produced, figned by the chairman of the committee of accounts.

61, That any fum, not exceeding TWELVE SHILLINGS, may be allowed for the burial of any poor perfon dying out of the houfe, on application being made to the next weekly committee, or to a magiftrate, on oath, that the deceafed did not leave effects fufficient for defraying funeral expences: but that nothing fhall be allowed when the perfon is not buried at the fole expence of the corporation, and in the ufual manner of fuch paupers; of which the officiating clergyman is defired to give a certificate.

70, That when it fhall be found neceffary to make ufe of any part, or the whole, of the fund of ONE THOUSAND POUNDS, which has been raifed from the favings of the average rates, and is vefted on bond from the treafurer, to anfwer any extraordinary demands the great extent of the buildings, and the various articles of furniture may require, beyond what can be fpared for the fame, from the average rates in any one year: fuch fum, fo ufed, fhall be re-placed from the firft favings that may be afterwards made.

The principal part of the building is 300 feet in length from eaft to weft, by 27 wide in the clear; having windows on both fides, for the advantage of a thorough draught of air: at the diftance of 200 feet from the weft end, a wing from the main building ranges fouthward, 170 feet by 24; from the end of which, are built work-fhops for the manufacturers and mechanics; and thefe, with a walk on the weft, form a fquare of 200 feet by 170.

On

On the eaft fide of the wing is a court, 170 feet by 50, formed by of-fices on the north; fuch as dairy, wafh-houfe, brew-houfe, wood-houfe, ftore rooms, &c. and a wall on the fouth. In the principal building is a large ftore-room, fteward's room, dining hall, 118 feet long by 27 wide, and a common fitting room, for the impotent and aged poor.

Under the eaft end theie are cellars for beer, meat, &c. Over this build-ing are the governor's and mation's lodging rooms, the laundry, nurferies, and fick waids.

In the wing on the ground floor are the fchool rooms, apothecary's fhop, kitchen, fcullery, bake-houfe, bread-room, governor's and mation's fitting room, and pantry; and over are the lying in rooms, fick wards, and 20 feparate rooms or apartments for married men and their wives, with two common fitting iooms adjoining, for the old and infirm, who are unable to go down ftairs. In front of the principal building is a large gate-way, on the eaft fide of which is a mafter weaver's room, and fpin-ning room, 96 feet long by 18 wide, with ftore-rooms over it; at the weft fide of this gate-way are the fhoe-maker's and tailor's fhops, with a fpinning room, 150 feet long by 18 wide, with weaving rooms and ftore-rooms over.

The chapel is erected on the north fide of the piincipal building: over it is a ftore-room. Four hundred yards diftance is a peft-houfe, with a buiying ground, walled in, clofe adjoining.

To the north of the peft-houfe a building has been lately erected for the admiffion of perfons under inoculation: it confifts of four rooms, each of about 15 feet by 14. On the fouth is a large garden, which fupplies the houfe with vegetables. On the eaft, behind the offices, are placed the hog-fties, barn, ftable, and other out-houfes[1].

The houfe can accommodate 700 people: the number of inmates, how-ever, feldom exceeds 550. The following is a lift of the prefent inmates: they amount to 495. (3d of April, 1796.)

86 men; from 20 to 90 years of age, confifting of cripples, blind, idiots, lunatics, &c.

115 women; from 20 to 90 years of age; of whom the younger part are blind, &c. or fent hither in cafes of baftardy.

[1] Warner's Hampfhire, iii. 73.

131 boys; from infants to 13 years; among whom are many cripples, who are ufually employed under the tailors, or fhoe-makers, in the houfe; or in knitting, &c. according to their ftrength, and ability.

163 girls; from infants to 13 years; cripples, &c. fome of whom can fpin worfted, yarn, or flax.

The manufacture carried on in the houfe chiefly confifts in making facks for coal, flour, and bifcuit; befides which, linfey, kerfeys, and other articles of that nature, are made, principally, for the ufe of the houfe. The quantity of each, annually manufactured during the laft 3 years, and in the years ending at midfummer 1783, may be feen in the annexed accounts; which alfo fpecify the falaries paid to the governor, matron, and other officers.

The baptifms in the houfe, during the laft 3 years were: 20—12—12: and the burials, 68—32—61.

The number of regular out-penfioners is, at prefent, 44: they receive, each, from 1s. to 3s. a week. The number of cafual weekly poor, and the amount of cafual weekly allowances, is very fluctuating; and depends much on the feverity of the weather, and other circumftances. In January, and February, 1795, the reliefs granted on Saturdays, amounted, for feveral weeks, to £ 130. £ 150. £ 170. and upwards. Laft winter the weekly reliefs, granted on Saturdays, were from £ 9. to £ 17.

The debt paid off amounts to £ 5250.: the debt now owing is £ 12,200. The land belonging to the corporation, amounting to near 80 acres, is laid down in a grafs farm. The produce is fold by a manager, and the receipts placed to the general account of the houfe.

The following ftatements of the receipts and expenditure for 4 years, are copied from printed papers, which are annually prepared and laid before the corporation. They are drawn up with great perfpicuity and accuracy, and afford a clearer view of the various circumftances connected with this inftitution, than any general obfervations could convey. Perhaps but few improvements could be made in the mode of framing up this annual amount; but I would venture to fuggeft to the guardians, that the quantity of flax, hemp, wool, and other materials purchafed, fhould be particularized, as well as the fums paid for them. The public would thereby be enabled to judge whether a houfe of induftry bought their raw
materials

materials dearer or cheaper than a common manufacturer. It is likewife extremely defirable that the average number of men, women, and children, in the houfe, each month in the year, fhould be annexed to the account, as is done, (in a geneial manner,) at St. Petei's hofpital in Briftol[1]; and that the average number of men, women, and children, employed weekly, or monthly, in the manufactoiy, and of the goods actually manufactuied in the year, fhould be piinted: it is only from comparing fuch particulars, with the amount of expenditure, that a fair eftimate can be formed of the woik annually peiformed in a houfe of induftry, and of the annual charge attending the maintenance of a Pauper, under thefe inftitutions.

The following table is extracted fiom the Returns made to Parliament in 1786:

Paiifhcs.	Expences for the Pooi in 1776.			Poor's Rates in 1783.			Poor's Rates in 1784			Poor's Rates in 1785.		
	£.	s.	d.	£.	s.	d.	£.	s.	d.	£.	s.	d.
Arreton	441	11	3	449	5	3	465	9	10	504	15	4
Binfted	51	5	0	60	14	0	61	2	0	61	0	0
Bonchurch	12	16	4	14	19	5	14	19	5	14	19	5
Brading	468	10	4	530	17	2	492	15	2	500	16	4
God's-hill	403	13	8	449	4	6	448	19	10	445	7	1
St. Helen's	88	8	0	101	8	3	100	19	6	100	10	9
S. Lawrence	13	0	0	17	18	1	17	14	3	15	19	10
Newchurch	541	16	8	585	10	8	582	11	8	603	6	3
Newport	452	0	0	487	6	9	482	11	0	483	17	0
Niton	74	10	8	96	8	3	98	8	10	85	8	0
Shanklin	20	18	0	38	8	7	23	13	4	23	13	4
Whippingham	232	5	0	271	11	6	278	0	11	292	14	5
Whitwell	71	14	8	83	8	0	86	17	0	79	18	7
Wooton	53	17	8	53	17	8	53	17	8	53	17	8
Yaverland	30	6	7	34	19	5	34	19	5	34	19	5
Brixton	129	0	8	129	0	8	129	0	8	129	0	8
Brooke	38	10	10	38	10	10	38	10	10	38	10	10
Calbourne	182	9	4	199	2	1	206	8	3	199	8	0
Carifbrook	465	15	10	499	8	0	502	13	3	501	1	0

Carried over, £ 3772 10 6 £ 4141 19 1 £ 4119 12 10 £ 4169 3 11

([1] See page 191)

Parishes.	Expences for the Poor in 1776			Poor's Rates in 1783.			Poor's Rates in 1784			Poor's Rates in 1785		
	£.	s.	d.	£.	s.	d.	£.	s.	d.	£.	s.	d.
Brought over,	3772	10	6	4141	19	1	4119	12	10	4169	3	11
Chale	137	15	8	145	18	7	145	18	7	145	18	7
Frefhwater	152	11	6	165	3	4	198	10	0	183	15	6
Gatcomb	64	4	0	77	19	8	76	5	10	48	4	4
Kingfton	13	1	0	13	5	10	13	5	10	13	5	10
Mottifton	18	14	8	28	6	9	28	6	9	28	6	9
St. Nicholas	60	1	8	77	12	7	79	6	7	82	4	5
Northwood	365	6	0	383	17	2	389	10	11	396	18	8
Shalfleet	306	13	10	330	7	4	330	19	2	348	2	2
Shorwell	179	10	0	194	4	1	194	4	1	194	4	1
Thorley	35	8	11	35	8	11	35	8	11	35	8	11
Yarmouth	38	18	0	47	4	0	47	4	3	46	14	9
	£5144	15	9	£5641	7	4	£5658	13	9	£5692	7	11

An Account of the Guardians of the Corporation of the Poor in the Isle of Wight, and of Monies received and paid, from Midsummer 1782, to Midsummer 1783.

RECEIPTS.

	£.	s.	d.
To cash in Treasurer's hands at Midsummer 1782	544	5	10
To cash received from the Treasurer of the county, being a moiety of the militia	29	3	0
To cash received, the moiety of a fine from a person destroying game	2	10	0
To cash for half a year's interest of one hundred pounds at £ 4. per cent.	2	0	0
To one quarter's average from Midsummer to Michaelmas	1285	10	6
To cash for half a year's interest of four hundred pounds at £ 4. per cent.	8	0	0
To cash received from two persons for stealing wood in coppices	0	5	2
To cash for bastardy	9	5	6

2   Carried over - £ 1881 0 0

	£.	s.	d.
Brought over -	1881	0	0
To one quarter's average from Michaelmas to Chriftmas	1285	14	9
To one hundred and feventy-four days intereft on three hundred pounds at £ 4 pei cent. - -	5	14	4
To eighty-three days intereft on one hundred pounds at £ 4. per cent. - - - -	0	18	2
To three hundred and fifty-feven days intereft on one hundred pounds at £ 4. per cent. - - -	3	18	2
To cafh for half a year's intereft of five hundred pounds at £ 4. per cent. - - - -	10	0	0
To cafh received from the Treafurers for intereft -	500	0	0
To one quarter's average from Chriftmas to Lady-day -	1285	10	6
To cafh received from a perfon as a final indemnification for a baftard child - - - -	30	16	0
To cafh received from a perfon on coming into the houfe to be fupported - - - -	6	9	0
To cafh received from three perfons in lieu of taking apprentices - - - - -	30	0	0
To half a year's intereft of two hundred and fifty pounds at £ 4. per cent. - - - -'	5	0	0
To cafh from the manufactory - - -	112	7	4
To one quarter's average from Lady-day to Midfummer	1285	10	6
	£ 6442	18	9

PAYMENTS.

	£.	s.	d.
By cafh paid the bond-holdeis - - -	500	0	0
By intereft - - - - -	627	0	0
By infurance - - - - -	10	17	0
By a year's rent due at Michaelmas 1782 - -	8	19	10
By chaplain - - - - -	50	0	0
By apothecaries - - - -	170	0	0
By fecretary - - - - -	30	0	0
Carried over - £ 1396	16	10	

		£.	s.	d.
Brought over -		1396	16	10
By governor - - - - -		40	0	0
By matron - - - - -		30	0	0
By conftant penfioners - - - -		256	6	6
By weekly Poor out of the houfe - - -		403	11	10
By militia - - - - -		71	12	6
By chapel-clerk and fchoolmafter - - -		8	0	0
By labourer, half to houfe and half to faim - -		13	0	0
By wheat, barley, and grinding - - -		1206	1	1
By cheefe - - - - -		196	16	7
By butcher's meat - - - - -		365	17	11
By pork - - - - - -		116	12	1
By malt and hops - - - -		305	14	9
By wine - - - - -		58	12	9
By butter - - - - - -		51	4	8
By peafe - - - - - -		62	18	3
By groceries - - - - -		139	8	11
By coals - - - - -		180	0	0
By drapery - - - -		186	1	7
By foap - - - - - -		25	0	3
By candles - - - - -		9	12	5
By leather - - - - -		101	11	2
By carpenter - - - - -		34	16	5
By ironmonger - - - -		15	19	2
By glazier - - - - -		7	8	0
By brazier - - - -		6	15	3
By printer - - - -		3	10	0
By bricklayer - - - -		13	2	8
By baker - - - - -		24	9	1
By incidental expences of the houfe, tailor, fhoe-maker, and labourer - - - -		167	0	0
By tradefmen's fmall bills - - -		33	10	7
By cafh at intereft - - - -		500	0	0
By furgeons, for inoculation, &c. - - -		7	17	0
Carried over -		£ 6039	8	3

		£.	s.	d.
Brought over -		6039	8	3
By frith, faggots, and wood - -	-	15	0	0
By ftationer - - - -	-	5	11	5
		£6060	2	7
To balance in Treafurer's hands - - -	-	382	16	2
		£6442	18	9

General Account of the Manufactory carried on at the Houfe of Induftry, from Midfummer 1782, to Midfummer 1783.

BOUGHT.

	£.	s.	d.
Goods and materials in the ftore-room at Midfummer 1782	316	2	10
Hemp, flax, mop-wool, and wages, to Meffrs. Kimber and Toomer, and gratuities to the children in the firft half-year	177	7	6
Flax, hemp, wages, and gratuities, as in the laft article, in the fecond half-year - - - -	171	8	6
	£664	18	10

SOLD OR USED IN THE HOUSE.

	£.	s.	d.
Sacks, mop-yarn, linfey, fhoe-thread, &c. in the firft half-year - - - - -	263	5	5½
Ditto in the fecond half-year - - - -	210	18	9

	£.	s.	d.		£.	s.	d.
Goods and materials in the ftore-room, at Midfummer 1783 { wrought	85	8	11½ }		291	2	11
{ unwrought	205	13	11½ }				

	£.	s.	d.
	£765	7	1½
Expended -	664	18	10
Gained -	£100	8	3¼

¹ There feems to be fome error in this account:

the items altogether amount to -	- £6059	19	8
Which, with balance - - -	- 382	16	2
amounts to	£6442	15	10

	£	s.	d.
Brought over -	100	8	3½
Earned clear of deductions, by spinning of worsted -	33	2	9½
Earnings and gains of the whole year - -	£133	11	1

An Account of the Corporation of the Guardians of the Poor in the Isle of Wight, and of Monies received and paid from Midsummer 1792 *to Midsummer* 1793.

RECEIPTS.

	£.	s.	d.
Cash in Treasurer's hands, Midsummer 1792 -	343	6	11
Cash in the Governor's hands, ditto - - -	25	5	4
Cash from the produce of the farm - -	27	19	4
Of the surveyors of Carisbrooke highways for maintaining the Forest Road, due Michaelmas 1792 -	5	0	0
Of the Reverend Henry Oglander in lieu of taking an apprentice - - - - -	10	0	0
Of John Delgarno Esquire ditto - - -	10	0	0
Of Mrs. Cooke ditto - - - -	10	0	0
Of Mr John Whitewood ditto - - -	10	0	0
Of Mr. James Harvey ditto - - -	10	0	0
For Joseph Brewer's board - - -	2	15	0
For Goodall Young's ditto - - - -	5	8	6
A moiety of a fine for selling corn by an unlawful measure	6	7	6
Of James James, towards the maintenance of his children	1	1	0
Of William Rowles, towards ditto - - -	1	10	0
Of Richard Ware, money advanced to his family -	0	12	0
Of Samuel Read, expences apprehending him for leaving his family chargeable to the Guardians of the Poor within the Isle of Wight - - -	0	7	6
Of Minson and Fry, part of a fine for hedge breaking - - - -	0	3	6
Carried over -	£469	16	7

	£.	s.	d.
Brought over -	469	16	7
Of Sir William Oglander, Baronet, part of Le Compts wages - - - -	0	14	0
John Phillips's penfion, three quarters - -	6	17	0
Of the reputed fathers of baftard children to reimburfe the money advanced from the houfe for the fupport of the faid children - - - -	42	5	0
One year's average rates due Midfummer 1793 -	5142	6	3

£ 5661 18 10

PAYMENTS.

	£.	s.	d.
One year's fee-farm-rent and poftage, due Michaelmas 1792	9	2	6
One year's infurance of the houfe and furniture, due ditto	10	2	6
One yeai's board and cloathing a lunatic in Bethlem -	15	18	7
One year's intereft or £12500, due Midfummer 1793 -	500	0	0

	£.	s.	d.			
Intereft in arrear due to the bond-holders from the late Tieafureis -	123	0	0			
Intereft of money depofited for baftardy in the hands of the late Treafurers -	18	0	0			
William Read, cafh depofited in the late Treafurer's hands for baftardy, the child being dead - - -	10	0	0			
Expences incurred in proving the debt due to this Corporation from the late Treafurers	2	2	0	153	2	0

	£.	s.	d.
Meff. Clarke, attorney's bill - - -	36	1	4
Surgeon for inoculation, attendIng women, &c. -	25	8	0
Dr. Bowen for reducing a fracture - - -	1	1	0

	£.	s.	d.			
Expences attending feffions and removing paupers to their refpective fettlements -	25	10	7			
Ditto apprehending men for baftardy and running away from their families -	10	13	5	36	4	0

Carried over - £ 786 19 11

		£.	s.	d.
Brought over -		786	19	11

			£.	s.	d.			
Chaplain's falary	-	-	-	50	0	0		
Surgeon and Apothecary's ditto		-	170	0	0		
Governor's ditto	-	-	-	50	0	0		
Matron's ditto	-	-	-	30	0	0		
Manufacturer's ditto		-	-	20	0	0		
Secretary's ditto	-	-	-	13	0	0		
Schoolmafter's ditto	-	-	-	8	0	0		
Chapel clerk's ditto		-	-	2	0	0		
						343	0	0
Flour, meal, and bran		-	-	905	6	11		
Baking and barm	-	-	-	22	14	0		
						928	0	11
Meat	-	-	-	-	506	4	2	
Salt	-	-	-	-	36	12	0	
						542	16	2
Peafe	-	-	-	-	56	2	0	
Potatoes	-	-	-	10	15	6		
Rice	-	-	-	-	47	9	8	
						114	7	2
Butter and cheefe	-	-	-	-	-	149	6	11
Malt and hops	-	-	-	183	9	0½		
Wine, brandy and geneva	-	-	33	14	6		
Vinegar	-	-	-	4	15	0		
						221	18	6¼
Groceries, tobacco, brufhes, &c.	-	79	16	7		
Candles, foap, and afhes	-	-	28	12	3½		
						108	8	10½
Drapery, thread, buttons, &c.	-	-	152	0	8		
Ditto from the manufactory	-	-	212	17	4		
Leather	-	-	-	-	156	1	1½	
Worfted, fhroud-wool, and fpindles	-	36	8	11		
						557	8	0½

Carried over -   £ 3752   6   6½

		£.	s.	d.
Brought over -		3752	6	6½

				£.	s.	d.			
Wharfage of coals	-	-	-	1	15	0			
Wood	-	-	-	33	14	6			
							35	9	6
Bricklayer and materials		-	-	20	19	10			
Carpenter	-	-	-	32	14	10			
Cooper	-	-	-	12	7	2			
							66	1	10
Ironmonger and fmith	-	-	-	4	9	7			
Brazier and cutler	-	-	-	8	8	7			
Plumber and glazier	-	-	-	20	18	2			
							33	16	4
Printer and ftamps	-	-	-	37	13	10			
Stationer, advertifements, &c.		-	-	6	1	0			
							43	14	10
Tradefmen's fmall bills under 40s.		-		-	-	-	36	9	8
Conftant penfioners		-	-	186	5	6			
Cafual Poor	-	-	-	522	3	11			
Militia men's families		-	-	58	3	6			
							766	12	11

		£.	s.	d.			
Money advanced to fupport baftard children out of that depofited in the Treafurer's hands	-	-		48	12	6
Gratuities to nurfes and others doing the laborious work of the houfe	-	£ 20	5	0			
Ditto to tailors and fhoemakers	-	2	2	0			
Ditto, apprentices ferving their time with a good character	-	-	23	0	0		
					45	7	0
Tailor and fhoemaker	-	-	46	16	0		
Bailiff and brewer	-	-	26	16	0		
Ann Stone the fpinner	-	-	7	1	0		
					80	13	0
Cafual labourers	-	-	-	-	-	13	13	5
Money advanced to Drayton's wife	1	0	0			
Ditto to Clarke's family	-	0	6	0			
					1	6	0

			£.	s.	d
	Brought over	-	4924	3	6½
Incidental expences of the house	-	-	31	1	1½
Total expences and arrears of interest	-	-£	4955	4	
Balance in the treasurer's hands	-	-	691	8	4
Balance in the governor's hands	-	-	15	5	10
		£	5661	18	10

*A General Account of the Manufactory carried on at the House of Industry,
from July 13th 1792, to July 25th 1793.*

STOCK.	DR.	£.	s.	d.
Goods and materials in store, July 13th, 1792 - -		318	6	2½
Materials bought, together with expences, viz.				
Flax - - - - - -		93	1	4
Hemp - - - - - -		109	18	1
Wool - - - - - -		29	3	9
Bleaching thread - - - -		14	4	6
Repairs - - - - -		3	8	0
Paid spinners out of the house - - -		32	7	7
Gratuities to the children - - -		17	12	9
Manufacturer's board and wages - - -		33	0	0
Dyeing materials - - - -		2	9	8½
	£	653	11	11

PER CONTRA.	CR.						
		£.	s.	d.	£.	s.	d.
GOODS SOLD, *viz.*							
Sacks and bags - - -		149	0	8			
Mops, yarn, thread and tow - -		21	14	9½			
					170	15	5½
GOODS USED IN THE HOUSE.							
Sheeting, 132½ ells, at 18d. ; 26 ells, at 15d. per ell -					11	11	3
Carried over -				£	182	6	8½

	£.	s.	d.
Brought over -	182	6	8½

	£.	s.	d.
Dowlas, 286 ells, at 18d. ; 651½ ells, at 15½d. per ell - - -	54	16	1
Linen, 614 yards, at 12d. per yard -	30	14	0
Linsey, 130 yards, at 22d. ; 550 yards, at 20d.; 331 yards, at 18d. ; 168 yards, at 16d. per yard - - -	93	15	6
Mops, yarn, shoe thread, oil, &c. -	22	0	6

	£.	s.	d.
	201	6	1

GOODS AND MATERIALS IN STORE.

	£.	s.	d.
Sacks, 10 loads 3 sacks, at 25s ; 2 loads, at 23s. per load - -	15	3	6
Coal bags, 71, at 2s. ; flax bags, 20, at 18d. ; biscuit bags, 300, at 11d. each -	22	7	0
Linsey, 88 yards, at 18d. per yard -	6	12	0
Sheeting, 60 ells, at 18d. per ell -	4	10	0
Dowlas, 72 ells, at 15½d. ditto -	4	13	0
Linen, 212½ yards, at 12d ; 124 yards, at 7d. per yard - - -	14	4	10
Bed bottoms, 9, at 5s. ; matts, 9, at 3s. each	3	12	0
Sacking, 13 yards, at 12d ; 18 yards, at 8d. per yard - - -	1	5	0
Mop yarn, 53 lbs. at 10d. ; doctors' tow, 96 lbs. at 6d. - - -	4	12	2
Thread for linen and sacking, 235 lbs. at 22d.; 1105 lbs at 18d ; 495 lbs. at 12½d.; 65 lbs. at 8d. ; 289 lbs. at 6d. ; 955 lbs at 3d. per lb. - -	151	10	6½
Shoe-thread, 230 lbs at 14d. - -	13	8	4
Dyed yarn, 40 lbs. at 16d. ; white, 39 lbs. at 14d. per lb. - - -	4	18	10
Flax, 99 dozen, at 7s. per dozen ; foreign ditto, 5 cwt. 2 qrs 7 lbs. at 40s. -	45	15	6
Hemp, 11 cwt. 2 qrs. 18 lbs. at 29s. 6d ; coarse ditto, 14 cwt 0 qrs. 3 lbs. at 13s.	26	6	4

K k 2   Carried over - £ 318 19 0½   £ 383 12 9½

	£.	s.	d.	£.	s.	d.
Brought over -	318	19	0½	383	12	9½

	£.	s.	d.
Dreſt flax, 174 lbs. at 9d.; dreſt hemp, 38 lbs. at 7d. per lb. - - -	7	12	8
Wool, 87 lbs at 9d. ; ditto, 29 lbs. at 6¼d per lb. - - - -	4	0	11½
Flax-tow, 912 lbs. at 3d.; hemp-tow, 3161 lbs. at 1½d. per lb. - - -	31	3	1½
Materials on the looms, valued - -	8	8	11
Ditto in ſpinning ſhops - -	5	1	4
Ditto at ſpinners out of the houſe -	3	1	9
Mop ſtaves, 8 groſs, at 16s. per groſs -	6	8	0
Logwood, 5 cwt. at 14s. per cwt. -	3	10	0

	£.	s.	d.
	388	5	9½
	771	18	7
Expended - - - -	653	11	11
Gained - - - -	118	6	8
Earned clear of deductions by ſpinning worſted -	74	17	0½
	£193	3	8½

An Account of the Corporation of the Guardians of the Poor, in the Iſle of Wight, and of Monies received and paid from Midſummer 1793, to Midſummer 1794.

RECEIPTS.

	£.	s.	d.
Caſh in the treaſurer's hands, Midſummer 1793, -	691	8	4
Caſh in the governor's hands, ditto, - - -	15	5	10
Of Mr. John Hills, from the produce of the farm -	55	17	5
Of John Toomer, from the manufactory - -	160	0	0
Of Mr. Budd, from the ſtock bag - - -	10	0	0
Of Mr. Cheek, in lieu of taking an apprentice - -	10	0	0
Of Mr. Deveniſh, in lieu of ditto - - -	10	0	0
3 Carried over, -	£952	11	7

	£.	s.	d.
Brought over -	952	11	7
Of Mr. Schuldt, in lieu of taking an apprentice -	10	0	0
Of Meffrs Thomas and Henry Way, in lieu of ditto -	10	0	0
Of the furveyors of Carifbrooke highways, for maintaining the Foreft Road, due Michaelmas 1793 - -	5	0	0
Of the treafurer of the county, money advanced to militia men's families - - - -	88	11	0
Of George and Ann Francis of Cowes, a fine for refufing to take in a foldier when billeted on them - -	2	0	0
Of John Lellow, for his father's board - -	2	0	0
Of John Nobb, for admitting his baftard child into the houfe - - - -	10	0	0
Of the reputed fathers of baftard children, to re-imburfe the money advanced for the fupport of the faid children -	24	8	9
John Dunverd's depofit to indemnify againft a baftard child forfeited - - - - -	10	0	0
John Phillips's penfion, five quarters - -	11	8	0
For fupport of part of the 78th regiment in the fmall pox	6	10	0
For Mrs. Woolgar's board, of Yarmouth - -	0	7	0
Of John Dore, for his board, three weeks - -	0	4	6
Of Le Compt's wages - - - -	0	4	0
Difcount on cheefe - - - -	0	0	10
A fine of hedge-breakers - - - -	0	5	0
Cafh, dividends claimed under the feparate eftate of Henry Roberts, one moiety of the houfe debt of £2073. 14. 6.	1036	17	3
Cafh on the fame account, from the feparate eftate of John Roberts - - - -	1036	17	3
One year's average rates, due Midfummer 1794 -	5142	6	3
	£8349	11	5

PAYMENTS.

	£.	s.	d.
One year's fee farm rent, due Michaelmas 1793 -	9	0	0
One year's infurance of the houfe and furniture, due ditto	10	2	6
Carried over -	£19	2	6

	£.	s.	d.
Brought over -	19	2	6

Board, cloathing, and funeral expences of James Rummond, a lunatic in Bethlem hospital - - 20 14 2

Cash to place in the treasurer's hands, the building fund[1] 1000 0 0

Cash to place in their hands, bastard money from Roberts and Co.[2] - - - - 540 0 0

Interest of money deposited in the late treasurer's hands for bastardy - - - - - 38 7 6

One year's interest of £12,500. due Midsummer 1794 - 500 0 0

Paid off bond-holder, £300. with interest - - 303 3 3

Messrs. Clarke, attornies' bill - - £44 12 6

Mr. Thomas Dickonson, attorney's bill - 73 14 6

                                                  118 7 0

Surgeon, for inoculation, attending women, &c. - 277 19 6

Expences attending sessions, and removing paupers to their respective settlements - 7 17 6

Ditto, apprehending men for bastardy, and running away from their families - 5 13 9

                                                  13 11 3

Chaplain's salary - - - £50 0 0

Surgeon and apothecary's ditto - - 170 0 0

Governor's ditto - - - 50 0 0

Matron's ditto - - - 30 0 0

Manufacturer's ditto - - - 20 0 0

Secretary's ditto - - - 13 0 0

Schoolmaster's ditto - - - 10 0 0

Chapel clerk's ditto - - - 2 0 0

                                                  345 0 0

Flour, meal, and bran - - 903 1 3

Baking and barm - - - 18 7 0

                                                  921 8 3

Meat - - - - 592 7 8

Salt - - - - 31 16 0

                                                  624 3 8

Carried over - £4721 17 1

[1] See 70th bye law
[2] A fund appropriated to the maintenance of bastards

		£.	s.	d.
Brought over -		4721	17	1
Peafe - - - -	£48 4 0			
Potatoes - - -	10 2 6			
Rice - - - -	29 5 10			
		87	12	4
Butter and cheefe - - - -		227	15	0
Malt and hops - - -	240 8 2			
Brandy, geneva, port wine, and raifins for wine - - - -	51 16 6			
Vinegar - - - -	5 6 6			
		297	11	2
Groceries, tobacco, brooms and brufhes -	75 19 5			
Candles, foap and afhes - -	32 15 5			
		108	14	10
Drapery, thread, buttons, &c. - -	111 13 11			
Ditto for the manufactory - -	219 19 2			
Leather - - -	142 12 2			
Worfted, fhroud-wool, cards and fpindles	35 18 11			
		510	4	2
Coals - - - -	203 12 9			
Wood - - -	33 6 0			
		236	18	9
The building for the reception of patients in the fmall pox		210	0	0
Carpenter, mill-wright and cabinet-maker -	£75 7 10			
Bricklayer and materials - -	5 12 1			
		80	19	11
Ironmonger and fmith - - -	7 11 3			
Brazier and cutler - - -	8 12 5			
Plumber and glazier - - -	29 19 5			
		46	3	1
Printer and ftamps - - -	11 5 10			
Stationer, advertifements, &c. - -	4 14 2			
		16	0	0
Tradefmen's fmall bills under forty fhillings - -		33	10	3
Conftant penfioners - - -	155 10 6			
Cafual poor - - -	588 11 2			
		744	1	8
Carried over -		£7321	8	3

	£.	s.	d.
Brought over -	7321	8	3
Militia men's families - - £284 16 2			
Bounties to men drawn in the militia - 36 0 0			
	320	16	2
Money advanced to fupport baftard children out of that			
depofited in the treafurer's hands - - -	53	14	3
Gratuity to Mr. Hills for fuperintending the			
farm - - - - £5 5 0			
Ditto to the matron, for extra-trouble by			
inoculation - - - 5 5 0			
Ditto to the nurfes and others doing the la-			
borious work of the houfe - - 23 1 6			
Ditto to tailors and fhoemakers - - 2 2 0			
Ditto, apprentices ferving their time with a			
good character - - - 15 0 0			
	50	13	6
With an apprentice, in lieu of cloaths - -	2	12	6
Tailors and fhoemakers - - 46 16 0			
Bailiff and brewer - - - 28 16 0			
Ann Stone the fpinner - - 7 4 0			
	82	16	0
Chiddy, for making fhoes - - - 4 10 8			
Cafual labourers - - - 22 19 6			
	27	10	2
Exton, for ftays - - - - -	2	7	0
Incidental expences of the houfe - -	32	9	8
Total expences, money paid off and intereft	7894	7	6
Balance in the treafurer's hands -	445	5	11
Balance in the governor's hands -	9	18	0
	£ 8349	11	5

A General

A General Account of the Manufactory carried on at the House of Industry,
from July 25th 1793, to July 28th 1794.

STOCK.   Dr.

	£.	s.	d.
Goods and materials in store, July 25th, 1793 -	388	5	9½

Materials bought, together with Expences, viz.

	£.	s.	d.
Flax - - - - - -	76	9	8
Hemp - - - - - -	70	11	4
Wool - - - - -	37	19	3
Bleaching thread - - - - -	5	11	3
Dying materials, oil, &c. - - - -	4	19	10
Paid spinners out of the house - - -	30	15	8
Manufacturer's board and wages - - -	33	0	0
Gratuities to the children - - - -	17	2	1

	£664	14	10½

PER CONTRA.   Cr.

GOODS SOLD, *viz.*	£.	s.	d.	£.	s.	d.
Sacks and bags - - -	137	9	4			
Mops, yarn, thread and tow - -	34	17	4			
				172	6	8

GOODS USED IN THE HOUSE.

	£.	s.	d.			
Linsey, 99 yards, at 20d.; 616½ yards, at 18d.; 307½ yards, at 16d. per yard -	74	19	9			
Dowlas, 408 ells, at 18d.; 708 ells, at 15½d.	80	19	6			
Sheeting, 175 ells, at 18d. per ell -	13	2	6			
Linen, 457 yards, at 12d.; 45 yards, at 8d. per yard - - - -	24	7	0			
Mops, yarn, shoe-thread, &c. - -	26	10	5			
				219	19	2

			£392	5	10
	Carried over, -				

	£.	s.	d.
Brought over, -	392	5	10

GOODS AND MATERIALS IN STORE.

	£.	s.	d.
Sacks, 4 loads, at 27s.—7 loads, 1 sack, at 25s.—16 loads, 1 sack, at 23s. per load	32	15	9½
Coal bags, 71, at 2s.—Wool bags, 14, at 3s. 6d. —Flax bags, 20, at 18d.—Biscuit bags, 60, at 11d. each - - -	13	16	0
Linsey, 45 yards, at 18d.—90 yards, at 16d. per yard - - - -	9	7	6
Sheeting, 31½ ells, at 18d. per ell -	2	7	3
Linen, 210 yards, at 12d.—54 yards, at 7d. per yard - - - -	12	1	6
Sacking, 22 yards, at 9d. per yard -	0	16	6
Thread, 849 lbs. at 18d.—134 lbs. at 13d. —482 lbs. at 12½d.—14 lbs. at 9d.—255 lbs. at 8d.—142 lbs. at 6d.—and 766 lbs. at 3d. per lb. - - -	118	3	9
Mats, 228 lbs. at 2½d. per lb. - -	2	7	6
Dyed yarn, 41 lbs. at 16d. per lb. -	2	14	8
Mop yarn, 33 lbs at 10½d. per lb. -	1	8	10½
Doctor's tow, 136 lbs. at 6d. per lb. -	3	8	0
Wool, 222 lbs. at 8½d.—132 lbs. at 8d.— 48 lbs. at 6d. per lb. - - -	13	9	3
Bed bottoms, 5, at 5s. each - -	1	5	0
Dreſt hemp, 143 lbs. at 6d. per lb. -	3	11	6
Hemp, 30 cwt. 2 qrs. 11 lbs. at 31s.—7 cwt. at 14s. per cwt. - - -	52	6	6
Flax, 113 dozen, at 7s 6d. per doz. -	42	7	6
Flax tow, 1331 lbs. at 3d. per lb. - -	16	12	9
Hemp tow, 2956 lbs. at 1½d. per lb. -	18	9	6
Mop ſtaves, 6 grofs, at 16s. per grofs -	4	16	0
Logwood, 4 cwt. at 14s. per cwt. -	2	16	0
Materials on the looms, valued - -	6	3	0

Carried over, - £361 4 4 £392 5 10

	£.	s.	d.	£.	s.	d.
Brought over -	361	4	4	392	5	10
Materials in the fpinning fhops - -	5	4	0			
Ditto at the fpinners out of the houfe -	1	16	6			
				368	4	10

	£.	s.	d.
	760	10	8
Expended - - - -	664	14	10½
Gained - - - -	95	15	9½
Earned clear of deductions, by fpinning woifted	72	10	3
Clear earnings - - - -	168	6	0½

An Account of the Corporation of the Guardians of the Poor of the Ifle of Wight, and of Monies received and paid, from Midfummer 1794, *to Midfummer* 1795.

RECEIPTS.

	£.	s.	d.
Cafh in the Treafurer's hands, Midfummer 1794 -	445	6	3
Cafh in the Governor's hands, ditto - -	9	18	0
Cafh of Mr. Hills, from the produce of the farm -	110	16	8
Cafh from the manufactory - - -	261	15	8
Fines of fundry perfons, in lieu of taking apprentices -	50	0	0
Received of the Governor, from the ftock bag - -	10	0	0
Half a year's intereft of £1000. due Michaelmas 1794	17	10	0
Half a year's intereft of £800. due Lady-day 1795 -	14	0	0
From the Building Fund - - -	1000	0	0
Mr. Phipps's penfion to Midfummer 1794, at £13. 6s. 8d. a year - - - - -	24	0	5
Ditto to Lady-day 1795 - - - -	10	0	0
John Phillips's penfion to Midfummer 1795 -	9	2	6
Of the Surveyors of Carifbrooke highways, for the maintaining the Foreft road, due Michaelmas 1794 -	5	0	0
Of Mr. Morris, for Goodall Young's boaid in the houfe	7	4	0
Carried over -	1974	13	6

	£.	s.	d.
Brought over -	1974	13	6
Of John Lellow, for his father's board, ditto - -	1	15	0
Of Mr. Hewett, for his servant's board, ditto, - -	0	14	0
Of Isaac Arnold, for his children's board, ditto - -	2	5	0
Of William Dell, for his wife's board, ditto - -	4	4	0
The balance of Mr. Budd's cash-book - -	4	8	8
Ditto of his incidental book - - -	2	13	11
Discount on cheese - - - -	0	2	11
Of the reputed fathers of bastard children, to reimburse the money advanced for the support of the said children	30	16	6
Received for Henry Frankise's cloaths, who died in the house - - - - -	1	11	6
A fine of an Overseer of the Poor of Brading, for non-attendance of the Committee - - -	2	0	0
Ditto of a Guardian of the Poor, for non-attendance of ditto	0	2	0
Ditto of sundry persons, for petty thefts - -	2	2	0
One year's average Rates, due Midsummer 1795 -	4642	6	3
Balance due to the Treasurers - - -	563	3	2
	£7232	18	5

PAYMENTS.

	£.	s.	d.
One year's fee farm rent and postage, due Michaelmas 1794 - - - -	9	2	10
One year's insurance of the house and furniture, due ditto	10	2	6
One year's interest of £12,200. due Midsummer 1795 -	488	0	0
Surgeon, for inoculation, attending women, &c. -	45	0	0

	£.	s.	d.			
Expences attending sessions, and removing Paupers to their respective settlements	20	7	2			
Ditto apprehending men for bastardy, and running away from their families -	1	5	6			
				21	12	8

2   Carried over - £573 18 0

		£.	s.	d.
Brought over - - -		573	18	0
Chaplain's falary - - -	£ 50 0 0			
Surgeon and apothecary's ditto - -	170 0 0			
Governor's ditto - - -	50 0 0			
Matron's ditto - - -	30 0 0			
Manufacturer's ditto - -	20 0 0			
Secretary's ditto .. - -	13 0 0			
Schoolmafter's ditto - -	10 0 0			
Chapel clerk's ditto - -	2 0 0			
		345.	0	0
Meal, 514 facks; bran, 21 bufhels -	1019 10 11			
Baking and barm - - -	13 3 6			
		1032	14	5
Pork, 91 fcore; beef, 1445 fcore; mutton, 2358 lbs. - - -	606 15 1½			
Salt, 114 bufhels - - -	34 4 0			
		640	19	1½
Peafe, 10 quarters - - -	40 0 0			
Potatoes, 500 bufhels - -	56 5 0			
Rice, 21 cwt. 3 qrs. - - -	35 19 3			
		132	4	3
Butter and cheefe - - -	-	129	5	6
Brandy, 12 gallons; geneva, 10 gallons; port wine, 37 dozen; and raifins to make wine, 5 cwt. 23 lbs. - -	61 3 6			
Malt, 82 qrs.; and hops, 3 cwt. 2qrs. 10 lbs.	220 14 2			
Vinegar, 1 hogfhead and a half -	6 14 0	288	11	8
Tobacco, 293 lbs; groceries, brooms, and brufhes - - -	79 15 0			
Candles, 11 dozen; foap, 57 dozen; and afhes - - - -	32 10 5½			
		112	5	5½
Drapery, thread, buttons, and flocks for beds - - -	128 1 7			
Ditto, from the manufactory - -	191 11 0			
Carried over £ 319 12 7		£ 3254	8	5

	£.	s.	d.	£.	s	d.
Brought over -	319	12	7	3254	8	5
Leather - - - -	188	11	6			
Worfted, fhroud-wool, cards and fpindles	23	12	8			
				531	16	9
Coals - - - -	394	16	6			
Faggots, 5875 - - -	39	0	6			
				433	17	0
Bricklayer and materials - -	13	12	6			
Carpenter, and timber for the houfe and farm - - - - -	97	9	6			
				111	2	0
Ironmonger and fmith - -	9	1	9			
Brazier and cutler - -	10	14	5			
Plumber and glazier - -	31	10	6			
				51	6	8
Printer and ftamps, £11. 6s. 1d.; ftationer, advertifements, &c. £8. 6s. - - - - -				19	12	1
Tradefmen's fmall bills, under 40s. - - -				44	10	2
Conftant penfioners - - £132 14 6	132	14	6			
Weekly relief out of the houfe - - 1949 0 9	1949	0	9			
				2081	15	3
Militia men's families - - - -				383	7	4
Money advanced to Robert Cooley's family, certificated - - £1 6 0	1	6	0			
Ditto to Jofeph Brewer's family, ditto - 1 10 6	1	10	6			
				2	16	6
Ditto to fupport baftard children, out of that depofited in the Treafurer's hands - - - -				43	7	0
Mr. Johnfon, for a horfe - - £20 0 0	20	0	0			
Mr. Attrill, for a mare and colt - - 21 0 0	21	0	0			
				41	0	0
Mr. Budd (late governor) on quitting his office -				10	10	0
Meffrs. Kirkpatricks, the balance of Budd's incidental book				2	13	11
Mr. Tucker, for taking an inventory of the ftock and furniture of the houfe - - - -				6	6	0
Carried over -				£7018	9	1

	£.	s.	d.
Brought over - - -	7018	9	1
Labourers, making the hedges of the farm £ 23 13 0			
Paid cafual labourers out of employ - 17 4 0			
	40	17	0
Paid William Smith, for making fhoes - - -	6	15	7
Gratuities to perfons affifting in extinguifhing the fire of the hay-rick - 3 10 0			
Ditto to Newport fire-engine men - 1 1 0			
Ditto to the Secretary for his extra trouble, occafioned by the militia and manufactory - - - - 2 0 0			
Ditto to nurfes and others doing the laborious work of the houfe - - 20 11 9			
Ditto to the tailors and fhoemakers - 2 2 0			
Ditto to apprentices ferving their time with a good character - • 12 0 0			
	41	4	9
Tailor and fhoemaker -, - 46 16 0			
Bailiff and brewer - - 27 0 0			
Ann Stone the fpinner - - 7 7 0			
	81	3	0
Incidental expenees of the houfe, (as by the Governor's incidental book,) examined by the Chairman of the weekly committee - - - -	31	15	4
	£ 7220	14	9
Balance in the Governor's hands -	12	3	8
	£ 7232	18	5

A General

A General Account of the Manufactory carried on at the House of Industry,
from July 28, 1794—to July 23, 1795.

STOCK.   DR.

	£.	s.	d.
Goods and materials in ftore, July 28, 1794 -	368	4	10

Materials bought, together with Expences, viz.

	£.	s.	d.
Flax -	33	15	2
Hemp -	22	12	2
Wool -	39	13	6
Bleaching thread -	14	9	0
Dyeing materials, oil, and tar -	5	4	8
Paid fpinners out of the houfe -	17	9	4½
Gratuities to the children -	15	13	1½
Manufacturer's board and wages -	33	0	0
	£ 550	1	10

PER CONTRA.   CR.

GOODS SOLD, viz.	£.	s.	d.	£.	s.	d.
Sacks and bags -	176	0	2			
Mops, yarn, thread, and tow -	42	4	1			
				218	4	3

GOODS USED IN THE HOUSE.

	£.	s.	d.			
Linfey, 678½ yards, at 18d.—251 yards, at 16d. per yard -	67	2	5			
Sheeting, 236 ells, at 18d. per ell -	17	14	0			
Dowlas, 375 ells, at 18d.—179 ells, at 15½d. per ell -	40	16	11½			
Carried over - £	125	13	4½	£218	4	3

	£.	s.	d.	£.	s.	d.
Brought over -	125	13	4½	218	4	3

Linen, 25 yards, at 15d.—545½ yards, at 12d.

—131 yards, at 10d. - -	34	5	11
Mops, yarn, fhoe thread, oil, &c. -	31	12	3

	191	11	6½

GOODS AND MATERIALS IN STORE.

Sacks, 12, at 2s 6d —wool bags, 14, at
3s. 6d.—flax bags, 7, at 1s. 6d.—and
bifcuit bags, 248, at 1s. each

	£.	s.	d.
Sacks... bifcuit bags, 248, at 1s. each - -	17	12	6
Sheeting, 61 ells, at 18d. per ell - -	4	11	6

Dowlas, 87 ells, at 18d.—48 ells, at 15½d.

per ell - - -	9	12	6
Linfey, 149 yards, at 18d. per yard -	11	3	6

Linen, 100½ yards, at 12d.—43 yards, at

9d. per yard - - - -	6	12	9
Sacking, 58 yards, at 9d. per yard - -	2	3	6

Thread, 205½ lbs. at 2s.—382 lbs. at 17d.
—88 lbs. at 14d.—152 lbs. at 9d.—287 lbs.
at 6d.—140 lbs. at 4d. and 1609 lbs. at 3d.

per lb. - - - -	88	1	3

Yarn, 123 lbs. at 17d.—61 lbs. at 15d.

per lb. - - - -	12	10	6
Bed bottoms, 6, at 4s 6d. each - -	1	7	0
Mats, 70 lbs. at 2½d. per lb. - -	0	14	7
Doctor's tow, 115 lbs. at 6d. per lb. -	2	17	6
Wool, 172 lbs. at 9d.—276 lbs. at 6d. per lb.	13	7	0
Flax, 2 cwt. 1qr. 1 lb. at 55s. per cwt.	6	4	3
Flax tow, 692 lbs. at 3d. per lb. - -	8	13	0
Materials on the looms, valued at - -	7	7	0
Ditto in fpinning fhops - -	4	14	0
Ditto at fpinners out of the houfe - -	1	6	6
Mop ftaves, 5½ grofs, at 16s. per grofs -	4	8	0
Mop nails, 16 lbs. at 8d. per lb. -	0	10	8

	£	s.	d.	£	s.	d.
Carried over -	203	17	6	409	15	9½

	£.	s.	d.	£.	s.	d.
Brought over -	203	17	6	409	15	9½
Red wood, ½ barrel - - -	0	15	0			
Tar, ½ barrel - - -	0	15	0			
Logwood, 3 cwt. - - -	2	2	0			
				207	9	6
				£617	5	3½
Expended - - - -				550	1	10
Gained - - - -				£ 67	3	5½
Earned clear of expences, spinning worsted -				64	16	5
				£131	19	10½

April, 1796.

HEREFORDSHIRE.

HEREFORD.

THE parish of All Saints, (one of the six, whereof the city of Hereford consists,) contains, by estimation, about 200 acres. The number of houses paying window-tax is about 160; but the number exempted cannot be ascertained: neither has the population ever been enumerated; but from the average of births and burials during the last 22 years, it may be reckoned at between 1500 and 2500 inhabitants: they consist of persons of independent fortune, tradesmen, mechanics, and labourers of various descriptions. There is one Roman Catholic chapel in this city, 1 Presbyterian, and 1 of Lady Huntingdon's congregations. The number of inns or ale-houses in Hereford is 60. The prices of provisions, at present, are: beef and mutton, from 4d. to 5d. the pound; veal, 6d.; pork, 5d.;

bacon,

bacon, 10d ; fresh butter, 1s. ; salt butter, 10d. ; wheat, from 11s. 6d. to 13s. for 10 gallons ; barley, from 5s. 6d. to 6s. for the same quantity ; oats, from 3s. 6d. to 4s. ; potatoes, 2s. the same quantity ; milk, 1½d. the quart.

The rent of land in the neighbourhood of the city is from 40s. to 80s. an acre : the land-tax in Hereford is from 6d. to 2s. in the pound ; the average about 1s. The land is let in small parcels, for pasture : there are no commons in this, or in the parish of St Nicholas : tithes are compounded for.

Here are 6 Friendly Societies, 5 of which have from 50 to 80 members in each : they have all had their Rules confirmed at the quarter sessions. One of them is chiefly for the benefit of widows, and has 250 members : in this club 26s are paid every year into the box ; a member of 3 years standing, when sick, receives 6s. a week ; and on the decease of a member, who has been 5 years in the club, his widow receives £ 20. a year for life ; £ 15 a year, if he has been a member 4 years ; and £ 10. a year, if he has not been more than 3 years a member, &c. The Rules of this Society are not printed.

Hereford is estimated to contain about 7500 inhabitants ; it furnished 10 men for the Navy, and therefore about 680 houses pay the window-tax : of these 10 men the proportion for the parish of All Saints was 2⅓, and for St. Nicholas 1½.

The Poor's Rate in the parish of All Saints is said to be the highest in Hereford. The Poor are, partly, maintained in the general work-house, and, partly, at home. 17 Paupers belonging to this parish, are, at present, in the work-house : about £ 3. a week are paid to 40 regular out-pensioners ; besides whom, there are 8 children, (mostly bastards,) at nurse, that cost the parish about 18s. a week. Several casual Poor receive occasional relief. About £ 65 (the amount of donations,) are annually distributed amongst indigent parishioners ; and 20 cottages, belonging to the parish, are occupied by distressed families. Great complaints are made in this country against monopoly and forestalling. The labouring classes, who usually bake their own bread, say, it is extremely difficult to procure a small quantity of corn from the farmer ; and that the millers and mealmen buy it in large quantities, and exact a large profit from the consumer.

A Table

Table of Baptisms, Burials, Marriages, and Poor's Rates, in the Parish of ALL-SAINTS, *Hereford.*

Years	BAPTISMS			Of which are marked Paupers	BURIALS			Of which are marked Paupers	MAR	Net amount of Poor's Rates £ s d	Total Expenditure £ s d.	Rate in the Pound s d
	Mal	Fem	Tot		Mal	Fem	Tot					
1766	—	—	—		—	—	—		—	101 3 5	107 11 11½	1 —
1767	—	—	—		—	—	—		—	152 10 10¹	154 18 5	— —
1768	—	—	—		—	—	—		—	167 15 9²	154 7 3	— —
1769	—	—	—		—	—	—		—	136 17 1	117 1 10	— —
1770	—	—	—		—	—	—		—	133 15 0	131 10 10	1 4
1771	—	—	—		—	—	—		—	166 18 7	163 17 8	1 8
1772	—	—	—		—	—	—		—	164 17 0	116 11 11	1 8
1773	25	25	50		33	28	61		—	166 15 2	160 14 6	1 8
1774	23	25	48	—	25	17	42	—	—	168 19 2	179 6 8	1 8
1775	25	19	44	—	14	19	33	—	16	168 9 3	184 11 3	1 8
1776	20	26	46	—	20	18	38	—	11	181 6 0	178 18 4	1 8
1777	22	24	46	—	20	26	46	—	14	143 0 4	152 4 10	1 4
1778	27	20	47	—	25	22	47	—	13	186 3 2	196 1 6	1 8
1779	17	28	45	—	37	33	70	—	9	302 0 2	338 4 3³	2 8
1780	19	25	44	—	24	26	50	—	16	266 10 11	258 15 6½	— —
1781	30	22	52	—	18	14	32	—	15	218 7 8	228 0 9	2 —
1782	13	15	33	—	31	25	56	—	7	219 14 9	236 4 2	2 —
1783	21	24	45	—	22	22	44	—	16	316 12 0	352 10 2	2 8
1784	27	22	49	—	15	21	36	9	16	366 5 8	362 0 4	3 4
1785	28	28	56	4	19	12	31	8	22	293 12 4	294 18 8	2 8
1786	27	28	55	5	17	15	32	10	9	336 13 4	346 15 0	3 2
1787	33	23	56	13	12	14	26	12	10	309 16 8	— — —	
1788	24	31	55	5	18	15	33	14	9	346 12 11	— — —	3 —
1789	36	23	59	4	11	11	22	7	13	— — —	— — —	
1790	30	28	58	6	15	19	34	6	17	272 8 7	276 7 11¼	2 4
1791	27	22	49	4	23	21	44	14	15	431 13 7	444 15 6	3 8
1792	32	32	64	2	24	30	54	18	16	317 4 1	345 3 11	2 8
1793	26	23	49	6	31	19	50	20	13	276 3 5	287 0 0	2 4
1794	21	34	55	—	43	35	78	—	16	391 4 11	533 16 0	3 4
1795	—	—	—		—	—	—		—	505 1 8	603 5 5	4 —

The affeffments are nearly on full rental ; the greateft part of the money, thus raifed, is expended on the Poor.

Donations amounting to about £ 65. are annually given to the Poor.

20 cottages belonging to this parifh are appropriated to the ufe of the Poor.

¹ ² Thefe fums are the total Receipts in their refpective years : the net Rates could not be procured.

³ This year, £ 36. 4s 6d were paid to militia men's families, which in fome degree accounts for the Rates being high : befides which, the overfeer was a clothier ; he cloathed the Poor, and paid himfelf out of the Rates.

The

The parifh of St. Nicholas contains about 260 acres : neaily 102 houfes pay the window-tax ; the number exempted could not be afcertained. The rent of land, land-tax, and general circumftances of the parifhioners, are much the fame as in All Saints parifh. Affeffments are nearly at the full rental.

About 12 years ago, the 6 parifhes, of which the city of Hereford con-fifts, agreed to maintain their Poor at a general woik-houfe, and to allow as few out-penfions as poffible. Every parifh has a power of fending as many Paupers into the houfe as it pleafes, upon paying a proportionable fum towards their fupport. The work-houfe rent is £ 26. a year; mafter's falary, £ 26. a year, and ¼ of the Poor's carnings ; veftry clerk's falary, £ 10. a year; doctor's bills about £ 10 a year, are all added to the gene-ral expences, and paid in certain proportions by the parifhes. The houfe is a good one, and in a good fituation ; the beds are of flocks, and kept tolerably clean. 56 Pooi perfons are in the houfe at prefent : they are chiefly old people, and children ; and are employed in fpinning mop-yarn, and carding wool for faddles ; a few are fent to work out of the houfe. The mafter fays their earnings-are about £ 50. a year. The leafe of this houfe, and the contract between the parifhes, expire at Chriftmas. 1796, when it is generally fuppofed that the union will be diffolved, and every parifh fup-port it's own Poor. The weekly charge of a Pauper, laft year, (including houfe-rent, &c) was about 4s. 6d. About £ 5. in donations are annually diftributed to the Poor of this parifh.

Table of Baptifms, Burials, Marriages, and Poor's Rates, in the Parifh of
St. Nicholas, Hereford.

Years	Baptisms			Burials			Marriages	Pooi's Rates.			Total Expenditure			Rate in the Pound	
	Males	Fem	Total	Males	Fem	Total		£.	s.	d.	£.	s.	d.	s.	d.
1772	—	—	23	—	—	14	6	58	9	8	56	15	8	—	
1773	—	—	15	—	—	23	4	58	6	4	62	12	2	—	
1774	—	—	7	—	—	14	10	61	17	4	52	5	1	—	
1775	—	—	15	—	—	13	5	76	18	8	94	13	2	1	3
1776	—	—	21	—	—	19	10	77	16	5	77	3	1½	1	3
1777	—	—	14	—	—	15	6	79	1	5	62	3	0	1	3
1778	—	—	18	—	—	14	8	47	1	2	62	1	8	0	9

Years.

Years.	Baptisms			Burials			Marriages	Poor's Rates			Total Expenditure			Rate in the Pound	
	Males	Fem	Total	Males	Fem	Total		£.	s.	d.	£.	s.	d.	s.	d.
1779	—	—	17	—	—	21	4	93	17	0	102	8	10	1	6
1780	—	—	13	—	—	18	6	109	9	2	122	9	11	1	9
1781	—	—	17	—	—	7	6	122	9	8	121	11	5	2	0
1782	—	—	10	—	—	10	4	61	8	7	63	4	4	1	0
1783	—	—	15	—	—	11	4	76	5	4	81	6	4	1	3
1784	9	10	19	7	6	13	3	137	7	10	138	9	11	2	3
1785	7	4	11	5	6	11	3	214	7	5	204	11	8	2	9
1786	7	4	11	6	9	15	1	205	2	8	212	16	7	2	9
1787	1	8	9	5	7	12	7	162	0	0	147	17	9	0	0
1788	8	6	14	6	2	8	5	105	2	5	125	15	7	0	0
1789	8	5	13	4	6	10	7	145	15	10	137	9	10	2	0
1790	7	3	10	5	3	8	4	146	17	11	133	12	1	2	0
1791	10	9	19	6	8	14	1	226	6	6	243	1	6	3	0
1792	5	9	14	6	3	9	9	119	19	0	127	13	10	1	6
1793	10	8	18	4	10	14	10	140	1	3	90	19	6	1	6
1794	8	16	24	10	7	17	16	161	15	4	132	15	1	2	0
1795	—	—	—	—	—	—	—	185	16	6	186	6	6	2	0

Table of Diet in the Work-house.

	Breakfast.	Dinner.	Supper.
Sunday,	Water gruel and bread.	Beef and vegetables	Bread, cheese, and beer.
Monday,	Broth and bread.	Bread and cheese.	Ditto.
Tuesday,	Ditto.	As Sunday.	Ditto.
Wednesday,	Ditto.	As Monday.	Ditto.
Thursday,	Ditto.	As Sunday.	Ditto
Friday,	Ditto.	As Monday.	Ditto.
Saturday,	Ditto.	Ditto.	Ditto.

About 7 oz. of beef are allowed each person : at bread and cheese meals about 6 oz. of bread, 1½ oz. of cheese, and 1 pint of beer are also allowed.

Six Paupers belonging to St. Nicholas's parish, are, at present, in the work-house ; 8 persons receive weekly allowances at home, to the amount of 12s. ; and several others have occasional relief.

November, 1795.

HERT-

HERTFORDSHIRE.

ST. ALBANS.

THE borough of St. Albans confifts of three parifhes.: in the pa-rifh of the Abbey-church 97 houfes pay the window-tax; and in the whole borough 268 houfes are taxed, but the number of thofe which are exempted could not be obtained. The parifhioners are moftly inn-keep-ers, fhop-keepers, common mechanics, and labourers. Formerly there were a great many women ftay-makers in this town.

The prices of provifions are : beef, from 5d. to 5½d. the pound; mut-ton, 6d. ; veal, 7d. ; butter, 1s.; bacon, 10d ; milk, 2d. a quart ; bread, 11¾d. the quartern loaf The common wages are 7s. a week, and a meal in winter; and 8s in fummer : in hay harveft 9s. a week, and during corn harveft 40s. a month. There is here a mill for fpinning candle-wicks, in which feveral children are employed, and earn from 1s. 6d to 2s. 6d a week The inhabitants are chiefly of the eftablifhed Church ; there is 1 Anabaptift chapel, and 1 Calvinift chapel, 1 Quaker's meeting-houfe, and a congrega-tion of Independents ; and once a week, a pious fhoemaker quits his awl, and expounds the Scriptures to an audience of old women ; after which, he and his congregation attend divine fervice at the church In the 3 parifhes in this borough there are 42 ale-houfes. Here are 2 Friendly Socie-ties containing about 100 members. The rent of land in this neighbourhood is about 50s an acre. The land-tax is paid by the landlord. Tithes are taken in compofition. The land-tax collected in the borough amounts annually to £ 774. 2s. and is about 3s. 8d. in the pound on the net rental.

The following is a Statement of the Affeffments, Expenditure, and Rates in the Pound.

Years.	Net Affeffments.			Total Expenditure.			Rate in the Pound	
	£.	s.	d.	£.	s.	d.	s.	d.
1762	302	18	3	364	12	6	3	0
1763	406	12	0	427	12	7	4	0
1775	399	12	4	387	13	9	4	0

Years.

Years.	Net Affeffments £. s. d.			Total Expenditure £. s. d.			Rate in the Pound s. d.	
1776	-	405 1	5	-	375 16	5	-	4 0
1777	-	391 13	8	-	465 10	6	-	4 0
1778	-	405 14	4	-	400 9	8	-	4 0
1779	-	494 9	3	-	574 15	5	-	5 0
1780	-	510 0	9	-	519 16	4	-	5 0
1781	-	516 5	6	-	505 15	1	-	5 0
1782	-	508 9	3	-	594 15	5	-	5 0
1783	-	470 17	1½	-	581 17	7½	-	4 9
1784	-	414 10	3	-	452 0	0	-	4 0
1785	-	438 0	2	-	461 6	9	-	4 0
1786	-	678 6	9	-	646 18	10	-	6 0
1787	-	458 17	6	-	494 19	1½	-	4 0
1788	-	481 5	6	-	461 11	0	-	4 0
1789	-	483 15	0	-	577 9	1	-	4 0
1790	-	489 1	0	-	491 14	0	-	4 0
1791	-	489 14	3	-	533 5	9	-	4 0
1792	-	495 8	0	-	536 4	7	-	4 0
1793	-	615 19	6	-	655 19	0	-	5 0
1794	-	750 8	9	-	838 5	10	-	6 0
1795	-	606 18	6	-	791 19	6	-	5 0

Houfes in this parifh are faid to be affeffed at ⁹⁄ₜₒ of their real rent; but it appears that feveral which have been rebuilt, and are occupied by their owners, continue to be affeffed at the old rental, which is not half of the real yearly value. The 2 other parifhes in this town, having a confiderable quantity of land, are not affeffed more than 2s 6d. or 3s in the pound, to the Poor's Rates. The parochial expenditure is £ 300. or £ 400. above what is actually expended on the Poor; but no fatisfactory account could be obtained how the furplus was difourfed. The parifh pays all incidental expences of militia men's families, who become chargeable; removals of vagrants, &c &c.; and alfo pays about £ 70. a year to the county ftock; to borough charges; towards repairing gaols, &c.; £ 10. are annually paid to a doctor, and £ 1 a year to the veftry-clerk.

The Poor of this parifh have generally been farmed, but during part of 1793, and in 1794, they were managed by the parifh-officers; fince which

which time they have been farmed for £ 400. a year. The contractor finds food, cloaths, fuel, &c ; and the parish provides the house and furniture, which the farmer is bound to leave in good condition. He has 39 poor people at present in the house, (10 of which are old women, 7 men, and the rest children.) To 15 out-penfioners he pays 18s. weekly, and gives occasional relief to casual Poor. In the course of the last year, there were, at times, 70 or 80 in the house. The farmer asserts, that he lost £ 100 by his bargain. The house is kept in very good order : the Poor are mostly employed in straw-work, and mop-making; no account is kept of their earnings. £ 50. are annually distributed in money, to 20 poor persons ; and a few other small donations are given away in bread.

Table of Diet in the Work house.

	Breakfast.	Dinner.	Supper
Sunday,	Gruel	Meat, pudding, &c.	Bread and beer.
Monday,	Broth, or gruel.	Cold meat	Bread and cheefe.
Tuefday,	As Sunday.	As Sunday.	Bread and beer.
Wednefday,	As Monday	As Monday	As Monday.
Thurfday,	As Sunday.	As Sunday.	Bread and beer
Friday,	As Monday.	As Monday.	As Monday.
Saturday,	Gruel.	Bread and cheefe.	Bread, and cheefe.

Every grown perfon receives a pint of small beer at dinner and fupper, and is allowed to eat till he is fatisfied

A List of Baptisms, Burials, and Marriages.

YEARS.	BAPTISMS.		BURIALS.		MARRIAGES.
1784	-	39	-	50	-	17
1785	-	55	-	34	-	11
1786	-	51	-	36	-	12
1787	-	61	-	42	-	18
1788	-	60	-	46	-	13
1789	-	50	-	29	-	10
1790	-	64	-	29	-	7
1791	-	44	-	18	-	20
1792	-	58	-	35	-	16
1793	-	36	-	39	-	7
1794	-	32	-	34	-	16

11) 550   11) 392   11) 147

Average - 50 $35\frac{7}{11}$ $13\frac{4}{11}$

About 6 poor perfons die annually at the work-houfe

September, 1795.

CHIPPING BARNET.

IN this parifh, the officers wholly refufed to give any information whatever, either refpecting the Poor or affeffments. The following is a lift of baptifms and burials:

Years	BAPTISMS.			BURIALS.		
	Males.	Females	Total.	Males.	Females.	Total.
1740	17	11	28	22	12	34
1760	22	17	39	19	22	41
1775	18	18	36	13	22	35
1776	32	56	88	23	13	36
1777	21	23	44	14	11	25
1778	16	22	38	17	12	29
1779	24	22	46	21	25	46
1780	23	24	47	20	16	36
1781	21	31	52	17	16	33
1782	19	20	39	8	9	17
1783	20	19	39	24	18	42
1784	27	28	58	19	7	26
1785	20	16	36	19	19	38
1786	23	30	53	29	28	57
1787	23	17	40	19	16	35
1788	26	23	49	13	19	32
1789	27	28	55	15	21	36
1790	25	22	47	12	11	23
1791	20	34	54	18	10	28
1792	33	19	52	15	14	29
1793	25	24	49	15	16	31
1794	34	31	65	22	29	51

24) 1054   22) 760

Average   48 nearly.   Average $34\frac{12}{22}$

From

From the information of a parishioner it appears, that the Poor are farmed at £23. a month; and that the Poor's rates are generally from £300 to £400 a year, and are from 2s. to 2s. 6d. in the pound. If this account is correct, farming the Poor keeps down the Rates. According to the returns made to Parliament in 1786, the net expences for the Poor in 1776 amounted to   -   -   -   £217 11   6
The Poor's Rates in 1783 to   -   -   -   386 12   3
            in 1784 to   -   -   -   466 10   0
            in 1785 to   -   -   -   418   9   7

This parish has a large tract of land belonging to it.   120 houses pay the window tax: the land-tax is £562. 7s. 6d. collected at 3s 4d. in the pound   *September*, 1795.

REDBOURN.

THIS parish is situated on the north road, and contains by estimation 4000 acres. No account of its population could be obtained. The inhabitants are farmers, inn-keepers, shop-keepers, straw-workers, and labourers. They are, (with the exception of 20 Anabaptists), all of the established Church.   107 houses pay the widow tax; the number exempted could not be ascertained. The prices of provisions are the same as at Markyate-street. The common wages of labourers in winter and summer are 7s. a week: this spring, wages were raised to 8s. a week, without board; in hay time they are 9s. a week; and in harvest 40s. a month, with board. Much piece-work is done here. The number of ale-houses is 15. Here are 3 Friendly Societies. The average rent of land is near £1. an acre; swarth or meadow land being £3. an acre, and plowed land about 15s. Farms are from £15. to £220. a year. Wheat, barley, oats, turnips, and clover, are the principal articles of cultivation. The tithes chiefly belong to Lord Grimstone, who takes a composition of nearly 2s 6d. in the pound. The land tax amounts to £379. 5s. 8d. and is collected at 9½d in the pound; it is partly paid by the landlord, and partly by the farmer. There are about 40 acres of common in this parish.

The

The Poor's Rates from 1773 to 1795 inclufive were as follow :

Years.	Net Affeffment.			Total Expenditure.			Rate in the Pound.	
	£.	s.	d.	£.	s.	d.	s.	d.
1773	262	8	8½	271	0	2	1	5
1774	289	3	6	273	15	11¾	1	6
1775	307	5	3	307	5	9	1	8
1776	355	3	4	330	12	5	1	11
1777	269	8	8	281	8	2	1	5
1778	394	3	3	346	6	6	2	0
1779	345	1	4	326	3	7	1	9
1780	282	8	10	316	8	8	1	5
1781	290	3	1½	361	5	3	1	6
1782	321	8	5	360	10	4½	1	7
1783	410	6	11	399	13	5	2	0
1784	416	6	5	452	0	0	2	0
1785	410	5	9	436	1	3	2	0
1786	417	12	5	399	3	3	2	0
1787	452	7	0½	452	9	5	2	2
1788	419	0	10	419	17	10	2	0
1789	420	5	5	476	10	10½	2	0
1790	422	9	2	434	10	4	2	0
1791	480	4	9½	470	6	4½	2	3
1792	640	8	8	601	9	7	3	0
1793	376	4	10	445	8	7½	1	9
1794	534	11	9	532	14	2	2	6
1795	542	12	5	550	19	3¾	2	6

Thefe affeffments are faid to be as near the net rent as can be afcertained. The expenditure includes the following difburfements, befides the charges for the Poor :

	£.	s.	d.
Towards the county ftock, about £28. or - -	30	0	0
To the furveyors of highways, about - -	100	0	0
To church-wardens, very variable, as from £18. to -	50	0	0
To conftables, about - - -	9	0	0
To the veftry-clerk - - - -	3	3	0
A common rent or fine of - - -	1	0	0
To the doctor for attending the Poor - -	10	10	0

The

The Poor have been farmed many years: for some years back they were farmed for £26. a month; laſt year a perſon contracted with the pariſh for three years, at £25. a month; but, on account of the late dear ſeaſon, the pariſh allowed him an addition of £3. a month, which was intended to be taken off after the harveſt.   The pariſh rents a houſe and furniture; the farmer provides fuel, victuals and cloaths, &c for thoſe in the houſe, and gives penſions to thoſe whom he can ſupport at a leſs expence out of it.   There are now 30 Poor in the houſe, who are chiefly children, and are principally employed in ſtraw work: 22 out-penſioners receive 30s. a week.   The farmer ſays he is not bound to give the Poor any particular diet, but generally obſerves the following bill of fare, viz.

	Breakfaſt.			Dinner.		Supper.
Sunday,	Broth or gruel.	—		Meat, pudding, &c.		Bread, cheeſe, and ſmall beer.
Monday,	Ditto.	—	—	Cold meat.	—	Ditto.
Tueſday,	Ditto.	—	—	Bread, cheeſe, and beer.		Ditto.
Wedneſday,	Ditto.	—	—	As Sunday.	—	Ditto.
Thurſday,	Ditto.	—	—	As Monday.	—	Ditto.
Friday,	Ditto	—	—	As Sunday.	—	Ditto
Saturday,	Ditto.	—	—	As Tueſday.	—	Ditto.

Rebuilding the workhouſe and veſtry-room partly occaſioned the increaſe in the Rates in the laſt 4 years.   *September*, 1795.

K E N T.

A S H F O R D.

THE pariſh of Aſhford is ſituated on the borders of, but juſt out of the weald of Kent: it contains about 2000 acres: the rental of the pariſh is eſtimated at £4000. a year.   The number of houſes is about 320; and of the inhabitants near 2000, of whom not above 100 are Diſſenters.   The land-tax is about 5s. 8d. in the pound on the half rental.   Rectorial tithes are

are moftly taken in kind; vicarial tithes are compounded for, on the average, at 15d. an acre: hops pay 10s. an acre.

Labourers are paid 1s 8d. a day in winter, and 2s. in fummer. Within thefe ten years, a market for cattle, (held at firft every month, but afterwards every fortnight,) was eftablifhed here, and has proved of great fervice to the fmall farmers: before that period they were entirely at the mercy of the butchers, but can now find a ready market, even for a few fheep, or a pig or. two. An annual fair for wool was likewife inftituted at this place laft year; and promifes to prove of great utility: till then, all the wool produced in Romney Marfh was fold at once, for the fame price, without the fmalleft regard being paid to the goodnefs or badnefs of it's quality: now, comparifons may be made at the fair, and various prices are given, according to it's excellence   Since the laft fhewing, the loweft price has been £ 8 10s. the pack; the higheft £ 9. 5s.   Before the prefent war, the higheft price was £ 15. the pack; but before the American war, the higheft price here was only £ 9 the pack; and near the end of the American war, the loweft price was £ 4. 10s. the pack. The price, during the reigns of George the Firft and Second, was, at times, as high as it has been at any period in the prefent reign, except during the 5 years between 1787 and 1793, in which it nearly doubled the ordinary. peace price.

Afhford has been paved fubftantially and fatisfactorily, at not more than double the expence of what an Act of Parliament for this purpofe ufually cofts.   The inhabitants, fortunately, were unanimous; and the fum neceffary for the work, amounting to £ 300. was obtained, partly from the highway cefs, and partly raifed by fubfcription.   There is very little turnpike road in the parifh.   About 7 years ago the highways were execrable, but are now excellent, in confequence of individuals paying great attention to the repairs of fuch parts as are contiguous to their houfes.   The cefs for the highway has never been higher than 9d. in the pound; it is now 6d.; and the debt incurred, in making the road, has been paid off, within £ 150.

Parochial bufinefs is managed by a committee of the principal inhabitants; one of whom attends, daily, at dinner, in the work houfe.   Some of the Poor are maintained at home; others are received into the parifh work-houfe.   There are, at prefent, about 60 perfons in the houfe: they earn, on an average, about 1s. a week, or about £ 150. a year. They are

I   chiefly

chiefly employed in a bleachery, which has been lately eſtabliſhed for bleaching Iriſh linen. The allowance to out-poor does not exceed 1s a week, to a ſingle perſon ; 2s. a week, to two in a houſe ; and 2s. 6d. to a family. About 2 removals take place every year : very few certificates are granted.

The only information obtainable relative to the Poor's Rates, was, that, from 1766 to 1786, they produced, annually, on an average, about £ 1050. at 4s. 3d in the pound ; and that laſt year, at 3s. in the pound, they amounted to £ 700.

Table of Baptiſms, Burials, and Marriages.

YEARS	BAPTISMS.	BURIALS.	MARRIAGES.
1774	32	36	10
1775	39	29	11
1776	44	46	10
1777	43	36	11
1778	41	32	17
1779	59	41	12
1780	36	44	13
1781	45	39	22
1782	37	36	13
1783	44	42	15
1784	44	33	9
1785	49	50	19
1786	34	26	9
1787	48	27	10
1788	55	45	8
1789	35	32	13
1790	47	33	11
1791	45	41	17
1792	49	30	13
1793	49	32	13
1794	32	29	14

There

There is one Friendly Society here, which was inftituted chiefly for the benefit of the widows of deceafed members; and a free grammar fchool, and a writing fchool for poor children.

Poverty here, is generally afcribed to the low price of wages, and the high price of provifions: they fuit each other very well in fummer, but not in winter. The Poor, in moft parts of Kent, ten years ago, always eat meat daily: they now feldom tafte it in winter, except they refide in a poor-houfe. Private brewing, even amongft fmall farmers, is at an end. The Poor drink tea at all their meals. This beverage, and bread, potatoes, and cheefe, conftitute their ufual diet. Labourers only eat barley or oat bread. Even houfhold bread is fcarcely ever ufed: they buy the fineft wheaten bread, and declare, (what I much doubt,) that brown bread difoders their bowels. Bakers do not now make, as they formerly did, bread of unfifted flour: at fome farmers houfes, however, it is ftill made of flour, as it comes from the mill; but this practice is going much into difufe. 20 years ago, fcarcely any other than brown bread was ufed.

January, 1795.

CHALK.

THIS parifh contains about 1700 acres, and 230 inhabitants. 15 houfes pay the commutation-tax; 27 are exempted, of which 6 are double tenements. The inhabitants are all employed in agriculture. The prefent prices of provifions are: beef, 6d. the pound; mutton, 6d.; pork, from 6d to 8d.; bread, 14½d. a quartern loaf; potatoes, from 8d. to 2s. the bufhel. Labourers are paid from 2s. to 2s. 6d. the day; by the great, they often earn from 2s. 6d. to 3s. 6d. a day: wages have been advanced within the laft 3 years, at leaft one-fifth. There are 3 ale-houfes in this parifh. The ufual diet of labourers is the beft wheaten bread, butter, cheefe, and meat.

The rent of land, upon an average, is from 10s to 15s. an acre. Nearly ⅓ of the parifh is marfh-land, near the Thames, and about half of it let at the very moderate rent of 23s. an acre; and the reft of it, (fuppofed

pofed to be of equal goodnefs,) for not more than about 12s. an acre.
The uplands are let equally low, and about half of them do not produce
more than 14s. an acre. Farms are from 60 to 300 acres: the tenure, in
general, is by leafe, or at will; the principal articles of cultivation are,
wheat, beans, barley, oats, peafe, and potatoes.

The tithes of coin, hay, and feeds, (which laft article includes fainfoin,
clover, and other artificial graffes,) are taken in kind ; the vicarial tithes are
paid by a compofition: the land-tax is about 2s. 3d. in the pound on
the net rental.

The Poor are, moftly, farmed in a poor-houfe, with the Poor of the
parifh of Northfleet, at the weekly expence of 3s. a head. The employers of labouring people, inftead of drawing the weekly pay, in confequence of the great price of provifions, have affifted them by various temporary expedients ; by felling them coin at a low rate, &c. This parifh
has always been confidered unhealthy : it is very fubject to agues in autumn.
The burials, therefore, as might be expected, are more numerous than the
baptifms : as to the number of marriages, no conclufions can be drawn
from them, becaufe many of the people marry here, who are inhabitants
of Gravefend.

Table of Baptifms, Burials, Marriages, and Poor's Rates.

Years.	Baptisms.			Burials.			Marriages.	Poor's Rates.			Net Expenditure			Rate in the Pound.	
	Males	Fem	Total	Males	Fem	Total		£.	s.	d.	£.	s.	d.	s.	d.
1700	—	—	—	—	—	—	—	34	3	0	34	19	5	—	—
1775	3	3	6	5	6	11	3	94	18	9	70	1	3	1	9
1776	4	2	6	3	1	4	0	80	19	6	59	1	10	1	6
1777	3	5	8	3	6	9	3	81	0	0	60	1	0	1	6
1778	5	6	11	8	4	12	3	81	6	0	45	1	8	1	6
1779	3	4	7	8	6	14	4	89	9	0	57	14	10½	1	6
1780	0	3	3	8	5	13	3	81	9	9	62	7	9	1	6
1781	4	4	8	7	8	15	3	108	17	0	76	4	4½	2	0
1782	4	3	7	6	5	11	2	121	8	3	94	5	1½	2	3
1783	4	5	9	9	7	16	6	125	7	3	97	1	11	2	3
1784	3	3	6	6	9	15	1	139	4	6	104	12	6	2	6

Years.	Baptisms			Burials.			Marriages.	Poor's Rate.			Net Expenditure.			Rate in the Pound.	
	Males	Fem	Total	Males.	Fem	Total.		£.	s.	d.	£.	s.	d	s.	d.
1785	3	2	5	4	1	5	2	137	2	6	108	11	0	2	6
1786	3	4	7	2	6	8	3	148	11	0	116	2	4	2	9
1787	4	4	8	5	3	8	5	136	0	0	105	14	8	2	6
1788	5	2	7	3	1	4	3	108	16	0	87	4	0	2	0
1789	4	1	5	2	4	6	10	138	19	0	78	13	8	2	0
1790	6	4	10	4	4	8	8	65	3	0	34	17	6	1	0
1791	3	2	5	1	2	3	9	64	17	0	43	8	8	1	0
1792	6	4	10	1	3	4	4	132	14	0	107	11	8	2	0
1793	10	2	12	3	4	7	0	64	17	0	88	19	0	1	0
1794	2	4	6	9	5	14	2	136	15	0	107	13	4	2	0
1795	1	2	3	11	8	19	8	137	14	0	98	12	8	2	0

$$21 \,)\, 149 \qquad 21 \,)\, 206 \quad 21 \,)\, 82$$

Average - $7\frac{2}{21}$ $\qquad$ $9\frac{17}{21}$ $\quad$ $3\frac{19}{21}$

It is cuſtomary to pay out of the Poor's Rates, the county Rate, the pariſh-clerk's ſalary, the veſtry-clerk's ſalary, and half the expences of providing ſubſtitutes for men who are drawn to ſerve in the militia, and many other incidental expences. The rents of a conſiderable part of the pariſh were advanced in the year 1790 ; ſo that the Rate ſince that time, although leſs in proportion to the rental, produces as much as a much higher nominal aſſeſſment did formerly.

April, 1796.

GREAT CHART.

THE pariſh of Great Chart is ſituated in the weald of Kent: it's inhabitants are all agricultural labourers, with the exception of one gentleman's family. The nominal rental of the pariſh is £ 2000. ; the actual rental £ 2500. There is no manufactory in this, or any other pariſh in the weald

weald of Kent: 300 years ago, the woollen manufacture here was very confiderable: it is fuppofed that the decreafe of fuel was the caufe of its migrating to the coal countries. Moft of the gentlemen's families in the weald fprung from the woollen manufacture; as in Suffex, many confiderable families have originated from the iron works; which, from the fcarcity of fuel, are now abandoned[1].

Arable land, in the parifh of Great Chart, lets from 8s. to 10s. an acre; pafture, from 16s. to £ 1. an acre.

A compofition is taken for tithes, of   5s. od. an acre for wheat,
                                2s. 6d. for Lent corn,
                                2s. 6d. for hay,
                                1s. od. for pafture,
                                10s. od. for hops,
                                3s. od. for potatoes.

There is no Friendly Society in the parifh.

According to the returns made to Parliament in 1786, the expences for the Poor, in 1776, were £ 266. 10s. 6d.; and the Poor's Rates, in 1783, £ 381. 10s.; in 1784, £ 382. 5s.; and in 1785, £ 381. The Poor's Rates, at prefent, are at 3s. 6d. in the pound on the full rental. A fixpenny affeffment produces £ 50. About £ 475. are annually expended on the Poor; who are partly maintained in a poor houfe, and partly at home. The paupers in the poor-houfe are chiefly old people and children. The parifh officers expect a labourer to maintain 3 children: they allow 1s. a week for every child beyond 3, or permit the parents to fend it to the poor-houfe.

Agricultural labourers receive 1s. 8d. a day, in winter; and 2s. in fummer: they earn, all the year round, about 11s. 6d. a week, on an average.

Table of Baptifms and Burials.

YEARS.		BAPTISMS.		BURIALS.
1725	-	8	-	—
1729	-	4	-	—
1742	-	9	-	—
1743	-	9	-	—

[1] All the iron work round the cathedral of St. Paul's was made in the parifh of Beckley, in that county.

Table

YEARS.	BAPTISMS.	BURIALS.	
1744 -	13 -	—	
1745 -	16 -	2	
1746 -	— -	6	
1747 -	— -	3	
1789 -	— -	5	
1790 -	— -	8	of whom 3 were paupers,
1791 -	17 -	15	4 paupers,
1792 -	22 -	7	4 paupers,
1793 -	11 -	8	
1794 -	19 -	8	4 paupers.

The adjoining parifh of Little Chart is partly fituated in the weald of Kent. There are 2 paper-mills in the parifh, which are fuppofed to be the caufe of a great influx of Poor. In 1793 the Poor's Rates were 7s., and in 1794 6s. in the pound on the nominal rental.

January, 1795.

COBHAM.

THE parifh of Cobham contains 2949 acres of land. The number of houfes which pay the window or commutation tax is 40, whereof 5 are double tenements: 29 are exempt, exclufive of the College, which contains 21 tenements. There are about 560 inhabitants, (all of the eftablifhed religion,) who are folely employed in agriculture. Labourers wages for many years were 18d. a day, but laft year they were advanced to 20d. and are now, (March, 1796,) 2s. a day. The wages of woodcutters, and of others who work by the piece, have lately advanced about one fixth. The rent of land varies, according to its goodnefs, from 5s. to £1. 1s. an acre: the land tax is about 2s. 9d. in the pound on the net rental. The tithe of corn is taken in kind; but all other produce is paid for by an ancient compofition. There are 3 ale-houfes in this parifh.
The

The farms are from 40 to 400 acres, and are moftly held by leafes for 14 or 21 years : corn of all forts is grown here, but wheat is the principal article of cultivation. About 1000 acres of this parifh, confifting of Cobham park and woods, belong to the Earl of Darnley. There is a charitable foundation, called the New College, in the village of Cobham, fituated near the church, built by truftees under the will of Sir William Biooke, Knt. Lord Cobham, for the reception, habitation, and fuppoit of 20 poor perfons fiom this and feveral adjoining parifhes[1]. There is one Friendly Society, confifting of about 75 members, the rules of which have been confiimed by the Magiftrates. Provifions, which in this part of the country ufually follow the prices of the London markets, have been advanced at leaft $\frac{1}{3}$ in the laft feven years, and many articles are doubled. Biead is now 15d. the quartern loaf ; cheefe, from 5d. to 8d. the pound ; falt butter, 10½d. ; beef, 6d. ; mutton, 6d ; pork, 7d. a pound.

About 3 or 4 years ago, a houfe was provided for the Poor, who were farmed at 2s. 9d. a week each ; the contractor received what they could earn : but this has been difcontinued, and it is now in contemplation to fet up an Houfe of Induftry. The ufual diet of labourers is, bread, butter, cheefe, pickled poik, and a little butcher's meat: potatoes, at this time, are a principal article in large families: wheaten bread, of the beft quality, is generally ufed heie ; milk is very fcarce.

Table of Baptifms, Burials, Marriages, and Poor's Rates, in the Parifh of COBHAM.

Years	BAPTISMS			BURIALS			Marriages	Total Expenditure.		
	Males	Fem	Total	Males	Fem	Total		£.	s.	d.
1740	5	5	10	5	4	9	—	—	—	—
1760	7	10	17	5	7	12	—	—	—	—
1775	8	5	13	9	10	19	6	—	—	—
1776	6	9	15	5	5	10	3	—	—	—
1777	4	3	7	7	7	14	4	—	—	—
1778	6	14	20	7	7	14	2	—	—	—
1779	8	9	17	8	10	18	3	—	—	—
1780	7	7	14	13	19	32	4	—	—	—
1781	8	9	17	8	9	17	4	170	10	10

[1] For further particulars relative to this College, fee Hafted's Hiftory of Kent, vol 1. page 505-6

Years.	BAPTISMS.			BURIALS.			Marriages.	Total Expenditure			Rate in the Pound.
	Males	Fem	Total.	Males	Fem.	Total		£.	s.	d.	
1782	6	5	11	7	10	17	5	213	6	11	
1783	13	6	19	12	9	21	4	259	18	0	
1784	10	5	15	6	4	10	4	272	0	11	
1785	12	7	19	6	6	12	3	217	17	6	
1786	7	6	13	8	9	17	5	222	16	1	
1787.	4	10	14	5	8	13	10	255	8	6	
1788	7	10	17	3	11	14	8	264	2	6	
1789	6	11	17	7	8	15	15	277	9	9	
1790	5	12	17	7	9	16	2	225	18	6	
1791	10	7	17	4	9	13	3	313	16	9	
1792	7	11	18	12	8	20	7	243	10	11	
1793	8	8	16	6	3	9	6	205	0	0	s. d.
1794	2	8	10	6	5	11	3	165	12	0	2 0
1795	7	7	14	10	12	22	6	191	0	0	— —
1796	—	—	—	—	—	—	—	330	0	0[2]	4 0

March, 1796.

HOTHFIELD.

THE parish of Hothfield is situated in the weald of Kent, and contains about 1244 acres of land. The number of houses that have annually paid the window tax, during the last 5 years, is about 40; about 10 are exempted. There are about 400 inhabitants in the parish; viz. 2 shoemakers, 1 tailor, 1 miller, 1 carpenter, 1 blacksmith, 4 shopkeepers who deal in groceries and chandlery, and the rest agricultural labourers. The grocers' and chandlers' shops have only been opened a few years: the articles they deal in were formerly sent for to Ashford, which is about 3 miles distant. The shopkeepers now procure their goods partly from Ashford, and partly from London, from whence riders frequently visit this place, and readily take orders for any article that may be wanted. There is no butcher in this parish.

[2] A sickness which prevailed amongst the labouring poor last autumn, and the dearness of provisions, were the causes of this advance.

Agricultural

Agricultural labourers earn 1s. 6d. a day in winter; and 2s. in summer. A boy, 14 years old, can earn 1s. a day, throughout the year. Women usually earn 8d. a day, except in summer, when their wages, for haymaking, weeding, &c. are 10d. a day; an industrious woman may earn 2s. 6d. or 3s. a day, in picking hops.

The average rent of land is 16s. an acre, including an unlimited right of intercommoning with the neighbouring parish of Westwell on a common of 500 acres. The yearly rental of land and houses in the parish, upon the average of the last 5 years, amounts to £1246: the land-tax produces £149. 4s. The Rector of Hothfield receives the following yearly compositions in lieu of tithe:

	s.	d.	
For the tithe of corn of all sorts	4	4	the acre.
For meadow land, from ⎱	2	0	
to ⎰	2	6	
For hop ground	10	0	

There is a modus of 2d. an acre, for pasture ground. Underwoods in this parish, and in other parts of the weald of Kent, are exempted from tithe. In the parish of Charing, situated on the borders of the weald, the composition for wheat is 8s. an acre, and for Lent corn, 5s,; besides 1s. in the pound, for other tithe, to the Vicar. A great part of this parish is let at 5s. an acre; but, although the land is naturally poor, it is rendered productive by the lime which is procured from a neighbouring chalk-hill.

The roads in this parish are maintained by statute labour. Waggons with four horses work 4 days, or pay £1. 10s.: a rental of £50. is deemed equivalent to keeping a waggon with 4 horses, and every rental exceeding £50. pays 6d. in the pound; a cottage is charged 2s. annually towards the roads. A turnpike road is now making from London to Ashford, which will pass through Hothfield. There is only one ale-house in the parish.

A decent brick cottage, with a garden and right of common, lets for £3. 10s a year.

The Poor's Rate, in 1770, was 1s. in the pound.

7

The

		£.	s.	d.	
The expences for the Poor in 1776 were		119	0	0	⎫ From the Returns made
The Poor's Rate in	1783 ——	175	3	9	⎪ to Parliament in 1786
Do. ——————— 1784 ——		174	9	3	⎬
Do. ——————— 1785 ——		161	0	9	⎭

		£	s.	d.	s.	d.
Do. from Michaelmas 1789						
to Michaelmas - - 1790 ——		166	15	9	at 2	9 in the pound.
Do to Michaelmas - 1791 ——		182	13	3	at 3	0
Do. to Michaelmas - 1792 ——		136	17	8½	at 2	3
Do. to Michaelmas - 1793 ——		136	16	4½	at 2	3
Do. to Michaelmas - 1794 ——		153	3	9	at 2	6

Lands left for the relief of the Poor of Hothfield, and for the putting out poor children apprentices; wood allowed for fuel, &c. altogether produce about £ 30 a year; which sum is diftributed by the fteward of Hothfield place, to fuch perfons as are thought to be moft neceffitous.

There is likewife a free fchool, (which was endowed by the Thanet family,) wherein a matron, whofe annual falary is £ 16. inftructs poor children in reading, &c. £ 4. a year were left for the repair of the fchool.

There is neither work-houfe, nor houfe of induftry, in the parifh: the indigent are relieved at home. Full half of the labouring poor are certificated perfons from other parifhes: the above-mentioned common, which affords them the means of keeping a cow, or poultry, is fuppofed to draw many Poor into the parifh; certificated perfons are allowed to dig peat. The inhabitants are, in general, healthy: in winter, however, agues are very common; they are, principally, afcribed to low diet. Bread is the chief food of labourers: in the winter they, ufually, eat meat about twice a week The little liquor they drink is procured from the neighbouring town of Afhford: they feldom, however, can afford to purchafe beer, and in it's place, have very generally, in this part of the country, fubftituted tea at every meal. Private brewing is gone much into difufe; fome farmers, however, ftill brew their own beer.

There are neither Diffenting chapels, nor Diffenters in the parifh.

Table

Table of Baptifms, Burials, and Marriages, in the Parifh of HOTHFIELD.

Years.	BAPTISMS			BURIALS.	MARRIAGES;
	Males.	Fem.	Total		
1724	—	—	11	—	3
1725	—	—	16	—	3
1726	—	—	6	—	4
1727	—	—	12	12	1
1728	—	—	9	7	2
1729	—	—	16	6	4
1730	—	—	14	7	2
1731	—	—	10	3	none.
1732	—	—	9	—	none.
1733	—	—	12	—	
1734	—	—	14	—	
1786	—	—	—	8	
1787	—	—	—	4	3
1788	5	2	7	5	2
1789	3	4	7	8	5
1790	3	8	11	6	none.
1791	5	5	10	1 infant; 2, upwards of 70 ; 1, accidental death.	1
1792	7	9	16	2 infants; 1, of 30; 2, upwards of 80.	none.
1793	7	9	16	3 infants ; 1, of 40 ; 2, of 70.	5
1794	2	10	12	3 infants; 1, accidental; 3, upwards of 70.	4

January, 1795.

MEOPHAM.

THE parifh of Meopham is fituated about 6 miles to the eaft of Farningham : it's extent is eftimated at 5697½ acres. It contains 117 families, confifting of 612 perfons, who are all of the Church of England and chiefly agricultural labourers and linen-weavers. 34 fingle, and 14 double houfes pay the window-tax. The prices of provifions are: beef, 6d. the pound; mutton, 6½d; veal, 7½d. The price of wheat flour is much the fame as at London. Labourers' wages were raifed, about May 1795, from 1s. 8d. to 2s. a day: threfhing corn is ufually paid at fo much the quarter. There are 4 ale-houfes in this parifh: and 1 Friendly Society, confifting of 60 members, who pay 4s. quarterly, each, towards the general fund; in time of ficknefs, or in cafes of accident, each member receives 7s. a week. The Society has £150. out at intereft: their rules have been confirmed by the Magiftrates. The rent of land varies from 5s. to 30s. an acre. The tithe of corn is taken in kind; but a compofition is paid for vicarial tithe. The land-tax is at 4s and amounts to about 3s. 6d in the pound. Farms, in general, are fmall; except one, which is held under the Dean and Chapter of Canterbury. The ufual tenure is by leafe, or at will; wheat, beans, barley, oats, clover, fainfoin, turnips, hops, fruit, and woad, are the principal articles of cultivation. There are not more than 6 acres of common in the parifh. Cafual Poor are relieved at home: orphans, and aged perfons, are provided for by the overfeer, in a poor-houfe, in which there are, at prefent, 6 aged perfons, and 11 children. Their diet is, generally, broth, or milk, for breakfaft; beef, for dinner; and bread and cheefe, or butter, for fupper, every day: the expence is about 3s. a week, for each perfon; or about £140. 8s. a year.

	£.	s.	d.
A labourer earns, at this time, 12s. a week during the whole year	31	4	0
Add 3s. a week for the harveft month -	0	12	0
Ditto 1s. 6d. a week the other 5 fummer months -	1	10	0
	£33	6	0

A boy, at the age of 10 years, earns 6d. a day; at 12 years, 9d; at 14 years, 1s.; at 16 years, 1s. 6d.; at 18 years, 2s. a day. Women earn from 10d. to 1s a day. The ufual diet of labourers confifts of bread, cheefe, butter, pudding, and fometimes beef or mutton.

A Table

A Table of Baptisms, Burials, Marriages, and Poor's Rates.

Years	Baptisms			Burials			Marriages	Poor's Rates			Net Expenditure			Rate in the Pound	
	Males	Fem	Total	Males	Fem	Total		£	s	d	£	s	d	s	d
1680	3	4	7				—	9	12	8	9	12	0	0	2
1685	9	6	15				1	20	11	8	19	7	8	0	4
1690	11	6	17				1	40	0	0	58	10	8	0	6
1691	10	5	15				2	16	4	4	14	11	4	0	2
1692	6	8	14				4	19	14	0	13	7	10	0	2
1693	11	10	21				—	27	16	0	14	19	6	0	4
1694	7	6	13	Register of Burials wanting			2	27	13	8	28	5	0	0	6
1695	6	7	13				4	40	0	0	58	10	8	0	6
1696	9	8	17				3	40	10	0	56	8	1	0	9
1697	10	13	23				1	81	13	0	54	9	11	1	0
1698	9	7	16				1	73	8	0	61	12	9	1	0
1699	12	9	21				—	94	16	8	72	15	0	1	0
1700	13	8	21				3	81	3	6	82	3	5	0	9
1720	7	7	14				1	—	—	—	Accounts lost				
1740	10	10	20				1	118	3	4½	109	10	4	1	3
1760	9	10	19	7	8	15	4	259	7	1¼	215	1	11	2	9
1775	8	13	21	8	6	14	5	211	3°	0	188	16	11	2	0
1776	14	10	24	3	7	10	3	212	6	0	194	15	3	2	0
1777	10	6	16	9	7	16	3	212	11	0	192	0	0	2	0
1778	10	16	26	7	9	16	7	212	12	6	225	0	0	2	0
1779	10	15	25	7	6	13	8	213	12	0	222	5	0	2	0
1780	19	11	30	3	9	12	4	212	8	0	230	10	1½	2	9
1781	10	11	21	11	16	27	5	283	4	1½	289	3	0	2	0
1782	8	10	18	4	4	8	4	328	10	6	242	10	7½	3	0
1783	13	8	21	7	6	13	5	319	13	0	354	9	5	3	0
1784	12	6	18	10	8	18	4	322	7	6	334	13	3	3	0
1785	10	12	22	5	5	10	6	324	0	6	323	11	1	3	0
1786	11	12	23	8	7	15	3	429	9	6	350	4	3¼	4	0
1787	7	18	25	7	7	14	6	432	8	6	438	10	3¼		0
1788	15	7	22	4	4	8	7	448	5	6	468	12	2½	4	0
1789	8	12	20	6	4	10	1	451	18	0	465	10	0	4	0
1790	9	14	23	5	5	10	7	339	0	6	349	8	5¼	3	0
1791	8	15	23	12	4	16	5	456	13	0	374	12	10½	4	0
1792	10	15	25	10	4	14	6	350	12	0	373	5	9	3	0
1793	4	15	19	7	8	15	8	349	11	0	415	6	2¼	3	0
1794	15	10	25	6	11	17	6	351	5	6	379	15	0	3	0
1795	10	11	21	7	8	15	5	352	2	6	365	19	2	3	0
1796	—							352	2	6	428	11	0	0	0

37)734   22)306 37)136

Average -   19⅓¾   14⅛⁸   3²⁵   April, 1796.

Pp 2

W E S T W E L L.

THE rental of the parifh of Weftwell, which is fituated on the bordeis of, but a little out of, the weald of Kent, is about £2150. a yeai. There are lands, which belong to a chaiity, and are ceffed at £8. Coin tithe is taken in kind; and £30. are paid out of them annually to the Vicar.

The Poor's Rates, during the laft 5 yeais, have amounted yeaily on an average to 4s. in the pound. The Poor in this paiifh are maintained at home: for three years they weie employed in a poor-houfe, in weaving, &c. This however, it was found, did not anfwer, and the poor-houfe was lately difcontinued. The Poor are not well managed, in this paiifh. 500 acres of common belong, jointly, to Weftwell and Hothfield. No gentleman refides in this parifh.

6d. in the pound is paid, almoft univerfally on the weald of Kent, towards the roads.

Prices in the Weald.

	£.	s.	d.
A coid of wood - - - -	1	0	0
100 faggots - - - - -	0	18	0
14 years ago they coft - - -	0	12	0
A waggon, 4 horfes, and 2 men by the day -	0	10	0

The general diet of the Poor in the Weald, is bread, milk, potatoes, tea, and cheefe: little or no meat is ufed; very little beer: and no butter. Rents, in general, have not much increafed: at the Revolution they were nearly the fame as at prefent. In Hothfield, however, they are fuppofed to have rifen about a fifth in the laft 20 years. In Romney Marfh, rents have doubled fince the Revolution.

Wood-land in the Weald, having feldom been let, is rated very low. The average Poor's Rate, taken indifcriminately, in 20 paiifhes in the Weald, amounted to 4s. 6d. in the pound on the nominal rental.

The price of labour in Kent is extremely various: Mr. Boys, the author of the General View of the Agriculture of this county, fays, that hufbandry-

labour

labour is nearly double what it was 30 years ago. He gives the following as the ordinary prices of labour in Kent, in the year 1795 [1] :

	£. s d		£. s. d.
Labourers, the day, of 10 hours, from - - -	0 1 6	to	0 2 0
Threshing wheat, the quarter (in 1795, some farmers on account of the badness of the crop, paid 10s a quarter.) - -	0 2 0	—	0 3 0
Threshing barley, beans, and oats, the quarter - -	0 1 2	—	0 1 8
Threshing pease, the quarter - - - -	0 1 6	—	0 2 0
Spreading dung, the 100 cart-loads, 24 bushels each - -	0 3 6	—	0 4 0
Making hedges, the rod - - - -	0 0 2	—	0 0 4
Hoeing beans, the acre, first time - - -	0 3 0	—	0 3 6
Hoeing pease, the acre - - - -	0 3 0	—	0 4 0
Dutch hoeing canary and barley, the acre - - -	0 1 8	—	0 2 0
Common hoeing, the acre - - - -	0 3 6	—	0 4 0
Hoeing turnips, the acre - - - -	0 5 0	—	0 6 0
Reaping wheat, the acre - - -	0 8 0	—	0 16 0
Mowing barley and oats, the acre - - -	0 1 8	—	0 2 6
Binding and shocking, the acre - - -	0 1 8	—	0 2 6
Cutting beans and binding, the acre - -	0 5 0	—	0 6 0
Mowing sainfoin, and clover seed, the acre - -	0 2 0	—	0 3 0
Mowing grass in the marshes and meadows, the acre - -	0 2 6	—	0 3 6
Waggoner's wages, with board, yearly - - -	10 0 0	—	13 0 0
If he is a married man, and boards himself, weekly, (with wheat and pork at reduced prices,) - - -	0 10 0	—	0 10 6
Second ploughman, yearly - - - -	9 0 0	—	11 0 0
Third ploughman, ditto - - - -	8 0 0	—	10 0 0
Waggoner's mate, ditto - - -	6 0 0	—	9 0 0
Second plough-boy, ditto - - -	4 0 0	—	6 0 0
Third plough-boy, ditto - - -	3 0 0	—	5 0 0
Bailiff, ditto - - - - -	12 0 0	—	16 0 0
Dairy maid, ditto - - - -	4 0 0	—	5 0 0
Cook-maid, ditto - - - -	4 0 0	—	5 0 0
Shepherd, weekly - - - -	0 9 0	—	0 10 0
Women's wages for weeding, daily - - -	0 0 8	—	0 0 10
Children, from 10 to 13 years old, daily - -	0 0 0	—	0 0 6
Ploughing an acre of land - -	0 7 0	—	0 10 0
Harvest-men, with board, weekly - -	3 10 0	—	4 0 0
Ditto, without board, weekly. - - -	5 5 0	—	0 0 0

Hop-Garden Labour.	£. s d.		£. s. d.
Common labourers by the day, from - - -	0 1 8	to	0 2 0
Digging, the acre - - - -	0 15 0	—	1 0 0
Cutting, the acre - - - -	0 5 0	—	
Poling, by the day - - - -	0 10 0	—	— — —
Sharping old poles, ditto - - -	0 2 0	—	— — —
Summer-hoeing, per acre - - -	0 5 0	—	
Picking by the basket, of 5 bushels - - -	0 0 7	—	0 2 0
Drying, per week, with a quart of strong beer the day - -	1 1 0	—	— — —
Thatching, the 100 square feet - -	0 3 0	—	0 3 6
Carpenters, the day; and 4d. allowance for beer - -	0 2 4	—	0 2 6
Bricklayer, ditto; with like allowance - -	0 2 6	—	0 2 8

[1] General View of the Agriculture of the County of Kent. 162.

December, 1795.

LANCASHIRE.

BURY.

THE extent of the townſhip of Bury is eſtimated at 3½ miles in length, by 1 mile in breadth. 325 houſes pay the window tax : the number exempted is, probably, greater, but could not be aſcertained. The inhabitants are employed in the cloth and in the cotton manufacture ; but, principally, in the latter, which is here carried on very extenſively in moſt of its branches.

There are in this townſhip, 1 Preſbyterian congregation, 1 Methodiſt ditto, and 1 Independent ditto.

The prices of proviſions are : beef, from 3½d. to 5d. the pound ; mutton, 5d. ; veal, from 5d. to 6d ; pork, 5d. ; bacon, 8d. ; freſh butter, 1s.; ſalt butter, from 8d. to 10d. ; potatoes, 6s. 6d. for 253 lb. ; ſkim-milk, 1½d. the quart ; new milk, 3d. the quart.

Manufacturers and other labourers are better paid here than at Mancheſter. 16s. a week are conſidered as moderate earnings. The wages in the woollen are much lower than in the cotton manufacture. Women, by ſpinning wool, do not earn more than 3s. or 4s. a week : common labourers receive from 2s. to 2s. 6d. a day ; common mechanics, from 2s. 6d. to 3s. a day [1].

Theſe

---

[1] It appears from the following account, which is taken from the report drawn up for the conſideration of the Board of Agriculture, that the wages of labourers in Lancaſhire have almoſt doubled within 30 years.

	In the year 1761.			In the year 1791.		
	£	s.	d.	£	s	d.
Head man-ſervant, wages, yearly, - - -	6	10	0	9	9	0
Maid-ſervant - - - -	3	0	0	4	10	0
Maſons and carpenters, the day -	0	1	2	0	2	2
Labourer's wages - - -	0	0	10	0	1	8

There are 29 ale-houfes in the township of Bury; and 9 Friendly Societies of men, and one of women. The former have all complied with the late Act : the number of members in the clubs varies from 50 to 200 : the average number is about 100 in each. A Friendly Society of women was fet on foot two months ago, and, as yet, confifts only of 35 members. They intend to apply to the next Quarter Seffions to have their rules confirmed. The Society is governed by a mafter, 2 ftewards, and 2 affiftants to the ftewards, who are to be chofen annually, by the members, from the hufbands or fathers of the women who are members : their duty is to collect the fubfcriptions, to make difburfements according to the rules, to vifit the fick, to endeavour to keep good order at the meetings, and in fhort to have the management of the whole concerns of the Society. The entrance money is 2s. 6d. to the fund, 4d. for articles, and 2d. to be fpent; the fubfcription to be paid at the meetings, (which are quarterly,) is 1s. 6d. to the box, and 2d. to be fpent. Every member of 2 years ftanding, on her lying-in, receives 10s. 6d. from the box, (paid on the firft notice of fuch an event,) and the farther fum of 1d. from each of the members, paid her at the next quarterly meeting after her delivery. This is all the relief allowed to a lying-in woman, during the firft month; but if her illnefs continues longer, fhe is entitled to the fame relief that is given to other fick, lame, or infirm members: and in cafe of death, thofe, who have the charge of her funeral, are entitled to the fame allowance from the Society, that is granted on the

	In the year 1761.			In the year 1791.		
	£.	s.	d.	£	s.	d.
Mowing, the acre -	0	3	0	0	5	0
Threfhing wheat, the fcore - -	0	5	0	0	7	6
Do barley and beans, the acre	0	2	6	0	4	0
Do oats, the acre - -	0	1	8	0	2	6
Tailor's wages, the day, and food -	0	0	6	0	1	2
Thatcher, the day - -	0	1	0	0	2	0
Butcher, for killing and cutting up a pig -	0	0	8	0	1	6
Do calf, and felling the carcafe - -	0	1	0	0	2	6
Butcher, for killing a cow, and felling the carcafe -	0	2	0	0	5	0
Price of a good cart horfe - -	10	0	0	25	0	0
Pair of men's fhoes - -	0	3	6 the fame perfon 0	7	0	
Set of horfe-fhoes - -	0	1	0	0	1	8

HOLT'S *General View of the Agriculture of the County of Lancafter.* 1804.

death

death of any other member. A member of two years ſtanding, rendered incapable of working at her daily calling, by ſickneſs, lameneſs,
or other infirmity, not occaſioned by an irregular courſe of life, is allowed
4s. weekly, during the firſt 3 months of her illneſs; 3s. a week for the
next 3 months; and 2s. a week during the remainder of her incapacity.
The allowance is to be paid by the ſtewards, who, by turns, viſit the ſick,
every week, if the place of reſidence is not more than 3 miles diſtant
from the club-room : but, if more than 3 miles off, the ſick perſon muſt ſend
once a month a certificate of her illneſs, ſigned by the miniſter and two of
her neighbours, in order to be entitled to the weekly allowance. Members, of two years ſtanding, are allowed 2 guineas on the death of a huſband, but cannot receive this allowance more than once : and upon a member's death, the perſons, who have the management of her funeral, are paid
2 guineas from the Society ; and, if ſhe has not received the allowance of
2 guineas on the death of her huſband, they are allowed 4 guineas for her
funeral, towards which every member is bound to contribute 6d. If the
ſtock, having once amounted to £ 20 ſhould be reduced to £ 10. the
quarterly payments are to be increaſed to 2s. ; and to continue at that
ſum, till the fund ſhall amount to £ 20. No perſon under 16 or above 35
years of age, can be admitted a member. The fines for diſorderly conduct
are from 2d. to 4d. In all caſes of diſpute reſpecting the articles, the determination of the officers is final.

The rent of land in the neighbourhood of this townſhip is from 15s.
to 90s. a ſtatute acre : the average is about 32s. an acre.

The land-tax in this townſhip is £ 61. 13s. and is collected at about
1¼d. in the pound on the net rental. Tithes are partly taken in kind, but
chiefly compounded for.

Farms are from £ 14. to £ 30. a year. The land-owners in theſe parts
find it advantageous to divide their farms into ſmall lots, to enable the labouring manufacturers to keep a cow or two. The land is principally in
graſs. There is no common in this townſhip.

The Poor are partly ſupported in the work-houſe, and partly at home.
37 perſons, (of whom 16 are children under 16 years of age, 3 young women, and the reſt old, and infirm,) are at preſent in the houſe. Six of the
boys are employed at a neighbouring cotton-printer's, and earn reſpectively,
3s.—2s. 6d.—2s.—2s—1s. 6d.—and 1s. 6d. a week. The earnings of
the

the other Paupers are very trifling. They are, chiefly, employed in the common work of the houfe. It is fituated on an open, airy, fpot, about a mile from the town. The beds are of flock; and are tolerably well provided with covering: there are 6 or 7 in each 100m; and upon the whole, the houfe feems kept neat, and clean. The diet is regulated according to the difcretion of the mafter: the following, however, is the moft ufual bill of fare:

	Breakfaft.	Dinner.	Supper.
Sunday,	Oat-meal pottage, or hafty-pudding, bread and beer.	Bread, broth, beef, potatoes, &c.	Hafty-pudding, as at breakfaft.
Monday,	Ditto.	Bread, butter, and potatoes.	Ditto.
Tuefday,	Ditto	Ditto.	Ditto.
Wednefday,	Ditto.	Ditto.	Ditto.
Thurfday,	Ditto.	As Sunday	Ditto.
Friday,	Ditto	As Monday.	Ditto.
Saturday,	Ditto	Ditto.	Ditto.

In the fummer, milk is eat with hafty-pudding: in winter, treacle is ufed inftead of milk. Bread and boiled milk are fometimes fubftituted for hafty-pudding.

The number of deaths in the houfe, in 1792, were 2; in 1793, 2; in 1794, 6; in 1795, 5.

Table of Baptifms, Burials, and Marriages, in the Parifh of BURY; *and of Poor's Rates in the Townfhip of* BURY.

Years.	Baptifms.	Burials.	Mar.	Net Rates £. s. d.			Total Expenditure. £. s. d.		
1770	—	—	—	644	12	10½	639	0	2
1771	—	—	—	566	9	6	522	4	7½
1772	—	—	—	491	5	8	543	5	1
1773	—	—	—	493	7	4	574	19	6
1774	—	—	—	650	14	3	676	14	2
1775	—	—	—	729	3	8	691	15	11
1776	—	—	—	691	6	7	670	9	0½
1777	—	—	—	577	5	1	566	7	11½
1778	—	—	—	658	4	9	620	3	4
1779	—	—	—	620	18	10	681	16	3

Years.		Baptifms.	Burials.	Mar.	Net Rates.			Total Expenditure.		
					£.	s.	d.	£.	s.	d.
1780		—	—	—	508	2	2	599	15	10
1781		—	—	—	627	15	10	604	14	8½
1782		—	—	—	610	1	3	555	15	4
1783		—	—	—	624	1	8	671	14	7
From July 1784 to July 1785		411	257	167	640	8	4	687	14	11
1785 — 1786		425	291	166	657	5	10	696	1	4
1786 — 1787		450	222	135	673	2	1	595	19	9
1787 — 1788		457	373	137	699	1	5	633	13	1
1788 — 1789		468	266	159	633	19	6	629	8	7
1789 — 1790		456	357	160	658	11	9	732	3	1
1790 — 1791		481	257	185	710	12	11	888	17	2
1791 — 1792		477	239	182	690	2	6	682	7	9
1792 — 1793		530	255	156	680	13	0	669	13	7
1793 — 1794		481	272	196	709	19	4	660	12	0
1794		—	—	—	960	4	0	—	—	—
1795		—	—	—	969	2	9	1056	8	9½

It fhould be obferved, that the baptifms and burials above inferted do not correctly fhew the progrefs of population in the townfhip of Bury. The parifh of Bury confifts of 5 townfhips, which infert their baptifms and burials, promifcuoufly, in the parifh regifter. The clergyman, who, with another gentleman, made an actual enumeration, about 6 or 7 years ago, fays, that, at that period, the town of Bury contained nearly 3700 inhabitants; the townfhip of Bury, 4500; and the whole 5 townfhips about 17,000. Since that time the population has much increafed. By an account taken in 1773, the number of houfes in Bury was found to be 463; of families, 464; and of inhabitants, 2090; or about 4½ perfons to a houfe. The excefs of baptifms above burials is eafily accounted for : many young married people, who are tempted by the demand for employment to fettle in and near the town, when they grew old, return to their native parifhes.

The Rate, in the years 1794, and 1795, was at 3s. in the pound, and is faid to be at half rental; but in feveral inftances, it does not appear to be laid on more than one third of the fair rental.

The following lift of out-poor, belonging to the townfhip of Bury, not refident

refident in the work-houfe, with the fums paid to each between 1 May 1793, and 1 May 1794, and account of other difburfements, are extracted from a Report publifhed by the parifh officers. It is much to be wifhed that fimilar ftatements may be publifhed annually.

A Lift of the Out-penfioners in the Townfhip of BURY.

	RELIEFS £ s. d	RENTS £ s. d		RELIEFS £ s d	RENTS £ s. d.
Afhworth, Betty	3 12 0	2 2 0	Brought over	91 9 2	31 6 0
Afhworth, James	3 16 0	1 11 6	Crompton, Ralph	3 12 0	
Afhworth, Ann	9 12 0	2 0 0	Davis, Samuel's wife (cafual,)	0 12 0	
Afhworth, Sarah and Ann	0 10 0		Duckworth, Deborah	0 11 0	
Afhworth, Samuel	1 4 0		Duckworth, William's wife	1 12 0	
Bucell, James		3 3 0	Diggle, John		0 19 6
Booth, John	0 11 0		Dawfon, Betty	0 16 0	
Blezard, Jane	0 14 0		Dawfon, John		2 10 0
Barlow, John	0 4 0		Davenport, Betty	3 6 0	2 12 0
Baterfby, Margaret	0 2 0		Eccles, Samuel	2 0 6	
Booth, Betty, widow	3 12 0		Fletcher, Richard's wife	4 18 0	
Booth, Betty, widow	2 0 6		Fitton, Ann	2 0 0	
Buckley, Betty, ditto	4 16 0		Fogg, Thomas	1 14 6	
Buckley, Alice, ditto	3 13 0	1 11 6	Gorton, James's wife	2 11 0	
Buckley, Ann, ditto	3 0 0		Greenhalgh, Jane	1 16 0	
Bucell, Richard, widow	4 6 0		Grant, John's wife	0 5 0	
Byrom, widow	6 0 0		Gorton, John	0 18 0	
Booth, John		1 10 0	Gregfon, Richard's wife	0 2 0	
Barlow, James	3 5 0	1 5 0	Hartley, Ann	3 18 0	1 5 0
Booth, Richard's wife	2 8 0	0 8 0	Hartley, Charles's child	5 8 0	
Bentley, Martha	2 13 10		Hartley, Cornelius	3 12 0	2 10 0
Barlow, John	3 0 0	2 15 0	Hall, Richard	0 3 0	
Buckley, Benjamin	1 2 5		Hind, Thomas		2 2 0
Bentley, John's wife	0 10 0		Horrox, Nathan	0 3 0	
Crompton, Betty	3 12 0		Holt, Alice	2 8 0	
Chadwick, widow	3 12 0		Hamer, James's wife	1 5 6	
Cheetham, James	1 16 0	1 10 0	Hopkin, Mary	4 16 0	
Chadwick, Jofeph	0 4 0		Hamer, Thomas's wife	0 6 0	0 5 •
Crompton, John's widow	1 6 0	3 0 0	Hardman, Ellen	4 16 0	
Chadwick, John	1 10 0		Heaton, Ralph's wife, jun	0 3 0	
Cheetham, Edward		2 0 0	Heywood, Mary	3 0 0	
Clegg, William	1 2 0		Hoyle, John	1 17 0	
Chadwick, Mary's children	6 6 0		Heywood, Jofiah	0 2 0	
Clayton, Alice, (cafual)	2 13 5		Howard, John	0 9 0	
Chadwick, Robert's widow	7 16 0	2 0 0	Heywood, John		3 3 0
Crompton, Ralph, hatter	0 16 0	3 3 0	Hickfon, Ann	0 9 0	
Cropper, Edmund		3 7 0	Howarth, Thomas	1 15 0	
Cropper, Job	0 4 0		Hollis, Mary	0 12 0	
Carried over	£91 9 2	31 6 0	Carried forward	£153 5 8	46 12 6

Holt,

	Reliefs. £ s d.	Rents. £ s d.		Reliefs. £ s d.	Rents. £ s d.
Brought forward	153 5 8	46 12 6	Brought over	254 13 0	74 4 0
Holt, Roger	0 8 8		Ratcliffe, Elizabeth	0 18 0	
Horrox, James's wife	2 11 0		Rothwell, Ann	1 4 0	·
Holt, James's wife	0 8 0		Rothwell, Margaret	1 8 0	
Hardman, Mary	1 16 6		Ryley, T.'s children	0 1 0	
Hatton, John, hatter	1 2 0		Scholfield, James	0 4 0	
Jones, John	1 17 0		Smethurst, Catharine	3 14 0	
Isherwood, George	0 7 0		Shaw, Betty	1 7 0	1 6 3
Jackson, Abraham	1 2 0	2 5 0	Shaw, John	1 18 10	1 11 6
Kay, widow	2 18 6		Scholfield, Jecho	2 8 0	
Kay, James	2 7 0	1 1 0	Smethurst, Betty	1 9 0	
Kay, John	1 10 0	1 11 6	Smith, Michael's widow	0 5 0	
Kenyon, Mary, widow	5 2 0	2 10 0	Scholfield, William	2 15 0	6 6 0
Kay, John's wife	8 15 0	0 15 9	Spencer, William	0 6 0	
Kay, John	2 1 0	1 6 3	Standering, Edmund	0 16 0	
Kay, Thomas	1 8 0		Shaw, Thomas		3 3 0
Kay, Ralph's wife	4 13 0		Taylor, Charles		3 10 0
Kay, Sarah	0 16 0		Taylor, Joseph	0 12 0	1 5 0
Kenyon, James	0 2 0		Taylor, Ann, widow	0 15 0	0 19 6
Leach, Mary		1 15 0	Thorpe, Zephaniah	3 12 0	2 7 6
Lomax, John	3 5 0	1 0 0	Thornley's widow	8 13 0	3 0 0
Lomax, Susannah	1 10 0	1 1 0	Tatterfall, Richard's wife	2 3 0	
Lomax, Thomas	8 1 0		Woolfenden, Mary	1 16 0	
Low, John's wife	3 12 0		Woolfenden, Alice	1 16 0	
Livsey, Peter	1 11 0	3 3 0	Wood, Susannah	3 2 0	
Livsey, James	2 5 0		Warburton, Esther	0 17 0	1 10 0
Leigh, Peter	0 3 6		Walmsley, Ann	3 9 0	
Linsey, John	0 3 0		Warburton, Samuel	2 8 10	3 0 0
Lomax, Samuel (casual,)	2 2 2		Wallwork, Samuel	1 13 0	
Maken, William's widow	4 8 6	1 11 6	Wood, Ellen	0 1 0	
Murry, William		2 12 6	Wardle, Cornelius's wife	0 10 0	
Meadowcroft, Robert	1 18 6		Walker, Esther	2 3 6	
Mills, John's wife	2 6 0		Wrigley, Rachel	2 16 0	
Morton, John	0 9 0		Wallwork, Mary	1 14 0	
Nuttall, John	2 8 0	2 10 0	Wood, James, hatter	1 3 0	
Nabb, Sarah	4 16 0		Wood, Richard, hatter	2 19 0	1 14 6
Nabb, James		3 3 0	Wild, James	1 3 0	2 0 0
Nuttall, James, miller	0 16 0		Whitworth, Wm. (casual,)	0 3 0	
Nuttall, widow	5 2 0		Yate, Thomas	5 4 0	1 10 0
Nuttall, widow	3 12 0		Yate, Martha	5 1 6	2 2 0
Nuttall, Robert's wife	0 1 0		Yate, James	0 8 0	
Nuttall, Joshua	1 18 0		Yate, Betty	0 2 0	
Ogden, John's son	3 9 0				
Pearson, Betty, widow	2 6 0	1 6 0	£ 327 11 8		109 9 3
Pickstones, Richard	6 0 0		Total - £ 447 0 11		
Carried over	£ 254 13 0	74 4 0			

Expen-

Expenditure for the Poor, from 1 May 1793, *to* 1 May 1794.

JONATHAN KENYON, Overseer, Dr.			
From May 1, 1793—to May 1, 1794			

	£.	s.	d.
In purse and uncollected leys at May 1793	185	14	4
First affeffment, 1s in the pound, is	318	5	11
Second ditto ditto ditto	323	2	6
Third ditto ditto ditto	320	15	10
By fundries, &c.	15	0	0

| | | | | £ 1162 | 18 | 7 |

CONTRA, *Cr.*

	£.	s.	d.	£.	s	d.
By meal and flour	35	17	3			
By milk and butter	39	15	9;			
By cheefe and treacle	11	10	11			
By beef, pork, and potatoes	28	5	5			
By coals, foap, and candles	24	11	7			
				140	0	11
By one year's out-penfioners, as per annexed lift				327	11	8
By difburfements for rents				109	9	3
By furgeon's bills and attendance				6	5	5
Paid feven militia-men's bounty				29	8	0
By journies, horfe-hire, and expences				8	18	0
Paid poftage of letters and paffes				7	5	3
Paid ringers, by order of the conftables				3	3	0
Paid to lunatic hofpital, for John Kay				20	14	9
Paid feven money warrants, (which are orders to pay money into the county ftock, and generally amount to about £ 100. a year)				135	14	10
Paid fubfcription to Manchefter Infirmary				5	5	0
By one year's cloathing in and out of the houfe				33	11	1
By fundries, &c.				15	8	8
Paid conftables wages, and joint charges				19	6	9
Paid funeral expences				4	8	1
By working materials, &c.				8	17	10
By governor's falary				17	8	0
By the ftanding overfeer's falary				30	0	0
In purfe and uncollected leys at May 1794				240	2	1
				£ 1162	18	7

115 out-poor, at prefent, receive relief.

December, 1795.

LAN-

LANCASTER.

THE townſhip of Lancaſter is eſtimated to contain a ſquare mile and a half in extent: it's population is ſuppoſed to amount to about 8000 ſouls: the number of houſes paying the window-tax may be computed at 612, as the townſhip furniſhed 9 ſeamen for the Navy, at the rate of 1 man for 68 rateable houſes: the number exempted could not be aſcertained; it probably exceeds the number of chargeable houſes. The occupations of the inhabitants are extremely various. Several perſons are employed in a ſail-cloth manufacture; a few in cotton-printing. Ship-building is carried on to a conſiderable extent. There are many artiſans and mechanics in the town. Various articles of upholſtery are made here, for cabinet-makers in London; a clear proof, notwithſtanding the great demand for labour in Lancaſhire, that ſuch kind of work can be performed cheaper here than in the metropolis.

Common labourers earn 2s. and 2s. 6d. a day; maſons, 3s.; common carpenters, 3s. The canal now cutting between Liverpool and Kendal, paſſes very near this town, and affords conſtant employment to all that are inclined to work.

The prices of proviſion are : beef, from 3½d. to 4½d. the pound ; mutton, from 4d. to 5d.; veal, from 4½d. to 5d. ; pork, 6d.; bacon, 8½d ; butter, 10d.; milk, 1d. the pint ; wheat, 4½ buſhels for 48s. 6d. ; barley, 4s. 6d. a buſhel; oats, 7½ buſhels for 20s.; potatoes, 1s. 8d. the buſhel ; coals, 1s. the cwt.; oatmeal, 6 lb. for 1s.

Farms in the neighbourhood are moſtly in graſs; and from £ 20. to £ 50. a year. The rent of land in this townſhip is from £ 2. to £ 6. the ſtatute acre. The land-tax is collected at about 1½d. in the pound on the net rental. The tithe of corn is taken in kind, and tithe of hay is compounded for at 5s. an acre. There are 2 or 300 acres of common, of which a ſmall part has been encloſed for the uſe of the work-houſe

There are 74 ale-houſes in the town.

4   The

The Poor are partly fupported in a work-houfe, and paitly at home. 57, (moftly old women and children,) are at prefent in the houfe, and are principally employed in picking cotton. One woman fpins filk; and one labouier is fent out to work: his weekly earnings, at prefent, amount to 12s.; and exceed what is eained by all the other Paupers in the houfe. Poor children are bound apprentices at 10 or 11 years old.

The following lift is piinted verbatim from an account, (the only one ever publifhed,) of the number of weekly out-penfioners in 1792:

No. of Family.	Names and Defciiptions.	£	s	d
1	Afhburner Ann, old woman - - -		1	0
1	Aitkin Rebecca, fingle woman - -		1	6
1	ArmerAnn, ditto - - - -		1	6
2	Atkinfon John and fon - - -		5	0
2	Afhton Peter and wife, old - - -		2	0
1	Airey, widow of Robeit - - -		1	0
1	Auftin Alice, fingle woman - - -		1	6
1	Addifon Betty, old- - - -		1	0
4	Burrow Betty, and 3 children - -		3	0
1	Blamer Ellin, baftard child - - -		1	0
1	Bailey Jane, a child - - - -		1	0
1	Beckett Ellin, widow - - - -		1	0
1	Batefon Sarah, baftard child - - -		1	0
2	Ball's two children - - - -		1	0
1	Batefon Catherine, baftard child - -		1	0
4	Baynes Nancy, and three children - -		2	0
1	Ball Sarah, wife of William - - -		2	0
1	Bamber Maiy, baftard child - - -		1	0
1	Batty Ann, widow - - - -		1	6
2	Baldeifton Mary and grand-child - -		1	0
1	Beck Sarah, old - - - -		2	0
1	Benfon Margaret, baftard child - -		1	0
3	Bland Elizabeth, two children - -		2	0
1	Bullan Sarah, a child - - -		1	0
1	Burrow Rebecca, old - - -		2	6
2	Butler Alice, children - - -		1	6

2 Bradley

No. of Family.	Names and Descriptions.	Weekly Relief. £ s. d.
2	Bradley John, lame, and wife	2 6
1	Bales Jane, old	1 0
1	Blacking Ann, ditto	1 0
4	Bland Molly and 3 children	3 0
3	Bell Nancy, widow, and 2 children	2 0
1	Beckett John, old	1 0
4	Bond Agnes and 3 children	3 6
1	Brockbank Betty, old	1 6
1	Blackburn John, old	1 6
1	Butler Mary, ditto	1 0
1	Baynes Ann, widow of Thomas	1 6
1	Birket Margaret, baftard child	1 0
3	Bulcock Elizabeth, two children	1 0
2	Clark John and wife	1 0
1	Clarkfon Elizabeth, widow	1 6
4	Cartmel Ann, three children	3 0
3	Cartmel Sarah, two children	2 0
1	Camm Ann, widow	1 0
2	Cartmel James, two children	2 0
1	Crofgill Betty, widow	1 6
2	Caton Thomas, two children	2 0
1	Chambers Margaret, old	2 0
1	Coats Betty's child	1 0
1	Coats Betty junior, baftard child	1 0
1	Cock Ifabel, widow	2 6
1	Corney Thomas, old	1 0
1	Clarkfon Molly, baftard child	1 0
2	Cawfon Richard and wife	2 0
1	Charnley Mary, baftard child	1 0
1	Davidfon Chriftopher, Hutton	1 0
1	Dawfon Hannah, baftard child	1 6
5	Dean Bryan and family	2 0
1	Ellot Betty, widow	1 0
1	Ethrington Mary, baftard child	1 0

1 Fair-

No. of Family.	Names and Defcriptions.	Weekly Relief. £. s. d.
1	Fairclough Alice, old	1 0
2	Fells, two orphans	1 6
1	Fenton Mary, old	1 0
1	Flemming Hannah, baftard child	1 0
1	Gardner Cornelius, old	1 0
1	Gardner Mary, old	1 0
1	Giles Grace, old	1 0
2	Giles Agnes, two baftard children	2 0
1	Gardner Alice, old	1 0
1	Holme Sarah, baftard child	1 0
1	Harling Mary, baftard child	0 8
1	Holme Ellin, old	1 0
1	Howfon Unice, ditto	1 6
1	Hull Elizabeth, ditto	2 0
1	Hunter Alice, baftard child	1 6
1	Higham Thomas, old	2 0
1	Hornby Peggy, baftard child	1 0
2	Hartley Ann and child	1 0
1	Hodgfon Molly, baftard child	1 0
3	Harrifon Ellin and two children	2 0
1	Hewetfon Alice, old	1 0
5	Holme William's wife and 4 children	3 6
1	Jackfon Alice, baftard child	1 0
2	Ifherwood Ellin, one child	1 0
3	Johnfon Nancy, two children	2 0
1	Jackfon Grace, baftard child	0 6
1	Jackfon Elizabeth, old	1 6
1	Kirkham Elizabeth, Liverpool	1 0
1	Lolly Ann, old	1 6
1	Ditto, for a child	1 0
1	Lord Betty, lame	1 0
1	Lamb Betty, a child	1 0
1	Larkin Alice, fon lame	2 0

No. of Family.	Names and Descriptions.	Weekly Relief. £. s. d.		
1	Mashiter Alice, single woman	-	-	1 0
1	Marchall Ann, bastard child	-	-	1 0
1	Mashiter Ann, wife of John	-	-	1 0
1	Mashiter Isabel, old	-	-	1 6
1	Mason Ann, bastard child	-	-	1 0
3	Mulvey Elizabeth, two children	-	-	1 0
2	Mackeral Thomas and wife	-	-	2 0
4	Maudsley Agnes, three children	-	-	2 6
1	Marshall Jane, old	-	-	1 0
1	Mason Jane, old	-	-	1 0
1	Nicholson Ann, bastard child	-	-	1 0
1	Nevill John, an orphan	-	-	2 0
4	Nutson John, widow, three children	-	-	3 0
5	Newsham Joseph and family	-	-	2 0
1	Oddey Ellin, old	-	-	1 0
1	Parkinson Edmund, lame	-	-	2 0
1	Parkinson Grace	-	-	1 0
1	Parkinson Margaret, old	-	-	1 0
3	Parkinson Jane, two children	-	-	1 0
1	Parkinson Catherine, widow	-	-	1 0
1	Parkinson Mary, ditto	-	-	1 0
1	Punder, widow, old	-	-	1 0
1	Parker Sarah, ditto	-	-	1 6
1	Parker Dolly, bastard child	-	-	1 0
1	Park Jane, ditto	-	-	1 0
2	Procter Richard and wife	-	-	2 0
2	Ralph Tamer and child	-	-	1 0
1	Robinson Alice, lame	-	-	1 6
1	Robinson Mary, blind	-	-	1 0
3	Richardson Ann, two children	-	-	1 6
1	Richardson Margaret, old	-	-	1 0
1	Ramsbotham Jane, Liverpool	-	-	1 6
5	Richmond Mary and 4 children	-	-	4 0

4

1 Ripley

No. of Family.	Names and Descriptions.	Weekly Relief. £. s. d.		
1	Ripley Peggy's child	– – –	1	0
3	Sill Susan, two children	– – –	2	0
1	Saul Jane, old	– – – –	1	0
4	Shaw Sarah and 3 children	– –	2	0
1	Smith Margaret, widow	– – –	2	0
1	Smith Mary, bastard child	– –	1	0
1	Speight Sarah, Liverpool	– – –	1	0
1	Stizaker Esther, Burnley	– – –	1	6
1	Stephenson Margaret's child	– –	1	0
1	Smith Mary, bastard child	– – –	1	0
2	Shires Mary, two bastard children	– –	2	0
2	Singleton Henry and wife	– – –	1	6
2	Stizaker Mary and child	– – –	1	0
1	Suttle Grace, old	– – –	1	0
1	Statters Betty, bastard child	– –	1	0
2	Singleton John and wife	– – –	1	6
1	Slater Jane, bastard child	– – –	1	0
3	Shaw Alice and 2 children	– – –	2	0
7	Speddy Robert, wife, and 5 children	– –	3	0
1	Turner Margaret, Ribchester	– – –	1	0
1	Taylor John, Lancaster	– – –	1	0
4	Taylor Mary, 3 children	– – –	2	6
2	Townley Sarah, two bastard children	– –	2	0
1	Tubman Jane, old	– – –	1	0
1	Turner Elizabeth, bastard child	– – –	0	8
1	Towers Mary, widow	– – –	1	0
1	Tristram John, old	– – –	4	0
2	Townley Thomas and wife	– – –	1	0
1	Thwaites Mary, old	– – –	1	6
1	Towers Mary, bastard child	– – –	1	0
1	Vickers Nancy, old	– – –	1	6
1	Woodhouse Betty, bastard child	– –	1	0
1	Walker Julian, old	– – –	2	0

1 Walmf-

No. of Family	Names and Descriptions.	Weekly Relief. £ s d
1	Walmsley Mary, ditto - - -	1 0
1	Ward Sarah, a bastard child - -	1 0
3	Witham Ann, two children - -	1 0
5	Wilson Ellin, four children - -	1 0
1	Wilson Margaret, old - - -	1 0
1	Woodburn Mary, old - - -	1 0
4	Warbrick Esther, three children - -	2 6
1	Winn Sarah, bastard child - -	1 0
1	Winder Jenny, ditto - - -	1 6
1	Wilkinson Lydia, ditto - - -	1 0
1	Witham Ellin, ditto - - -	1 0
1	Winder Ann, ditto - - -	1 0
1	Walker Margaret, infirm - - -	1 0
3	Winder Mary, two children - - -	1 6
1	Wright Jenny, old - - -	2 0
4	Walling Ann, 3 children - - -	3 0
1	Woodhouse Mary, bastard child - -	1 0
1	Wittingham Ann, bastard child - -	1 0
1	Williams Jane, ditto - - -	1 0
2	Worswick Alexander and wife, old - -	2 0
1	Woodburn Jane, bastard child - -	1 0
1	Wilson Charles, old - - -	1 6
5	Waller Williams, widow, and 4 children -	2 0
1	Yates Peggy, old - - - -	1 0

Total, 296 persons, paid weekly - £ 13 5 4

There are at present 158 names, or families, on the out-pension list: their weekly allowances amount to £11. About £30. a month are paid to casual poor, including militia-men's families, &c.

The work-house, which was built a few years ago, stands on an elevated healthy situation on the common, whereof about 13 or 14 acres
have

have been enclofed for the ufe of the Poor. In each room there are 2 beds, which are partly filled with chaff, and partly with ftraw : neatnefs and regularity are much attended to.   4 cows are generally kept, from which near £20. are annually made by fale of the butter ; none of which is ufed in the houfe, except for the fick, and the governor and governefs.   The average number of Poor in the houfe is from 55 to 60 : about 6 die annually out of the houfe, but no regifter is kept of deaths.   The building coft £2000 ; near £1500. of which were paid by a feparate Rate : £550. were paid out of the laft 6 years Poor's Rates.

About 120 lb of beef are ufed weekly in the work-houfe.

It is ftated in an old book, that in 1740 there were 10 perfons in the work-houfe, and that, in 1727, 20 perfons were relieved ; but it does not appear whether they were in, or out of, the houfe.

The bill of fare is occafionally altered by the mafter of the work-houfe : the following, however, is the moft ufual courfe of diet :

	Breakfaft		Dinner.		Supper.
Sunday,	Milk pottage.		Bread, broth, beef, and vegetables.	—	Milk pottage.
Monday,	Ditto.	—	Broth, bread, and hafhed meat.	—	Ditto.
Tuefday,	Ditto.	—	Same as Sunday.	—	Ditto.
Wednefday,	Ditto	—	Same as Monday.	—	Ditto.
Thurfday,	Ditto.	—	Same as Sunday	—	Ditto.
Friday,	Ditto.	—	Same as Monday.	—	Ditto.
Saturday,	Ditto.	—	A fort of hafh, made of the meat left unconfumed in the week, and butter milk.		Ditto.

The above is the general diet in fummer, and at other times while they have plenty of milk : when milk is fcarce, the Poor have 3 broth breakfafts, and 4 milk-pottage breakfafts, a week ; and hafty-pudding for fupper every night.   Oat-cake leavened is the common bread ufed in Lancafhire.   It is preferred to any other.   Very little cheefe is confumed in labourers' families.   Their breakfaft ufually confifts of milk pottage or hafty-pudding, which is here called water pottage : and dinner, of potatoes with a little butter, and falt : fifh, bacon, or butcher's meat are added, according to the feafon, and circumftances of the family.   Ironed clogs, which are much cheaper, more durable, and more wholefome, than fhoes, are very generally worn by labouring people.

In

In this townfhip there are 18 Friendly Societies, all which have had their rules confirmed by the Magiftrates: the following is an account of them :

1, The Good Intent Society, inftituted March 3, 1788 ; number of members 90 : expences in relieving the fick amounted laft year to £41. 1s. 6d. : no funeral.

2, Friendfhip and Unity Society, inftituted January 1, 1789 ; number of members 109 : expences in relieving the fick laft year amounted to £9. 1s. : no funeral.

3, Unity Society, inftituted February 4, 1789 ; members 90 : expences in relieving the fick laft year, including one funeral, amounted to £47. 16s.

4, Unanimous Society, inftituted January 1, 1789 ; members 70 : expences in relieving the fick laft year amounted to £5. 17s : no funeral.

5, Loyal Union Society, inftituted April 8, 1793 ; members, 60 : expences in relieving the fick laft year, £3. : no funeral.

6, Provident Society, inftituted January 21, 1794 ; members, 58 : no expences or funeral laft year.

7, Benevolent Society, inftituted March 22, 1767 ; members, 176 : expences laft year in relieving the fick, including 2 funerals, £53. 12s.

8, Friendly Society, inftituted November 6, 1777 ; members, 173 : expences laft year in relieving the fick, including 4 funerals, amounted to £108. 19s. 2d.

9, Union Society, inftituted March 4, 1782 ; members, 160 : expences laft year in relieving the fick, including 4 funerals, amounted to £81. 15s. 4½d.

10, Humane Society, inftituted June 2, 1783 ; members, 125 : expences laft year in relieving the fick, including 2 funerals, amounted to £66. 4s. 6d.

11, Amicable Society, inftituted Auguft 5, 1783 ; members, 119 : expences laft year in relieving the fick, £31. 16s. : no funeral.

12, Brotherly

12, Brotherly Society, inftituted December 6, 1784; members, 82 : expences laft year in relieving the fick, £13. 3s. : no funeral.

13, Samaritan Society, inftituted December 17, 1787; members, 224 : expences in relieving the fick laft year, £32. 1s. 2d : no funeral.

14, Female Benefit Benevolent Society, inftituted September 2, 1792 ; members, 50: expences in relieving the fick laft year, £2. 4s. 10½d.: no funeral.

15, Female Benefit Benevolent Society.

16, Female Amicable Society, inftituted June 4, 1792.

17, Female Sifterly Society, inftituted June 25, 1792.

18, Female Friendly Society, inftituted July 3d, 1792.

The following are the moft material of the rules of the Loyal Union Society : they appear to have been drawn up with great attention ; and are, in many refpects, extremely judicious. Moft of the Societies in this part of England are fenfible of the advantage refulting from regular forms, for declarations of members on admiffion, applications from the fick, and certificates of death, &c. : they are therefore printed at the end of the articles, for the information of the members. I have tranfcribed a few of the moft perfpicuous; and think they might be adopted, with great advantage, in the Friendly Societies in the South of England; perhaps too, it might be advifeable for Clubs to provide printed forms, (for the ufe of fick members, &c.) of fuch fhapes and dimenfions, that they might be regularly entered, and folded in the general accounts of the Society.

2, This Society fhall confift of one prefident, two ftewards, one clerk, two wardens, two treafurers, three auditors, and as many members as the Society fhall think proper.

That no perfon be admitted into this Society who is under the age of eighteen or above the age of thirty-fix years ; and if any perfon fhould gain admittance by concealing his age, he fhall be excluded ; and any member that is, or may hereafter become acquainted with fuch fraud, fhall immediately make it known to the officers, or pay a fine of five fhillings.

It is further agreed, that any perfon who is admitted into this So-

ciety,

ciety, being above the age of thirty-fix, fhall pay the fame entrance as others, and five fhillings for every year above thirty-fix, and in proportion for the odd parts of the year if it fhould fo happen, and fhall be fubject to the fame rules as the other members.

N. B No perfon fhall be admitted into this Society who is above forty years of age.

3, The officers, viz. the prefident, ftewards, clerk, wardens, treafurers, auditors, and committee, fhall be chofen as follows : the prefident, by a majority of the Society on a quarterly meeting ; the declining prefident to put up one member, and the declining ftewards, each, one, out of which three the Society by votes fhall elect one ; and he, who has the greateft number of votes, fhall ferve as prefident, or forfeit five fhillings, to continue in office fix months, and fhall not be elected again for the fpace of eighteen months after. If he choofes to pay the fine, the fecond in number of votes fhall ferve, or pay five fhillings ; and the third to be governed by the fame rule.

The wardens fhall ferve as they ftand on the lift of enrolment, or forfeit two fhillings and fixpence ; the declining wardens fhall ferve as ftewards, or forfeit five fhillings All committees fhall be chofen by the officers ; the prefident to choofe two, the ftewards each one, the clerk one, and the wardens each one. The treafurers fhall be chofen by a committee on the firft Monday in March. The auditors alfo fhall be chofen at the fame time, and in the following manner : the prefident to put up two, and the ftewards each two, out of which the Society, by votes, fhall elect three ; if any of thofe elected refufe to ferve, he fhall forfeit one fhilling ; and the next in number of votes fhall be fubject to the fame regulation. The clerk fhall be elected annually, on the firft Monday in March, by a majority of members then prefent.

4, The office and power of the prefident is to furnifh the room with all things neceffary, and not to bring any expence upon the Society that can be avoided. All emergency fhall be fettled by a committee on a month or quarterly night, and no bufinefs done but the whole Society to know of it the firft month night ; to fee that each officer does his duty, and, by the affiftance of the other officers, to keep the Society

o   in in good oider, demand filence, and fee the reckoning paid. And if any member applies for relief, he fhall within twenty four hours after fuch application, inform one or both of the ftewards, or forfeit one fhilling.

5, The office of the ftewaids is to receive the entrance-money of every new member, the Society's monthly collections and fines, command filence, pay the reckoning, and fine any member who behaves contrary to the rules of this Society; to vifit thofe members twice a week, who refide within the townfhips of Lancafter or Skerton, and have applied to the prefident for relief.

And that the piefident may be rightly infoimed of the fick member's fituation, the acting fteward, when he receives the money to pay the fick, fhall deliver to the prefident, a note figned by the fick member, (if able,) othei wife, by fome perfon in his prefence, fignifying, to the beft of his judgment, the fituation of the fick member, the date on which each vifit was made, or forfeit fixpence for each neglect. That all members under this defcription be paid their full dues every Friday from twelve o'clock till fix at night; that the acting fteward be fined two-pence for every hour he neglects payment paft thefe hours; which fhall be paid to the box, and given to the fick member. But if any fick member has neglected to pay his quarterly dues, the ftewards fhall deduct fuch arrears from his firft payment.

6, The office of the clerk is to keep the Society's accounts, and write their agreements, in the Society's books, and, in the courfe of the laft month of each quarter, fummon thofe members who refide within the townfhips of Lancafter or Skerton, whofe turn it is to ferve as wardens; and their reply at that time fhall be a final anfwer. If any fhould confent to feive, and neither appear at the time, nor fubftitute another to reprefent him in receiving the office, he fhall pay a fine of five fhillings. Should the clerk be abfent, and fail to appoint a proper perfon to do the bufinefs, within an hour after the club begins, he fhall forfeit two fhillings and fixpence. His falary fhall be paid him quarterly after the rate of four-pence for each member annually. If the clerk, by way of fubftitute, fhould bring any member's money, he fhall be fined one fhilling for each offence.

7, The office of the wardens is to obferve the rules of the Society, and impartially give every prefent member an equal fhare of liquor, and to the utmoft of their power fhall detect all members who mifbehave; and if either the wardens neglects to give in his name, the warden who was guilty of the neglect fhall pay the fame as the offender.

And, for the regulation of the club-room, a warden fhall be ftationed at either end, to ferve the members there with liquor, and notice their behaviour.

8, A committee fhall be chofen each quarter night, and to continue three months in office, or pay a fine of one fhilling each, who, together with the treafurers and officers, fhall have the management of all money bufinefs belonging this Society, which fhall be entirely confined to the treafurers, and they fhall be allowed reafonable expences, each three penny-worth of liquor, and fhall, if required, give fecurity according to the ftatute as the committee fhall direct.

9, In the courfe of the firft month of each quarter, the auditors fhall examine the Society's accounts, and fhall on the quarter night report to the Society in what ftate they were found.

10, If the prefident and ftewards, in the courfe of their bufinefs, find any thing difficult, a committee may be chofen agreeable to the articles, who together with the officers fhall determine fuch matters, if the fine be ten fhillings or under; but if it exceeds that, or any thing that immediately tends to exclufion, they fhall have it in their power to refer it to a quarter night.

If any party thinks himfelf injured, he may apply for redrefs on the next quarter night; but if the decifion of the committee be then confirmed, the party fo convicted fhall pay double the award.

13, Any perfon offering to become a member of this Society, fhall appear at the club-room on a month night, and depofit one fhilling; on the month night following, a committee fhall be chofen to examine him; if he be rejected, his fhilling fhall be returned him; but, if admitted, he fhall pay two fhillings and fix-pence for entrance, fix-pence for an article, two-pence for the reckoning, and fix-pence for every ten pounds the box is worth at his admiffion.

14, Any perfon following a pernicious bufinefs fhall not be admitted into this

this Society; or any in actual service in the army, navy, or militia; and all shall be excluded who shall hereafter enter into the army, navy, or militia, who are subject to be reinstated, and, if found in body and health when they demand their reinstatement, they shall again become members, if they make their demand within three months after their discharge.

15, —It is further agreed, that if any member shall go to sea, he shall forfeit all claim upon the box until he returns, when, if found in body and in good health, he shall become a member as before; or if he should stay at the West Indies, or at any part beyond the seas, and should follow any business or occupation, and should fall sick or die, and proof be made to satisfy the Society that he did not get his sickness, or death, at sea, his heirs will be entitled to the same as in case of death at Lancaster.

16, There shall be a box provided with five locks, wherein shall be deposited all such things as may be thought necessary to be kept there; three locks shall be fixed on the out-side, all of different sorts, the keys of which shall be kept by the stewards and clerk; one inside key to be kept by the president, and the other by the person who gives security for the box. The box shall not be opened but in the presence of the stewards and clerk, or whom they may appoint; but if any officer should substitute another, who keeps a key, he shall be fined ten shillings and six-pence.

17, On each club night every member present shall pay one shilling and two pence to the box, and will be entitled to two penny-worth of liquor.

18, Any member residing within the townships of Lancaster or Skerton, having paid his dues to the box for the space of eighteen months, and becoming afflicted with any disorder, he shall send a note to the president drawn in the form prescribed, and he will then be entitled to ten shillings per week from the time he declares on the box till the time he declares off, providing such indisposition continues no longer than ten months; but, if it should, he will then be entitled to four shillings per week, by making quarterly, (if required,) a declaration appointed for that purpose; and he will be allowed to follow

S s 2
any

any lawful employment for the fupport of himfelf and family till recovered from the infirmity that he labours under.

20, Any member refiding out of the townfhips of Lancafter or Skerton, having paid his dues to the box for the fpace of twenty months, and becoming afflicted with any diforder, he fhall fend a certificate, figned by a minifter, churchwarden, or a juftice of the peace, and alfo by a phyfician, furgeon, or an apothecary, if any attend him, declaring to the beft of his knowledge the fick member's complaint; and if this Society have a communication with another, at or near the place where the fick member refides, they fhall immediately write, requefting them to vifit, and pay him, according to the articles of this Society; but if this Society have no fuch communication convenient, his money fhall be paid to his order. Any member receiving relief from the box, more than one month, fhall fend a certificate, figned as above, or it will be rejected. If he dies, his heirs fhall be entitled to the fame as the heirs of thofe who die at Lancafter. Any member, defrauding or attempting to defraud the Society by a falfe certificate, fhall be excluded.

21, When any member dies within the townfhips of Lancafter or Skerton, who has paid his dues to the box for the fpace of twenty months, the fum of ten pounds fhall be paid to his widow, if he left one; if fingle, to be paid to whom he has ordered by his laft will and teftament; if he left no wife, to be paid to his heir at law. The prefident, ftewards, clerk, wardens, and feven members, who fhall take it by rotation, fhall, if duly fummoned, attend the funeral, or forfeit one fhilling. Each to carry a black ftaff or rod, and the prefident to wear a black fcarf, and a pair of black gloves, or white as occafion requires, to meet at the houfe where the club is kept, and to be allowed each three penny-worth of liquor. Every member will be allowed four pounds at the death of his wife; and, in that cafe, he will only have fix pounds to difpofe of at his deceafe. It is alfo agreed, that every member fhall pay one fhilling extraordinary to the box on the firft quarterly night after the death of each member, or a fine of fix-pence for each neglect.

N. B. The benefits included in this article fhall in no wife extend
to

to any member who fhall, on any account or in any ftate of mind, commit felf-murder.

22, If any member fhould go to a parifh woik-houfe, his pay fhall not be with-held, fo long as he continues fick, or lame ; but the officers fhall difpofe of it, at their difcretion, in fuch a manner as they think moft proper for the recovery of his health fo long as he continues there; and although he does not pay his dues to the box, he fhall be. reinftated when he quits the fame; but if he fhould happen to die in a paiifh woik-houfe, he fhall not be entitled to any thing out of the box towards his funeral expences.

23, If any member be found at work, or feen intoxicated, or doth not come home by eight o'clock in winter evenings, and nine in fummer, during any part of the time he receives relief from the box, he fhall pay a fine of ten fhillings, or be excluded. And if any member commits wilful murder or felony, and be convicted by due courfe of law, he fhall be excluded.

24, If any member, not fiee of this Society, fhould be fick, lame, or other-wife difordered, fo as to render him incapable of working, he fhall, if he defires it, be excufed paying his contributions during fuch illnefs, by fending a written notice thereof to the prefident ; if he fhould recover, he is to pay his regular monthly payments to this Society, till he has paid twenty calendar months befides his entrance money, before he fhall be free : but if any member of this Society be fick, lame, &c. who has received the weekly allowance for ten fucceffive months without intermiffion, his weekly payments fhall be ieduced to four fhillings per week : if he fhould declare off the box before the expiration of ten months, with an intent to evade the reduction of the weekly allowance, not being recovered from the infirmity with which he was afflicted ; fuch member, on full proof thereof by the examination of a phyfician, furgeon, or other profeffional man, or otherwife, fhall be deemed an impoftor, and treated with accordingly, that is to fay, to be tiied before a committee, and their determination, to be final.

25, Every member is to pay to the box one fhilling and two-pence per month from the time of his admiffion, and, when fiee, fhall receive, if fick, lame, or otherwife difordered, the fum of ten fhillings per
week,

week, while the flock of this Society is above fifty pounds fterling;
but when it fhall be above one hundred and fifty, and under two
hundred and thirty, they fhall receive eleven fhillings per week, and
when above two hundred and fifty pounds, they fhall receive twelve
fhillings per week and no more. If at any time the flock of this Society fhould be reduced to fifty pounds fterling or under, to prevent
effectually the box from ever being fhut, every member not indifpofed, both in town and elfewhere, fhall contribute an extra two-pence
per week during the time the member fhall receive the benefit of
this Society, and to advance an extra penny for every member above;
and if a free member, or his wife, fhould die whilft the flock is fifty
pounds fterling or under, each member fhall contribute one fhilling
towards the funeral expences paid by the Society, to be paid into the
flock at two quarterly payments, fix-pence each quarter: the fum of
ten fhillings per week is by no confideration to be withheld from fuch
fick or lame members entitled to receive the fame, or the funeral
money ever to be difcontinued.

26, If any member of this Society fhould offer to enter into any other Society or club whatfoever, out of which relief is paid to the fick, he fhall
be excluded.

37, That at fome quarterly meeting a fuitable perfon fhall be elected
and appointed into the office of treafurer, or truftee, of and for this
Society, to be approved of by the faid Society, at fuch meeting; and
fuch treafurer or truftee fo elected and appointed, fhall, whenever
thereunto requefted by a majority of the faid Society, become bound
with two fufficient fureties for the juft and faithful execution of fuch
office or truft, to the fatisfaction of the faid Society; and fuch bond
fhall be given to the clerk of the peace of the town of Lancafter, in
manner directed by act of parliament for that purpofe; and the
landlord or occupier of the houfe where the box is kept, and the
fteward or ftewards, or other perfon or perfons, intrufted with
the box money, or other property of this Society, or any part thereof
befides what is committed to the care of the treafurer, fhall give fuch
fecurity for the fame to the treafurer as this Society fhall think fit and
neceffary.

Form

Form of a Note to be fent to the Prefident by a Member, when indifpofed, who refides within the Townfhips of Lancafter or Skerton.

" I ———— ———— do declare I am fo indifpofed as to render me incapable of following my bufinefs.

Yours,

Lancafter or Skerton. 17 ."

Form of a Certificate from an abfent Member, requefling Relief from the Society.

" I A. B. do declare, that I am fo afflicted with (here mention the complaint) that I am incapable of following my bufinefs.

We whofe names are hereunto fubfcribed believe the above to be true,
Minifter, Church-Warden, or Juftice.
Phyfician, Surgeon, Apothecary."

Form of a Certificate to be fent on the Death of a Member or his Wife.

" This is to certify, that ———— ———— died on the (here infert the date)

Witnefs, Minifter. Clerk."

Form of a Certificate to be fent at the Death of a Member, who died in any Part beyond the Seas.

" This is to certify, that ———— ———— died on the (here infert the date) and we do certify that he has not been at fea thefe laft two years.

Witnefs, Minifter, Juftice, or Governor of the Ifland."

The Prefident's Declaration.

" I A. B. do folemnly declare and fincerely promife, in the prefence of God and this Society, that I will act in all things for the fafety and wellbeing of this Society ; and, to the beft of my power, with the advice of my ftewards, clerk, and committee, will faithfully difcharge the truft repofed in me as prefident, according to the orders and rules of this Society, without favour or affection, malice or ill will to any, to the end of my continuance in the faid office ; and at the end thereof will give a juft and fair account,

2 and

and deliver up all that of right belongs to this Society, to my immediate fucceffors."

The Steward's Declaration.

" I W. N. do folemnly declare, and fincerely promife, in the prefence of God and this Society, that I will act in all things for the fafety and well-being of this Society ; and, to the beft of my power, by order of the prefi-dent and advice of my committee, will faithfully difcharge the truft repofed in me as fteward, according to the rules and orders of this Society, without favour or affection, malice or ill-will to any, to the end of my continuance in the faid office ; and then, will give a juft and fair account, and deliver up all, that of right belongs to this Society, to my immediate fucceffors."

The Warden's Declaration.

" I W. N. do folemnly declare, and fincerely promife, in the prefence of God and this Society, that according to my judgment I will act in all things for the good and well-being of this Society, and to the beft of my power difcover and detect every member who behaves contrary to the articles; and will impartially diftribute the liquor committed to my care."

The Clerk's Declaration.

" I W. N. do folemnly declare, and fincerely promife, in the prefence of God and this Society, that I will act in all things for the fafety and well-being of this Society, and that I will faithfully difcharge the truft repofed in me as clerk to this Society ; and to the beft of my knowledge I will not fuffer the Society to be wronged, but will forthwith let and make known the fame to the prefident, ftewards, and committee. God be my helper !"

A Declaration to be made by every Perfon on being admitted a Member of the Loyal Union Society.

1, " I W. N. do folemnly and fincerely declare, before God and this So-ciety, that I am not, to the beft of my knowledge, above the age of thirty-fix, nor under the age of eighteen years.

2, " That I am not joined with any other Society or Club of this kind.

3, " That

3, " That, to the beft of my knowledge, I am healthy, found in conftitu-
tution of body, and I have not any private diforder or ailment.

4, " That, to the beft of my power, I will act in all things for the good
and well-being of this Society ; and, by God's affiftance, will con-
form to the rules and orders of the fame whilft I continue a member
thereof : and, if I happen to be excluded, I will refign all my right to
all things belonging to the Society whatever.

" And I do declare, that I will not complain of ficknefs, fo as to be
troublefome to the box, without a juft caufe ; and if it fhould pleafe
God to vifit me with ficknefs or lamenefs, which obliges me to have
recourfe to the box for fupport, I will, to the beft of my judgment,
ufe the beft means poffible to regain my ftrength ; and, as foon as it
fhall pleafe God to give me my health and ftrength, fo as to become
capable of following my bufinefs or occupation, I will immediately
declare off the box."

*A Declaration to be made by Members who are rendered incapable of
getting a living.*

" I W. N. do folemnly and fincerely declare, before God and this Society,
that I am fo afflicted with [*Here mention the complaint.*] that I am not able
to gain four fhillings per week by all the honeft endeavours I am able to
make; and I do likewife declare, if it fhould pleafe God to return me my
former health and ftrength, I will make it known to the prefident and
ftewards, as foon as I can follow my trade or occupation, and will not be
on the box any longer."

The age of admiffion to this Society, is from 20 to 30. In the club
called the " Friendly Society," the age of admiffion is from 20 to 35.
This club is managed by a prefident, ftewards, wardens, and a clerk for
fettling their accounts. The entrance money varies in proportion to the
ftock, but cannot exceed 10s. 6d. The monthly payment to the box is 1s.
and 2d for the meeting. Members of 18 months ftanding, if fick, are
entitled to 1s. a day for the firft 12 months, and 6d. a day afterwards :
if a member, who has received 12 months pay, recovers fufficiently to
work for 18 months, he is allowed his 1s. a day if he falls fick again.
On the death of a married member, £ 3. are paid to his widow ; and on

the death of an unmarried member, £ 3. are paid to his legatee, or next of kin.

The Rules of moſt of the other Clubs for men, in Lancaſter, are very ſimilar to the above, except that, in the Samaritan Society, any member making a declaration, and producing a certificate ſigned by his employer, that, by infirmities of old age, he is not able to earn more than 6s. a week, is entitled to 2s 6d a week from the ſtock. The following Rule fixes a ſtandard, according to which a member's allowance is to be increaſed or diminiſhed.

12, Any member who ſhall have paid his dues for the ſpace of eighteen months, and who ſhall become ſick or lame, ſhall be entitled to relief as follows : If the Society's ſtock be under the ſum of thirty-five ſhillings per member, the ſick ſhall be paid each fourteen-pence per day ; but ſhould the Society's ſtock be increaſed to thirty-five ſhillings or upwards per member, then the ſick ſhall be paid fifteen-pence per day, and one penny per day more, for every additional five ſhillings per man, the Society's ſtock may amount to; which payment ſhall be made him weekly, from the day he ſhall declare himſelf ſick or lame, to the day he ſhall declare himſelf well; but ſhould his indiſpoſition continue above twelve months, without an intermiſſion of more than four weeks at one time, he ſhall then be reduced to half pay, and ſhall be allowed to earn what he can, provided it does not exceed the ſum he receives from the Society per week, and he ſhall make quarterly a declaration for that purpoſe, if required.

23, All members in the club-room ſhall behave decently and reſpectfully to each other, (and particularly to the preſident, ſtewards, and other officers, by addreſſing them by the title of their reſpective offices, and giving them the honour and reſpect due to their ſeveral ſtations,) or forfeit one penny.

The Female Benefit Benevolent Society are managed by a preſident, ſtewards, wardens, and committee, choſen from the members, much in the ſame manner as in the men's clubs. They pay a ſmall ſalary to a man for executing the office of clerk : he attends on club nights, and enters agreements, receipts, and diſburſements, in their books. They meet once a a month, pay 9d. to the box, and ſpend 1d. in liquor. No member

is

is entitled to an allowance during the time of pregnancy, or in child-bed ; but if, in confequence of lying-in, fhe is incapable of working, fhe is allowed, from the end of two months after her delivery, 5s a week, or 8½d. a day, provided her indifpofition continues no longer than 12 months. On the death of a member, who has paid her dues to the box for the fpace of 18 months, £ 5 are paid to her hufband, if living ; but if he dies firft, £ 2. are paid to his widow, and fhe is entitled to difpofe of £ 3. by will. From the difficulty of afcertaining whether an indifpofition may arife merely from pregnancy, no perfon can claim any allowance till fhe can convince the Society what her diforder is ; in which cafe, fhe is entitled to 5s. a week, during her illnefs ; but if it continues above 12 months, the allowance is reduced to 2s. 6d. If a member marries, fhe muft give notice of her nuptials within a month, in order that her proper name may be regiftered on the Society's books. An unmarried woman, having a child, is not entitled to an allowance during any illnefs arifing from pregnancy ; and for a fecond offence, of this nature, fhe is excluded. If a member goes to a parifh work-houfe, fhe forfeits all claim to the box during her continuance there, but may be re-inftated when fhe quits it, on paying up her arrears to the time fhe entered the work-houfe. If fhe dies there, the fum of £ 5. is paid to her heir-at-law, or to whomfoever fhe may appoint. The age of admiffion is from 18 to 36, in all the female clubs in Lancafter.

The Female Sifterly Society is alfo governed by a female prefident, ftewards, wardens, and committee : a man likewife officiates for them as clerk, upon an annual falary of 3d. from each member : the monthly payment is 9d. The allowance to fick members, in the cafes above-mentioned, is 6s. a week, for a twelve-month ; and, after that period, 2s. 6d. a week, with a permiffion to work, provided the earnings do not exceed 2s. 6d. a week. The allowances on deaths are nearly the fame with thofe in the firft-mentioned Female Society. On the deceafe of a member of 18 months ftanding, the officers and 7 other members, (taken by rotation,) are bound to attend the funeral, or to forfeit fixpence. Twelve hoods, (fix of white muflin, and fix of black filk,) and thirteen pair of gloves, belonging to the Society, are worn by the members who attend.

Ia

In the Female Friendly Society, the monthly payment is 1s., and the weekly allowance, in cafes of ficknefs, 7s.; the payment, on the death of a member, £ 8.; on the death of a member's hufband, £ 5. to his widow, and £ 5. to her heirs. This Society has an annual feaft on the 7th of Auguft, towards which every member is allowed 1s. 3d. from the box. Every new member, befides paying 2s. 6d. entrance money, and 6d. for the articles, contributes 6d. for every £ 10 the box is worth. The falary of the man who officiates as clerk, is 4d. a year from each member, paid quarterly.

In the Female Amicable Society the monthly payment to the box is 8d. Neither in this, nor in the laft-mentioned Society, is any thing allowed for drinking on club-nights. The allowance for deaths, &c. are the fame as in the Female Benevolent Society. Each member is allowed 1s. 3d. from the box towards the annual feaft, on the 4th of June. The penalty for not addreffing the prefident, ftewards, and other officers, in the club-room, by the title of their refpective offices, and omitting to pay them the refpect due to their feveral ftations, is one penny.

The Female Benevolent Benefit Society is managed by a committee confifting of 11 perfons, namely, 2 auditors, (the hufbands of members,) the prefident, 2 ftewards, and 2 wardens, who are chofen quarterly, and are fimilar officers to thofe of the fame name in other Societies; and 4 members chofen by a majority of the whole Society, from 7 of the fenior members felected by the officers. All matters in difpute are fettled by 5 arbitrators, chofen by ballot, from the committee. The auditors receive a fmall falary, and infpect the Society's books once a quarter. A man, who officiates as clerk, is allowed 16s. a year, for entering agreements and certificates in the books, and attending the auditors, &c. The monthly fubfcription is 9d. but nothing is paid for liquor. Sick members, of 2 years ftanding, are allowed 5s. a week, and more in proportion to the amount of the ftock. The Society holds an annual feaft, on Eafter Monday, towards which, each member who attends, receives 9d. from the box: abfentees are fined 4d. The reft of the Rules are fimilar to thofe in the other Female Friendly Societies. Their printed regulations are all accompanied with forms for admiffions, declarations, and certificates.

Table

The following ſtatement of the Poor's Rates aſſeſſed, and total Expenditures, were obligingly communicated by the overſeer.

Years.	Poor's Rates.			Total Diſburſements.		
	£.	s.	d.	£.	s.	d.
1736	83	2	4	94	19	8
1739	94	15	8	117	11	0¾
1740	88	11	2	102	17	1
1741	144	13	7	176	11	9
1742	179	15	3	223	17	9
1743	174	17	11	189	13	3
1744	142	15	5	175	15	10¼
1745	146	2	7	153	9	2
1746	153	1	7	148	13	10
1747	103	17	7	159	10	10
1748	104	14	5	143	1	6
1749	132	17	5	190	6	8
1750	220	11	6	222	9	5
1751	155	18	3	223	6	11
1752	185	8	6	260	2	0
1753	234	5	7	220	1	0
1754	226	11	9	286	2	5
1756	246	4	9	310	16	6
1760	345	16	8	391	4	2
1765	428	16	1	499	5	8
1770	547	1	9	650	1	8
1771	644	1	2	733	3	4
1772	676	11	2	770	0	1
1773	681	14	5	772	2	0
1774	692	19	4	836	4	0
1775	746	0	1	861	14	1
1776	699	1	9	756	18	4
1777	662	14	4	645	17	3
1778	514	6	5	832	10	5
1779	703	0	10	783	12	0
1780	535	14	7	866	16	6
1781	728	17	3	900	17	1
1782	866	4	2	1052	10	0
1783	922	7	9½	1197	9	8
1784	1248	8	11	1474	12	0
1785	1148	16	11	1085	13	0¼
1786	—	—	—	1163	1	3
1787	986	13	10	1201	16	5
1788	1246	0	10	1798	0	10
1789	2065	14	8	1592	17	4
1790	1419	17	7	1483	17	3
1791	1439	11	1	1606	13	0
1792	1443	12	1	1801	11	1
1793	1449	0	3	1442	3	11
1794	1469	9	3½	1697	6	1
1795	1487	1	11	1645	13	9

In the expences of 1795 are included £ 219. 4s. 1d. paid for raifing 9 men for the navy.

The affeffments for the laft 6 years were at 3s. 4d. in the pound, at ½ rental on land, and ⅔ on houfes.

The ftanding overfeer's falary is - £ 50. a year.
Mafter and miftrefs of work-houfe d°. -   £ 25. a year, and board.
Doctor's falary - - - £ 10. a year.

Table of Baptifms, Burials, and Marriages.

Years.	BAPTISMS			BURIALS			MARRIAGES
	At the Church	At the Chapel	Total.	At the Church	At the Chapel	Total	
1776	208	33	241	234	16	250	83
1777	209	41	250	177	5	182	88
1778	208	32	240	152	6	158	82
1779	213	36	249	228	10	238	99
1780	183	41	224	256	14	270	101
1781	238	33	271	226	10	236	107
1782	207	42	249	184	10	194	114
1783	228	38	266	226	16	242	115
1784	237	30	267	175	7	282	114
1785	258	35	293	202	12	214	143
1786	254	29	283	201	13	214	134
1787	269	7	276	173	18	191	130
1788	254	21	275	245	20	265	118
1789	266	20	286	164	8	172	119
1790	256	17	273	194	8	202	105
1791	259	20	279	288	11	299	117
1792	256	18	274	170	10	180	144
1793	285	8	293	223	14	237	148
1794	309	7	316	228	8	236	136
1796	306	12	318	236	11	247	142

The Diffenters of various denominations in this town[1], keep regular re-gifters of their baptifms and burials; but the marriages at the parifh-church of Lancafter include thofe from feveral chapelries in the parifh, which is very extenfive. The great increafe of baptifms, for the laft three years, is owing to the influx of labourers to work at the canal now cutting in this neighbourhood.   *January*, 1796.

[1] There are, in Lancafter, 1 Quaker, 1 Methodift, and 2 Prefbyterian congregations, and one Catholic chapel.

LIVER-

LIVERPOOL.

THE parish of Liverpool contains, by admeasurement, 2102 acres. Mr. Simmons, the general overseer, took the number of houses and population in 1790, of which the following is an account:

Number of Front houses 6540, containing 39188 inhabitants.

Back houses	1608,	-	7955
Cellars	1728,	-	6780
In the work-house	-	-	1220
Charity school	-	-	300
Infirmary	-	-	150
Seamen's hospital	-	-	83
Alms-houses	-	-	126

Total - 55732

Houses inhabited, exclusive of cellars,   8148
Empty houses   -   -   -   717

Total number of houses   -   8865

Since that period, it is supposed that 300 or 400 houses have been built. Dr. Aikin mentions an enumeration having been made in 1773, the result of which is as follows :—

Inhabited houses	-	-	5928
Untenanted houses	-	-	412
Families	-	-	8002
Inhabitants	-	-	34407
Number of persons to a house			$5\frac{4}{5}$
Number to a family	-	-	$4\frac{1}{3}$ [1]

It appears from the subjoined bills of mortality, that 1397, the number of christenings in 1773, was to 34407 the number of the then existing inhabitants, as 1 to $24\frac{3}{4}$ nearly; and that 1109, the number of burials in

[1] Aikin's Descript of Manchester, 343.

1773, was to the number of inhabitants as 1 to 31. From thefe proportions, we are, in fome degree, enabled to calculate the population of Liverpool, at the two fucceeding periods of 1790, and 1794.

2244 chriftenings in 1790 × by 24¾ = 55539 inhabitants.
1763 burials   in 1790 × by 31   = 54653 inhabitants.
2527 chriftenings in 1794 × by 24¾ = 62544 inhabitants.
2009 burials   in 1794 × by 31   = 62279 inhabitants.

Thefe proportions tally very well with Mr. Simmons's enumeration,
and are, probably, near the truth.

75 feamen were raifed by the town of Liverpool, in purfuance of the
late Act for manning the Navy; fo that reckoning one man for 68 rateable houfes, (the proportion which has been obferved in moft parts of
England,) we may eftimate the number of houfes fubject to the window-
tax at 5100; and the number of houfes exempted at about 4000.
The number of inns and ale-houfes is 917; fo that every tenth houfe, at
leaft, is a public-houfe. The magiftrates, however, are certainly extremely attentive to this branch of police, and reduce the number of unneceffary
public-houfes, whenever a fair opportunity offers. It is faid that a few
years ago, there were 1500.

The fubjoined tables exhibit the growth of population in Liverpool;
the great progrefs of it's commerce; and the ftill more rapid increafe of
its Poor's Rates. It is, however, confoling to reflect, that, notwithftanding this apparent difproportion, the refources of wealth are more than ade-
quate to the calls of charity; and that the Poor of Liverpool, although
more numerous, and proportionably more expenfive than they were 30
years ago, are yet lefs burthenfome to the town, than when it's trade was
lefs flourifhing, and it's parochial expenditure more contracted.

It is hardly neceffary to add, that every branch of employment, connected with foreign commerce, is here carried on with great exertion, and
great fuccefs. The neighbourhood of Manchefter is, perhaps, more congenial to manufactures; but fome, very important ones, that are not peculiar to
a fea-port, may be found at Liverpool. The moft confiderable are, glafs-
houfes, falt-works, copperas-works, copper and iron-works, fugar-houfes,

ı   rafping

rafping and other mills, breweries, roperies, watch-movements, and ftocking manufactories.

The rent of land, in the neighbourhood of the town, is from £ 4. to
£ 6. the ftatute acre. The land-tax is very low, and is fuppofed to amount
to about 6d. in the pound on the net rental.

No correct information could be obtained relative to Friendly Societies
in Liverpool: their number is about 12 ; and the members, in each,
are from 80 to 100. In one of the Societies, the members meet once a
fortnight, fpend 3d. and pay 1s. into the box : members of 2 years ftanding are allowed, when fick, 15s. a week ; fuperannuated members, 8s. a
week during life. From £ 10. to £ 20. according to the time a man has
been a member, are paid, on his deceafe, to his widow, if there is one ;
or to his children ; or, in default of children, to his legal reprefentatives.
The Society is governed by a prefident and ftewards, with the affiftance of
a committee of four members ; bye-laws are made by a majority of the
whole body.

The Poor are partly maintained in the work-houfe, and partly relieved
at home. The work-houfe is well fituated, on a rifing ground, in a detached fituation ; and is, in many refpects, conftructed upon an eligible
plan. The old people, in particular, are provided with lodging, in a moft
judicious manner : each apartment confifts of three fmall rooms, in which
are 1 fire-place and 4 beds, and is inhabited by 8 or 10 perfons. Thefe habitations are furnifhed with beds, chairs, and other little articles of domeftic ufe, that the inmates may poffefs ; who, being thus detached from the
reft of the Poor, may confider themfelves as comfortably lodged as in a
fecluded cottage ; and thus enjoy, in fome degree, (even in a work-houfe,)
the comforts of a private fire-fide. The moft infirm live on the ground
floors : others are diftributed through two upper ftories. They all dine
together in a large room, which ferves occafionally for a chapel.

The children are, principally, employed in picking cotton, but are too
much crowded together : 70 or 80 work in a fmall room. About 50
girls are bound apprentices to a perfon who attends in the houfe, and employs them in fprigging muflin. The houfe receives a fmall weekly fum
for their work during their apprenticefhip. The fum is from 1s. to 2s. 6d.
a week, according to their proficiency in tambour-work. They are
bound for 3 years, and provided with victuals by the parifh. A few old

VOL. II. U u

men are employed in boat-building: tailors', and other trades, are carried on in the houfe. The women pick and fpin cotton, for houfhold ufe: linen, and moft other articles of domeftic confumption, are manufactured within. The following table, extracted verbatim from the treafurer's ftatement of accounts of the parifh of Liverpool for the year 1783, exhibits the various trades and occupations ufually carried on in the workhoufe.

State and Employment of People in the Work-houfe, 25th March 1794.

Governor - - - - - -	1
Matron and chamberlain - - -	2
Houfe fervants - - - - -	3
Hall and ftair-cleaners - - -	5
Keeper of Lock and fervants - - -	4
Two cooks and fix fervants - - - -	8
Two falters and 10 wafherwomen - -	12
Milk-miftrefs and porter - - -	2
Bread-cutter and doctor's affiftant - -	2
Miftrefs and kneaders of bread - - -	11
Nurfes and fervants for infants - -	6
Nurfes for lying in women, for fick, infirm, venereal, fever and lunatic wards - - -	14
Brewer, warehoufeman and affiftants - - -	4
Two carters, two fwine-herds - - -	4
One coal-man, ten labourers - - -	11
Bell-ringer, clerk and meffengers - -	5
Gardener and affiftant, ten pumpers - -	12
Keeper of Lock's family - - - -	6
Schoolmafters and miftreffes - - -	4
Book-keepers - - - - -	2
Barber and painter - - - -	2
Bricklayer, plaifterer and blockmaker - -	5
Flax-dreffer, leather-cutter, and glazier - -	3
Shoemakers - - - - -	9
Boys ditto - - - -	9
Weavers - - - - -	3
Boys ditto - - - -	4

Ropers and knotters   -   -   -   -   9
Coffin-makers, joiners, and boys   -   -   6
Boat-builders   -   -   -   -   4
Two fmiths and eighteen boys, making nails for fale
    and own ufe   -   -   -   -   -   20
Yeomen of the fmithies   -   -   -   2
Spinners of wool, thread, and linen   -   -   59
Knitters and feamftieffes   -   -   -   51
Four fawyers, feven tailors   -   -   11
Cotton-pickers   -   -   -   -   266
Ditto fpinners, &c.   -   -   -   -   42
Tambour-workers   -   -   -   -   45

            Total of working people   -   668

Matron's family   -   -   -   -   4
Turnkey   -   -   -   -   -   1
Working people   -   -   -   -   668
Lunatics, idiots, fick, lame, infirm, very old, and very
    young   -   -   -   -   -   524

In the houfe   -   -   -   -   -   1197

Average number from 21ft March 1793, to 21ft
    March 1794   -   -   -   -   1032
Ditto, 29th March 1792, to March 1793   -   -   826

Average increafe   -   -   -   -   206

9th, 10th, and 12th June 1794, on the parifh committee's examining
    the people in the houfe, there appeared as follows :

		Under	2 years				80
From	2	to	10	-	-	-	273
	10	to	20		-	-	113
	20	to	30		-	-	88
	30	to	40	-		-	122
	40	to	50	;	-	-	90

U u 2   Carried over   -   766

	Brought over	-	766.
From 50	to	60.	76
60	to	70	88
70	to	95	107

	1037
Governor, matron, and other officers and family	16
	1053
Decreafed fince 25th of March laft - -	144
	1197

The following lift fhews the number of Paupers in the houfe on the 25th of March, in each of the under-mentioned years:

Years.	Number in the Houfe.	Deaths.	Births.
1782	783		
1783	920		
1784	963		
1785	985		
1786	946		
1787	966		
1788	1018		
1789	1098		
1790	1164		
1791	909		
1792	1003	Deaths.	Births.
1793	885	230	—
1794	1197	240	182

The following has been the expençe of cloathing the in and out-poor for a few years:

	£.	s.	d.
1790 - - -	2442	12	1
1791 - - -	1948	2	8
1792 - - -	1746	16	$5\frac{1}{2}$
1793 - - -	1682	9	6
1794 - -	1844	15	$6\frac{1}{2}$

In

In the year 1790, the parifh owed, on feveral accounts, the fum of £11,709, befides a debt to the corporation of £4000. The greateft part, however, of thefe debts have been paid off; and, notwithftanding the average increafe of people in 1793 within the work-houfe, and ftill more without doors, the great advance in the price of the neceffaries of life, and the expence of feveral additional buildings, it appears from the treafurer's accounts, that a furplus of £4000. was expected at the clofe of the year 1794.

From the following comparifon of the houfe expences in 1792 and 1793, with thofe of the two preceding years 1790 and 1791, it is obvious, that the annual expence of a Pauper in the work-houfe does not exceed £7.; a fum, which may be deemed moderate, when compared with the heavy charges of fimilar eftablifhments in other parts of England.

1790.	£.	s.	d	1791.	£	s	d	Average £	s.	d.
Milk and butter, -	935	13	8	Ditto -	923	4	6	929	9	1
Coals - -	360	6	0	Ditto -	374	7	6	367	6	9
Further expences -	8726	14	4	Ditto -	6801	18	10 }			
Tradefmen unpaid } were paid in 1791				Do of this year, paid off in 1792 }	2936	8	3¼	9232	10	8½

1792	£.	s.	d.	1793.	£.	s.	d.	Average. £.	s.	d	Lefs per Ann. £.	s.	d.
Milk and butter,	398	19	3	Ditto -	479	9	11	439	4	7	490	4	6
Coals - - -	213	7	9	Ditto -	241	19	5¼	227	13	7¼	139	12	10¾
Farther expences	5128	6	5¼	Ditto -	5878	18	10½						
Tradefmen paid in 1793 }	1491	18	0	Ditto unpaid }	1530	0	0 }	7014	5	2	2218	5	6½

Houfe expences leffened in each year - - - £2848 2 11¼

	Ton.	C.	Q.	Lb.
Beef ufed in the houfe, from 6th June 1789, to 5th June 1790, was - - - - -	47	19	2	16
Pork, fame time - - - - -	4	10	2	3
	52	10	0	19
Beef ufed from 25th March 1791, to 25th March 1792,	29	0	1	6
Salt beef - - - - -	1	0	0	0
Pork, ditto - - - -	1	16	0	0
	31	16	1	6

Salaries

Salaries paid out of the Rates.   £.   s.   d.

	£.	s.	d.
To the treafurer and his fon -	280	0	0
Standing overfeer - - -	133	10	0
Another overfeer - - -	73	10	0
Mafter and matron - - -	80	0	0
5 tax-collectors, at £80. each - -	400	0	0
The officiating clergyman - -	22	0	0
Total - £989	989	0	0

Weekly Bill of Fare in the Work-houfe.

	Breakfaft.	Dinner.	Supper.
Monday,	Burgo and milk 1.	Milk pottage, and bread.	Milk pottage, and bread.
Tuefday,	Ditto.	Lobfcoufe 2.	Milk pottage, and bread.
Wednefday,	Ditto.	Broth, beef, and bread.	Broth, beef, and bread.
Thurfday,	Ditto.	Lobfcoufe.	Milk and bread.
Friday,	Ditto.	Milk pottage and bread.	Milk and bread.
Saturday,	Ditto.	Lobfcoufe	Milk pottage, and bread.
Sunday,	Ditto.	Broth, beef, and bread.	Broth, beef, and bread.

Diet ufed in Liverpool Work-houfe in one week.

		lbs.	d.	£.	s.	d.	£.	s.	d.
	Oatmeal - -	118	at 2½	1	4	7			
40	Loaves, houfhold bread, at 2s.	1040	—	4	0	0			
	Beef, 570 lbs. paupers—beef,								
	17 lbs. governor, &c. -	587	3	7	6	9			
	Ale and beer - -	142½	1	0	11	10½			
							13	3	2½
		1887½							
	Oatmeal - -	118	2½	1	4	7			
41	Loaves, houfhold bread, at 2s.	1066	—	4	2	0			
	Beef, governor, fick, &c. -	60	3	0	15	0			
99	Gallons fweet milk -	792	2¼	1	2	8¼			
61¼	Gallons butter ditto -	490	1⅓	0	6	2			
	Ale and beer - -	142½	1	0	11	10½			
							8	2	11¼
		2668½							

Carried over   -   £21   6   2¼

¹ Burgo is oatmeal hafty-pudding.
² Lobfcoufe is beef cut in fmall pieces, and boiled with potatoes.

Brought over - £ 21 6 2¼

		lbs.	d.	£.	s.	d.
	Oatmeal - -	118	2½	1	4	7
24	Loaves, houshold bread, at 2s.	624	—	2	8	0
	Beef, 102 lbs. for scouse— beef, 60 lbs. governor, sick, &c. - -	162	3	2	0	6
14	Measures potatoes for ditto	420	18	1	1	0
	Onions for ditto - -	20	1	0	1	8
64	Gallons sweet milk -	512	2¾	0	14	8
58½	Gallons butter ditto -	468	1⅓	0	6	6
	Ale and beer - -	142½	1	0	11	10½

                                                                  8 8 9½

2466½

		lbs.	d.	£.	s.	d.
	Oatmeal - -	118	2½	1	4	7
25	Loaves, houshold bread, at 2s.	650	—	2	10	0
	Beef, 566 lbs. paupers—beef, 27 lbs. governor, &c. -	593	3	7	8	3
16	Measures turnips - -	384	12	0	16	0
49¼	Gallons sweet milk - -	394	2¾	0	11	3
70¼	Gallons butter ditto -	562	1⅓	0	7	10
	Ale and beer - -	142½	1	0	11	10½

                                                                  13 9 9½

2843½

		lbs.	d.	£.	s.	d.
	Oatmeal - -	94	2½	0	19	7
25	Loaves, houshold bread, at 2s.	650	—	2	10	0
	Beef, 101 lbs. for scouse— beef, 57½ lbs. governor, sick, &c. - -	158½	3	1	19	7½
14	Measures potatoes for ditto	420	18	1	1	0
	Onions for ditto - -	20	1	0	1	8
66	Gallons sweet milk -	528	2¾	0	15	1½
69	Gallons butter ditto -	552	1⅓	0	7	8
	Ale and beer - -	142½	1	0	11	10½

                                                                  8 6 6½

2565

Carried over - £ 51 1 3¾

			Brought over	-			£ 51	11	3¾
		lbs.	*d.*	*£.*	*s*	*d.*			
	Oatmeal - -	160	2½	1	13	4			
46	Loaves, houſhold bread, at 2s.	1196	—	4	12	0			
	Beef, 43 lbs. governor, ſick, &c.—beef, 24 lbs. common	67	3	0	16	9			
	Molaſſes for pottage for dinner and ſupper - -	38	3½	0	11	1			
48½	Gallons ſweet milk -	388	2¾	0	11	1½			
93¼	Gallons butter ditto -	746	1⅓	0	10	4½			
	Ale and beer - -	142½	1	0	11	10½	9	6	6½
		2737½							
	Oatmeal - -	94	2½	0	19	7			
26	Loaves, houſhold bread, at 2s.	676	—	2	12	0			
	Beef, 101 lbs. for ſcouſe—Do. 60 lbs. governor, ſick, &c.	161	3	2	0	3			
	Do. 14 lbs. officers, &c. -	14	3	0	3	6			
14	Meaſures potatoes for ſcouſe	420	18	1	1	0			
	Onions for ditto, and uſed weekly - -	28	1	0	2	4			
	Molaſſes uſed weekly -	60	3½	0	17	6			
	Cheeſe ditto - -	12	3	0	3	0			
	Butter, ſugar, ditto -	—	0	1	5	0			
	Wine and ale for ſick ditto, extra - - -	—	—	1	13	6			
8	Meaſures potatoes, do. do. -	240	18	0	12	0			
107	Gallons ſweet milk -	856	2¾	1	4	6¼			
100	Gallons butter ditto -	800	1⅓	0	11	1½			
	Ale and beer - -	142½	1	0	11	10½	13	17	2¼
		3503½					£ 74	15	0½

Beſides the number of Poor in the work-houſe, (amounting at preſent to 982,) 900 families in the pariſh receive a weekly allowance. The number in each family is about 3 perſons; ſo that there are, altogether, 2700 out-penſioners. Their weekly allowances amount to £ 56. 9s. About 180 families of Sick and caſual Poor, receive, on an average, £ 9. or £ 10. a week. 19 militia-men's wives are allowed £ 2. 11s. a week. The pariſh-committee

committee have very judicioufly adopted a regulation of withholding relief from fuch Poor as keep dogs. The war has certainly much increafed
the Poor's Rates, as a confiderable number of the out-poor are the wives
or children of parifhioners, who have entered the navy or army.
Common labourers, in Liverpool, earn from 2s. to 2s. 6d. a day. Ship-
carpenters, from 2s. 6d. to 4s. : and other artificers in proportion.

*A Table of Chriftenings, Burials, and Marriages, from the earlieft date of
Regifters in LIVERPOOL.*

In the Year	Chriftened.	Buried.	Married.	In the Year	Chriftened.	Buried.	Married.	In the Year	Chriftened.	Buried.	Married.	In the Year	Chriftened.	Buried.	Married.
1660	3	0	0	1694	126	69	9	1728	355	429	79	1762	1077	1014	375
1661	22	5	0	1695	130	88	10	1729	335	536	91	1763	1057	849	559
1662	30	31	7	1696	120	96	20	1730	397	307	129	1764	1255	1102	472
1663	57	35	11	1697	150	97	23	1731	398	289	149	1765	1241	1169	495
1664	56	35	6	1698	114	80	14	1732	460	406	143	1766	1309	955	516
1665	75	62	15	1699	136	105	36	1733	407	346	132	1767	1305	1175	461
1666	69	37	10	1700	132	124	35	1734	457	347	117	1768	1329	967	465
1667	68	69	6	1701	168	146	47	1735	451	578	122	1769	1349	983	403
1668	53	42	5	1702	208	131	45	1736	472	435	116	1770	1347	1562	433
1669	62	58	2	1703	172	126	52	1737	495	479	131	1771	1470	951	465
1670	67	48	5	1704	224	140	55	1738	464	422	169	1772	1375	1103	497
1671	24	15	2	1705	243	149	73	1739	522	599	132	1773	1397	1109	500
1672	41	11	0	1706	209	147	47	1740	485	608	137	1774	1451	1166	539
1673	82	22	8	1707	201	117	39	1741	478	593	177	1775	1498	1352	572
1674	79	32	0	1708	239	167	52	1742	561	613	183	1776	1541	1113	541
1675	74	65	3	1709	243	209	41	1743	594	569	210	1777	1578	1186	481
1676	79	42	9	1710	258	211	40	1744	658	587	192	1778	1616	1511	474
1677	65	41	1	1711	273	171	71	1745	677	755	215	1779	1648	1489	526
1678	101	60	7	1712	304	169	46	1746	696	753	247	1780	1709	1544	606
1679	89	55	7	1713	304	315	62	1747	742	602	255	1781	1760	1383	607
1680	106	51	3	1714	346	247	57	1748	781	796	308	1782	1766	1687	580
1681	123	109	8	1715	363	304	58	1749	893	778	337	1783	1872	1696	800
1682	99	98	2	1716	334	222	73	1750	972	1075	290	1784	2068	1635	816
1683	82	75	3	1717	392	383	76	1751	923	617	258	1785	2007	1778	767
1684	100	61	5	1718	391	194	73	1752	917	763	319	1786	2143	1772	791
1685	98	131	6	1719	396	204	72	1753	984	936	365	1787	2267	1773	804
1686	140	134	11	1720	410	293	58	1754	907	643	238	1788	2332	1564	822
1687	113	95	5	1721	376	482	62	1755	918	681	277	1789	2366	1662	819
1688	119	91	7	1722	412	242	70	1756	910	878	296	1790	2244	1763	805
1689	171	262	13	1723	367	262	56	1757	936	833	312	1791	2491	2166	854
1690	116	158	10	1724	337	275	88	1758	862	885	346	1792	2606	1767	946
1691	141	92	11	1725	368	410	100	1759	1042	1015	363	1793	2500	1464	846
1692	110	101	12	1726	357	305	91	1760	986	599	408	1794	2527	2009	753
1693	133	134	7	1727	360	367	111	1761	1064	945	391	1795	2251	2394	799

PAROCHIAL REPORTS.

A General Bill of Mortality,

For the Town and Parish of Liverpool.

Comprising an Annual and a Monthly Table of the Births, Burials, and Marriages, as enumerated from the several Registers of the Parish Church of St. Peter, the Parochial Chapel of St Nicholas, St. George's, St. Thomas's, St. Paul's, St. Ann's, St. John's, Trinity, St. James's, and St. Stephen's Churches: including those likewise from the several Chapels of Dissenters, &c.

From the 25th of March 1795, to the 25th of March 1796.

ANNUAL TABLE.

	Births Males	Fem.	Total	Burials Males	Fem.	Total	Marriages
At St. Peter's,	156	140	296	171	186	357	229
St. Nicholas's,	510	525	1035	127	159	286	250
St. George's,	7	9	16	2	3	5	8
St. Thomas's	43	26	69	25	26	51	56
St. Paul's,	34	38	72	82	88	170	55
St. Ann's,	9	5	14	11	10	21	96
St. John's,	40	31	71	680	565	1245	40
Trinity,	21	16	37	11	11	22	31
St. Stephen's,	5	3	8	0	0	0	0
St. Catharine's,	0	0	0	0	0	0	0
St. James's,	86	46	132	72	105	177	33
Baptists, Byrom-street,	15	12	27	14	14	28	0
Ditto, Matthew-street,	0	0	0	0	0	0	0
Dissenters, Paradise-street,	22	11	33	0	0	0	0
Ditto, Benn's Garden,	13	19	32	0	0	0	0
Ditto, Toxteth Park,	8	6	14	7	9	16	0
Independents, Renshaw-street,	17	14	31	3	5	8	0
Methodists, Mount Pleasant,	22	19	41	0	0	0	0
Scotch Kirk, Oldham-street,	22	32	54	0	0	0	0
Roman Chapel, Lumber-street,	77	89	166	0	0	0	0
Ditto, Sir Thos. buildings,	13	20	33	0	0	0	0
Ditto, Seel-street,	33	30	63	0	0	0	0
Quakers' meeting, Hunter-str.	6	1	7	4	4	8	1
Total	1159	1092	2251	1209	1185	2394	799

MONTHLY TABLE.

	Births Males	Fem.	Total	Burials Males	Fem.	Total	Marriages
March	24	25	49	14	29	43	1
April	107	104	211	83	88	171	6
May	94	108	202	111	107	218	6
June	107	80	187	92	68	100	5
July	89	90	179	72	69	141	5
Aug.	107	105	212	98	63	161	6
Sept.	97	87	184	110	102	212	6
Oct.	88	90	178	116	123	239	8
Nov.	109	81	190	120	133	253	7
Dec.	94	63	157	128	140	274	8
Jan.	97	110	207	106	112	218	6
Feb.	84	90	174	93	82	175	7
March	62	59	121	66	63	129	2
Total	1159	1092	2251	1209	1185	2394	79

Decreased in Births, 276.
Increased in Burials, 385.
Increased in Marriages, 46.

Of the Number of Burials, in the above List, there have died

Under	2 Years	1074	Between 30 and 40	137	Between 80 and 90	37
Between	2 and 5	384	40 and 50	122	90 and 100	3
	5 and 10	134	50 and 60	111	Above 100	1.
	10 and 20	88	60 and 70	108		
	20 and 30	117	70 and 80	78	Total	2394

Tabl

Table of the Shipping employed in the Foreign Trade of Liverpool[1].

Years	British ships	Tons	Foreign ships	Tons	Total of shipping	Total of Tonnage
1709	——	13238	——	277	354	13515
1716	——	17118	——	977	389	18095
1723	——	17810	——	796	414	18606
1730	——	17834	——	730	426	18564
1737	——	17230	——	2691	418	19921
1744	——	19336	——	3068	414	22404
1751	555	30181	20	2521	575	32702
1758	621	37382	59	6786	680	44168
1763	637	53418	85	8972	722	62390
1772	938	74950	70	9842	1008	84792
1779	825	60969	142	18501	967	79470
3 yrs av ending with 1786	4070	125944	435	25403	4505	151347
3 yrs. av. ending with 1792	6058	218561	670	41819	6728	260380

There belonged to the Port of Liverpool,

in the year 1565   12 barks of   223 tons
in —— — 1709   84 ships of   5789
in —— — 1792   584 ships of   92098

The following table was, obligingly, furnished by the Treasurer and Governor of the work-house. It exhibits the Poor's Rate, annual collection, the produce of cotton weft to the work-house, the disbursements of the overseers to out-poor, and the house disbursements, during the last twenty-nine years.

[1] I am indebted for this table, (which is constructed on the average of the inward and outward shipping,) to Mr Chalmers's Estimate, Dedication, p. xi.;—to Dr. Aikin's Description of Manchester, p. 365 ;—and to Enfield's Liverpool, p. 67 I must, however, remark, that the three accounts do not perfectly agree with each other.

Years	Rate in the Pound		Money collected.			Cotton Weft, &c			Overseers.			House Disbursements		
	s.	d.	£.	s.	d.	£.	s.	d.	£.	s.	d.	£.	s.	d.
1767	—	—	2703	10	8	171	1	3	425	1	1	1968	6	2
1768	—	—	2867	3	0½	180	16	6	385	0	11	2655	12	0
1769	—	—	3431	0	0½	189	14	6	349	10	0	3565	19	6½
1770	3	2	6400	9	4¾	95	17	6	480	1	1	3256	9	4
1771	3	2	5877	10	1¼	285	10	8	363	9	0	2723	17	8¾
1772	3	2	6682	4	1½	172	12	0	460	11	1	2980	18	8¾
1773	3	2	6819	9	6	182	16	0	572	18	3	3469	4	4½
1774	3	2	6942	16	2½	338	1	5	410	18	7	3851	10	3
1775	3	10	8317	4	11	252	2	8	428	10	3	3514	18	0½
1776	—	—	8312	1	8½	213	11	5	495	12	11	3532	2	5½
1777	3	2	9130	1	2	274	17	3½	457	15	1	4378	18	4
1778	3	2	8653	10	4½	240	0	7	289	19	2	4489	15	5½
1779	3	2	8500	16	8½	394	0	7	339	4	0	4749	5	1½
1780	3	4	7957	17	5	579	13	7	411	5	0	4801	5	10
1781	3	8	8428	11	2	283	16	10	433	11	6	4499	13	3
1782	3	8	8374	15	2½	642	9	1	932	7	4	6841	9	0
1783	2	0	9256	6	10	451	12	1	744	7	1	7117	7	1
1784	2	0	9535	7	10	410	9	11	748	7	10	7653	1	3
1785	2	0	8692	5	7	516	5	6	812	3	3	7471	17	2
1786	—	—	10631	7	5	508	9	0	952	1	4	7041	9	3
1787	2	5	7316	14	11	495	17	6	1325	6	9	7408	9	4
1788	2	5	[1]473	0	0	271	16	0	2187	13	0	8528	14	3
1789	2	6	[1]865	9	2	449	9	0	2527	13	0	8800	19	8
1790	3	0	5612	9	7	274	3	0	3416	18	6	10127	14	0
1791	3	0	8272	2	9	103	5	0	2874	2	0	8304	10	10
1792	3	0	15791	11	10	67	10	4	2877	3	7	5831	4	10¾
1793	3	0	13647	8	8½	—	—	—	3075	9	1	5342	7	2½
1794	2	6	19658	17	2½	564	15	6	4010	1	0	7177	19	5½
1795	2	0	17442	13	1	337	0	5½	4562	19	9	5841	1	9

Ending March 25th 1795.

[1] The smallness of the collections mentioned for these two years was occasioned by the want of a confidential treasurer, and by the orders of the then managers to pay the money into a bank, from whence it was again drawn as the wants of the parish required; what those collections were, there are no means of ascertaining, but it is supposed they were not less than usual in such rates of assessment. The system, however, adopted by these Magistrates, was, luckily for the parish, given up; for, in the 2 or 3 years that it prevailed, a debt was contracted to the amount of near £ 12,000.; of which between 3000 and 4000l. still remain unpaid.

From

From the following account, (which is printed in the Report concerning the Slave Trade,) it appears that the inland navigation to and from Liverpool has kept pace with it's foreign trade.

On the Lancashire end of the Leeds canal, there are employed, between Liverpool and Wigan, 89 boats, of 35 to 40 tons burthen each; which brought to Liverpool, in the years

		1786,	1787,	1788,
Coals	tons	91249	98248	109202
Flags, flates, and mill-ftones	tons	3944	2561	3613
Merchandize	tons	347	393	405
Oak timber	feet	17403	17986	13589
Took back Merchandize	tons	3836	4610	4257
Lime-ftone, and bricks	tons	2245	2064	1429
Lime, and manure	tons	10213	11129	12224
Pine timber	feet	160766	193706	153006

Between Liverpool and the river Douglas,

36 boats brought Coals	tons	16724	22592	20706
Lime-ftone	tons	4589	6164	5921

The tonnage of the boats on the Sankey Canal, between Liverpool, Northwich, and Warrington, amounted to

tons	74289	98356	115828

Between Liverpool on the river Merfey, and Northwich and Winsford on the Weaver, 110 veffels are employed, in carrying timber, falt, coals, and other commodities, to the amount of 164,000 tons annually.

Between Liverpool and Manchefter, on the old navigation, are employed 25 boats of 55 tons each: they generally make 3 trips every two fpring tides; or, upon an average, allowing for delays from bad weather, 36 trips each in a year[1].

On the Duke of Bridgewater's canal, which communicates with the Staffordfhire canal, 42 boats, of 50 tons each, are employed. They make 3 trips to Liverpool every 14 days.

[1] Aikin's Defcript of Manchefter, p. 370.

December, 1795.

M A N-

MANCHESTER.

IN the great manufacturing town of Manchester, the preservation of parochial records has been almost wholly neglected ; and, of course, very little correct information, relative to the Poor, can be obtained. The following is the substance of various accounts from the parish officers, who seemed to be very willing to make every communication in their power. It should, however, be remarked, that Manchester is much divided into parties respecting the administration of parochial concerns ; and that strong charges of negligence and misconduct have been made against many of the persons vested with the management of the Poor. Many pamphlets have been published on both sides of the question ; but, whether the complaints of the associated Ley-payers[1], or the defence of the parish officers, will afford the public much useful information, relative to the actual state of the Poor in Manchester, or to the excellencies or defects of the system there adopted for their maintenance and relief, the little knowledge I have acquired on the subject does not enable me to determine.

		£.	s.	d.
In the year 1776 the Expences for the Poor in Manchester were -	according to the	3322	15	1
1783 the Poor's Rates - -	Returns made to Parliament	4741	12	2
1784 the Poor's Rates - -	in 1786.	5462	4	11
1785 the Poor's Rates - -		5721	17	4

	£.	s.	d.			
1789 to 1790 The Rate on land, and houses, at 3s. 8d. in the pound	5476	0	0			
The Rate, or Ley, as it is here called, on personalty	253	16	0			
				5729	16	0
1790 to 1791 The Rate at 5s. in the pound £7965	17	0				
Personalty - - 256	14	0				
				8222	11	0
1791 to 1792 The Rate at 5s. in the pound £8363	1	0				
Personalty - - 268	4	0				
				8631	5	0

[1] A *ley*, or *lay*, in Lancashire, signifies a tax : see p. 90.

1792

1792 to 1793 The Rate at 5s. in the pound and Perfonalty   £.   s   d.
         together   -   -   -   -   9191 18   0
1793 to 1794 The Rate at 5s. in the pound and Per-
         fonalty   -   -   - -   9250   0   0

The affeffments have been made upon a very ancient valuation, perhaps of 60 years ftanding; in fome inftances houfes were rated at a third, and in others at a fourth of the real rent: however in 1794 a new regulation took place, and it was found that a 3s. Rate upon houfes and land at ½ rental produced   -   -   -   -   £ 10,931   0   9
Perfonalty, (not including ftock in trade,)   -   728 17   0

                                  £ 11,659 17   9

A fecond Rate of 3s. was levied between Eafter 1794 and Eafter 1795, but a great proportion of each Rate ftill remains uncollected. In the latter Rate, the perfonalty was not attempted to be collected. The prefent annual expenditure on the Poor may therefore be ftated at near £ 20,000.

The Poor of Manchefter are partly maintained in a work-houfe, and partly at home. 319 perfons, principally old women and children, are at prefent in the houfe.

	Average Number in the Houfe.	Their Earnings.
		£. s. d.
From Eafter 1791 to Eafter 1792	200	224 12 2½
Eafter 1792 to Eafter 1793	250	204 18 9
Eafter 1793 to Feb. 1794	400	99 7 7

The Poor within are principally employed in winding yarn: particulars of their work and diet are not eafily attainable at prefent, as a malignant fever now rages with great violence in the houfe, and renders it unfafe to enter it. A detached houfe or apartment is much wanted for perfons infected with contagious diforders; and it is faid to be in contemplation to build one next year.

The following are the moft material of the Rules, lately publifhed, for the government of the houfe.

                                          Rules

Rules for the Governor and Matron.

1, No Pauper shall be received into the house without an order from one of the church-wardens or overseers.

2, The following books shall be accurately kept, according to the forms prescribed in each:

    No. 1. The admission and discharge book.

        2. A book of receipts and disbursements.

        3. Ditto ditto, abstracted under various heads.

        4. A weekly account of all the provision received into the house, and from whom received.

        5. A list of the In-poor, with their ages, &c.

        6. A ledger, Dr and Cr. for the house.

3, The relations and friends of Paupers shall not be permitted to visit them without an order as aforesaid.

4, No Pauper shall be placed in the wards without previous careful examination—clean washing—and (if the church-wardens and overseers think necessary) new cloathing—the old cloaths to be well cleansed and fumigated, and laid by against the Pauper's discharge (if such discharge is probable) to be then exchanged for the house cloaths.

5, That for the more effectually maintaining perfect order and good government in the house, if any person shall profanely curse or swear, or appear to be in liquor, he shall be immediately confined in the stocks, by order of the visiting committee or governor, for any time not exceeding four hours : or if any persons having permission to go out of the house, shall not return within the time allowed, or shall return drunk or disorderly, or shall be otherwise refractory or disobedient to the reasonable orders of the governor or matron ; or if they shall pretend sickness, or make any false excuse in order to avoid working ; or if they shall wilfully destroy or spoil any materials or implements ; or if they shall be guilty of dishonest practices, breach of trust, lewd, indecent, immoral or disorderly behaviour, or of any other mischief or transgression repugnant to the peace and well-being of the house, they shall be admonished or confined, according to the magnitude of their offences, at the discretion of the visiting committee or governor, and the case

o

be

be reported to the next weekly board, when the offender, upon conviction, shall be sentenced to suffer such corporal punishment, confinement, task-work, distinction of dress, abatement of diet, or loss of gratuity, as the board shall judge proper, agreeably to the powers vested in them by the act.

6, The doors of the house and court shall not be opened before six in the morning, nor after eight in the evening, from Lady-day to Michaelmas: From Michaelmas to Lady-day, opened at eight in the morning; shut, at six in the evening

7, An accurate list of each Pauper in the house shall be made every quarter; two, or more of the church-wardens and overseers being present.

8, All the beds shall be sheeted once a month, and in proper weather they shall be beaten and brushed in the open air.

9, The children's heads, hands, cloaths, and beds, shall be kept clean: clean linen shall be given to each Pauper every Saturday evening, and the foul linen received every Sunday morning. All the Poor shall be in bed by nine in the summer, and eight in the winter; at which hours, all fires and candles shall be put out, except in the sick-ward.

10, No tea, tobacco, or spirituous liquors shall be brought into the house, without an order from the surgeon, or weekly board.

11, Immediate notice of sickness shall be given to the surgeon, and his directions respecting the diet of the sick shall be strictly followed.

12, The men poor shall be shaved, at least, once a week: the children's hair cut, as often as necessary.

13, The linen and wearing apparel shall be made and mended by the Poor.

14, The coals shall be locked up, and the key intrusted to a proper person, who shall deliver out the same as the governor and matron shall direct.

15, No person filling any station in the house shall either directly or indirectly take any fee or gratuity from any tradesman dealing with the township, on pain of dismission: and any tradesman offering such fee or gratuity, shall be disqualified from serving the house in future. This rule shall be advertised twice every year, the first week in January, and first week in July, in the Manchester papers; as also a caution to the keepers of lodging-houses, not to take in and harbour single pregnant women who do not belong to the town; and offering a reward to any person giving information where such women are harboured and concealed.

16, The men and boys shall not enter the women's or girls' apartments: nor *vice versa*.

17, The governor, or matron, shall not on any occasion be absent at the same time, or go out of town without leave from the weekly board ; neither shall they, or any other officer or officers in the poor-house, encourage any person or persons to come or remain there, but on the business of the township.

18, The quantity of provisions shall be allotted according to the bill of fare agreed upon from time to time by the weekly board. The Poor shall breakfast, dine, and sup together in the dining-hall, except such only as are by age and infirmity rendered unable, or improper objects to attend in that place, of whom proper care must be taken in separate apartments.

19, The governor and matron shall take care that the larder, kitchen, back-kitchen, and other offices, together with the utensils and furniture thereof, be kept sweet, clean and decent : that the dining-hall, tables and seats be cleaned immediately after each meal, and the several wards or dormitories every morning before, or immediately after breakfast, when the windows thereof shall be thrown open, the doors locked, and the keys delivered to them ; and the strictest cleanliness and decency shall be observed in every part of the house.

20, The governor shall take care that grace be said before and after meat ; read, or cause to be read, prayers every morning before breakfast, and every evening before supper ; that every person in the house, not necessarily engaged elsewhere, be required to attend ; and that a list of absentees, if any, be laid before the next weekly board.

21, The Poor shall be called up by ring of bell, and set to such work as their several abilities will permit, from six o'clock in the morning to six in the evening, from the first of March to the middle of October ; and from seven in the morning till such hour at night as the directors may appoint, from the middle of October to the first of March ; being allowed half an hour at breakfast, and an hour at dinner. That nevertheless they shall not work on Sundays; Saturday afternoons from four o'clock;

o'clock ; Good Friday; Chriftmas-day and the two following days, and Monday and Tuefday in Eafter and Whitfun weeks. That in order to excite the Poor to induftry, fuch rewards and gratuities fhall be diftributed to the induftrious and fkilful, in proportion to the quantity and perfection of their work, as to the church-wardens and overfeers fhall feem reafonable. (*Manchefter Act*, § 39.)

22, On every Sunday morning and afternoon all the able Poor fhall attend divine fervice at the collegiate church, preceded by the governor, and after fervice fhall return in the fame order to the work-houfe.

23, The matron fhall deliver to the laundrefs an inventory of articles to be wafhed, by which the articles returned from wafhing fhall be compared, and the account laid before the weekly board.

24, The matron fhall take care that fuch girls as are of proper age be, by rotation, employed and inftructed, as much as may be, in cookery, houfewifery, wafhing, fcouring, and fuch other work as may beft qualify them for fervice.

25, An inventory and appraifement of all the fixtures, furniture, and working implements, fhall be laid before the weekly board once in each year, by the governor; in which fhall be particularly fpecified fuch new furniture and implements as have been purchafed within the year. And a clear ftate of the year's account fhall be then made out by him.

26, The governor and matron fhall fee that all the fervants, and perfons employed in the houfe, perform their duty in their refpective departments; and that thefe laws, rules and ordinances be carried into full effect.

The chaplain of the houfe fhall read prayers, and preach a fermon to the Poor at the time appointed by the weekly board ; adminifter the facrament, once a quarter; catechife the children and others, once a week ; vifit the fick ; fuperintend the fchoolmafters, and perform the other duties of his function.

An apothecary fhall be annually appointed, who fhall, by himfelf, or his approved deputy, duly attend and adminifter proper medicines to fuch fick Poor within the houfe as may be put under his care : he fhall remark what nurfes are wanted, and note their conduct; and fhall make a weekly report to the board of their names and cafes, in a book provided for that purpofe.

As the perfonal comfort of the Poor, the inftruction and morals of the younger part of them, their attention to labour, and the œconomical management of the houfe, depend much upon a conftant and vigilant infpection into its interior concerns, there fhall be always two or more overfeers appointed by written notice from the weekly board, as a vifiting committee, each to act a fortnight, and then to be fucceeded by others in rotation; but that no new overfeer may, from want of experience, be at a lofs how to execute the office of vifitor, at the end of every week one of them to go out, and another be affociated with the remaining vifitor appointed the week before, by whom he will be attended the week enfuing. The vifiting committee are daily, or as often as poffible, to attend the houfe, to fee that the Poor, particularly the fick, be taken care of, and regularly attended by the apothecary and nurfes; that all infectious perfons be removed to the apartments appointed for their reception; that the fchoolmafters and miftreffes do their duty; that the working Poor be diligent in their refpective employments; that the houfe be kept clean, the windows of the dormitories be kept open in the day-time, and the doors of thofe rooms be locked. That they compare the flour fent in with the famples; examine the bread, beer, and other provifions; enquire into the complaints and the offences of the Poor; and enter in a book kept for that purpofe, whatever obfervations ftrike them as material.

One or more fchoolmafters and miftreffes fhall be appointed, who fhall keep the children in good order, and inftruct them in reading and other ufeful branches; fuch as are not employed in the manufactory or work of the houfe, to be taught from eight to eleven in the morning, and from one to four in the afternoon; and fuch as are fo employed, at thofe hours when they can be beft fpared from their work.

I. The overlooker fhall keep the following books for the infpection of the weekly board:
    1. A lift of the perfons employed in the different branches.
    2. A weekly account of goods manufactured.
    3. Ditto of the amount of the labour.
    4. The winder's, warper's, and weaver's account.

II. Shall obferve the 5th rule, the 17th, the 21ft, and the 26th.

III. No goods manufactured or unmanufactured fhall be bought or fold,
                                            without

without the confent of two or more church-wardens, or affiftant overfeers.

IV. An inventory of all working implements, wrought and unwrought goods, fhall be made out once a year by the overlooker, and alfo a clear ftate of the year's accounts.

An overfeer, to be appointed by the weekly board, fhall attend one or more days in every week, to keep the accounts of the cloathing, and of the manufactory; which accounts fhall be laid before the weekly board, from the books provided for that purpofe.

Rules for the Poor in the Houfe.

1, That they obey the governor and matron in all their reafonable commands.

2, That they demean themfelves orderly and peaceably, with decency and cleanlinefs.

3, That they never drink to excefs.

4, That they be diligent at their work.

5, That they work from fix o'clock in the morning till fix at night, in fummer; and from feven o'clock in the morning till fuch hours in the evening as the directors fhall appoint, in the winter; except Saturday afternoons, from four o'clock; and on Good-Friday, Chriftmas-day, and the two days following; and Monday and Tuefday in the Eafter and Whitfun weeks, which are to be regarded as holidays.

6, That they do not pretend ficknefs, or other excufes, to avoid their work.

7, That they do no wilful damage, but execute their work to the beft of their abilities: fuch rewards and gratuities fhall be diftributed to the induftrious and fkilful, in proportion to the quantity and perfection of their work, as to the church-wardens and overfeers fhall feem reafonable. (*Manchefter Act*, § 39.)

8, That they regularly attend divine fervice on Sundays, and prayers before breakfaft and fupper every day.

9, That they go to breakfaft, to dinner, and to fupper, in the dining-hall, when fummoned by ring of bell.

10, That they be allowed half an hour at breakfaft, and an hour at dinner.

11, That

11, That no ftrong or fpirituous liquois be allowed in the houfe, except by oider of the phyficians or apothecary.

12, That they do not cuife, nor fwear, nor lie.

13, That they do not fteal, fell their provifions, or fell or pawn their cloathing, nor be guilty of any othei bieach of truft.

14, That they never go out during woiking houis, nor at any other time, without leave

15, That when permitted to go out, they do not ftay longer than the hour appointed.

Whoever fhall offend againft the above rules, will be punifhed, eithei by confinement in the ftocks, or in the dungeon, or elfewhere; or by diftinction of drefs, by abatement of diet, lofs of giatuity, or by fuch corporal or other punifhment as may be deteimined and adjudged by the weekly board of overfeeis, according to the powers vefted in them by the Act of Parliament.

Thefe rules fhall be read to the Poor in the houfe, by the governor, on the firft Monday in every month.

Manchefter is divided into 14 diftricts, in each of which there are from one to four overfeers; whofe bufinefs is to diftribute immediate relief to fuch perfons as require it; to collect information ielative to fingle women in a ftate of pregnancy; to vifit the Poor fiequently, and report the ftate of them to the weekly board, held at the poor-houfe. A full account of the number of out-poor, in all the diftricts, could not be obtained; but fome general idea of their number may be formed from a printed ftatement of the overfeers of the third diftrict, which is one of the moft populous. From thence it appears, that the number of perfons in the vaiious families relieved, between 14th May and 1ft October 1795, was 957; and that the fum diftributed amongft them amounted to £565. 9s. 3d. Three-fourths of the perfons in the lift are females. The weekly allowances to each are not ftated; but in the printed rules, drawn up by the church-wardens and overfeers in May 1794, it is obferved, as a fort of general direction to the diftrict overfeers, that in the moft extreme cafes of fick-nefs, and however numerous the family may be, the relief had not, for any one family, exceeded feven fhillings and fixpence a week, and a fmaller fum in proportion to the family. From the information of Mr.

4   Edgley,

Edgley, the general overfeer, it appears, that 1s. 6d. a week is the ufual out-pay to a grown perfon, and 1s a week to a child. Except in cafes of ficknefs, which demand immediate relief, the diftrict overfeers furnifh fuch claimants, as they think proper objects, with an order upon Mr. Edgley. He pays moft of the out-poor, and fays that the number of families receiving a weekly allowance is about 1190, and that the weekly difburfements, on their account, amount to about £150. About 150 of thefe families, however, belong to other parifhes, for which Manchefter is reimburfed, as well as for feveral militia families, 68 of which here receive parochial aid.

The ftagnation of bufinefs, fince the war, has induced many thoufand manufacturers to enter his Majefty's fervice: this, in a great meafure, accounts for the late increafe in the Poor's Rates, and the exceffive number of neceffitous females, who have no longer their hufbands here to maintain them.

The prefent treafurer, who has not been many months in office, has formed the following eftimate of the probable future expenditure for the Poor :

	Weekly Expence.					
	£.	s.	d.	£.	s.	d.
Baftardy and orphans	25	0	0			
Regular and cafual Poor	145	0	0			
Removals	6	0	0			
				176	0	0
Work-houfe Expences.						
Butcher's meat	10	0	0			
Potatoes and falt	3	0	0			
Malt	3	0	0			
Flour, meal, butter, and cheefe	25	0	0			
Milk	6	0	0			
Soap and candles	1	6	0			
Coals	3	4	0			
Groceries	3	10	0			
				55	0	0

Total weekly expence - £231 0 0

According to this calculation, the annual expenditure will amount to £12,012. exclufive of cloaths for the Poor in the work-houfe, repairs, &c. Thefe articles have not been calculated, as the treafurer is not yet in pof-
feffion

feffion of fufficient data to enable him to form an eftimate with any degree of accuracy.

Exclufive of the above charges, the following annual expences are defrayed fiom the Poor's Rate: they chiefly regaid the intereft of a confiderable debt, which has been incurred by the townfhip, upon mortgage, and by way of annuity.

			£.	s.	d.
Annuity	-	-	513	6	8
Mortgage	-	-	120	0	0
Salaries	-	-	353	0	0
Chief rent	-	-	100	0	0
Infurance	-	-	11	5	0

$£1097$ 11 8

The following particulars, copied from a printed account of the expenditure for the Poor in the year ending at Eafter 1785, appear to merit infeition, as the account is feldom to be met with, and affords fome infight into the general management of the Poor:

	£.	s.	d.
By late church-warden's balance of accounts -	500	19	2½

William Beynon's difburfements.	£.	s.	d.			
Cafh for weekly relief - -	664	12	9			
Cafual payments - -	163	8	2			
Rents - -	229	12	6			
Extra-payments - -	115	5	3			
Apprentices - -	6	10	0			
Cloathing - -	4	10	4			
Law charges - -	24	9	5			
Burials - -	16	13	11			
Salary - - -	45	0	0			
				1270	2	4

Thomas Bradbury's difburfements.						
Weekly relief - -	751	3	0			
Cafual payments - -	145	4	3			
Rents - - -	227	8	2			
Extra payments - -	75	10	8½			
Law charges - -	20	10	0			
Burials - - -	14	1	6			
Salary - - -	45	0	0			
				1278	17	7½

Carried over - $£3049$ 19 2

	£.	s.	d.
Brought over -	3049	19	2
Nurfing orphan children - - -	320	15	7
Nurfing baftard children - - -	576	6	11
Flour and meal - - - -	297	0	0
Butcher's meat - - - -	173	5	0½
Governefs; work-houfe bills - -	495	6	8½
Do. falary - - - -	36	1	0
Thomas Harper - - - -	5	0	0
Apothecary - - - -	54	12	0
Attorney's notes - - - -	92	6	4
Linen, woollen, hats, fhoes, and leather -	355	4	8
Malter - - - -	23	14	0
Stationary, including 1784 - -	16	9	8
Brick, fand, and lime - - -	7	5	2
Bricklayer - - - -	5	11	5
Pump - - - - -	1	3	4
Porterage - - - -	0	4	6
Releafing James Samuel from gaol -	1	4	0
Infurance - - - -	0	17	6
Conftable's difburfements - -	594	8	3
Widows - - - - -	5	0	0
Coffins - - - - -	59	2	0
Ironmonger - - - -	11	9	0
Glazier - - - -	2	0	0
Fanny Worthington and fureties - -	5	15	6
Infirmary - - - -	10	10	0
Coals - - - - -	44	17	0
Balance for next church-warden - -	462	12	6½

$$£6708 \quad 1 \quad 3½$$

From the lift of regular out-poor inferted in the above account, it appears that 530 families received, in weekly relief, in 1785, £1415. 15s. 9d.

The following ſtatement of expenditure for the Poor in the year ending at Eaſter 1793, is taken from the Report of the aſſociated Ley-Payers
in Mancheſter, publiſhed laſt year [1] :

	£	s.	d
By caſh paid at the work-houſe, viz			
For ſhoes	240	15	0
Meal and flour	228	0	6
Milk	148	11	10
Tea and groceries	90	11	9
Butcher's meat	367	4	1
Coals	169	9	0
Butter	27	0	6
Cheeſe	26	12	0
Snuff and tobacco	39	10	6
Stockings	12	1	0
Candles and ſoap	49	19	6
Huckſter	193	5	0
Malt	49	6	6
Potatoes	13	5	0
Drugs	12	13	0
Cloth	105	15	7
Leather	9	11	0
Warps	38	19	0
Yarn	1	1	0
Weft	23	4	11
Inſurance	3	15	0
Apothecary's ſalary	25	0	0
Mr Taylor's do governor	48	8	0
Sundries	201	12	6½

	£.	s	d.
	2125	12	2½
By caſh paid on baſtardy account	973	13	0
Do. orphans	692	17	6
Do conſtables	1080	4	5¼
[2] Do. S. Edgley, for caſual and regular Poor, &c.; his ſalary, law charges, &c.	2275	18	7
Do. ſubſcription to Infirmary	31	10	0
Do. do. Lying in-Hoſpital	5	5	0
Do. bills for coffins	61	13	6
Do. Jones, Barker, and Co. commiſſion and intereſt	95	10	6
Daniels	27	15	5
Do. ſundries, loſs on light gold, premium on bills, rents, &c.	57	5	4
Do Mr. Hallows on ſalary account	85	10	0
Do Mr. Wharmby, 1 year's ſalary (the collector)	70	0	0
Do. from Mr. Unite, charged in D. Locke's balance	17	0	0
	£7599	15	6

[1] P. v. vi.

[2] The following are the particulars of Mr. Edgley's general account, but do not ſtrictly agree
with the above ſtatement :

	£.	s.	d.
By caſh paid weekly for regular Poor	1373	12	8
By do. caſual payments	490	13	10
By do. extraordinary payments	277	4	4¼
By apprentice bonds	7	10	0
By dues	16	12	0
By law payments	112	7	0
By a year's ſalary	100	0	0
	£2377	19	10½

It is fcarcely neceffary to add, that every branch of bufinefs connected with the cotton manufacture, of which Manchefter is the centre, is carried on either in the town, or in the neighbourhood. The increafe of population, in confequence of the great extenfion of trade and manufacture, may, in fome degree, be eftimated from the following table of births, burials, and marriages, from the year 1580 to the prefent period:

Bill of Mortality for Manchefter.

Years.	Baptifms.	Burials.		Marriages.	Years.	Baptifms.	Burials.	Marriages
1580	206	158		50	1772	1127	904	427
1590	201	264		25	1773	1168	923	383
1600	210	141		72	1774	1245	958	422
1605	175	1078	Plague Year.	61	1775	1359	835	473
1610	275	172		63	1776	1241	1220	494
1620	297	284		96	1777	1513	864	577
1630	310	195		71	1778	1449	975	484
1640	303	297		86	1779	1464	1288	448
1645	143	1212	Plague Year	67	1780	1566	993	456
1650	144	182		35	1781	1591	1370	495
1660	162	135		37	1782	1678	984	567
1670	188	149		176	1783	1615	1496	682
1680	185	264		66	1784	1958	1175	843
1690	173	183		64	1785	1942	1734	893
1700	231	229		133	1786	2319	1282	872
1710	211	235		128	1787	2256	1761	903
1720	290	273		148	1788	2391	1637	968
1730	305	548		210	1789	2487	1788	920
1740	552	700		194	1790	2756	1940	1120
1750	740	902		279	1791	2960	2286	1302
1760	793	818		380	1792	2660	1605	1657
1770	1050	988		429	1793	2579	1491	1234
1771	1169	993		429	1794	2041	1241	1066[1]

[1] Aikin's Defcript. of Manchefter, 584

An enumeration of the inhabitants in the town, (which comprehends part of Manchefter and Salford townfhips,) was made in 1773, and produced the following refults[1] :

	MANCHESTER.	SALFORD.	Total
Inhabited houfes	3402	866	4268
Families	5317	1099	6416
Males	10548	2248	12796
Females	11933	2517	14450
Of both fexes	22481	4765	27246

Perfons to a houfe, $6\frac{1}{3}$: to a family, $4\frac{1}{4}$.

At Chriftmas 1788, there were in the townfhip of Manchefter, (a fmall part of which is detached from the town,) 5916 houfes, 8570 families, and 42821 perfons; in the townfhip of Salford, about 1260 houfes. The whole number of perfons, therefore, at that period, in the town of Manchefter, might be eftimated at near 50000 ; a very rapid increafe of numbers in 15 years. A ftill more aftonifhing increafe took place in the following years, which, though it cannot be accurately afcertained, I fhall endeavour to compute from the foregoing bill of mortality ; in which, however, it is probable that many baptifms and burials of Diffenters are omitted.

The number of births in Manchefter, in 1773, is to the number of inhabitants as 1 to $19\frac{1}{4}$; and the number of burials to the number of inhabitants as 1 to $24\frac{1}{3}$: if we therefore multiply 2960, the number of births in 1791, by $19\frac{1}{4}$, the population of Manchefter, (exclufive of Salford,) will be found to have increafed to 56980 perfons ; and to 55626, if 2286, the number of burials in 1791, be multiplied by $24\frac{1}{3}$ the proportion of burials in 1773.

The number of inhabitants in Salford[2] may be eftimated at 10000 and

---

[1] Aikin's Defcript. of Manchefter, 156.

[2] The Baptifms in Salford in

				Burials		Marriages	
1775	were	138		193		108	
1780		173		250		108	
1785		240		350		249	
1791		375		517		276	
1794		415		600		157	

upwards ;

upwards; fo that, upon the whole, it feems probable that the population of Manchefter, 3 years ago, exceeded that of Liverpool; but fince the commencement of the war, it has confiderably decreafed. Before the year 1793, it is fuppofed that 20000 perfons were employed in preparing warp and weft cotton.

In Manchefter, 3879 houfes pay the window-tax; and in Salford, 693 : total 4572. The number exempted in the two towns cannot be af-certained.

The prices of piovifions are: beef, fiom 3½d to 5d. the pound; mutton, 5d.; veal, from 5d. to 6d.; poik, 5d.; bacon, 8d.; frefh butter, 1s; falt butter, from 8d. to 10d.; wheat flour, 3s. 3d. for 12 lb; oatmeal floui, 1s 11d for 10lb.; potatoes, 6s. 6d. for 253 lb.; fkim milk, 1½d. the quart; new milk, 3d. the quait; coals, 6d. to 7d the cwt: houfe-rent is high here; 2 fmall 100ms let fiom £4 to £6. a year.

Wages vary much in the different branches of manufacture; and even in the fame employment, accoiding to the fkill and induftry of the workmen. From the accounts of well-informed perfons, I think the average weekly earnings of manufacturing laboureis in Manchefter, may be ftated at about 16s.; but it is to be obferved, that they rarely work on Mondays, and that many of them keep holiday, two or three days in the week. It muft, however, be confeffed, that at prefent, conftant and regular employment cannot be piocured by all who are inclined to work. The town would have fuffered much more feverely than it has done, by the ftagnation of bufinefs, had not the Navy and Army carried off thofe fuperfluous labourers, who, had they iemained in Manchefter without employment, muft have ultimately fallen on the parifh, and greatly increafed the heavy burthens already fuftained by the maintenance of their families.

Women and children are employed in winding cotton, reeling, ending and mending, cutting fuflian, picking cotton, managing the fpinning jennies, &c. Women earn from 6s. to 12s. a week: their clear weekly eainings may be ftated at 8s. Children, of 7 or 8 yeais old, can eain 2s. a week; of 9 or 10 yéars, 4s. a week; printers of cotton, fiom £1. 1s. to £2. a week; common laboureis, fiom 2s. to 2s. 6d a day.

The rent of land, in the neighbourhood of Manchefter, is about £4. an acre: the land-tax, in the townfhip, amounts to £877. which is about 1½d. in the pound on the net rental.

There

There are 238 ale-houfes in the townfhip of Manchefter: in the year 1787, there were 177: they may be confidered as few, in comparifon with the number of public-houfes in Iiverpool.

There are about 12 places of worfhip for different fects of Diffenters, confifting of Prefbyterians, Roman Catholics, Methodifts, Quakers, Calvinifts, and a congregation called the New Jerufalem.

The following is a ftatement of the earnings and expences of a dyer; an intelligent, honeft man; who, in the account he gave of himfelf, feemed defirous of communicating the truth.

He is 65 years of age, receives 13s a week, ftanding wages, befides being allowed a houfe, and firing His wife, befides taking care of the houfe, winds cotton, and earns about 3s. 6d. a week. Their whole annual earnings are £ 42. 18s.

	£.	s.	d.
Their expences are: Bread, 3s. 6d. a week, annually	9	2	0
Butcher's meat, 2s. 3d. a week - - -	5	17	0
Beer, about 6d. a week - - -	1	6	0
Cheefe, 8d. a week - - - -	1	14	8
Butter, 2s. a week - - - -	5	4	0
Milk, 4d. a week - - - -	0	17	4
Tea and fugar, 2s. 6d. a week - - -	6	10	0
Potatoes, and other vegetables, 1s. a week -	2	12	0
Soap, candles, and falt, annually, about - -	2	12	0
Cloaths, annually, about - - -	4	0	0

Total expences - £ 39 15 0

The man has no perfon, except his wife, to provide for at home; but has feveral children, and grand-children, who, although able to fupport themfelves, are frequently in want. They often partake of his meals, and folicit pecuniary affiftance from him, fo that he finds it impoffible to lay up any part of his earnings.

The following is a ftatement of a labourer's earnings and expences. He is carter to a gentleman in Manchefter, is 39 years old, has a wife aged 35, and 5 children; viz. a girl of 12 years, another of 9; a boy of 5, another of 3, and another of 5 months old. The 3 youngeft children cannot earn any thing.

	£.	s.	d.
The man has 12s. a week, conftant wages - -	31	4	0
The wife earns, by roving cotton, about 6d. a week -	1	6	0
The eldeft girl nurfes for a neighbour, and earns 2s. 6d. a week	6	10	0
The fecond girl earns, in the fame manner, 2s. a week -	5	4	0
Total earnings -	£ 44	4	0

The annual expences of the family are :

	£.	s.	d.
Houfe-rent, 2s. a week - - - -	5	4	0
Fuel, about 7d. a week - - - -	1	10	4
They have lately begun to ufe oatmeal bread, which cofts 5s. a week - - - - -	13	0	0
Butcher's meat, 1s. 6d. a week - - -	3	18	0
Potatoes, 1s. 6d. a week - - - -	3	18	0
Tea and fugar, 1s. 3d. a week - - -	3	5	0
Milk, 1s. 2d. a week - - - -	3	0	8
Cheefe, 1s. 6d. a week - - - -	3	18	0
Butter, 1s. a week - - - - -	2	12	0
Soap, candles, groceries, &c. annually - -	2	10	0
Cloaths, and other cafual expences, are eftimated annually at	5	0	0
Total expences -	£ 47	16	0
Total earnings -	44	4	0
Deficiency -	£ 3	12	0

Here appears to be a deficiency of £ 3. 12s. ; it muft, however, be obferved, that the man occafionally carries parcels for his mafter, to different
parts of the town, where he fometimes receives a little beer, or fome
other perquifite : he has alfo now and then a little beer at his mafter's
houfe. He has a good character, both for honefty and fobriety, and has
lived many years with the fame employer. He has one daughter, 15 years
old, out at fervice: the reft of his family board at home. He has loft
two children. *December*, 1795.

PRES-

PRESTON.

THE extent of this townſhip is about 4 ſquare miles: the population was taken in 1791, when the number of inhabitants was found to be 6490: it is ſuppoſed that now they amount to 7000. As 7 men were raiſed for the Navy, the number of aſſeſſed houſes may be eſtimated at 476. About two-thirds of the inhabitants are employed in ſpinning, weaving, printing cottons, muſlins, &c. The reſt are chiefly tradeſmen, common meehanics, and labourers. Several perſons of fortune reſide here. The Diſſenters are, a large Roman Catholic congregation, 1 Anabaptiſt ditto, 1 Methodiſt ditto, and 1 Preſbyterian ditto.

The prices of proviſions are: beef, 4½d. a lb.; mutton, 5d; veal, 4½d.; pork, 5d.; bacon, 9d; butter, 11d.; new milk, 2d. a quart; beſt flour, 3½ lb. for 1s.; houſhold bread, 4 lb. for 1s.; oatmeal, 240 lb. for 41s.; wheat, 3½ buſhels, Wincheſter meaſure, for 41s.; barley, from 15s. 6d. to 17s. for the ſame quantity; potatoes, 22d. a buſhel; oats, 3s 6d. a buſhel, Wincheſter meaſure.

A common labourer earns 2s. a day, ſometimes 2s. 6d; maſons and bricklayers, 3s. a day; carpenters have 15s. or 16s. a week; the wages in the cotton line are as high, at leaſt, as at Bury or Mancheſter.

There are 63 ale-houſes in this townſhip.

The rent of land is from £ 2. to £ 4. the ſtatute acre. Farms in this neighbourhood are from £ 15. to £ 50. a year; and conſiſt chiefly of graſs land. Tithes are taken partly in kind, and partly by compoſition. The amount of the land-tax is £ 202., and is collected at 2¾d. in the pound: in this townſhip there are 170 acres of common, Cheſhire meaſure[1].

There is a priſon or penitentiary houſe, upon Mr. Howard's plan, for the reform of criminals, at Preſton. Each priſoner has a daily allowance of one pound and a half of bread, a lump of butter, and one halfpenny-worth of potatoes. This allowance may be exchanged for tea and ſugar; but no ſpirituous liquors are permitted.

[1] One Cheſhire acre contains two acres and eighteen perches and a half of the ſtatute meaſure.

Table

Table of Baptisms, Burials, and Marriages.

Years.	Baptisms.	Burials.	Marriages.
1781	142	184	51
1782	149	250	78
1783	170	159	80
1784	139	266	81
1785	168	180	96
1786	206	214	97
1787	204	277	83
1788	220	189	73
1789	202	209	73
1790	197	179	72
1791	209	279	84
1792	224	282	77
1793	243	218	72
1794	223	———	91

On the subject of Poor's Rates, the parish officers either could not, or would not, furnish any satisfactory account. They say they settle their accounts quarterly, and do not preserve their old books. The few books that were visible, appeared to be kept in a very confused manner. The subjoined statements of parochial expenditure, from January 1, 1794, to July 1, 1795, were furnished by the vestry-clerk; and the Poor's Rates of 1793, 1794, and 1795, supplied by one of the tax-gatherers. I have added the years 1776, 1783, 1784, and 1785, from the Returns made to Parliament in 1786.

Statement of Expenditure from January 1, to June 30, 1794.

	£.	s.	d.
Occasional relief	303	5	0
Militia, Preston	22	9	0
Ditto, sundry townships	33	5	0
Ditto, county	39	16	0
Provisions	273	3	11
Apparel	1	1	7
Work-shop	25	16	8½
Sundries	142	3	5
Coals and wood	16	9	9
Old account	188	18	9
	£1046	9	1½

Statement of Expenditure for the use of Poor from July 1, 1794, to January 1, 1795.

No. of Weeks.	Relief.	Milltia of Preston.	Militia of sundry townships.	Militia of County.	Provisions.	Apparel.	Work-shop.	Sundries.	Coals and Wood.	Old Account.
	£. s. d.	£. s. d.	£. s. d.	£. s. d.	£. s. d.	£. s. d.	£. s. d.	£. s. d.	£. s. d.	£. s. d.
July 4	11 4 3	— 17 —	1 8 0	1 4 0	—	—	0 13 0	2 14 0	—	—
11	8 3 9	— 17 —	1 8 0	1 4 0	—	—	1 1 10	4 4 0	—	63 15
18	9 1 3	— 17 —	1 8 0	0 15 0	1 6 11	—	0 13 0	—	—	—
25	9 3 9	— 19 —	1 6 0	0 15 0	10 15 1	—	0 13 0½	0 10 1	—	1 0 1
Aug. 1	8 4 3	— 13 —	0 16 0	1 15 0	31 11 3	—	0 13 2½	4 10 8	—	40 4
8	9 10 6	— 13 —	0 12 0	1 13 0	11 6 2	—	0 14 9½	6 3 1	—	31 13
15	9 17 0	— 13 —	1 2 0	1 17 0	10 1 3	—	0 13 3½	5 12 4	—	38 19
22	8 1 6	— 13 —	0 14 0	1 16 0	5 1 8	—	0 13 3	0 8 10	—	14 11
29	11 1 0	— 13 —	0 12 0	1 9 0	15 11 11	—	0 12 9½	0 13 5	—	34 12
Sept. 5	7 19 0	— 13 —	0 16 0	1 16 0	11 12 2	—	0 19 3½	4 4 0	—	33 9
12	8 3 10	— 13 —	1 2 0	1 11 0	4 9 11	—	1 16 0	1 12 0	—	8 1
19	9 17 6	— 13 —	0 14 0	1 11 0	8 18 11	—	1 16 3	—	—	2 10
26	6 13 6	— 13 —	0 18 0	1 14 0	2 6 8	—	2 14 7	—	3 5 0	3 19
Oct. 3	8 13 6	— 13 —	0 16 0	1 14 0	12 3 9	—	1 2 0	2 14 7	0 9 0	—
10	9 5 0	— 13 —	0 14 0	1 11 0	11 15 3	—	1 10 11	10 7 3	—	28 5
17	10 3 0	— 13 —	0 7 0	1 9 0	12 13 8	—	1 13 8	0 18 7½	—	32 15
24	9 5 0	— 13 —	0 11 0	1 7 0	13 10 0	—	1 5 0	12 11 6	—	5 0
31	10 12 0	— 13 —	1 6 0	1 7 0	11 15 0	—	2 6 2	11 8 9	—	14 13
Nov. 7	9 15 6	— 13 —	0 18 0	1 7 0	12 19 6	4 0 0	1 3 6½	7 14 7	—	5 0
14	10 7 6	— 13 —	0 16 0	1 7 0	21 9 9	9 2	2 7 0	21 0 4½	—	14 7
21	8 16 0	— 13 —	0 14 0	1 7 0	7 5 8	—	2 3 2	11 18 3	—	10 0
28	8 8 6	— 13 —	0 14 0	1 7 0	8 0 0	2 8 0	1 2 6	26 6 10	—	—
Dec. 5	9 1 6	— 13 —	1 4 0	1 7 0	11 8 6	—	1 3 9	1 16 8	—	3 8
12	7 3 0	— 13 —	0 14 0	1 7 0	6 8 0	—	1 17 8	7 18 6	13 4 0	—
19	9 6 0	— 13 —	0 13 0	1 7 0	13 1 0	—	1 3 2	6 6 6	—	—
28	7 14 6	— 13 —	0 13 0	1 3 0	18 10 6	—	2 18 8	13 13 3	1 0 0	—

Suppose the potatoes used in the house be 3 loads per week, then, for 26 weeks, there will be 78 loads, at 5s. per load   -   -   19 10 0

£. 235 12 1 | 17 16 0 | 22 16 0 | 37 0 0 | 293 12 6 | 6 17 2 | 35 11 6½ | 178 8 1 | 17 18 0 | 386 6

TOTAL.

	£. s. d.	
Occasional relief to out-poor	235 12 1	Thefe difburfements for occafional relief to the Poor of Prefton, on an averaâ€¦ amount to £9. 14s. 11d. a week.
Militia of Prefton -	17 16 0	
Militia of other townfhips	22 16 0	
Militia of the county -	37 0 0	
Provifions -	293 12 6	The number in the houfe this half-year was 148: the expence of provifior therefore £11. 5s. 10¾d. weekly for the houfe; or 1s. 6¼d. weekly for c perfon; annually £3. 19s. 1d.
Apparel - - -	6 17 2	
Work-fhop - -	35 11 6½	
Sundries - .	178 8 1	The article of Sundries, on an average, amounts to £6. 17s. 2¾d. weekly.
Coals and wood - -	17 18 0	
Old account - -	386 6 1¼	
	£ 1231 17 6	

Stat

Statement of Expenditure reſpecting the Work-houſe and Poor of this Town, from January 1, to July 1, 1795.

No. of Weeks.	Relief.	Militia of Preſton.	Militia of ſundry townſhips.	Militia of county.	Proviſions.	Apparel.	Work-ſhop.	Sundries.	Coals and Wood.	Old Account.
	£. s. d.	£. s. d.	£. s. d.	£. s. d.	£. s. d.	£. s. d.	£. s. d.	£. s. d.	£. s. d.	£. s. d.
an. 2	8 9 6	0 13 0	1 1 0	2 6 0	6 11 6	— — —	1 3 5	3 3 0	— — —	102 5 6½
9	9 11 6	0 13 0	0 15 0	1 9 0	2 18 0	— — —	1 2 2	1 9 11	— — —	67 12 2
16	9 4 0	0 13 0	0 13 0	1 9 0	— — —	— — —	1 2 8	9 16 8	— — —	0 3 10
23	8 5 9	0 13 0	0 15 0	0 11 0	— — —	8 0 7½	— — —	1 5 6	— — —	— — —
30	11 8 6	0 9 0	— — —	1 9 0	— — —	— — —	1 9 9	3 16 1	— — —	— — —
.b. 6	9 15 0	0 17 0	1 12 0	2 7 0	— — —	— — —	2 13 4½	23 13 7	1 5 4	5 18 0
13	15 5 0	0 13 0	0 13 0	1 9 0	— — —	— — —	1 5 0	7 3 6	— — —	— — —
20	8 5 7½	0 13 0	0 17 0	1 9 0	36 12 6	— — —	1 4 6	3 7 9	1 18 1	12 0 0
27	7 5 0	0 13 0	0 11 0	1 9 0	28 13 5	4 0 6	1 3 8	1 0 0	— — —	12 15 0
arch 6	8 11 3	0 13 0	0 19 0	1 9 0	20 6 6	1 14 10	1 17 0½	5 8 6	2 14 0	3 16 0
13	8 10 6	0 13 0	0 13 0	1 9 0	27 9 2	0 17 11½	1 13 11	28 16 10	— — —	2 19 8
20	8 10 0	0 13 0	0 15 0	1 9 0	25 9 3	0 4 11	1 4 4	5 13 4	1 3 6	— — —
27	8 1 0	0 13 0	0 11 0	1 9 0	11 16 6½	9 2 3	1 9 9	9 0 5	0 12 0	3 4 8
pril 3	8 6 6	0 13 0	0 17 0	1 9 0	16 8 1	— — —	1 17 1	7 9 1½	0 5 8	— — —
10	8 0 3	0 13 0	0 19 0	1 9 0	9 18 2½	16 17 3	1 18 7	62 17 7½	— — —	1 18 1
17	7 2 6	0 12 0	0 13 0	1 9 0	15 1 1½	— — —	1 8 7	3 17 1½	— — —	— — —
24	8 14 9	0 12 0	0 17 0	1 9 0	6 8 0	0 4 9	4 0 1½	8 18 6	14 16 10	— — —
ay 1	9 14 6	0 12 0	0 13 0	1 9 0	19 0 1	2 18 0	1 9 11½	3 13 1	1 11 0	— — —
8	6 3 0	0 5 0	0 9 0	1 7 0	32 14 3	0 7 0	1 3 8½	15 13 0½	— — —	— — —
15	11 10 1	0 19 0	1 3 0	1 7 0	10 6 6½	— — —	1 3 8	1 6 0	1 5 10	— — —
22	8 12 0	0 12 0	1 1 0	1 6 0	12 0 10	— — —	1 3 5	2 12 0	— — —	— — —
29	10 19 0	0 12 0	0 13 0	1 10 0	20 1 0	0 17 9	0 9 2	20 8 4½	— — —	2 16 11½
ie 5	8 10 7½	0 12 0	0 15 0	1 6 0	14 13 2	1 0 11	0 15 8	1 17 3	— — —	9 15 0
12	7 2 8½	0 12 0	0 13 6	1 10 0	11 9 8	11 9 6	1 3 0	31 7 1	— — —	5 4 0
19	6 3 6½	0 12 0	0 15 6	1 8 0	14 19 9½	2 7 6	0 13 9	0 16 0	— — —	— — —
26	9 13 3	0 12 0	0 11 6	1 8 0	20 15 9	0 12 1½	0 11 11	4 18 5	— — —	8 12 3
	£.231 15 4	16 7 0	19 15 6	38 1 0	363 13 4½	60 15 10½	35 8 2½	269 8 8½	25 12 3	239 1 2

TOTAL.

	£.	s.	d.
Relief to out-poor -	231	15	4
Militia of Preſton -	16	7	0
Militia of other townſhips	19	15	6
Militia of the county -	38	1	0
Proviſions - -	363	13	4½
Apparel - -	60	15	10½
Work-ſhop -	35	8	2½
Sundries - -	269	8	8½
Coals and wood -	25	12	3
Old account - -	239	1	2
Total of 26 weeks	£1299	18	5

} Theſe diſburſements for occaſional relief to the Poor of Preſton, on an average, amount to £9. 10s. 10¼d. a week.

— The number in the houſe was 154; the expence of proviſions, on an average, is £13. 9s. 9d. a week, for the whole houſe; 9¾d. for the weekly maintenance of each perſon: yearly, £4. 14s. 3d.; excluſive of ſundries, coals, &c. The article of Sundries, on an average, amounts to £10. 7s. 3d. a week.

Years.

Years.	Poor's Rate.				
	£.	s.	d.		
1776	894	17	6	Net expences for the Poor	From the Returns made to Parliament, in 1786.
1783	1304	13	6	The other sums denote the gross amount of money raised by assessment.	
1784	935	6	2		
1785	1342	19	8		

				s.	d.		
1793	1692	13	4	at 4	0	in the pound	From the tax-gatherer
1794	2412	14	11	at 5	6	on the no	
1795	2244	13	4	at 5	0	minal rent	

Houses are assessed at ½ rental; land at ⅓ of the real rent. About £ 40. each year, may have been uncollected, from houses being empty.

A new work-house was lately erected near the town, on which occasion the following paper was published, which it is thought proper to insert; as it in some degree points out the mode of maintaining the Poor hereafter intended to be pursued in the township of Preston :

" The motives for the erection and establishment of the work-house at Preston, are to train up the children of the Poor to habits of industry, religion and virtue, that they may be useful members of society; to furnish employment for the Poor of all ages, and oblige them to earn their own support, so far as their strength and ability will admit; to prevent idleness, dissipation and vice; and to provide a comfortable asylum for the deserving, whom age, disease or infirmity, have disabled from pursuing their various employments.

To effect these purposes, the following rules and regulations are adopted:

1, That the present committee of seven act as directors, who shall continue in office six calendar months, when seven others shall be proposed by them, and elected by a majority of the poor tax-payers, who are rated at £15. per annum, at a parish meeting to be convened for that purpose; and that each committee, so to be from time to time elected, shall remain in office for six calendar months; such half-yearly elections to take place on the first Monday in January, and first Monday in July, in every year.

2   2, That

2, That a steward or master of the work-house, and also a matron, shall be appointed and removable by a majority of the committee for the time being.

3, That William Smith shall be appointed clerk, to keep the accounts and enter the proceedings of the committee in the book kept for that purpose, and be removable by a majority of the committee for the time being, at a special meeting to be called for that purpose, in case of his misconduct.

4, That two overseers of the Poor shall be yearly appointed, who shall lay and collect the rates, and deposit the amount where the majority of the committee shall from time to time determine at a special meeting.

5, That the overseers, and also the clerk, or, in case of sickness or absence on necessary business, another officer in his place and stead, attend each weekly court before the hour of 10 in the forenoon.

6, That they make themselves acquainted with the situations, circumstances and characters of persons applying for relief, and report the same to the committee.

7, That they do not pay any rents whatsoever, and that they do not defray any lying-in expences, or relieve any Pauper whatsoever, but by the written order of the magistrates, or the weekly court.

8, That they do not order or engage to defray the expence of any coffin or other funeral charges, without the written consent of three of the committee.

9, That they give notice to the weekly court, of all persons likely to become chargeable, who may come to reside within the township, not belonging thereto, nor bringing certificates from their last legal places of settlement, within forty days of their so coming to reside therein, according to the directions of the Act.

10, That they use their utmost endeavours to obtain the earliest information of all single women in a state of pregnancy resident within the township, and give notice thereof to the next weekly court.

11, That they keep regular accounts of their weekly pay, occasional relief, and other incidental expences, and produce the same once a week to the committee at their meeting, in order to their being examined and allowed.

12, That

12, That they infert in their books, the names, ages, number of family, ftate of health and refidence of the Poor relieved by ordei of the magiftiates or the committee, as before mentioned.

13, That they deliver all certificates, paffes, orders of removal, orders of filiation, letters, and all other papers refpecting the Poor, to the next weekly couit after receiving the fame, in oider to their being filed by the cleik.

14, That no Pauper fhall be removed to the place of his oi her fettlement, or any appeal made againft any oider of iemoval, without having the cafe fiift confidered and recommended by the committee at theii weekly couit.

15, That no weekly pay be allowed to the out-poor, (childien at nurfe excepted,) unlefs in cafes of lunacy, ficknefs, or wheie their admiffion into the houfe fhall be judged improper by the weekly court.

16, That childien fhall not be taken into the houfe before they are two years old, or continued at nurfe, (except in very particular cafes,) after the age of four

17, That where families are too large to maintain themfelves by their own labour, the mode of relief fhall be by taking one or moie of the children into the houfe, or binding them apprentices, at the difcretion of the committee.

18, That no Pauper whatfoever be admitted into the houfe without a written order of the magiftrates or weekly couit, or in cafes of emeigency the like order from three of the committee.

19, That no cloathing whatfoever be allowed to the out-poor, except in cafes of ficknefs, when the weekly court, or, if immediately neceffary, three of the committee may exercife a difcretionary power.

20, That Paupers admitted into the houfe, for temporary relief only, fhall not be deprived of their houfhold goods or other property.

21, That an apothecary be half-yearly appointed, and removable by a majority of the committee, who fhall, by himfelf, or his approved deputy, duly attend, and adminifter proper medicines to fuch fick poor, both within and out of the houfe, who may be put under his care by the committee; and that he fhall make a weekly report to the court of their names and cafes in a book provided for that purpofe.

22, That

22, That a caution be given twice every year, the firſt week in January and fiiſt week in July, by advertiſement, that no perſon take in and harbour ſingle women pregnant or not, who do not belong to the townſhip, and offering a reward to any perſon giving information where ſuch women are harboured and concealed.

23, That the ſteward and matron reſide within the houſe. That they both be not abſent on any occaſion at the ſame time; and that neither of them be out later than eight o'clock at night, without written leave fiom three or more of the committee."

A debt of £ 2200 ſtill remains, in conſequence of the erection of this houſe; beſides which, the pariſh owes ſeveral bills, amounting, in the whole, to near £ 1000. The eſtimate of the weekly expences of proviſions for a Pauper in the houſe, which was furniſhed by the veſtry-clerk, does not comprehend the whole chaige of each perſon: beſides proviſions, the articles of apparel, ſundrics, woik-ſhop, coals and wood, as far as they relate to the work-houſe, and the expence of the building, ſhould be taken into the account.

Suppoſing the whole expence of erecting the work-houſe was £ 2200. the intereſt may be fairly reckoned at 6 per cent, and will amount in the half-year between

	£.	s.	d.
January and July 1795, to · 〃 -	33	0	0
Proviſions - · 〃 -	363	13	4½
Apparel - · - -	60	15	10½
Work-ſhop - - 〃 -	35	8	2½
Sundries, (if they all relate to the work-houſe,)	269	8	8½
Coals and wood 〃 〃 -	25	12	3
	£787	18	5

This ſum is £ 30. 6s. 1d. a week, on an average, for the houſe, which amounts to 3s. 11¼d. a week, or £ 10. 4s. 8d. a year, for eveiy individual in the work-houſe, (ſuppoſing there are 154,) as ſtated in the account ending July 1795.

The

The number of Poor in the work-houfe, a few weeks ago, was as follows:

Men	26
Women	39
Boys	47
Girls	40
Total -	150

At prefent there are 158 or 159 in the houfe. The number of out-poor at prefent is 70 ; they coft about £ 10. a week.

The work-houfe is built on a tolerable plan, but wants apartments for the fick. There are 4 or 5 beds in a room : the bed-fteads are made of iron, and the beds are ftuffed with chaff : white-wafhing and other means of keeping the houfe clean, feem rathei neglected. It is faid that about 15 die in a year in the houfe. About 20 acres of land were inclofed from the common, for the ufe of the houfe, for keeping cows, hoifes, and pigs ; raifing potatoes, &c. : this plot of ground is much impioved by culti-vation. Nothing is manufactured for the ufe of the houfe. The boys and girls are employed in weaving callicoes, till they are able to earn their living elfewhere. Old women wind cotton ; a few, who can work, aie employed in hufbandry, gardening, and other occupations : no account of their earnings could be obtained.

The following is the Bill of Fare.

	Breakfaft	Dinner	Supper.
Sunday,	Broth and bread	Beef, bread, vegetables, and beer.	Bread, broth, and bread
Monday,	Hafty-pudding and beer, or milk	Beef hafhed with onions, &c.	Beer or milk-pottage.
Tuefday,	As Sunday.	As Sunday	As Sunday.
Wednefday,	As Monday.	As Monday.	As Monday.
Thurfday,	As Sunday.	As Sunday	As Sunday.
Friday,	As Monday.	As Monday.	As Monday.
Saturday,	Ditto.	Ditto	Ditto.

The following is an extract from a printed account of the laft year's ex-penditure, of the Friendly Societies in Prefton : they have an annual feftival every Whit-Monday, and parade through the town after divine fervice, accompanied by bands of mufic, with the flags of the different companies. They have all had their rules confirmed by the magiftrates.

1. Union

1. Union Society, inftituted 11th February 1788; confifts of 64 members; expences laft 12 months £6. 10s.: no funerals.
2. Friendly Society, inftituted 12th January 1789; confifts of 43 members; paid to the fick, the laft 12 months, £4. 11s.: no funerals.
3. United Weavers' Society, inftituted 8th January 1791; confifts of 69 members; expences laft year, including 2 funerals, £4. 9s. 6d.
4. Beneficent Society, inftituted 6th June 1791; confifts of 58 members; expences laft 12 months, including 1 funeral, £4.
5. Amicable Society, inftituted 20th March 1762; confifts of 154 members; expences laft 12 months, including 4 funerals, £87. 7s.
6. Humane Society, inftituted 7th Auguft 1780; confifts of 51 members; paid to the fick, the laft 12 months, £15. 5s.: no funerals.
7. Unanimous Society, inftituted 1ft March 1792; confifts of 21 members: no expences.
8. Commendable Society, inftituted 4th March 1793; confifts of 17 members: no expences
9. Conftitutional Society, inftituted 21ft March 1793; confifts of 30 members: no expences.
10. A Society lately eftablifhed.

December, 1795.

WARRINGTON.

THE town and townfhip of Warrington, in 1781, contained 1941 houfes, and 8791 inhabitants[1]: fince that period, the population has not increafed. The parifh regifter affords the following annual averages:

	Marriages	Baptifms	Burials
From 1750 to 1769 inclufive; annual average	73	237	199
From 1770 to 1772 inclufive; annual average	95	331	258

In 1773, bills of mortality were begun to be kept: they comprehend Diffenters of all kinds, and are publifhed every year.

[1] Aikin's Defcript. of Manchefter,

Years	Baptifms.	Burials.	Marriages		Sums expended for the ufe of the Poor.	
1773	356	473	93			
1774	398	208	69			
1775	370	199	. 50			
1776	378	234	101			
1777	415	364	78			
1778	400	214	96			£.
1779	392	295	105	From 1 May 1783 to 1 May 1784	1595	
1780	413	362	93	1 May 1784 to 1 May 1785	1296	
1781	435	270	93	1 May 1785 to 1 May 1786	1094	
1782	387	267	84	1 May 1786 to 1 May 1787	1091	
1783	325	265	87	1 May 1787 to 1 May 1788	928	
1784 to 1789 } yearly aver	430	315	—	1 May 1788 to 1 May 1789	1002	
				1 May 1789 to 1 May 1790	973	
1790	418	407	102	1 May 1790 to 1 May 1791	1033	
1791	444	286	127	1 May 1791 to 1 May 1792	983	
1792	478	314	127	1 May 1792 to 1 May 1793	1025	
1793	514	361	103	1 May 1793 to 1 May 1794	1233	
1794	423	319	81	1 May 1794 to 1 May 1795	1381	

From hence it appears that the total expenditure of the laft eleven years amounts to £12039. If the total of the expenditure be taken for 11 years, at the rate of £1595, the fum paid in 1783, it will amount to £17545.; fo that there has been a faving of £5506 fince that time, which is £500. a year.

In the Returns made to Parliament, the expences for the Poor in 1776 are ftated at

		£.	s.	d.
for the Poor in 1776 are ftated at	-	831	3	10
The Poor's Rate in 1783 - -	-	1617	11	4
1784 - -	-	1468	1	11
1785 - -	-	1273	19	1

The Poor are partly maintained in a work-houfe, and partly relieved at home. 95 perfons, (50 of whom are children under 9 years of age, and the reft moftly old and infirm people,) are at prefent in the houfe. They are employed in fpinning hair for hair-cloth, winding warp for fail-cloth, &c. Dr. Aikin fays, that the manufacture of fail-cloth, or poldavies, a few years ago, was carried on to fuch an extent, that half of the heavy fail-cloth, ufed in the Navy, has been computed to be manufactured here[1]. It rather declined before the prefent war, but is now carried on with great fuccefs.

[1] Aikin's Defcript. of Manchefter.

The

The following accounts of the expenditure for the Poor, during the laſt 3 years, exhibit the earnings of the Poor in the houſe, the particulars of their diet, the charges of out-penſioners, &c. It is much to be wiſhed that ſimilar accounts were publiſhed annually by every work-houſe in the kingdom.

JOHN WILLIAMSON, Overſeer and Governor of the Work-houſe.
From 1ſt May 1792 to 1ſt May 1793.

	Dr.				*Cr.*		
	£	s	d		£	s.	d.
To balance from laſt year	11	17	1½	By illegitimate children, paid more than received	12	3	8
To work done in one year in the houſe	85	5	4	By out-poor, paid more than received	9	11	2
To caſh received for ſundries	10	6	11	By proviſions (average 68½ in the houſe, is near 1s. 6¾d. each a week,) viz.			
To do. from William Smart, collector	910	0	0	Flour, £23 12s. 8d —meal and peaſe, £80. 3s. 7d.—butter and cheeſe, £37. 16s. 2d —beef, &c £38. 1s. 5d —potatoes, £33 9s. 9d.—milk, &c. £40. 3s. 5d — treacle, £23. 5s. 10¼d	276	12	10¼
				By paid Mr. Heath for medicine and attendance	30	0	0
				By bounty, governor's bill of ſundries for ſick, &c. and ſalary	62	7	1½
				By coals, ſoap, candles	53	1	10
				By one year's cloathing in and out of the houſe	127	5	3
				By incidents	26	1	6
				By one year's out-penſioners, as per liſt	294	0	3
				By law charges	5	9	6
				By goods and repairs	27	7	6
				By apprentice fees	32	0	0
				By removals of Paupers	4	2	8
				By burials	14	14	9
To balance due to John Williamſon	8	8	2½	By militia, paid more than received	50	19	6
	£1025	17	7		£1025	17	7

The number of perſons in the liſt of out-penſioners is 188, of whom 65 are men; 113, women; and the reſt are children.

From

From 1st May 1793 to 1st May 1794.

	Dr.	£.	*s.*	*d.*
To work done in one year in the house	- - -	80	5	7½
To cash received for sundries	-	21	18	9
To do. from William Smart, collector	- - -	1130	0	0
To balance	= = =	8	16	7
		£1241	0	11½

	Cr.	£.	*s.*	*d.*
By balance from last year	-	8	8	2½
By illegitimate children, paid more than received	- -	9	19	1
By out-poor, paid more than received	- - -	42	8	0
By provisions, (average in the house 84, which is 1s. 6d. each a week,) viz. Flour, £44. 19s. 4d.—meal and pease, £92. 13s.—butter and cheese, £53. 6s. 4d —beef, &c. £41. 3d.—potatoes, £32. 5s. 3d. —milk, &c. £38. 5s. 11d.— treacle, £25. 4s 1d.	- -	327	14	2
By paid Mr Heath for medicine and attendance	- -	30	0	0
By bounty, governess's bill of sundries for sick, &c. and salary	-	63	9	3½
By coals, soap, and candles	-	57	4	5½
By one year's cloathing in and out of the house	-	120	12	8
By incidents	- -	18	11	0
By paid to Liverpool Infirmary for 2 years	- - -	4	4	0
By paid insurance	- -	0	14	0
By one year's out-pensioners, as per list	- - -	393	4	0
By law charges	- - -	41	1	11
By goods and repairs	- -	39	13	4
By apprentice fees	- -	20	11	0
By removal of paupers	- -	8	4	8
By burials	- -	22	13	2½
By militia, paid more than received	32	8	0
		1241	0	11¼

The number of persons, in the list of out-pensioners, amounts to 273, of whom 111 are men; 154, women; and the rest are children.

1st May

1st May 1795.	Dr. £. s. d.		Cr. £. s. d.
To work done in one year in the house	57 17 7	By balance from last year -	8 16 7
To cash for sundries - -	6 11 6	By illegitimate children, paid more than received -	40 7 4
To do. from William Smart, collector - - -	1310 0 0	By out-poor, paid more than received -	0 19 6
To militia, received more than paid	11 8 0	By provisions (average in the house 94½, which is 1s. 4d. each a week,) viz.	
		Flour, £29. 12s. 1d.—meal and pease, £127. 18s.—butter and cheese, £58. 17s. 9½d.—beef, &c. £50. 0s. 3d.—potatoes, £36. 4s. 7d.—milk, &c. £46. 5s. 4d.—treacle, £26. 8s. 9d. -	375 6 9½
		By paid Mr. Heath for medicine and attendance - -	30 0 0
		By bounty, governess's bill of sundries for sick, &c. and salary -	64 16 2
		By coals, soap, and candles -	59 11 8
		By one year's cloathing, in and out of the house - -	136 3 1½
		By incidents - -	25 0 11
		By one year's out-pensioners, as per list - - -	498 10 0
		By paid insurance - -	0 14 0
		By law charge - -	54 9 3
		By goods and repairs -	39 9 1
		By apprentice fees -	30 7 6
		By removal of paupers -	7 11 7
To balance - - - 3 12 0		By burials -	17 5 7
	£1389 9 1		£1389 9 1

The number of persons, in the list of out-pensioners, amounts to 285, of whom 104 are men; 174, women; and the rest children.

Table of Diet in the Work-house.

	Breakfast.	Dinner.	Supper.
Sunday,	Pottage and butter-milk, sweetened with treacle.	Broth, beef, and vegetables.	Bread and cheese.
Monday,	Bread and broth.	Thick pottage or hasty-pudding.	Boiled milk or milk pottage.
Tuesday,	Milk pottage.	Potatoes and cold meat.	Do. do.
Wednesday,	Do.	Do.	Do.
Thursday,	Do.	As Sunday.	Do.
Friday,	Bread and broth.	Cold meat and potatoes.	Do.
Saturday,	Milk pottage.	Butter milk and potatoes.	Do.

The

The work-houfe is an old one, but is kept very clean, and the Pool there feem very contented. The beds are filled with chaff, and well pro-vided with covering. About 10 deaths occur annually in the houfe.

December, 1795

LEICESTERSHIRE.

ASHBY DE LA ZOUCH.

Ashby DE LA ZOUCH is a fmall market-town, in the parifh of the fame name, which contains, by eftimation, about 11200 acres. 195 houfes pay the window or commutation tax. The inhabitants are fhop-keepers, inn-keepers, manufacturers of woollen and cotton ftockings, and hats, farmers, and labourers. The prefent war has been very injurious to the commercial intereffs of this town.

There is here 1 of Lady Huntingdon's chapels, 1 Methodift chapel, and 1 Prefbyterian chapel; but the parifhioners are chiefly of the eftablifh-ed Church.

The prices of provifions are : beef, 3½d. to 5d. the pound; mutton, 5d. ; veal, 3d. to 4d.; butter, 9d. to 10½d ; bread flour, 4s. a ftone ; pota-toes, 5d. the gallon ; about autumn, they are generally 2d. or 3d. the gal-lon; milk, 1½d. the quart. Spinners of wool earn from 1s. 6d. to 3s. a week; wool-combers, from 12s. to 14s. a week; ftocking-weavers, in general, from 7s. to 17s. a week; but a few earn £ 1. 1s. a week; hat-ters, from 12s. to 20s. a week; labourers in hufbandry, till within the laft year, had 4s. a week in winter, and 6s. in fummer ; but they now have 6s. in winter, and from 7s to 9s. in fummer, and victuals. The number of ale-houfes in the parifh has been reduced fince laft winter, from 25 to 21. Here are 8 Friendly Societies, which have from 40 to 80 members in each ; only 2 have had their rules confirmed by the magiftrates.

3   The

The rent of land, on large farms, is from 20s. to 30s an acre; one small farm near the town is let at £ 2. an acre: the land-tax is 1s. 6d. in the pound. About 24 years ago, when the common fields were inclofed, the Vicar had an allotment of land given in lieu of tithes. Farms are from £ 40 to £ 300, a year; but, chiefly, from £ 50. to £ 90. a year: wheat, barley, oats, turnips and clover, are cultivated. There is much pafture ground. Lord Moira claims the principal right to between 3 and 4000 acres of wafte land in this parifh. A feam of coal lies under this common, and, (it is expected,) will foon be worked. In the year 1770, about 1040 acres were enclofed, part of which was common, and part common field.

The Poor are partly maintained in the work-houfe, and partly at their own homes: there are at prefent 52, who are chiefly old women and children, in the work-houfe: the children are taught to read, to fpin jerfey, to do common houfe-work; fpinning, knitting, fewing, working in the fields, &c by which means they become early attached to induftrious principles, and are thereby made truly ufeful and valuable fervants. The bedding and wearing apparel are chiefly manufactured in the houfe, exclufive of which work, the Poor generally earn, by fpinning jerfey, &c. about 10s. 6d. a month. The bill of fare has been much varied of late, on account of the dearnefs of bread, &c.: 2 pudding dinners in a week were formerly allowed; and the fupper, every day, was about 1 lb. of bread, and 1 pint of fmall beer for each grown perfon; children had a proportionable allowance: potatoes and vegetables are now generally fubftituted for bread; as will appear by the following general bill of fare:

	Breakfaft.	Dinner	Supper.
Sunday,	Milk-pottage, water-pottage, or gruel	Hot meat and vegetables, and broth.	Mafhed potatoes, with milk or hafhed meat.
Monday,	Ditto	Cold meat, vegetables and broth	Ditto.
Tuefday,	Ditto	As Sunday	Ditto
Wednefday,	Ditto.	Ditto	Ditto.
Thurfday,	Ditto	As Monday.	Ditto.
Friday,	Ditto.	As Sunday.	Ditto.
Saturday,	Ditto	Ditto.	Ditto

33 weekly penfioners receive allowances, amounting to £ 3. 5s. a week.

The

The following is a Table of Baptisms, Burials, Marriages[1]*, and Poor's Rates.*

Years.	Baptisms Mal	Baptisms Fem	Baptisms Tot.	Burials Mal	Burials Fem	Burials Tot	Marriages	Net amount of Assessments. £.	s.	d.	Total Expenditure. £.	s.	d	Rate in the Pound. s.	d.
1680	30	24	54	(inclusive)		55	15								
1685	26	24	50	—	—	66	6								
1690	23	18	41	—	—	44	8								
1691	26	30	56	—	—	42	2								
1692	22	20	42	—	—	34	4								
1693	27	17	44	—	—	38	6								
1694	13	13	26	—	—	26	2								
1695	22	18	40	—	—	46	7								
1696	26	16	42	—	—	60	6								
1697	22	12	34	—	—	32	10								
1698	22	15	37	—	—	30	5								
1699	23	15	38	—	—	32	10								
1700	23	20	43	—	—	22	14								
1720	24	16	40	—	—	35	10								
1740	24	20	44	—	—	27	Reg lost								
1760	29	36	65	—	—	39	Ditto								
1775	42	42	84	23	22	45	20								
1776	39	43	82	32	24	56	23								
1777	37	36	73	23	23	46	20								
1778	43	32	75	29	31	60	24								
1779	34	37	71	30	21	51	18								
1780	35	37	72	12	24	36	19								
1781	42	37	79	20	29	49	19								
1782	31	36	67	27	26	53	21	457	5	$3\frac{3}{4}$	456	12	$6\frac{1}{2}$	2	3
1783	36	33	69	20	16	36	22	379	18	$9\frac{1}{4}$	374	4	$8\frac{3}{4}$	1	$10\frac{1}{2}$
1784	35	36	71	28	23	51	27	455	0	10	460	19	3	2	3
1785	30	33	63	19	22	41	14	378	14	$11\frac{1}{2}$	424	14	8	1	$10\frac{1}{2}$
1786	31	32	63	36	38	74	19	404	4	$8\frac{1}{2}$	427	15	$3\frac{1}{2}$	2	0
1787	31	31	62	17	20	37	21	379	13	1	475	1	$2\frac{1}{2}$	1	$10\frac{1}{2}$
1788	28	31	59	32	29	61	16	451	19	5	546	1	$10\frac{1}{4}$	2	3
1789	31	36	67	35	26	61	22	405	0	$7\frac{1}{2}$	510	12	$11\frac{1}{2}$	2	0
1790	38	34	72	27	18	45	22	460	14	$10\frac{1}{2}$	529	9	$11\frac{1}{2}$	2	3
1791	34	33	67	28	32	60	13	510	16	$1\frac{1}{4}$	611	8	3	2	6
1792	32	43	75	33	32	65	18	506	3	$5\frac{1}{2}$	662	19	$3\frac{3}{4}$	2	6
1793	30	30	60	36	36	72	31	406	13	5	520	16	9	2	0
1794	28	31	59	35	23	58	28	510	5	$2\frac{1}{2}$	739	11	9	2	6
1795	—	—	—	—	—	—	—	559	0	$7\frac{1}{2}$	764	6	$7\frac{1}{4}$	2	9
			2096			36) 1685	34) 522							14) 1 10	$10\frac{1}{2}$
		Average	$58\frac{1}{4}$		Average	$46\frac{5}{6}$	Ave. $15\frac{1}{3}$ nearly							Average 2	$2\frac{1}{2}$ nearly

The net expences for the Poor in 1776 were £305. 9s. 8d. See Returns to Parliament.

These Rates are at fixed about 30 years ago, at ¾ of the net rent: at present, perhaps, they may not much exceed ½ of the net rental.

[1] The registers are extremely perfect.

No account of the Rates could be obtained prior to 1782, but, by information, they appear to have been nearly the same for a few years previous to that period : about 30 years back they were very low, and are said to have risen, as manufactures increased It is observed, that near $\frac{4}{5}$ of the now chargeable inhabitants here belong to manufactories ; and that, notwithstanding they have higher wages than the labourers in husbandry, the latter maintain their families much better than the former: the labourer is more economical, and does not so much frequent the public-house, by which means he can support a family, of 3, 4, or 5 children, without any parochial assistance ; while the manufacturer, being more exposed to temptation, and too often connected with drunken associates, generally spends that money in ale-houses, which ought to be appropriated to domestic purposes ; and having once applied to the parish for relief, he becomes totally regardless of that sense of shame, which is the best preservative of independence. That the Poor might not experience any inconvenience from the inclosing of the commons, and common fields, the lanes were reserved exclusively for their use : they pay 2s. 6d. a year for a horse or cow-gait therein. About £10. a year are paid out of the Poor's Rates towards the county stock. A doctor, who attends the work-house, receives a salary of £10. a year ; and the vestry-clerk is paid £15. a year.

August, 1795.

CARLTON CURLIEU.

THIS parish contains 1160 acres, and about 40 inhabitants, consisting of one gentleman's family, two farmers, a few shepherds, and labourers. 5 houses pay the window-tax ; 3 are exempted. The 2 farmers rent 400 acres ; the remainder of the parish is farmed by persons who reside at a distance. Not one acre is ploughed land ; nor are there any commons or waste lands in the parish : it has been enclosed many years. The average rent of land is one guinea an acre. The landlord pays tithe and land tax.

There are neither ale-houses, nor Friendly Societies in the parish. There are seldom any Poor here. The persons at present chargeable are, 2 orphan

phan children, that coft, weekly, 4s.; a man, aged 55, infane, whofe weekly allowance is 5s. 6d.; and a reduced grazier, aged 70, who receives 2s. a week. Graziers, and their families, are the people moft ufually chargeable.

Years.	Affeffments.			Parochial Difburfements.			Rate in the Pound.	
	£.	s.	d.	£.	s.	d.		
1783	19	7	2	34	15	3		
1784	33	2	0	25	7	5		
1785	57	17	8	34	10	6½		
1786	57	17	6	56	8	8		
1787	No Affeffment this year.			37	6	4½		
1788	28	13	1½	38	12	6		
1789	57	17	6	65	19	5½		
1790	79	11	6	77	16	1½		
1791	57	17	6	54	17	7½		
1792	57	6	6	59	4	7	s.	d.
1793	86	8	2½	86	13	9½	1	4½
1794	86	8	2½	82	14	7	1	4½
1795	86	8	2½	—	—	—	1	4½

The difburfements principally relate to the church, conftables, and high roads. The conftable, on an average, receives £ 8. a year; about £ 7. are annually expended on the church; and on high-ways, from £ 15. to £ 30. The latter charge, however, this year, amounted to £ 66.

Auguft, 1795.

KIBWORTH-BEAUCHAMP.

THIS parifh is divided into 3 townfhips, viz. Kibworth-Beauchamp, Kibworth-Harcourt, and Smeeton-Wefterby. Kibworth-Beauchamp contains about 1300 acres; Kibworth-Harcourt, 1500 acres; and Smeeton-Wefterby, 1200 acres. 43 houfes in Kibworth-Beauchamp, 41 houfes in Kibworth-Harcourt, and 40 houfes in Smeeton-Wefterby, pay the window-tax: in the firft,

firft, the number of houfes exempted is 50; in the fecond, 40; and in the third, 45. The inhabitants are chiefly agricultuiifts: fome few are manufacturers. In the firft divifion, there was formerly a tammy manufacture, which is now nearly laid afide; in the other divifions a little ftocking-weaving is carried on; fpinning worfted, with the two-handed wheel, is very generally ufed here. In the fiift divifion, theie are 2 Independent chapels; and 1 in Smeeton-Wefterby.

The prices of provifions are: beef, fiom 4½d. to 5d. the pound; mutton, 5d.; veal, 3½d.; butter, 9½d. and 10d.; bread, 3½d. a lb. or 4lb. for 1s.; coals, 13d. the cwt; potatoes, 6d. the gallon; milk, ½d. the pint; but of this little is fold.

The wages of labour vary much; a common labourer in hufbandiy earns about 8s. 6d. a week, in winter; and from 10s. to 12s. a week in fummer, without victuals: women fpin worfted, and can earn from 6d. to 10d. a day; children, of 12 or 14 years of age, earn about 6d. a day, by fpinning. In the firft divifion, there are 2 ale-houfes; in the fecond, 4; and in the third, 2. There is one Friendly Society in the parifh, confifting of about 110 members, who have had their rules confirmed by the magiftrates.

The average rent of land is about 25s. an acre. The land-tax, in the firft divifion, is £ 90. 7s. 6d.; in the fecond, £ 82. os. 3d.; and in the third, £ 92. 11s. 10d. Farms are from £ 20. to £ 300. a year; but generally about £ 100. a year. About ⅖ of the land are pafture; oats, barley, and wheat are cultivated. There are no commons nor wafte land in the parifh: about the year 1780, 3600 acres were enclofed, when the rector had ⅐ part of the enclofuie allowed him, in lieu of tithes.

The Poor of this parifh are maintained either by a weekly allowance, or by occafional relief, at their own houfes: in the divifion of Kibworth-Beauchamp, 18 poor perfons, (fome of whom have families,) receive £ 2. 11s. 11½d. weekly, and feveral more have cafual relief: in Kibworth-Harcourt, 20 poor families have about £ 5. weekly, and otheis receive cafual payments: in Smeeton Wefterby divifion, 21 penfioners receive £ 3. 3s. 6d. weekly; and about £ 2. 12s. a week is, at prefent, paid to others, in cafual payments. The following is an account of the regular

3 C 2   penfioners

penfioners on the lift in Kibworth-Beauchamp divifion, and may feive as a fpecimen of the Poor in the other divifions.

	Age.	Receive weekly, In money. s. d.	In coals. d.
A weaver's widow ; aged -	50	3 6	7½
A man, and 2 grand-children, orphans ; he	65	10 0	11½
A ftocking-weavei ; - - -	60	1 0	7½
A labourer and family ; - -	40	0 0	7½
A ftocking-weaver ; - -	55	0 0	7½
A labouier ; - - -	50	0 6	7½
Ditto ; - - - -	50	1 6	7½
Ditto ; - - - -	55	2 0	7½
A labourer's widow ; - -	55	0 0	7½
A foldiei's child - - -	7	2 6	
A fpinfter ; - - -	40	1 6	
A baftard child ; - - -	—	1 6	
2 old men at Leicefter ; - -	—	4 0	
A fpinfter ; - - -	55	5 0	
A weaver and family ; - -	40	4 0	
A weaver and 3 children ; - -	40	2 c	
A weaver and 4 children ; - -	30	3 0	
A labourer and 6 children ; - -	35	4 0	

Weekly payments in money   -   £ 2   6   0
Ditto for coals   -   0   5   11½

Total weekly payments   -   £ 2   11   11½

The following is a ftatement of the earnings and expences of a labourer's family in this parifh.

The labourer is 40 years of age ; has a wife and 5 children, whofe ages are ; a girl, 14 years old ; ditto, 12 ; a boy, 8 ; a girl, 6 ; and a boy, 18 months old. The man faid, that his earnings were fo uncertain that he could give no accurate ftatement of them, but, as near as he could calculate, they were as follows, for one year, beginning at Michaelmas.

For

	£.	s.	d.
For about half a year he worked at the canal, and had 2s. a day, when the weather permitted him to work; but when it did not, the parifh allowed him 1s. 2d. a day. Upon the whole, he computes his receipts by that means at 8s. 6d. a week, for 26 weeks - - -	11	1	0
The fucceeding 13 weeks, about 9s a week - -	5	17	0
The fummer quarter, 8s. 6d. a week and victuals -	5	10	6
13 weeks victuals may be eftimated at 6s. a week, annually	3	18	0
Father's earnings - - - - -	£26	6	6
Eldeft girl earns, on an average, by fpinning, 2s. a week	5	4	0
Total earnings -	£31	10	6

The fecond girl is fubject to fits; the mother, and other children, earn nothing. The parifh pays this man's houfe-rent, finds him coals, occafionally gives him articles of wearing apparel, and, for the laft 2 weeks paft, has given him an allowance of 2s. a week.

This family ufes 6 lb. of bread a day; (which lately fold for 2s. and was formerly about 10d.; at prefent, 1s. 6d.;) which is for the year £27. 6s.

He could give but little account of their other expences, but fays, that they ufe little or no milk or potatoes; that they feldom get any butter; neither do they ufe any oatmeal; that they occafionally buy a little cheefe, and fometimes have meat on a Sunday; that his wife and daughters confume a fmall quantity of tea; but that bread is the chief fupport of the family, and that they have far from a fufficiency of that article at prefent; that they fhould ufe much more, if they could procure it; and that his children are almoft naked, and half ftarved. He adds, that he has lately worked many days with only bread diet, and that many weeks have elapfed fince he has tafted any beer.

A Table of Baptifms, Burials, Marriages, Poor's Rates, Difburfements, &c.

Years	BAPTISMS.			BURIALS.			Marriages.	Poor's Rates.	Difburfements.	Rate in the Pound.
	Males.	Fem.	Total	Males	Fem	Total.				
1680	—	—	31	—	—	37	6			
1685	—	—	40	—	—	20	5			
1690	—	—	20	—	—	21	5			

Years	Baptisms			Burials			Marriages	Poor's Rates			Disbursements			Rate in the Pound	
	Males	Fem.	Total.	Males	Fem.	Total.									
1691	—	—	23	—	—	26	5								
1692	—	—	24	—	—	18	4								
1693	—	—	28	—	—	15	2								
1694	—	—	19	—	—	16	3								
1695	—	—	25	—	—	25	cut out								
1696	—	—	23	—	—	19	4								
1697	—	—	18	—	—	22	3								
1698	—	—	19	—	—	26	4								
1699	—	—	18	—	—	23	10								
1700	—	—	25	—	—	16	7								
1720	—	—	21	—	—	30	9								
1740	20	8	28	9	8	17	5								
1760	12	20	32	10	19	29	13								
1775	21	19	40	14	16	30	8								
1776	18	21	39	15	14	29	5								
1777	17	19	36	8	10	18	14								
1778	18	20	38	7	15	22	5								
1779	19	19	38	10	6	16	9								
1780	12	20	32	11	23	34	9								
1781	15	19	34	10	16	26	7								
1782	20	20	40	11	6	17	6	£.	s.	d.	£.	s.	d.	s.	d.
1783	16	12	28	8	12	20	8	91	1	10	87	8	10	1	9
1784	13	19	32	14	16	30	not inserted	148	19	7½	147	14	4	2	9
1785	17	14	31	12	16	28	10	131	4	10	133	5	4¾	2	6
1786	24	9	33	8	10	18	10	159	19	2¼	153	18	7	3	0
1787	14	17	31	5	13	18	6	121	0	10½	128	13	7	2	4
1788	15	13	28	8	12	20	4	132	1	8	144	14	0	2	6
1789	18	12	30	9	9	18	8	132	4	2	118	6	11½	2	6
1790	9	14	23	15	11	26	14	79	6	9	94	3	1¼	1	6
1791	13	16	29	16	12	28	10	141	15	6	145	10	0	2	8
1792	15	20	35	14	18	32	10	119	2	6	119	6	5	2	3
1793	16	14	30	13	16	29	12	131	13	0	137	4	8¼	2	6
1794	15	11	26	11	12	23	11	157	17	4	158	10	9	3	0
1795	—	—	—	—	—	—	—	210	11	8	205	12	1¼	4	0

These Rates and Disbursements, &c relate only to the township of Kibworth-Beau-champ.

The Pound-rate was fixed when the fields were enclosed; so that, (allowing the land to have been then set at the full value,) the Assessments may not be, at present, upon much more than ⅘ of the net rent.

The

The Rates and Diſburſements, which could be obtained relating to the townſhip of Smeeton, or Smeeton-Weſterby, were as follows:

Years	Net amount of Aſſeſſments.			Diſburſements.			Rate in the Pound.	
	£.	s.	d.	£.	s.	d.	s.	d.
1790	178	1	2	173	17	8	3	9
1791	140	14	6	150	7	10½	3	0
1792	199	9	8¼	197	10	1	4	0
1793	164	5	7½	172	6	4	3	6
1794	199	9	8¼	201	4	2½	4	0
1795	281	12	4	277	16	5½	6	0

The books of Kibworth-Harcourt are preſerved with leſs care than in the other diviſions: the only accounts of the Rates were thoſe of the year ending in 1791, which amounted to £ 158. 4s. 5d., and were raiſed at 2s. 6d. in the pound; and thoſe of the year ending in 1795, which amounted to £ 199. 8s. 6½d. and are ſaid to have been raiſed at 2s. 6d in the pound.

The County Rates are paid out of the Poor's Rates in this pariſh; they vary in different years, but from the beſt information which could be obtained, it appears, that from £ 10. to £ 15 a year are paid out of each diviſion for that purpoſe. A great number of cottages, belonging to the different diviſions of this pariſh, are inhabited by ſome of the Poor; others have their houſe-rents paid by the pariſh; and ſeveral have cloaths, &c. found them by their reſpective townſhips. The Poor complain of hard treatment from the overſeers, and the overſeers accuſe the Poor of being ſaucy.

No account of the Rates, in any of the diviſions, previous to the encloſure of the fields, could be obtained; but it is ſaid, that they were not one-third of what they are at preſent[1]; and the people attribute the riſe of them

[1] This ſeems to have been the fact, if the Returns made to Parliament in 1786 were tolerably correct: however, I find they ſeldom agree with the pariſh-books.

	Kibworth-Beauchamp.			Kibworth-Harcourt.			Smeeton-Weſterby		
	£.	s.	d.	£.	s.	d.	£.	s.	d
1776 Net expences for the Poor	65	13	3	54	9	6	78	6	8
1783 Money raiſed by diſburſement	151	14	6	107	2	0	187	12	8
1784 Ditto	131	4	10	126	11	8	140	14	6
1785 Ditto	158	19	3	126	11	9	154	3	7

to the enclofure ; for they fay, " that before the fields were enclofed, they were folely applied to the production of corn ; that the Poor had then plenty of employment in weeding, reaping, threfhing, &c , and could alfo collect a great deal of corn by gleaning ; but that the fields being now in pafturage, the farmers have little occafion for labourers, and the Poor being thereby thrown out of employment, muft, of courfe, be fupported by the parifh." There is fome truth in thefe obfervations : one-third, or perhaps one-fourth of the number of hands, which were required 20 years ago, would now be fufficient, according to the prefent fyftem of agriculture, to perform all the farming work in the parifh. However, with regard to the collective intereft of the nation, and not the particular benefit of the parifh, I much doubt, whether the wool now produced from the Leicefterfhire enclofures does not employ more hands, (though, perhaps, not in Leicefterfhire,) than it's arable fields did formerly.

Many labourers can, at prefent, get work at a canal cutting in the neighbourhood ; otherwife, the Rates muft have been much higher than they even now are. In the winter, and at other times, when a man is out of work, he applies to the overfeer, who fends him from houfe to houfe, to get employ : the houfe-keeper, who employs him, is obliged to give him victuals, and 6d. a day ; and the parifh adds 4d. ; (total, 10d. a day ;) for the fupport of his family : perfons working in this manner, are called rounds men, from their going round the village or townfhip for employ[1]. As the work is here moftly done by the great or piece, earnings are very variable, and fluctuating ; fo that it is not poffible to give a very correct ftatement of them : a day-labourer has about 1s a day, and breakfaft, in winter ; and in hay and corn harveft, (which is very fhort,) 1s. 2d. a day, and board. The tradefmen, fmall farmers, and labourers, are very loud in their complaints againft thofe, whom they call monopolizing farmers, and graziers ; an evil, which they fay increafes every year.

Auguft, 1795.

[1] See p 29

LEI-

LEICESTER.

THE parifh of St. Martin, Leicefter, confifts entirely of buildings : in 1792 it contained 565 inhabitants, and about 2825 fouls. 520 houfes pay the window tax : very few are exempted, as the parifh is fituated in the centre of the town, and principally confifts of good houfes. The land-tax is about 10d. in the pound. A confiderable manufacture of worfted ftockings is carried on here; ftocking-weavers earn from 7s. to £1. 1s. a week; wool-combers, from 9s. to 12s. a week ; worfted-fpinners, from 4d. to 8d. a day; agricultural labourers, at prefent, receive 1s. 6d. a day, with victuals.

The prices of provifions are: beef, 4½d. the pound ; mutton, 5d. ; veal, 4½d. ; butter, 10½d. or 1s. the pound ; bread, 1 lb. 11 oz. for 6d.; milk, 1½d. the quart, fhort meafure.

In the town of Leicefter there are 143 public-houfes, of which, 40 are inns ; and 14 Friendly Societies, of which, 3 are in this parifh. Almoft all have had their rules confirmed by the Magiftrates. Thefe inflitutions are much liked here, and are increafing in number very rapidly.

In Leicefter, the Calvinifts, Prefbyterians, Methodifts, Anabaptifts, Roman Catholics, and Quakers, have each a feparate houfe of worfhip.

The following extracts from the Hiftory of Leicefter [1] exhibit the progreffive increafe of population in this town.

Parifhes.	1558		1600		1650		1700		1750		1787	
	Bapt.	Bur	Bapt.	Bur	Bapt.	Bur	Bapt.	Bur.	Bapt.	Bur	Bapt.	Bur.
St. Mary	—	—	26	18	19	14	26	24	70	73	120	112
St. Nicholas	—	—	6	6	10	7	13	9	13	16	23	16
St. Leonard	—	—	—	—	—	—	—	—	—	—	12	9
All Saints	—	—	23	24	24	15	24	21	44	50	86	88
St. Martin	41	38	38	35	46	35	62	53	56	71	73	77
St. Margaret	—	—	38	30	35	37	53	40	56	83	139	117

[1] Throfby's Leicefter, 408 He makes an addition of 50, for Diffenters, annually, to the Burials

	1712		1785			1792	
	Families	Inhabitants	Families	Inhabitants	Houfes.	Families	Inhabitants
St Mary	250	1250	668	3090	604	687	3435
St. Nicholas	90	450	180	900	138	187	935
St Leonaid	omitted.		97	450	90	95	475
All Saints	220	1100	501	2428	470	551	2755
St. Martin	350	1750	524	2620	533	565	2825
St. Maigaiet	380	1900	756	3296	800	850	4250
Totals	1290	6450	2726	12784	2635	2935	14675

The Poor of this parifh are farmed by a man, who ieceives from the parifh £14. a week, or £728 a year. There are 42 peifons, (piincipally old women and children,) at prefent, under his caie : fome out-poor receive £4. 11s. a week : the farmer is a ftocking-manufacturer, and employs the Poor in fpinning worfted, &c : they woik, in the fummer, from 6 o'clock in the moining till 8 at night; and in wintei, from 7 in the morning till 9 at night; the time of meals excepted. The houfe is not well fituated, nor aired in the beft manner; but appears to be kept very clean; the beds are of flocks, and much infefted with bugs. A woman teaches the children to read and fpin. In cafes of baftardy, the farmer does not take care of fuch as were not chargeable, or not born befoie his agreement with the parifh. His agreement is renewed annually.

Table of Diet in the Poor-houfe.

	Breakfaft.	Dinnei.	Supper
Sunday,	Milk pottage or gruel.	Broth, meat, and vegetables.	Bread, cheefe, and bee:
Monday,	Broth and biead.	Cold meat, vegetables, and beer.	Do
Tuefday,	As Sunday.	As Sunday.	Do
Wednefday,	As Monday.	As Monday.	Do.
Thurfday,	As Sunday.	As Sunday.	Do.
Friday,	As Monday.	As Monday.	Do.
Saturday,	Milk pottage.	Bread, cheefe, and beer.	Do

About £16. a year, from different donations, are annually diftributed among the Poor of this parifh. There are in Leicefter 5 hofpitals, in which there are, ufually, about 200 Poor.

The war has had no other effect upon the manufactures of this town than by taking off a great number of hands: several soldiers' families of course became burdensome. The manufactures of Leicester are sent to different parts of the kingdom, and to America.

Table of Baptisms, Burials, Marriages, and Poor's Rates in the Parish of St. Martin, LEICESTER.

Years	Baptisms			Burials			Marriages	Net amount of Poor's Rate			Total disbursements, including balances in the hands of officers, &c			Rate in the Pound	
	Males	Fem	Total	Males	Fem	Total		£.	s	d.	£.	s.	d.	s.	d.
1680	—	—	54	—	—	63	—								
1685	—	—	53	38	29	67	—								
1690	—	—	62	15	19	34	—								
1691	—	—	54	27	18	45	—								
1692	—	—	55	20	21	41	—								
1693	—	—	56	17	24	41	—								
1694	—	—	53	21	19	40	—								
1695	—	—	44	34	31	65	—								
1696	—	—	56	30	21	51	—								
1697	—	—	44	14	28	42	—								
1698	—	—	46	23	20	43	—								
1699	—	—	58	17	19	36	—								
1700	—	—	62	32	21	53	—								
1720	30	25	55	39	26	65	—								
1740	28	29	57	29	27	56	—	244	17	3¼	245	18	11	—	—
1760	28	24	52	46	59	105	—	736	18	8	737	12	7	—	—
1775	43	43	86	24	38	62	27	714	9	0½	808	4	1	3	0
1776	48	42	90	42	42	84	31	735	19	4	736	6	7	3	0
1777	37	48	85	28	30	58	27	744	1	3	715	6	2	3	0
1778	31	43	74	29	43	72	25	693	9	8½	740	16	5	2	9
1779	36	47	83	33	46	79	28	897	3	11	937	5	7	3	6
1780	37	43	80	31	34	65	32	971	13	9	1110	12	4½	3	9
1781	46	51	97	51	56	107	29	962	17	7	1018	15	7	3	9
1782	35	39	74	22	48	70	41	926	14	3	967	18	8	3	9
1783	45	47	92	38	38	76	—	889	16	5	1008	15	8	3	5
1784	52	36	88	35	39	74	—	931	1	10	1003	17	3	3	7
1785	40	42	82	35	38	73	—	980	16	9	1027	14	5	3	9
1786	35	47	82	40	45	85	—	983	18	7	1083	3	6	3	9
1787	40	42	82	28	31	59	—	870	5	9½	1012	3	10	3	3
1788	44	35	79	41	53	94	—	919	7	1	1012	15	4	3	5
1789	44	29	73	35	42	77	—	950	14	8	1132	14	8	3	6
1790	34	43	77	34	36	70	—	1028	1	3	1109	2	8	3	10
1791	42	37	79	38	31	69	—	955	7	10	1106	6	4	3	6
1792	30	32	62	46	39	85	—	963	17	9	1119	5	1	3	6
1793	32	40	72	23	40	63	—	923	2	10	1015	16	6	3	4
1794	45	45	90	—	—	—	—	1109	14	6	1301	3	11	4	0
1795	—	—	—	—	—	—	—	Not settled this year.						Rate 5	5

It appears from an old parish book, mentioned in Throsby's Leicester, (p 258,) that in the year 1677 a Rate, of 1½d in the pound, was raised, for the maintenance of the Poor.

Houses in this parish are usually assessed at about 2-thirds of the net rent.

3 D 2

Baptisms,

Baptifms, from 1680 to 1700 inclufive,   590—Yearly average 53$\frac{7}{11}$
Do.   from 1775 to 1794 inclufive, 1629—Do.   -   81$\frac{9}{20}$
Burials,   fiom 1680 to 1700 inclufive, 491—Do.   -   44$\frac{7}{11}$
Do.   fiom 1775 to 1794 inclufive, 1422—Do.   -   71$\frac{2}{20}$

Money for repairing bridges, &c. called Borough Rates, is paid out of
the Poor's Rates : it was geneially about £70. per annum, but now
amounts to £200. and upwaids, in confequence of the floods laft winter
having cailied away feveral bridges.

Every parifh in the town fuppoits it's own Pooi fepaiately : the Rates
in the other paiifhes, it is faid, are, on an aveiage, neaily fimilar to thofe
in this parifh ; fome are a little higher, and fome a little lower.

The following is an account, given by a woolcomber, of his earnings and
expences. He is 50 years old; has a wife and 2 fons, the eldeft 13, the
youngeft 9 years of age.

		£.	s.	d.
The man earns, on an average, 9s. a week; annually	-	23	8	0
The oldeft boy feives a brieklayer : he earns about 4s. 6d. a week in winter; and 2s. a week in fummer : upon an average, 3s. 3d. a week ; annually	- - -	8	9	0
The woman earns, by fpinning, and feaming ftockings, 1s. 6d. a week; annually - - - - -		3	18	0
Total annual earnings of the family	-£	35	15	0

Annual Expences.

		£.	s.	d.
In bread, 3s. a week, before the prefent fcarcity; at prefent 7s. a week : the former fum amounts annually to	-	7	16	0
10 lb. of butcher's meat weekly, at 3d. the lb.	-	6	10	0
Potatoes and vegetables, 1s. 6d. weekly	-	3	18	0
Milk, 2d. a day - - -	-	3	1	4
Ale and beer, about 1s. 6d. weekly	annually -	3	18	0
Butter, 2 lb. weekly, at 9d. the lb.	-	3	18	0
Cheefe, 3½ lb. weekly, at 6d. the lb.	-	4	11	0
Tea, fugar, &c. weekly about 1s. 6d.	-	3	18	0

                      Carried over   -   £37 10 4

		£.	s.	d.
Brought over	-	37	10	4
Cloaths and fuel, eftimated at	- - - -	6	0	0
Houfe-rent	- - - - - -	3	18	0
Total annual expences	£	47	8	4
Deduct earnings	-	35	15	0
Deficiency	£	11	13	4

This account, it is probable, is erroneous in fome particulars, for the man has not lately received any affiftance from the parifh. He ftated his various expences with every appearance of veracity. That he does not earn more than 9s. a week, in a place where wages are high, is eafily accounted for: he often fpends 2 or 3 days in the week, in an ale-houfe, lamenting the hardnefs of the times. Some inferences may be drawn from this account, refpecting the proportion of the different kinds of food ufed by people of this defcription in manufacturing towns. The improvidence of the family is glaring: not a fixpence is laid by, to provide againft ficknefs, or old age; and it is probable, that the temporary incapacity arifing from the one, or the inevitable effects of the other, will ultimately throw them on the parifh.

Auguft, 1795.

LINCOLNSHIRE.

ALFORD.

THIS parifh contains by eftimation 1300 acres, a confiderable part of which is common-field. In the fmall market town of Alford, there are

188 families, confifting of tradefmen, inn-keepers, common mechanics, fhop-keepers, a few farmers, and labourers. No manufactory is carried on in this parifh. The inhabitants are of the Church of England, with the exception of one fmall congregation of Calvinifts, and one of Methodifts. 48 houfes pay the window-tax; and 90 are exempted.

The prices of provifions are: beef, from 4¼d to 5d. the pound; mutton, 5½d; veal, 4d. and 4½d.; bacon, 8d the pound; potatoes, 16 lb. for 6d.; butter, 6d. the lb; flour, from 2s. 2d to 2s 6d. the ftone; wheat, £3. 10s. a quarter; barley, £2 a quarter; oats, 26s a quarter; malt, 54s. a quarter; coals, 28s. a chaldron of 32 bufhels; milk, ½d. a pint.

The wages of common labourers are from 1s. 4d to 1s. 6d a day, without victuals: women, for weeding corn, have 8d. or 10d a day, without victuals: in the harveft, wages are often as high as 5s a day. There are 11 ale-houfes in this parifh; and 2 Friendly Societies, containing together 64 members.

The rent of land is from 15s. to 30s. an acre; the average is about 20s. Tithes are generally taken in kind. The land-tax raifes nearly £167.

Before the year 1791, the Poor were taken care of by the overfeers of the parifh, who rented a houfe, wherein moft of the Poor were kept, and thofe who were able to work were employed. A fchool of induftry was kept up for a few years; but having been thought to be difadvantageous to the parifh, it was wholly difcontinued laft year. Till lately, this parifh joined with another parifh in the maintenance of their Poor, fo that the net expenditure for the Poor could not be afcertained: fince the year 1791, the Poor have been farmed, and maintained in a poor-houfe. The prefent number in the houfe is 15; of whom 3 are under 7 years of age; 3 between 7 and 15 years old: and the reft chiefly old people. There are no baftards in the houfe: no information could be obtained of earnings; it is probable, they are very infignificant; as an old woman, who is almoft a pauper, is the governefs of the houfe; fhe is often oppofed by very clamorous competitors for power, and is fcarcely able to retain the reins of government; much lefs to enforce good order and induftry. The following is the general rotation of diet:

Breakfaft,

	Breakfast.	Dinner.	Supper.
Sunday,	Bread and milk.	Bread, potatoes, broth, dumplins, and butcher's meat.	Broth and bread.
Monday,	Do.	Bread, cold meat, and milk.	Bread and milk.
Tuesday,	Do.	As Sunday.	As Sunday.
Wednesday,	Do.	As Monday.	As Monday.
Thursday,	Do.	As Sunday.	As Sunday.
Friday,	Do.	As Monday.	As Monday.
Saturday,	Do.	Bread and butter, or cheese, and milk.	Do.

One pound of bread a day is allowed to each adult: the beds are, mostly, filled with feathers : that neatness, which discovers itself in some work-houses, is not to be found here.

Several small donations, amounting to £ 6. a year, are annually distri-buted amongst such Poor as do not receive parochial assistance. The officers of this parish do not grant certificates, except to such parishioners as reside within the limits of the county; about 3 or 4 are generally granted in a year : there are usually 2 or 3 removals in a year; a removal, which was lately contested, cost the parish between £ 60. and £ 70.

A Table of Baptisms, Burials, Poor's Rates, &c.

Years.	Baptisms.	Burials.	Assessments. £. s. d.			Rate in the Pound. s. d.	
1774	34	29	—	—	—	—	—
1775	32	30	116	9	1½ ending April, 1775.	1	6
1776	33	18	91	18	2	1	2
1777	29	34	101	18	3	1	3
1778	39	30	144	16	3	1	9
1779	35	32	147	19	9	1	10
1780	36	36	163	0	3	2	0
1781	31	35	195	4	8½	2	4
1782	—	—	211	6	5	2	9
1783	28	36	328	12	8	4	6
1784	35	34	298	4	5	4	0
1785	42	28	No accounts this year.			0	0
1786	38	23	209	4	0	2	8
1787	33	25	228	5	8½	2	11
1788	49	19	276	14	4½	3	6

Years.

Years.	Baptisns.	Burials.	Affessments £. s. d.	-	-	Rate in the Pound. s. d.
1789	22	18	276 4 1¾	-	-	3 5
1790	40	16	228 18 0	-	-	2 10
1791	30	21	- -	-	-	2 2
1792	30	16	- -			2 2
1793	37	13	The Poor were let these years: the farmers received the affess-			2 4
1794	45	27	ments			2 4
1795	—	—	-	-	-	2 4

A parcel of land belongs to this parish, the rents of which are annually added to the Poor's Rate, but not included in the above account; the amount of the rent from 1774 to 1783 was £15 a year; since that period, it has not exceeded £12. a year: this rent is paid to the farmers of the Poor, who, on the other hand, pay £16. a year for a sort of work-house, and a parcel of land.   *June*, 1795.

COCKERINGTON.

THIS parish contains about 1400 acres: the inhabitants are all employed in agriculture, either as farmers or labourers. 22 houses pay the window tax; and 10 are exempted. There are no ale houses in this parish. The rent of land is from 5s. to 25s. an acre. The average rent is about 16s. The land-tax is £93. and is 1s. 6d. in the pound. The greatest part of the land in this parish was, formerly, common-field; it was enclosed 25 years ago. A confiderable portion of most of the parishes in Lincoln-shire is common-field. Upon the enclosure, land was given in lieu of all tithes.

The prices of provisions are: beef, 4d. and 5d the pound; mutton, 5d.; veal, 3½d. to 5d.; bacon, 8d.; wheat, 7s. 6d. the bushel; malt, 50s. to 55s. the quarter; barley, 36s. to 39s. the quarter; butter, 8d. the pound of 18 oz.; milk, 1d. the pint.

                                                    The

The wages of labour are: for common labourers, with diet, 1od. the day in winter, and 1s. 6d. the day in fummer.

The following were the annual difburfements for the Poor, from the year 1774:

	£.	s.	d.
Year ending at Eafter 1774	78	5	9
1775	93	6	10
1776	82	5	5
1777	50	6	2
1778	50	3	9
1779	57	13	10
1780	No accounts.		
1781	85	18	9
1782	67	5	9
1783	83	4	8
1784	82	12	2
1785	82	5	9
1786	52	10	6
1787	97	4	9
1788	74	1	9
1789	85	17	8
1790	No accounts.		
1791	70	13	6

No accounts of affeffments or difburfements fubfequent to 1791 are preferved; a few balances only are inferted in the book: the officers, however, fay, that the difburfements for the Poor have not varied much during the laft eight years; and that in the year ending at Eafter 1795, the affeffments for the Poor, and the quota towards hiring a man for the Navy, amounted to £95. 6s. which were collected at 1s. 8d. in the pound on the full rental.

The Poor belonging to this parifh have an allowance at home; the following is a lift of the Paupers, who receive weekly penfions:

	Ages.	Weekly Allowance s.	d.
1 A labourer's widow	70	2	0
2 A fpinfter; lame	24	1	6

3 The

		Ages.	Weekly Allowance.	
			s.	d.
3	The parish clerk; lame	60	3	0
4	A soldier's wife and child	23	2	6
5	An orphan	8	2	0
6	Do.	9	1	6
7	A labourer's widow	70	1	6
8	A bastard	---	1	6
9	Do.		1	6
10	A spinster; lame	20	1	0

Besides the above, there are some others who receive casual relief. This parish grants a certificate about once in 2 years; a removal occurs about once in 5 or 6 years: no contest can be remembered.

Cottages in this and several of the neighbouring parishes are very small: they are made of clay, and thatched with straw. Labourers appear to be much more cleanly in their persons and habitations, than persons of a similar description in the northern parts of England.   *May,* 1795;

L O U T H.

THIS parish contains about 3000 acres: it's population in 1782 was 3300; and, at present, it is generally supposed to amount to 4000 inhabitants; consisting of a few farmers, and other persons of the description usually found in a small market town, that has no manufacture.   Louth is a small market for cattle, grain, butcher's meat, and other provisions; but is not a thoroughfare of any consequence.   Coal is now brought by a canal from the Humber to within ½ a mile of this town, which has considerably lessened the prices of fuel.   It is hoped, that the introduction of coal will induce the inhabitants to desist from their ancient practice, not yet entirely disused, of using the dung of their cattle for fuel[1].   In this parish 392 houses

---

[1] " They brenne also cowe-dung dryed with the hete of the sunne," was the remark of Leland, near 300 years ago, respecting the inhabitants of the Isle of Portland. Itin. iii f. 50.

This

houfes pay the commutation tax; the number exempted could not be obtained.

The prices of provifions are: beef, from 4d. to 5d the pound; mutton, 5d.; veal, 3½d. to 5d.: bacon, 8d.; flour, 2s. 6d. to 2s. 10d. the ftone; oat-meal, 2s. the ftone; potatoes, 6d. to 9d. a peck; wheat, 7s. 6d. a bufhel; malt, 50s. to 55s. a quarter; barley, 36s. to 39s. a quarter; butter, 8d. for 18 oz.; milk, 1d a pint. The wages of common labourers are from 20d. to 2s. a day, in fummer; and 16d. in the winter; or throughout the year, 1s. 6d. a day, without victuals. In this parifh there are 22 ale-houfes, (8 of which fell wine;) and four Friendly Societies, containing, together, 190 members.

The rent of land is from 10s. to £3. an acre, on an average about £1. 1s. Moft of the land belonging to this town lies in 2 large common fields, which are fallowed and cropped alternately: in feveral parts of thefe common fields there are large tracts of wafte land, upon which a great number of poor people fummer each a cow, which in winter go at large in thefe fields. The Poor complain heavily of the farmers, faying, "That they encroach on their property;" and the farmers fay, "That the Poor take the opportunity of eating their corn with their cattle." Tithes are here taken in kind. The land-tax amounts to £356. 16s.; and is about 1s. 3d. in the pound.

Donations, of the annual value of about £100. are diftributed amongft fuch Poor of this parifh as do not receive parochial aid. Here is an hofpital or alms-houfe, in which apartments are provided for 12 decayed widows; befides which, a penfion of £3. 7s. and 7 pecks of coals, is given to each of them annually.

In 1791 a new houfe of induftry was erected, which coft £700.; towards the payment of which, £260. (which arofe from the fale of a houfe, and a piece of land, belonging to the parifh,) were paid; the remaining debt is to be difcharged by annual inftalments of £50. from the farmer of the Poor, till the whole debt is difcharged. The houfe is not erected on a good plan; the only entrance to the houfe, yard, &c. is through a door not

This cuftom ftill continues, as well as another of ufing pig-dung, inftead of foap; whence the following, rather coarfe, couplet, has become proverbial—

In the Ifle of Portland, in fam'd Dorfetfhire,
The pigs fh ~ foap, and the cows fh— fire

3 F 2   4 feet

4 feet wide, and only 8 feet high, which is very inconvenient for the taking in of hay, or bringing out manure, &c : the ftair-cafe is narrow and fteep ; there are no regular working rooms, or detached apartments for the reception of the fick. There is one large lodging-room for the men, and another for the women, each containing 14 beds, which are partitioned from each other by deal boards at each end, and on one fide : the view of a fick neighbour is thereby, in a great meafure, obftructed; but, to a feeling mind, the fenfe of hearing muft frequently convey very difagreeable ideas ; the fmell muft, alfo, be frequently offenfive : yet, upon the whole, and under all thefe unpleafant circumftances, the houfe is kept as clean as it well can be. The gentlemen of this town are now aware of the inconvenience of trufting, to inexperienced people, the execution of a project of fuch importance ; and feem to be convinced that the advantages derived from houfes of induftry are very inconfiderable.

The prefent farmer of the poor houfe of induftry, is a woolcomber and manufacturer of worfted ; he employs fome of the Poor in combing wool, fpinning and knitting worfted, and fome in common labour out of the houfe: he fays, that he provides places for thofe boys and girls who do not like his bufinefs. At prefent, there are 39 Paupers in the houfe; confifting of 15 children, (under 12 years of age,) 9 men, and 15 women. The farmer adds, that not more than 8 or 9 people are conftantly employed : the others are either young children, old, or infirm ; or are engaged in attending their fick companions in other neceffary offices in the houfe. The farmer of the Poor pays, at this time, about 22s. a week to 28 poor people out of the houfe, and about £65. a year to the families of 5 militia-men ferving for this parifh ; and he is at the expence of all neceffary medicinal affiftance.

Bill of Fare ufed in this Poor-houfe.

	Breakfaft.	Dinner.	Supper.
Sunday,	Milk, or water-gruel, and 6 oz. of bread.	Flour puddings, butcher's meat, bread, broth, and potatoes, or greens.	Bread and milk.
Monday,	Bread and broth.	Milk, or cheefe, and bread.	6 oz. of bread, and 2 oz. of cheefe or butter, with beer.
Tuefday,	Same as Sunday.	Same as Sunday.	Same as Sunday
Wednefday,	Same as Monday.	Same as Monday.	Same as Monday
Thurfday,	Same as Sunday.	Same as Sunday.	Same as Sunday
Friday,	Same as Monday.	Same as Monday.	Same as Monday.
Saturday,	Same as Sunday.	Dumplins and treacle fauce.	Bread and milk.

Small

Small beer is allowed at every dinner and fupper, when cheefe is ufed: thofe, who work out of the houfe, have often cold meat allowed them for dinner on bread-and-milk days. On meat-days about 28 lbs. of meat are boiled for 40 people.

About £100. being the amount of feveral donations, are annually diftributed amongft fuch Poor as are not otherwife chargeable to the parifh.

Table of Baptifins, Burials, Annual Difburfements, &c.

Years	Baptifms	Burials	Difburfements.			Rate in the pound, net rent.		
			£.	s.	d.	s.	d.	
1774	88	69	224	12	0	1	0	There was a common Poor houfe in thefe years.
1775	87	71	280	18	0	1	3	
1776	101	61	340	0	0	1	5	
1777	97	75	401	10	0	1	8	In thefe years a woollen manufacture was carried on in the houfe; but from the unfkilfulnefs of the directors, it proved unfuccefsful.
1778	99	85	314	19	0	1	4	
1779	92	55	488	13	0	2	0	
1780	90	96	270	1	0	1	1	In thefe years, the Poor and Poorhoufe were let to a manufacturer.
1781	100	83	302	3	0	1	2	
1782	94	75	506	1	0	2	0	In thefe years, the houfe was under the direction of a hired mafter, who was not much acquainted with the manufacturing bufinefs.
1783	87	155	459	6	0	1	9	
1784	109	121	439	5	0	1	9	
1785	103	98	441	19	0	1	9	In thefe years, the Poor, workhoufe, furniture, &c. were let to a woollen-manufacturer, who fuftained every expence relative to the Poor in this parifh, (law contefts excepted,) and employed the Poor as he pleafed, and had their earnings.
1786	101	83	369	8	0	1	5	
1787	121	80	402	0	0	1	5½	
1788	92	73	372	12	0	1	5	
1789	111	128	376	17	0	1	5	
1790	112	113	399	18	0	1	5	
1791	127	68	431	16	0	1	5½	
1792	133	67	394	8	0	1	5	
1793	142	64	399	18	0	1	5	
1794	117	134	798	17	0	2	8	The Poor were not let this year.
1795	—	—	510	2	0	1	9	The Poor, and houfe, &c. let this year, as before.

It muft be noticed, that, in 1782, about £70. which were paid for the erection of a new building belonging to the parifh, are included in the difburfements

ments of that year: in that, and the fubfequent years, are likewife included the different fums of money paid to the conftables, which the contractors for the Poor, &c. are obliged to pay out of the above fums; the money paid on that occafion is various, of late it has amounted to about £25 a year. It is worthy of remark, that, in 1794, when the Poor were managed by the parifh-officers, the expence was double of what it was the year before, when they were farmed   *June*, 1795.

SPILSBY.

THE parifh of Spilfby contains, by eftimation, 1200 acres. By an account of the population, taken 3 years ago, the number of inhabitants was found to be 850. They are, chiefly, common tradefmen, fhop-keepers, farmers, and labourers. 121 houfes pay the window-tax; and about 50 are exempted. There is no manufacture of confequence in the parifh, and only 1 Friendly Society.

The wages of common labourers, without diet, are about 1s. a day in winter; and 2s. in fummer. In harveft, men receive 2s. 6d. a day; and inftances are not wanting of 6s. and 7s a day being earned at that feafon. The women have very little employment at home, except in taking care of their family. A few endeavour to get work in wafhing, and in affifting at public-houfes, (of which there are 9 in the parifh,) and receive from 6d. to 8d. a day.

The prices of provifions are: beef, 4½d. and 5d. the pound; mutton, 5d.; veal, 4d. and 4½d.; bacon, 8d.; butter, 6d.; potatoes, 5d. and 6d. the peck; milk, ½d. the pint; wheat, 63s. to 70s. the qr.; oats, 28s. the qr.; barley, 42s. the qr.; malt, 52s. the qr.; coals, 1s. 6d. the bufhel

The labouring people are not very thrifty, or parfimonious in their diet; and, confequently, often very poor. Tea, milk, and potatoes, are much ufed; to which are added, butter, and butcher's meat, whenever they can poffibly be obtained.

The high-ways are maintained by ftatute labour, without a Rate. The average rent of land is about 24s. an acre. The land-tax amounts to

I   £151.

£ 151. 2s. 4d. The greateſt part of the pariſh belongs to Lord Gwydir, who is likewiſe impropiiator of the great tithes. His tenants pay no tithes; from other farmers, a ſmall modus is collected.

The inhabitants of Spilſby are, principally, of the Eſtabliſhed Religion. A ſmall number, however, of Methodiſts, have a congregation in the town.

At the concluſion of the American war, the Rates in this pariſh were ſo high, and the poverty of the labouring claſſes in this part of the county of Lincoln ſo great, that the Magiſtrates for the ſouthern diviſion of Lindſay were induced to publiſh orders for purchaſing materials, providing proper places to ſet the Poor to work in, and teaching all poor children in the diſtrict to knit before they were ſix, and to ſpin before they were nine years of age. Towards the end of the year 1783, theſe laudable views were much aſſiſted by the eſtabliſhment of a Society, for the promotion of induſtry, by diſtributing premiums, in various articles of cloathing, amongſt ſuch children, of certain ages and deſcriptions, within the diſtrict, as ſhould, within a given time, produce the greateſt quantity of work, of different kinds, and of the beſt quality. To carry this project into execution, the pariſhes within the diſtrict were to ſubſcribe a ſum equal to one per cent of their laſt year's Poor's Rates; and individuals, within the diſtrict, to ſubſcribe 5s. each annually. From theſe funds, and ſeveral private benefactions, ſchools were ſoon provided in the ſeveral pariſhes in the diviſion, for the inſtruction of children in the ſpinning of jerſey: and premiums have been, ſince, annually diſtributed among the moſt induſtrious, who were farther diſtinguiſhed by the appellation of King, or Queen, of the ſpinners of their diſtrict; innocent devices to encourage induſtry; which, if they animate the Poor, as much as ribbons and gaiters ſtimulate the Rich, to active and honeſt exertion, muſt render it deſirable that the titles of royalty ſhould grace the brow of every induſtrious cottage child in the kingdom.

In the year 1786 the Society eſtabliſhed a dyer and hot-preſſer, at Louth.

From a full account of the proceedings of the Society, publiſhed a few years ago, at Louth, it appears that between January 1786 and the middle of 1790, 222 knitting premiums were diſtributed, for which the number of candidates were 400 children, all under eight years of age. The following is an account of the number of premiums adjudged to ſpinners,

of

of the number of candidates, and of their earnings, in the two trial months each year, during the above period.

1786.   150 candidates for 103 spinning premiums.
Total of their work, in the two trial months, 464 grofs, 8 dozen, 11 hanks; worth £ 139. 8s

N. B. A grofs is 12 dozen hanks; a hank is 7 lees, and one lee 80 yards.

Each candidate's daily earning, upon an average, was fomewhat more than 4d. Average of their ages, eleven years four months.

1787.   128 candidates for 90 spinning premiums.
Total of their work, in the two trial months, 398 grofs, 2 dozen, 8 hanks; worth £ 119. 9s 4d.

Each candidate's daily earning, upon an average, was fomewhat above 4¼d. Average of their ages, eleven years five months.

1788.   142 candidates for 105 spinning premiums.
Total of their work, in the two trial months, 460 grofs, 2 dozen, 5 hanks; worth £ 138. 1s. 2½d.

Each candidate's daily earning, upon an average, was 4½d. Average of their ages, ten years eleven months.

1789.   136 candidates for 101 spinning premiums.
Total of their work, in the two trial months, 505 grofs, 3 dozen; worth £ 150. 16s. 6d.

Each candidate's daily earning, upon an average, was fomewhat more than 5d. Average of their ages, eleven years eleven months.

1790.   112 candidates for 70 spinning premiums.
Total of their work, in the two trial months, 438 grofs, 10 dozen, 5 hanks; worth £ 131. 13s. 2½d.

A candidate's daily earning, upon an average, was 5½d. Average of their ages, eleven years eleven months.

The spinning schools are now wholly laid afide; and the opinions of well informed men on the subject, with refpect to their utility, are extremely various. Many perfons thought that schools, conducted on the plan propofed by the Society of Induftry, were not only expenfive to the parifh, but detrimental to the children themfelves; for, by being fo long confined to a fedentary employment, at an early period of life, they were
often

often rendered puny and weak; and at the age of 12 or 13, when they ought to go out to fervice with the farmers, or become apprentices, they were fo extremely ignorant of every thing, except fpinning, that it was a long time before they could be of any fervice to their mafters; befides which, the gieat and fudden change of employment was often injurious to the children. Otheis were, and are, of opinion, that, had the Society been properly encouraged, and the fpinning fchools continued, the country would, ultimately, have been much benefited, the rates confidciably reduced, and the children of the Poor rendered ferviceable members of the State, from being trained, by conftant and orderly employment, to virtue and induftry. The unfavourable opinion formed of thefe parifh working fchools, although, perhaps, originating, with fome, from piejudice, was, it may be prefumed, in many, the refult of faii conviction, that the inconveniencies would, ultimately, more than counterbalance the benefits of fuch inftitutions; for it cannot be fuppofed, that either gentlemen or farmeis fhould be inclined to difcountenance a fyftem, from which there was any probabil ty of theii inteiefts being effentially promoted, by a reduction of the Poor's Rate. The experience, however, of 8 years, has proved, that, although fchools of induftry may flourifh for a while, under the active zeal of their firft promoters, yet, when, after a few years trial, they are left to the fuperintendance of lefs interefted adminiftrators, they dwindle into the ordinary ftate of paiifh poor-houfes.

A poor-houfe has exifted for feveral years at Spilfby, and to it are fent fuch Poor as do not receive relief at their own homes. They are under the direction of a worfted manufacturer, who lives in the woik houfe, and, by an agieement made laft Eafter, provides cloaths and-other neceffaries for every one the parifh fends thither; foi which he is allowed 3s. 6d. a week for each perfon, together with their eainings; thefe, however, aie very inconfiderable. There are in the houfe, at prefent, 8 children, under 12 years of age; one man and woman, each about 70 years old; and a woman, 35 years of age: foui of the children aie baftaids. The overfeers alfo pay 28s. weekly to 14 out-penfioners, moft of whom have families; to 2 militia men's families, 6s. a week; and to feveial others, occafional relief. Amongft the weekly penfioneis 6 baftards aie included Before the Poor were contiacted for, 5 guineas a year and victuals weie allowed to a perfon who fupeiintended the woik-houfe. An apothecaiy was alfo paid £ 6. a year for his attendance on the Poor. The houfe is a good building, but much out of repair: it is not kept fo clean as it ought to be: the beds are filled with feathers, and well provided with covering. The prefent undertaker is bound to obferve the following table of diet:

	Breakfaft.	Dinner.	Supper
Sunday,	Milk or broth.	Beef, mutton, or pork.	Bread and cheefe.
Monday,	Broth.	Cold meat.	Ditto
Tuefday,	Milk pottage.	Bullocks' or fheep's heads.	Bread, cheefe, and milk,
Wednefday,	Broth.	Light dumplins.	Bread and cheefe.
Thurfday,	Milk pottage.	As Sunday.	As Tuefday.
Friday,	Ditto.	Bread and cheefe, puddings, or dumplins.	As Sunday.
Saturday,	Broth.	Puddings, or dumplins.	Ditto.

From Lady-day to Michaelmas, the Poor, in the houfe, rife at 6 in the morning, and go to reft at 9 at night: the doors are fhut at half paft 8.

From Michaelmas-day to Lady-day, they rife at 8 in the morning, and go to reft at 8 at night: the doors are fhut at 6 o'clock in the evening.

This parifh, on an average, grants about 4 or 5 certificates in a year, and has about 1 removal in the fame time; a contefted removal feldom occurs above once in 10 years.

A Table of Baptifms, Burials, and Difburfements for the Poor.

Years.	Baptifms.	Burials.	Expenditure.			Rate in the Pound	
			£.	s.	d.	s.	d.
1720	—	—	59	4	6	1	2
1721	—	—	69	16	7	1	4
1722	—	—	50	8	6	1	3
1723	—	—	55	8	8	1	3
1740	—	—	59	16	11	1	0
1760	—	—	104	8	3	1	6
1766	—	—	85	5	8½	1	0
1774	24	16	160	5	9	2	1
1775	33	17	181	10	10½	2	6
1776	16	10	191	15	0	2	1
1777	28	19	183	14	5½	2	0
1778	27	20	179	5	10¾	1	10

Years.

Years.	Baptisms.	Burials.	Expenditure.			Rate in the Pound.	
			£.	s.	d.	s.	d.
1779	21	12	244	11	3	2	7
1780	20	27	195	5	8¾	2	0
1781	29	19	269	3	8	3	0
1782	26	18	233	1	8	2	4
1783	28	13	270	0	3½	3	0
1784	27	27	175	14	3½	1	9
1785	25	15	222	8	5	2	9
1786	33	14	198	13	9½	2	5
1787	19	12	165	14	8½	2	0
1788	23	22	174	0	10	2	1
1789	29	18	164	18	11	2	0
1790	23	17	194	3	9	2	3
1791	32	13	176	9	9½	2	0
1792	25	14	136	19	0	1	8
1793	25	16	187	0	7	2	0
1794	26	14	205	5	2½	2	2
1795	—	—	244	15	11	2	8

The rent of a few houses, amounting to £ 30. a year, is annually given to poor house-keepers, who receive no parochial aid. The same benefactor, who bequeathed these houses to the Poor, also founded a school, for the education of 15 poor children, with a salary to the master. A Sunday school is established in this town, for 50 scholars.

June, 1795.

SWINESHEAD.

THIS parish contains, by estimation, 4400 acres, and 1550 inhabitants; consisting of a few shop-keepers, publicans, tradesmen, and mechanics ; the rest are farmers, and labourers. The parishioners are principally of the Church of England ; but a small congregation of Methodists have a

3 F 2   chapel

chapel here. 166 houfes pay the commutation-tax ; the number exempted could not be obtained.

The prices of provifions are : beef, 5d. the lb ; mutton, 5d. to 5½d ; pork, 5d. ; bacon, 9d ; butter, 7d or 7½d ; potatoes, 4d. a peck ; wheat, £ 3. 10s. the quarter ; barley, £ 1. 16s. the quarter ; malt, £ 2 12s. the quarter ; flour, 2s. 4d. to 2s. 10d. the ftone ; milk, ½d the pint, but little is fold, as the farmers moftly flock their paftures with fheep. The Poor ufe much tea, and water-pottage ; the latter is made of water, oatmeal, onions, falt, and pepper, with the addition of butter, when it can be procured. Labourers' wages, in winter, are from 1s. 2d. to 1s 6d a day ; and in fummer, 2s. a day, without victuals. In harveft, from 3s. to 4s. a day, and fometimes, confiderably more. Women receive 1s. or 1s. 2d. a day, for weeding corn ; but in winter they have little or no employ, except in fpinning jerfey, or worfted, in which the earnings are fo extremely low that fcarcely one perfon in ten will apply to it. It is generally remarked, that the poor people, in thefe extenfive fens, are moftly fluggifh, and have an averfion to induftry ; whether this circumftance in any degree accounts for the general diflike of Mr. Bouyer's plan, of fchools of induftry, I fhall not pretend to determine.

In this parifh there are 10 ale-houfes, 3 of which fell wine. There is no Friendly Society in the parifh. The rent of land, upon an average, is about 20s. or 21s. an acre. Farms are from £ 10. to £ 200. a year, but moftly from £ 40. to £ 100. a year. When the fens were divided, about 27 years ago, a quantity of land was given in lieu of all tithes. The land-tax amounts to £ 470. 12s. The Poor have been farmed for more than 20 years back : the farmer finds a houfe for fuch Paupers as are willing to come into it ; and the parifh furnifhes it with beds, filled with chaff, and bedding : at prefent, only 5 Paupers are in the houfe ; viz. a fhoe-maker, 46 years of age, (who is deaf and dumb) ; an old woman, and 3 baftard children, who are from 6 to 9 years of age. The regular weekly out-penfioners are as follow :

		s.	d.
1 A labourer's widow, and 4 children, who received 6s. a week in winter ; now - - - - -		4	0
2 A tailor's ditto, aged 70 ; - - - -		2	0
3 A labourer's ditto, aged 68 ; - - - -		2	0

4 A

		s.	d.
4 A labourer's widow, aged 30, and 1 child; - -		1	6
5 A lame man, aged 28 ; - - - -		1	0
6 A woman and 2 children, in Lincoln hofpital ; - -		2	0

Befides thefe, theie are fome who receive cafual relief'; and, in general, it muft be confideied, that, at this feafon, the Poor are moft eafily maintained, from the work which they can procure in the fields. The farmer of the Poor, this year, is to receive £130. for which he agrees to fupport the Poor belonging to this parifh with food : the parifh-officers are to fuinifh cloaths, pay the doctor's bills, (which may amount to £ 20. a year ;) and to be at all expences of meetings, journies, removals, appeals, and the maintenance of cafual Poor who do not belong to the paiifh ; alfo to give occafional relief to indigent parifhioners, as it was thought the farmer had too hard a bargain for fome yeais paft : his allowance laft year was £ 120.

A fubfcription, made heie laft winter, for the neceffitous, amounted to £ 50. : upon the whole, the Pooi are well fupported in this parifh. Several donations, charities, or doles, amounting to about £ 60. a year, are annually diftiibuted among poor houfe-keepers. Here is alfo a charity fchool for the education of 25 poor children. Certificates are granted and received, without fcruple. There are about 3 removals from this parifh in a year; an appeal fcarcely happens once in 7 years.

A Table of Baptifms, Burials, and Poor's Rates.

Years.	Baptifms.	Burials.	Difburfements.			Rate in the Pound.
			£.	s.	d.	
1774	57	36	188	16	9½	
1775	55	47	181	11	11½	
1776	48	48	155	14	0½	
1777	63	44	152	17	11¼	
1778	60	105	184	16	5¾	s. d.
1779	49	73	236	5	1½	0 10
1780	59	45	225	4	11	0 11
1781	46	51	279	7	5	— —
1782	59	44	222	17	4	1 0
1783	64	64	239	16	3	— —
1784	54	67	314	19	8½	1 4

Years.

Years.	Baptifms.	Burials.	Difburfements.			Rate in the Pound.	
			£.	s.	d.	s.	d.
1785	68	59	287	11	1½	1	2
1786	43	42	247	3	10½	1	2
1787	52	29	231	19	10¾	1	2
1788	50	37	244	8	0¼	1	0
1789	65	53	349	7	7¼	1	6
1790	64	45	207	7	8¼	1	5
1791	56	48	241	3	0½	—	—
1792	73	41	242	13	6¼	1	1
1793	67	46	328	2	1½	1	6
1794	67	57	321	9	7	1	4

The accounts for the laft year, ending at Eafter 1795, are not yet paffed, or inferted in the book: affeffments were that year 1s. 3d. in the pound, and were faid to be on the rack or net rent. Exclufive of the above dif-burfements, a fum is paid to the conftables, which amounts annually to about £ 35.

According to the Returns made to Parliament, £. s. d.

The Expences for the Poor in 1776 were	172	8	5
The Affeffments in 1783	225	11	11
in 1784	332	8	11
in 1785	296	14	10

June, 1795.

TATTERSHALL.

TATTERSHALL is a fmall market-town, in which there is no manu-facture: a great proportion of the inhabitants are farmers; a few mecha-nics and fhop-keepers; the reft are chiefly labourers. The population has not varied much for the laft 20 years. 50 houfes pay the commutation-tax; the number of thofe exempted could not be obtained. The prices of provifions here are nearly fimilar to thofe at Spilfby There are 4 ale-houfes, but no Friendly Society in Tatterfhall. The land-tax amounts to

o £ 144.

£ 144. 2s. 6d. a year. The Poor receive an allowance at their own houfes of about 2s. a week, each. Very little information could be obtained refpecting them : the parifh-officers would not permit the parifh-books to be infpected ; but furnifhed the following extract of the Rate on the net rental, and the amount of the Affeffments for the laft 21 years.

Years.	Affeffment			Rate in the Pound.	
	£.	s.	d.	s.	d.
1774	77	0	0	1	8
1775	91	15	0	2	1
1776	138	1	6	3	0
1777	113	0	0	2	6
1778	100	3	8	2	3
1779	97	15	2	2	2
1780	110	0	0	2	3
1781	130	0	0	2	10
1782	105	1	8	2	4
1783	90	15	9	2	0
1784	152	15	4	3	5
1785	137	10	0	3	0
1786	110	6	0	2	3
1787	85	11	2½	1	11
1788	82	10	1	1	11
1789	100	1	1	2	3
1790	109	10	0	2	5
1791	166	0	0	3	8
1792	153	0	0	3	5
1793	169	14	6	3	9
1794	174	0	0	3	10
1795 Eafter	177	8	6	3	10

I much doubt the correctnefs of thefe extracts. According to the Returns made to Parliament,

		£.	s.	d.
The Expences for the Poor in 1776	were	129	4	11
The Affeffments in 1783		181	1	0
in 1784		158	2	3
in 1785		127	5	0

June, 1795.

WILLOUGHBY.

THIS parifh contains 5647 acres, of which 536 are common-field. The inhabitants are almoft all agicultural labourers : their number, by an enumeration taken in 1788, was found to be as follows :

	59 married couple	118
	fingle men -	10
	fingle women -	11
Children at home with {	boys - -	61
their parents - {	girls - -	73
	men - -	18
	women - -	19
Servants - - {	boys - -	19
	girls - -	10
	inmates - -	39
	Total inhabitants -	378

There is here a fmall congregation of Methodifts. 41 houfes pay the commutation tax. There are 2 ale-houfes in the parifh, but no Friendly Society. Wages in hufbandry are from 20d. to 2s. a day, without victuals : in hay and corn harveft, wages are moftly 3s. or 4s a day. Moft of the land here is in fheep pafture ; the average rent of land is about 9s. or 10s. an acre. Corn land, of every defcription, pays 6s. an acre, compofition for tithe ; grafs, from 1s. to 2s. 6d. an acre : the average is about 1s. 6d. an acre. The land-tax raifed produces £184.

The Poor have an allowance at home ; there are, at prefent, 14 weekly penfioners, chiefly old labourers and widows, who receive £1. 1s. a week ; one militia-man's family is allowed 3s. a week : the reft of the money raifed by the Poor's Rates is paid, at the difcretion of the officers, for coals, houfe-rents, repairing houfes for the Poor, &c. The overfeer receives

ceives 4 guineas, as an annual falary : upon an average, about 2 certificates have been annually granted for fome years back : about 1 removal occurs every three years : no perfon can recollect a contested one.

A Table of Baptifms, Burials, and Difburfements on account of the Poor.

Years	Baptifms.	Burials	Difburfements
1774	7	6	
1775	10	5	
1776	6	5	£. s. d.
1777	7	8 ending at Eafter	169 10 4¾
1778	17	6	216 16 6
1779	11	7	206 8 6
1780	11	15	195 12 0½
1781	9	21	190 18 4¼
1782	8	9	180 17 11
1783	12	12	220 15 6¼
1784	6	5	257 18 10½
1785	9	9	251 0 6½
1786	15	7	266 16 11½
1787	6	12	266 12 2¾
1788	11	8	249 6 9
1789	10	9	227 12 6½
1790	10	6	211 1 7½
1791	5	4	223 8 9
1792	14	5	304 1 4
1793	6	16	229 16 9¾
1794	10	8	232 17 10½
1795	—	—	241 3 1

In the above difburfements is included the money paid towards the county ftock ; it is generally from £ 15. to £ 20. a year. In the laft year's expenditure £ 24. are included, which were paid towards hiring a man for the Navy. The affeffment was raifed at 2s. in the pound.

The parish of Willoughby is situated in the district of Alford, one of the four districts, in which the schools of industry were introduced. Several poor children from Willoughby, have been succefsful competitors for the spinning and knitting premiums, which are distributed every spring. The following lift of premiums, appointed to be distributed in the year 1795, and of the regulations, and conditions, impofed on the candidates, is copied, verbatim, from a paper published by the general committee of the Society of Industry, at the clofe of the year 1794.

The following Premiums to be allowed to the beft Spinners of Jerfey.

FIRST RATE PREMIUM

Boys	Girls.
Coat, waiftcoat, and breeches	Hat and ribband
Three fhirts and ftocks	Two fhifts, two pair of fleeves, two caps
Three pair of ftockings	Gown, quilted and flannel petticoat
Two pair of fhoes	Stays
Pair of buckles	One white apron
Two pocket handkerchiefs	One check ditto
Hat	Two pair of ftockings
Medal, No, 1	One pair of fhoes and buckles
	Two pocket handkerchiefs
	Two neck ditto
	Medal, No. 1.

To each of the four firft of their refpective diftricts will alfo be given a pair of knit worfted gloves.

SECOND RATE PREMIUM.

Boys.	Girls.
Coat, waiftcoat, and breeches	Hat and ribband
Shirt	Gown and durant petticoat
Stockings	Check apron
Shoes and buckles	Neck handkerchief
Hat	Pocket ditto
Medal, No. 2.	Stockings and fhoes
	Medal, No. 2.

THIRD RATE PREMIUM

Shirt	Hat and ribband
Breeches	Gown and woolfey petticoat
Stockings	Check apron
Shoes and buckles	Neck handkerchief
Hat	Stockings
Medal, No 3.	Shoes
	Medal, No. 3.

FOURTH

FOURTH RATE PREMIUM.

BOYS.	GIRLS.
Breeches	Hat and ribband
Stockings	Check apron
Shoes and buckles	Neck handkerchief
Handkerchief	Pocket ditto
Hat	Stockings
Medal, No. 4.	Shoes
	Medal, No. 4.

FIFTH RATE PREMIUM.

Breeches	Hat and Ribband
Stockings	Check apron
Shoes and buckles	Neck handkerchief
Hat	Pocket ditto
Medal, No. 5.	Stockings
	Shoes
	Medal, No. 5.

SIXTH RATE PREMIUM.

Breeches	Hat and Ribband
Stockings	Check apron
Shoes and buckles	Neck handkerchief
Medal, No. 6.	Stockings and shoes
	Medal, No. 6.

SEVENTH RATE PREMIUM.

Breeches	Ribband
Stockings	Check apron
Shoes	Neck handkerchief
Medal, No. 7.	Stockings and shoes
	Medal, No. 7.

The following Premiums to be allowed to the best Knitters.

EIGHTH RATE PREMIUM.

Stockings	Ribband
Shoes	Check apron
Hat	Stockings and shoes
Medal, No. 8.	Medal, No. 8.

NINTH RATE PREMIUM.

Stockings	Ribband
Shoes	Stockings and shoes
Medal, No. 9.	Medal, No. 9

TENTH RATE PREMIUM.

Shoes	Ribband, shoes
Medal, No 10.	Medal, No. 10.

Regu-

Regulations and Conditions to be observed by the Candidates for the
Premiums above mentioned.

1, FIVE fets of premiums, each confifting of ten premiums of the refpective rates above defcribed, will be adjudged, at one meeting, to be held
at Alford, in the courfe of the next Spring; and the diftribution of the
faid fifty premiums fhall be at Alford, in the beginning of May next:
the fuccefsful candidates from other diftricts being paid their travelling expences in the fame manner as heretofore.

2, All the fpinners of fubfcribing parifhes fhall be admitted candidates
for any of the above premiums, without any diftinction of diftricts.

3, No fpinner of jerfey will be admitted a candidate for any of the firft-
rate premiums, who fhall not, within the months of December 1794,
and January 1795, have fpun 40 dozen of hanks.

4, No fpinner of jerfey will be admitted a candidate for any of the fecond
or third rate premiums, who fhall not, within the time above limited,
have fpun thirty-fix dozen of hanks.

5, No fpinner of jerfey will be admitted a candidate for any of the in-
ferior rates of premiums, who fhall not, within the time above limited,
have fpun twenty-four dozen of hanks.

6, No candidate, who fhall have been a fpinner more than three years,
fhall be capable of receiving a premium of a fourth, or any lower rate,
in preference to any qualified candidate, who fhall only be in the firft
or fecond year of fpinning; unlefs fuch fenior fpinner fhall have thirty
dozen, clear of all deductions.

7, No one parifh fhall be allowed to receive two, either of the firft, fecond, or third-rate premiums, to the prejudice of any qualified candidate of another parifh.

8, Every candidate, who fhall be convicted before the committee, of
having been employed in jerfey-fpinning, during the time above limited, before feven o'clock in the morning, or after eight o'clock in
the evening, fhall be fet afide, and forfeit every chance of a premium.

9, Where fpinning-houfes or rooms are provided, the work is expected
to be all reeled by the teacher or overlooker, or at leaft under his or
her immediate infpection.

10, Where

10, Where no fuch houfe or room is provided, the work of all the candidates within the fame hamlet or parifh, muft be brought to be reeled by fome one perfon, who muft be authorifed, under the hand of a truftee of this Society ; and it is hereby requefted of every truftee, not to appoint, (unlefs in cafe of abfolute neceffity, and where they are well fatisfied of the good character of the party,) the parent or near relation of any of the candidates to be the reeler of any fuch hamlet or parifh.

11, All fpinners, not employed in fchools, and intending to become candidates for any of the premiums of this Society, muft, at leaft ten days before the beginning of the trial months, give notice of fuch their intentions to fome truftee of this Society, refiding in or near their parifh, and requeft him to appoint a reeler as aforefaid.

12, At the time of making the general returns of the work done in the trial months, complaint may be entered, by the employers, or any other perfon, againft any of the candidates, for coarfe or bad fpinning ; and fuch complaints will be referred to the confideration of the refpective diftrict committees, againft the time of adjudication.

13, At the faid adjudication meetings, a fample of the wool given to fpin, and three or more pounds of the jerfey complained of, muft be laid before the committee, who will compare the jerfey with the produce of fuch candidate's fpinning in the hour's trial, and with the report of the examiner, and determine accordingly ; provided that where any complaint fhall be entered, the employer fhall not be the examiner.

14, All the jerfey fpun in fubfcribing parifhes, during the time abovementioned, muft go to and from the fpinner, through the hands of the overfeer of the poor, or fome perfon of good character fpecially appointed by him, or fome truftee of this Society, for that purpofe : and fuch jerfey muft be ticketed with the name of the fpinner, by fuch overfeer or deputy, or by the teacher, reeler, or overlooker.

15, The perfon, who reels, is expected to make affidavit of the truth of the tickets, if required.

16, The overfeer of every parifh where there are any candidates for jerfey-fpinning premiums, or fome other perfon of reputable character in the fame parifh, muft, on the firft day of February next, or eight days after, produce to one of the truftees of this Society, a return of the
candidates

candidates in fuch parifh, who fhall have performed, within the two trial months, the quantities of jerfey above fpecified ; which truftee is hereby defired to examine and fign fuch return, and to direct the fame to be forwarded to the reverend Thomas Pennington, treafurer of the Society of Induftry at Alford, fo that the fame may be received on or before Tuefday the 24th day of February next ; and in cafe of failure of tranfmitting the return to the faid treafurer, by the faid laft day of February, the candidates to lofe all chance of the premiums

17, Printed blank forms of fuch returns will be fent with this paper to every fubfcribing parifh, to be filled up by the minifter, parifh officers, and principal inhabitants : and to prevent irregular and uncertain returns, notice is hereby given, that no other form will on any account be received.—N. B. A number of fuch blank forms will alfo be left in the hands of every diftributor, to be delivered gratis to any fubfcriber who fhall apply.

18, Whereas a doubt has arifen, whether the miftreffes of fchools, or any other affiftants, may pull twitches or pluckings for the premium fpinners, and by the permiffion of this practice in fome fchools, and the forbearance of it in others, an undue advantage may be obtained; it is hereby declared, that the pulling twitches or pluckings is part of the candidate's own work, and cannot be fuffered to be done by any one elfe.

19, Perfons of fkill will be employed by the committee, after the 26th day of February 1795, to go round to the qualified candidates, and to fee each of them fpin for the fpace of one hour precifely, taking an exact account of the number of hanks, lees, and rounds, belonging to each candidate, in fuch hour's work ; which account, with the produce of fuch trial, properly ticketed, fhall be immediately tranfmitted to the chairman, to be laid by him before the general committee, and before the feveral diftrict committees, when they fhall meet for the purpofe of adjudication.

20, The jerfey fpun before the examiners, fhall be of the fame wool, that was given to each candidate refpectively in the trial months.

21, The candidates fhall be examined, with the wool of their refpective employers ; and the examiner fhall leave in the hands of the overfeer

of

of each parish, the price of the wool so spun, for the benefit of the said employers, after the rate of two-pence per ounce.

22, No person shall be admitted a candidate for a jersey-spinning premium, above the age of seventeen; if a sufficient number of candidates under that age shall appear.

23, No candidate for a knitting premium shall be admitted above eight years old; and the trial of candidates shall be made during the sitting of the adjudication committee, as usual.

24, If, at the knitting trial, ten country children shall appear as candidates, the whole number of 15 premiums shall be adjudged: but if a smaller number of country candidates should attend, then it shall be at the option of the adjudging committee to reduce those premiums to any number not less than eight.—N. B By country children are here meant, those of any subscribing parish not belonging to the parish of Alford.

25, It will be a qualification indispensably required of all the candidates, to be able to answer every question in the Church catechism, without hesitation; and whereas great default hath been made in this condition, it is ordered by the committee, that the spinning candidates shall be asked their catechism in the morning of the distribution day, and before the procession, and that any gross deficiency shall immediately be reported to the committee, which shall thereupon order the medal, and such other part of the deficient candidate's premium as shall be thought proper, to be detained until such candidate shall be perfect in saying the catechism.

26, Every premium will be open, not only to the parish Paupers, or their children, but also to all such persons, and their children, who subsist chiefly by their manual labour, provided that they submit their work to be weekly taken account of by the overseer of their parish, and go through all such other examinations as are above specified, or may hereafter be appointed by the committee.

27, Any person discovering an attempt to obtain any premium by fraudulent or false pretences, shall, upon proving such fraud, to the satisfaction of the committee, receive double the value of the premium so attempted to be gained, if the success of such fraud shall be prevented

2   by

by the difcovery; and if the fraud is fully proved, but too late for
prevention, the difcoverer fhall, neverthelefs, be handfomely rewarded, and the perfon or perfons guilty of fuch fraud fhall be profecuted
according to law, and be declared for ever incapable of receiving any
of the premiums, rewards, or encouragements, given by this Society.

The above premiums, and the conditions thereof, were fettled and agreed
upon, at a general committee of the Society of Induftry, held at Alford,
on Friday the 19th day of September 1794.   R. G. BOUYER, Chairman.

June, 1795

LINCOLN.

SOME years ago, the gentlemen of feveral parifhes in, and adjoining
to the city of Lincoln, purchafed a houfe, very well fituated for the purpofe for which it was intended; and, after undergoing feveral neceffary
alterations, it was opened for the reception of Paupers. At firft, a certain
fum per head was paid for the maintenance of each perfon; but this having been found to be productive of great inconvenience, an affociation
was formed of feveral parifhes in and near the city, about four years ago.
It was agreed to pay the proprietors of the houfe a certain rent, for receiving all fuch Poor as fhould be fent thither; and that the houfe, and
out-poor expences, fhould be paid out of the general ftock; towards
which, each parifh is bound to contribute the average of their annual expenditure for five years preceding the union. This average is divided
into 4 quarterly payments; but the refult of the inftitution has been fuch,
that, hitherto, feldom more than 3 of the quarterly fums have been called
for in one year; and, confequently, a reduction of one fourth of the average rates has been effected: befides which, there is now a furplus in
hand, amounting to £400. with which it is propofed to defray the expences of an intended application to Parliament, for an Act to incorporate
the united parifhes, and to make fome additional improvements in the
work-houfe.

At

At preſent, the Union conſiſts of 19 ſmall pariſhes. The number in the houſe is, 40 males, and 41 females; of which, 30 are children, under 12 years of age; and 25, above 60 They are chiefly employed within doors, in ſpinning flax and wool; and in making ſtockings, and other cloaths, &c. The worſted ſpinners earn about £25. a year The houſe is kept clean: it's ſituation is very healthy. Of 4 Paupers, who died laſt year, 3 were above 80 years of age.

The following is a ſtatement of the expences of the houſe for three years:

From 18th May 1792, to 11th May 1793	£	s.	d	From May 1793, to May 1794	£	s	d	From May 1794, to May 1795	£	s	d
Butcher - -	64	6	2	Butcher -	70	12	11	Butcher - -	74	10	5½
Baker - -	115	8	0	Baker - -	136	11	1	Baker - -	150	16	5
Brewer - -	28	15	9	Brewer - -	28	15	9	Brewer - -	28	6	7½
Milk - -	57	9	0	Milk - -	56	9	1	Milk - -	57	4	0
Tailor - -	5	11	2	Cheeſe - -	31	17	7½	Cheeſe - -	35	11	10½
Mercer, and draper	67	15	6½	Groceries -	33	7	1½	Groceries -	37	18	0¼
Shoemaker -	19	3	2	Oatmeal -	3	19	0	Oatmeal - -	5	15	1
Furniture -	4	16	9	Vegetables -	20	10	9½	Potatoes -	12	7	6½
Cheeſe - -	20	5	10½	Tailor - -	5	6	11	Tailor - -	5	0	7½
Groceries -	39	14	3	Mercer and draper	42	5	0½	Mercer and draper	41	14	11
Oatmeal -	1	16	0	Shoes - -	21	15	11	Shoes - -	23	1	3
Vegetables -	10	9	2	Furniture -	3	0	2	Furniture -	2	15	9½
Funerals -	18	5	10	Funerals -	7	10	6	Funerals -	5	13	2
Sundries - -	33	9	8	Sundries - -	2	0	1	Sundries -	17	7	5
Repairs - -	17	9	2½	Repairs - -	20	15	5	Repairs - -	61	10	0½
Apothecary, mid-				Coals - -	50	8	7	Coals - -	32	12	2
wife, &c. -	22	12	8	Apothecary, &c -	45	15	4	Apothecary, &c -	20	16	6
Coals and faggots	46	15	11½	Rent, ſalaries, &c	95	17	5½	Rent, ſalaries, &c	99	2	6
Rent, ſalaries, &c	92	15	11	Paid to out-paupers	59	0	4	Paid to out-paupers	41	18	10½
Paid to out-paupers	102	6	2¼								
Total -	£769	16	3¼	Total -	£735	15	1½	Total -	£754	3	3¼
Average number of Paupers in the houſe this year not preciſely known; ſuppoſed to have been about 85				Average number of Paupers this year was 80				Average number of Paupers this year was 81			

Bill of Fare in the Work-houſe.

	Breakfaſt	Dinner	Supper
Sunday,	Milk pottage	Bread, broth, beef, potatoes, &c	Maſhed potatoes.
Monday,	Ditto	Bread, cheeſe, and beer	Bread, cheeſe, and beer.
Tueſday,	Ditto	Peaſe pottage, or boiled beer	Ditto
Wedneſday,	Ditto	Same as Sunday	Same as Sunday
Thurſday,	Ditto	Rice milk, and bread	Same as Monday.
Friday,	Ditto	Beef, and ſtewed potatoes	Ditto.
Saturday,	Ditto	Bread, cheeſe, and beer	Ditto.

The city of Lincoln contains about 5000 inhabitants. The Poor's Rates vary from 2s. to 4s. 6d. in the pound on the net rental. In the neighbouring farming country they are from 1s. 4d. to 1s. 6d. in the pound. The land-tax in Lincoln is from 9d. to 2s. in the pound.

May, 1795.

MIDDLESEX.

EALING.

THE parifh of Ealing forms nearly a regular oblong, of 3 miles and a half by 2 miles; and, confequently, contains about 4480 acres, of which 1560 are grafs-land; about 1220 arable; about 250 are cultivated by market-gardeners; and about 70 are common: the remainder is laid out in roads, private gardens, pleafure grounds, &c. The inhabitants are gentlemen, fhop-keepers, gardeners, labourers, and of fuch other defcriptions as are ufually found in a village within feven miles of London. From the average number of births during the laft 10 years, the population may be eftimated at between 4000 and 5000 fouls. No accurate conclufions can be drawn from the burials, as they include many parifh children that have been fent from the London parifhes to be nurfed at Ealing. The number of houfes rated to the window, or commutation-tax, appears, from the Surveyor's books, to be 355; and the number exempted, 33[1]. 49 houfes have above 25 windows each. There are 38 ale-houfes in this parifh.

[1] The total of thefe two numbers is 388; which, when compared with the baptifms and burials, appears to be much too low for the whole number of houfes in the parifh Upon examining the Rate book, in which every houfe paying to, and exempted from, parochial taxes, is accurately fet down, the number of houfes in the parifh was found to be 729; which, multiplied by 5½ inhabitants to a houfe, gives a population of 4009 fouls.

4 The

The price of provisions is much the same here, as in the metropolis. A garden labourer can earn 10s. a week, all the year round ; and 3s. a day, by piece-work.

The price of agricultural labour here, and in most parts of Middlesex, (near the metropolis,) is as follows :

Mowers of grass receive from	3s. to 6s.	an acre.
Mowers of oats and barley -	3s. to 4s.	ditto.
Reaping wheat, including bind- ing and shocking - - }	10s. to 12s.	ditto.
Hoeing turnips - -	10s. to 12s.	ditto.
Threshing oats, including bind- ing - - - }	2s. 6d.	ditto.

Labourers, near London, are paid 18d. or 20d. a day. An able man, however, can earn 2s. a day, both in summer and winter. During the fruit season, a great many women are employed by the market-gardeners in this parish, in gathering, and carrying fruit, pease, &c. to London. Their wages seldom exceed half of what men receive for the same work. A woman is only paid 6d. for carrying a very heavy basket of fruit from Ealing or Brentford to Covent Garden, near 9 miles. They, however, sometimes make two trips in a day. Most of the women, who are thus employed, are Welsh.

The rent of land is from £ 2. to £ 4. an acre. The average rental of the whole parish, it is probable, is now near £ 3. an acre; for, in an estimate, made in 1780, of the amount of the gross rental charged to the Poor in each parish within the hundred of Ossulston, in order to fix their respective quotas towards the sum recovered against the hundred for the damages occasioned by the riots in 1780, the gross rental of Ealing and Old Brentford was stated at £10491. The soil is gravel and clay ; chiefly the latter, towards the Brentford extremity of the parish, in which there are several considerable brick-kilns. The great tithes are annexed to the chancellorship of St. Paul's, and are now held upon a lease for three lives. A farmer rents them of the lessees of the Rector, for £ 600. a year. The small tithes are compounded for by the Vicar.

From the best information that could be obtained, the number of Friendly Societies in the parish appears to be 9 ; of which, 3 are in Ealing, properly so called, and 6 in Old Brentford.

3 H 2   The

The Poor of this parish are partly relieved at home, and partly maintained in a work-house, which belongs to the parish. The following copy of the pensions, ordered to be allowed at a Vestry on the 14th of last May, shews the usual description of out-poor :

"Cross House, Ealing, *May* 14, 1795.

" AT a public Vestry held this day in pursuance of notice given in the church and chapel, the persons receiving collections of the parish were called over, and their reasons of taking relief were examined, and thereupon the following list was made :

When admitted to Relief	Names of Persons receiving Pensions.	Weekly Allowance.	Occasion of Relief.
		£. s. d.	
May 14, 1796	Abraham Bartlett	0 1 0	Aged and infirm.
	Soundy's two children	0 ' 5 0	Destitute.
	William Jackson	0 4 0	Paralytic.
	John Ingram	4 qr. loaves	Four children.
	Hannah Hughes	0 2 6	An illegitimate child.
	John Wigley	3 qr. loaves	Five children.
	Stephen Biggins	1 qr. loaf	Old and infirm.
	Ann Fold	0 1 0	Old and infirm.
	William Beazley	{ 0 2 0 } { 1 qr. loaf }	Old and infirm.
	Mary Dairy	{ 0 1 0 } { qr. loaf, and } { 1 lb. of meat }	A widow, old and infirm.
	Mary West	2 qr. loaves	Deserted by her husband, and daughter, ill of the dropsy.
	Sarah Hole	0 1 0	Lame and infirm.
	Elizabeth Hedges	0 2 6	A widow and 3 children.
	Mary Cook's child	0 1 6	Left destitute on the parish, lame and infirm.

Isaac

When admitted to Relief	Names of Persons receiving Pensions.	Weekly Allowance. £. s d.	Occasion of Relief.
May 14, 1796.	Isaac Hannaway	2 qr loaves, 4 lb. of meat	Five children.
	Jane Hope	0 1 0	A child by a former husband.
	Elizabeth Crofs, now Merrett	0 1 0	A child by a former husband.
	Sarah Humphrys	0 1 0	Infirm.
	Ann Mazey	0 1 0	Lame and infirm.
	Ann Durham	0 5 6	A widow with 3 children.
	Samuel Gilbert	0 1 6	A widower, with 3 children.
	Francis Bryant's grand-child	0 1 6	Left deftitute.
	Jane Mitchell	0 2 6	Left deftitute by her hufband, with 2 children.
	Sarah Haywood	0 1 6	An illegitimate child.
	John Terry	0 2 6	Two children, infirm.
	John Blackall	0 3 0	Himfelf and wife, old and infirm.
	Samuel Wheeler	0 2 6	Two children, lame.
	Samuel Coxen	0 3 6	Old and infirm.
	Widow Cranage	0 1 6	Aged and infirm.
	Widow Green	0 2 6	Aged and infirm.
	Charles Yates	3 qr loaves	Aged, and in diftreffed circumftances.
	George Tame	0 2 0 1 qr. loaf	Himfelf and wife, aged and infirm.
	Elizabeth Howfon	0 1 6	Aged and infirm.
	Sarah Ball	0 1 6	An illegitimate child by Wm. Burt.
	Amy Carter	0 1 0	Old, & unemployed.
	Widow Ward	0 1 6	Ditto.

Elizabeth

When admitted to Relief.	Names of Perfons receiving Penfions.	Weekly Allowance.	Occafion of Relief.
		£. s. d.	
May 14, 1796.	Elizabeth Manfey	1 qu. loaf	Old, & unemployed.
	Widow Hayley	0 1 0	Infirm, and aged.
	Elizabeth Atlee	0 1 6	Two children.
	John Terry	2 qu. loaves	{ Infirm, and has 2 children.
	Ann Ware	0 1 6	An illegitimate child.
	Sarah Hope	0 1 0	An orphan child.
	Ann Dean	0 1 0	{ Two children, and her hufband in the militia.
	Thomas Gregory	0 3 0	{ His wife bed-ridden, and 3 children.
	John Philby	0 3 6	{ Has 5 children, and is a widower.
	Sarah Sheriff	0 1 0	{ Elderly and infirm, a widow.
	Widow Hawkins	0 5 0	{ Four children, and now with child.
	Ann Armitage	0 1 0	For her child.
	Widow Franklyn	0 1 6	Aged, and infirm
	Elizabeth Render	0 1 6	A widow, with a child.
	Elizabeth Tame	0 2 0	Old, and infirm.

The defcription of perfons fent to the work-houfe, confifts of infirm and aged parifhioners, and poor perfons, who meet with accidents in paffing through the parifh. It is a fmall, inconvenient building, very ill adapted to the purpofe to which it is applied. When the houfe is full, four men fleep in a bed: at prefent, three men fleep in a bed; four boys in a bed; and three women in a bed. The beds are of feathers. The average number of perfons in the houfe, and the annual mortality, may be eftimated from the following table:

Table

Table of the Number of Poor in EALING Work-house, and Burials.

Years.		Grown Persons.		Children.		Totals.	Deaths.	
		Males	Fem	Males.	Fem			
1781	in February	17	36	18	18	89	—	
1782	in January	20	42	20	21	103	—	
1783	in January	17	37	27	27	108	—	
1784	in January	21	44	37	30	132	—	
1785	in January	27	51	33	31	142	—	
1786	in January	19	46	24	18	107	—	
1787	in January	26	43	27	20	120	—	
1788	Account confused : the present master came this year							
1789	in July	12	26	11	11	60	9	about a 7th.
1790	in January	21	50	21	18	110	6	—— an 18th.
1791	in January	24	43	8	11	86	14	—— a 6th.
1792	in January	24	44	14	12	94	· 12	—— an 8th.
1793	in January	19	41	17	18	95	4	—— a 24th.
1794	in January	21	40	18	18	97	15	—— a 6th.
1795	in January	27	38	31	22	118	—	
1796	in January	28	38	35	25	126	—	

Table of Diet in EALING Work-house.

	Breakfast	Dinner.	Supper.
Sunday,	Bread and cheese.	Half a pound of beef, 5th part of a quartern loaf, and a pint of small beer to each person.	Bread and cheese, and a pint of small beer.
Monday,	Broth from the beef of the preceding day.	Milk pottage, 4th part of a quartern loaf, and a pint of small beer.	Ditto.
Tuesday,	Milk pottage.	Same as Sunday.	Ditto.
Wednesday,	Same as Monday.	Suet pudding, 4th part of a quartern loaf, and a pint of small beer.	Ditto.
Thursday,	Same as Tuesday	Same as Sunday.	Ditto.
Friday,	Same as Monday	Same as Monday.	Ditto.
Saturday,	Same as Tuesday	Pease soup, 4th part of a quartern loaf, and a pint of small beer	Ditto.

Men, who work out of the house, are allowed, each, a pint of small beer at breakfast. Each person receives 2 ounces of cheese at breakfast and supper. The allowance of small beer to children is only half a pint at each meal. On Easter-day, mutton is served, instead of beef; and, during

two.

two days at Chriftmas, the Poor in the houfe are treated with ftrong beer, and tobacco. The fick, only, are permitted to ufe tea and fugar.

The men received into the work-houfe are, chiefly, employed on the common, and in other work out of doors: while they are at work, out of the houfe, they are allowed each 6d. a week for tobacco money. The boys beat hemp, weave bed facking and facks, and make ropes. They are put to work at 5 or 6 years old: a boy, 10 or 11 years old, learns to weave tolerably well in about a month, and weaves a fack worth 2s 6d in two days. Many of them run away: the parifh provides for others, by fending them to a manufactory, when they are fufficiently fkilful. Out of work hours, they are taught to read, by a fchoolmafter who attends for the moderate falary of 2s a month. The women and girls are employed in fpinning hemp, and dreffing fine flax for fheeting, &c. The children are cloathed, by the parifh. The boys receive a hat and coat, every two years; a waiftcoat and breeches, every year; and other articles of drefs, as they want them. The flax and hemp manufacture, which is now carried on at the work-houfe, was fet on foot in the beginning of laft year. Previous to that period, the Poor in the houfe were employed in carding wool, making mops, and other trifling articles of woollen, under the fuperintendance of the man who is now mafter of the work-houfe. He and his wife receive, each, £10. a year, befides board and lodging. He fays, that, one year, the houfe cleared from the woollen bufinefs, £90. after paying the expence of raw materials, cards, and other machines. From this account, it fhould feem, that the prefent manufacture is not likely to prove equally profitable to the parifh; for, from the information of the teacher at the manufactory, it appears, that the ropes, lines, facks, nets, &c. fold between May and December 1794, produced   -   -   -   -   -   - £219   0   0

Raw materials, falary of the teacher, fpinning, and other
    expences, were   -   -   -   -   243   0   0

Lofs to the parifh   -   £24   0   0

The lofs this year, (1795,) is likely to be much more confiderable, as
hemp

hemp and flax have rifen 25 per cent. and the manufactory continues to fell at the old prices.

The following ftatement, which is copied verbatim from an account prefented to the Veftry, appears to me to be worthy of infertion ; as, although it is in fome particulars rather obfcure and unintelligible, it clearly evinces that the parochial manufacture is a lofing concern.

State of the Sack Manufactory, March 1794, to 29th of February 1796.

	£.	s.	d.		£.	s.	d.
1794. May 15 Due to George Burchett for hemp, &c - - -	63	0	9	Received by Mr. Child for goods fold by Mr. Blackall - -	1	17	7½
Ditto for utenfils, £23 6s. 10½d				Received by Mr. Child for goods fold			
Paid by Mr. Child, for hemp, wages, work-people, &c. -	194	16	2	at the work-houfe, to 24th June 1795 - - -	79	15	8½
Paid by Mr Strudwick, ditto -	180	6	4	Received by Mr. Strudwick, ditto,			
Due to Meffrs J Atkinfon, and Co.	104	15	2	to 29th February 1796 -	179	1	10
Cafh loft by a boy (J. Hughes) -	1	2	2	Outftanding debts, Feb 29, 1796	151	1	9
A bill due to Meffrs J Atkinfon,				Stock of goods at the work-houfe,			
paid by Mr. Strudwick - -	184	13	7	Feb 29, 1796 -	236	2	0
				Stock of goods at Mr. Blackall's,			
				unfold, February 29, 1796 -	12	0	11½
				Due from Mr. Blackall, for goods			
				fold - - - -	28	14	2¼
				Lofs on the trade from 15th March			
				1794, to 29th February 1796 -	40	0	0¾
	£728	14	2		£728	14	2

The total amount of goods fold, from 15th March 1794, to 29th February 1796 - £440 11 1¾
Goods manufactured, but not fold - - - - 75 3 1½

Total of the return £515 14 3¼

George Burchett expended, March 15th, to May 17th, 1794,
as under :

	£.	s.	d.	£.	s.	d.	
Mr. Nicholl's wages - - - -	8	8	0				
Size, oil, &c. - - - -	2	11	0				
				10	19	0	

Mr C Child expended, May 1794, to April 9th, 1795 :

	£.	s.	d.	£.	s.	d.	
Thomas Nicholl's wages - -	55	16	0				
Work-people - - -	65	0	5½				
Flour and oil, &c. - - -	8	16	9				
				129	13	2½	243 16 5

Mr. Strudwick expended, April 9, 1795, to February 29, 1796 :

	£.	s.	d.	
Thomas Nicholl's wages - -				
Work-people - - -				
Flour, oil, &c. - - -	103	4	2½	

The

The teacher is allowed 52 guineas a year, and a shilling in the pound on all articles sold. The sacks made here are sold 2d. a piece under the usual price at which they may be purchased in Brentford.

There is a charity school for 20 girls in this parish, and another for 20 boys: into which children are admitted between the ages of 6 and 7. They are taught to read and write, and are cloathed once a year: at 14 years of age, the girls are sent to service; and the boys put out apprentices with a fee of £5. The following is a list of the principal benefactions to these charities, and to the Poor of the parish in general:

Years		£	
1612	Edward Vaughan Esq gave -	20	and 4 acres to the Poor
1629	John Bowman Esq. -	60	per annum for the good of the parish, i e £40 for a Lecturer—£20 for the Poor
1633	Mr and Mrs. Need, a house at Old Brentford -		for the Poor there
1685	John Taylor Esq gave some ground to the Poor.		
1712	Lady Rawlinson -	500	for teaching 20 poor girls of the parish
1714	Lady Derby -	500.	for a yearly distribution to Poor of Old Brentford, not receiving alms of the parish.
1715	Richard Taylor gave a tenement and malt house, to provide coals annually for 16 poor persons.		
1721	Lady Capell—some land in trust for the boys' charity school.		
1752	Jonathan Gurnell jun. Esq. by will -	500	to the boys' charity school.
1753	Jonathan Gurnell sen Esq -	200	3 per cents to ditto
1753	Jonathan Gurnell sen Esq -	500	3 per cents to provide coals for the Poor.
1759	Mrs. Elizabeth Barns, the interest of -	400.	to 4 widows, annually
1774	Mrs. Mary Bertrand, by will -	20	to the girls' charity school
1777	Rev P Courayer, by will -	200	laid out in the purchase of freehold lands for do.
1783	Mrs Martha Sparrow, left by will -	21. 13s	to the girls' charity school
1783	William Adair, Esq. the interest of -	100.	for poor widows
1795	Mrs Harman -	20	to the girls' charity school

There are several Sunday schools in this parish.

Very considerable subscriptions were raised, the last and preceding winter, for the relief of the Poor; and brown bread was made, which distressed families were allowed to purchase at a reduced price. I am, however, credibly informed, that many labourers thought the bread so extremely coarse and unpalatable, that they returned the tickets which had been

granted

gianted them to entitle them to purchase a quartern loaf at 10½d. although the ordinary price of the wheaten quartern loaf in the baker's shop was at that time near 15d.

A great many children from the parishes of Mary-le-bone and St. George's, Hanover Square, are nursed by the cottagers on Haven Green, and in other parts of this parish. They remain there till 7 or 8 years old. Mary-le-bone parish pays at present 3s. 10d. a week, for a child at the breast; and 3s 6d. a week, for others.

Table of Baptisms, Burials, and Marriages, in the Parish of EALING.

Years	BAPTISMS.			BURIALS.		
	Males	Females	Total	Males	Females	Total.
1582	9	9	18	15	7	22
1583	19	9	28	10	8	18
1584	19	12	31	12	9	21
1585	8	16	24	7	9	16
1586	16	15	31	10	14	24
1587	19	11	30	18	13	31
1588	10	11	21	6	10	16
1589	30	16	46	13	10	23
1590	16	11	27	12	9	21
1591	14	15	29	23	20	43
1592	12	16	28	22	18	40
1593	—	—	25	—	—	39
1594	—	—	28	—	—	22
1595	—	—	26	—	—	27
1596	—	—	17	—	—	40
1597	—	—	21	A plague year: the Burials in		74
1598	—	—	19	July were	4	23
1599	—	—	37	August ——	12	27
				Sept ——	14	
1600	—	—	45	Oct. ——	4	30
1601	—	—	28	——	—	26
1602	—	—	31			18

	Baptisms			Burials				
Years	Males	Females	Total	Males	Females	Total		
1603	—	—	32	In 1603, no burials occur in the Register between 10th of May and 17th of August. This was a plague year: 29 died in Sept. — In 1604, there is a chasm between 22d May and 11th of Nov. except that one burial occurs on 22d of July — In 1605, Register wanting — In 1606, there is an interval in the burials, of 2 months between April and July. — In 1609, there is a chasm of 2 months, at the same period of the year. — In 1610, there are no burials in May. — In 1611, March and April are omitted.		54		
1604	—	—	39			16		
1605	—	—	—			22		
1606	—	—	28			14		
1609	—	—	59			27		
1610	—	—	40			27	One man, aged 110	
1611	—	—	37			44		
1612	—	—	53			39		
1613	—	—	43			39		
1614	—	—	43			38		
1615	—	—	—			38		
1616	—	—	—			52		
1617	—	—	—			28		
1618	—	—	53			19		
1619	—	—	46			—		
1640	—	—	63			69		
1643	—	—	48			—		
1644	—	—	54	—	—	51		
1645	—	—	63	—	—	76		
1677	—	—	53	—	—	61		
1685	—	—	60	—	—	82		
1688	—	—	82	—	—	97		
1689	—	—	100	—	—	113		
1704	—	—	70	—	—	87		
1707	—	—	87	—	—	102		
1708	—	—	80	—	—	93		
1709	—	—	84	—	—	121		
1715	—	—	105	—	—	81		
1725	—	—	121	—	—	123		
1740	—	—	90	—	—	153	Marriages.	
1760	—	—	113	—	—	131	—	29

Years.

Years.	Baptisms			Burials			Number marked P (Paupers) in the Burials	Number of Infants included in the Burials	Marriages.
	Males	Females	Total	Males	Females	Total			
1775	86	83	169	77	68	145	—	—	52
1776	75	78	153	67	68	135	—	—	54
1777	72	66	138	99	91	190	—	—	60
1778	74	85	159	78	102	180	—	—	52
1779	75	61	136	67	67	134	—	—	50
1780	64	66	130	93	100	193	—	—	42
1781	90	76	166	134	123	257	—	—	49
1782	72	65	137	79	71	150	—	—	49
1783	66	72	138	95	93	188	—	—	51
1784	68	65	133	86	71	157	44	—	62
1785	84	73	157	95	94	189	62	66	53
1786	66	64	130	104	81	185	49	80	52
1787	67	95	162	63	75	138	43	46	63
1788	82	79	161	77	77	154	43	69	60
1789	79	94	173	64	69	133	40	66	57
1790	76	74	150	85	79	164	48	85	61
1791	76	77	153	80	72	152	37	88	53
1792	78	90	168	80	83	163	35	92	67
1793	97	88	185	83	91	174	52	92	71
1794	85	84	169	107	97	204	66	155	57
1795	103	80	183	100	85	185	72	93	59

The inhabitants are chiefly of the Eftablifhed Church : there are, however, Prefbyterians, Anabaptifts, and Methodifts, in the parifh : they have each a place of worfhip at Brentford. The average annual number of burials in the Prefbyterian burying-ground is about 2. The regifters of this parifh are very clear for the firft 40 years. In the latter part of the laft, and beginning of the prefent century, they are very imperfect; but, fince the Marriage Act, they have been kept with great care and regularity.

A State-

A Statement of the Rates made and collected in, and the Disbursements of, the Parish of EALING *in the County of Middlesex, from the year* 1774, *inclusive, to the year* 1796.

	RATES				DISBURSEMENTS			
	RATES MADE.			RATES COLLECTED.	ON ACCOUNT OF			
Years.	Rate when made. What in the Pound.		Amount.	Amount.	The resident Poor.		Casual Poor, and casual Expences [1].	Total.
Commencing from Easter in the one year, and ending at Easter in the other.		s. d.	£. s. d.	£. s. d.	Poor-house Acct. £. s. d.	Pensions. £. s. d.	£. s. d.	£. s.
1774—1775	24 Aug. 1774 at	1 6	480 16 6					
	22 Feb. 1775 —	1 2	374 5 4					
			855 1 10	840 10 2	609 3 11¼	— — —	247 16 0¾	857 0
1775—1776	23 Aug. 1775 —	1 6	503 11 6					
	21 Feb. 1776 —	1 0	337 18 0					
			840 9 6	831 7 0	591 5 0	— — —	246 15 0½	838 0
1776—1777	21 Aug. 1776 —	1 6	508 7 0					
	19 Feb. 1777 —	0 9	254 19 3					
			763 6 3	753 4 6	535 9 10½	— — —	229 5 0¾	764 14
1777—1778	3 Sept. 1777 —	1 6	508 7 0					
	4 March 1778 —	1 0	349 11 0					
			857 18 0	846 9 6	652 13 8¾	— — —	241 15 6½	894 9
1778—1779	9 Sept. 1778 —	1 6	531 13 6					
	10 March 1779 —	1 0	353 3 0					
			884 16 6	863 7 6	554 13 2¾	— — —	312 12 4¼	867 5
1779—1780	24 June 1779 —	1 6	534 9 0					
	8 March 1780 —	1 4	466 5 4					
			1000 14 4	973 19 4	698 8 9	— — —	368 19 11	1067 8
1780—1781	23 Aug. 1780 —	1 6	529 2 6					
	14 March 1781 —	1 8	571 8 4					
			1100 10 10	1080 19 8	768 9 10½	— — —	427 9 11	1195 19

[1] It is impossible to divide these two classes of expenditure in the manner that might be wished, as the Overseers, in their ca book, (from whence the total amount of the same here set down is taken,) enter indiscriminately monies given to travelling P the apothecary's account for the resident Poor, occasional charges of the Coroner, and, in short, all expences to which, by law, are liable. The *casual book*, however, although it specifies every sum *paid*, is totally silent as to the least sum *received*. *total* amount of the sums paid, and the particular amount of those received, are entered in the general Rate-book, in which entry is made, when the Overseers pass their accounts. In this general Rate-book, the totals of the manufactory account ov to have been entered, all along, distinct; but this has not been the case: some of the Overseers have set down in their private ca books the several sums they have paid for the manufactory, and have added the amount to the common casuals of the year; a consequently, when this has happened, the total amount has been entered in the Rate-book under the head of Casuals. Thus
pa

RATES MADE. Years.	Rate when made.	What in the Pound. s. d.	Amount. £. s. d.	RATES[2] COLLECTED. Amount. £. s. d.	Poor-house Account. £. s. d.	Pensions. £. s. d.	Casual Poor, &c. £. s. d.	Total. £. s. d.
81—1782	22 Aug. 1781	at 1 8	582 18 4					
	6 Feb. 1782	— 2 6	877 5 0					
			1449 15 4	1386 3 8	714 12 9½	194 3 6	425 5 10½	1334 2 2
82—1783	7 Aug. 1782	— 2 0	702 2 0					
	29 Jan. 1783	— 1 10	637 7 2					
			1339 9 2	1297 2 8	826 11 5¼	198 6 6	473 1 3	1497 19 2¾
83—1784	20 Aug. 1783	— 2 0	707 4 0					
	11 Feb. 1784	— 2 0	703 2 0					
			1410 6 0	1348 4 6	844 17 6	194 9 0	446 13 7	1486 0 1
84—1785	25 Aug. 1784	— 2 6	879 7 6					
	16 Feb. 1785	— 2 4	811 1 4					
			1690 8 10	1646 6 10	952 15 0¾	227 16 6	557 3 5½	1737 15 0¼
85—1786	20 July 1785	— 2 6	869 5 0					
	25 Jan. 1786	— 2 8	935 14 8					
			1804 19 8	1740 18 0	738 3 5	196 10 0	774 8 4	1709 1 9

ing the account of Mr. Burchett, overseer, (who was the proposer of the manufactory,) in 1794, there is regularly entered the of £86. 7s. 7½d. expended in the manufactory; but in the account of Mr. Child, in 1794-5, after the entrance in the Rate-k of the house account, casuals, and pensions, there is the following note: "N. The amount of the money expended in the ma-ıcture is included in the above casuals." It was therefore thought necessary to find what the casuals for 1794 and 1795 were; ch being deducted, the sums found to have been expended on the manufactory in the year 1794 were £127. 6s. 5½d.; and in 5, £243. 17s. 11½d. These sums do not quite agree with the account laid before the Vestry; but, taken together with it, rly prove that the manufacture is a losing concern.

'he totals of sums paid by the parish, on account of the manufactory, as stated in the casual book, are as follows:

		£. s. d.	
	1794.		
Child	May, June	12 10 5	£186 10 10.— This is stated in the account delivered in to the Vestry at £194. 16s. 2d.
	July, August	15 11 6	
	August, September, October	77 15 8	
	October, November, December	21 8 10½	
		127 6 5½	
	1795.		
	January	26 10 0½	
	February, March	32 14 4	
Strudwick	August	184 13 7	
		243 17 11½	

se are the whole of the sums advanced, within the above period, to the manufactory.

[2] In the printed account of the returns made to Parliament in 1786,

		£. s. d.
The net expences for the Poor in 1776 are stated at		719 18 3
Money raised by assessment in	1783	1295 18 2
	1784	1348 4 6
	1785	1646 6 10

RATES

Years.	Rate when made.	What in the Pound.	Amount.	RATES COLLECTED. Amount.	Poor-house Account.	Pensions.	Casual Poor, &c.	Total.
		s. d.	*£. s. d.*					
1786—1787	2 Aug. 1786 —	2 0	711 10 0					
	14 Feb. 1787 —	1 8	597 11 8					
				£. s. d.	*£. s. d.*	*£. s. d.*	*£. s. d.*	*£. s.*
			1309 1 8	1275 11 10	702 17 4	96 17 0	541 5 0	1340 19
1787—1788	22 Aug. 1787 —	2 0	759 0 0					
	20 Feb. 1788 —	1 8	643 10 0					
			1402 10 0	1353 13 10	873 6 1¾	59 15 6	641 6 9¾	1574 8
1788—1789	30 July 1788 —	2 0	788 8 0					
	18 Feb. 1789 —	1 8	682 10 0					
			1470 18 0	1433 14 3	1046 2 11½	115 0 6	416 18 0½	1578 1
1789—1790	11 Aug. 1789 —	2 0	806 14 0					
	11 March 1790 —	2 0	808 10 0					
			1615 4 0	1554 19 0	908 14 2¼	150 16 0	607 8 11	1656 19
1790—1791	7 July 1790 —	2 0	807 4 0					
	2 March 1791 —	2 0	815 10 0					
			1622 14 0	1583 8 0	820 11 6¼	160 7 6	587 11 11¾	1568 11
1791—1792	15 Oct. 1791 —	1 6	1220 12 6					
	21 March 1792 —	0 9	610 9 0					
			1831 1 6	1666 9 9	727 10 9	145 18 6	885 9 4½	1758 18
1792—1793	15 Aug. 1792 —	1 0	804 16 0					
	20 Feb. 1793 —	0 9	609 0 0					
			1413 16 0	1373 2 9	802 16 1½	205 12 6	541 4 6	1549 13
1793—1794	23 Aug. 1793 —	1 0	816 18 0					
	5 Feb. 1794 —	0 9	610 5 6					
			1427 3 6	1399 18 0	911 11 4½	257 4 6	606 13 1½	1775 8
1794	16 May 1794 —	1 0	823 3 0					
	12 Dec. 1794 —	1 6	1261 16 9					
			2084 19 9	1971 18 6	1056 12 7	216 3 6	694 8 7¾	1967 4
1795—1796	10 July 1795 —	2 0	1679 3 0					
	15 Jan. 1796 —	2 0	1656 3 0					
			3335 6 0	3076 8 6	1753 17 3	264 4 0	968 15 4	2986 16

T

The following is a ſtatement of the earnings and expences of a labourei, (aged about 40,) who is employed, regulaily throughout the year, in a gentleman's fields and gaiden. His weekly wages, both in ſummer and winter, are 11s ; or 1s. 1od. a day: ſometimes, however, his employer ſets him to woik by the piece; at which time, his uſual wages are ſtopped, and he is paid according to the woik he perfoims. On theſe occaſions he eaſily earns 3s a day. His extra-receipts fiom his maſter, on this account, amounted laſt year to £6. or £8. Beſides which, he eains ſomething by little jobs for other people, out of woik-hours; which, in ſummer, are fiom 6 till 6 ; and, in winter, from day-light till dark.

This man has a wife, and 4 children, viz. a boy, 8; another, 6: a girl, 4; and another, 1½ year old.

EARNINGS.	£.	s.	d.
Regular weekly wages 11s. annually - - -	28	12	0
Extra earnings from his maſter, annually about - -	6	0	0
Ditto from other people, (ſuppoſe about) annually -	3	0	0
The wife does a little work in the hay harveſt ; it may perhaps amount to - - - - -	1	0	0
Total income	£38	12	0

EXPENCES.	£.	s.	d.
He pays for the rent of a cottage and ſmall garden, 1s. 6d. a week ; annually - - - -	3	18	0
His family conſumes, daily, a quartern loaf of wheaten-bread, which, at the preſent price 1od. amounts annually to - - - - -	15	3	4
His uſual weekly conſumption of meat is 1s. 6d. or 2s. : ſuppoſe 1s. 9d. : which amounts annually to - -	4	11	0
The weekly expence of ſmall beer is 6d. for 4 quarts ; annually - - - - -	1	6	0
A ſmall quantity of cheeſe is uſed in the family ; ſuppoſe annually - - - - -	1	0	0
Carried over -	£25	18	4

	£.	s.	d.
Brought over -	25	18	4

The confumption of tea, fugar, candles, and foap
could not be afcertained ; but may be reckoned, at a moderate calculation,

2 oz. of tea a week, at 4s. the lb.
    annually   -   -   - £0 19 6 ⎤

2 lb. of fugar a week, at 9d. the lb.
    annually   -   -   3 18 0 ⎬ Total annually 6   7   0

Soap, about ½ lb. a week, at 9d.
    the lb. annually   -   -   0 19 6 ⎪

Candles, annually about   -   -   0 10 0 ⎦

His expence of coals in winter is one bufhel weekly, which,
    at 1s. 6d. for 26 weeks, is, annually   -   -   1 19 0

He ufes 2 pair of fhoes in a year, which (at 7s. 6d. each pair,
    and 1s. mending,) coft annually 16s.   3 pair of ftock-
    ings, (at 2s. a pair,) 6s ; an old coat, about 7s.; the
    yearly expence of fhirts may be eftimated at 10s.; and
    of other articles at the fame fum at leaft : total annually   2 9 0

His wife's cloaths are not fuppofed to coft annually more than   1 1 0

The 2 eldeft children learn to read at a day-fchool at 3d. a
    week, each; annually   -   -   -   - 1 6 0

                             £ 39 0 4

Nothing is charged for cloathing the children; as the wife contrives to
provide them from her hufband's old cloaths, and from the prefents of
linen, &c. which fhe receives on lyings-in, &c. Befides his regular pay,
the man is allowed, from his mafter's garden, what potatoes and other vegetables he has occafion for, and about a quart of fkim-milk every morning
from the dairy: notwithftanding which, he complains heavily of the hardnefs of the times; he fays, that his earnings are barely fufficient to pay
his expences, and is now foliciting his mafter for an increafe of wages.
A Cumberland labourer, who was as well fupplied with vegetables, would
make himfelf many a palatable difh, with onions, potatoes, and milk, and
                                                 not

not expend above £15. a year in house-keeping. With all the advantages above enumerated, it is astonishing that this family should consume so large a quantity of the best wheaten bread. This is however considered to be so essential a part of the diet of a labourer in the Southern parts of England, that I am convinced, that any farmer, who attempted to vary the diet of his men, by the introduction of various palatable and nutritious soups and puddings, would be considered as a very hard-hearted fellow, whose only view, in so doing, was the promotion of his own interest. If the wife of this man was as economical in her kitchen, as her husband is industrious in the field, I have no doubt, that half their income might be laid by, and their family as well fed as it is at present, upon a diet not less wholsome, and what, I think, (from the variety of dishes that might be prepared,) would soon prove more palatable, than bread for dinner, six days in the week, and a small piece of plain roast beef on a Sunday.

June, 1796.

HAMPTON.

IN this parish the Poor are partly relieved at home, and partly maintained in a poor-house, which is situated on Hampton Common, in an airy situation, on a gravelly soil. The number of Paupers, at present, in the house, are, 7 girls, 5 boys, 4 women, and 1 man; total, 17: there are generally more in winter. In the last winter, there were 21 in the house; of which there died, chiefly owing to the inclemency of the weather, 4 old persons, and 1 child. The house is under the direction of a man and his wife, who receive a small salary from the parish; besides which, they are allowed 2s. 8d. per week, for every Pauper whom they feed. The food seems wholsome and good; and is, certainly, much better than a labouring man could afford his family: meat is served every day, with vegetables from the garden, which the man is chiefly employed in cultivating. The female Paupers in this house are not content with the ample allowance of food that is furnished them, and would be riotous without tea every morning: this, however, is not allowed them by the master; who, when they go out to work, which is not often, is entitled to their earnings. Notwithftanding this, they contrive means of obtaining tea and fugar, cups and tea-pots. The houfe feems clean and neat. It can contain about 40 Paupers: there are 6 rooms appropriated to them; each contains 3 feather beds: feldom more than 2 fleep in a bed. An apothecary receives £ 15. per annum, for attending the fick in the houfe. The children are taught to read and fay their prayers, but no kind of work feems going forward in the houfe. Previous to May 1795, the man who keeps this houfe farmed all the poor of the parifh of Hampton, at £ 300. a year; but fince that period, the parifh has either relieved diftreffed families at home, or fent them to the poor-houfe. The allowance for each perfon, at 2s. 8d. a week, amounts to £ 6. 18s. 8d. per annum. The Poor in this houfe are cloathed once a year; every perfon wears a red badge on their fhoulder, marked P. H. (Parifh of Hampton.)

Table of the Diet ufed in the Poor-houfe.

	Breakfaft	Dinner.	Supper
Sunday,	Broth, or water gruel: and fometimes bread and milk for the children: bread and cheefe for the men and women.	Hot boiled beef, (half a pound to each perfon;) fometimes dumplins, and 1 pint of beer: the children are not limited to any certain quantity.	Bread, and 2 oz of butter or cheefe, and 1 pint of beer for each man and woman Bread, and a piece of cheefe, and fometimes a little treacle, in lieu of cheefe, for the children.
Monday,	Ditto.	Cold boiled beef.	Ditto.
Tuefday,	Ditto.	Hot boiled beef.	Ditto
Wednefday,	Ditto	Same as Monday	Ditto.
Thurfday,	Ditto.	Same as Tuefday.	Ditto.
Friday,	Ditto.	Same as Monday.	Ditto.
Saturday,	Ditto.	Same as Tuefday.	Ditto.

One pound of bread is given out every morning to each man and woman; and ferves them the whole day.

Table of Baptifms, Burials, and Marriages.

Years.	Baptisms				Burials			Marriages.
	Males	Females	Total	Twins	Males	Females	Total.	
1657	13	7	20					
1658	7	9	16					
1659	8	8	16					
1660	11	6	17					
1661	8	8	16					
1662	7	10	17					
1663	16	14	30					
1664	10	12	22					
1665	9	17	26					
1666	7	13	20					
1667	14	13	27					
1668	15	19	34					
1669	18	5	23					

Years

Years.	Baptisms.				Burials.			Marriages.
	Males.	Females.	Total.	Twins.	Males.	Females.	Total.	
1670	17	10	27					
1671	10	12	22					
1672	13	13	26					
1673	10	7	17					
1674	14	9	23					
1675	12	10	22					
1676	12	6	18					
1677	11	6	18					
1678	8	7	15					
1679	7	10	17					
1680	19	10	29					
1681	9	8	17					
1682	13	12	25					
1683	16	16	32					
1684	9	11	20	4				
1685	20	12	32	—				
1686	16	15	31	—				
1687	14	12	26	—				
1688	13	15	28	—				
1689	24	15	39	—				
1690	24	25	49	—				
1691	14	18	32	—				
1692	22	22	44	—				
1693	20	13	33	—				
1694	19	11	30	—				
1695	14	18	32	4				
1696	22	18	40	4				
1697	14	14	28	—				
1698	26	11	37	—				
1699	18	23	41	—	—	—	30	12
1700	28	19	47	—	—	—	30	5
1701	22	15	37	—	—	—	31	11
1702	20	27	47	2	—	—	30	9
1703	19	13	32	—	—	—	36	5
1704	28	20	48	6	—	—	43	7
1705	15	13	28	2	—	—	49	9
1706	23	20	43	—	—	—	38	15
1707	17	20	37	—	—	—	52	8
1708	25	23	48	—	—	—	44	10
1709	19	22	41	—	—	—	38	11
1710	19	15	34	—	—	—	47	5
1711	19	20	39	—	—	—	42	5
1712	18	25	43	—	—	—	45	8
1713	23	20	43	—	—	—	47	7
1714	19	15	34	2	—	—	54	6
1715	25	22	47	—	—	—	38	7
1716	18	16	34	—	—	—	32	12
1717	23	29	52	—	—	—	39	—
1718	16	24	40	—	—	—	43	—
1719	22	10	32	2	—	—	45	—
1720	14	24	38	2	—	—	38	—
1721	12	12	24	—	—	—	49	—
1722	27	18	45	2	—	—	45	—
1723	18	16	34	—	—	—	47	—
1724	20	18	38	—	—	—	42	—
1725	15	27	42	2	—	—	37	—
1726	20	17	37	2	—	—	—	—
1727	18	15	33	—	—	—	—	—
1728	17	13	30	2	—	—	—	—
1729	13	17	30	2	—	—	—	—

| | BAPTISMS. | | | | BURIALS. | | | |
Years.	Males.	Females.	Total.	Twins.	Males.	Females.	Total.	Paupers.
1730	12	18	30	4				
1731	11	18	29	—				
1732	26	10	36	—				
1733	17	15	32	—				
1734	17	17	34	—				
1735	13	17	30	—				
1736	13	20	33	—				
1737	18	21	39	—				
1738	21	14	35	—				
1739	13	12	25	4				
1740	20	16	36	—				
1741	16	13	29	—				
1742	13	16	29	—				
1743	7	12	19	—				
1744	9	18	27	—				
1745	7	11	18	—				
1746	16	11	27	—				
1747	13	13	26	—				
1748	14	8	22	—				
1749	14	10	24	—				
1750	11	18	29	—				
1751	9	14	23	—				
1752	13	15	28	—				
1753	11	15	26	—				
1754	15	14	29	—				
1755	21	15	36	4				
1756	15	17	32	—				
1757	7	12	19	—				
1758	10	16	26	—				
1759	9	17	26	—				
1760	10	12	22	—				
1761	15	16	31	—				
1762	14	10	24	—				
1763	21	17	38	2				
1764	14	15	29	—				
1765	23	19	42	—				
1766	18	18	36	—				
1767	20	12	32	—				
1768	16	23	39	—				
1769	22	12	34	—	—	—	53	
1770	19	24	43	—	—	—	63	
1771	21	19	40	—	—	—	46	
1772	13	22	35	—	—	—	45	
1773	18	13	31	—	—	—	61	
1774	20	16	36	—	—	—	46	
1775	25	17	42	—	—	—	49	
1776	18	16	34	—	—	—	56	
1777	18	25	43	—	—	—	63	
1778	10	23	33	—	—	—	53	
1779	21	25	46	—	—	—	39	
1780	20	25	45	2	—	—	57	
1781	14	22	36	—	—	—	71	
1782	22	26	48	2	—	—	48	
1783	20	21	41	2	—	—	55	
1784	26	20	46	2	—	—	49	8
1785	22	17	39	—	—	—	41	4
1786	15	15	30	—	—	—	52	7
1787	28	16	44	—	—	—	59	11
1788	15	13	28	—	—	—	46	4
1789	24	17	41	—	—	—	50	4
1790	18	25	43	—	—	—	55	1
1791	26	20	46	—	—	—	53	4
1792	19	12	31	—	—	—	34	—
1793	19	21	40	2	—	—	52	—
1794	24	25	49	2	—	—	58	—

On Hampton Common are feveral nurfe children from the parifh of St.
Martin's in the Fields, Weftminfter: a woman that had 5 of them told me,
fhe was allowed 3s. a week, for each, by the parifh; that fhe had brought
them all up by hand; and that a parifh-officer came fiom town twice a
year, to fee that they were well taken care of. They are fent back to
London, when 8 or 9 years old. She teaches them to read: and the
parifh clothes them once a year. The allowance for each, amounts,
per annum, to £7. 16s.

The Rates have continued nearly the fame for many years. The fmall
rife in 1795 is principally owing to the expence of furnifhing men to the
Navy. According to the returns made to Parliament,'

The expences for the Poor in 1776 were	- £356	4	0
The affeffments -	1783 -	412 19	6
	1784 -	416 14	4
	1785 -	417 8	6

The following was the amount of the Poor's Rates of Hampton, from
1788 to 1796:

		When made.			Amount of each Rate.		
					£. s. d.		
1789.							
3 Rates, at	First,	April	14	-	- 141 11 0		
8d. in the	Second,	May	7	-	- 140 6 6		
pound.	Third,	Auguft	27	-	- 140 9 0		
							422 6 6
1790.							
	First,	January	8	-	- 141 19 0		
4 Rates,	Second,	April	28	-	- 141 17 6		
at 8d.	Third,	Auguft	5	-	- 144 19 4		
	Fourth,	Dec.	16	-	- 146 10 0		
							575 5 10
1791.							
2 Rates,	First,	May	2	-	- 224 9 0		
at 1s.	Second,	Nov.	30	-	- 224 8 6		
							448 17 6
1792.							
2 Rates,	First,	April	19	-	- 223 17 6		
at 1s.	Second,	Oct.	31	-	- 227 17 6		
							451 15 0

7

	When made.				Amount of the Rate.		
					£.	s.	d.
1793.							
2 Rates,	Fiift,	April	17	- - -	227	6	0
at 1s.	Second,	Oct.	31	- - -	229	4	0
						456 10 0	
1794.							
2 Rates,	Fiift,	May	12	- -	231	18	0
at 1s.	Second,	Nov.	14	- - -	234	17	0
						466 15 0	
1795.							
2 Rates,	Fiift,	Apiil	28	- -	237	5	0
at 1s.	Second,	Nov.	12	- - -	249	0	6
						486 5 6	

January, 1796.

ST. MARTIN IN THE FIELDS.

THE Pooi of this paiifh are paitly relieved at home, and partly maintained in the woik-houfe in Caftle ftreet, Leicefter Fields There are, at prefent, about 240 weekly out-penfioners, befides a confiderable number of Poor on the cafual lift. Of 573, the number of Poor at prefent in the work-houfe, 473 are adults, and 1co, children; of which, 54 are boys, 21 giils, able to work, and 25 infants. Their principal employment is fpinning flax, picking hair, carding wool, &c. : their annual earnings, on an average of a few years paft, amount to about £150. It was once attempted to eftablifh a manufacture in the houfe; but the badnefs of the fituation for bufinefs, the want of room for workfhops, and the difficulty of compelling the able Poor to pay proper attention to work, rendered the project unfuccefsful. Between 70 and 80 childien belonging to this parifh are, generally, out at nuife in the country : a weekly allowance of 3s. (lately advanced to 3s. 6d.) is paid with each child. At 7 or 8 years of age, the childien are taken into the houfe, and taught a little reading, &c. for 3 or 4 years, and then put out apprentices.

The following tables exhibit various particulars, ielative to the number and expence of the Poor of this paiifh : they aie, I hope, as accurate as

accounts

accounts of this nature can be expected to be. The apprehension of creating alarm, prevented me from being more minute in my enquiries[1].

Table of Poor annually admitted into the Work-house, &c.

Years	Nº admitted	Nº discharged, removed, put out apprentices, &c	Average Nº in the house.	Births in the house	Deaths in the house	Nº of parish apprentices bound out annually.	Nº of burials paid for by the parish, exclusive of those from the house
1767	—	—	—	—	—	9	—
1768	—	—	—	—	—	29	—
1769	—	—	—	—	—	18	—
1770	652	582	—	—	—	37	—
1771	728	550	—	35	158	55	—
1772	1171	779	—	43	236	24	—
1773	1322	1043	—	48	235	26	—
1774	981	804	—	49	162	27	—
1775	967	764	—	53	178	34	—
1776	1023	865	—	49	166	35	65
1777	1099	863	—	46	221	34	94
1778	1183	903	—	64	237	26	69
1779	1101	894	—	45	237	27	85
1780	1007	810	—	62	290	27	76
1781	1022	870	—	48	228	29	101
1782	1142	813	723	54	238	16	65
1783	1195	963	781	67	264	23	80
1784	1519	1247	800	56	294	37	86
1785	1535	1484	765	63	247	68	56
1786	1276	1146	698	50	203	55	72
1787	1105	978	664	43	205	67	86
1788	1249	949	706	40	249	16	57
1789	1084	989	719	31	176	42	65
1790	1178	1033	717	45	209	41	49
1791	1048	969	680	39	174	83	64
1792	998	895	633	30	198	24	56
1793	949	762	634	31	197	13	—
1794	945	757	642	38	191	25	—

Table

[1] I made similar enquiries in Mary-le-bone parish; but was told by the Vestry-clerk, that the Directors and Guardians of the Poor were of opinion, that my request could not be complied

Table of Poor's Rates and Disbursements.

Years.	Rate affessed. £.	Deficiency uncollected. £.	Rate collected. £.	Total Expenditure. £.	Rate in the Pound. s. d.
1771	- - - - - - - - -		7565	7777	s. d.
1772	- - - - - - - - -		8526	8961	2 6
1773	- - - - - - - - -		8570	9439	2 6
1774	- - - - - - - - -		10739	10838	3 0
1775	- - - - - - - - -		10609	10828	3 0
1776	- - - - - - - - -		9493	9947	2 8
1777	- - - - - - - - -		8600	10983	2 4
1778	- - - - - - - - -		8441	9859	2 4
1779	- - - - - - - - -		9764	10104	2 8
1780	- - - - - - - - -		9657	16162	2 8
1781	- - - - - - - - -		9515	10446	2 8
1782	- - - - - - - -		9510	10347	2 8
1783	11874	1972	9902	10780	2 10
1784	12051	2127	9914	11203	2 10
1785	12292	1759	10533	11270	2 10
1786	11441	1529	9912	9686	2 8
1787	11268	1143	10125	10072	2 8
1788	10551	1192	9359	10986	2 6
1789	11048	912	10136	10168	2 7
1790	10802	1042	9760	10531	2 6
1791	10939	1197	9742	9830	2 6
1792	10172	936	9424	9719	2 4
1793	10339	990	9456	11048	2 4
1794	- - - - - - - - - - - - - - - - - - -				2 7

plied with. This refusal to communicate information respecting a parish, where the cleanly and orderly management of the work-house led me to hope that the accounts of receipts and disbursements would bear the test of fair examination, has, I confess, deterred me from attempting the Herculean task of investigating the Augean mass of parochial expence in other parishes of the metropolis.

Expences of the Work-house in St. MARTIN's in the Fields.

Years	Linen		Woollen			Coals		Flour		Beer		Cheese and Butter		Grocery		Meat		Total Expenditure	
	£	s	£	s	d	£	s	£	s.	£	s	£	s.	£	s	£	s.	£	s
1782	384	16	237	13	6	266	9	1292	7	528	17	664	12	273	17	985	17	4624	12
1783	265	11	192	1	0	294	4	985	5	402	13	739	17	203	10	938	5	4071	6
1784	345	5	239	8	0	207	3	1212	0	573	12	805	14	159	3	1221	9	4914	9
1785	329	15	229	8	0	305	0	1215	19	601	1	774	1	202	9	1169	0	4827	12
1786	350	4	277	6	0	161	0	806	17	579	17	622	17	280	10	1079	5	4157	17
1787	376	16	217	9	0	274	0	864	0	446	11	596	0	304	12	1055	11	4134	19
1788	361	18	208	13	0	230	10	1291	10	626	13	636	19	249	3	1271	11	4946	18
1789	205	1	162	0	0	294	17	1372	5	634	4	644	7	250	9	1262	4	4825	7
1790	250	5	258	18	0	283	11	1425	7	531	8	725	3	289	10	1133	4	4947	7
1791	293	4	215	13	0	214	19	1135	12	529	11	676	4	263	15	1045	11	4379	10
1792	310	10	171	6	0	251	5	1034	11	448	6	629	2	286	1	1189	19	4321	0
1793	321	8	217	6	0	305	10	1221	10	481	10	551	8	231	4	1232	11	4562	7
1794	417	0	426	6	0	336	15	1345	0	527	13	656	8	205	10	1296	13	5251	10

Twenty men were raised by this parish for the Navy; and as 68 houses furnished one man, the number of houses paying the window-tax may be estimated at about 1360: the number exempted is about 1800, in which are included about 200 uninhabited houses.

The full rental of this parish is £250,563[1]. The number of ale-houses is 179. Removals, appeals, advertisements, &c. on account of the parish, seldom exceed £44 a year. The salaries of parish-officers amount to £499. a year. 108 militia-men belong to the parish: about one third of that number have families.

Bill of Fare for the Poor in the Work-house of St. MARTIN's in the Fields.

	Breakfast.	Dinner.	Supper.
Sunday,	Bread and butter.	Six oz. of meat, (without bone,) and greens.	Bread and cheese, or butter.
Monday,	Milk-pottage.	Pease soup	Bread and butter.
Tuesday,	Ditto.	Beef and greens.	Bread and cheese, or butter.
Wednesday,	Ditto	Pease soup	Bread and butter
Thursday,	Ditto	Beef and greens.	Bread and cheese, or butter
Friday,	Water gruel sweetened and spiced.	Barley-gruel, with milk.	Bread and cheese.
Saturday,	Milk-pottage	One pound of plum-pudding.	Bread and butter

Fourteen oz. of bread, and one quart of beer, a day, are allowed to each person; mutton and broth for the sick, every day; to each married lying-in woman, one pot of porter for caudle the first 9 days, and a pint for 7 days

[1] I think the following Table worthy of insertion It affords a comparative view of the Rentals charged to the Poor in every parish in Westminster, and the adjoining parishes, in the year 1780

after;

after; others, half that quantity; baked mutton with potatoes once in 6 weeks; peafe and beans with bacon, and mackerel and falmon, once in the feafon; grey peafe and bacon, on Shrove Tuefday; bunns, on Good Friday; roaft beef on Chriftmas-day; pork and peafe-pudding on New-Year's-day; plum-cake on Holy Thurfday.

The donations to the Poor, laft winter, on account of the fcarcity of bread, amounted to £832. 8s. 6d.

The Amount of the Grofs Rentals charged to the Poor in each Parifh within the Hundred of Ossulston, for the year 1780, together with the Quotas to be levied on thefe Parifhes refpectively, towards the Sum of £21133. 2s. 3d. recovered by different Actions againft the faid Hundred, at £1. 6s. 3¼d. per centum, on

£ 1607598. ============ £ 21133. 4s. 3¼d.

PARISHES, &c.	Rentals.	Quotas.			PARISHES, &c.	Rentals.	Quotas.		
		£.	s.	d.		£.	£.	s.	d.
					Brought forward -	945102	12424	2	9¼.3
Acton - - -	4375	57	10	3 7/100	Liberty of Glafs Houfe Yard	2445	32	2	9¼.9
Artillery Old - -	3378	44	8	1½ 16/100	Liberty of the Tower, within - - -	1167	15	6	9¼.54
St. Ann's, Soho - -	53936	709	0	8 7/100	Liberty of the Tower, without - - -	1704	22	8	0 .4
St. Ann's, Limehoufe - -	4799	63	1	8¼ 78/100	Liberty of Well Clofe -	2544	33	8	10¼.28
St. Andrew's Holborn, and St. George the Martyr -	74291	976	12	4 42/100	St. Leonard, Shoreditch -	32903	432	10	8¼.86
Bethnal Green, St. Matthew	20876	274	8	7¾ 12/100	St. Leonard, Bromley -	3322	43	13	4¼.64
St. Clement Danes, including the Duchy of Lancafter -	53072	697	13	6 64/100	St. Margaret and St. John, Weftminfter -	61257	805	5	5¼.34
Chrift Church, Spitalfields -	27286	358	13	11¼ 10/100	St. Martin in the Fields -	124063	1630	18	2¼.06
St. Catharine -	5733	75	7	3¼ 19/100	St. Mary Le Strand - -	6892	90	12	0¼.0
Chelfea - - -	13596	178	14	7¼ 16/100	St. Mary Le Bone * - -	210195	2763	3	9 .09
Chifwick - -	7636	100	6	0¼ 6/100	St. Mary, Whitechapel -	30235	397	9	3¼.07
Ealing and Old Brentford -	1049	137	18	3 42/100	Mile End, Old Town - -	10520	138	5	10¼.02
Eaft Smithfield - -	12600	165	12	9	St. Mary Bow, Stratford -	3273	43	0	6¼.2
Ely Rents, Saffron Hill, and Hatton Garden - -	15627	205	8	7 72/100	Mile End, New Town -	6183	81	5	4 .8
Finchley - - -	4422	58	2	7¼ 44/100	Minories, Trinity -	1879	24	14	6 .9
Fryern Barnett - -	2333	30	13	4¼ 66/100	Norton Falgate -	4541	59	3	10¼.4
Fulham - - -	11231	147	12	9¼ 72/100	St. Paul, Covent Garden -	32102	422	0	1¼.2
St. George, Hanover Square	17409	2288	12	2¼ 78/100	St. Pancras - -	38115	501	1	0¼.0
St. Geo. Bloomfb. & St. Giles	101300	1331	13	5¼	Paddington - -	4400	57	16	10 .
St George, Middlefex - -	2666	350	10	11 7/100	Precinct of the Savoy - -	1837	24	2	11¼.9
Hornfey - -	8261	108	11	11¼ 10/100	Poplar and Blackwall -	7533	99	0	6¼.4
Hackney - - -	28937	380	8	0 64/100	St. Paul, Shadwell -	14000	184	0	10 .
Hammerfmith - -	9440	124	1	11 10/100	Rolls Liberty -	8347	109	14	6¼.1
St. John, Hampftead - -	14277	187	13	7¼	Radcliffe -	7732	101	12	10¼.8
St. John the Evangelift -	18405	241	18	11¼ 10/100	St. Sepulchre -	9337	122	14	10 .9
St. James, Weftminfter -	133760	1758	7	8¼ 20/100	Stoke Newington -	4875	64	1	8¼.0
St. John, Wapping - -	12458	163	15	4¾ 100/100	Wilfdon -	5850	76	18	0¾.
St. James and St. John, Clerkenwell - - -	33879	445	7	4 9/100	St. Mary, Iflington - -	24746	325	6	1¼.5
Kenfington - - -	24240	318	13	1 10/100	Twyford - - -	500	6	11	5¼.
St. Luke, Old-ftreet - -	33709	443	2	7¼ 50/100		1607598	21133	3	8¼
	945102	12424	2	9¼ 3/100					

* Memorandum. In 1704, the whole Rental charged to the Poor was £3440; and in 1772, £125000. Average increafe, the laft 10 ye... £100c0. per annum. The prefent Rental muft greatly exceed £300000.

5

Since the preceding accounts were obtained and printed, the following statement has been publifhed by the parifh-officers: it is much to be wifhed other parifhes in the metropolis would favour the Public with fimilar accounts, though a little more detailed: I much miftake, if fuch details, fairly given, would not aftonifh the warmeft advocates for Poor fyftems: various abufes would appear, which are now enveloped in the thickeft obfcurity. As an inftance, it may be mentioned, that one of the Overfeers of St. Clement Danes abfconded a few months ago, with above £300. of the parifh money.

" *Parifh of St. Martin in the Fields.*

" THE Church-warden and Overfeers of the Poor of this parifh, for 1795 and 1796, with the concurrence and approbation of the Magiftrates, and feveral other refpectable inhabitants, have thought proper to publifh a fhort ftatement of their accounts during the year that they were in office, as a fatisfaction to the parifhioners at large, as well as to lay before them, at one view, a clear and precife account of that *feeming* enormous fum that is collected yearly for the maintenance of the Poor ; although, in fact, only about five parts out of fix of it are appropriated in reality for that purpofe ; the remainder being for various mifcellaneous fervices, and all paid out of the Poor's Rate, as will appear by the following Table:

	£.	s.	d.
Paid to the Out-door or Settled Poor - - - -	886	1	0
—— Cafual Poor - - - - - -	171	3	6
—— Paffes - - - - -	37	1	1
—— To the families of militia-men - - -	245	7	0
- —— To ditto, extra expence this year - - -	90	0	0
—— County Rate - - - -	759	7	6
—— To binding apprentices - - -	95	0	0
—— Children at nurfe in the country - - -	521	17	6
—— Cloathing ditto - - - -	60	0	0
Paid the Poor in the houfe in lieu of their bread and meat - -	350	0	0
Paid various poor perfons at the time they were difcharged from the houfe, and various other expences in the houfe - - -	130	0	0
Expences in vifiting the children in the country - - -	36	0	0
Paid fearchers for infpecting the dead - - -	7	16	0
To bearers, for conveying the dead to be buried - - -	18	18	0
Paid for coffins and fhrouds for ditto - - -	80	0	0
Repairing the houfe and furniture - - - -	100	0	0
Expences of a law fuit with the parifh of St. Mary le Bone ; the verdict being given againft them - - - -	96	0	0
Paid for tools and utenfils in eftablifhing the woollen manufactory in the workhoufe - - - - -	40	0	0
Paid for wool for ditto - - - -	236	4	0
Paid poor families not belonging to the parifh - -	40	0	0
Expences of removals and appeals, and various other contingencies -	278	12	0
Expences attending fire engines - - -	51	11	6
Paid Mr. Booth, veftry clerk, for making the return of the Infant Poor -	30	0	0
Paid to ditto, out of the fines for overfeers - - -	46	4	0
To yearly payments to the different annuitants - - -	220	0	0

Brought over   -   £4627 3 1

"HOUSE ESTABLISHMENT.

	£.	s.	d
Mr. Harding, apothecary - - - -	120	0	0
To ditto for attending Out-door Poor - -	20	0	0
Mr. Lemage, clerk; and the principal part of his board	150	0	0
Mr. Simmonds, furgeon - - -	80	0	0
Mr Sherriff, chaplain - - -	30	0	0
Mr. Conno, mafter - - -	50	0	0
Mrs. Ellis, matron - - -	20	0	0
Mr. Feezie, porter - - -	10	0	0
To mafter-baker - - -	20	0	0
Paid nurfes in the different wards - -	205	0	0

705 0 0

	£.	s.	d
Expences of the Mafter's table, &c - - -	150	0	0
To Mr. Beavan, for flour, as part of his bill for 1796 -	100	0	0
To expences for rate-making - - -	30	0	0
To arrears of annuitants - - -	40	0	0
To Rev. Mr Sherriff (his falary for the previous year being £42) -	12	0	0

To 620 Poor in the houfe, at £12. 10s. 6d each, being the average number
that year   -   -   -   -   -   - 7765 10 0

The whole paid   -   -   -   -   - 13429 13 1
Balance in hand, paid over to the fucceeding Overfeers   -   - 504 12 4

13934 5 5

The whole collection of the different Rates, the firft half-
year, at 1s. 6d.   -   -   -   -   } 12282 5 0
The fecond half-year, at do.   -   -   -
Sundries received   -   -   -   -   - 1652 0 5

13934 5 5

*** "Early in the year 1796, when flour was at twelve fhillings the bufhel, the Church-warden and Overfeers of the Poor came to a refolution to fubftitute rice inftead of flour, for puddings and other ufes in the houfe. The following Table will fhew the difference of ex-pence in the two articles, per week.

" PLUM-PUDDING.	£.	s.	d.	" RICE-PUDDING.	£.	s.	d.
4 bufhels flour - -	2	8	0	100 lb. rice - -	0	19	0
4 do. barley at 7s. -	1	8	0	18 gallons of milk -	1	4	0
42 lb raifins - -	0	12	0	14 lb. of fugar - -	0	8	2
30 lb. fuet, at 6d. -	0	15	0	10 lb of butter - -	0	6	8
8 gall. milk, 1s 4d. -	0	10	8	1 lb fpices - -	0	3	6
All-fpice and ginger -	0	3	9				
					3	1	4
	£5	17	5	Difference in faving -	2	16	1
					£5	17	5

" This quantity will dine fix hundred people

" Admitted into the houfe in the year 1795—6 - -	797 perfons,
" Difcharged - - - -	710
" Died - - -	112

" December, 1796."

MONMOUTHSHIRE.

ABERGAVENNY.

THIS parifh contains, by eftimation, 4 fquaie miles. The vicar eftimates the population at about 2500 fouls. 302 houfes pay the window-
tax; the number exempted could not be obtained: the number of ale-
houfes is 25. The inhabitants are, a few gentlemen, mechanics, publicans, fhop-keepeis, farmers, common aitificeis and labourers. Here are
1 Anabaptift, 1 Roman Catholic, and 2 Methodift chapels.

The piices of provifions are: wheat, from 12s. to 13s. for 10 gallons;
barley, 5s. 6d. do.; beef, 4d. the pound; mutton, 4d.; veal, 4½d.; bacon,
1od.; milk, 1½d. a quait.

Common laboureis have 9s. a week, and beer; and in hay and corn harveft, 9s. a week, and board: in the neighbouring country parifhes, labourers
are paid 6s a week in winter, and 7s. in fummer; befides which, the farmer
allows them to have corn, &c. rather lower than the market piice. The rent
of land is fiom 10s. to £3 10s. an acre. Farms are from £25. to £170.
chiefly about £40. or £50. a yeai: wheat, barley, oats, turnips, and clover,
are chiefly cul.ivated; but a great proportion of the land is in pafture.
Theie is no common: the uncultivated hills in the parifh are private pro-
peity Tithes are compounded for. Here is a fort of poor-houfe, in
which foimeily a woollen manufaclure was attempted; but, not being
found to anfwei, it was difcontinued; and for the laft 6 or 7 years, no
mafter has been kept in the houfe, but fuch Poor as cannot procuie a refidence elfewhere are put into the houfe, with an allowance to fupport
themfelves. 70 iegular out-penfioneis receive, at prefent, about £7. a
week; and about 30 poor people, 30s. a week, in cafual payments.

A Table

A Table of Baptisms, Burials, Marriages, and Poor's Rates.

Years.	Baptisms	Burials	Marriages	Poor's Rates.			Net Expenditure			Rate in the Pound		
				£.	s.	d.	£.	s.	d.	s.	d.	
1654	43											
1655	44											
1680	74											
1681	83											
1692												
1693												
1694												
1695												
1697	The register badly kept these years.											
1698												
1699												
1700												
1720	—	—	—	—	—	—	—	—	—	1	0	
1722	—	—	—	—	—	—	—	—	—	0	8	
1723	—	—	—	—	—	—	—	—	—	1	2	
1724	—	—	—	—	—	—	—	—	—	1	2	
1740	49	59	—	—	—	—	—	—	—	1	10	
1759	—	—	—	—	—	—	—	—	—	3	3	
1760	42	40	—	—	—	—	—	—	—	3	0	
1765	44	42	—	—	—	—	—	—	—	2	0	
1770	—	—	—	—	—	—	—	—	—	3	6	Deficiency
1775	39	29	8	—	—	—	—	—	—	5	0	of rates ow-
1776	49	42	13	—	—	—	374	0	0[1]	—	—	ing to empty houses, &c
1777	42	99	15	—	—	—	-	—	—	4	0	£. s. d.
1778	64	48	20	290	16	2	486	8	6	3	6	3 17 2
1779	46	40	20	372	13	3	576	4	0	4	6	8 17 2
1780	44	35	10	—	—	—	—	—	—	5	0	
1781	37	45	10	—	—	—	—	—	—	0	0	
1782	39	40	21	—	—	—	—	—	—	3	9	
1783	51	52	16	503	3	1	—	—	—	4	0	
1784	48	57	20	446	2	10 }[2]	—	—	—	5	3	
1785	46	29	21	482	0	4	—	—	—	4	9	
1786	41	54	11	—	—	—	—	—	—	5	0	
1787	42	49	18	—	—	—	—	—	—	5	0	
1788	49	40	23	—	—	—	—	—	—	5	0	
1789	63	71	18	—	—	—	—	—	—	5	0	
1790	58	50	13	—	—	—	—	—	—	6	0	
1791	61	46	23	—	—	—	—	—	—	6	0	
1792	65	59	28	—	—	—	—	—	—	6	9	
1793	61	67	16	367	10	0	—	—	—	5	0	
1794	57	56	23	—	—	—	—	—	—	6	0	
1795	—	—	—	—	—	—	—	—	—	6	0	

[1] From returns to Parliament.   [2] Ditto.

The

The accounts of this parifh were heretofore kept on loofe paper; moſt of which were in the poſſeſſion of a perſon, who lately became inſane, and in one of his fits deſtroyed them. The Rate is extremely irregular; nor has any alteration in the mode of aſſeſſment taken place for ſome time back : ſo that it is probable that, on an average, land is not aſſeſſed at more than one third of its real value. From an old book it appears, that, in 1722, there were 33 penſioners, who received weekly £1. 18s. 9d.; in 1723, 32 penſioners received £1. 17s. 1d. a week.

November, 1795.

MONMOUTH.

THIS parifh is ſaid to be a ſquare of about one mile and a quarter : the population has never been taken. The inhabitants are ſhop-keepers, inn-keepers, agriculturiſts, &c. Here is one Catholic, and one Methodiſt congregation. 351 houſes pay the window tax; 30 are ſtated in the ſurveyor's books as exempted; and the officer thinks 30 or 40 more may be exempted.

The prices of proviſions are : beef, 3¾d. to 4½d. the lb.; mutton, 4d. to 4½d.; veal, 6d. to 7d.; bacon, 10d. to 1s.; freſh butter, 1s.; ſalt do. 9d. the lb.; potatoes, 8d. a peck; bread, 8d. the quartern loaf, or 5½ lb. for 1s.; coals, 12s. the ton; wheat, 11s. 6d. to 12s. for 10 gallons; barley, 4s. 6d. to 5s. for 10 gallons; oats, 4s. for do.; milk, 1½d. the quart.

The wages of common labourers are, 1s. a day, and victuals; or 1s. 6d. with only a dinner. There are 45 ale-houſes in this pariſh; and five Friendly Societies, each of which has about 80 members; all of them have had their rules confirmed. One of theſe Societies is ſomewhat ſingular; the members each pay a guinea a year into the box, for which a proviſion is made for their widows; a copy of their rules could not be obtained.

The rent of land, near the town, is from £3. to £4., 10s. an acre; but, at a diſtance, about £1. an acre. The farms let from £25 to £250. a year; wheat, barley, and oats, are cultivated here in ſome degree; but the greateſt part of the land is chiefly in graſs. The tithes belong to the Duke of Beaufort, and are compounded for. The land-tax amounts to £354. 10d.

o

and

and is collected at about 1s. 2d. in the pound. There is no common nor waste land in the parish.

The Poor are partly maintained in a work-house, and partly at home: there are 24 persons, at present, in the work-house; of which 3 are children, under 7 years of age; 12, between 7 and 30; and 9, between 30 and 79 years old. They are chiefly employed in manufacturing linen and woollen cloaths for the house. The house is convenient, and well aired, and appears to be kept very clean: the beds, which are good, are furnished with coarse sheets: there are no blankets at present; but some are preparing against next winter. 45 out-pensioners receive, at present, £3. 18s. 3d a week; 4 or 5 receive occasional relief. It is supposed that the Poor of this parish do not really cost the parish more than 1s in the pound on the fair rental: yet it is generally thought that the Rates are high. Several people belonging to the parish are employed in fisheries on the river Wye, on which Monmouth is situated, and in navigating barges to and from this place.

The following is the bill of fare in the house:

	Breakfast	Dinner	Supper.
Sunday,	Milk pottage	Meat and vegetables.	Bread and beer.
Monday,	Broth	Bread and cheese.	Ditto
Tuesday,	As Sunday	As Sunday.	Ditto.
Wednesday,	As Monday.	As Monday.	Ditto.
Thursday,	As Sunday.	As Sunday	Ditto.
Friday,	As Monday.	As Monday.	Ditto
Saturday,	As Sunday.	Ditto.	Ditto

Statement of a Labourer's Earnings and Expences.

Samuel Price, a labourer, 52 years old, has a wife and 9 children, viz. a girl aged 17, who is subject to fits, and not able to work; a boy, aged 16, at service; a boy, 15, at home; another boy, 14, at home; 3 girls, 12, 10, and 8 years old; a boy, 3, and another boy, $1\frac{1}{2}$ years old; the wife is now pregnant.

	£.	s.	d.
The father, mostly, works for a gentleman at 8s. a week, and beer; except in hay and corn harvest, when he has 1s. 6d. a day, and victuals; annual amount about - -	21	3	0
The boy, who is 15 years old, earns, by going on errands, &c. about 1s. a week - - - -	2	12	0
The other children earn nothing, but pick sticks for fuel in the winter - . - - -	0	0	0
The wife earns, by baking bread for sale, annually about -	1	5	0
Total income - £25	0	0	

EXPENCES.

	£.	s.	d.
The man fays, bread at prefent cofts him about 9s. a week throughout the year, and that he could ufe more if he could get it - - - - -	23	8	0
Butter and cheefe, about 6d. a week; he ufes neither meat nor beer - - - - - - -	1	6	0
Tea and fugar, about 4d. do. - - -	0	17	4
Potatoes, 6d. a week - - - - -	1	6	0
Fuel - - - - - - -	0	8	8
Houfe-rent - - - - - -	2	2	0
Soap, candle, thread, &c. about - - -	1	6	0
Total expences -	£30	14	0

Heie appears a deficiency of £5. 14s.; yet, the man fays, his children moftly go without fhoes and ftockings, and that the cloaths woin by him and his family are, moftly, if not wholly, given them by charitable people The gentleman, for whom this labouier works, allows him about 3 pints of milk a day, which, with a little bread, ferves his children for breakfaft; his wife drinks tea: their dinner is, bread, potatoes, and falt, fometimes a little fat or dripping, if it can be piocured cheap: their fupper, generally, bread, or potatoes. The man fays, his family is little more than half fupplied with what they could eat. He rents his houfe of the corporation of Monmouth, at 2 guineas a year; but not being able to pay his rent, he fays, they lately feized on all his working tools, fome of his furniture, &c. and fold them, fo that he is obliged to borrow fpades, axes, &c: he applied to the parifh for relief; which they offered, on condition that he would come into the poor-houfe with all his family; which he has hitherto refufed to do. From farther enquiry, it appears, that the man is honeft and induftrious. He is determined to remain in his houfe, in defiance of the corporation. His childien, having been bred up in idlenefs, and in the moft abject illiterate ftate, (although feveral of them have been at fervice,) are fo faucy, that no perfon will employ them.

In this town there are 20 alms-houfes, 10 for men, and 10 for women, each of whom receives 3s. 6d. a week, and 15s. a year for coals; and one suit of cloaths every 2 years : 16s. a week are paid for militia-men's families.

A Table of Baptisms, Burials, Marriages, and Poor's Rates.

Years.	Baptisms.			Burials			Marriages.	Poor's Rates			Rate in the Pound.	
	Males.	Fem.	Total.	Males.	Fem.	Total.						
1723	—	—	68	—	—	66	11					
1740	—	—	49	—	—	29	5					
1760	37	32	69	41	42	83	—					
1775	35	50	85	40	25	65	28					
1776	49	38	87	49	34	83	24	—No Return from Monmouth for this				
1777	34	43	77	28	21	49	22	year is inserted in the Returns to Parliament.				
1778	31	37	68	33	51	84	29					
1779	48	42	90	42	31	73	34					
1780	39	52	91	61	41	102	22					
1781	37	34	71	41	34	75	35					
1782	42	34	76	34	31	65	20	£.	s.	d.		
1783	45	43	88	26	27	53	22	375	8	7	From Returns	
1784	40	39	79	26	38	64	21	377	7	4	to Parliament.	
1785	33	40	73	37	30	67	31	377	3	5		
1786	44	37	81	31	28	59	23					
1787	37	31	68	24	31	55	15					
1788	36	36	72	41	28	69	23					
1789	43	33	76	48	40	88	16				s.	d.
1790	38	22	60	25	28	53	24	422	16	11	5	6
1791	24	35	59	25	32	57	16	380	17	9¾	5	0
1792	31	32	63	31	30	61	21	381	18	1	5	0 [1]
1793	37	39	76	32	31	63	16					
1794	37	35	72	41	36	76	17					
1795	—	—	—	—	—	—	—					

[1] These three lines contain all the information given by the parish-officers respecting parochial expenditure. From the information of the Gentlemen of the town it appears, that, for some years back, the affairs of the parish have been badly managed, and that their books are in great confusion.

In

In the above account are included the fums paid to the county ftock, and for building a gaol, &c.; but the precife fums, thus expended, could not be afcertained.

The people complain, that the farmers do not bring their corn to maiket, and afcribe the high price of corn to badgeis, or corn-dealers. In the neighbouring foreft of Dean, colliers collected together by thoufands, and came to Monmouth market, where they obliged the faimers to fell their corn at a reafonable price, on which account a party of dragoons have been ftationed here for fome time.

November, 1795.

N O R F O L K.

D O W N H A M.

DOWNHAM is a fmall market town, fituated on the weftern boideis of Norfolk, about 12 miles from Lynn: the accounts of the parifh are kept in fo confufed a manner, that much information from them cannot be expected. The following table, however, of Parochial Expenditure, and Poor's Rate, (though, peihaps, not very accurate,) may afford fome general idea of thefe matters here:

		Expenditure £.		Rate affeffed. s.	d.
April 1782	-	214	-	1	8
1783	-	324	-	2	9
1784	-	332	-	2	9
1785	-	210	-	2	0
1786	-	265	-	2	8
1787	-	231	-	2	8
1788	No accounts.		-	—	—
1789	-	168	-	—	—
1790	-	231	-	—	—

3 M 2

		Expenditure.		Rate affeffed.	
		£		s.	d.
April 1791	-	280	-	—	—
1792	-	230	-	—	—
1793	-	209	-	—	—
1794	-	200	-	—	—
1795	-	276	-	2	6

The Poor are partly farmed. The contractor has the ufe of 4 acres of land, and a work-houfe, in which he maintains fuch Poor as the parifh pleafe to fend him. They find beds, &c. and cloathe the Poor, when they go into the houfe; but the farmer provides cloathing, during their refidence with him. He is paid £ 95. a year, provided their number does not exceed 20; and for all above that number, 2s. a week each; he is likewife entitled to their earnings. They are employed in fpinning jerfey or woifted; one man weaves hemp-cloth. At prefent, there are 26 Paupers in the houfe; of which 7 are under 9 years of age; 4 from 9 to 20 years old; and the others from 25 to 70 years of age. There are 4 baftards, and 3 foldiers' wives. The officers give weekly allowances to fuch Poor as can fupport themfelves upon a lefs fum than what is charged by the mafter of the poor-houfe.

There are no manufactures here. The price of provifions is nearly the fame as in Lincolnfhire; but the wages of agricultural labour are here confiderably lower[1]

In Helgay, a fmall farming parifh, 3 miles from Downham, the Poor's Rates are 6d. in the pound. Farms there are from £ 10. to £ 100. a year.   *June*, 1795.

                                                                    G R E S-

---

[1] The wages of agricultural labour, in this county, are thus fet down in Mr. Kent's Survey of Norfolk, lately publifhed, p.159.

			Yearly wages.					
			£	s.	d.		£	s.	d.
A head carter	-	from	-	9	9	0	to	10	10	0
An under carter	-	——	-	5	5	0	—	7	7	0
A fhepherd	-	-	-	10	0	0				
A dairy-maid	-	-	-	4	4	0				

Daily wages

A common labourer, without diet, in fummer	0	1	6	in winter 0 1 2
A carpenter, thatcher, or bricklayer,	-	-	0	1	8
Men hay-makers	-	-	-	0	1	6

GRESSINGHALL.

THE House of Industry, belonging to 50 incorporated parishes of the Hundreds of Thetford and Launditch[2], stands in this parish. The house is excellently situated; being built on a rising ground at some distance from the village, half surrounded by a common, with no obstructions near it, to impede the free circulation of air. The house was finished, and made ready for the reception of Paupers, in July 1777. The total expence of purchasing 63 acres, 3 roods, and 3 perches of land, an dof building and furnishing the house, &c. was £ 15,442. 6s. 11d.[3], of which £ 5442. have been repaid; and, therefore, the house has still a debt of £ 10,000.

The following table shews the births and burials, with the average number of Paupers each year, in the house, since it's commencement :

Years.

	£.	s.	d.	
Women hay-makers, by the piece, and three pints of beer	o	o	6	
Threshing wheat, the quarter	o	2	o	and two pints of beer, per day.
——— barley and oats, ditto	o	1	o	ditto
——— peafe, ditto	o	1	4	ditto.
——— clover feed, the bushel	o	5	o	ditto.
Reaping and binding wheat, the acre, - from	o	5	o	to £ 0 7 0
Mowing barley or oats, the acre	o	2	o	to 0 2 6
New banking, and ditching, per rod of 70 yards	o	1	o	to 0 1 6
Making open drains, of 2 feet wide, and 2 feet deep, per rod	o	o	3	
Larger ditto, of 9 feet wide, and 6 feet deep, per rod	o	2	6	
Thatching, with fea or marfh-reed, the fquare	o	4	2	
Wafhing and clipping fheep, the fcore	o	1	4	

[2] Incorporated by 15 Geo III. c 59.

[3] Viz

	£.	s.	d.
Building the house	10000	0	0
Furniture	1600	0	0
Purchafe of land	1400	0	0
Farming ftock	200	0	0
Improving farm	280	0	0
Printer's bills	42	0	o
Sundry articles	860	0	o
Expence of obtaining the Act of Parliament, to which there was much oppofition	1060	6	11
Total - £ 15442	6	11	

Years.					Births.	Burials.	Av No of Paupers in the houfe.
1777 (only half a year)			-	-	5	26	221
1778	-	-	-	-	17	85	352
1779	-	-	-	-	17	53	388
1780	-	-	-	-	22	85	412
1781	-	-	-	-	18	124	459
1782	-	-	-	-	7	107	470
1783	-	-	-	-	16	68	410
1784	-	-	-	-	15	69	437
1785	-	-	-	-	14	48	460
1786	-	-	-	-	21	71	466
1787	-	-	-	-	20	46	460
1788	-	-	-	-	14	71	491
1789	-	-	-	-	17	54	497
1790	-	-	-	-	14	65	506
1791	-	-	-	-	10	44	467
1792	-	-	-	-	22	38	436
1793	-	-	-	-	16	43	446
1794	-	-	-	-	18	36	451

$$17)278 \qquad 17)1107 \qquad 17)7608$$

Av. of 17 yrs. from 1778 to 1794 inclufive $16\frac{6}{17}$ $65\frac{2}{17}$ $447\frac{9}{17}$
Annual deaths, 1 in $6\frac{9}{11}$ nearly.

The prefent number in the houfe is 539: the whole number admitted fince the firft inftitution, 3776. An exact account of the men, women, and children, admitted every year, could not be obtained; and, perhaps, fuch an account would not enable us to draw a correct conclufion refpecting the number of the Poor; as it often happens, that the fame perfons quit and re enter the houfe 2 or 3 times in the courfe of a year. The following lift of the number of men, women, and children, in the houfe, was taken at Midfummer, in each of the under-mentioned years:

1780.		1781.		1782.	
Men	73	Men	91	Men	75
Women	105	Women	127	Women	111
Boys	111	Boys	115	Boys	131
Girls	101	Girls	132	Girls	149
	390		465		466

1783.

1783.	Men	59	1787.	Men	74	1791.	Men	72
	Women	89		Women	101		Women	124
	Boys	113		Boys	127		Boys	146
	Girls	124		Girls	125		Girls	102
		385			427			444
1784.	Men	70	1788.	Men	84	1792.	Men	79
	Women	90		Women	122		Women	116
	Boys	128		Boys	131		Boys	116
	Girls	127		Girls	122		Girls	97
		415			459			408
1785.	Men	66	1789.	Men	81	1793.	Men	82
	Women	105		Women	120		Women	127
	Boys	137		Boys	139		Boys	119
	Girls	131		Girls	122		Girls	87
		439			462			415
1786.	Men	72	1790.	There are no accounts of this year respecting the numbers in the house at Midsummer.		1794.	Men	85
	Women	114					Women	133
	Boys	127					Boys	106
	Girls	123					Girls	84
		436						408

There is no particular account of baftards; but, from the information of the governor, it appears, that there are about 100 in the houfe. The boys and girls, mentioned in the above account, are almoft all under 14, as at that age they are drafted out to the parifhes to which they belong. If a perfon, to whofe lot a child falls, fhould refufe to take him or her for a year, (which is the ftated term,) he forfeits 20s. which goes to the mafter, who accepts his allotment; if he fhould likewife refufe, he alfo forfeits the fame fum, which is then paid to the third perfon, upon his accepting the child : when the year is expired, the child is again put by lot to another mafter, in cafe his old mafter does not wifh to keep him, and he is not able to provide for himfelf.

The average amount of 7 years difburfements for the Poor, beginning 10 years before the inftitution, was the quota fixed, at the commencement of the bufinefs, to be furnifhed annually, by each of the incorporated parifhes.

7

The

The Rates paid by the different parifhes, in proportion to their prefent rentals, are very different, and vary from 6d. to 3s in the pound. The average may be ftated at 20d. The whole fum, thus produced from the quotas of 50 parifhes, is regularly paid by quarterly payments, and amounts annually to £ 3965. 18s. 1d. But, notwithftanding £ 5422. of the debt incurred at the firft eftablifhment, have been paid off fome years, the receipts have, of late, been found to be not only infufficient to enable the incorporated diftricts to clear off any part of their remaining debt; but, from the dearnefs of provifions, interruption of trade, feverity of feafons, and heavy charges of foldiers' and militia-men's families, they have been proved to be even inadequate to defray the difburfements incurred from a great influx of Poor. Laft winter, the treafurer was obliged to advance £ 1000. to the houfe; fo that it has been refolved, by the corporation, to apply to Parliament, to authorize them to increafe the Rates; a cir-cumftance, which has occafioned confiderable difcontent inthe incorpora-ted parifhes.

The following table exhibits the quarterly payments of each of the 50 incorporated parifhes:

MITFORD HUNDRED.

Towns' Names.	Sum affeffed.		
	£.	s.	d.
Cranworth - -	20	0	0
E. Dereham, with			
Dilington - -	104	0	11¾
Garvefton - -	23	8	6
Hardingham - -	37	16	2
Hockering - -	14	15	9¾
Letton - -	9	1	6¼
Mattifhall - -	46	12	6
Mattifhall Bergh -	9	5	4¼
Reymerftone - -	9	7	4
Carried over -	£ 274	8	2

Mitford Hundred continued.

	£.	s.	d.
Brought over -	274	8	2
Shipdham - -	95	0	0
South Bergh - -	18	5	4¼
Thuxton - -	9	11	7½
E. Tuddenham -	19	10	0½
N. Tuddenham -	19	6	5½
Whinbergh - -	5	12	4¾
Weftfield - -	5	8	2
Woodrifing - -	9	19	2½
Yaxham - -	24	7	1½
Total Mitford -	£ 481	8	6½

LAUN-

LAUNDITCH HUNDRED.				Launditch Hundred continued.			
Towns' Names.	*Sum affeſſed.*				£.	s.	d.
	£.	s.	d.	Brought over	309	10	0½
Beeſton with Bitteĩing	29	18	11¼	Mileham - -	19	15	9
Beetley - -	14	3	0½	Oxwich cum Patch-			
E. Bilney - -	8	2	6	ley - -	8	0	0¼
Briſly - -	21	0	6	Rougham - -	9	0	1
Colkirk - -	18	5	6	Scarning - -	36	0	1
Great Dunham -	15	3	0½	Stanfield - -	11	8	10¼
Little Dunham -	14	17	11	Swanton Morley -	31	16	5
N. Elmham - -	57	12	8¾	Tittleſhal cum God-			
Great Franſham -	13	1	8¾	wick - -	25	14	7
Little Franſham -	15	6	5	Weaſenham St. Peter	11	15	1½
Gately - -	6	8	1	Weaſenham All Saints	14	15	2¼
Greſſenhall - -	27	0	0	Wellingham -	2	14	2¼
Hoe - - -	13	5	8¾	Wendling - -	10	10	0
Horningtoft - -	13	14	0¼	Whiſſönſet - -	15	6	10¼
Kempſon - -	4	14	2¾	Worthing - -	3	13	9
E. Lexham - -	2	10	8				
W. Lexham - -	7	7	10½	Total Launditch £	510	0	11¾
Litcham - -	14	16	7	Total Mitford £	481	8	6½
Longham - -	12	0	6½				
				Total - £	991	9	6¼
Caĩried over £	309	10	0½				

The men, belonging to the Houſe of Induſtry, aĩe employed in cultivating 60 acres of fields and gardens belonging to the houſe ; in combing
wool, dreſſing flax and hemp ; and in weaving theſe aĩticles into vaĩious
manufaδures, which are principally deſtined for the uſe of the houſe. A
few alſo work on the public roads. The women and children are moſtly
employed in ſpinning worſted for the Norwich manufaδories ; ſome knit
and ſew ; others inſtruδ girls in theſe different branches of work. The
boys and girls work in ſeparate apaĩtments ; and every claſs has a maſter, or
miſtreſs, to ſuperintend and inſtruδ the learners in their work. Tow
and hemp are alſo ſpun by the women.

There is a dairy of 10 cows belonging to the houfe ; and a wind-mill on the farm, at which all their corn is ground. They grind fometimes for their neighbours. Baking and brewing are carried on in the houfe.

The following table exhibits the earnings of the houfe from Midfummer 1780 :

				£.	s.	d.
Midfummer 1780 to Midfummer 1781 the earnings were				615	11	6¾
Midfummer 1781 to Midfummer 1782	ditto			670	3	8¼
Midfummer 1782 to Midfummer 1783	ditto			693	3	9½
Midfummer 1783 to Midfummer 1784	ditto			668	9	7
Midfummer 1784 to Midfummer 1785	ditto			785	9	10¼
Midfummer 1785 to Midfummer 1786	ditto			839	5	9¼
Midfummer 1786 to Midfummer 1787	ditto			812	10	10¼
Midiummer 1787 to Midfummer 1788	ditto			859	11	9
Midfummer 1788 to Midfummer 1789	ditto			878	9	5¼
Midfummer 1789 to Midfummer 1790	ditto			812	8	11½
Midfummer 1790 to Midfummer 1791	ditto			—	—	—
Midfummer 1791 to Midfummer 1792	ditto			911	7	5
Midfummer 1792 to Midfummer 1793	ditto			813	18	11¾
Midfummer 1793 to Midfummer 1794	ditto			666	7	5

In the above earnings are included wages for fpinning, weaving, &c. for the ufe of the houfe. No perfons above 60 years of age are obliged to work. Men are allowed 1d. out of every fhilling they earn ; young women, 2d. from every fhilling ; and women above 60 years of age, 4d. from every fhilling. Children, alfo, receive various little rewards, according to their merit and induftry

The following Rotation of Diet is obferved:

	Breakfaft.	Dinner.	Supper
Sunday,	Milk-broth, or onion gruel.	Boiled meat, dumplins, vegetables, and beer	Bread and cheefe, or treacle, and beer.
Monday,	Bread, cheefe, and beer.	Peafe pottage, boiled in meat broth, and milk-broth.	Bread and cheefe, or butter, and beer
Tuefday,	Onion or plain gruel	The fame as Sunday	Broth and bread
Wednefday,	Bread and cheefe, or treacle, and beer.	Frumenty; or thick milk with bread	Bread and cheefe, or butter, and beer.
Thurfday,	Bread and cheefe, or butter, with beer	Baked fuet puddings, and beer.	Bread and cheefe, or treacle.
Friday,	The fame as Tuefday	The fame as Tuefday.	The fame as Tuefday.
Saturday,	Bread and cheefe, or treacle, and beer.	Milk-pottage ; or onion gruel.	Bread and cheefe, fome butter, or treacle, and beer.

Cab-

Cabbages, carrots, turnips, potatoes, beans, &c. are ſerved in great plenty, during the ſeaſon. The quantity of food allowed at each meal could not be aſcertained; but the ſhares of dumplin, for dinner, ſerved up on Thurſday, (June 18, 1795,) and ſhares of bread, at ſupper, (although the pieces of cheeſe were ſmall,) ſeemed abundantly ſufficient.

The following is the annual amount of expenditure for victuals to the houſe, and payments to the out-poor:

	Houſe Proviſions.			Out Penſioners.		
	£.	s.	d.	£.	s.	d.
From 24th June 1777 to ditto 1778	1215	11	2½	354	10	7
1779	1571	16	1½	269	2	4¼
1780	——	—	—	278	11	2½
1781	1455	14	10	283	3	8½
1782	1433	7	10	518	19	4
1783	1369	10	0¼	317	5	4
1784	1283	9	5¼	700	11	11
1785	1303	3	2¾	501	12	5½
1786	1332	8	10¾	410	4	4½
1787	1349	19	9½	408	9	8
1788	1423	8	3	385	18	4
1789	1500	1	3	448	17	11
1790	1748	9	2½	614	12	4
1791	1589	6	4½	395	10	11
1792	1372	6	10½	467	5	7½
1793	1288	9	2½	617	18	1½
1794	1486	1	11¼	615	18	6
1795	——	—	—	1183	2	6

In the above account, the expence of cloathing is not included; nor could any ſtatement reſpecting this article be obtained: neither do coals, nor the governor's incidental expences, form any part of the above diſburſements. The latter, it is ſaid, amount to about £100. a year.

 The

The following Salaries are paid annually :

			£.	s.	d.
To the Chaplain	-	-	40	0	0
Houfe Surgeon	-	-	63	0	0
4 Out-furgeons	-	-	176	10	0
Committee Clerk	-	-	44	0	0
Goveincr	-	-	65	0	0
Mation	-	-	25	0	0
Baker	-	-	15	12	0
Shoemaker	-	-	15	12	0
Tailor	-	-	10	8	0

$$£ 455 \quad 2 \quad 6$$

The inteieft of the money owing by the houfe, viz £10,000. is £450.

The houfe was oiiginally intended to have had two wings; but want of funds prevented this projeſt being carried into execution ; and, from the number of Paupers in the houfe at prefent, there is veiy little fpaie 1oom. The different apaitments are lofty, well aiied, and feem well adapted to the different purpofes for which they are intended. The boys and girls have feparate lodging-rooms, and generally fleep 3 in a bed; about 20 beds aie in each room. Old people, and a few otheis, are allowed to iefide in cottages; and fome are provided with rooms on the giound-floor. The beds are of flocks ; each has 2 fheets, 2 blankets, and 1 coverlet ; and, upon the whole, the houfe feems to be as clean as can be expeſted. The goveinors are ceitainly veiy attentive to this objeſt; notwithftanding which, it is faïd, that, from the continual influx and efflux of Paupeis, it is found impoffible to keep the houfe clear from veimin.

The following are the bye-laws and regulations for the goveinment of the Poor in the houfe. They are taken from a printed copy, that was publifhed in 1787 :

1, THAT no poor perfon be admitted into the houfe for the Poor, without the order of the weekly committee, on every Tuefday in every week, except in cafes of broken limbs, fudden ilknefs, or other extraordinary cafes, when, for the benefit of the Pauper, an earlier admiffion may be neceffary. In fuch cafes, admiffion may be had at any
other

other time, by an order from one director, or one acting guardian, under a certificate from the surgeon of the division, that such Pauper is removable.

2, That all single and married persons, with or without families, who shall be thought by the weekly committee to be unable to maintain themselves, be taken into the house, and not supported out of it, by any settled allowance or pension, except in extraordinary cases, such as lunacy, epilepsy, epidemical distempers, &c.

3, That persons, whose families are too large to be maintained by their own labour, may have one or more of their children received into the house, at the discretion of the weekly committee.

4, That all persons wanting relief, are to apply to the churchwardens and overseers of their parish, when one of them is to attend the committee on a Tuesday, with such poor person for his admission into the house; and in case any doubt shall arise, touching the settlement of such poor person, he or she shall immediately be examined by two justices, and if the settlement appear to be out of the two Hundreds, then shall be immediately removed by order of two justices.

5, That the house surgeon shall visit the house every Tuesday and Saturday, (and oftener if required by the governor or weekly committee,) and regularly make a report, every Tuesday, of the sick, in writing, entered in a book kept for that purpose.

6, That the out surgeons, when they do not attend in person, shall send their reports in writing, every Tuesday, of the state of the Poor under their care, in their respective divisions, to the governor, that the same may be entered in a book kept for that purpose, and shewn to the weekly committee, that the corporation may be thereby constantly possessed of the state of the sick out-poor, as well as of those within the house; and if Paupers live out of the Hundreds, under lawful certificates, the surgeon of the division nearest the parish where such Paupers are resident, (if within a reasonable distance,) shall attend such Paupers in their illness or accidents, and shall be paid for his journey by the corporation. And that in cases of midwifery, or sudden accidents happening to persons out of the house, which require instant relief, and cannot by any means be otherwise provided for; the out surgeons, within the respective divisions, are enjoined, on no pretence whatever,

whatever concerning pay, or otherwise, to neglect such poor persons, but carefully to attend them; and should it be doubted by the surgeons, whether the parties themselves are to be confidered as persons able to pay them, or as Paupers entitled to corporation relief, such doubtful cafes shall be finally determined by the quarterly committee.

7, That the governor shall place no person whatever in the wards, until carefully examined, washed, and cleaned, and, if thought necessary by the weekly committee, new cloathed, when the old cloaths shall be well cleaned, hung up, and ticketed with the Pauper's name, in a room provided for that purpose; and upon the difcharge of such poor person from the house, such old cloaths shall be delivered in exchange for the cloaths furnished by the house.

8, That poor persons received into the house for temporary relief only, shall not be deprived of their houfhold goods, or other property, but shall be permitted to enjoy the fame.

9, That the governor and matron shall execute all bye-laws made by the directors and acting guardians under the authority of the said Act, and also such temporary orders as they, or either of them, shall receive from the weekly committee, the fame being firft entered in the committee book; such temporary orders to continue in force until altered by fome fucceeding committee.

10, That the governor shall fee the meal, flour, and other things, weighed and meafured, and keep an account of the quantity and price thereof, and give an account, every Tuefday, of all provifions and other things brought in, ufed, and expended the preceding week, and of all work done in the house, and make his complaint of all perfons who shall mifbehave.

11, That the governor shall at all times keep a book in the committee room, with pen and ink near it, which shall be called the obfervation book, that in cafe any guardian or other, perfon vifiting the house shall perceive any thing amifs, or can fuggeft any new propofal for the better conducting the management of the house, he may write his thoughts or obfervations therein, that the weekly committee may confider the fame, and report it to the next quarterly committee, if they think proper.

12, That

12, That nothing ſhall be brought into the houſe without notice being given to the governor, or, in his abſence, to the matron.

13, That a book ſhall be kept, in which the governor ſhall enter the admiſſion of every poor perſon admitted into the houſe, expreſſing their names, age, place of ſettlement, the reaſon of their admiſſion, and the day when admitted; with blank columns to enter the time and manner of their diſcharge, deaths, &c.

14, That an inventory ſhall be taken of all the goods and furniture belonging to the houſe; and the committee, on the firſt Tueſday next after the twenty-fourth day of June, yearly, ſhall cauſe a new inventory to be made, and compare it with that of the preceding year.

15, That the matron ſhall deliver out ſoap and candles, and ſee all the linen waſhed and got up, and that the beds be ſheeted once a month, and that no linen be hung to dry in the lodging wards, but in the drying room prepared for that purpoſe.

16, That the nurſes ſhall deliver the apparel of perſons dying in the houſe, mended, clean, and neat, to the governeſs, to be laid up in the wardrobe, and ſhall deliver an account thereof to the next weekly committee.

17, That neither the governor, matron, or any other officer, ſhall buy or ſell, or ſuffer any diſtilled liquors to be brought into the houſe, without leave of the committee or houſe ſurgeon.

18, That for the encouragement of thoſe who ſhall reſide in the houſe, and diſcharge the buſineſs to which they ſhall be appointed with care and diligence, rewards ſhall be given to them from time to time, at the diſcretion of the weekly committee; and all perſons going to work out of the houſe by leave of the weekly committee, and bringing in the produce of their labour, ſhall be allowed two-pence in the ſhilling for their induſtry; and that all children, who are reported by the chaplain to have ſaid their catechiſm, or to have read in the Bible or Teſtament in the beſt manner, ſhall be rewarded with a new Bible, Teſtament, or other book, at the diſcretion of the weekly committee.

19, That the chaplain ſhall read the Liturgy of the Church of England, and preach to the Poor in the houſe, in the morning on one Sunday, and afternoon on the following Sunday, and ſo continue; and ſhall catechiſe the children once a month, viſit ſuch ſick as ſhall require it, adminiſter adminifter the Sacrament four times in the year at leaft, and do the other duties of his office.

20, That no perfon whatever, who fhall be appointed to any ftation in this houfe, fhall prefume at any time to take, of any tradefmen, ftranger, or other perfon, any fee or reward, or gratuity of any kind, directly or indirectly, for any fervices done or to be done on account of this corporation.

21, That the governor fhall read fuch prayers as fhall be directed by the chaplain, or caufe them to be read every morning immediately after the ringing of the bell, and in the evening after fupper ; and fhall, every Sunday morning, between the hours of eight and ten o'clock, call over the names of all the Poor, and all the abfentees fhall be punifhed at the difcretion of the next weekly committee ; and fhall, once in every month, read, or caufe to be read to the Poor, the bye-laws, rules, and orders to be obferved by them, that none may pretend or plead ignorance thereof ; and that the fame, and all other bye-laws, rules, and orders, fhall be read every year, at the general meeting to be held on Tuefday next after the 24th day of June, immediately after the election of the officers of this corporation.

22, That a chairman fhall be chofen by every committee, to prefide and regulate the proceedings ; and every member of any committee, who fhall not appear in the committee room within one hour of the time appointed for their meeting, fhall, if a director, forfeit three fhillings, if an acting guardian, two fhillings ; and no member, under the fame penalty, fhall leave the committee when fitting without leave of the chairman, and on no account if there are not members remaining fufficient to conftitute the committee ; and in cafe of entire non-attendance in either director or acting guardian, then the penalty fhall be paid purfuant to the Act of Parliament.

23, That the out-doors of the houfe fhall not be opened before fix in the morning, and the fame fhall be locked by eight in the evening, from Lady-day till Michaelmas-day ; and not opened before day-light in the morning, and locked at fix in the evening, from Michaelmas till Lady-day ; except on fpecial occafions.

24, That the governor and matron fhall keep peace and good order in the houfe, and permit none to fight, quarrel, or give abufive or rude language.

guage. They fhall fee that all the Poor are in bed by nine o'clock in the summer, and eight in the winter, and be careful to have all the fires and candles put out, except in the fick wards; and that no candles be ufed in the evenings of the months of May, June, July, and Auguft, (except by the governor, and in the infirmaries)

25, That the governor and matron fhall keep all the able Poor to fuch work or employment as they are fit for, and fhall call them to it, by ringing the bell, at the following hours, viz. from Lady-day to Michaelmas-day, from fix in the morning to fix in the evening; from Michaelmas to Lady-day, from feven in the morning to fix in the evening; and they fhall allow to the working Poor half an hour for breakfaft, an hour and an half for dinner and recreation, in the fummer time, and an hour for thofe purpofes in the winter; and fhall oblige the children to play abroad, if the weather will permit; and alfo fhall allow the children a fufficient time for learning to read, and being inftructed in their catechifm, &c.

26, The governor and matron fhall make ready the provifions in a clean and wholfome manner, and fee that breakfaft be ready at eight o'clock, dinner at twelve, and fupper as foon as the work of the day is finifhed.

27, That the governor and matron fhall caufe grace to be faid before and after dinner and fupper; and fhall keep all the rooms clean and neat, fhall fee them fwept every day by ten o'clock in the morning, and wafhed as often as conveniently can be: they fhall caufe the windows to be fet open every day, (except in rainy or windy weather,) and fuffer no victuals to be eaten out of the dining-room, by any but the fick, and fuch as officiate as fervants in the houfe; and that the whole houfe fhall be yearly white-wafhed, at leaft a week before the 24th day of June.

28, That the governor and matron fhall caufe the children's heads and hands to be kept clean, and alfo all the cloaths and beds; and fhall deliver to every one of the Poor, clean linen on every Saturday evening, and take in their foul on Sunday morning.

29, That no perfon fhall be admitted to fee the Poor without leave of the governor.

30, That no poor perfon fhall be admitted to go out of the houfe at any time, without leave of the governor in writing; and that none be permitted to be abfent in the night, without leave of the weekly committee.

31, That the governor and matron, with the approbation of the weekly committee, fhall appoint nurfes and fervants to do the neceffary bufinefs of the houfe, who, if they behave well, and be recommended, fhall be encouraged, and advanced by the weekly committee; they fhall alfo fee the provifions cut, and properly delivered to each Pauper, and take care that no wafte be made, nor any bread be cut or eaten before it has been baked one entire day.

32, That the governor fhall immediately give notice to the furgeon of the houfe whenever any Pauper fhall fall fick or lame, that proper diet may be allowed, and care taken of the Pauper.

33, This rule fpecifies the bill of fare; but as it has fince been altered, it is not thought neceffary to tranfcribe it.

34, That no perfon[i] whatfoever fhall be allowed out of the houfe, except in cafes of neceffity, and at the difcretion of the weekly committee.

35, That there fhall be a fchool in the houfe, where all children above two years of age fhall be kept under proper fchoolmafters or dames until they are five years old, and inftructed in reading, learning their catechifm, and other plain rudiments of the chriftian religion, and, after that age, fhall be employed in fpinning, and fuch other work as they fhall be able to perform; and alfo, there fhall be another fchool for inftructing, in the fame manner, at feafonable times when not at work, all the other children or Paupers who may want inftruction.

36, That girls of proper age fhall be inftructed and employed in cookery, houfewifery, fcouring, wafhing, and all other works, to qualify them for fervice.

37, That the governor fhall provide wormwood, from time to time, to fumigate the rooms, which fhall alfo be ufed in wafhing the linen, and be laid in the beds.

38, That the governor fhall keep an exact account of all the houfhold goods, furniture, cloaths, linen, and apparel, belonging to the houfe, in a book kept for that purpofe.

[i] So in the original: qu. penfion?

9

39, That

39, That boxes be provided, and fixed in fome confpicuous place in the dining-room, for occafional donations; to which there fhall be two locks, and the key of one of them fhall be kept by the governor, and the other by the clerk; and the money put into the faid box fhall be at the difpofal of the weekly committee, for the benefit of the deferving Poor, and no poor perfon fhall be permitted to afk alms.

40, That in all advertifements to tradefmen, and others, for the delivering propofals, to contract for any kind of goods for the ufe of the houfe, it fhall be particularly fpecified, that all propofals will be rejected by the committee, which are figned by the propofer's name, or marked with any character, by which it may be known from whom fuch propofals come; and all committees are enjoined to reject the fame; and that every tradefman fhall deliver with his goods a bill of parcels thereof, and every workman fhall deliver to the weekly committee his bill of work done.

41, That where any perfon fhall apply for a certificate to live out of the Hundreds, the clerk fhall and may, under the direction of the weekly committee, by a note under his hand, certify that fuch perfon belongs to the corporation, and, (if fuch perfon be forced to afk relief,) he may be maintained at the expence of the corporation until the next quarterly meeting, when the directors and acting guardians may, (if it fhall appear that fuch perfon's fettlement is within either of the faid Hundreds,) grant a certificate under the feal of the corporation.

42, That the directors and acting guardians upon the weekly committee, fhall meet every Tuefday, at the Houfe of Induftry, precifely at ten o'clock in the morning.

43, That no director fhall be fubject to penalties for non-attendance, provided another director fhall attend for him; and that no acting guardian fhall be fubject to penalties for non-attendance, provided another acting guardian fhall attend for him.

44, That no director or acting guardian whatever, fhall, at any time, without the confent and concurrence of the weekly committee for the time being, give any orders or directions relative to the employment, relief, or management of the Poor, which fhall be in the Houfe of Induftry.

45, That

45, That four gentlemen fhall be named and chofen from amon ft the directors and acting guardians, two for Mitford, and two for Laun-ditch Hundreds, for the remaining three quarters of the year, commencing from the twenty-ninth day of September, and ending the twenty-fourth day of June next, and fo in fucceffion if neceffary, who fhall be called the general overfeers for the Hundreds, whofe bufinefs fhall be, at times moft convenient to themfelves, in perfon to vifit the fick, and penfioned out-paupers, (of which lifts fhall be delivered,) refident in the feveral divifions of the out furgeons, to make enquiries about baftard children, non-certificated perfons, and of perfons who have deferted their families, and left them an expence to the corpora-tion, and then fhall make their reports in writing, at the weekly or quarterly meetings, as they find it neceffary.

The following are the Rules and Orders to be obferved by the Poor in the Houfe.

1, THEY fhall not be guilty of profane curfing or fwearing, or of any lewd, indecent, or diforderly behaviour, or fhall neglect or refufe to perform the work or fervices, which he, fhe, or they fhall be required to do, or fhall be remifs therein, (fuch work or fervice being fuited to his or their age, ftrength or ability,) every fuch offender, if under the age of twelve years, fhall be punifhed by moderate correction, or abatement in diet ; if above twelve years, then either by abatement of diet, or diftinction in drefs and diet, or by fetting in the ftocks, or to be without any other diet than bread and water for any fpace not exceeding twenty-four hours; fuch punifhments to be inflicted by or-der of the major part of the directors and acting guardians prefent at the weekly meeting. See Public Acts, 15 G. III. c. 59.

2, If any of the Poor purloin, fell, or pawn any of the materials or im-plements of work intrufted to them, belonging to the corporation, or fhall fell or pawn any of the apparel with which they fhall be clothed at the expence of the corporation, upon complaint before any juftice of the peace for the faid county, by any of the guardians, or gover-nor, or fteward for the time being, fuch juftice fhall iffue his warrant for apprehending fuch offender, and, being convicted on oath of one

or

or more witneffes, or confeffion of the party, fhall be committed to the houfe of correction, for the firft offence, any time not exceeding feven days, and for the fecond, and every other offence, if a man, to be publicly whipped, and, if a woman, to be kept to hard labour for fourteen days, and then difcharged. See Act.

3, If any perfon or perfons fhall knowingly buy, receive into pawn, or fecrete any of the cloaths or wearing apparel of any poor perfon received into or maintained in the faid houfe, or any of the goods, materials, or implements of work carried into the faid houfe, to be wrought up, manufactured, or ufed by the Poor there, or any of the goods or furniture of the faid houfe ; or fhall buy or receive any of the provifions allotted to or provided for the Poor in the faid houfe ; every offender fhall forfeit, on conviction, five pounds, by oath of one or more credible witnefs or witneffes before any juftice of the faid county, to be levied by diftrefs and fale of fuch offender's goods, one moiety to the informer, and the other moiety to the treafurer, as part of the common ftock, and to be applied to the purpofes of the Act ; if no goods, then fuch offender to be committed to the houfe of correction, to be kept to hard labour, for any time not exceeding three months. See Act.

4, They fhall at all times behave peaceably and quietly ; they fhall not quarrel or give rude language ; they fhall attend prayers morning and evening, eat their victuals orderly in the dining room, carry none out, nor depart till after grace be faid, on pain of lofing their next meal.

5, They fhall not ftrike or abufe the governor or matron, or their affiftants, but fhall obey them at all times ; and if they think themfelves aggrieved, they fhall make complaint to the weekly committee, who fhall examine into the truth of it, and redrefs him if it be proper ; but if any poor perfon, maintained in the houfe, fhall ftrike, or threaten or attempt to ftrike, abufe, or even behave difrefpectfully to the governor or matron, or fhall excite any mutiny, or difturbance, the governor fhall, for fuch offence, of ftriking, threatening or attempting to ftrike, immediately complain to the next juftice of the peace, that the delinquent may be dealt with according to law.

6, They are to take their clean linen from the matron every Saturday evening, and bring their foul linen to her every Sunday morning.

7, They are not to go out without leave, nor ftay beyond the time allowed

ed them, on pain of losing their next meal, and such other punishment as the weekly committee shall inflict.

8, They are to be in bed by nine o'clock in the summer, and eight in the winter ; and the fire and candles are to be put out before that time.

9, They are not to smoke but in the working rooms, and by no means above stairs, on pain of severe punishment.

10, If any of the nurses, or other persons employed in the service of the house, go out without leave of the governor or matron, they shall be severely punished.

11, If any of the Poor presume to beg money or drink from any person attending, or coming to view the house, for the first offence they shall be deprived of their next meal.

12, That slothful people, who pretend ailments to excuse themselves from work, be properly examined, and if it appears they make false excuses, then they shall be punished by order of the next weekly committee.

13, They are not to throw water or other things out of the windows of the Poor's houses, on pain of severe punishment.

14, The sick, on their recovery, are to attend divine service, and publicly to return thanks to Almighty God for their recovery, according to the form of the Church of England.

15, Persons convicted of lying, to be set on stools in the most public place of the dining-room, and have a paper fixed on their breasts, with these words written thereon :

INFAMOUS LIAR.

The inhabitants of the incorporated parishes are chiefly farmers, agricultural labourers, a few necessary mechanics, publicans, and shop-keepers.

The prices of provisions, at present, are : beef, 5d. the pound ; mutton, 5d. ; pork, 6d. ; bacon, 8d. ; butter, 7d. ; flour, 2s. 6d. to 2s. 10d. the stone ; wheat, £ 3. 10s. the qr. ; malt, £ 2. 10s. the qr. ; barley, £ 1. 12s. the qr. ; milk, (of which little is sold,) 2d. the gallon.

The wages of labourers are : for husbandry work, 1s. 2d. a day, in winter, and 1s. 6d. in summer, without victuals ; women weeding corn are paid 6d. and 8d. a day, without victuals ; bricklayers, 2s. 6d. to 3s. a day ; their assistants, 1s. 6d. to 2s.

The

The land-tax varies much in the different parishes. Instances may be found of a few small tracts of land paying 5s. or 6s. in the pound; and of other parts not charged more than 2d. in the pound. From the best information obtainable on this subject, 1s. in the pound appears to be the average.

Both in this, and in the adjoining county of Lincoln, small shop-keepers, manufacturers, publicans, and labouring people, complain heavily against those, whom they call monopolizers of corn, farming clergymen, (who are not rare,) and the consolidators of small farms. To the conduct of men of this description, the high price of provisions, the increase of the Poor's Rates, and almost every evil, that attends, or is likely to attend the nation, are not unfrequently attributed.

June, 1795.

HECKINGHAM.

THE House of Industry at Heckingham, was erected in 1767. The original sum borrowed was £ 7500. The annual assessments to be paid by 41 incorporated parishes, in the Hundreds of Loddon and Clavering, were fixed at the average expenditure of the 7 years immediately preceding their incorporation. In 1786 the whole debt was paid off. The total Rates fixed on the several parishes, amounted to £ 2132. 6s. 3d. annually; but after the debt was paid off, they were lowered to £ 1986. 1s. and some time afterwards to £ 1866. The high price of provisions, the lowness of wages for spinning, and the late severe seasons, have so much increased the number of necessitous, that it was found necessary to augment the Rates; and, about three months ago, they were raised to their original standard.

The following table exhibits the number of Paupers, yearly earnings and expences of the house, for a few years back.

Years.

Years.	Number in the House		Earnings.			Total Expenditure.		
			£.	s.	d.	£.	s.	d.
1789.	199	By spinning wool	204	2	3			
		By spinning tow	9	16	7			
		By other work	5	9	0			
		Total earnings	219	7	10	2230	11	8
1790.	233	By spinning wool	220	13	$2\frac{3}{4}$			
		By spinning tow	20	12	0			
		By other work	15	8	7			
		Total earnings	256	13	$9\frac{3}{4}$	2324	10	5
1791.	245	By spinning wool	217	12	$8\frac{1}{2}$			
		By spinning tow	19	11	11			
		By spinning silk	54	9	4			
		By other work	13	8	9			
		Total earnings	305	2	$8\frac{1}{2}$	2223	11	11
1792.	224	By spinning wool	280	19	9			
		By spinning tow	19	6	8			
		By other work	1	18	0			
		Total earnings	302	4	5	2047	2	6
1793.	214	By spinning wool	228	8	8			
		By other work	5	12	2			
		Total earnings	234	0	10	2094	10	$8\frac{1}{2}$
1794.	239	By spinning wool	140	13	10			
		By spinning tow	14	14	$11\frac{1}{2}$			
		By other work	34	7	4			
		Total earnings	189	16	$1\frac{1}{2}$	2261	4	11

Bill

Bill of Fare in the House of Industry.

	Breakfast.	Dinner.	Supper.
Sunday,	Bread and cheese, and butter, or treacle	Dumplins, butcher's meat, and bread.	Bread and cheese, or butter.
Monday,	The same as Sunday.	Broth and bread	Ditto.
Tuesday,	Milk and water gruel, and bread.	Baked fuet puddings.	Ditto.
Wednesday,	The same as Sunday.	Dumplins and milk broth; or milk and water gruel.	Ditto.
Thursday,	The same as Tuesday.	The same as Sunday.	Ditto.
Friday,	The same as Sunday.	The same as Monday.	Ditto.
Saturday,	The same as Tuesday.	Bread and cheese, or butter.	Ditto.

The men are, each, allowed a pint of beer at every meal, except when they have broth, or gruel. Women, with children at the breast, have the same allowance. Others have two-thirds of a pint.

The Poor, here, are not subject to any peculiar disorder. A very fatal putrid fever, however, is now raging in the neighbourhood; but this place has hitherto escaped the contagion. Mr. Howlett informs us, that, in 1774, 126 persons in this house died of that disorder[1], out of an average of about 220. He adds, that the average of Paupers in the house during 20 years, before 1788, was 216; and that the average annual deaths of children in the house had been $7\frac{95}{100}$, or about 1 in 8.

In the year 1791, in consequence of representations having been made to the directors and guardians, that the weekly charges for provisions, &c. for the preceding three or four years, appeared very high, when compared with those for the corresponding weeks in former years, without sufficient reason appearing to account for such excess; a special committee was appointed, for the purpose of examining into the expenditure of the corporation. From a statement of their proceedings, which was published in 1793[2], it appeared, that the books of the house had been kept in a very vague and loose manner; that no entries were made of the cloaths delivered to the different Paupers; and that the only way in which the amount of

[1] See " The Insufficiency of the Causes to which the Increase of our Poor, and of the Poor's Rates, have been commonly ascribed," &c. 1788, p 87, 96.

[2] Entitled, " An Account of the Proceedings of the Special Committee, appointed by the Corporation of the Hundreds of Loddon and Clavering, in the County of Norfolk, in the year 1791, to enquire into the Expenditure in the House of Industry at Heckingham. By the Committee." Norwich, 1793.

provifions delivered out every week was afcertained, was, by taking ftock every Sunday night, and charging the deficit as the weekly expenditure. The committee, therefore, recommended to the directors to difmifs the governor of the houfe, as a perfon perfectly incompetent to fulfil the duties of his office. The recommendation, however, was not attended to ; but foon after, the governor fignified his intention of refigning, becaufe he " too well knew the inveterate prejudices which fome few entertained againft him, to expect any peace or happinefs from a continuance in his prefent fituation ;" and quitted his office at Michaelmas 1792.

Not much information is to be derived from the printed ftatement of the committee, as feveral of the facts brought forward by them, relative to the number of the Paupers, and expenditure in former years, were difputed by the oppofite party. Some idea, however, of the weekly charges may be formed from the following extracts :

The Weekly Charge from the 15th to the 22d of March 1790.

Number of Paupers 246.

	St.	lb.		s.	d.
Meal	91	0	at	1	6
Flour	26	0	—	2	0
Beef	21	0	—	4	1½
Pork	6	7	—	4	0
Cheefe	23	7	—	2	0

168 0. Charge for the week, exclufive of coals, £22 18 10¼

The Week from the 29th of March to the 5th of April 1790.

Number of Paupers 243.

	St.	lb.		s.	d.
Meal	86	0	at	1	6
Flour	25	0	—	2	0
Meat	27	0	—	4	0
Cheefe	22	7	—	2	0

160 7.   Charge, exclufive of coals, £22 5 2½

The Week from the 17th to the 24th of May 1790.

Number of Paupers 253

	St.	lb.		s.	d.
Meal	81	0	at	1	6
Flour	25	0	—	2	1¾
Meat	28	0	—	4	0
Cheefe	22	0	—	2	0

156   0.   Charge, exclufive of coals, £21 19 10½

The Week from the 5th to the 12th of July 1790.

Number of Paupers 258.

	St.	lb.		s.	d.
Meal	84	0	at	1	6
Flour	25	0	—	2	1¾
Beef	28	7	—	4	0
Pork	1	0	—	4	0
Cheefe	24	0	—	2	0

162   7   Charge, exclufive of coals, £22 17 8

The committee were furnifhed with the following account of the annual
confumption of meal, flour, meat, and cheefe, from the firft inftitution
of the houfe to Midfummer 1791, by the clerk, from the books of
expenditure[1].

Dates	Quantity			Average Number in the Houfe	Confumption of each Pauper pʳ week
	St.	lb.	oz.		lb.
From Mich. 1767 to Midf. 1768	5318	2	4	244	8
—— Midf. 1768 to Midf. 1769	5974	10	8	208	7¾
—— Midf. 1769 to Midf. 1770	6073	4	0	210	7¾
—— Midf. 1770 to Midf. 1771	6117	6	12	205	8
—— Midf. 1771 to Midf. 1772	6005	4	8	217	7¼

[1] P 31

From

Dates.	Quantity. St. lb. oz.			Average Number in the House	Consumption of each Pauper p' week. lb.
From Midf. 1772 to Midf. 1773	7521	7	0	260	7½
—— Midf. 1773 to Midf. 1774	6845	9	0	273	6½
—— Midf. 1774 to Midf. 1775	5845	1	0	244	6¼
—— Midf. 1775 to Midf. 1776	5792	10	0	224	6½
—— Midf. 1776 to Midf. 1777	5556	7	0	207	7
—— Midf. 1777 to Midf. 1778	5265	4	0	188	7½
—— Midf. 1778 to Midf. 1779	5240	0	8	185	7½
—— Midf. 1779 to Midf. 1780	4873	0	0	165	8
—— Midf 1780 to Midf. 1781	5067	0	0	167	8
—— Midf. 1781 to Midf. 1782	6815	15	0	220	8¼
—— Midf. 1782 to Midf. 1783	7261	0	0	237	8¼
—— Midf. 1783 to Midf. 1784	8061	0	0	264	8¼
—— Midf. 1784 to Midf. 1785	7598	0	0	235	8½
—— Midf. 1785 to Midf. 1786	7090	0	0	211	9
—— Midf. 1786 to Midf. 1787	6332	0	0	189	9
—— Midf. 1787 to Midf. 1788	7260	0	0	192	10
—— Midf. 1788 to Midf. 1789	7298	0	0	199	9¾
—— Midf. 1789 to Midf. 1790	7945	0	0	233	9
—— Midf. 1790 to Midf. 1791	8273	0	0	245	9

The Governor laid before the Committee the following average of the number of Paupers in the houfe, in different years[1].

	Adults.		Boys and Girls.
From 1784 to 1785	—	104	—	130
—— 1785 to 1786	—	96	—	105
—— 1786 to 1787	—	82	—	105
—— 1787 to 1788	—	91	—	103
—— 1788 to 1789	—	100	—	98
—— 1789 to 1790	—	111	—	119
—— 1790 to 1791	—	114	—	130

[1] P. 41.

June, 1795.

NORWICH.

THE city of Norwich, comprehending 32 parishes, and 3 or 4 hamlets, and containing, in extent, about 8 square miles, is incorporated for the maintenance of it's Poor. It's population was ascertained in 1693, when it was found to amount to 28,881 souls; and again in 1752, when it was found to have increased to 36,169 : it's present population is estimated at 40,000 inhabitants; but that number appears, from the subjoined tables of baptisms and burials, to be rather exaggerated.

The number of houses, &c. assessed to the window tax is 2200 : the number exempted could not be ascertained, but must be more considerable.

There are 370 ale-houses in Norwich.

The land-tax produces £ 8518. 11s. 11d. The rent of land, in some places near Norwich, is £ 5. an acre; but farms in general, in the vicinity of the city, let at about £ 1. an acre.

A cotton manufactory was established here about 7 years ago; but the staple manufactures of Norwich are camblets, and other worsted stuffs, of various denominations. It is probable, that more hands without the city, than within it, are employed in the manufactures; for, in 1771, Arthur Young calculated the number of looms in and near Norwich, at 12,000; and, allowing 6 persons to a loom, reckoned the number of people employed in this manufacture to be 72,000, and the amount of the stuffs sent annually from Norwich to exceed a million sterling [1].

The Norwich trade has for some years been in a declining state, which is ascribed to the following causes : to the prevalent taste for wearing cottons, which has necessarily lessened the consumption of stuffs [2];
the

---

[1] Eastern Tour, ii 79.

[2] The woollen manufacture, considering all it's branches, is, no doubt, a more important national concern than the cotton manufacture. It would seem, however, that the cottons of Manchester create more employment than the Norwich stuffs. The general languor of the woollen business seems to have been principally owing to the difficulty of introducing machinery; the improvements of which have given cottons a decided advantage The author of a pamphlet, written in 1788, asserts, that, not above twenty years before his time, the whole cotton trade of Great Britain did not return £ 200,000l to the country, for the
raw

the low wages of the weavers and spinners, who are, in a considerable degree at the mercy of the manufacturers, and are not supposed to receive better pay than they did 20 years ago ; and, lastly, to the war, which has put a stop

raw materials, combined with the labour of the people; and at that period, before the introduction of the water-machinery, and hand-engines, the power of the single wheel could not exceed 50,000 spindles, employed in spinning the cotton-wool into yarn ; but, at that mo ment, the power of spindles thus employed, amounted to two millions ; and the grofs return for the raw materials and labour, exceeded seven millions sterling It was about the year 1784, that the expiration of Sir Richard Arkwright's patent caused the erection of water-machines for the spinning of warps, in all parts of the country ; with which the hand-engines, for the spinning of weft, kept proportion At the time he wrote, he estimated the number of

Water-mills, or machines, at - - - -	143
Mule-jennies, or machines, consisting of 90 spindles each -	550
Hand-jennies, of 80 spindles each - - -	20,070

Of the water-mills, 123 are in England, and 19 in Scotland.

Of those in England,

Lancashire has	41	Cheshire has	8
Derbyshire —	22	Staffordshire -	7
Nottinghamshire -	17	Westmorland -	5
Yorkshire —	11	Flintshire —	3

These establishments, when in full work, are estimated to give employment to about 26,000 men, 31,000 women, and 53,000 children, in spinning alone ; and, in all the subsequent stages of the manufacture, the number of the persons employed, is estimated at 133,000 men, 59,000 women, and 48,000 children ; making an aggregate of 159,000 men, 90,000 women, and 101,000 children ; in all, 350,000 persons employed in the cotton manufacture

Cotton Wool remaining in the Country after Exportation in			Grofs Value of Cotton Goods made in		
Years.		lb.	Years		£.
1783	-	9,546,179	1783	-	3,200,000
1784	-	11,280,238	1784	-	3,950,000
1785	-	17,992,888	1785	-	6,000,000
1786	-	19,151,867	1786	-	6,500,000
1787	-	22,600,000	1787	-	7,500,000

See a pamphlet published in 1788, entitled, " An important crisis in the callico and muslin manufactory in Great Britain, explained :" and Aikin's Descript of Manchester, 178

The increased import of cotton since 1787, more especially when compared with the imports previous to 1783, is very astonishing

Cotton wool imported, on the average of 5 years, to 1783 inclusive, was 7,000,000 lb.
Ditto   to 1794 inclusive, — 28,000,000 lb

Lord Auckland's Speech in the House of Lords on the 2d May 1796

stop to the exportation of stuffs to France, Flanders, and Holland, and, from the high price of insurance, much reduced the trade to other countries The merchants and manufacturers are now overstocked with goods; and the weavers are, consequently, very ill supplied with work, and, what is worse, are obliged to work up the worst materials. While business was brisk, an industrious weaver might earn £ 1. 1s. a week, from fine work; and from coarser work, 12s. a week. The average earnings of weavers, at present, are thought not to exceed 7s. or 8s. a week. Women weavers earn from 5s. to 6s. a week. Females, however, are principally employed in spinning, reeling, winding, &c., in which they earn from 2s. to 4s. a week. Children, in spinning, winding, &c. earn about 2s. a week. Of late, the wages, both of women and children, have been very low; but business, since the beginning of this month, has been rather brisk, from a notion that peace is not very distant.

The prices of provisions, at present, are: beef, 5½d. the pound; mutton, from 5d. to 6d; veal, from 4d. to 5d.; pork, from 7d. to 8d.; bacon, 10d.; milk, ¾d the pint; eggs, two for 1d.

The Poor of the 32 parishes of the city of Norwich, are, principally, maintained in two large work-houses[1]; one of which, was formerly a palace, belonging to the Duke of Norfolk; and the other, a monastery. It is, therefore, not surprising, that they should, in many respects, be extremely unfit for the purpose to which they are now applied. The latter, more especially, is dark and confined; and, from the great number of Paupers in it, (about 700,) exhibits rather an uncleanly appearance.

There are about 40 beds, (generally of straw,) in each chamber. The room, where the victuals are served out, has two doors; through one of which, the Poor enter, one by one, to receive their allowance; go out by the other door; and carry their victuals up to their bed-rooms, where they are allowed to dine, sup, &c. The Poor in the house are chiefly women and children: they are employed in schools, under the superintendance of task-masters, in spinning worsted.

[1] "Previous to the year 1727, the Rates throughout the city were immoderately burthened with weekly allowances to the Poor, of 1s. 6d ; 2s ; 2s 6d ; or 3s. a family; in which manner, £ 1200 a year, was given. A resolution was taken, in that year, to strike them all off; it was accordingly done, and nothing ensued but murmuring; no ill consequence at all." Young's Eastern Tour, ii. 76.

The

The mortality in the work-houfes has been confiderably leffened, by feveral improvements, made in the year 1783, for ventilating the rooms, removing nuifances, and newly-arranging the offices.

About the fame period, in confequence of the fuggeftions of Mr. Rigby, a member of the court of guardians[1], a fpecial provifion committee was appointed, through whofe exertions feveral judicious alterations, refpecting the diet of the Poor in the two work-houfes, were effected; though not without confiderable clamour, on the part of the Poor, who were unhappily perfuaded, that no change could be made, which had economy for it's principal object, without rendering their allowances lefs ample, lefs wholfome, or lefs palatable, than they were before.

As the reforms which took place in the purchafing and delivering of provifions, in confequence of this enquiry, may be, (perhaps,) fuccefsfully applied in other work-houfes, where fimilar abufes exift, I fhall briefly ftate the points to which the attention of the committee was directed, and the fteps which their reports induced the court of guardians to adopt[2].

In the article of bread, it was found, that the baker's bread was infinitely fuperior to the work-houfe bread, which, (the Report ftates,) feemed to be made principally of bran, and to be much too ordinary for common food; and that, notwithftanding this, the former was confiderably the cheaper: it was therefore refolved, that the practice of buying corn, and baking bread, at the work-houfes, fhould be difcontinued; and that, in future, the bread fhould be bought, by contract, of the baker; and the flour, of the flour-merchant.

[1] The court of guardians, which has the management of the work-houfes, and other concerns relative to the Poor in the 32 incorporated parifhes, confifts of fixty perfons, of whom the mayor, recorder, fteward, the two fheriffs, and twenty-three aldermen, are perpetual guardians: the remaining thirty-two are elected every two years, half of them being chofen by the court of aldermen, and the other half by the common council

[2] See a pamphlet, containing much information, entitled, "Reports of the Special Provifion Committee, appointed by the Court of Guardians, in the City of Norwich; with an Account of the Savings which have been produced by the late Regulations in the Diet of the Work-houfes: exhibiting fome important facts refpecting the œconomy of thofe eftablifhments. By Edward Rigby." Norwich, 1788.

The

The following agreements were, therefore, entered into, by the provision committee, in February, 1794 :

1ft, With the flour-merchant, to furnifh ftandaid flour, for the workhoufes, and infirmary, for three months, at £ 1. 13s. per fack, weighing 20 ftone, during the continuance of the affize at 23s. per comb ; and to vary 1s. 6d. per fack, as the affize fhall rife or or fall 1s. per comb.

2d, With feveral bakeis, to fupply the houfes with bread, of the following defcription, for fix months :

	lb	oz		lb	oz	
The meal loaf, when baked, to weigh	2	3	or	43	12	per fcore,
The white loaf - - -	1	10	or	32	8	per fcore,

at 4s. per fcore, while the affize of bread remains at 23s. per comb of wheat ; and to advance or abate 2d. per fcore for every variation of 1s. in the affize.

In the articles of butter and cheefe, it was calculated, that an allowance of four ounces of butter a week to each perfon, inftead of the ufual allowance of cheefe, which was 12 oz. a week to each perfon, (except in particular inftances, when they were allowed 3½ ounces of cheefe,) would produce an annual faving of £ 356. : cheefe was therefore difcontinued ; and the weekly fhares of butter, were increafed to 4 ounces.

In the articles of beef, flour, and beer, it was found that great abufes exifted ; of which the following ftatement was an evincing proof :

In January 1774, 1478 Paupers confumed, of beef,   496 ftone.
of bread, 9370 quartern loaves.
of flour,   552 ftone.
of beer,   128 barrels.

The total expence of provifions for one month was - £ 532. 10s. 8d.

In January 1784, 1231 Paupers confumed, of beef,   466 ftone 7 lb.
of bread, 9250 quartern loaves.
of flour,   580 ftone.
of beer,   135 barrels.

The total expence of provifions for one month was £ 548. 18s. 11¼d.

To correct this evil, the court of guardians directed, that the quantity of provisions for one week, for 692 persons, (the number then in the new work-house,) should be as follows; and should be increased, or diminished, according to the number in the house:

Bread 1917 coarse loaves, ⎫ 2130 total[1].
       213 fine loaves, ⎭
Flour 67 stone.
Oatmeal 10½ pecks.
Beer 15 barrels.
Beef 60 stone.

And for 579, the number of persons in the old work-house:

Bread 1440 coarse loaves, ⎫ 1680 total.
     240 fine loaves, ⎭
Flour 53 stone.
Oatmeal 9½ pecks.
Beer 12 barrels.
Beef 48 stone.

From the 4th Report of the committee, it appears, that, in April 1784, when the number of persons in the new work-house was 677, 486 dumplins, weighing 13 ounces each, were the usual quantity consumed three times in a week. The expence of them was as follows:

	£.	s.	d.
19 stone of flour, at 1s. 9½d.	1	14	2½
3 gallons of yeast, at 1s.	0	3	0
1 pound of salt	0	0	2
3 persons' time, who make them, and who have each a dumplin extraordinary allowed them	0	1	6
	£1	18	10½

[1] I suppose the coarse loaves weighed 2 lb. 3 oz. each, and the fine loaves 1lb 10 oz. each: see p. 481. The weight, therefore, of 1440 coarse loaves was 4193 lb 7 oz.; and of fine, 346 lb. 2 oz.; total, 4539 lb. 9 oz, or nearly 6 lb. 9¾ oz. a man, weekly The allowance of bread in the old work-house, (where the number of boys and young men is proportionably smaller than in the new work-house,) is less than the above.

A re-

A reputable baker offered to fell 20 lb. of dough for 2s. [1]; and from trials made with it, it appeared, that eleven ounces of it would make a dumplin, weighing full $13\frac{1}{2}$ oz.; and of which, to make 486 such dumplins as the above-mentioned, it would take 334 lb. 2 oz., which, at 2s. per 20 lb. would come to £ 1. 13s. 5d.; which, (although each dumplin would weigh full half an ounce more than the work-houfe dumplin,) would coft 5s. $5\frac{1}{2}$d. lefs than thofe made at the work-houfe did. This multiplied by 3, (the number of times this quantity was confumed every week,) amounted to 16s. $4\frac{1}{2}$d.; which being again multiplied by 52, (the number of weeks in the year,) amounted to £42. 11s. 6d. In the fame manner, the faving at the old work-houfe, where the confumption was one-fourth lefs, was calculated at £ 31. 19s.: and the court of guardians was induced to direct, that, for the future, the dough fhould be bought of the bakers, at the rate of 21 lb. for 2s. (the affize being at £1. 5s. for 4 bufhels of wheat,) to increafe or decreafe 1d. for 21 lb. of dough, for every variation of 1s. in the affize of corn.

In the 5th Report, the committee reprefented, that the manner in which the different articles of provifion were ferved in the work-houfes was a great fource of wafte and extravagance, and that the total quantity of meat diftributed in fhares much exceeded what was ufually eaten by perfons in perfect health. The following ftatements, by which they exemplified the truth of their affertions, in the inftance of *beef* are extremely curious; and afford many conclufions worthy of attention by thofe who are defirous of inveftigating the domeftic economy of work-houfes.

" *Account of Beef,* Sunday, April 11, 1784.

77 perfons had each	10	ounces	
26	-	-	11
42	-	-	12
26	-	-	8

} 1768 oz.

171

[1] It may feem extraordinary that the bakers, who muft have a profit upon making dough, fhould be able to fell it cheaper than it can be made at the work-houfe. This is, however, owing to the baker being able, from a more perfect knowledge of the art, to produce a larger quantity of dough, from a given quantity of flour, than thofe who were employed to do this bufinefs at the work-houfe could do; as it appeared from their ignorance of the matter, that a great wafte of flour had been made, an extravagant quantity of yeaft had been ufed, and the dough fo improperly compounded, and fo imperfectly fermented, as not to admit of the due increafe.

This

This fum of 1768 oz. divided by 16, gives 110 lb. 8 oz. and which is of beef cooked, and without bone ; and which, according to the butchei's and mafter's account, being to beef uncooked, and with bone, only as 8 lb. to 14 lb. amounts to 193 lb. of meat, as bought from the butcher; and which, being biought into ounces, and again divided by the number of perfons, namely, 171, gives the average fhare of uncooked meat for each perfon, and is 18 oz. which, at 4d. per lb. comes to 4½d. each perfon ; to which being added, bread, beer, and the expence of cooking, it amounts at leaft to 6d. each perfon.

Account of Beef, Tuefday, April 13, 1784.

81 perfons had each	10 ounces		
24	-	-	11
74	-	-	12
13	-	-	8

} 2066 oz.

192

This, from the fame operation of figures, turns out to be 18¼ ounces for each perfon, which, in biead, &c. as before, may be eftimated at full 6d. each perfon's meal.

Account of Beef, Thurfday, April 22, 1784.

71 peifons had each	10 ounces		
19	-	-	11
123	-	-	12
4	-	-	8

} 2427 oz.

217

This, likewife, by the fame operation of figures, turns out to be 19½ oz. for each perfon, which, with biead, &c. as before, may be eftimated at almoft 7d. for each perfon's meal.

In the old work-houfe, no account has yet been taken, in the above manner, of the quantities which all the different claffes of the Poor have ; but it appeared to this court, from actual fhares produced and weighed in court, that the weavers' allowance in that houfe confifted of 17 ounces of boiled beef, with a large bone and fome fragments upon it, for each perfon ; and which, (according to the foregoing allowance of one ftone of meat uncooked and with bone, to eight pounds cooked, and without bone,) muft be, uncooked, at leaft, 1¾ lb. which, at 4d. per pound, comes to 7d. each

fhare ;

share ; and to which being added bread, beer, and the expence of cooking, the meal must come to 9d. each person.

From the above account, the truth of which cannot be controverted, it is evident, that the dinners of the above number of persons, three times a week, cost more than if the Poor were to dine at a cook's shop, or a public house ; as it is well known, that many respectable artificers dine at such places for less money ; and that the quantity, for each person, exceeds, considerably, the proportion of what is usually eaten at the tables of most private families. The extravagance of this will be further proved by observing, that these three meals cost more than twenty-one meals in several houses of industry, in this county, do."

To prevent this superfluous consumption of provision, the committee proposed, that the Poor should, in future, all dine together in two large rooms in the work-house, by which they would be more equally fed ; the general consumption of food considerably lessened ; the practice of selling provision put a stop to ; and, instead of the custom of eating upon the beds, (which was a source of dirt in both houses,) the whole number of Paupers would be collected together, once a day, in a decent and orderly manner, and the real number in the house more easily ascertained.

The plan of making the Poor dine together was not adopted ; but an alteration was made in the meat dinners, in consequence of the statements of the committee ; from whence it appeared, that the Sunday dinner in the new work-house, for 171 persons, was 1768 ounces of boiled beef without bone, which, (reckoning 8 lb. of such beef to be equal to 14 lb. with bone, and uncooked,) amounted to 13¾ stone, and, at 4s. the stone, cost £2. 15s. The soup recommended to be adopted, and which was approved of by the guardians, in lieu of the Sunday meat dinner, was as follows :

	s.	d.
70 lb. of cheeks, at 2s. the stone -	10	0
43 gallons of water		
2 pecks of old pease, at 1s. - -	2	0
4½ lb. of onions, at 1d. - -	0	4¾
4¾ pints of oatmeal, at 1½d. - -	0	7
3¾ ounces of pepper, at 1½d. -	0	5½

| Carried over - | 13 | 5 |

	s.	*d.*
Brought over -	13	5
5 crufts of loaves burnt - -	0	1¾
1¾ lb. of falt - - -	0	2
Thyme - - - -	0	1
	13	9¾

In the 6th Repoit of the committee, it was ftated, that the *beer* brewed at the woik-houfe coft 7s. 3d. a barrel, and that a brewer would furnifh beer at 5s. the barrel, which, after a fair trial, had been found to be equally good, and would produce a faving of £210. 12s. a yeai. This plan was immediately adopted, and a contraɛt made with a brewer, foi the fupply of beer at 5s. the barrel.

Of the favings refulting from thefe reforms, in the aiticle of provifions confumed in the work-houfes, the following table exhibits a convincing proof:

Years, from 1 May 1783 to	Average Nº. of Poor in the work-houfes.	Total Expences, omitting fraɛtions. £.	What the Expence would have been in proportion to the Expence of 1783-4.	Annual Saving.
1 May 1784	1301	7058	£.	£.
to 1785 11 months	1430	6400	7757	1357
to 1786	1612	6387	8745	2358
to 1787	1488	5833	8072	2239

Total faving in three years - £5954

It fhould be obfeived, that the reform took place in January 1784, and, confequently, effeɛted a reduɛtion, even in the firft year of the above account: had the books of preceding years been forthcoming, when the committee made their enquiry, it is probable that the favings, from the new regulations, would have appeared more confiderable. This deficiency, however, may be in a great meafure fupplied from a week's account of the expence of provifions in each work-houfe, prior and fubfequent to the ieform taking place.

A Week's

A Week's Expence for Proviſions in the New Work-houſe, Norwich, Sept. 21, 1783.

	£.	s.	d.
71 ſtone 6 lb of meat, at 4s.	14	5	9
80 ſtone of flour, at 2s	8	0	0
1120 brown loaves, at 6¾d. each, weighing 4 lb. 7 oz.	31	2	6
140 white loaves, at 6¾d each, weighing 3 lb. 5 oz.	3	18	9
24 ſtone of cheeſe, at 5s. ¼d.	5	16	5¼
80 pints of butter, at 8d.	2	13	4
308 pints of milk, at ¾d	0	19	3
8 pecks of oatmeal, at 1s. 10d.	0	14	8
5½ ditto of wheat, at 1s 9d.	0	9	7½
4 ſtone of ſalt, at 1s. 7½d.	0	6	6
7 tubs of lees, at 9d.	0	5	3
11 lb of brown ſoap, at 6½d.	0	8	8
6 lb of white ſoap, at 7d.	0	3	6
6 lb. of candles	0	3	4
18 barrels of beer, at 6s 6d.	5	17	0
Grocery	1	1	3
	£76	5	9¾

649 perſons in the houſe.

A Week's Expence for Proviſions in the New Work-houſe, Norwich, Sept 22, 1787.

	£	s	d.
6 ſtone of cheeks	0	11	0
40 ſtone of meat	7	17	11
30 ſtone of flour, at 34s. the ſack	2	16	1
69 ſtone 7 lb of dough	4	1	1
117 ſcore brown loaves, at 3s. 6d	19	14	6
14 ſcore white loaves, at 3s 4d.	2	6	8
78 lb of butter, at 9d	2	18	6
3¼ firkins of butter, at 34s.	5	10	6
6 lb. of ſoap, at 1s. 6d.	0	4	0½
18 lb of ſoap, at 8d.	0	11	0
8 lb of candles, at 8d.	0	5	4
1¾ peck of peaſe, at 2s 4d.	0	4	1
6 pecks of wheat, at 1s. 6¾d:	0	9	4½
10 pecks of oatmeal, at 1s. 6d.	0	15	0
5 ſtone of ſalt, at 1s 6d.	0	7	6
7 tubs of lees, at 9d.	0	5	3
19 barrels of beer, at 4s. 6d.	4	5	6
464 pints of milk, at 1¼d. a quart	1	4	2
2¼ ſacks of potatoes, at 4s.	0	9	0
Grocery	1	9	0½
	£56	5	6½

714 perſons in the houſe.

A Week's Expence for Proviſions in the Old Work-houſe, Norwich, Sept. 20, 1783.

	£	s	d.
62 ſtone 7 lb. of meat, at 4s.	12	10	0½
60 ſtone of flour, at 2s.	6	0	0
780 brown loaves, at 6¾d.	21	18	9
140 white loaves, at 6¾d	3	19	2
10 ſtone of cheeſe, at 5s. 3½d.	4	16	2¼
63 pints of butter, at 8d	2	2	0
378 pints of milk, at ¾d.	1	3	6
5 pecks of wheat, at 1s. 9d	0	8	9
8 pecks of oatmeal, at 1s 6d.	0	12	0
4 ſtone of ſalt, at 1s 10d.	0	7	4
20 lb. of ſoap, at 6¾d.	0	11	3
3 tubs of lees, at 6d.	0	1	6
6 lb. of candles, at 6¾d.	0	3	4½
15½ barrels of beer, at 6s. 6d.	5	0	9
Grocery	1	1	0½
	£60	15	7¾

547 perſons in the houſe.

A Week's Expence for Proviſions in the Old Work-houſe, Norwich, Sept. 21, 1787.

	£	s	d.
6 ſtone of ox cheeks	0	11	0
20 ſtone 7 lb. of meat, at 3s 11d.	4	0	1½
25 ſtone of flour, at 34s the ſack	2	2	6
56 ſtone 7 lb of dough, at 1s 9d for 21 lb.	3	4	9
94 ſcore of brown loaves, at 3s 6½d	17	0	0
12 ditto white loaves, at 3s 4½d.	2	0	6
4½ firkins of butter, at 1l. 14s.	7	4	6
3 pints of ditto, at 8½d.	0	2	1½
5 ſtone of cheeſe, at 2s.	0	10	0
384 pints of milk, at 1¼d. the quart	1	0	0
2 pecks of peaſe, at 1s 3d.	0	2	6
5½ pecks of wheat, at 1s 6¾d.	0	9	1½
20 pecks of potatoes, at 5¼d	0	8	9
8 pecks of oatmeal, at 1s. 4d.	0	12	0
4 ſtone of ſalt, at 1s. 6d.	0	6	0
5¾ ſtone of treacle, at 3s.	0	17	3
24 lb of ſoap, at 8½d.	0	17	0½
4 tubs of lees, at 1s.	0	4	0
6 lb. of candles, at 8½d.	0	4	3
16 barrels of beer, at 4s. 6d.	3	12	0
Grocery	0	5	8
	£45	14	1

618 perſons in the houſe.

Notwithſtanding the ſavings, which, from Mr. Rigby's account, ſeem to have been evidently the reſult of the above enquiry, the expences for the

 Poor

Poor of this city, have, in general, of late, confiderably increafed. This, it is probable, may be attributed to the War, and other caufes, which have occafioned a great ftagnation of trade in Norwich. The reliefs to out-poor, which, in 1784, coft £2318. 10s. 11d. in 1794 called for £7327. 9s. 11d. ; but, although the number of Paupers in the work-houfes and infirmary was increafed from 1301, (the number in 1784,) to 1406, (in 1794) it appears from the fubjoined tables, that, in the former period, the expence of their cloathing and maintenance was £10,204. 13s ; and in the latter, notwithftanding the high price of every article of fubfiftence, only £9240. 9s 2d.

Since the year 1783, the court of guardians have annually publifhed an account of their general receipts and difburfements relative to the Poor of Norwich. From thefe printed accounts, fome ufeful information is to be collected, refpecting the detail of parochial concerns in a large city. It is, however, to be regretted, that in laying the particulars of their difburfements before the public, the guardians fhould not have fpecified the *quantity* of articles purchafed within the year, as well as the fums expended on each article : in this refpect, the annual ftatements of the Corporation for the Poor of the City of Briftol, and of the Governors of the Houfe of Induftry in the Ifle of Wight, are more fatisfactory[1].

General State of Receipts and Difburfements of the Court of Guardians in the City of NORWICH, from May 1ft, 1783—to May 1ft, 1784.

RECEIVED,

	£.	s.	d.
For the militia - - - -	234	18	0
Earnings at the feveral workhoufes - - -	1029	10	3
Bran - - - - - -	43	0	8
Balance of rents - - - -	43	3	1
Earnings at fpinning fchools for nine months - -	185	18	4
Money lent overfeers - - - -	423	3	0
Mulcts - - - - - -	18000	0	0
Deficiencies of rates added to mulcts - - -	210	2	5
Total received	£.20169	15	9

[1] See p. 185. and p. 261.

PAID.

PAID.

	£.	s.	d.
For wheat, bread, flour, and baking office expences -	3500	19	6

N. B. There remains due £190 for flour, besides the above; the bill for which not being delivered, it must be added to the next year's account.

	£.	s.	d.
Malt, hops, and brewhouse expences - - -	635	9	9
Minister, clerks, furgeons for attendance, and medicines, and fervants' falaries - - - -	450	0	0
Printer and ftationer - - - -	32	10	0
Infurance - - - - - -	11	15	7
Intereft on £5000. money borrowed by the corporation of guardians, at 5 per cent - - - -	250	0	0

N. B. Over and above the intereft ftated, there is a running account of intereft due to the treafurer, Roger Kerrifon, Efq which cannot appear in this year's account, amounting to £52. 11s.

	£.	s.	d.
Manufacturing implements - - - -	43	3	3
Sword-bearer, for orders of removal, &c. - -	36	3	0
Removal-officer's expences - - - -	68	13	7
Apprehending vagrants - - - -	14	17	6
High Conftable for King's Bench and Marfhalfea - -	60	6	0
Seffions' orders - - - - -	200	0	0
Bridewell expences - - - -	84	5	6
Man-midwife, 1782, £7. 5s.; 1783, £10. 5s. - -	17	10	0
Non-refident poor - - - -	133	3	8
Cafual Poor - - - - -	183	2	11
Money lent overfeers, repaid as per credit account -	423	3	0
Apprentices binding - - - -	73	16	0
Spinning-fchool expences - - - -	64	0	4
Water rent - - - - - -	10	0	0
Horfe keeping at the infirmary - - -	6	14	1
Out-door allowances - - - -	2318	10	11
Deficiencies of Rates by empty houfes, &c. -	1497	16	6
Ditto by Rates made fhort of the mulcts, errors, &c re turned upon each parifh, repaid as per credit account -	210	2	5
Peafe - - - - - -	49	8	1
Oatmeal - - - - -	98	0	6
Beef - - - - - -	1291	3	8
Cheefe - - - - - -	571	3	7

Carried over - £12335 19 4

	£.	s.	d.
Brought over -	12335	19	4
Butter - - - - - -	391	15	2
Milk - - - - - -	97	12	2
Groceries - - - - -	165	4	11
Candles - - - - -	35	0	8
Salt - - - - - -	59	10	1
Soap - - - - - -	93	14	6
Oil - - - - - -	64	0	0
Men's, women's, boys', girls', and infants' shoes -	457	4	6
Breeches - - - - -	113	1	6
Wool and yarn for outward apparel - - -	223	17	8
Ditto for stockings - - - -	88	0	10
Ditto for burials - - - -	6	16	3
Casual expences, in which sundry articles are included, which will in future be arranged under the different heads - - - - - -	640	16	8
Linen cloth for shirts and shifts - - -	402	5	4
Ditto for sheets - - - -	54	11	8
Check for handkerchiefs and aprons - -	100	16	8
Leather for mending shoes - - -	167	0	3
Coals - - - - - -	336	1	10
Coffins - - - - - -	50	2	3
Funeral expences - - - -	82	4	2
Blankets and coverlets - - -	88	18	0
Flock - - - - -	49	4	8
Haberdashery - - - -	38	6	2
Extra expences for washers, nurses, additional food for the sick, and sundry contingencies - - -	194	14	8
Whitesmith - - - -	23	11	7
Carpenter - - - -	173	12	4
Bricklayer - - - -	78	6	4
Ironmonger - - - -	36	19	0
Plumber and glazier - - - -	35	3	5
Brazier and tinman - - -	38	12	4
Cooper, two years - - -	64	9	11
Rents - - - - -	111	0	0
Bed-tick - - - - -	44	14	10

	£.	s.	d.
Expended	16943	9	8
Balance applied towards paying off money borrowed -	3226	6	1
	£20169	15	9

₊ The average number of Paupers in the several work-houses is 1301.

July 30, 1784. The posting of each article in the Ledger, of which this account is an extract, was examined, and every folio cast up by us, and we find it exact.

ROBERT PARTRIDGE,   J. G. BASELEY,
S. HARMER,   JAMES CHASE.
JAMES ALRIC,

General State of Receipts and Disbursements of the Court of Guardians in the City of NORWICH, from May 1, 1784, to April 1, 1785.

RECEIVED.

	£.	s.	d.
Earnings at the several work-houses — — —	1133	15	4
Ditto at spinning-schools — — — —	503	12	7
Mulcts — — — — —	18000	0	0
Deficiencies of Rates added to mulcts — —	207	14	0
Cash paid the Treasurer, on account of rents of the work-house estates — — — — —	65	7	9
Money lent the Overseers — — — —	105	0	0
	£20015	9	8

PAID.

	£.	s.	d.
For bread, flour, and baking-office expence, including £197. 13s. 6d. omitted in last year's account — —	3527	13	0
Beer, malt, hops, and brew-house expences — —	516	8	5
Minister, clerks, surgeons for attendance, medicines, and servants' wages — — — — —	435	0	0
Printer and stationer — — — —	42	4	11
Insurance — — — — —	13	1	0
Interest money — — — —	122	13	6
Manufacturing implements — — —	8	3	10
Sword-bearer, for orders of removal, &c. — —	43	14	0
Removal-officer's expences — — —	94	9	8
Apprehending vagrants — — —	23	1	10
High Constable for King's Bench and Marshalsea	60	6	0
Sessions' orders — — — —	200	0	0
Bridewell expences — — — —	36	8	8
Man-midwife — — — —	18	17	6
Carried over —	£5142	2	4

3 R 2

	£	s.	d.
Brought over -	5142	2	4
Non-refident Poor - - - - -	108	11	8
Cafual Poor - - - - -	14	7	0
Apprentices binding - - - -	61	4	0
Spinning-fchool expences - - - -	230	17	6
Water rents - - - - -	10	0	0
Horfe-keeping at the Infirmary - - -	11	17	7
Out-door allowances - - - -	2763	16	0
Deficiencies of Rates by empty houfes - - -	1784	17	9
Ditto by Rates made fhort of the mulcts returned upon each parifh, repaid as per credit account - -	207	14	0
Peafe - - - - - -	50	19	4
Oatmeal - - - - - -	88	15	2
Beef - - - - - -	1096	4	4
Cheefe - - - - -	307	18	2
Butter - - - - -	699	12	5
Milk - - - - - -	98	8	7
Groceries - - - - -	138	2	10
Candle - - - - -	34	12	8
Salt - - - - - -	32	13	3
Soap - - - - - -	101	1	9
Oil - - - - - -	70	1	1
Men's, women's, boys' and girls' fhoes - -	365	18	4
Breeches - - - - -	86	17	4
Wool for ftockings - - - -	47	19	7
Ditto for burials - - - - -	2	10	8
Cafual expences for fundry fmall articles, fuch as earthen ware, brufhes, bafkets, fand, wooden ware, greens, &c. &c. bought weekly - - - -	330	1	5
Linen for fhirts and fhifts - - -	368	16	7
Ditto for fheets - - - -	64	18	9
Check for aprons and handkerchiefs - - -	67	16	6
Leather for mending fhoes - - -	179	13	1
Coals - - - - -	373	0	8
Coffins - - - - -	55	6	4
Funeral expences - - - -	82	17	1
Coverlets and blankets - - - -	93	7	7
Flock - - - - -	43	13	4
Haberdafhery - - - - -	22	12	1
Whitefmith - - - - -	22	6	11
Carpenter - - - - -	14	19	0
Carried over -	£15276	12	8

	£.	s.	d.
Brought over -	15276	12	8
Bricklayer - - - - -	9	7	0
Ironmonger - - - - -	25	6	5
Plumber and glazier - - - -	5	17	6
Brazier and tinman - - - -	15	16	7
Cooper - - - - - -	8	5	0
Bed tick - - - - - -	50	0	0
Help in the houses - - - -	85	18	0
Law charges - - - - -	38	13	0
Potatoes - - - - - -	41	3	9
Money lent Overseers, repaid as per credit account -	105	0	0
Rents and repairs of the work-house estates -	345	10	1
Cash paid Roger Kerrison, Esq. - - -	2000	0	0
Wool and yarn for outward apparel -	173	6	6

	£.	s.	d.
	£18170	16	6[1]
Balance in Treasurer's hands -	1844	13	2
	£20015	9	8

** The average number of Paupers in the several work-houses is 1430.

The posting of each article in the ledger, of which this account is an extract, was examined, and every folio cast up by us, and we find it exact.

ROBERT PARTRIDGE,   JOHN ROBINSON,
S. HARMER,   BARTLETT GURNEY,
JAMES ALRIC,   JAMES CHASE.
J. G. BASELEY,

N. B. The above is stated for eleven months only, in order that the future accounts may tally with the yearly audited accounts of the Treasurer.

A General State of Receipts and Disbursements of the Court of Guardians in the City of NORWICH, from the 1st of April 1785, to the 1st of April 1786.

RECEIVED.

	£.	s.	d.
To balance in the Treasurer's hands -	1844	13	2
Earnings at the two work-houses -	417	19	10
Carried over -	£2262	13	0

[1] There is an error of £10 in this account : the various items, altogether, amount to £18180. 16s 6d. and not to £18170. 16s 6d.

o

	£.	s.	d.
Brought over -	2262	13	0
Earnings at the fpinning-fchools - - -	527	12	6
Mulcts - - - - - -	17000	0	0
Arrears of Rates added to mulcts, and arrears of 1784 received in 1785 - - - -	543	11	5
Levies for penalties and arrears - - -	219	17	10
Cafh paid to the Treafurer, on account of rents of the work-houfe eftates - - - -	207	10	4
	£20761	5	1

PAID.

	£.	s.	d.
Bread, flour, and baking-office expences - -	3437	15	4
Beer - - - - - -	539	6	9
Minifter, clerks, furgeons, and fervants' wages - -	447	10	0
Printers and ftationers - - - -	42	14	0
Infurance - - - - -	12	3	6
Intereft money - - - - -	158	2	11
Manufacturing implements - - -	28	3	10
Sword-bearer for removal orders, &c. - -	56	16	0
Tyler, removal officer's expences - -	90	4	5
Apprehending vagrants - - -	19	5	0
High Conftable for King's Bench - -	60	6	0
Seffions' orders - - - -	450	0	0
Bridewell expences - - - -	68	17	6
Man-midwife, and woman in the houfe - -	26	3	1
Non-refident Poor - - - -	134	19	6
Cafual Poor - - - -	34	9	4
Apprentices binding - - -	45	1	0
Spinning-fchool expences - - -	126	16	8
Water rents - - - - -	11	10	0
Horfe-keeping at the Infirmary - -	9	19	4
Out-door allowances - - - -	3954	14	6
Deficiencies of Rates by empty houfes - -	2740	15	6¾
Peafe - - - - - -	68	15	6
Oatmeal - - - - -	103	5	0
Beef - - - - - -	875	18	5
Cheefe - - - - -	153	10	11
Butter - - - - -	843	5	9
Milk - - - - - -	118	8	7
Carried over -	£14658	18	4¾

	£.	s.	d.
Brought over	14658	18	4¾
Groceries	157	15	4¼
Candle	35	17	5
Salt	39	19	10
Soap	115	5	6
Oil	56	19	0
Men's, women's, and children's shoes	422	6	8
Breeches and leather aprons	110	10	9
Wool and yarn for outward apparel	263	5	6
Wool for stockings	77	1	0
Wool for burials	7	8	10
Casual expences for sundry small articles—earthen ware, wooden ware, baskets, sand, and greens, bought weekly	143	8	10
Cloth for shirts and shifts	321	2	4
Ditto for sheets	103	6	4
Check for aprons and handkerchiefs	104	16	8
Leather for mending shoes	264	16	0
Coals	461	15	1
Coffins	62	6	7
Funeral expences	92	6	1
Blankets and coverlets	96	8	0
Flock and straw	17	4	9
Haberdashery	41	12	10
Whitesmith	42	0	4
Carpenter	17	3	2
Bricklayer	25	2	8
Ironmonger	45	14	1
Plumber and glazier	6	16	3
Brazier and tinman	20	14	6
Cooper	14	13	9
Bed tick	61	10	6
Help in the houses	84	2	9
Law charges	187	16	4
Potatoes	49	13	1
Rents and repairs for work-house estates	911	17	2
	£19121	16	4
Balance in the Treasurer's hands	1639	8	9
	£20761	5	1

⁎ Average number of Poor in the several work-houses and infirmary, 1612.

The posting of each article in the Ledger, of which this account is an extract, was examined, and every folio cast up by us, and we find it exact.

ROBERT PARTRIDGE,   J. G. BASELEY,
S. HARMER,   JOHN ROBINSON,
J. ALRIC,   J. CHASE.

N. B. £480, part of this year's earnings, not being paid into the Treasurer's hands till after this account was balanced, it is not included therein.

A General State of Receipts and Disbursements of the Court of Guardians of the City of Norwich, from April 1, 1786, to April 1, 1787.

RECEIVED.

	£.	s.	d.
Balance in the Treasurer's hands - - -	1639	8	9
Earnings at the two work-houses - -	1024	10	8
Ditto at the spinning-schools - -	583	8	3
To mulcts - - - - -	15319	5	7
Earnings not paid to the Treasurer last year -	479	5	11
For rents of work-house estates - -	125	17	6
Arrears from sundry overseers - -	291	0	5
	£ 19462	17	1

PAID.

	£.	s	d.
Wheat, flour, bread, and baking expences -	2847	8	1
Beer - - - - -	510	13	9
Minister's, clerk's, surgeon's, and servants' salaries	457	10	0
Printer and stationer - - -	55	5	0
Insurance - - - -	12	3	6
Interest and principal money - -	765	0	0
Manufacturing implements - - -	27	8	4
Sword-bearer, for removal warrants -	62	15	0
Removal-officer - - -	90	17	5
Apprehending vagrants - - -	17	15	0
Sessions' orders - - - -	660	6	0
Bridewell expences - - -	86	3	0
Man-midwife, and woman in the house -	24	3	1
Non-resident Poor - - - -	131	0	6

Carried over - £ 5748   8   8

	£.	s.	d.
Brought over -	5748	8	8
Casual poor - - - - -	58	14	0
Binding apprentices - - - -	29	4	0
Spinning-school expences - - -	112	13	1
Water rents - - - -	11	10	0
A new horse, and keeping at the Infirmary - -	23	5	10
Out-door allowances - - - -	4137	11	8
Deficiencies of Rates, by empty houses and arrears -	1453	6	11
Pease - - - - - -	64	6	1
Oatmeal - - - - -	90	17	0
Beef - - - - - -	908	16	9
Butter - - - -	903	2	0
Cheese - - - - -	122	14	7
Groceries - - - -	218	0	6
Candles - - - - -	34	2	6
Salt - - - - -	12	16	9
Soap - - - - -	123	16	9
Oil - - - - -	66	0	6
Breeches - - - - -	99	12	9
Shoemaker - - - -	414	12	11
Wool and yarn for outward apparel - -	281	6	0
Wool for stockings - - - -	74	10	2
Wool for burials - - - -	11	7	7
Casual expences - - - -	176	7	2
Cloth for shirts and shifts - - -	402	9	1
Ditto for sheets - - - -	19	13	4
Check for aprons and handkerchiefs - -	112	13	9
Leather for mending shoes - - -	301	8	5
Help in the houses - - - -	89	17	9
Funeral expences - - - -	102	1	2
Blankets and coverlets - - -	55	7	6
Brazier and tinman - - -	10	9	9
Coals - - - - -	464	19	5
Coffins - - - - -	66	7	3
Milk - - - - -	121	11	8
Haberdashery - - -	34	16	3
Whitesmith - - - -	21	3	0
Carpenter - - - - -	30	4	2
Bricklayer - - - -	74	7	0
Ironmonger - - - -	13	18	0

	£.	s.	d.
Brought over	17098	11	8
Glazier	44	3	4
Cooper	9	11	1
Bed-ticks	38	10	0
Potatoes	33	4	3
Law charges	59	7	0
Flock and ftraw	4	4	0
Rents and repairs of the work-houfe eftate	648	18	7

	£.	s.	d.
	17936	9	11
Balance in the Treafurer's hands	1526	7	2
	£ 19462	17	1

** The aveiage number of Poor in the feveral work houfes, and in-firmary, is 1488.

The pofting of each article in the Ledger, of which this account is an extiact, was examined, and every folio caft up by us, and we find it exact.

> J. G. BASELEY,
> S. HARMER,
> JOHN ROBINSON.

A General State of Receipts and Difburfements of the Court of Guardians of the City of NORWICH, from April 1ft, 1787—to April 1ft, 1788.

RECEIVED.

	£.	s.	d.
Balance in the treafurer's hands	1526	7	2
Earnings at the two woik-houfes	1056	2	11
Ditto at the fpinning-fchools	539	6	8
To mulcts	14211	2	3
For rents of the woik-houfe eftate	122	4	0
Paid by J. Abuin, for fundries received by him	51	1	11
Due from J. Abuin	3	15	5

	£.	s.	d.
	£ 17510	0	4

N. B. Befides the above earnings, the Poor in the houfes manufacture almoft all their cloathing, for which no fum is carried to account.

5

Part of the money expended for cloathing is repaid by the court of feffions, and accounted for amongft the fundry receipts.

PAID.

	£.	s.	d.
Wheat, flour, bread, and baking expences	2942	15	8
Beer	498	3	9
Minifter's, clerk's, furgeon's, and fervants' falaries	455	18	0
Printer and ftationer	32	14	2
Infurance	12	3	6
Intereft and principal money	814	11	10
Manufacturing implements	31	19	4
Sword-bearer, for removal warrants, &c.	55	3	6
Removal officers	124	2	4
Apprehending vagrants	12	15	0
Seffions' orders	590	6	0
Bridewell expences	37	18	0
Midwives	16	14	4
Non-refident Poor	118	18	6
Cafual Poor	64	3	10
Binding apprentices	12	8	0
Spinning fchool expences	124	12	11
Water rents	11	10	0
Horfe-keeping at the Infirmary	15	16	3
Out-door allowances	3903	5	10
Empty houfes, and arrears by deficiencies of Rates	1274	10	5
Peafe	62	17	8
Oatmeal	90	15	11
Beef	930	16	4
Butter	917	8	8
Cheefe	114	11	6
Groceries	180	14	3
Candle	48	18	0
Salt	42	18	6
Soap	134	17	6
Oil	40	19	0
Breeches	106	15	0
Wool and yarn for outward apparel	257	3	1
Shoemakers	464	11	10
Wool for ftockings	80	16	8
Wool for burials	9	3	2

3 S 2   Carried over - £ 14633 18 3

	£.	s.	d.
Brought over -	14633	18	3
Cafual expences - - - - -	164	12	3
Cloth for fhirts and fhifts - - - -	285	11	9
Ditto for fheets - - - - -	35	0	0
Check for aprons and handkerchiefs - -	54	0	0
Leather for mending fhoes - - - -	295	11	0
Help in the houfes - - - -	92	3	11
Funeral expences - - - -	70	7	4
Blankets and coverlets - - - -	71	3	1
Brazier and tinman - - - -	11	0	7
Coals - - - - -	366	3	2
Coffins - - - - - -	42	1	1
Milk - - - - - -	122	8	11
Haberdafhery - - - - -	35	7	2
Blackfmiths - - - - -	44	16	2
Carpenters - - - - -	18	7	9
Bricklayer - - - - -	101	19	0
Ironmonger - - - - -	15	16	1
Glaziers - - - - -	2	13	0
Coopers - - - - - -	11	12	6
Bed-tick - - - - -	43	10	2
Potatoes - - - - -	37	12	0
Law charges - - - - -	103	10	3
Flock and ftraw - - - - -	5	9	0
Rents and repairs of the work-houfe eftate - -	599	0	0
	£ 17263	14	5
Balance in the Treafurer's hands -	246	5	11
	£ 17510	0	4

*** The average number of Poor in the feveral work-houfes, and infirmary, is 1490.

The pofting of each article in the Ledger, of which this account is an extract, was examined, and every folio caft up by us, and we find it exact.

ROBERT PARTRIDGE,   J. G. BASELEY,
S. HARMER,   JAMES CHASE.
JOHN ROBINSON,

A General

*A General State of Receipts and Disbursements of the Court of Guardians
of the City of* NORWICH, *from April* 1*st*, 1788 — *to April* 1*st*, 1789.

RECEIVED.

	£.	s.	d.
The balance in the Treasurer's hand — —	246	5	11
Earnings at the two work-houses — — —	944	13	9
Ditto at the two spinning-schools — —	507	0	5
By the four quarters' mulcts — — —	15378	15	6
By John Aburn, due last year — —	3	15	5
By ditto, for sundry receipts — — —	83	19	3
By ditto, for rents of the work-house estate —	128	2	6
Balance due to the Treasurer — — —	194	7	2
	£ 17486	19	11

N. B. Besides the above earnings, the Poor in the houses manufacture
almost all their cloathing, for which no sum is carried to account. Part
of the money expended for cloathing is repaid by the court of sessions,
and accounted for amongst the sundry receipts, as above.

PAID.

	£.	s.	d.
Wheat, flour, bread, and baking expences — —	3326	1	7
Beer — — — —	513	18	9
Minister's, clerk's, surgeon's, and servants' salaries —	456	16	0
Printers and stationers — — —	39	9	9
Insurance — — — —	12	3	6
Interest money — — —	37	10	3
Manufacturing implements — —	11	18	5
Sword bearer, for removal warrants —	51	18	0
Removal officer and mayor's constable —	113	2	1
Apprehending vagrants — —	14	15	0
Sessions' orders, and chief constable —	460	6	0
Bridewell expences — —	36	0	8
Man-midwife, and women in the houses — —	16	5	1
Non-resident Poor — — —	136	6	6
Casual Poor — — — —	98	12	6
Binding apprentices — — — —	26	19	9
Spinning-school expences — — —	94	13	0
	Carried over - £ 5446	16	10

		£.	s	d.
Brought over —	—	5446	16	10
Water rents — — —	—	11	10	0
Horse-keeping at the Infirmary —	—	13	6	6
Out-door allowances — —	—	4692	11	5
Empty houfes, and arrears by deficiencies of Rates	—	1267	14	9
Peafe — — — —	—	53	9	4
Oatmeal — — — —	—	83	15	0
Beef — — — —	—	912	8	10
Butter — — — —	—	857	16	9
Cheefe — — — —	—	113	12	8
Groceries — — —	—	181	0	5
Candle — — — —	—	40	19	4
Salt — — —	—	43	7	6
Soap — — — —	—	135	19	1
Oil — — — —	—	51	7	9
Breeches — — —	—	101	12	0
Wool and yarn for outward apparel —	—	294	8	8
Shoemakers — — —	—	459	5	6
Wool for, and knitting flockings —	—	66	1	4
Wool for burials — —	—	11	7	6
Cafual expences — — —	—	126	11	0
Cloth for fhirts and fhifts — —	—	476	19	9
Ditto for fheets — — —	—	33	14	4
Check for aprons and handkerchiefs —	—	75	0	0
Leather for mending fhoes — —	—	279	19	10
Help in the feveral houfes — —	—	93	19	7
Funeral expences — — —	—	83	9	3
Blankets and coverlets — —	—	71	16	9
Braziers and tinman — — —	—	8	11	4
Coals — — — —	—	402	10	4
Coffins — — — —	—	56	6	1
Milk — — — —	—	121	7	3
Haberdafhery — —	—	31	18	2
Carpenters — — —	—	24	15	0
Bricklayers — — —	—	28	12	0
Whitefmiths — — —	—	29	18	8
Ironmonger — — —	—	23	10	8
Glaziers — — — —	—	23	12	9
Coopers — — — —	—	9	3	6
Bed tick — — — —	—	24	6	8

Carried over - £ 16864 14 1

	£.	s.	d.
Brought over —	16864	14	1
Flock and ftraw — — —	4	17	0
Law charges — — —	20	16	5
Potatoes — — —	39	11	2
Rents and repairs of the work-houfe eftate	557	1	3

£ 17486 19 11

*** The average number of Poor in the feveral work-houfes, and infirmary, is 1481.

The pofting of each article in the Ledger, of which this account is an extract, was examined, and every folio caft up by us, and we find it exact.

J. G. BASELEY,   JAMES ALRIC,
S. HARMER,   JOHN ROBINSON.

A General State of the Receipts and Difburfements of the Court of Guardians of the City of NORWICH, from April 1ft, 1789—to April 1ft, 1790.

RECEIVED.

	£.	s.	d.
To mulcts — — —	16490	15	0
Earnings — — —	1584	8	5
Rents for the work-houfe eftate — —	125	15	0
Receipts by J. Aburn — — —	16	9	0

£ 18217 7 5

N B. Befides the above earnings, the Poor in the houfes manufacture almoft all their cloathing; for which no fum is carried to account.

PAID.

	£.	s.	d.
Wheat, flour, bread, and baking office expences —	3700	1	5
Out-door allowances — — —	4500	8	10
Empty houfes, and arrears by deficiencies of Rates —	1298	16	3
Minifter's, clerk's, furgeon's, and fervants' falaries —	461	8	0

Carried over — £ 9960 14 6

		£.	s.	d.
Brought over —		9960	14	6
Beer — — — —		490	10	9
Butter — — — —		827	10	5
Beef — — — —		964	2	7
Coals — — — —		428	7	1
Shoemakers — — —		474	12	1
Leather for mending shoes — — —		271	18	1
Cloth for shirts and shifts — —		372	18	2
Wool for outward apparel — —		294	18	7
Sessions' orders, and chief constable — —		410	6	0
Non-resident Poor — —		141	17	3
Removal-officer and mayor's constable —		104	3	2
Cheese — — —		111	19	6
Milk — — —		118	10	4
Groceries — —		163	7	10
Soap — — —		125	1	2
Breeches — — —		106	14	0
Law charges — —		120	0	0
Printers and stationers — —		36	0	8
Casual Poor — — —		71	12	1
Insurance — — —		12	3	6
Interest money — —		25	4	0
Manufacturing implements —		39	15	5
Sword-bearer, for removal orders, &c. — —		44	19	6
Apprehending vagrants — —		21	2	6
Midwives for the houses — —		22	7	10
Bridewell expences — —		34	5	8
Casual expences — — —		124	12	11
Binding apprentices — —		55	18	6
Spinning-school expences — —		82	5	9
Water rents —		11	10	0
Horse-hire at the Infirmary — —		7	12	9
Pease — —		61	11	6
Oatmeal — —		80	7	4
Candle — — —		38	18	11
Salt — — —		51	0	3
Oil — — —		35	2	8
Wool for knitting stockings —		74	16	8
Wool for burials — —		9	8	0
Cloth for sheets — —		43	16	8

Carried over — £ 16472   4   7

	£.	s.	d.
Brought over —	16472	4	7
Check for aprons and handkerchiefs — —	81	0	0
Help in the feveral houfes — — —	96	15	1
Funeral expences — — —.	61	16	4
Braziers and tinman — —	14	18	1
Coffins — — —	41	9	2
Haberdafhery — —	35	18	6
Carpenters — —	29	0	0
Bricklayers — —	19	19	0
Glaziers — — —	20	0	0
Ironmongers — —	21	8	5
Coopers — — —	13	8	5
Potatoes — — —	35	14	6
Blankets and coverlets — —	43	1	9
Bed-tick — — —	33	19	8
Flock and ftraw — —	5	6	0
Rents and repairs of the work-houfe eftate —	721	3	7
Balance due to the Treafurer laft year — —	194	7	2
	£17941	10	3
Balance in the Treafurer's hands —	275	17	2
	£18217	7	5

*** The average number of Poor in the feveral work-houfes, and infirmary, is £ 1473.

The pofting of each article in the Ledger, of which this account is an extract, was examined, and every folio caft up by us, and we find it exact.

> J. G. BASELEY,   JAMES ALRIC,
> S. HARMER,   JOHN ROBINSON,
>   JAMES CHASE.

A General State of the Receipts and Difburfements of the Court of Guardians of the City of NORWICH, from April 1ft, 1790—to April 1ft, 1791.

RECEIPTS.

	£.	s.	d.
Balance in the Treafurer's hand laft year — —	275	17	2
To affeffments — —	16326	18	10

	£.	s.	d.
Brought over —	16602	16	0
To earnings — — —	1601	11	5
To rents of the work-houfe eftate — —	119	18	0
To fundry receipts by John Aburn the beadle —	30	0	9
To part of the capital ftock of the linen manufactory paid in	80	0	0

	£ 18434	6	2

N. B. Befides the above earnings, the Poor in the houfes manufacture almoft all their cloathing, for which no fum is carried to account.

Part of the money expended for cloathing is repaid by the court of feffions, and accounted for amongft the fundry receipts, as above.

PAID.

	£.	s.	d.
Ironmonger — — —	24	8	6
Blackfmith — — —	14	7	9
Brazier and tinman — —	11	17	11
Water rents — —	11	10	0
Coopers — — —	8	11	10
Midwives — —	30	16	10
Printers and ftationers — —	42	8	9
Law charges — — —	526	3	10
Bridewell expences — —	58	2	0
Manufacturing implements — —	73	6	0
Seffions' orders, and chief conftable —	260	6	0
Candles — — —	28	16	0
Salt — — —	45	0	0
Breeches — —	75	8	2
Wool for burials — —	11	17	1
Coffins — — —	51	10	1
Straw and flock — —	7	0	0
Funeral expences — —	83	16	5
Horfe-hire at the infirmary —	7	16	0
Infurance — —	12	3	6
Cafual poor — —	59	18	3
Sword-bearer, for removal orders, &c. —	41	1	6
Spinning-fchool expences —	197	18	1
Potatoes — —	31	11	10
Out-door allowances — —	4612	4	7

		Carried over — £ 6328	0	11

		£.	s.	d.
Brought over	—	6328	0	11
Empty houfes, and arrears by deficiencies of rents	—	1325	10	10
Haberdafhery	—	24	13	8
Help in the feveral houfes	—	75	7	11
Binding apprentices	—	42	6	6
Cafual expences	—	161	11	6
Peafe	—	56	10	6
Milk	—	110	18	5
Minifter's, clerk's, furgeon's, and fervants' falaries	—	494	11	0
Groceries	—	139	13	9
Intereft money	—	1	5	0
Shoemakers	—	407	1	6
Cloth for fhirts and fhifts	—	273	11	11
Butter	—	788	17	2
Coals	—	370	18	3
Soap	—	110	2	4
Blankets and coverlets	—	15	2	0
Removal officer and mayor's conftable	—	98	17	2
Check for aprons and handkerchiefs	—	57	0	0
Cheefe	—	86	16	6
Oil	—	48	4	11
Sheeting	—	31	6	4
Bed-ticks	—	7	6	8
Oatmeal	—	65	14	1
Beer	—	476	15	3
Rents and repairs of the work-houfe eftate	—	540	4	6
Beef	—	891	1	7
Wool for knitting ftockings	—	74	17	1
Non-refident Poor	—	148	5	0
Apprehending vagrants	—	14	5	0
Leather for mending fhoes	—	276	14	4
Wheat, bread, flour, and baking	—	3200	18	3
Wool for outward apparel	—	255	7	3
		£16999	17	1
To balance in the Treafurer's hands	—	1434	9	1
		£18434	6	2

N. B. The above law-charges are large, on account of arrears of feveral years back being now paid off.

3 T 2   *⁎* The

*** The average number of the Poor of the feveral work-houfes, and infirmary, is 1356.

The pofting of each article in the Ledger, of which this account is an extract, was examined, and every folio caft up by us, and we find it exact.

ROBERT PARTRIDGE,	JOHN ROBINSON,
S. HARMER,	JOHN HERRING,
J. CHASE,	J. C. HAMPP.

A General State of the Receipts and Difburfements of the Court of Guardian of the City of NORWICH, *from April* 1, 1791—*to April* 1, 1792.

RECEIPTS.

			£.	s.	d.
Balance of cafh in hand	—	—	1434	9	1
Mulcts	—	—	13268	2	6
Earnings at fpinning-fchools	—	—	929	10	2
Ditto by the weavers and work abroad	—	—	610	1	1
Cafh received by linen and utenfils	—	—	584	7	0
Ditto, rents of the work-houfe eftate	—	—	126	4	0
By Aburn, for fundry receipts	—	—	36	4	2
			£16988	18	0

N. B. Befides the above earnings, the Poor in the houfes manufacture almoft all their cloathing, for which no fum is carried to account.

Part of the money expended for cloathing is repaid by the court of feffions, and accounted for amongft the fundry receipts as above.

PAID.

				£.	s.	d.
Whitefmith	—	—	—	4	15	5
Braziers	—	—	—	10	14	5
Coopers	—	—	—	7	1	3
Midwives	—	—	—	21	12	1
Printers and ftationers	—	—	—	34	13	6
Bridewell expences	—	—	—	46	14	10
Seffions' orders, and chief conftable	—	—	—	410	6	0
		Carried over -		£535	17	6

	£.	s.	d.
Brought over —	535	17	6
Flock and straw — — —	9	6	0
Horse-hire at the Infirmary — —	7	16	0
Insurance — — —	12	3	6
Spinning-school expences — —	210	19	5
Out-door allowances — —	3892	4	11
Empty houses and arrears — —	1090	15	7
Haberdashery — — —	30	10	5
Apprentices binding — — —	49	7	6
Minister's, clerk's, surgeon's, and servants' salaries —	496	16	0
Groceries — — —	152	15	3
Coals — — — —	334	10	2
Blankets and coverlets — — —	51	14	11
Removal-officer and mayor's constable —	94	6	11
Check — — — —	70	6	7
Cheese — — — —	80	11	1
Bed-ticks — — —	6	3	4
Oatmeal — — —	49	1	1
Beer — — —	434	18	9
Non-resident Poor — —	119	0	6
Apprehending vagrants — —	13	15	0
Leather for mending shoes — —	253	11	0
Casual expences, and to the Treasurer's clerk —	154	16	10
Milk — — —	96	6	4
Butter — — —	697	12	0
Beef — — —	839	3	4
Shoemakers — — —	341	13	0
Cloth for shirts and shifts — —	251	9	1
Breeches — — —	76	15	0
Burial wool — — —	8	0	5
Coffins — — —	46	17	8
Stockings — — —	58	7	8
Funeral expences — —	67	7	8
Potatoes — — —	29	6	9
Candles — — —	24	4	9
Salt — — — —	37	6	0
Casual Poor — — —	71	6	0
Rents and repairs of the work-house estate —	427	7	11
Soap — — —	102	11	1
Wool and materials for apparel — —	220	12	3
Wheat, bread, flour, and baking — —	2254	14	11
Carried over - £13802	1	0	

				£.	s.	d.
		Brought forward	—	13802	1	0
Ironmongers	—	—	—	16	1	4
Oil	—	—	—	57	0	11
Sword-bearer, for removal orders, &c.	—	—	42	4	3
Help in the houfes	—	—	—	75	10	5
Cloth for fheeting	—	—	—	108	6	10
Water rents	—	——	—	11	10	0
Law charges	—	—	—	52	14	3
Peafe	—	—	—	44	19	0

		£.	s.	d.
		£14210	8	0
To balance in the Treafurer's hands	-	2778	10	0
		£16988	18	0

*** The average number of the Poor in the feveral work-houfes, and infirmary, is 1141.

The pofting of each article in the Ledger, of which this account is an extract, was examined, and every folio caft up by us, and we find it exact.

ROBERT PARTRIDGE,	S. HARMER,
E. NORGATE,	JOHN HERRING,
J. CHASE,	JOHN BRITTAN,
J. C. HAMPP,	STARLING DAY, jun.

A General State of the Receipts and Disbursements of the Court of Guardians of the City of NORWICH, from April 1, 1792—to April 1, 1793.

RECEIPTS.

			£.	s.	d.
Balance of cafh in hand	—	—	2778	10	0
Mulcts	—	—	10129	15	11
Earnings at fpinning fchools	—	—	832	8	7
Ditto by the weavers and work abroad	—	568	11	3
Rents of the work houfe eftate	—	—	124	2	0
By Aburn, for fundry receipts	—	—	38	1	0

		£.	s.	d.
		£14471	8	9
Balance of cafh due to the Treafurer	-	1620	16	11
		£16092	5	8

N. B.

N. B. Befides the above earnings, the Poor in the houfes manufacture almoft all their cloathing, for which no fum is carried to account.

A confiderable part of the money paid for the militia is due from the feveral counties which have fubftitutes from the city.

Part of the money expended for cloathing is repaid by the court of feffions, and accounted for amongft the fundry receipts, as above, by John Aburn.

PAID.

	£.	s.	d.
Coopers — — —	16	4	1
Midwives — — —	28	18	4
Printers and ftationers — —	36	1	1
Law charges — — —	36	10	7
Bridewell expences — —	51	14	8
Seffions' orders, and chief conftable — —	460	6	0
Flock and ftraw — — —	13	13	0
Horfe-hire at the Infirmary — —	7	16	0
Infurance — — —	12	3	6
Spinning-fchool expences —	191	15	0
Haberdafhery — — — —	25	6	7
Apprentices binding — — —	47	15	0
Peafe — — —	49	14	9
Minifter's, clerk's, furgeon's, and fervants' falaries —	496	16	0
Groceries — — —	144	13	10
Braziers — — — —	8	2	11
Intereft money — — —	16	16	4
Blankets and coverlets — —	90	19	9
Mayor's conftable — —	59	16	7
Removal officer — —	51	12	7
Cheefe — — —	79	7	0
Oil — — —	50	0	3
Bed-ticks — — —	22	8	3
Oatmeal — — —	44	3	2
Non-refident Poor — — —	125	13	0
Apprehending vagrants — —	20	5	0
Water rents — — —	11	10	0
Sword-bearer, for removal orders, &c. — —	44	0	0
Leather for mending fhoes — —	287	5	8
Cafual expences, and to the Treafurer's clerk —	162	15	10
Milk — — —	90	9	2

Carried over — £ 2784 13 11

	£.	s.	d.
Brought over - -	2784	13	11
Breeches - - - - -	80	15	6
Burial wool - - - -	11	15	10
Coffins - - - - - -	44	12	3
Wool for ftockings - - - - -	74	4	8
Funeral expences - - - - -	63	19	11
Potatoes - - - - -	28	17	5
Coals - - - - - -	335	1	0
Candles - - - - - -	23	18	11
Salt - - - - -	34	10	6
Cafual Poor - - - - -	82	1	9
Soap - - - - -	100	19	10
Ironmongers - - - -	15	10	7
Cloth for fhirts and fhifts - - -	262	15	8
Cloth for fheeting - - - -	86	6	8
Shoemakers - - - -	363	1	8
Check - - - -	49	0	11
Beer - - - - - -	397	2	3
Help in the houfes - - -	76	15	6
Beef - - - - - -	929	17	1
Butter - - - - -	663	1	0
Rents and repairs of the work-houfe eftate - -	517	19	3
Out-door allowances - - - -	4730	4	11
Empty houfes and arrears - - -	986	3	7
Wool and materials for apparel - - -	132	9	1
Wheat, bread, flour, and baking - - -	2110	6	0
Money to pay the militia - - - -	1100	0	0
	£ 16092	5	8

*** The average number of the Poor in the feveral work-houfes, and infirmary, is 1133.

The pofting of each article in the Ledger, of which this account is an extract, was examined, and every folio caft up by us, and we find it exact.

        ROBERT PARTRIDGE,   S. HARMFR,
        J. G. BASELEY,   JOHN BRITTAN,
        JOHN HERRING,   JOHN WEBB.
        J. C. HAMPP.

A General

A General State of the Receipts and Disbursements of the Court of Guardians of the City of NORWICH, *from April 1st, 1793—to April 1st, 1794.*

RECEIPTS.

	£.	s.	d.
Mulcts — — — —	18664	17	5
Received for militia payments —	2088	6	4
Earnings at the spinning-schools —	909	0	3
Ditto by weavers and work abroad —	400	10	5
Rents of the work-house estate — —	124	2	0
Receipts by John Aburn — —	55	16	5
	£ 22242	12	10
Balance of cash due to the Treasurer —	416	13	7
	£ 22659	6	5

N. B. The Poor in the houses manufacture almost all their cloathing, for which no sum is carried to account.

Part of the money expended for cloathing is repaid by the court of sessions, and accounted for amongst the sundry receipts as above.

Part of the above sum received for militia payments was due last year from sundry counties.

PAID.

	£.	s.	d.
Wheat, bread, flour, and baking — — —	2877	9	0
Minister's, clerk's, surgeon's, and servants' salaries —	496	16	0
Printers and stationers — — —	52	11	11
Insurance — — — —	10	4	9
Removal officer — — —	64	1	6
Mayor's constable — — — —	61	3	0
Apprehending vagrants — — —	20	10	0
Sessions' orders and chief constable —	360	6	0
Bridewell expences — — —	58	15	3
Midwives — — — —	21	3	10
Non-resident Poor — — — —	124	10	2
Casual Poor — — — —	89	2	7
Apprentices binding — — —	27	2	0
Spinning school expences — — —	290	18	8
Water-rents — — — —	11	10	0
Horse-hire at the Infirmary — — —	7	16	0

Carried over - £ 4574 0 8

			£.	s.	d.
Brought over	—	—	4574	0	8
Out-door allowances	—	—	7327	9	11
Empty houfes and arrears	—	—	1776	0	0
Peafe	—	—	83	6	9
Oatmeal	—	—	56	10	4
Beef	—	—	973	13	2
Cheefe	—	—	106	1	4
Butter	—	—	1012	3	1
Milk	—	—	99	19	3
Groceries	—	—	168	19	6
Candles	—	—	24	7	7
Salt	—	—	44	11	3
Soap	—	—	113	11	10
Oil	—	—	59	3	11
Shoemakers	—	—	502	15	0
Breeches	—	—	111	16	6
Wool and materials for apparel	—	—	213	15	4
Burial Wool	—	—	13	0	7
Wool for ftockings	—	—	63	2	8
Cafual expences and the treafurer's clerk	—	—	196	5	5
Cloth for fhirts and fhifts	—	—	254	10	11
Cloth for fheets	—	—	100	4	8
Check	—	—	114	4	5
Leather for mending fhoes	—	—	185	18	1
Coals	—	—	374	11	0
Coffins	—	—	57	12	0
Funeral expences	—	—	91	15	11
Blankets and coverlets	—	—	151	16	3
Flock and ftraw	—	—	18	18	0
Haberdafhery	—	—	29	3	4
Help in the houfes	—	—	76	15	8
Ironmongers	—	—	20	18	0
Rents and repairs of the work-houfe eftate	—	1104	0	0
Coopers	—	—	9	19	3
Braziers	—	—	14	15	10
Bed-ticks	—	—	70	16	7
Law-charges	—	—	48	6	2
Beer	—	—	453	5	6
Potatoes	—	—	30	11	0
Sword-bearer	—	—	54	1	0
Cafh to pay militia	—	—	1797	0	0

4   Carried over - £ 22584 17 8

		£.	s.	d.
Brought over —		22584	17	8
Interest money — — —	—	57	1	3
Interest on militia account — —	—	17	7	6
		£ 22659	6	5

*** The average number of Poor in the feveral work-houfes, and infirmary, are 1406.

The pofting of each article in the Ledger, of which this account is an extract, was examined, and every folio caft up by us, and we find it exact.

ROBERT PARTRIDGE,   JOHN ROBINSON,
ELIAS NORGATE,   JOHN BRITTAN,
S. HARMER,   JAMES ANGIER.

A General State of the Receipts and Difburfements of the Court of Guardians of the City of NORWICH, from April 1ft, 1794— to April 1ft, 1795.

RECEIPTS.

			£.	s.	d.
To mulcts for this year — — —		—	20349	3	8
Received by militia payments — —	—	—	1321	18	0
Earnings at fpinning-fchools — —	—	—	701	19	6
Ditto by weavers and work abroad —	—	—	437	12	6
Rents of the work-houfe eftate —	—	—	124	2	0
Receipts by John Aburn — — —	—	—	36	12	6
Ditto by public fubfcription for the Poor	—	—	1000	0	0
			£ 23971	8	2

N B. The Poor in the houfes manufacture almoft all their cloathing, for which no fum is carried to account.

Part of the money expended for cloathing is repaid by the court of feffions, and accounted for amongft the fundry receipts as above.

PAID.

			£.	s.	d.
Balance to the Treafurer — —		—	416	13	7
Wheat, bread, flour, and baking — —	—	—	3195	18	9
Minifter's, clerk's, furgeon's, and fervants' falaries	—	—	496	16	0
Printers and ftationers — —	—	—	38	0	4
Infurance — — — —	—	—	9	17	9
3 U 2 Carried over -			£ 4157	6	5

	£.	s.	d.
Brought over —	4157	6	5
Sword-bearer for removal orders — —	45	13	6
Mayor's conftable — — — —	63	2	0
Removal officer — — — —	60	19	5
Apprehending vagrants — — —	23	0	0
Chief conftable and feffions' orders — — —	760	6	0
Bridewell expences — — —	39	2	9
Midwives — — — —	14	13	4
Non refident Poor — — — —	148	19	0
Cafual Foor — — — —	252	19	3
Binding apprentices — — —	17	18	0
Spinning fchool expences — — —	223	14	3
Water-rents — — — —	11	10	0
Horf -hire at the Infirmary — — —	8	0	6
Out-door allowances — — — —	7463	14	3
Empty houfes and arrears — — —	1898	0	7
Peafe and rice — — — —	93	17	11
Oatmeal — — — — —	61	9	0
Beef — — — — —	1025	8	0
Cheefe — — — — —	111	9	1
Butter — — — — —	854	11	11
Milk — — — — —	116	18	4
Grocery — — — —	180	11	6
Candles — — — —	22	6	6
Salt — — — — —	41	13	4
Soap — — — —	115	12	7
Oil — — — — —	67	0	10
Shoemakers — — — —	398	8	2
Breeches — — — — —	101	7	6
Wool and yarn for apparel — — —	256	16	10
Wool for ftockings — — —	66	18	0
Burial wool — — — —	9	8	11
Cafual expences and the treafurer's clerk —	247	3	10
Cloth for fhirts and fhifts — — —	230	17	1
Cloth for fheets — — — —	38	14	4
Check for aprons and handkerchiefs — —	111	1	9
Leather for mending fhoes — — —	221	14	2
Coals — — — —	397	5	4
Coffins — — — —	44	8	0
Funeral expences — — — —	63	2	6
Blankets and coverlets — — —	98	15	0
Flock and ftraw — — — —	19	19	0
Carried over — £ 20185	18	8	

		£.	s.	d.
Brought over	—	20185	18	8
Haberdafhery — — — —	—	28	1	4
Help in the houfes — — — —	—	77	6	3
Ironmongery — — — —	—	16	19	9
Beer — — — —	—	442	6	0
Brazier and tinman — —	—	12	4	0
Coopers work — — —	—	18	5	4
Rents and repairs of the work-houfe eftate — —	—	375	10	6
Bed ticks — — —	—	55	17	6
Potatoes — — —	—	35	18	0
Law-charges — — —	—	24	18	8
Whitefmith — — —	—	20	8	1
Paid to militia families — — —	—	1884	15	0
Intereft on militia account — —	—	26	8	9
Ditto for the corporation — —	—	10	4	4
		£ 23215	2	2
Balance in the Treafurer's hands — —	—	756	6	0
		£ 23971	8	2

*** The average number of Poor in the feveral work-houfes, and in-firmary, are 1316.

The pofting of each article in the Ledger, of which this account is an extract, was examined, and every folio caft up by us, and we find it exact.

ROBERT PARTRIDGE,   JAMES CHASE,
S. HARMER,   JOHN BRITTAN.
JOHN ROBINSON,

A General State of the Receipts and Disburfements of the Court of Guardians in the City of NORWICH, *from April* 1, 1795 — *to April* 1, 1796.

RECEIPTS.

		£.	s.	d.
Balance of laft year in the Treafurer's hands	—	756	6	0
Mulcts for this year — — —	—	21216	6	7
Received by militia payments — —	—	1467	9	10
Earnings at the fpinning-fchools — —	—	701	13	10
Ditto by weavers and work abroad — —	—	655	0	5
Rents of work-houfe eftate — —	—	119	18	0
Receipts by John Auburn — —	—	60	19	10
		£ 24977	14	6
Balance due to the Treafurer — —	—	4729	2	2
		£ 29706	16	8

N. B. The Poor in the houses manufacture almost all their cloathing, for which no sum is carried to account.

Part of the money expended for cloathing is repaid by the court of sessions, and accounted for amongst the sundry receipts as above.

PAID.

	£.	s.	d.
Wheat, bread, flour, and baking[1] — —	9126	2	3
Minister's, surgeon's, clerk's, and servants' salaries —	496	16	0
Printers and stationers — — —	38	2	7
Insurance — — — —	9	17	6
Sword-bearer for removal orders — —	48	15	6
Mayor's constable — — — —	64	10	6
Removal officer — — — —	63	15	0
Apprehending vagrants — — —	30	15	0
Chief constable and sessions' orders — —	810	6	0
Bridewell expences — — — —	61	14	9
Midwives — — — —	11	18	5
Non-resident Poor · — — —	159	13	0
Casual Poor — — — —	160	17	6
Binding apprentices — — —	10	18	0
Spinning school expences — — —	199	3	3
Water-rents — — — —	11	10	0
Horse-hire at the Infirmary — —	9	16	0
Out-door allowances — — —	6608	14	3
Empty houses and arrears — — —	1866	12	0
Pease and rice — — — —	167	3	0
Oatmeal — — — —	85	14	5
Beef — — — — —	1413	7	8
Cheese — — — — —	108	14	6
Butter — — — —	1024	14	0
Milk — — — — —	112	3	10
Grocery — — — — —	200	9	9
Candles — — — — —	31	15	10
Salt — — — — —	44	16	2
Soap — — — — —	141	16	0
Oil — — — — —	82	2	7
Carried over — £ 23202		15	3

[1] I am informed, that the enormous difference in the article of wheat, &c in the two last years, was chiefly produced by the late high price of provisions; and that the large sum due to the Treasurer at this time, is, in a great measure, owing to the same cause An increasing debt, however, notwithstanding a large increased Rate, is, (as my correspondent justly observes,) an alarming circumstance; and I sincerely wish, with him, that the cause of it may be only a temporary one.

					£.	s.	d.
Brought over	—			—	23202	15	3
Shoemakers	—	—	—	—	392	1	1
Breeches	—	—	—	—	105	4	10
Wool and yarn for apparel	—	—	—	253	12	2
Wool for stockings	—	—	—	93	2	10
Wool for burials	—	—	—	—	11	14	10
Casual expences and treasurer's clerk	—	—	368	11	10
Cloth for shirts and shifts	—	—	—	372	2	9
Cloth for sheeting	—	—	—	—	41	17	8
Check for aprons and handkerchiefs	—	—	156	10	1
Leather for mending shoes	—	—	—	289	14	0
Coals	—	—	—	—	—	411	11	11
Coffins	—	—	—	—	—	46	15	3
Funeral expences	—	—	—	63	10	11
Blankets and coverlets	—	—	—	131	19	10
Flock and straw	—	—	—	—	27	13	6
Haberdashery	—	—	—	—	32	7	8
Help in the houses	—	—	—	76	15	0
Ironmongery	—	—	—	—	13	1	10
Beer	—	—	—	—	—	461	2	6
Brazier and tinman	—	—	—	24	6	9
Coopers work	—	—	—	—	10	2	0
Rents and repairs of the work house estate	—	—	761	15	0
Bed-ticks	—	—	—	—	—	2	10	6
Potatoes	—	—	—	—	23	4	0
Law-charges	—	—	—	—	65	10	3
Whitesmith	—	—	—	—	30	11	4
Paid to militia families	—	—	—	2142	0	0
Interest money on the militia account	—	—	34	6	10
Interest ditto on running account	—	—	60	4	3
Disbursed	-	£	29706	16	8

There remains due from the militia-account, and from the barracks, £ 1000 and upwards, towards the payment of the Treasurer's balance.

⁎ The average number of Poor in the several work-houses, and infirmary, is 1403.

The posting of each article in the Ledger, of which this account is an extract, was examined, and every folio cast up by us, and we find it exact.

JAMES ANGIER,   J. C. HAMPP,
JOHN BRITTAN,   JAMES CHASE.
JOHN WEBB,

Number in the Work-houses at different Periods.

Years.			Persons.	Years.			Persons,
1795.—Jan.	6th		1295	1795.—Oct.	6th		1218
Feb.	3d		1316	Nov.	3d		1203
March	3d		1342	Dec.	1ft		1262
April	7th		1328	1796.—Jan.	5th		1408
May	12th		1305	Feb	2d		1446
June	2d		1272	March	1ft		1425
July	7th		1236	April	5th		1441
Aug.	4th		1232	May	16th		1334
Sept.	1ft		1188	June	7th		1331

Number of Deaths in the New Work house [1]

			Years			Years.		Deaths.
From Jan.	5th	1790	to	Dec.	28th	1790		64
—— Jan.	11th	1791	to	Dec.	28th	1791		50
—— Jan.	4th	1792	to	Dec.	26th	1792		35
—— Jan.	8th	1793	to	Dec.	23d	1793		80
—— Jan.	2d	1794	to	Dec.	29th	1794		61
—— Jan.	2d	1795	to	Dec.	9th	1795		61
—— Jan.	5th	1796	to	June	6th	1796		29

Number of Deaths in the Old Work-house [1]

		Years.				Years.		Deaths.
From Jan.		1789	to	Jan.		1790		73
—— Jan.		1790	to	Jan.		1791		83
—— Jan.		1791	to	Jan.		1792		62
—— Jan.		1792	to	Jan.		1793		117
—— Jan.		1793	to	Jan.		1794		63
—— Jan.		1794	to	Jan.		1795		70
—— Jan.		1795	to	Jan.	14.	1796		69
—— Jan.		1796	to	June	12	1796		30

The Rate of Mulcts or Affeffments in the 1ft, 2d, and 3d quarters in 1795, was at 2s. 3½d. in the pound on the net rent; and for the 4th quarter, at 2s 9d. in the pound on the net rent. In 1796, the 1ft and 2d quarters were 2s 9d. in the pound.

[1] Page 521 was printed off, before this lift of deaths, and the accounts of 1795 and 1796, were received: the omiffions, however, in the Tables in that page, are eafily fupplied, by referring to this and the five preceding pages.

From

From the above Annual Accounts, and from other documents, the following Tables have been formed:

TABLE I.

Years.	Amount of Mulcts or Affeffments [1].			Total Receipts			Total Expences for the Poor			Relief to Out-Poor		
	£.	s.	d.	£.	s	d.	£.	s.	d.	£.	s.	d.
From 1 May, 1783, to 1 May, 1784.	18000	0	0	20169	15	9	16943	9	8	2318	10	11
April 1, 1785.	18000	0	0	20015	9	8	18170	16	6	2763	16	0
April 1, 1786.	17000	0	0	20761	5	1	19121	16	4	3954	14	6
April 1, 1787.	15319	5	7	19462	17	1	17936	9	11	4137	11	8
April 1, 1788.	14211	2	3	17510	0	4	17263	14	5	3903	5	10
April 1, 1789.	15378	15	6	17486	19	11	17486	19	11	4692	11	5
April 1, 1790.	16490	15	0	18217	7	5	17941	10	3	4500	8	10
April 1, 1791.	16326	18	10	18434	6	2	16999	17	1	4612	4	7
April 1, 1792.	13268	2	6	16988	18	0	14210	8	0	3892	4	11
April 1, 1793.	10129	15	11	16092	5	8	16092	5	8	4730	4	11
April 1, 1794.	18664	17	5	22659	6	5	22659	6	5	7327	9	11

TABLE II.

Years.	Average number of Poor in the work-houfes	Deaths in the work-houfes	Earnings of the Poor in the work-houfes			Cloaths and Provifions in the work houfes			Weekly Expence of Paupers[2]	
			£.	s.	d.	£.	s.	d.	s.	d.
1784	1301	128	1215	8	7	10204	13	0	3	$4\frac{1}{2}$
1785	1430	170	1637	7	11	10624	9	2	2	10
1786	1612	267	1424	18	3	9533	0	0	2	7
1787	1488	117	1607	18	11	8579	17	0	2	8
1788	1490	183	1595	9	7	9261	7	2	2	10
1789	1481	155	1451	14	2	9014	19	11	2	$8\frac{1}{2}$
1790	1473	148	1584	8	5	9289	8	5	2	10
1791	1356	———	1601	11	5	8133	13	6	2	9
1792	1141	———	1539	13	3	6711	3	5	2	$9\frac{1}{2}$
1793	1133	———	1400	19	10	6920	11	9	2	$9\frac{3}{4}$
1794	1406	———	1439	1	2	9240	9	2	2	11

Table

[1] In the Returns made to Parliament in 1786, the money raifed by affeffment,

　　　　　　　　　　£.　s.　d.
in 1783 is ftated at 13414　2　8
　　1784　-　-　-　13985　14　8
　　1785　-　-　-　13541　16　9

[2] This calculation of the weekly expence of each Pauper was furnifhed by one of the Guardians of the Poor: it nearly agrees with the preceding column, but not exactly: for,

　　　　　　　　　　　s.　d.　　　　　　　　　£.　s.　d.
1301 Paupers, at 3　4¼ a head, coft annually 11416　5　6
1430 ———　　　　2　10　-　-　-　10534　6　8

Table of Baptisms, Burials, and Poor's Rate, in the City of NORWICH.

Years.	Baptisms.	Burials.	Rate in the Pound [3] s.	d.	Years.	Baptisms.	Burials.	Rate in the Pound. s.	d.
1774	1090	1055	10	4	1776	1212	1358	9	8
1775	1241	952	10	4	1777	1289	996	7	10

		s.	d.		£	s.	d.
1612	Paupers, at	2	7	a head, cost annually	10827	5	4
1488	———	2	8	- - -	10316	16	0
1490	———	2	10	- - -	10976	6	8
1481	———	2	8½	- - -	10428	14	2
1473	———	2	10	- - -	10851	2	0
1356	———	2	9	- - -	9695	8	0
1141	———	2	9½	- - -	8281	15	2
1133	———	2	9¼	- - -	8285	1	3
1406	———	2	11	- - -	10787	3	4

The following seems to be nearly the weekly expence of each Pauper in cloaths and provisions, exclusive of lodging, &c. Their earnings should be deducted, in order to obtain the net weekly expence of each

		s	d		£	s	d.
1301	Paupers, at	3	0¼	a head, cost annually	10218	5	5
1430	———	2	10¼	- - -	10611	15	10
1612	———	2	3¼	- - -	9517	10	4
1488	———	2	2½	- - -	8543	12	0
1490	———	2	4½	- - -	9200	15	0
1481	———	2	4	- - -	8984	14	8
1473	———	2	5	- - -	9255	7	0
1356	———	2	3¾	- - -	8152	9	0
1141	———	2	3¼	- - -	6737	1	5
1133	———	2	4¼	- - -	6934	18	1
1406	———	2	6½	- - -	9215	3	2

These sums nearly agree with the amount of cloaths and provisions as stated in Table II

[3] The Poor's Rate is assessed on half the rack rental, and on stock: so that 1s. 6d. in the pound, is, in fact, 9s. 3d in the pound, on the fair rental*.

* In the parish of Hethersall, which, from it's proximity to Norwich, is burthened with the maintenance of a numerous Poor, more especially of journeymen weavers, the following has been the amount of only two taxes paid by a Gentleman for a small farm of 63 acres of arable and pasture, the rack-rent whereof is £66 a year It is rated at ¾ of the rack rent

			£	s.	d
The Poor and Church Rates in the year ending in	1785	were	15	17	7½
	1786	——	10	18	7½
	1787	——	12	16	6
	1788	——	11	9	6
	1789	——	13	12	3
	1790	——	11	18	3
	1791	——	13	12	2½
	1792	——	11	3	1½
	1793	——	10	2	1½
	1794	——	11	13	1½

The average rent of land in this parish is from 16s. to 20s. an acre.

Years.	Baptisms.	Burials.	Rate in the Pound. s. d.	Years.	Baptisms.	Burials.	Rate in the Pound. s. d.
1778	1229	1060	9 9	1787	1151	1063	12 4
1779	1257	1214	10 0	1788	1154	1192	12 6
1780	1132	1167	9 0	1789	1050	1138	14 6
1781	1150	1617	11 0	1790	1055	1219	14 6
1782	1022	1027	11 4	1791	1096	1112	13 0
1783	1125	1049	15 0	1792	1166	973	8 0
1784	1164	1180	15 0	1793	1094	1161	17 8
1785	1227	1041	15 0	1794	963	1064	18 6
1786	1185	1363	14 0	1795	——	——	18 6

140 Aged people are maintained in three hofpitals; and a fmall number of boys and girls in two other hofpitals. The donations by which this is effected, amount to about £ 3000. a year. The Norfolk and Norwich hofpital for fick perfons is fupported by voluntary fubfcriptions : between it's inftitution in October 1770, and 16th July 1794, it's receipts were £ 50,343. 3s. 4d. ; and it's difburfements, £ 49,448. 13s. 0½d., or rather more than £ 2000l. a year. The following is a general account of the Patients admitted and difcharged, from the firft opening of the hofpital, for out-patients, July 11, 1772 ; and for in-patients, November 7, 1772; to July 16, 1794 :

		In.	Out.	Total.
Patients admitted	-	8624	6363	14987
Discharged, { Cured	- -	5629	3534	9163
Relieved	- -	1248	1194	2442
Not likely to receive benefit		100	44	144
Incurable	-	177	108	285
For non-attendance	-	——	1268	1268
At their own requeft	-	398	224	622
Went away without leave		157	——	157
For irregularity	- -	44	9	53
Deaths	- -	444	190	634
Remaining on the books	-	84	135	219
		8281	6706	14987

It appears there were 343 in-patients lefs, and 343 out-patients more, difcharged, than admitted; becaufe 343, who were admitted as in-patients, were afterwards made out-patients.

There are about 40 Friendly Societies in the city of Norwich; moft of which have taken the benefit of the late Act. The number of members in each, is from about 18 to 30 and 40. They are not much encouraged by honorary members.

Under

Under the article of Friendly Societies, may be mentioned a Club which was eftablifhed in Norwich, in the year 1775, under the title of the "Scots Society," for the purpofe of relieving any poor Scotchman who might come to Norwich in diftrefs. The chief motive of the inftitution was to fupply an omiffion in the Englifh law, relative to the natives of Scotland, and of other countries; refpecting whom it is faid, that "a ftranger coming into England, and not having obtained a proper parifh fettlement, is not entitled to parifh relief; that nobody is obliged to relieve him, but that they might let him ftarve."[1] In the year 1778, it was agreed that the charity of the Society fhould be extended to all fubjects of Great Britain, and the natives of foreign countries, refiding in England, when in diftrefs; and in 1784, the Society took the additional name of the "Society of Univerfal Good-will." By an account publifhed in 1784, it appears that the following objects, of different nations, who, having no fettlement here, were not entitled to relief, by the laws of England, had been relieved by the Society:

	1778.	1779.	1780.	1781.	1782.	1783.	1784.	Total.
Natives of Scotland	5	7	6	11	13	27	42	111
Ireland	—	3	3	3	5	10	5	29
France	—	—	—	—	—	—	1	1
America	—	—	—	—	5	4	5	14
Germany	—	—	—	—	—	—	5	5
Italy	—	—	—	—	—	—	8	8
Turkey	—	—	—	—	1	—	1	3
Pruffia	—	—	—	—	—	—	2	2
Barbary	—	—	—	—	—	2	—	2
Norway	—	—	—	—	—	1	—	1
Hungary	—	—	—	—	—	—	1	1
Sweden	—	—	—	—	—	—	1	1
Jeweffes	—	—	—	—	—	—	2	2
Perfons who could give no pofitive account to what parifhes they belonged				1	1	1	1	4
The wives and children of the above objects, and fingle women				—	—	—	—	172
						Total number	—	356

51 annually on an average.

Since the year 1784, many other fimilar objects of charity have been relieved by the Society.   *June*, 1796.

[1] Burn's Juftice, Title Settlements.

7   Y A R-

YARMOUTH.

THE extent of this parifh is about 24 furlongs by 4. The population in 1784 was accurately taken, and found to be 12,608 fouls; but, at prefent, is fuppofed to amount to 13,000. There are 137 ale-houfes in Yarmouth. About 40 of the inhabitants are employed in making fail-cloth; there is no other manufacture of importance in the parifh. The principal employments are thofe connected with a fea-faring life.

Here are 3 Prefbyterian, 1 Methodift, 1 Quaker, and 2 Anabaptift congregations: the number of Diffenters is eftimated at 2000. 750 houfes pay the window-tax; the number exempted could not be afcertained.

The prices of provifions are: beef, mutton, and lamb, from 5d to 6d. the pound; veal, from 4d. to 5d.; pork, 6d. to 7d.; bacon, 1od.; butter, 1s. for 20 oz.; milk, 1d. the pint; wheat, £3. 15s. the qr.; barley, £1. 13s.; oats, £1. 11s.; flour, from 2s. 6d. to 2s. 1od. the ftone.

Common labourers have from 1s. to 1s. 6d. a day, and victuals. Men employed in fifhing, in loading and unloading veffels, &c. work by the piece, and fometimes earn 3s. or 4s. a day: fhip-carpenters, &c. earn from 3s. 6d to 4s. a day. It is thought that 20 Friendly Societies exifted here, before the late Act refpecting them took place: they were chiefly compofed of the pooreft claffes. Unfortunately they conceived that their feveral funds were intended to be at the difpofal of the magiftrates; they, therefore, moftly, agreed to break up, and divide their ftock. Of thefe clubs, only three are now remaining: and they have not taken the benefit of the Act. The number of members in each club, is about 30 or 40.

Little land is rented here, except in fmall parcels for gardens. Tithes are thus taken; horfes and cows pay 6d. a head, a year; and windmills, each, 1os. a year. The land-tax amounts to £2820. 3s. 1d. and is about 3s 8d. in the pound. The principal part of this parifh lies along the fhore, and is common, or wafte land, and not very fertile; a great part of it being covered with fand and furze.

There is here, one charity-fchool for the maintenance and education of 30, and another for 50 poor children. The latter adjoins to the workhoufe,

houfe, and is fupplied with victuals from thence, at the rate of 1s. 9d. a week, for each child.

There is an hofpital at Yarmouth for 20 poor fifhermen, who have, each, two rooms, and coals, allowed them, together with 2s. a week in fummer, and 2s 6d. a week in winter.

Wheaten bread is univerfally ufed in Norfolk. The Poor, in Yarmouth, and all along this coaft, live much upon fifh, which is, generally, very cheap.

The Poor are chiefly maintained in a poor-houfe, where they are employed in making nets for taking mackerel, and other fmall fea-fifh; a few fpin worfted. There are about 15 or 16 beds in each room; they have, moftly, feather beds; and are placed clofe together. Boys, girls, men, and women, have all feparate apartments. The married people have fingle rooms; but there are not many of that defcription. There are two rooms for the reception of the fick; which are well aired, but not diftinct from the main building. The poor-houfe has a good dining-room, and fuitable conveniences for cooking, &c. but the lodging-rooms and ftair-cafes do not feem to be well planned, or to be in the beft order. From the great number of people fleeping in a room, clofe together, many dif-agreeable circumftances muft frequently happen, befides the general injury arifing from thence on the fcore of health. At prefent, there are 65 men, 148 women, 40 boys, and 42 girls (in the whole, 295) in the houfe.

Table of Diet.

	Breakfaft.	Dinner.	Supper
Sunday,	Bread and butter	Suet pudding.	Bread and cheefe.
Monday,	Bread and treacle.	Boiled meat, dumplins, and vegetables.	Ditto.
Tuefday,	Bread and broth.	Peafe foup, and bread.	Ditto.
Wednefday,	Same as Sunday.	Milk, or gruel, and bread.	Ditto.
Thurfday,	Same as Monday.	Same as Monday.	Ditto.
Friday,	Same as Tuefday	Same as Tuefday.	Ditto.
Saturday,	Same as Wednefday.	Same as Wednefday.	Ditto.

At every meal, except when there is milk, broth or gruel, one pint of beer is allowed to every perfon, who wifhes to have it: rice, milk, wine, &c. are allowed to the fick: mutton and veal are alfo provided for the fick every Sunday.

Table

Table of Baptisms, Burials, Poor's Rates, Expenditure, &c.

Years	Bapt	Burials		Poor's Rates. £.	s.	d	Total Receipts in the year, exclusive of balances remaining in hand from former years. £.	s	d	Total Expenditure, exclusive of balances £.	s.	d.	Work-house. Earnings £.	s	d	Work-house. Provisions £	s	d
1774		—	end Ap 1774	2218	5	0	2500	11	7	2463	15	7	—	-	-	886	15	6
1775		235	—	1923	13	0	2295	1	8	2294	10	10	—		-	996	6	2½
1776		282	—	2168	19	0	2242	10	3	2109	4	1	—	-	-	1052	15	6½
1777		273	—	1910	12	7	2413	10	6½	2546	11	5	—	-	-	1050	16	1¾
1778		284	—	2458	10	5¼	2608	11	5	2636	9	5	—	-	-	1137	10	11½
1779		404	—	2677	13	1	2766	15	9½	2677	6	1	—	-	-	1300	15	0
1780		425	—	2707	16	0	2819	10	6½	2926	4	1	—	-	-	1359	7	3½
1781		313	—	2988	8	9¾	3090	15	0	3061	19	11	—	-	-	1540	7	0
1782		431	—	3361	4	6¾	3479	16	0¾	3537	0	1	—	-	-	1792	8	11
1783		366	—	3877	4	1½	4086	14	4	4001	7	4	—	-	-	2325	17	10½
1784		302	—	3915	10	1	4397	17	5	4356	8	5	188	9	4½	2332	17	3½
1785		307	—	4429	2	0	4880	16	0	4996	8	0	214	5	11	2615	19	3½
1786		368	—	4451	18	0	4916	4	1	4881	10	5	227	1	10½	2640	3	9
1787		302	—	4646	7	9	5131	6	3¾	5110	1	2	220	15	10¾	2572	17	2¾
1788		270	—	4628	5	10½	5218	4	3	5330	2	9	152	9	5½	2617	2	9
1789		350	—	3970	1	10½	4340	2	3	4311	18	2	124	12	4	1814	3	0
1790		336	—	2868	12	7	3526	13	7¾	3660	1	7	254	3	4	1733	9	1
1791		287	—	3191	6	6	3864	8	9½	3857	8	7	375	0	7	1726	16	6½
1792		339	—	3406	10	5	4121	2	10	3892	5	10	255	18	1	1761	2	11
1793		373	—	3086	2	3	3697	0	3	3832	2	7	229	10	0	1672	1	11½
1794		316	—	3428	14	0	4053	6	6	4078	14	0	148	6	9	1677	11	4
1795	The Rate, for the year ending in 1795, was 4s 9d in the pound on the net rent.			3500	0	0	No account.			No accounts.								

The births, from 1776 to 1781 inclusive, are 2423.

The accounts ending in 1795, are not inserted in the books, nor passed; but the Collector says, that the Rates amounted to nearly £3500, as stated above. The following are the particulars of one year's receipts and disbursements:

RECEIPTS		£	s	d	DISBURSEMENTS.		£	s	d
1794	By balance received -	110	18	7	1794	Provisions for work-house -	1677	11	4¾
	Rates - - -	3128	14	0		Removals, out-pensions, &c.	1117	6	9
	Benevolences - -	1	12	0		Cloathing - -	279	11	11
	Composition for bastardy -	176	1	0		Salaries - - -	205	0	0
	Rents - - -	2	17	0		Repairs, &c - -	193	19	6
	Money reimbursed, earnings, &c. - -	444	2	9		Fuel - -	117	14	6
						Special payments - -	486	10	2
						Balance - -	86	11	1¼
		£4164	5	4			£4164	5	4

June, 1795

NORTH-

NORTHAMPTONSHIRE.

BRIXWORTH.

THIS parish contains 3300 acres; 150 houses; and 800 inhabitants; who are graziers, agricultural labourers, and spinners. Excepting a few Methodists, they are all of the Established Church. 36 houses pay the window-tax; about 114 are exempted.

The prices of provisions are: beef, 5d. the pound; mutton, 5d.; veal, 4d.; bacon, 10d.; milk, 1d. the quart; potatoes, 3s. the bushel; butter, 9d. the lb.; and near 4 lb. of bread for 1s. Coals are 20d. the cwt.

Labourers, in winter, have generally 14d. a day, with a little beer, or bread and milk: in spring, and part of the summer, they have 8s. a week, with beer, &c.; and for the harvest month, they are paid 45s. Women earn from 4d. to 6d. a day, by spinning jersey; some years ago, they earned from 6d. to 10d. a day; but the wages are much lower than they were formerly.

Here are 6 ale-houses; and one Friendly Society, consisting of about 60 members; but they have not yet had their rules comfirmed.

The average rent of land is about 27s an acre. Farms are chiefly from £ 40. to £ 100. a year; some, however, are as high as £ 500. About ⅓ of the parish is arable land, and produces wheat, barley, oats, and turnips. There are no commons. In the year 1780, the common-fields, of which the parish almost entirely consisted, were enclosed. At that time, there were about 100 acres of ancient enclosure. Upon the enclosure taking place, land, (in the proportion of about one seventh,) was given in lieu of tithe. The land-tax amounts to £ 225. 2s. 4d., and is about 13d. in pound on the net rental: it is paid by the landlord.

The Poor have, mostly, an allowance at their own homes: at present, 34 poor people, most of whom have families, receive £ 3. 10s. 9d. weekly.

12 fa-

12 families have cafual relief, which laft week amounted to 12s. About a year ago, a fort of poor-houfe was eftablifhed, in which fome of the Poor refide, without the controul of a mafter: the parifh allows them neceffaries; there are 5, at prefent, in the houfe; they coft the parifh about 12s. a week. Exclufive of the Rates, about £60. were collected for the ufe of the Poor, laft winter. They likewife receive the rent of a fmall eftate, which amounts to £20.; and coals, to the value of £40. are annually bought, and then fold to them at reduced prices. The money thus expended by the parifh, is added to the annual difburfements; and receipts from the Poor, for the coals fold, added to the Affeffments.

A Table of Baptifms, Burials, Marriages, and Poor's Rates.

Years	Baptifms			Burials			Marriages
	Males	Females	Total	Males	Females	Total	
1683	12	7	19	6	6	12	8
1685	9	7	16	5	11	16	5
1690	9	12	21	5	4	9	4
1691	8	7	15	5	12	17	5
1692	10	17	27	6	9	15	6
1693	5	7	12	6	13	19	2
1694	8	11	19	6	5	11	1
1695	7	10	17	12	10	22	2
1696	10	8	18	13	12	25	1
1697	10	8	18	3	5	8	6
1698	13	15	28	7	7	14	5
1699	4	2	6	10	7	17	3
1700	8	17	25	12	15	27	8
1720	1	6	7	5	5	10	2
1740	14	9	23	7	10	17	3
1760	8	13	21	8	10	18	1
1775	8	4	12	6	9	15	5
1776	19	7	26	3	3	6	5
1777	7	5	12	10	3	13	4
1778	5	7	12	5	2	7	10
1779	12	17	29	9	10	19	5
1780	6	15	21	14	7	21	4
1781	19	14	33	8	12	20	5
1782	10	9	19	8	5	13	2
1783	14	9	23	8	7	15	4
1784	12	10	22	8	10	18	9
1785	13	14	27	8	4	12	3
1786	15	17	32	10	10	20	3
1787	10	12	22	3	10	13	4
1788	12	7	19	11	8	19	2
1789	9	7	16	14	11	25	3
1790	12	10	22	11	11	22	4
1791	8	8	16	6	5	11	4
1792	15	14	29	14	5	19	10
1793	10	13	23	12	9	21	10
1794	13	14	27	11	12	23	3
1795	—	—	—	—	—	—	

36) 734   36) 584   36) 160

Average 20 4/8   Average 16 11/18   4 16/36 Average.

In the years 1787 and 1790, it was not poffible to feparate the total receipts from the net affeffments; I have therefore given the former

The parifh books could not be found farther back than 1782: they are in a very irregular and confufed ftate.

From the rates, two guineas are paid annually to an infirmary The conftables receive about £16 a year: a few years ago they did not receive more from the rates than £4. or £5 a year

£121 6s Net expences for the poor; from the returns to parliament.

Net affeffments			Total difburfements			Rate per£. nominal	
£.	s.	d.	£	s.	d.	s.	d.
155	15	8¼	177	4	5	1	0
233	4	1¹	203	13	8¼	1	6
193	5	6¹	222	18	11	1	3
212	9	2¹	220	16	4	1	4
244	1	8	351	18	11	1	7
323	14	11	282	7	0	0	0
253	3	5	321	8	3½	1	8
312	15	0	324	13	8¼	2	0
305	14	8	301	18	5¼	0	0
391	1	1	350	18	1	2	6
234	11	9¾				1	6
273	11	11	The difburfements of thefe			1	9
332	4	5	years could not			2	2
312	16	0	be obtained			2	0

¹ Thefe fums tally with the Returns made to Parliament

Auguft, 1795.

KETTERING.

THE Poor in this town are very numerous; the Rates very high, and expected to increase: it is thought, that, next year, they will be 13s. or 14s. in the pound on the net rental. From the overseer's accounts, which are kept at the work-house, it appears, that 145 families received relief at home, last week: the usual allowance, to each individual, is 1s. a week. The above relief amounted, last week, to £11. 3s. Besides these families, 64 militia-men's wives receive £9. 13s. 10d a week.

Of about 600 houses, in Kettering, above 250 are exempted from the window-tax.

The trade of the town is, chiefly, in woollens. Tammies, lastings, calimancoes, and fine serges, are made here; but, since the war, business has considerably declined: for 1s. work, a spinner is now only paid 8d. A man, who could earn, in the woollen business, 14s a week, 3 years ago, cannot now get more than 7s. About 400 men from Kettering have entered into the militia; and nearly as many have enlisted in the army.

The lands about Kettering are chiefly open-field: they produce rich crops of corn. The people of the town seem averse to enclosures, which they think will raise the price of provisions, from these lands being all turned to pasture, when enclosed; as was the case in Leicestershire, which was formerly a great corn country, and is now, almost entirely, converted into pasture.

Near 100 persons, (men, women, and children,) are maintained in the work-house; which is under the care of a man, who is allowed 8s. a week, (besides his board,) and a matron, who is allowed 2s. a week, (besides her board.) The house can contain 200. Three, usually, sleep in a bed. The boys and girls are employed in spinning wool, which is afterwards made use of in a neighbouring manufactory of tammies, where this business has been carried on, some years; and was modified, on a new plan, about 3 years ago, when £300. were borrowed to carry the projected improvements into execution. The loss on the business amounts to about £40. a year, and is paid by the parish.

Table

Table of Diet in the Work-houfe.

	Breakfaft.	Dinner.	Supper.
Sunday,	Gruel, or milk-porridge.	Hot boiled beef, ½ pound, ½ pint of beer, ¼ lb of bread, and vegetables, to each perfon.	3 quarters of a lb. of bread, ⅓ of an ounce of cheefe, and ½ a pint of beer, to each perfon.
Monday,	Ditto.	½ oz. of cheefe, ¼ lb. of bread, ¼ pint of fmall beer, and milk-porridge, to each perfon.	Ditto.
Tuefday,	Ditto.	Same as Sunday.	Ditto.
Wednefday,	Ditto.	Baked fuet puddings: no bread; ¼ pint of beer.	Ditto.
Thurfday,	Ditto.	Boiled meat, &c. as Sunday.	Ditto.
Friday,	Ditto.	Same as Monday.	Ditto.
Saturday,	Ditto.	Sometimes baked fuet puddings; or bread and cheefe; or ftewed legs, and fhanks of beef.	Ditto.

The bread of the work-houfe is made at home. About 6 weeks ago, in confequence of the dearnefs of wheat, barley bread was fubftituted; which, in colour, much refembles the black bread of France: it's tafte, however, is fuperior. Beef, mutton, and veal, are ufed occafionally; and, as all the beer drank in the houfe is brewed at home, hogs are kept, and the Poor fometimes have falt pork for dinner. There is a fmall garden adjoining, which fupplies them with cabbages, and potatoes. An apothecary receives £ 40. a year, for attendance and medicines to all that receive relief; fractures and broken bones not included.

The Poor of Kettering were farmed from 1763 to 1769.

As money is wanted for the Poor, it is raifed by a levy of 1s. in the pound.

	£.	s.	d.
In 1776 a levy of 1s. in the pound, produced about -	131	0	0
The earnings of the Poor in the work-houfe, this year, were - - - -	57	18	3
1789 a levy of 1s. raifed - -	131	0	0
1792 the work in the houfe produced -	180	6	0¼
1794 a levy of 1s. raifed - -	153	0	0

3 Y 2   The

The man who farms the great tithes of Lord Sondes, (which amount to near £ 300. a year,) paid laſt year towards one levy, £ 11. 5s.; and in the whole year, above £120. for Poor's Rate. The whole of the under-mentioned ſums appear, from the books, to have been applied to the maintenance and relief of the Poor, but the conſtables' bills, amounting to £ 20. or £ 30. a year, are included in the pariſh expenditure. Neither church nor highway Rate are included.

Years.	Rate in the Pound.		Levies in the Year.			Total Poor's Rate.		
From	*s.*	*d.*	£.	*s.*	*d.*	£.	*s.*	*d.*
1774 to 1775	7	0	700	3	10			
			599	8	5	1299	12	3
1775 to 1776	8	6	899	19	9½			
			399	1	1	1299	0	10½
1776 to 1777	6	0	574	18	1¼			
			308	14	2½	883	12	3¾
1777 to 1778	9	0	749	3	8¼			
			651	3	6	1400	7	2¾
1778 to 1779	9	0	810	3	3½			
			640	16	8½	1451	0	0
1779 to 1780	7	0	1150	1	4¼	1150	1	4¼
1780 to 1781	8	0	599	8	1¾			
			568	0	0	1167	8	1¾
1781 to 1782	8	1	609	4	10¾			
			608	18	1	1218	2	11¾
1782 to 1783	8	0	1119	12	7¼	1119	12	7¼
1783 to 1784	8	0	430	10	7			
			570	8	2½			
			458	9	4	1459	8	1½

Years.

Years.	Rate in the Pound.		Levies in the Year.			Total Poor's Rate.		
From	s.	d.	£.	s.	d.	£.	s.	d.
1784 to 1785	10	0	559	1	9½			
			471	19	0½			
			629	4	10¼			
						1660	5	8¼
1785 to 1786	11	9	566	3	7½			
			432	14	0½			
			567	0	11			
						1565	18	7
1786 to 1787	9	0	101	9	10			
			657	10	10½			
			524	16	3½			
						1283	17	0
1787 to 1788	9	0	654	14	5			
			523	17	6¼			
						1178	11	11¼
1788 to 1789	9	0	655	13	1¾			
			526	1	0¾			
						1181	14	2½
1789 to 1790	9	0	649	13	11			
			692	1	1¼			
						1341	15	0¼
1790 to 1791	9	0	818	8	2½			
			875	2	2½			
						1693	10	5
1791 to 1792	9	0	794	11	3¼			
			820	11	1			
						1615	2	4¼
1792 to 1793	8	0	562	12	4¼			
			893	5	1			
						1455	17	5¼
1793 to 1794	11	4	559	0	0			
			136	8	8			
			593	11	3			
			1007	2	10½			
						2296	2	9½
1794 to 1795	10	8	1070	8	4¼			
			911	18	7¼			

About 120 more expected—2102 6 11½

There

There is a charity, in Kettering, of about £ 15. a year, for binding boys apprentices. A Friendly Society, or two, meet in Kettering : they allow 6s. a week, to members, when fick ; but if their illnefs lafts above a year, they are thrown on the parifh. The labouring people feem anxious that gentlemen fhould encourage the clubs, by becoming honorary members.

July, 1795.

NORTHAMPTON.

THE parifh of All Saints, in the town of Northampton, confifts almoft entirely of buildings. Of 792 houfes, 408 are rated to the window-tax ; 384 are exempted. The number in the whole town charged with the window tax is 680 ; but the whole number of exempted houfes could not be afceitained. It, probably, does not exceed 500. An account of the prefent population could not be obtained ; but the fubjoined tables of baptifms and burials indicate that it has been nearly ftationary for fome years.

In the parifh of All Saints, an account has been kept, ever fince the year 1735, of the ages at which all have died there; from which, and the accounts of the baptifms and burials in the other 3 parifhes, Doctor Price has formed very ufeful tables on the probabilities and values of lives, and the number of inhabitants in towns, whofe bills of mortality are given. The following particulars, which he has noticed, refpecting the population, &c. merit an infertion in this place.

In 1746, (he fays[1],) an account was taken of the number of houfes, and of inhabitants in the town. The number of houfes was found to be 1083 ; and the number of inhabitants, 5136. In the parifh of All Saints and St. Giles, the number of male and female heads of families, fervants, lodgers, and children, was particulaly diftinguifhed. The heads of families were 707 males, and 846 females. Children, males, 624; females, 759. Servants, males, 203 ; females, 280. Lodgers, males, 137;

---

[1] Obfervations on Reverfionary Payments, 5th edit. i. 349.

females,

females, 287. In St. Peter's, males, 99; females, 129 In St. Sepulchre's, adults, 638; children, 427. In the laſt pariſh the ſexes were not diſtinguiſhed.

The chriſtenings and burials in the whole town, for 40 years, from 1741 to 1780, have been as follows:

Chriſtened, $\left\{\begin{array}{l}\text{Males,} \quad 3218 \\ \text{Females, } 3108.\end{array}\right\}$ 6326 —Annual medium, 158.

Buried, $\left\{\begin{array}{l}\text{Males,} \quad 3757 \\ \text{Females, } 3823.\end{array}\right\}$ 7580.—Annual medium, 189$\frac{1}{2}$.

In the pariſh of All Saints, from 1735 to 1780, or 46 years:

Chriſtened, $\left\{\begin{array}{l}\text{Males,} \quad 2152. \\ \text{Females, } 2068.\end{array}\right\}$ 4220.—Annual medium, 91$\frac{3}{4}$.

Buried, $\left\{\begin{array}{l}\text{Males,} \quad 2377. \\ \text{Females, } 2312.\end{array}\right\}$ 4689.—Annual medium, 102.

Of theſe died, under 2 years of age	- -	1529
Between 2 and 5	- -	362
Between 5 and 10	- -	201
Between 10 and 20	- -	189
Between 20 and 30	- -	373
Between 30 and 40	- -	329
Between 40 and 50	- -	365
Between 50 and 60	- -	384
Between 60 and 70	- -	378
Between 70 and 80	- -	358
Between 80 and 90	- -	199
Between 90 and 100	- -	22
	Total -	4689

From theſe dates, it appears, that the proportion of the inhabitants to the annual deaths, (on the ſuppoſition that all who die in Northampton are born there,) is, as 28.83 to 1. I have ſubjoined tables of baptiſms and burials, from the year 1768 to the year 1794, incluſive, for the information of ſuch perſons as may be deſirous of forming ſimilar calculations.

Northampton

Northampton was formerly a very manufacturing town. A confiderable quantity of fhoes was made here, but that bufinefs is much declined : very little is done in the woollen manufacture at prefent. Theie are a few wool-combeis in the town, and jerfey-fpinneis ; and about 100 women and childien are employed in a cotton manufactory, wheie they earn from 2s. to 5s. a week; fhoemakers earn from 10s. to 15s. a week; wool-combers, from 9s. to 12s ; lace-makers, of which theie was once a great number in Northampton, can earn, by hard working, fiom 1d. to 1½d. an hour; but their wages have, of late years, much decreafed. Common labourers receive from 14d. to 18d. a day.

The prices of piovifions are : beef, from 4½d. to 5d. the lb ; mutton, 5d. ; veal, 4½d. ; bacon, 10d. ; butter, 10d. ; milk, 1d. the quart, fhoit meafuie ; potatoes, 4d. the gallon ; coals, 15d. the bufhel.

The land and window-taxes are collected in wards : towards the land-tax, the whole town of Noithampton raifes £830. 7s. 10d　In one of the waids, it is collected at 1s. 6d. in the pound ; in another, at 2s. 10½d. ; in the third, at 1s. 10d. ; in the fourth, at 1s. ; and in the fifth, at 2s. 2½d. : this laft-mentioned ward is in All Saints parifh. Thefe affeffments are of a very old date, and veiy iiregular : it is fuppofed, that, upon an average, they do not fall on more than ¾ of the net rental.

There are 29 inns, and 42 ale-houfes, in Noithampton : and 7 Friendly Societies; all of which have had their rules confirmed by the magiftrates.

The Poor of this parifh are partly maintained in a work-houfe, and partly at their own homes : the average number in the houfe is eftimated at 70 ; at prefent, there are only 40, (moftly old infirm people, lunatics and children,) in the houfe. The children are employed in fpinning jerfey ; and the old men in making fhoes : their earnings altogether amount to about £85. or £90. a year. The children are taught to read : the boys, at 12 or 14 years old, are bound apprentices, (generally to fome of the northern cotton manufacturers,) till they are 21 years of age ; and the girls, at a proper age, are fent to fervice. The work-houfe was not originally defigned for the purpofe to which it is now applied ; and is, therefore, (as might be expected,) in fome refpects, very inconvenient : it is, however, very clean and neat ; and the Poor, there, live comfortably, under the direction of a very proper perfon. The beds are filled with flocks and ftraw. The high walls, which encompafs the narrow courts, being capped with fpikes, give

the

the place a great refemblance to a prifon. In this work-houfe, as in moſt others, the earnings feem to be chiefly produced by children.

The following is the Weekly Bill of Fare.

	Breakfaſt.	Dinner.	Supper.
Sunday,	Milk-pottage.	Broth, beef, bread, and vegetables	Bread, cheefe, and beer.
Monday,	Broth and bread.	Bread, cheefe, and beer	Ditto.
Tuefday,	Same as Sunday.	Same as Sunday	Ditto.
Wednefday,	Same as Monday	Same as Monday	Ditto
Thurfday,	Milk-pottage	Broth, mutton, bread, and vegetables	Ditto
Friday,	Broth and bread	Same as Monday.	Ditto.
Saturday,	Milk pottage	Ditto.	Ditto

The victuals are not weighed, but I am told, the Poor have generally as much bread and meat as they can eat ; one pint of beer is allowed to each adult, at bread and cheefe meals ; children are allowed in proportion to their age.

137 Poor people, moſt of whom have families, receive, at prefent, £ 10. 6s. 6d. weekly, from the parifh. £ 2. 8s. 4d. are paid weekly to militia-men's families ; of which fum, 7s. are paid to the families of militiamen ferving for this parifh ; and 16s. 4d. are paid to ferjeants, drummers, fifers, &c. of the militia.

The baptifms and burials in the following table were taken from the annual bills of mortality, publifhed in Northampton : the marriages were extracted from the regifter of All Saints parifh.

Years	Parifhes.	Baptisms.				Burials.			Marriages.
		Males	Females	Total		Males	Females	Total	
1768.	All Saints	48	53	101		48	55	103	38
	St. Sepulchre	14	14	28		16	18	34	
	St. Giles	20	15	35		16	18	34	
	St Peter	4	2	6		6	9	15	
	At a Meeting Houfe	—	—	—		10	5	15	
1769.	All Saints	55	55	110		66	55	121	44
	St. Sepulchre	18	11	29		16	11	27	
	St. Giles	25	17	42		19	17	36	
	St. Peter	2	4	6		5	5	10	
	The Meeting Houfe	—	—	—		9	7	16	

Years.	Parishes.	Baptisms.			Burials.			Marriages.
		Males	Females	Total.	Males.	Females	Total	
1770.	All Saints	55	49	104	77	99	176	43
	St. Sepulchre	13	15	28	31	27	58	
	St. Giles	22	21	43	25	23	48	
	St. Peter	3	5	8	5	18	23	
	The Meeting Houfe	—	—	—	8	16	24	
1771.	All Saints	46	36	82	49	45	94	66.
	St. Sepulchre	18	11	29	11	23	34.	
	St. Giles	17	13	30	12	22	34	
	St. Peter	4	1	5	4	4	8	
	The Meeting Houfe	—	—	—	7	2	9	
1772.	All Saints	55	47	102	52	34	86	38
	St. Sepulchre	12	23	35	20	38	58	
	St. Giles	16	13	29	15	21	36	
	St. Peter	3	6	9	6	3	9	
	The Meeting Houfe	—	—	—	7	4	11	
1773.	All Saints	64	43	107	59	44	103	35
	St. Sepulchre	22	19	41	16	13	29	
	St. Giles	12	16	28	11	13	24	
	St. Peter	4	7	11	6	3	9	
	The Meeting Houfe	—	—	—	6	7	13	
1774.	All Saints	51	56	107	44	35	79	23
	St. Sepulchre	18	15	33	15	17	32	
	St. Giles	19	15	34	18	13	31	
	St. Peter	6	2	8	1	4	5	
	The Meeting Houfe	—	—	—	5	3	8	
1775.	All Saints	44	51	95	49	40	89	36
	St. Sepulchre	12	22	34	15	29	44	
	St. Giles	14	9	23	15	17	32	
	St. Peter	3	11	14	5	7	12	
	The Meeting Houfe	—	—	—	6	1	7	
1776.	All Saints	61	49	110	33	30	63	24
	St. Sepulchre	30	9	39	16	20	36	
	St. Giles	15	10	25	11	14	25	
	St. Peter	2	7	9	6	11	17	
	The Meeting Houfe	—	—	—	5	2	7	

Years.

Years	Parishes.	BAPTISMS.			BURIALS.			Marriages.
		Males	Females	Total.	Males.	Females	Total	
1777.	All Saints	62	54	116	75	77	152	32
	St. Sepulchre	15	25	40	34	32	66	
	St. Giles	12	18	30	28	18	46	
	St. Peter	3	5	8	7	11	18	
	The Meeting House	—	—	—	7	6	13	
1778.	All Saints	63	40	103	33	39	72	42
	St. Sepulchre	20	16	36	28	9	37	
	St. Giles	9	20	29	20	14	34	
	St Peter	4	1	5	5	4	9	
	The Meeting House	—	—	—	3	2	5	
1779.	All Saints	42	31	73	62	41	103	36
	St. Sepulchre	7	13	20	24	26	50	
	St. Giles	10	11	21	13	17	30	
	St. Peter	3	2	5	6	4	10	
	The Meeting House	—	—	—	—	8	8	
1780.	All Saints	32	51	83	62	64	126	44
	St. Sepulchre	12	23	35	13	16	29	
	St. Giles	12	16	28	19	14	33	
	St. Peter	3	3	6	5	4	9	
	The Meeting House	—	—	—	2	3	5	
1781.	All Saints	40	40	80	39	48	87	54
	St. Sepulchre	17	22	39	15	12	27	
	St. Giles	17	7	24	28	17	45	
	St. Peter	2	5	7	2	3	5	
	The Meeting House	—	—	—	2	5	7	
1782.	All Saints	52	41	93	57	32	89	44
	St. Sepulchre	12	14	26	18	20	38	
	St. Giles	7	15	22	15	24	39	
	St. Peter	5	1	6	3	6	9	
	The Meeting House	—	—	—	1	1	2	
1783.	All Saints	58	55	113	70	50	120	41
	St. Sepulchre	17	21	38	15	13	28	
	St. Giles	14	9	23	16	13	29	
	St. Peter	—	1	1	2	6	8	
	The Meeting House	—	—	—	3	8	11	

Years.	Parishes.	Baptisms.			Burials.			Marriages.
		Males	Females	Total	Males	Females	Total	
1784.	All Saints	42	39	81	98	79	177	40
	St. Sepulchre	18	9	27	34	28	62	
	St. Giles	13	15	28	32	23	55	
	St. Peter	2	2	4	5	7	12	
	The Meeting Houfe	—	—	—	5	4	9	
1785.	All Saints	54	54	108	53	43	96	34
	St. Sepulchre	12	25	37	10	15	25	
	St. Giles	19	17	36	17	17	34	
	St. Peter	3	3	6	5	9	14	
	The Meeting Houfe	—	—	—	3	3	6	
1786.	All Saints	49	53	102	65	52	117	42
	St. Sepulchre	13	15	28	20	22	42	
	St. Giles	11	13	24	21	20	41	
	St. Peter	1	—	1	3	5	8	
	The Meeting Houfe	—	—	—	2	11	13	
1787.	All Saints	50	36	86	46	48	94	35
	St. Sepulchre	11	12	23	11	10	21	
	St. Giles	22	18	40	14	24	38	
	St. Peter	2	3	5	3	5	8	
	The Meeting Houfe	—	—	—	3	4	7	
1788.	All Saints	52	55	107	73	65	138	27
	St. Sepulchre	20	11	31	23	25	48	
	St. Giles	14	17	31	24	38	62	
	St. Peter	2	3	5	6	4	10	
	The Meeting Houfe	—	—	—	5	3	8	
1789.	All Saints	36	44	80	37	42	79	36
	St. Sepulchre	13	18	31	14	18	32	
	St. Giles	22	19	41	24	19	43	
	St. Peter	3	2	5	3	5	8	
	The Meeting Houfe	—	—	—	3	7	10	
1790.	All Saints	61	47	108	49	33	82	45
	St. Sepulchre	11	18	29	15	16	31	
	St. Giles	14	12	26	8	18	26	
	St. Peter	2	3	5	4	4	8	
	The Meeting Houfe	—	—	—	6	4	10	

Years.

Years.	Parishes.	Baptisms.			Burials.			Marriages.
		Males	Females	Total	Males	Females	Total	
1791.	All Saints	45	39	84	44	47	91	42
	St. Sepulchre	18	13	31	8	18	26	
	St Giles	14	18	32	15	19	34	
	St. Peter	2	5	7	4	3	7	
	The Meeting House	—	—	—	Omitted.			
1792.	All Saints	56	59	115	49	50	99	35
	St. Sepulchre	12	18	30	23	49	72	
	St. Giles	25	20	45	27	24	51	
	St. Peter	3	4	7	4	5	9	
	The Meeting House	—	—	—	—	13 in all.		
1793.	All Saints	65	50	115	42	49	91	40
	St. Sepulchre	18	13	31	21	22	43	
	St. Giles	24	17	41	32	26	58	
	St. Peter	1	3	4	9	7	16	
	The Meeting House	—	—	—	Omitted.			
1794.	All Saints	36	53	89	27	35	62	55
	St. Sepulchre	12	11	23	11	19	30	
	St. Giles	30	24	54	20	20	40	
	St. Peter	1	—	1	2	1	3	
	The Meeting House	—	—	—	—	—	—	

In the above accounts, the chriftenings and burials at the different meeting houfes are omitted, except the burials at one meeting-houfe in St. Peter's parifh, which are inferted in moft years. The burials from the infirmary, and the other meeting-houfes, may amount to about 20 annually.

A Table of Receipts and Difburfements for the Poor in the Parifh of
ALL SAINTS, Northampton.

Years.	Total Receipts.			Total Difburfements.		
	£.	s.	d.	£.	s.	d.
1769	884	0	0	989	6	11
1773 to 1776	2474	7	6	2413	4	1¾
1776 to 1778	1533	7	7	1641	8	5
1779	1333	10	10½	1388	19	0
1780	No Settlement inferted			——	——	——

Years.	Total Receipts			Total Disbursements.		
	£.	s.	d.	£.	s.	d.
1781	1318	2	7¾	1230	9	1¼
1782	1000	5	6¼	997	9	5¼
1783	1560	8	10½	1443	17	9½
1784	1663	17	0	1538	5	3
1785	1644	16	5	1632	19	9
1786	1386	0	8¾	1335	6	2½
1787	1133	4	8	1033	18	0¼
1788	1251	4	4½	1153	8	5¼
1789	1333	19	10¾	1208	17	6
1790	1470	17	8¾	1368	14	5¼
1791	1461	3	0	1320	4	10¾
1792	1248	13	1½	1080	10	11¾
1793	1395	2	5¾	1301	3	1
1794	1767	8	7¼	1859	3	4¼
1795	1350	0	0	—	—	—

In the year ending 1794, the net assessments were nearly £1260 at 7s. in the pound.

Net rates, at 7s 6d. in the pound.

The net assessments in All Saints' parish could not be procured. The amount of the receipts includes the earnings of the Poor; money received for militia-men's families, belonging to other places; balance of last year's accounts; money received for bastardy, &c. The earnings of the Poor, it is said, for the 2 last years, have not exceeded £50 each year, as the sweepings of the streets, which formerly produced about £45. a year, have lately been taken from this parish.

The master of the work-house (who is also vestry-clerk,) has a salary of £36. a year. A doctor receives £12. 12s a year, for attending the Poor. 5 guineas are paid annually from the Rates to the county infirmary; and £90. have been paid, annually, for the last 3 years, out of the Rates, towards building a new gaol.

The parish of St. Giles, Northampton, contains, by estimation, 400 acres of land, which were enclosed, from the common fields, in 1779; and 205 separate houses.

I

Table

Table of Assessments and Parochial Expenditure in St Giles.

Years.	Net Money raised by Assess- ments for the Poor.			Total Expenditure.			Rate in the Pound.	
	£.	s.	d.	£.	s.	d.	s.	d.
1740	97	7	0	98	7	7	1	6
1760	149	13	5½	145	5	11	0	0
1775	269	10	0	276	5	7	2	6
1776	228	3	0	214	8	11	2	3
1777	174	5	0	189	9	10¾	1	9
1778	211	19	1	249	19	7	2	1
1779	262	0	0	249	12	11½	2	6
1780	279	0	0¾	304	10	1	2	6
1781	346	9	3	347	6	8	3	4
1782	360	15	3	349	2	7¼	3	6
1783	356	5	11	379	15	2¼	3	6
1784	369	14	6	379	4	0	3	6
1785	393	12	11	422	6	11¼	4	0
1786	402	1	1	403	9	4¼	4	0
1787	400	16	8	427	3	4½	4	0
1788	376	4	1	441	16	4	3	10
1789	447	5	2½	487	2	11½	4	6
1790	371	5	11	406	7	3	3	9
1791	435	4	3	466	10	0	4	3
1792	427	10	1	500	16	8	4	3
1793	444	3	6½	481	5	8	4	6
1794	526	7	3	566	10	1¼	5	3
1795	600	0	0	Not settled.			6	2

These assessments are said to be at $\frac{3}{4}$ of the rack rent; but it may be doubted whether more than $\frac{2}{3}$ of the net rent are rated.

Out of the Poor's Rates, £51. were paid to the constables last year; formerly the constables only received about £18. a year. £40. a year have been paid out of the Rates, for the last 3 years, towards building the new gaol. In 1791, this parish had a law-suit respecting some land, which cost £300. of which £80. still remain unpaid; the rest was paid out of the Rates.

Of the Poor, 39 out-pensioners receive £3. 11s. 7d. a week; £1. 10s. a week, is also paid to militia-men's families. There are 8 Paupers at pre-

sent

fent in the work houfe: they are employed in fpinning jerfey, &c. and earn, on an average, about £20. a year. Their bill of fare is fimilar to that obferved in the work-houfe in All Saints parifh. The average rent of land in this parifh is about 40s. an acre.

Auguft, 1795.

R O D E.

THIS parifh contains, by eftimation, 1300 acres; and about 370 inhabitants, who are chiefly agriculturifts. A few women and children are employed in lace-making. There is here a fect of Anabaptifts: it is conjectured, that about ⅙ of the parifh is of that perfuafion; the remainder is of the Eftablifhed Church. 21 houfes pay the window tax; and 54 are exempted. There are 3 ale-houfes in the parifh.

The prices of provifions are the fame as at Northampton. The wages of labour are various; but, generally, in the winter and fpring, about 1s. a day, with breakfaft and beer; in hay harveft, 10s. 6d. the week, with beer; in corn harveft, 40s. the month, and board; and if the harveft exceeds the month, then the wages are 1s. a day, and board, till it is concluded: lace-workers earn from 6d to 1s. or 1s. 2d. the day; but generally 8d. or 10d. a day. Women here are never employed in reaping; and it is even very rare to fee them milk a cow. A fervant-maid, of 20 years of age, has about £3. a year, in a farmer's fervice; a man of the fame age has £6. to £9. a year; mafons, 2s. a day, with beer; joiners, from 12s. to 15s. the week; a common carpenter, 1s. a day, and board.

The greateft part of this parifh belongs to the Duke of Grafton, and is let at 8s. an acre; the average rent of the whole parifh is about 10s. 6d. or 12s. an acre. Farms are from £12. to £90. a year, but chiefly about £30. or £40. a year. The parifh, (excepting about 160 acres,) is common field; which is divided into three parts, one of which is fallow; another, wheat or barley; and the third, beans or peafe: this is the conftant rotation of crops. Tithes are taken in kind. The land-tax is £70. 10s. 5d. and is about 1s. 11d. in the pound. There is a fmall common of about 100 acres, on which this and two other parifhes intercommon.

The

The Poor receive an allowance at home : the following lift exhibits their number, ages, and weekly pay :

			Age	Weekly Pay.
				s. d.
1	A fpinfter, who has been a lace-maker ;	- -	70	2 0
2	Ditto, - do.	- -	60	1 6
3	A labourer's widow, and 3 children ;	- -	34	5 0
4	A fpinfter, infane ;	- - -	38	2 6
5	An old farmer, and his wife ; they are about	-	80	3 0
6	A labourer's widow, and 2 children ;	- -	30	2 0
7	An inn-keeper's widow ;	- -	70	2 2
8	A farmer's widow ;	- - -	60	1 6
9	A labourer's widow ;	- -	66	2 0
10	A labourer, and wife ;	- -	60	4 0
11	A fpinfter, was a lace-maker ; now almoft blind ;		70	2 6
12	An innkeeper's widow ;	- -	70	2 0
13	A labourer, and his wife ;	- -	70	1 6

£1 11 8

To families of militia-men, ferving for this parifh, weekly   0 4 8

Total - £1 16 4

Befides the above regular penfioners, feveral have occafional relief.

Table of Poor's Rates and Difburfements in the Parifh of RODE.

Years.	Net Affeffments.			Total Difburfements		
	£.	s.	d.	£.	s.	d.
1769	67	16	2	68	1	9¼
1772	82	13	4	85	1	6½
1773	86	17	0	82	16	5¼
1775	86	14	3½	84	6	8
1776	76	3	4	81	0	4
1777	90	18	9	88	0	11
1779	127	6	1¼	125	6	5¼
1780	76	4	0	75	2	11
1781	95	19	4½	98	17	1
1782	91	14	5	88	10	11
1783	118	4	6½	116	6	6

Years.	Net Affeffments.			Total Difburfements.			Rate In the Pound.	
	£.	s.	d.	£	s	d.	s.	d.
1784	109	1	7¼	122	14	11¼	3	3
1785	—	—	—	131	1	11	—	—
1786	121	10	5½	127	0	11½	3	6
1787	110	4	8¾	110	17	5¼	3	3
1788	101	2	9½	93	12	2	3	0
1789	122	14	6½	121	0	9	3	6
1791	81	9	9¼	90	13	6¾	2	3
1793	96	3	4	97	6	6	2	9
1794	82	10	0	71	0	11	2	3
1795	123	17	3	119	10	6	3	6

The years, of which the accounts do not appear above, are either erafed, or torn out of the book.

The following is a ftatement of the earnings and expences of a labourer's family in this parifh :

Richard Walker, 36 years of age, has a wife and 5 children, viz a girl, 9 years old ; a boy, 7 years ; another boy, 6 years ; another, 3 years ; and another child, 1 year old.

The man, in the winter and fpring, earns about 1s. a day, and his breakfaft and beer, when he works by the day ; when he works by the piece, 1s. 6d. or 2s. a day ; in hay time, 10s. 6d. a week, with beer ; harveft, 40s. a month.

EARNINGS.

	£.	s.	d.
He eftimates his earnings, annually, at - - -	20	0	0
He rings the church-bell twice a day, for which he receives annually - - - - - -	1	6	0
He earns a little as a barber ; and digs graves at the diffenting chapel : his earnings, annually, by thefe employments, are eftimated at - - - - -	1	0	0
His wife is a lace-worker, and, befides taking care of the family, earns about 6d. a week ; annually - -	1	6	0
Three of his children are at the lace-fchool, and, befides paying for the thread and fchooling, earn about 6d. a week	1	6	0
His family, by gleaning in harveft, collect corn, worth about	1	10	0

Total receipts - £26 8 0

EXPENCES.

	£.	s.	d.
The bread ufed in this family cofts, at prefent, 7s. or 8s. a week; it formerly coft 5s. - - -	13	0	0
Butcher's meat, now 2s. 6d.; was, till lately, about 2s. a week	5	4	0
Beer, about a gallon a week, at 4d. - - -	0	17	4
Butter, ½ pound a week, at 8d. the lb. - - -	0	17	4
Tea and fugar, about 11d. a week - - -	2	7	6
Cheefe, potatoes, and milk, (of which very little is ufed,) annually	1	10	0
Soap, candles, &c. annually, coft about - -	0	15	0
Shoes, 25s.; fhirts, about 12s.; other cloaths, about 10s. -	2	7	0
Houfe-rent (the houfe is the Duke of Grafton's) -	0	8	0
Wife's lyings-in (fay once in two years) coft annually about	0	10	0

	£.	s.	d.
Total expence - -	27	16	2
Total earnings - -	26	8	0
Deficiency of earnings -	1	8	2

Notwithftanding every thing is taken at the laft year's prices, here is a deficiency of £1. 8s. 2d. This man does not receive any parochial affiftance; but his neighbours, who know him to be induftrious and careful, are very kind to him, and give him old cloaths, &c. He has alfo, fometimes, been affifted by his landlord. His expence for fuel, (wood,) which, he fays, cofts him about 50s. a year, is not included in the above ftatement; fo that his deficiencies muft be £3. 18s : he has the character of an honeft, induftrious man.

The Poor make a great deal by gleaning here; feveral families will gather as much wheat as will ferve them for bread the whole year; and as many beans as will keep a pig. Agriculture, here, is in a wretched ftate, from the land being in common-fields: the farmers are often at a great lofs for hay: their cows, in the fummer, muft be herded on the head-lands in the day-time, and confined in the night: their crops of corn are fcanty; and their land, by conftant tillage, becomes almoft exhaufted. In fhort, they are of opinion, that were their lands enclofed, and their rents doubled, they fhould be confiderable gainers: it is faid, however, that fome great proprietors object to the meafure.

4 A 2

The

The produce of the Rates is all applied to the ufe of the Poor, with the exception of 2 guineas a year, which are paid to the county infirmary. Moft of the parifhes in this neighbourhood confift of open-field. In fome, where the land is old enclofure, the Rates are from 10d. to 1s. 6d. in the pound.

A donation of £4. a year is annually diftiibuted to the Poor of this parifh. The affeffments are faid to be at full rental.

September, 1795.

YARDLY-GOBEN.

THE townfhip of Yaidly-Goben is fituated in the parifh of Perry: it contains, by eftimation, 1100 acres; and about 500 inhabitants, who are agriculturifts, and lace-makers.: they are chiefly of the Church of England; feveral Diffenters, however, of the fect of Independents, refide in this townfhip. 24 houfes pay the window tax; and 79 are exempted.

The prices of provifions are: beef, 4d. and 4½d. the pound; mutton, 5d.; bacon, 9d.; and butter, 10d. and 11d.; of milk veiy little is fold; potatoes, 2s. 6d. the bufhel: coals are 1s. 11d. the cwt.

Common labourers' wages are from 1s. to 1s. 6d. a day in winter, without diet; and nearly the fame in fpring: in hay time, 20d. or 2s. a day: in harveft, 40s. or 44s. a month, with board; carpenters are paid 2s. a day; mafons, 2s. a day. Wages have rifen very confiderably this year. Much work is done by the piece; a mode of working, which labourers here generally prefer. In the winter, fometimes 9 or 10 labourers, out of employ, go round from houfe to houfe for work; the rule is, that every perfon whofe rent is £20. and upwards, fhall, in his turn, employ a man one day, and give him 1s. but no victuals. Women do very little out of doors, except during the harveft, when they go out to glean in great numbers. Laceworkers earn from 6d. to 14d. a day; upon the average, about 8d. Here are 2 ale-houfes.

The rent of land is from 18s. to 20s. an acre. Farms are from £40. to £200. a year, chiefly about £100 or £140. Wheat, barley, oats, and

beans,

beans, are principally cultivated. Nearly the whole of this townſhip was encloſed 19 years ago, when one ſeventh of the land was allotted to the church in lieu of tithe. The land-tax amounts to £136. 18s. and is 2s 5½d. in the pound. The inhabitants of this townſhip, and of ſeveral other adjoining pariſhes, claim a right of depaſturing cattle on Wickle-wood Foreſt, a tract of about 7 or 8000 acres.

In this townſhip is a ſort of work-houſe, in which there are, at preſent, only 2 perſons. The manager of the houſe finds ſuch Poor, as the town-ſhip may ſend him, in victuals, and fuel, for which he receives 3s. a week for each perſon. The townſhip provides cloaths, beds, and other furniture. 28 poor People, moſt of whom have families, receive, weekly, at preſent, £2. 17s. 7d. ; among them are 13 widows : a few perſons have occaſional relief.

Table of Poor's Rates.

Years.	Net Aſſeſſments.				Net Expences for the Poor			
	£.	s.	d.		£	s.	d.	
1776	—	—	—		109	6	9	from the Returns to Parliament.
1783	169	5	11	From the Returns to Parliament.				
1784	165	11	9		Total Diſburſements			Rate at full Rental nearly
1785	169	2	10		£.	s.	d.	s. d.
1788	216	0	6		216	9	10	4 0
1789	229	10	0		225	19	9½	4 3
1790	220	1	0		203	13	9	4 1
1791	230	8	6		232	15	4	4 3
1792	202	10	7		213	3	4	3 9
1793	216	0	0		243	10	8½	4 0
1794	243	0	0		256	0	7	4 6
1795	216	0	0		217	3	11	4 0

About £10. or £12. are paid annually from the Poor's Rate to the conſtable : the remainder is expended on the Poor.

It is ſaid that the Poor's Rates, between 30 and 40 years ago, were about £30. a year. A great number of women are lace-workers, and generally, in their younger days, earn a good livelihood ; but, being a buſineſs which requires a good ſight, it, at length, much affects the eyes ; ſo that when they grow old, not being accuſtomed to any other work, they often be-come neceſſitous. Many people of this pariſh attribute the riſe in the Rates to the encloſure of the common-fields ; " becauſe, (ſay they,) before " the encloſure took place, farms were from £10. to £40. a year, and any
" perſon

" person could then rent a small tenement: but now, the parish being
" moftly thrown into large farms, it requires a very confiderable capital
" to ftock one. This circumftance reduces numbers to the neceffity of
" living in a ftate of fervile dependence on the large farmers ; and, as they
" have no profpect to which their hopes can reafonably look forward, their
" induftry is checked ; economy is deprived of its greateft ftimulative ;
" and their only thought is to enjoy the prefent moment."

It was thought unneceffary to make any extracts from the parifh regifters, as the births and burials from two other townfhips are intermixed ;
and one third of the inhabitants of Yardly-Goben are Diffenters.

September, 1795.

NORTHUMBERLAND.

NEWCASTLE.

NEWCASTLE contains, exclufive of the out-townfhips, the four
parifhes of All Saints, St. Andrew, St. John, and St. Nicholas. Very
little land, unbuilt on, belongs to either of the parifhes ; fo that the
Poor's Rates are chiefly raifed from houfes. The number of affeffed
houfes, (according to the proportion of 68 feamen for one houfe, which
was generally adhered to, in raifing men for the Navy, laft year,) is,

in All Saints'	1224
St. Andrew's	476
St. John's	476
St. Nicholas's	340
	2516 ;

The number of exempted houfes muft be confiderably greater.

Every occupation, derived from, or connected with, the coal trade, or
mines, is here carried on with great vigour. There are glafs-works, pot-

o   teries,

teries, founderies, forges, a fail-cloth and other manufactories, in and near Newcaftle. It is alfo noted for it's grind-ftones, of which great quantities are exported   The inhabitants confift of failors, coal-mineis, keelmen, feamen, fhopkeepers of various defcriptions, merchants, and gentlemen of independent fortune.

Pit-men earn from 1s. 6d. to 3s. 6d. a day; on an average, about 16s. a week; befides which, they are allowed rye from their mafters, at 4s. the bufhel. Notwithftanding thefe high wages, they are feldom richer than their neighbours. They ufe a great deal of butcher's meat, during the three or four firft days of the week; but, towards the clofe of it, as their earnings of the preceding week become nearly exhaufted, they are generally obliged to live more frugally and abftemioufly. All accounts ftate, that few of them ever contrive to be beforehand in the world. Keelmen, (of whom 6000 or 7000 are conftantly employed in navigating keels with coal, from the collieries on the Tyne to Shields,) are paid from 15s. to 20s. a week. Sailors, in time of war, are paid, from 6 to 11 guineas, for a voyage to London, which is often performed in a month, or lefs. Common labourers earn 9s. a week.

The price of butcher's meat is from 4d. to 6d. the lb.; of butter, from 14d. to 15d. for 21 oz. The price of other articles is mentioned in the account of North and South Shields.

The land-tax is faid to be very low: on this fubject, however, no accurate account could be obtained. This is, in many places, a very tender fubject; and many, (in other refpects enlightened) perfons have refufed to give any information refpecting it.

In the vicinity of Newcaftle, land lets from 15s. to £3. an acre. There is a common of 1000 acres belonging to the corporation; from which, 100 have been enclofed; which, after being cultivated for 7 years, are to be laid down: 100 acres more are then to be reclaimed in the fame manner; and fo on, till the whole is improved.

In May 1795, at the general licenfing, 196 ale-houfes were licenfed: fince that period, three or four have been difcontinued.

Each parifh maintains it's own Poor feparately. In All Saints, 150 Paupers, (of whom 55 are children, under 12 years of age,) are relieved in a poor-houfe. The children are chiefly employed in a pin-manufactory, and earn 1s. each, a week: the others, (who are moftly old people, or proftitutes,)

proftitutes,) pick oakum, and earn, weekly, 4d. or 5d. a head. Of out-penfioners, 231 families receive £ 59. 7s. a month; 65 families of im-preffed feamen, £ 23. 11s. 3d. a month; and 64 families of militia-men, £ 35. 3s a month.

The following is the Bill of Fare, at prefent obferved in the Poor-houfe in ALL SAINTS Parifh.

	Breakfaft.	Dinner.	Supper
Sunday,	Hafty pudding, and milk, or beer: the allowance is 1 pint of beer, or ¾ of a pint of milk, to each perfon.	Beef, peafe pudding, broth, and bread.	Broth, and 7 oz. of bread
Monday,	Ditto.	Peafe-foup, and 7 oz of bread, to each perfon.	Milk and water, and oat-meal boiled.
Tuefday,	Ditto.	Barley-milk : no bread.	Milk, or beer, and bread.
Wednefday,	Ditto.	Same as Sunday.	Same as Sunday
Thurfday,	Ditto	Same as Monday.	Same as Monday.
Friday,	Ditto.	Same as Sunday.	Same as Sunday.
Saturday,	Ditto.	Same as Tuefday.	Same as Tuefday.

The allowance of bread was lately reduced from 10 oz. to 7 oz. each perfon. About 23 ftone of butcher's meat are ufed, weekly, in this houfe.

In St. Andrew's parifh, there are 27 perfons in the poor-houfe; and 131 weekly penfioners.

34 Paupers are maintained in the poor-houfe of St. John's: of out-poor there are 39 families, exclufive of 15 families of militia-men.

In the parifh of St. Nicholas, 56 perfons are, at prefent, in the poor-houfe; and are principally employed in picking oakum. Their earnings are very fmall.

The houfe is remarkably clean: each Pauper cofts about 2s. 6d. a week.

The following is the ufual Courfe of Diet in the Poor-houfe in ST. NICHOLAS' Parifh:

	Breakfaft.	Dinner.	Supper.
Sunday,	Hafty-pudding, and milk.	Beef and potatoes.	Bread and broth.
Monday,	Ditto.	White bread and milk.	Milk, boiled with oat-meal.
Tuefday,	Ditto.	Cold milk and bread.	Ditto.
Wednefday,	Ditto.	Same as Sunday.	Same as Sunday.
Thurfday,	Ditto.	Same as Monday.	Same as Monday.
Friday,	Ditto.	Cold milk and bread.	Ditto.
Saturday,	Ditto.	Same as Monday.	Ditto.

7

The

The weekly confumption of rye-bread, (exclufive of wheaten bread to boil with the milk,) is 3 cwt.

There are 148 families of out-penfioners belonging to this parifh ; but very little information concerning them, could be gained from the parifh-officers.

As each parifh is divided into 4 quarters, and the accounts of each quarter are fettled once a month ; it was neceffary to fearch for 48 different fums, in order to afcertain the amount of the Poor's Rates, for one year, in a fingle parifh. I have, therefore, only given the amount of two years affeffments in All Saints' parifh, collected in this manner ; from whence, on referring to the column of pound rates, the amount of affeffments in the fubfequent years may be tolerably well afcertained.

ALL SAINTS.

Years.			Affeffments.				Rate in the Pound.		
			£.	s.	d.		s.	d.	
1767 to Eafter	1768		370	0	0	– –	1	0	This is laid on
1768 ———	1769		370	0	0	–	1	0	about 4-5ths
1771 ———	1772		——	—	—	– –	1	6	of the net rental.
1772 ———	1773		——	—	—	– –	1	6	
1773 ———	1774		——	—	—		1	6	
1776 ———	1777		698	1	1	Expences for the Poor from the Returns to	0	0	
1782 ———	1783		——	—	——	Parliament.	4	0	
1783 ———	1784		1814	0	6	Affeffments from the	4	0	
1784 ———	1785		1572	6	9	Returns to Parliament.	0	0	
1785 ———	1786		1740	1	0		4	0	
1793 ———	1794		——	—	—	– –	4	4	
1794 ———	1795		——	—	—	– –	5	2	
1795 to Eafter	1796		——	—	—	– –	6	0	

Four-fifths of the parifh rental amount to £ 11,268. : a fix-penny Rate comes to £ 281. 14s. ; but, owing to the deductions for empty houfes, which amounted to £ 19. 6s. 6d., the money collected was £ 262. 7s. 6d. This fum muft fluctuate according to circumftances.

In St. Andrew's parifh, the Poor's Rates, from 1794 to 1796, varied from 2s. 6d. to 3s. 6d. in the pound. The rental of the parifh, in 1794, was £ 5329.; in 1795, £ 5533.; in 1796, £ 5573.

In St. John's parifh, the Pooi's Rates are 3s. 3d. in the pound, and produce near £ 1200. About 4 yeais ago, the Rates were only 1s. 9d. in the pound. They are not levied on the full iental; but the propoition of rent affeffed could not be afceitained. I fuppofe, that the Rate may be laid, as in All Saints' paiifh, on four-fifths of the net rental.

In St Nicholas's parifh the Rates are about 4s. 4d. in the pound on four-fifths of the net rental. A fixpenny Rate amounts to £ 160. 18s. 4d. In 1793, the Rates were 3s 4d. in the pound.

The great iife of the Rates, in the above three parifhes, may be eftima- ted from the Returns made to Parliament, in 1776, and 1786. According to them,

		St Andiew's			St John's			St Nicholas's		
		£	s	d	£	s	d.	£.	s.	d.
The Expences for the Poor, in 17;6 amounted to		321	0	0	190	12	1	529	0	0
The money raifed by affeffment, in 1783 ———		542	1	4	574	14	11	640	17	0
Ditto - - - 1784 ———		591	15	3	483	11	1	660	0	0
Ditto - - - 1785 ———		638	19	8	600	4	0	864	4	7

The parifh of GATESHEAD, although fituated in the county of Durham, may be confidered as part of Newcaftle, from which it is only feparated by the Tyne

In 1773, the Poor of this parifh, exclufive of cafual Poor, were farmed for £ 250. The cafual Poor, it is fuppofed, coft about £ 100 more. At prefent, the Rates are 3s. in the pound on the full rental, and produce, annually, about £ 1500. According to the Returns made to Parliament, the

				£.	s.	d.
Expences for the Poor,	in	1776	were	350	13	10
Money raifed by affeffment,	in	1783	—	757	6	7
Ditto - - -		1784	—	684	13	0
Ditto - - -		1785	—	754	6	7

The contractor is allowed 2s. a head, for each Pauper in the poor-houfe, and their earnings. The parifh have, in addition, given him, this year, a gratuity of £ 10.; but it is fuppofed that he will be a confideiable lofer by his bargain.

The

The poor-houfe was formerly an alms-houfe: it is neither very convenient, nor very clean. The beds are chiefly of ftraw: there are 6 or 8 in each room.

The following is the Bill of Fare obferved in the Poor-houfe:

	Breakfaft	Dinner.	Supper
Sunday,	Bread, and frumenty.	Beef, and peafe pudding; or mutton, and potatoes	Bread and broth.
Monday,	Bread, and broth.	Wheaten bread, and milk, boiled	Bread, and milk-pottage
Tuefday,	Crowdie, and milk.	Rye bread, and cold milk.	Frumenty, and bread.
Wednefday,	Same as Sunday	Same as Sunday	Same as Sunday.
Thurfday,	Same as Monday.	Same as Monday.	Same as Monday.
Friday,	Same as Tuefday.	White-peafe-pottage, and bread.	Milk-pottage, and bread
Saturday,	Same as Tuefday.	Same as Monday.	Frumenty, and bread.

There are, at prefent, 48 Paupers in the houfe. 261 poor families, eftimated to contain 2½ perfons each, (exclufive of militia-men's families,) receive weekly penfions.

There are about 26 Friendly Societies in Newcaftle; the average number of members, in each, is fuppofed to be about 100. 13 have had their rules confirmed by the magiftrates. The following are the rules of the Society of Flaxdreffers, eftablifhed in 1772:—thofe of other Societies are very fimilar.

1, No flaxdreffer fhall be admitted into this Society that is above the age of thirty-four years, and fhall pay, at entrance, two fhillings and fix-pence, to be put into the fund, and three-pence to fpend in the meeting-hours. No perfon, of any other trade or calling, fhall be admitted above the age of twenty-eight years, and fhall pay at entrance five fhillings, to be put into the fund, and three-pence to fpend; and no more than thirty of any other trade or calling to be in the Society at any one time[1]. Any perfon who offers himfelf as a member, and is fufpected to be above the age fpecified, muft produce a certificate of his age before he can be admitted.

Every perfon entering this Society fhall bear a fair character, and, at that time, be free from all infirmities and deformity of body.

No apprentice to enter this Society on any account, nor any perfon that cannot earn feven fhillings per week by his proper employment;

[1] Not very grammatical: I do not alter the language

and,

and, if any belonging to this Society enter into any other, he fhall be excluded this. Each member fhall fign his name to the articles on being admitted, and will be prefented with a book of the articles, at the fame time, for his own perufal. Any member that introduces any perfon to enter, contrary to the tenor of this article, fhall be fined five fhillings, to be paid the firft fix weeks meeting after fuch default

2, Regulations of the meeting; held every fix weeks: fine for non-attendance, 2d.: fix weeks' contribution money, 1s. 6d.; of which 3d. to be fpent

3, Power in the ftewards to call a bye or occafional meeting, if neceffary.

4, New members may be entered at the fix weeks, or bye-meetings.

5, There fhall be two half-yearly meetings for choofing the ftewards and affiftants, balancing the books, &c viz. the 29th of May, and the 25th of November, when the two ftewards and two affiftants fhall be chofen, according to their feniority on the roll, and to continue for half a year, and then the two affiftants fhall take the office or place of ftewards, and other two affiftants fhall be chofe next in feniority: and he that refufes to ftand fteward, fhall be fined two fhillings and fix-pence; and for refufing to ftand affiftant, five fhillings. The meeting hours, on the 29th of May, to begin at two o'clock in the afternoon, and continue two hours. The roll fhall be called by the ftewards at the appointed hour, and each member refiding within one mile of Newcaftle, fhall (on being called) anfwer to his name, and fpend three-pence with the new ftewards, or be fined two-pence; and for not coming within the meeting-hours, fix-pence; and three-pence for each abfent member fhall be taken out of the box, to fpend with the new ftewards.

The meeting on the 25th of November to be at one o'clock in the afternoon, when a dinner fhall be provided at the houfe where the Society's box is kept: each member prefent paying one fhilling for dinner, and one fhilling for drink; and each abfent member paying one fhilling for dinner, and three-pence to fpend with the new ftewards.

After dinner is over, the ftewards fhall call the roll, and collect in the cafh for dinner and drink; alfo, fee the books fettled, the new ftewards and affiftants chofe, and the Society's cafh counted over and delivered

delivered to the new ftewards; they fhall likewife fee the reckoning after dinner fettled and paid off, &c. Every member refiding
within feven miles of this town, whofe dinner and drink money, one
fhilling and three-pence, is not paid on calling the roll, fhall be fined
two-pence; and if it is not paid before four o'clock, fix pence: and
one fhilling and three-pence for each abfent member fhall be taken out
of the box, to pay for their dinners and drink.

6, The ftewards and affiftants, or their fubftitutes, fhall attend every
meeting at the hours appointed, or be fined one fhilling.

Likewife, if any member falls fick or lame, and fends to acquaint
the ftewards that he is not able to follow his trade or calling, one, or
both of them, fhall vifit him the fame day he acquaints them therewith, and twice a week, at leaft, during fuch time as he continues
indifpofed, provided the fick member refides within one mile of Newcaftle, or for each negled fhall be fined fix-pence.

They fhall likewife pay to every fick member his weekly fick money
(according to the 7th article) the day it is due, or the fteward that has
the payment of the money fhall be fined one fhilling; and if he negled or withhold payment of fick money for the fpace of twenty-four
hours after the day it is due, he fhall be fined five fhillings.

They fhall likewife pay to the heir or affign of a deceafed member
the fum of forty-three fhillings, to defray his funeral expences; and
if the member, deceafed, had paid his contribution money and fines
for one year, the heir apparent is entitled to a legacy of three pounds:
if the deceafed was a member two years, the heir apparent is entitled
to a legacy of five pounds: laftly, if the deceafed was a member
three years, the heirs or affigns are entitled to a legacy of feven pounds,
over and above the faid forty-three fhillings allowed for the funeral of
a member.

The fum of three pounds fhall be paid for the funeral of a member's wife or widow, if the member had paid contribution above one
year: but this part of the article is not meant to extend to the widows
of deceafed members before the date of thefe articles; fuch widows
are entitled only to the fums expreffed in the articles that were in
force at the time of their hufbands' deaths.

The

The funeral-money and legacies to be paid by the stewards within twenty-four hours after it is legally demanded; the steward or stewards, acting to the contrary, shall be fined five shillings. The stewards to collect, the first six weeks meeting after every funeral, six-pence from each member, to be put into the fund. No member shall be entitled to any benefit from this Society, (his own funeral-expences excepted,) nor bear any office, until he has paid his contribution and fines for one whole year.

When a member dies, or the wife or widow of a deceased member, the stewards and assistants shall provide two decent members for bidders, who shall deliver the mourning, the day before the funeral, to four bearers, eight mourners, and two mutes, all members of this Society; the mutes to be the two last entered members. The bearers and mourners to be chosen out of the members residing in town, by the heir apparent of the deceased member, wife, or widow; or if the heir aforesaid make no choice, the stewards must do it. And if any member refuse to come, or send a substitute when so chosen, or misbehave when at the funeral, he shall be fined sixpence.

The bidders to be paid two shillings each, and the bearers, mourners, and mutes, six-pence each, for loss of time at the funeral, the money to be taken out of the box.

The stewards' assistants, or their substitutes, shall attend at every funeral, to see proper regulations.

They shall likewise see the mourning properly taken care of, after each funeral; and if any of the mourning be lost, they shall make such loss good.

They shall keep just and regular accounts in every thing that concerns the box, or be fined two shillings and six-pence.

For non appearance at a funeral, shall be fined half a crown.

The stewards to be allowed from the fund two shillings each every half year, for defraying their expences; and the assistants, one shilling each.

7, Every member that is not able to follow or work at his trade or calling, on giving notice to the stewards, shall be paid every week (see article 6th) five shillings, during the space of twenty-six weeks; but

but if he continue any longer, and be not able to follow his bufinefs, he then fhall only receive three fhillings per week, whilft fuch time as he recovers, or to the time of his death; and thofe members that receive only three fhillings per week, may endeavour to get what they legally can, provided it do not interfere with their trade or calling; but if any member be known to work at his trade, and at the fame time receives the benefit of the Society, he fhall be excluded.

Any country member, that happens to fall fick or lame, muft fend a certificate of his indifpofition to the ftewards, figned by the minifter of the parifh, an overfeer of the Poor, a church-warden, and the doctor that vifits him, or any two of them, and they fhall pay their weekly allowance to any perfon they fhall appoint, every week, from the date of the certificate.

8, Whenever the Society's cafh does not amount to thirty pounds, then the weekly money allowed to fick members fhall not be taken out of the box, but each member that is fick fhall receive from the reft of the members one penny per week; and if the fick member dies, or the wife or widow of a member, every member fhall pay one fhilling to defray his (or her) funeral expences; and if the fhillings do not amount to the fum allowed by article for burying a member, wife, or widow, what is wanting muft be taken out of the Society's cafh; but if above, the overplus fhall be put to it. The penny per week to be collected from the members every fix weeks meeting; and the fhilling, the firft fix weeks meeting after the funeral. The legacy (in cafe of a member's death) to be the fame as expreffed in article 6th.

9, The perfon in whofe hands the Society's cafh is lodged, fhall give fecurity for the fame, to the fatisfaction of the faid Society, or it fhall be no longer lodged in his hands.

10, Difputes to be fettled by a committee of nine members: their award to be final.

11, The clerk—his power, duty, and falary.

12, Felons excluded.

13, The Society not to be diffolved, as long as three members are willing to fupport it.

14, No

14, No member can be fined, if fix weeks have elapfed fince his offence was committed.

15, Stewards finable for excufing a member's fine.

The following additional Rules were made in 1778 :

16, A member entering the army or navy, (except if impreffed, or ballot-ted in to the militia,) to be excluded.

17, To prevent evafions of the feventh article, it was agreed, that if any member, after having received fick money for any period under 26 weeks, fhould declare off the box, he fhould earn, at leaft, 7s. a week for 3 weeks, or otherwife be excluded, for 26 weeks, from receiving the ufual benefit from the box ; and that the weeks of his former fick-nefs fhould be reckoned up with thofe of his fecond declaration, till they amounted to 26 weeks; after which period, he was only to re-ceive 3s. a week during life, or until his recovery : but, that, if any member, after declaring off the book, fhould earn 7s. a week for 3 weeks, he fhould be entitled to the ufual benefit, on falling fick again. The ftewards were to enquire, whether the 7s. a week were truly earned; and if a member deceived the Society in this point, he was to be excluded.

18, Refolved, on the 30th of June 1794, that the fick money fhall be ad-vanced one fhilling per week extra, until the 29th of May 1795.

The above rules were confirmed at the Michaelmas feffions in 1794.

The ufual diet of miners, keelmen, and other labourers, in, and near Newcaftle, is hafty-pudding and crowdie for breakfaft; butcher's meat, (whenever they can purchafe it,) much butter, bread made of wheat, and rye, or barley, and malt liquor, for dinner, and fupper.

Some idea of the population of Newcaftle may be formed from the fol-lowing table of baptifms and burials : fome additions, however, are to be made for the burials, at the Ballaft Hills, (an extenfive unconfecrated burial-ground,) which are not regiftered, but have been found to vary from 400 to 500 for feveral years paft. It is probable, that the number of inhabitants in the town, and fuburbs, (including Gatefhead,) exceeds 40,000.

Table of Baptisms and Burials.

Years From 1770 to	ALL SAINTS. Baptisms.			ALL SAINTS. Burials.			ST. ANDREW. Burials.			ST. ANDREW. Baptisms.			ST. JOHN. Baptisms.			ST. JOHN. Burials.			ST. NICHOLAS. Baptisms.			ST. NICHOLAS. Burials.			GATESHEAD. Baptisms.			GATESHEAD. Burials.		
	Mal.	Fem.	Tot.	Mal.	Fem.	Tot.	Mal.	Fem.	Tot.	Mal.	Fem.	Tot.	Ma.	Fem.	Tot.	Ma.	Fem.	Tot.	Ma.	Fem.	Tot.	Ma.	Fem.	Tot.	Mal.	Fem.	Tot.	Mal.	Fem.	Tot.
1771	170	162	332	73	80	153	47	48	95	54	49	103	27	32	59	54	45	99	47	47	94	62	55	117	98	95	193	127	120	247
1772	143	163	306	70	92	162	45	41	96	29	39	68	53	37	90	44	45	89	52	38	90	50	59	109	87	107	194	105	142	247
1773	131	154	285	60	81	141	47	37	84	50	59	109	38	22	60	74	52	126	47	39	86	63	57	110	83	92	175	95	108	203
1774	162	153	315	60	64	124	35	47	82	40	43	83	49	45	94	54	47	101	54	49	103	46	51	97	94	79	173	95	96	191
1775	139	141	280	89	100	189	46	53	99	47	50	97	39	31	70	58	60	118	46	51	101	54	64	118	87	87	174	121	148	269
1776	179	152	331	100	97	197	42	47	89	47	44	91	36	36	72	37	62	99	43	52	95	59	57	116	102	85	187	90	97	187
1777	140	168	308	80	105	185	53	44	97	61	54	115	45	31	86	56	52	108	51	45	96	53	43	96	86	84	170	100	104	204
1778	187	178	365	75	72	147	47	51	98	40	55	95	35	44	79	47	43	90	49	39	88	46	47	93	88	130	218	91	78	169
1779	180	160	340	78	78	156	49	37	86	45	62	107	41	50	91	42	55	97	58	43	101	55	53	108	111	93	204	97	94	191
1780	163	154	317	77	92	169	51	40	91	75	57	132	34	38	72	59	68	127	45	50	95	46	58	104	112	99	211	124	121	245
1781	171	200	371	76	87	163	41	42	83	33	54	87	43	34	77	42	56	98	46	46	92	38	50	88	96	105	201	121	118	239
1782	144	143	287	108	107	215	36	52	88	56	54	110	39	44	83	58	55	113	43	57	100	59	57	116	106	106	212	111	126	237
1783	160	182	342	89	82	171	53	52	105	51	49	100	41	43	84	64	70	134	62	40	102	43	50	93	104	97	201	119	87	206
1784	173	170	343	89	88	177	50	43	93	53	58	111	43	39	82	71	69	140	44	66	110	57	63	120	112	90	202	143	154	297
1785	212	187	399	93	68	161	47	49	96	55	61	116	50	58	108	54	60	114	33	28	61	32	51	83	99	103	202	110	115	225
1786	192	187	379	95	111	206	33	55	88	53	63	116	53	43	101	58	84	142	31	23	54	42	56	98	105	114	219	138	111	249
1787	176	172	348	52	75	127	52	48	100	39	42	81	38	40	78	68	58	126	58	43	101	42	42	84	128	114	242	118	151	269
1788	184	162	346	50	63	113	53	44	97	35	52	87	54	54	108	51	57	108	49	43	92	44	38	82	89	121	210	84	107	191
1789	187	173	360	68	91	159	38	52	90	56	64	120	54	48	102	59	69	128	40	48	88	54	44	78	107	110	217	140	132	172
1790	203	210	413	55	52	107	55	50	105	62	58	120	45	48	93	55	42	97	54	43	97	32	35	67	104	102	206	117	116	233
1791	212	146	358	59	61	120	42	52	94	53	50	103	48	53	101	59	61	120	54	43	97	46	73	101	101	202	103	117	220	
1792	160	166	326	51	46	97	53	40	93	46	45	91	50	42	102	51	69	120	59	45	104	50	57	107	94	89	183	107	114	221
1793	211	229	440	62	63	125	66	65	131	43	57	100	63	58	121	69	52	121	41	55	96	37	58	95	114	91	205	127	100	227
1794	186	199	385	73	80	153	43	53	96	61	51	112	62	59	121	70	69	139	57	49	106	41	44	85	98	108	206	116	121	237
1795	222	209	431	74	84	158	38	46	84	50	41	91	51	68	119	58	44	102	56	71	127	41	42	83	112	95	207	134	116	250
1796	178	175	353	55	87	142	41	39	80	51	53	104	—	—	119	—	—	119	49	44	93	45	42	87	108	85	193	118	124	242

BALLAST HILLS.

Year ending in				Burials.		Christenings at Meeting-houses.
1777	—	—	—	about	400	—
1780	—	—	—	about	400	
1783	—	—	—	about	300	—
1784	—	—	—	about	200	—
1785	—	—	—	about	400	200
1786	—	—	—	about	400	260
1787	—	—	—	about	500	—
1788	—	—	—	about	500	
1789	—	—	—	about	400	—
1790	—	—	—	about	400	
1791	—	—	—	about	500	—
1792	—	—	—	about	500	
1793	—	—	—	about	1000	—
1796	—	—	—	about	500	—

March, 1796.

NORTH

NORTH SHIELDS.

THE extent of the townſhip of North Shields is almoſt ſix hundred acres: the population has never been taken, but, from the amount of births and burials, may be eſtimated at 10,000 ſouls[1]. About 740 houſes pay the window-tax; the number exempted could not be aſcertained. The number of ale-houſes is 97.

The inhabitants are ſailors, ferrymen, coal-heavers, coal-miners, keelmen, common mechanics, and tradeſmen of the various deſcriptions uſually found in a ſea-port town. Common labourers receive 12s a week, in ſummer; and 10s in winter; maſons, 15s. a week; joiners, 15s. a week; colliers, from 15s. to 18s. a week.

The prices of proviſions are: mutton, 5d. the lb; veal, 6d.; butter, 14d. for 22 oz; oatmeal, 2s. 6d. the ſtone; fine flour, 4s. 2d. the ſtone; ſecond ſort of flour, 3s. 11d. the ſtone; potatoes, 11s. for 20 ſtone; new milk, ¾d. the pint; old milk, three pints, 1d.; in ſummer, it is rather cheaper.

There are four Friendly Societies in North Shields, containing about 100 members each.

[1] We have the following account of the origin of North and South Shields, in a plea between the Burgeſſes of Newcaſtle and the Prior of Tynemwe, in the year 1290, (18 E 1)

" Et poſtea dicunt quod in itinere Johannis de Vallibus, et ſociorum ſuorum in Com Northumbr. anno regni regis Edwardi nunc vii preſent fuit per jur quod Prior de Tynemuth levavit unam villam ſuper ripam aque de Tyne, apud Sheles, ex una parte aque, et Prior Dunolmie levavit aliam ex altera parte aque, ubi nulla villa debet eſſe, niſi tantummodo Logges in quibus piſcatores poſſent hoſpitari Et quod piſcatores ibi piſcem vendiderunt qui vendi deberent apud Novum Caſtrum, ad magnum nocumentum totius burgi, et ad detrimentum priſarum Domini Regis ad caſtrum ſuum, quia piſcis, & alia mercimonia de quibus Dominus Rex ſolebat habere priſas, et que ibidem modo venduntur, deberent vendi apud burgum de Novo Caſtro, ubi Dominus Rex habet priſas ſuas; et quod idem Prior ſimiliter fecit braciare apud Sheles, et habuit magnas naves piſcatorum ubi non deberet habere niſi batellos tantum, unde Dominus Rex perdit priſas ſuas, et burgus Novi Caſtri cuſtumam ſuam, ad grave dampnum Domini Regis & burgi prediċti: Et ſimiliter, quod Prior Dunelm ex altera parte aque de Tyne, fecit braciare et naves habuit ubi niſi batellos habere deberet: et quod prediċtus Prior de Tynemuth fecit furnire in furno ſuo proprio panem alienum, qui forniri debuit apud burgum de Novo Caſtro, per quod burgus perdit furnagium ſuum, videlicet de quolibet quarterio quatuor denarios "—Rot. Parl 1. 29.

The

The Methodifts, Prefbyterians, and Quakers, have, each, a houfe of worfhip in the town.

The rent of land is from £2. to £3. an acre: farms in the neighbourhood are from £100. to £200. a year: barley, oats, and wheat, are cultivated; but turnips and graffes are the principal articles of produce There are no commons in the townfhip. Tithes are chiefly compounded for.

The Poor of this townfhip, and feven others in the parifh, are farmed by a contractor, for £600. a year; for which fum he undertakes to maintain all the Poor in and out of the poor-houfe. In confequence of the late dearnefs of provifions, this fum was found inadequate; and the townfhip made him a prefent of £60 The houfe ftands in an airy fituation, and is built upon a pretty good plan; but feems to be dirty. The beds are of chaff. The number of inmates, at prefent, is 96, of whom 53 belong to this townfhip. The annual deaths vary from $\frac{1}{8}$ to $\frac{1}{10}$ of the average number of Paupers in the houfe. A fever prevails here at prefent; and has carried off feveral perfons.

Exclufive of feamen and militia-men's families, 123 families out of the houfe, of whom 60 belong to this townfhip, receive £11. weekly. This townfhip is alfo burthened with the families of 76 imprefled men: their ufual weekly allowance is 9d. for the wife, and 1s a week for each child The whole weekly charge, at prefent, arifing from their maintenance, amounts to £8. Tinmouth townfhip fupports 33 families of imprefled men, at the rate of £3. 10s. a week. In the account of South Shields, I omitted to mention, that 74 wives, and 113 children, of imprefled feamen of that port, coft £8. 6s. 3d. a week; and feven wives, and 14 children, of militia-men, £1. 6s. 3d. a week.

The Poor's Rates in the townfhip of North Shields were 2s. 6d. and 3s. in the pound, (on $\frac{2}{3}$ of the net rental,) for feveral years previous to the commencement of the war: fince that period they have been 4s. in the pound, till about nine months ago; when they rofe to 6s. in the pound, and have continued at that height ever fince. A Rate of 6s in the pound produces about £1200 From the information of a refpectable perfon, it appears, that, about 24 years ago, the Poor's Rates in this townfhip did not exceed £340. a year.

Every townfhip in the parifh feparately maintains it's own Poor; and

4 C 2   of

of courfe, from local circumftances, there is great vaiiation in their refpective difburfements. In the townfhip of Tinmouth, the Rates are about
3s. in the pound. In the townfhip of Collour-cotes, which has little land
belonging to it, and is moftly inhabited by fifhermen, the Rates are 9s. in
the pound. Another townfhip, chiefly agricultural, (the name of which
I do not recollect,) fupports it's Poor for 1s. in the pound.

*The following is the Bill of Fare at prefent obferved in the Poor-houfe in
NORTH SHIELDS.*

	Breakfaft.	Dinner	Supper.
Sunday,	Hafty-pudding and milk.	Beef, broth, bread, and vegetables	Bread and broth.
Monday,	Bread and broth.	A hafh ; or milk boiled with white bread.	Bread and milk.
Tuefday,	Same as Sunday.	Dumplins and puddings, or fifh and bread.	Ditto.
Wednefday,	Ditto.	Peafe foup and meat.	Milk, potatoes, and bread
Thurfday,	Ditto.	Same as Sunday	Same as Sunday
Friday,	Same as Monday.	Same as Monday.	Same as Monday.
Saturday,	Ditto.	Milk boiled with white bread.	Bread and milk.

Table of Baptifms and Burials in the Townfhip of NORTH SHIELDS.

Years.	Baptifms.	Burials.	Marriages.
1680	152	140	27
1685	139	74	33
1690	165	104	17
1710	140	110	30
1720	162	144	33
1750	174	194	62
1770	273	219	80
1771	220	274	—
1780	271	280	123
1785	303	310	128
1794	350	357	119
1795	383	367	135

March, 1796.

NOT-

NOTTINGHAMSHIRE.

NEWARK.

THE parifh of Newaik contains 800 acres. The population is eſtimated at about 7000 inhabitants; who are, chiefly, tradeſmen, inn-
keepers, and a few gentlemen of independent fortune. A fourth or fifth
of the inhabitants diſſent from the Eſtabliſhed Church, and are either Cal-
viniſts, or Methodiſts: they have, each, a place of worſhip at Newark.
605 houſes pay the window tax; and about 500 are exempted.

The cotton manufacture is the principal buſineſs of conſequence carried
on in this pariſh: a mill, for making cotton-thread for ſtockings, employs
about 300 hands; chiefly women and children: they earn, at preſent,
from 1s. to 5s. a week. A canal in the neighbourhood has lately occaſioned a gieat demand for men in various branches of work: they receive,
each, 2s. a day, and 3 pints of beer. There are ſeveral conſiderable
breweries in Newark.

The prices of proviſions are: beef and mutton, from 5d. to 5½d. the lb.;
veal, 4½d.; bacon, 8d.; butter, from 7d. to 8d. the lb.; flour, 2s. 6d. to
2s. 10d. the ſtone; very little oatmeal is uſed here; potatoes, 7d. the peck;
milk, 2d. the quart; barley, 40s. and 42s. the quarter; malt, 54s. to 56s.
the quarter.

Here are 49 ale-houſes; and 10 Friendly Societies, conſiſting, altogether,
of about 800 members. The following are the principal iules of the
Society held at the White Hart: thoſe of other Clubs, in Newark, aie veiy
ſimilar.

1, The title of this club ſhall be " The Friendly Society ;" the members whereof ſhall be under the government and inſpection of a father
   and two ſtewards: and it is hereby declared to be inſtituted ſolely for
   the purpoſe of diſpenſing pecuniary relief to each and every member
   of this Society, who ſhall at any time, by ſickneſs or accident, (except
   such

fuch as fhall be hereinafter excepted,) being rendered incapable of procuring his fubfiftence by his ufual vocation.

2, That on the firft Monday in every month, from Michaelmas to Lady-day, the members meet at the hour of fix in the evening, and clofe the book by eight; and from Lady-day till Michaelmas, at feven, and clofe at nine; and every member fhall pay one fhilling to the box, and two-pence to be fpent.

3, That for the good government of this Society, two ftewards fhall be chofen, and they to hold their office one year, and at their going out fhall make a feaft for the Society, and every member fhall pay on the month-night before the feaft, one fhilling, or be excluded the Society; the feaft to be kept on the firft day of January yearly, except on a Sunday, and then to be kept on the day following; and that a fermon fhall be preached on the feaft-day, and the charge paid out of the box; and every member that neglects attending the club houfe, between nine and ten o'clock on the day before mentioned, fhall forfeit one fhilling, except upon a lawful occafion.

4, That the box fhall have three locks of different wards, to keep the money and books, &c; the father of the club fhall keep one key, and each of the ftewards one.

5, That on the month night before the feaft, the old ftewards fhall nominate fix members, two whereof, to be chofen by the majority then prefent, to be ftewards for the year enfuing; and whoever refufes to ftand, fhall forfeit two fhillings and fixpence to the box; and the faid new ftewards fhall choofe fix members for their affiftants for the year, and if any refufes to ftand, fhall forfeit one fhilling to the box.

12, That this Society fhall confift of no more than eighty-one members, and each new member to pay five fhillings to the box, four-pence for orders, and two-pence to be fpent; and no perfon to be admitted into this Society above thirty years of age, nor under eighteen, nor any that is troubled with the king's evil, falling ficknefs, lamenefs, venereal difeafe, or any other diftemper whatfoever, that may render him incapable of getting his living; and if any perfon fhall be entered as a member, and it appears afterwards that he had any infirmity upon him, as above mentioned, at the time of his firft ad-

mittance,

mittance, which he then concealed, it fhall be deemed a fraud, and he fhall be excluded.

13, That no member of this Society fhall be entitled to any benefit, relief, or advantage from the box, but fuch as have belonged to it the fpace of twelve months; after that time, if any member fall fick or lame, he fhall receive fix fhillings weekly during his illnefs, except it be occafioned by quarrelling or the venereal difeafe, which if proved upon him, he fhall not only be denied the benefit of the box, but be for ever expelled the fame.

14, In cafe of a rebellion or invafion, any members who enter into the army, fhall immediately quit the Society, and providing they return again to the town of Newark, with a difcharge from the army, (excepting for theft,) and under 40 years of age, free from lamenefs and diftempers, fhall be entitled to the benefit of the box, on paying his next monthly payment

15, If any member fhall receive charity, (whether weekly or otherwife,) from any parifh, and at the fame time fhall declare himfelf upon the box, whether upon full or half-pay, he fhall be expelled the Society; and if any member fhall go into the work-houfe, or to his refpective parifh, he fhall immediately quit the Society; but on taking himfelf from the parifh, and free from lamenefs or diftemper, he fhall be entitled to the benefit of the box, immediately after paying his next monthly payment.

18, If any perfon fall fick or lame, he fhall give notice to the clerk of the Society, who fhall fend out a written roll, within twenty-four hours, on forfeiture of 6d. ; and the faid clerk fhall vifit the faid fick member once a week, and pay him his money, on forfeiture of 6d. ; and fhall warn as many members as the ftewards think proper, to vifit the fick perfon daily ; and they fhall deliver the vifiting roll, from one to another, in courfe, or forfeit 6d. for every member's name on the roll fucceeding them ; and the fick perfon fhall give, or caufe to be given, to the clerk, an account, at each week's end, of every perfon who vifited him, or forfeit 6d. each.

19, If the fick perfon is fo well as to walk abroad, he fhall leave in word, or writing, at his dwelling-houfe, where he is to be found by the vifiting member, or be excluded the Society.

20, If any member, during the time he receives the benefit of the box,

5

fhall

fhall be known to drink in any public-houfe more than the value of 2d. at any one time to refrefh himfelf, he from that time fhall be excluded the benefit of the box : but any member, during the time he is on the box, is allowed to write, mark, or give orders.

21, If any member of this Society die, there fhall be allowed for his widow or executor, £ 6., and fhe or they to bury him in a decent manner, and the money fhall be paid the club night after; and the clerk to pay to the widow or executor, the weekly pay, if any, up to the day the perfon died; and every member, the quarter night following, to pay 1s. extra, on account of the funeral, or be excluded; and each member that dies to be fung to church, and the expence paid out of the box.

22, That when the wife of any member of this Society fhall die, he fhall be allowed £ 2. towards the expences of her funeral, if at her death he has been a member of this Society twelve months, to be paid out of the box the club-night after; and each member fhall pay 6d. the next quarter night, towards making good the fame.

23, If any member of this Society be chofen into the alms-houfe, or other public charity, he fhall receive, when junior in the alms-houfe, 3s. per week; and when fenior, 2s. per week, and to be vifited with a roll as another member.

25, If any member of this Society fhall abfent himfelf from the club two months, and does not come or fend his contribution money, and forfeits, he fhall be excluded; and each member fhall clear the book the firft Monday in March, June, September, and December, or be excluded.

27, That at the funeral of any member of this Society, the clerk fhall warn the father and ftewards, and fix affiftants of this Society, to meet in the club-room, to attend the corpfe to the grave, and to return to the club-room in the fame order; upon neglect, fhall forfeit 6d. to the box, except on a lawful occafion; and to go to church, on the feaft-day, in a decent and reverent manner by two's, and by feniority, on forfeiture of 6d.; and there fhall be allowed, at the funeral of each member, 3s. 6d. to be fpent by the attending members, and the charge paid out of the box; and the clerk fhall be allowed 1s. for warning the Society.

28, If any member have occafion to leave the town, and go into any part

of

of the kingdom, he fhall caufe to be paid his club-money regularly during his abfence; and in cafe of ficknefs or lamenefs, that he declares himfelf on the box, he fhall fend a ceitificate weekly, figned by the minifter and church-wardens of the parifh where he lives, certifying an account of his ficknefs or lamenefs to the Society, and he fhall be entitled to the benefit of the box, and he may have a printed ceitificate from the box for a copy.

30, Whereas eight of the Societies in the town of Newark, have, at their joint expence, purchafed a corn wind-mill, for the mutual benefit of themfelves and families, and appointed Mr. George Stevenfon as their agent to the fame ; and whereas it may be ufeful to the members of the faid Societies, to have flour on credit from the agent ; it is therefoie agreed, that any debt which may be contracted for flour, by any member of this Society, with the faid George Stevenfon, or any future fervant or agent to the faid Societies, fhall be deducted from fuch monies as he or they may be entitled to receive from the Societies, as their fhare of money, to be divided ; and if any fuch member fhall happen to die before fuch debt fhall be difcharged, the remainder of the debt fhall be deducted from the allowances paid by the club at the death of fuch member.

31, If any member of this Society, by ficknefs or lamenefs, fhall prove incurable, he fhall be allowed 2s. 6d. per week for life ; and if any member be found earning money, the time he is on the box, he fhall be excluded, except on half-pay.

32, That this Society fhall not be diffolved, or broken, fo long as any three members will ftand by it, and the ftock fhall not be reduced under foity pounds.

36, That if any member or members fhall be thought to impofe on this Society, by ficknefs or lamenefs, the ftewards then being fhall be empowered to employ a furgeon or apothecary, to examine him or them concerning fuch ficknefs or lamenefs ; and if fuch furgeon or apothecary fhall deem it a fraud and impofition on the Society, he or they fhall be for ever expelled the fame, and fuch furgeon or apothecary fhall be paid for his trouble out of the box.

37, That in cafe the father or ftewards, or any of them, or any other officer or officers of this Society, fhall, at any time or times during the continuance thereof, divert or misapply any of the monies subscribed, paid, or given, or to be subscribed, paid, or given, to, or for the benefit of this Society, and wherewith they, or any of them, shall, or may be entrusted, then every such person so diverting or misapplying the the same, shall immediately repay to the stewards of this Society, a sum of money equal to that which he may have so diverted or misapplied, and shall, besides such re payment as aforesaid, forfeit and pay, for every such diversion or misapplication, the sum of five shillings.

38, That in case any doubt or dispute shall arise between or amongst any of the members of this Society, or any person or persons acting under them, touching or concerning the construction or meaning of any of the aforesaid Rules, or any defect or imperfection therein, or any thing relating thereto, then every such doubt or dispute shall be referred to, and be determined by, such three persons as the major part of the members of this Society shall, at any general meeting, elect or appoint for that purpose; and whatever award or determination the said three persons, so to be appointed as aforesaid, shall make, either by writing or word of mouth, touching the doubt or dispute so to them referred, the same shall be binding and conclusive, to all intents and purposes.

39, That if any member or members of this Society shall, by sickness or lameness, be thought incurable, and he or they shall be put on half-pay, that is, 2s. 6d. per week, and if after that time, the said member or members shall be able to earn his living as before, under forty-five years of age, the said member or members shall give up his 2s. 6d. per week, and be entitled to full pay, when sick or lame, during such time as the major part of the Society think proper.

The above Rules were confirmed at the Quarter Sessions in November 1794.

The rent of land, near Newark, is from 15s. to £6. an acre: the average is about £2. 2s. the acre. Tithes are generally taken in kind. The land-tax raised in this parish is £463. 3s.

The Poor are maintained partly at a work-house, and partly at their own homes. The number of Paupers, at present, in the work-house, is 54; of whom, 20 are under 15 years of age, (including 3 bastards;)

70 of the children work at the cotton-mill lately erected here: the other Paupers are employed in such work as suits them, in different parts of the town: grown people are allowed 2d. in the shilling from their earnings; children have no regular perquisites, but are now and then paid an halfpenny: the whole earnings, at present, from the Poor in the house, amount to about £ 90. a year. 42 regular pensioners, (including 12 bastards,) receive £ 3. 2s. a week: several house-rents are likewise paid; and a large sum is expended by the parish, every week, in discretionary payments; but, of these, the amount could not be ascertained. The badge appointed by the Act of King William, is worn by the Paupers of this parish: it was laid aside a few years ago, but the Poor having increased very much, it was resumed last year; and the consequence has been, that several persons, who had before made regular applications to the parish, have now declined asking for relief.

The work-house, here, is one of the very best in England: it is sufficiently capacious, and well aired: the men are lodged on one side, and the women on the other: 2, 3, 4, or 5 beds, (some of chaff, but mostly of feathers,) are in each room: the house is well supplied with vegetables from a good garden; and, in all other respects, both within and without, it exhibits a degree of comfort, and cleanliness, that is seldom to be met with. A few apartments, rather neater than the rest, are appointed for the reception of such persons as have been unfortunately precipitated from an easy station in life, to the humiliating condition of subsisting on a parochial allowance; and their situation receives every attention, that humanity can dictate.

The following is the Bill of Fare observed in the Work-house:

	Breakfast.	Dinner.	Supper.
Sunday,	Milk-pottage.	Bread-puddings, beef, bread, broth, and roots.	Beer and bread, with cheese, or butter.
Monday,	Ditto.	Bread, and pease-pottage.	Ditto.
Tuesday,	Ditto.	Boiled meat, broth, roots, and bread.	Ditto.
Wednesday,	Ditto.	Frumenty of wheat, and milk.	Ditto.
Thursday,	Ditto.	Same as Tuesday.	Ditto.
Friday,	Ditto.	Suet-pudding.	Ditto.
Saturday,	Ditto.	Dumplins, with sauce, composed of vinegar, sugar, and water.	Ditto.

At

At fupper, 1 pint of beer, and 2 ounces of cheefe, or butter, are allowed to each adult ; and to children in proportion : at dinner, all have as much bread and meat as they can eat ; but they are not fuffered to take any away.

The mafter has a falary of £ 24. a year, and a furgeon has £ 20. a year for attending the Poor in the houfe : about £ 8. a year are fpent in meetings for fettling the Rates, &c.

Certificates are allowed here without fcruple : about 3 are granted in a year. There are nearly the fame number of removals : but one has been contefted thefe 7 years.

A Table of Baptifms, Burials, and Expences for the Poor in the Parifh of NEWARK.

Years.	Baptifms.		Burials.		General Expenditure.		
					£.	s.	d.
1774	———	-	———	-	458	18	11½
1775	128	-	84	-	331	10	6
1776	115	-	108	-	279	13	0¼
1777	131	-	127	-	352	2	0
1778	98	-	124	-	517	3	6½
1779	126	-	115	-	562	15	4
1780	135	-	130	-	624	3	6½
1781	126	-	126	-	690	13	10½
1782	120	-	113	-	727	15	1
1783	133	-	225	-	916	10	9½
1784	212	-	118	-	926	12	5¼
1785	164	-	126	-	745	4	2
1786	192	-	104	-	904	18	10
1787	197	-	136	-	983	16	0
1788	202	-	166	-	880	17	7
1789	205	-	148	-	707	19	3
1790	196	-	155	-	907	8	9½
1791	233	-	181	-	1068	4	7
1792	243	-	134	-	866	12	8½
1793	230	-	150	-	924	0	11½
1794	230	-	129	-	1321	4	1

1795—The account of the Expenditure of this year, ending in May 1795, could not be procured ; but the amount of the affeffments was about £ 820. which was collected, upon the net rental, at about 2s. 6d. in pound, for land ; and 1s. 6d. in the pound, for houfes.

In

In the above fums are included the expences of conftables, militia-men's families, baftard children, &c. the greateft part of which is reimburfed to the parifh. The conftables receive, for County Rates, about £ 25. a year, out of the Rates. At prefent, 18 militia-men's families receive £ 3 1s. 8d. weekly.

The donations and charities are, moftly, under the direction of the corporation; from the beft information obtainable relative to thefe matters, it appears that about £ 120. a year, aiifing from various charities, doles, &c. are diftributed among the Poor, in money, coals, corn, bread, &c. There are 2 hofpitals, or alms-houfes, in Newark, for the reception of 14 decayed tradefmen, and 10 widows; they have coals and cloathing, and an allowance from 2s. 6d. to 4s. 6d. a week, each, according to their age, and time of refidence in the houfe.

About £ 140. were collected, laft winter, from voluntary fubfcriptions, for the relief of the Poor.

May, 1795.

NOTTINGHAM.

THE town of Nottingham contains 3 parifhes. The population was taken in 1779, and was as follows:

	Houfes inhabited.	Houfes empty.	Families.	Souls.
In St. Mary's parifh	2314	57	2584	12637
St. Peter's	446	10	497	2445
St. Nicholas's	431	9	475	2502
	3191	76	3556	17584
Brew-houfe-yard, (extra parochial,)				127
			Total	17711

It is generally fuppofed, that, fince the above period, the population has increafed to about 22,000 fouls; and nearly proportionally in each parifh.

The parifh of St. Mary contains, by eftimation, 1200 acres of land,

9   exclufive

exclufive of about 100 acres of wafte land. 1200 houfes pay the win-dow-tax; and about 1822 are exempted.

There are, here, feveral mills for twifting and fpinning filk and cotton : the filk mills are worked by horfes: many lace-workers belong to this parifh ; but the frame work knitters, or ftocking-weavers, form, by much, the moft numerous branch of manufacturers in Nottingham. There are, alfo, in this town, a white-lead work ; a foundery for making caft-iron-ware from the pigs, which are brought from Colebrook Dale; dyeing and bleaching works ; and a manufacture of Britifh lace by frame-work. A confiderable brewery is eftablifhed here : and the malting-bufinefs is carried on to a great extent, both at Nottingham, and Newark.

Exclufive of the 3 parifh churches, here are, alfo, 1 Methodift chapel ; 2 Prefbyterian ditto ; 1 Roman Catholic ditto ; 1 Anabaptift ditto ; 1 General Baptift ditto ; 1 Sandimonian ditto ; and 1 Quaker meet-ing-houfe.

The prices of provifions are : beef, from 5d. to 6d. the lb. ; mutton, and veal, 5d ditto ; bacon, 9d ; potatoes, 9d or 10d. the peck ; but-ter, 9d the lb ; flour, from 2s. 6d. to 2s. 10d. the ftone ; oatmeal, 6s. the bufhel ; wheat, 9s. 4d. ditto ; barley, £ 2. 2s. the quarter ; malt, 5s. the bufhel ; milk, 1½d. the quart.

The price of labour is very variable in this town, particularly in the ftocking line : fome weavers earn 40s. a week, and others only 8s. : this difparity is occafioned, in fome, through want of induftry ; but, chiefly, arifes from the nature of the different branches of the manufacture. It is thought ⅔ of the weavers do not, upon an average, earn more than 10s. weekly. Lace-workers earn from 20s. to 40s. a week. The women and children are, chiefly, employed in manufacturing cotton and filk ; and earn from 10d. to 4s. weekly ; common labourers have 10s. and 10s. 6d. a week, in fummer ; and in winter, 8s. : hands cannot be eafily procured in winter.

In this town there are 152 ale-houfes, and 51 Friendly Societies : the number of members is limited to 41, or 51, in each club.

There is, likewife, in Nottingham, a Society called the Charitable Society; the principal intention of which is, to extend relief to fuch cafes as it is impoffible general laws can reach ; in purfuance of which plan, the funds have been applied, as far as their prefent confined amount will admit, principally to the following objects : To strangers in distress, and to persons labouring under temporary disease, or other casual misfortune ; either in loans, donations, or both, as circumstances required : in a small annual subscription to Sunday Schools ; and, in a few instances, they have been extended to pay for the education of children of poor and deserving families. The Society originated with a few of the people called Quakers, and has been continued principally under their management ; it has since been joined by many others. The Rules are :

1, That the meetings be held at the house of George Bott, on the first Sunday in every month, at seven o'clock in the evening ; which meetings are competent to transact all business, except choosing a secretary and treasurer, which shall only be done at the first meeting which happens in each year respectively.

2, That the secretary shall keep a record of the transactions of the Society in a book provided for that purpose, which may be inspected by the members at every meeting, or by calling on, or sending to the treasurer for the same.

3, That any person desirous of becoming a member, shall send his name to the treasurer or secretary, together with a subscription for every month unexpired of the current year ; and it is understood, that every member continues to subscribe, till he acquaints the secretary or treasurer to the contrary, by letter ; and when a person declines, it is expected that the subscription be paid up to that time, and that, by the resignation, all claim to the fund of the Society is relinquished.

4, That the subscription be 1s. per month, or 6d. at the pleasure of the subscriber.

5, That a member may recommend an object of charity to the Society, by sending a note to the secretary or treasurer, mentioning the name and place of abode of the person distressed ; the note to contain an avowal, that the writer believes the person applying to deserve the sum asked for ; or, if the facts cannot be stated from personal knowledge, two of the members (the secretary or treasurer being one,) are to visit the petitioner, and increase or diminish the sum ; or totally reject the application, as they shall think proper.

6, That if any member omits paying his subscription for a year together, he shall be apprised of the neglect, by a letter from the secretary ; and

if

if it is not paid in three months from the date of such notice, he shall be deemed to have excluded himself, and his name shall be erased from the records of the Society accordingly.

The average rent of land is about £ 3. an acre. A modus is paid in lieu of tithes

The work-house, in which the Poor of this parish are maintained, is surrounded by other buildings, most of which are much higher than it, so that the free current of air is compleatly obstructed. The rooms are close : the beds are, partly, of flocks, and partly of straw. The present overseers have ordered a few more beds, as the number is too small for the family, particularly in summer, when 3, and sometimes 4 persons, are obliged to sleep in one bed : this probably may be the reason why vermin are found to prevail here ; although the floors, stair-cases, &c. seem to be kept clean. A spotted fever, at this time, rages in the house.

There are, at present, 168 Paupers in the work-house ; of which number, 42 are boys, between the ages of 6 months and 14 years ; 35 girls, under 20 years of age ; 30 men, from 20 to 60 years old ; and 61 women, from 20 to 80 years of age : in the above number, 8 bastards are included. 456 weekly out-pensioners receive £ 23. 2s. 6d. a week : about £ 11. a week are paid to casual Poor ; their number could not be ascertained : besides these, 39 Paupers, belonging to other parishes, receive a weekly allowance ; for which this parish is reimbursed. 136 militia-men's families are allowed about £ 24. a week.

The earnings in the work-house are trifling : most of the women are employed in nursing the young children: few men, who are able to work, enter the house : the earnings, therefore, are, chiefly, from such of the children as work at the cotton-mills: they amount to rather more than £ 60. a year.

The Weekly Bill of Fare in the Work-house.

	Breakfast	Dinner.	Supper.
Sunday,	Milk pottage.	Broth, beef, and potatoes.	Bread and beer.
Monday,	Water gruel	Cold meat, broth, and potatoes.	Ditto.
Tuesday,	As Sunday.	As Sunday.	Ditto.
Wednesday,	As Monday.	As Monday.	Ditto
Thursday,	Bread and gruel.	Puddings, and sauce, made of water, flour, alegar, and sugar.	Bread, cheese, and beer.
Friday,	As Sunday	As Sunday.	As Sunday.
Saturday,	As Monday.	As Monday.	As Monday.

Table

Table of Butcher's Meat and Beer confumed weekly in the Work-houfe.

	1795.	Meat. St.	Meat. lb.	Beer. Gallons.	No. of Paupers
Week ending April	12th	58	12	104	189
	19th	47	8	170	190
	26th	49	5	33	190
May	3d	66	8	68	187
	10th	36	10	75	185
	17th	56	6	33	168

		6)315 7	6)483	6)1109
Average	-	52 8⅙	80½	184⅚
		14	8	

lb. 736   0⅙   pints 644.   paupers 184⅚

This amounts to 4 lb. of meat, and 3½ pints of beer, a week, for each Pauper.

About 70 ftone of fecond flour, at 2s. 6d. the ftone, are made into bread weekly; about 11 oz. of brown bread are allowed to each grown perfon for fupper, and ⅔ of a pint of beer: 5 pecks of potatoes, at 9d. the peck, are ufed daily, on meat days. About 1 bufhel of oatmeal is ufed weekly. Children, and fick people, are often indulged with puddings, &c. and flour hafty-puddings. At Thurfday's fupper, about 2¾ oz. of cheefe are allowed to each adult; and a proportionable quantity to children.

In the following table, (which was not colle&ed without confiderable trouble, from different perfons, and different books,) the fourth column fpecifies the annual amount of parochial affeffments; the fifth and fixth columns, the rate on the net rental of houfes and land, by which the affeffments were levied; the feventh column denotes the total receipts of the year, whether arifing from affeffments, reimburfements from other pa-rifhes, compofitions for baftardy, balances in the hands of parifh offi-cers, &c.: the laft column fpecifies the total difburfements.

	Years.	Bap-tiſms.	Burials.		Amount of Aſſeſſments. £.	s.	d.	Rate on houſes: at net rental. s.	d.	Rate on land: at net rental. s.	d.	Total Receipts. £.	s.	d.	Diſburſements. £.	s.	d.
From 25 March	1773			ending in													
to 25 March	1774	460	326	May 1774	1070	16	7	1	4	3	2	1413	18	2½	1293	13	7½
	1775	442	249		1042	7	4	1	2	2	8	1386	7	7	1312	5	2
	1776	426	326		1082	0	8½	1	4	3	2	1334	3	10½	1248	2	1
	1777	502	411		1103	14	5½	1	4	3	2	1436	10	4	1422	10	6
	1778	517	275		1425	8	1	1	8	4	2	1686	5	7½	1631	2	3½
	1779	431	292		1731	1	1	2	0	5	2	2088	4	6½	2000	13	11
	1780	471	407		1756	16	1	2	0	5	2	2141	6	6	2079	5	6½
	1781	491	332		2068	19	4	2	4	6	2	3008	18	0	2698	18	0
	1782	475	439		1759	14	7½	2	0	5	2	2812	0	9	2717	1	3
	1783	523	315		1920	9	7	2	2	5	6	2615	9	9	2578	14	1
	1784	—	413		1920	5	11	2	2	5	6	2324	0	3½	2308	1	1
	1785	554	334		2074	18	10	2	4	6	0	2383	12	6¼	2479	0	2
	1786	589	453		2503	0	4½	2	10	7	6	2930	9	6	2911	15	10¾
	1787	595	387		2529	14	3	2	10	7	6	2942	1	2	2834	3	4½
	1788	653	514		2270	19	6	2	6	6	6	2764	8	0	2561	13	6
	1789	656	471		2476	3	7	2	8	7	0	3396	9	1	3156	16	4½
	1790	659	317		2493	12	4	2	8	7	0	3276	0	9	3171	16	10½
	1791	746	506		2881	8	0	3	0	8	0	3405	2	9	3414	12	3
	1792	749	474		2924	8	0	3	0	8	0	3358	9	11	2901	1	9
	1793	839	602		2686	6	11	2	8	7	0	3657	14	3½	2976	6	1
	1794	862	502		3683	9	4	3	8	10	0	6044	4	2½	5892	4	7
to 25 March	1795	837	502														

The accounts for 1795 were not made up, nor ſettled; but the aſſeſſments were £600. more than laſt year; and were at the rate of 4s. 4d. in the pound, on houſes; and 12s. on land; excluſive of the Rate for raiſing men for the Navy. Theſe aſſeſſments were profeſſedly made at 4d. in the pound, on ⅔ of the real rent, on houſes; and 1s. in the pound, on the real rent of land: however, on minute enquiry, it was found, that, in general, houſes were aſſeſſed at half value; and land, in moſt inſtances, ſomewhat below the real rent: and therefore, in the above ſtatement, the houſes are taken at half, and land at about ⅞; which is near the truth.

Out of the Poor's Rates are paid the ſalaries of the ſtanding officers, maſter of the work-houſe, and ſurgeon, &c. which amount annually to £165.

Certificates are not willingly granted: about 4 or 5 are allowed in a year. About 14 or 15 removals occur in the ſame time; one or two are conteſted in a year.

Several ſmall donations, amounting to about £80. a year, are annually diſtributed to ſuch Poor, as do not, otherwiſe, receive parochial aſſiſtance.

The

The other parishes in Nottingham are burdened with Poor nearly in the same proportion with St. Mary's. Some years back, it was in contemplation to erect a house of industry, which was to have been built and maintained at the joint expence of the different parishes in this town; but the very great difference of opinion which then prevailed, and the discordancy of interests, caused this scheme to fall to the ground: the project is likely to be brought forward again; but it may be doubted whether it will succeed: the town is split into parties; and neither this, nor any other measure, that must materially affect the inhabitants, will be allowed to be carried into execution, without undergoing a very rigorous investigation.

No satisfactory reason could be ascertained for the late rapid rise of the Rates: the principal stocking-manufacturers say, that the war has not very materially affected them, as their chief exportation is to America: it is true, that the population of Nottingham has increased considerably, of late years, but not in proportion to the Rates. Their rise is, here, generally attributed to the high price of provisions, the scarcity of common labour, and the great number of soldiers' and militia-men's wives and families, who have, of late years, become burthensome to their parishes. *May*, 1795.

OVERINGHAM.

THIS parish, which contains about 800 acres, is situated on the river Trent, half way between Nottingham and Newark: it contains 240 inhabitants, who, (excepting 40 stocking-weavers, of whom 3 are women,) are all agriculturists; and are chiefly of the Established Church. 24 houses pay the window-tax; and 19 are exempted.

The provisions consumed here, are, chiefly, milk, butter, cheese, tea, butcher's meat, &c.: the labouring classes use much tea, milk, butter, and bread. Prices are mostly regulated by the neighbouring markets: milk, when new, is sold, here, for $\frac{1}{2}$d. a pint; and a quart, for $\frac{1}{4}$d. when old.

The wages of labourers are, in harvest, generally 2s. a day, and victuals; and, at other times of the year, 1s. a day, and victuals: stocking-

weavers

weavers earn about 12s. a week. There are 2 ale-houfes in the parifh ; and one Friendly Society, which confifts of 95 members.

The rent of land is fiom 15s. to 40s. an acre; the average is about 25s. the acre. This parifh chiefly belongs to one proprietor; and is moftly tithe-fiee. The land-tax amounts, annually, to £43. 4s.

The Poor are allowed a maintenance at home: the following is a lift of the prefent weekly penfioners, viz.

	Weekly Allowance.
	s.	d.
A baftaid child receives - - -	1	6
A labourer's widow, aged 70 yeais; befides her houfe rent, and 1 ton of coals yearly, has - - -	1	6
An old blind man, (who is married to a young woman, by whom he has 5 children,) befides houfe-rent, has -	4	0
A young woman, a lunatic - - -	3	0
A woman, and 3 children, deferted by the father, has, for fome weeks paft, received - - -	6	0

Exclufive of the above regular weekly allowances, feveral other difcretional payments are made, occafionally, to the moft neceffitous.

Table of Baptifms, Burials, and Expences for the Poor in the Parifh of OVERINGHAM.

Years.	Baptifms.	Burials.		Total Expenditure.		
				£.	s.	d.
1774	10	8				
1775	10	3				
1776	10	7				
1777	9	5				
1778	7	6				
1779	7	5				
1780	9	6	May 1780 to			
1781	6	7	May 1781 -	22	18	0½
1782	7	3	—	27	5	8
1783	2	1	—	26	7	3½
1784	8	6	—	31	1	1
1785	4	8	—	36	6	3
1786	4	5	—	31	18	8½
1787	Regifter imperfect this year.		—	23	8	5

Years.

Years.	Baptifms.	Burials.	Total Expenditure.		
			£.	s.	d.
1788	8	—	—	17	8	8
1789	9	8	—	30	0	3
1790	10	8	—	22	5	0
1791	8	3	—	28	17	3½
1792	10	7	—	35	17	7½
1793	13	5	—	29	8	3½
1794	9	9	—	32	14	6
to May 1795	—	—	—	36	1	0

The fum of £36. is collected in this parifh, at about 9¼d. in the pound, on the net rent. About one removal happens in a year; a conteft occurs about once in 4 years.

In a neighbouring farming parifh, containing about 1000 acres of land, the Poor Rates at prefent are 7d. in the pound; they have no work-houfe: and in another farming parifh, half a mile from Overingham, a donation of £10. a year, to the ufe of the Poor, has prevented any Poor's Rates being collected for the laft 50 years, excepting in the two laft years, when they were very trifling : the parifh contains about 800 acres, and 13 families. In many of the parifhes between Overingham and Newark, which are all in a farming country, the Poor's Rates are, at this time, not more than from 6d. to 9d. in the pound.   *May,* 1795.

WORKSOP.

THERE is a fmall work-houfe in this parifh. The number of Poor at prefent in the houfe is 18. Very little work is done within; but the out-poor of the parifh, who are in want of work, are fupplied with flax for fpinning; and are paid 1d. for every 300 yards of thread fpun : a pound of flax is, ufually, fpun into 6 leas, each of 300 yards. A good fpinner will fpin a pound into 8 leas. With the above pay, few can earn above 4d. a day. The woman, who attends the work-houfe, is allowed

3   5 guineas.

5 guineas a year, and her bed and board. An inspector has a salary of 20 guineas a year. The diet in the house is as follows:

	Breakfast.	Dinner.	Supper, every day in the week.
Sunday,	Milk-porridge.	Boiled beef, suet puddings, and greens, and a slice of bread.	Milk porridge, and ½ pint of beer to each person
Monday,	Ditto.	Bread, light suet dumplins, and treacle sauce.	No beer is allowed at
Tuesday,	Ditto.	Meat with the broth, cabbage, and bread.	dinner.
Wednesday,	Ditto.	Same as Monday.	When the women wash, they are allowed bread and
Thursday,	Ditto.	Same as Tuesday.	cheese, and ¼ pint of beer,
Friday,	Ditto.	Same as Tuesday.	each, for supper.
Saturday,	Ditto.	Same as Monday.	There is no garden belonging to the house.

Poor's Rates, from the Parish Book, which commences in 1722.

Years.	Poor's Rates.			Years.	Poor's Rates.		
	£.	s.	d.		£.	s.	d.
1722	88	13	8	1746	111	14	10
1723	113	19	2¾	1747	116	12	10
1724	113	6	3½	1748	178	1	6
1725	105	4	11	1749	113	10	9¼
1726	109	15	5	1750	135	2	5¾
1727	115	19	0½	1751	117	14	3½
1728	107	9	8¾	1752	106	13	1
1729	117	1	1¼	1753	115	6	9½
1730	117	10	5¾	1754	113	1	0¼
1731	121	1	8½	1755	107	2	5¼
1732	108	8	8¼	1756	143	10	1
1733	102	14	10½	1757	167	15	10¼
1734	112	2	5¾	1758	139	19	0¼
1735	149	13	5¾	1759	137	1	2
1736	77	18	11¾	1760	122	11	7
1737	75	9	3¾	1761	128	13	5½
1738	65	17	5	1762	159	5	9½
1739	73	0	6¼	1763	196	18	6¼
1740	69	8	8	1764	209	0	9
1741	114	9	6¾	1765	252	12	10
1742	122	13	0	1766	288	19	6½
1743	124	13	8	1767 & part of 1768 }	302	14	6¼
1744	133	16	5¼				
1745	86	1	8¾	1769	241	10	5

Years.	Poor's Rates.			Years.	Poor's Rates.		
	£.	s.	d.		£.	s.	d.
1770	310	14	$2\frac{1}{2}$	1783	443	5	$5\frac{3}{4}$
1771	349	0	2	1784	391	16	5
1772	342	4	0	1785	347	5	1
1773	340	7	$7\frac{1}{2}$	1786	316	11	6
1774	361	5	$11\frac{1}{2}$	1787	317	7	7
1775	411	10	6	1788	165	18	10
1776	335	15	5	1789	283	13	$5\frac{1}{2}$
1777	342	5	$2\frac{1}{2}$	1790	317	2	$4\frac{1}{2}$
1778	478	18	0	1791	317	2	$4\frac{1}{2}$ } 951 7 $1\frac{1}{2}$
1779	—	—	—	1792	317	2	$4\frac{1}{2}$
1780	—	—	—	1793	318	8	$9\frac{1}{2}$ } 636 17 7
1781	501	0	$2\frac{1}{2}$	1794	318	8	$9\frac{1}{2}$
1782	499	10	10				

Workfop pays £421. to the land-tax.

Table of Baptifms and Burials.

Years	Baptifms	Burials	Years.	Baptifms	Burials.
1654	54	59	1780	82	60
1655	66	35	1781	77	51
1656	48	37	1782	79	61
1657	57	58	1783	80	43
1688	46	31	1784	65	49
1689	59	67	1785	64	52
1690	48	31	1786	63	40
1691	51	49	1787	72	55
1692	43	35	1788	72	47
1693	54	47	1789	97	61
1694	37	35	1790	88	48
1775	82	35	1791	82	43
1776	79	45	1792	111	Not yet entered in the clerk's copy of the re
1777	87	46	1793	87	gifter, from whence
1778	85	70	1794	98	the births and burials were taken
1779	91	48			

There are feveral Catholics in Workfop. They have the ufe of a cha-pel belonging to the Duke of Norfolk.

July, 1795.

O X—

OXFORDSHIRE.

BANBURY.

THIS borough confifts almoft entirely of houfes: the fmall portion of land, that is not built on, is laid out in gardens: the inhabitants are tradefmen, and manufacturers, principally, of worfted, and hair-fhagg, or plufh. Here are one of Lady Huntingdon's chapels, one Prefbyterian, one Methodift, and one Quaker's meeting-houfe. The number of houfes paying window-tax is 228; the number exempted is fuppofed to be much the fame. The prices of provifions are: beef, 5d. the lb.; mutton, 5d.; bacon, 10d.; milk, 1d. the pint; bread, 1s. 10d. the half-peck loaf. Weavers, in full bufinefs, earn from 8s. to 30s.; and fome even 40s. a week: common labourers have 8s. or 9s. a week, during the whole year: children and women in the manufactories earn about 3s. a week. There are 42 inns and ale-houfes in this town: and four Friendly Societies, confifting, each, of about 100 members; the rules of three have been confirmed by the magiftrates. The land-tax is £200.; and is about 1s. 1d. in the pound. The Poor are partly maintained in a work-houfe, in which there are at prefent 39, viz 6 from 1 to 7 years of age; 6 from 7 to 8 years; 11 from 8 to 15 years; 4 from 15 to 30 years; and 12 from 30 to 74 years of age. Of thefe, one is blind; one infane; and four are lame. The Poor in the houfe are chiefly employed in fpinning, and twifting for the manufacturers of the town. Their earnings amount to about £40. a year. No account of the annual mortality in the houfe could be obtained.

Table of the Diet ufed in the Poor-houfe.

	Breakfaft	Dinner.	Supper.
Sunday,	Bread and broth.	Meat and vegetables.	Bread, cheefe, and beer.
Monday,	Ditto.	Cold meat.	Ditto.
Tuefday,	Bread and cheefe	Same as Sunday.	Ditto.
Wednefday,	As Monday.	Same as Monday.	Ditto.
Thurfday,	Bread, cheefe, and beer.	Bread, cheefe, and beer.	Ditto.
Friday,	As Sunday.	Same as Sunday.	Ditto.
Saturday,	Bread and broth.	Cold meat.	Ditto.

The

The Poor here, in general, appear to be in a very miferable ftate. The following is a ftatement of the earnings and expences of a labourer's family, viz. He is a widower, between 50 and 60 years of age; has one daughter 21 years old, another 13 years, and a fon 7 years old.

	£.	s.	d.
He works as a common labourer, in carting, digging, &c. and, generally, with the fame mafter; his earnings are 8s. a week for 48 weeks; and, in one of the fummer months, 9s. a week; annually - - -	21	0	0
The eldeft daughter is fubject to fits; and is otherwife very fickly: fhe cannot earn any thing, but takes care of her father's houfe. The youngeft daughter is at a charity-fchool, where fhe is provided with cloaths, but her father finds victuals. The boy earns nothing. The parifh allows the father 2s. a week, for his children - -	5	4	0
Total income - £ 26		4	0

EXPENCES.

	£.	s.	d.
This family ufes 4½ half-peck loaves in a week, or 234 annually, which fell at prefent for 22d. each, £ 21. 9s; but taking the average price of laft year, 1s. 2d.; they coft annually - - - -	13	13	0
Tea and fugar, about - - -	2	10	0
Butter and lard - - - -	1	10	0
Beer and milk - - - -	1	0	0
Bacon, and other meat; about - -	1	10	0
Soap, candles, &c. about - -	0	15	0
Houfe-rent - - - -	3	0	0
Coals - - - -	2	10	0
Shoes and fhirts - - -	3	0	0
Other cloaths, &c. - - -	2	0	0
Total expences - £ 31		8	0

In

In this account the expences exceed the income by £5. 4s.; on enquiry, it was found, that the man was in debt between £3. and £4.; and that his neighbours were very kind to him, and often supplied him with old cloaths, &c. Perhaps, too, as he could only give a certain account of his annual income, and the quantity of bread used in his family, he may have calculated his other expences too high. He has a garden of 160 square yards, on which he grows about three or four bushels of potatoes; he only bought two gallons more last year.

The following is an account of the earnings and expences of another labourer, who lives in Banbury. He is about 50 years of age; has a wife, and six children at home, viz. a girl 15; a boy 13; a girl 11; a girl 9; another girl 7; and a boy 4 years old.

EARNINGS.

	£.	s.	d.
The father says, he earns on an average 8s. a week, throughout the year - - - -	20	16	0
Eldest girl spins, and earns about 1s. 6d. a week -	3	18	0
Eldest boy goes to plough, and earns about 3s. a week -	7	16	0
The second girl is lame: the three youngest earn nothing -	0	0	0
Total earnings - £32		10	0
The man receives 1s. a week, from the parish, to support his lame daughter - - - -	2	12	0
Total income - £35		2	0

EXPENCES.

	£.	s.	d.
This family uses 9 half-peck loaves in a week, at 1s. 2d. annually - - - -	27	6	0
House-rent - - - - -	2	12	0
Fuel, about 1s. a week - - - -	2	12	0
Carried over - £32		10	0

£. s. d.

Brought over - 32 10 0

The man could give but little account of his other articles of
expence; but in order to balance his income, it will appear, that he muſt procure cloathing for his family, as well
as every other neceſſary article of food, for the trifling
ſum of   2 12 0
                                              ————————
                    Total expences - £35 2 0
                                              ————————

The labourers in this part of the country complain, heavily, that the
farmers, inſtead of ſelling their milk to the poor, give it to their pigs.
Of the difficulty of ſubſiſting with their preſent earnings, on a bread diet,
the above ſtatements afford a convincing proof.   The family, which
receives about 13s. 6d. a week, in earnings and parochial aid, has uſually
conſumed 9 half peck loaves in a week, which, at 1s. 10d. each, the
preſent price, would coſt 16s or 2s 6d. a week, more than their receipts.
They muſt, therefore, reduce their conſumption of the moſt neceſſary, and,
indeed, almoſt their only, article of ſubſiſtence.   It is much to be lamented,
that, in a country where wages are not high enough to enable the poor to
ſupply themſelves with wheaten bread, ſtrong beer, and butcher's meat,
they have not the means of eking out their ſcanty portions by culinary
contrivances.   No doubt, a labourer, whoſe income was only £20. a
year, would, in general, act wiſely in ſubſtituting haſty-pudding, barley
bread, boiled milk, and potatoes, for bread and beer; but, in moſt parts
of this county, he is debarred, not more by prejudice, than by local
difficulties, from uſing a diet that requires cooking at home.   The extreme
dearneſs of fuel, in Oxfordſhire, compels him to purchaſe his dinner at the
baker's; and, from his unavoidable conſumption of bread, he has little left
for cloaths, in a country where warm cloathing is moſt eſſentially wanted.

Some ſlight attempts to prevent the removal of corn, which have lately
been made at Banbury, are certainly atcribable to the pinching wants of the
people: the arrival of the military prevented more ſerious conſequences
taking place.

Table of Poor's Rates, and Expences for the Poor.

Years	Poor's Rates £. s. d.			Net Expenditure £ s. d.			Rate in the Pound s. d.	
1680	57	17	11	57	11	10		
1740	278	13	5¼	258	0	9		
1760	340	11	0	365	11	6		
1781	705	18	0	827	3	6¾		
May, 1782	762	19	6	788	16	10	13	6
1783	769	5	11½	970	8	6¼	13	6
1784	809	5	2	845	14	9½		
1785	823	5	0	977	4	3½		
1786	935	2	6	995	7	4½		
1787	885	4	4	1091	0	4¼		
1788	782	10	0	890	7	11¼		
1789	839	0	6¼	946	16	7		
1790	866	1	10½	824	2	10½		
1791	970	9	7½	1226	8	0		
1792	1052	12	0	1271	10	10¾		
1793	880	12	9	1046	17	11		
1794	1025	13	6	1128	5	9		
1795	1151	12	0	1304	9	8½	19	0

N B The Rate in the the pound (which is marked in those years of which the accounts could be obtained,) is on the nominal rental, and is said to be at ⅓ of the rack rent One house, however, is rated at near half the real rental

The books for the years from 1775 to 1781, could not be found. The fums under the title " Poor's Rates," are the net affeffments ; and are feparated from the total receipts, which include compofitions for baftardy, &c. and £ 26. an annual donation of the Earl of Guilford.

In the above difburfements are included the following annual payments, viz. 16 guineas to watchmen ; £ 17. 10s. to the gaoler ; houfe-rent, £2. 2s. ; governor of the work-houfe, 20 guineas ; conftables, in time of peace, for removing foldiers' families, &c. receive, yearly, about 20s. or 30s. ; and in time of war, £ 40. or £ 50. The manufactures of this town are chiefly exported to Ruffia. The trade has been very dull for fome years, but has lately revived : fome confiderable orders have been received, and trade is a little brifk again, though ftill the weavers have not full employment. July, 1795.

D E D-

DEDDINGTON.

THIS parish contains, by eſtimation, 4000 acres. The number of houſes that pay the window-tax is 102 ; the number exempted near 300. The inhabitants, (who, with the exception of a ſmall congregation of Preſbyterians, are of the Eſtabliſhed Church,) are moſtly employed in agriculture There are ten inns, or ale-houſes, in the pariſh : the number, a few years ago, was 21. Farms are from £ 15. to £ 315 a year ; but are, chiefly, about £ 100. a year. The principal articles of cultivation are wheat, barley, and beans. There are about 45 acres of common in the pariſh. The tithes are farmed at £ 750. a year, and taken in kind.

The prices of proviſions are : beef, 5d. the lb. ; mutton, 5d. ; veal, 5d. ; bacon, 10d. ; butter, 9d. 10d. ; milk, 1d. the pint ; bread, 1s. 10d. the half-peck loaf Common labourers earn 7s. a week in winter ; 8s. in ſpring ; and 12s. in hay and corn harveſt : women are paid 6d. the day, for weeding corn ; 8d. for hay making ; and 1s. in corn harveſt, without victuals.

There are two Friendly Societies in this pariſh. The number of members in each, amounts to 120. They pay 8d. into the box, monthly ; allow 6s. a week, to ſick members, during the firſt twelve months ; and 3s. a week, after that period. Both Societies have taken the benefit of the late Act of Parliament.

The Poor are farmed, in the pariſh work-houſe, for £ 1000. year. The pariſh, however, defrays all expences ariſing from baſtardy, ſmall pox, broken bones, diſlocations, and law concerns. The number of perſons in the houſe, at preſent, is 18. Out-penſioners receive about £ 7. a week ; beſides which, the rounds-men,[1] (or labourers who cannot get employment,) are often chargeable, and ſupported by the pariſh. In winter, their number is ſometimes 40, or 50 ; the pariſh employs them in the ſtone-quarries in the neighbourhood. No regular bill of fare is obſerved in the work-houſe. The Poor were not all farmed till the preſent year ; but were chiefly ſupported by weekly penſions. In general, however, about 20 perſons have been maintained in the work-houſe, under a contractor, who was allowed 2s. 6d. a head for their weekly maintenance.

[1] See pp 29, & 548.

Table

Table of Baptisms, Burials, Marriages, and Poor's Rates[1].

Years	Baptisms			Burials			Marriages	Total Income, including receipts for bastardy, &c	Expenditure on Poor	Rate in the pound, nearly on the full rental
	Mal	Fem	Tot	Mal	Fem	Tot				
1680	—	—	—	18	21	39	10			
1685	—	—	—	18	29	47	3			
1690	22	26	48	14	10	24	2			
1691	22	26	48	9	14	23	4			
1692	24	24	48	17	17	34	6			
1693	20	20	40	10	18	28	0			
1694	13	16	29	22	18	40	4			
1695	32	28	60	14	21	35	6			
1696	25	9	34	9	25	34	14			
1697	26	23	49	17	12	29	6			
1698	19	23	42	22	16	38	5			
1699	23	15	38	8	15	23	1			
1700	25	18	43	25	19	44	4			
1720	22	20	42	12	14	26	8			
1740	17	28	45	20	21	41	10			
1760	28	26	54	18	8	26	11			
1775	22	27	49	7	16	23	10		*£. s. d*	
1776	12	28	40	19	18	37	10	— — —	463 3	
									From the Rate made to Parliament	
1777	21	28	49	18	22	40	6			
1778	27	18	45	15	17	32	12			
1779	22	23	45	11	13	24	13			
1780	26	19	45	10	31	41	12			
1781	24	35	59	20	23	43	10			
1782	24	32	56	7	15	22	6	*£. s. d*		
1783	24	27	51	15	16	31	12	637 11 2	Money ... by settlement, from the Returns to Parliament	
1784	24	16	40	14	17	31	14	796 1 9		
1785	25	29	54	30	39	69	8	952 8 11		
1786	26	25	51	17	21	38	11	989 17 5	1126 3 8	
1787	31	25	56	22	22	44	11	997 16 9	985 18 2¼	
1788	33	25	58	20	12	32	7	1015 15 4¼	1100 13 1¾	
1789	24	22	46	10	10	20	11 }			
1790	28	15	43	24	13	37	12 }	2605 8 5	2622 19 6'	
1791	35	24	59	8	15	23	8	1181 0 2½	1202 17 2½	
1792	—	—	—	19	15	34	4	1315 9 2½	1314 7 2	
1793	28	18	46	14	17	31	5	1251 3 6¼	1181 1 8	
1794	13	15	28	16	24	40	11	1487 14 4½	1463 7 5¼	6 0
May 1795	—	—	—	—	—	—	—	1548 19 8¼	1343 16 7¼	6 6

No accounts could be procured, of either receipts or expenditure, farther back than the year ending in 1786; but it is said, that, for some years previous to that period, the Rates were as high as they were in that

[1] The Rate and Expenditure, of 1789 and 1790, are inserted together in the books

    year;

year; and that account is corroborated by the Returns made to Parliament, of the expences for the Poor in 1776, and the Affeffments in 1783, 1784, and 1785 An old farmer adds, that he has heard his father fay, that, 55 years ago, he paid £ 3. 12s. Poor's Rates for a farm, which now pays £ 26.; and that, in 1740, the year after the great froft, 9 gallons of wheat, at one time, coft 11s.; but fell, in a few months, to 3s.

In the country between Oxford and Deddington, the Rates are from 1s. 3d to 3s. 6d. in the pound, in feveral parifhes, which are almoft entirely agricultural. The high Rates, in this parifh, are afcribed to the common-field, of which the land principally confifts; whereas the neighbouring parifhes have been inclofed many years, and many fmall farms in them have been confolidated; fo that many fmall farmers, with little capitals, have been obliged, either to turn labourers, or to procure fmall farms in Deddington, or other parifhes, that poffefs common-field. Befides this, the neighbouring parifhes are, many of them, poffeffed by a few individuals, who are cautious in permitting new comers to obtain a fettlement.

The general opinion, here, is, that canals are a great injury to the Poor, by enabling farmers to fend their corn abroad: fuch erroneous ideas do not merit a refutation; but the farmers are very apprehenfive that they will produce ferious confequences. A boat laden with flour was lately feized by the populace; but was reftored, on the miller's promifing to fell it at a reduced price.

According to the prefent price of bread, a family here, which confifts of a man, his wife, and three children, (the eldeft of which is 4 years of age,) will expend, in that article alone, from laft Michaelmas to Michaelmas next, £ 16. 18s. The whole earnings of the man, provided he continues in health during the year, and can obtain conftant work, will not exceed £ 22. 15s.; and as his wife and children earn nothing, there will only remain £ 5. 17s. to provide him and them with lodging, fuel, cloaths, and every other neceffary of life; and his deficiencies muft be made up by the parifh.

July, 1795.

O X -

OXFORD.

ELEVEN parifhes of the city of Oxford were incorporated in 1771, for the maintenance of their Poor, who are principally relieved in the geneial work-houfe[1]. The average number of Paupers in the houfe, duiing the laft feven years, has been 160, in fummer ; and 200, in winter: The prefent number is 167, confifting chiefly of children, women, and old men. Their earnings aie about £300. a year, and arife from a facking manufactory, and from fweeping the ftreets ; for which the Corporation of Guardians is paid £100. a year. The work-houfe is under the fuperintendance of acting Guaidians, who are chofen annually. This fyftem of government appears to be a very bad one : many perfons, who aie chofen guardians, are too much engaged with their own private concerns, to attend to the affairs of the work-houfe : others, who enter into their office, with a zealous defire to promote the inieeft of the paifhes, by a regular attendance at the woik-houfe, have fcaicely acquiied the knowledge that is neceffary for parochial adminiftraois, when the teim of their office expires ; and they are fucceeded by guardians, who cntiiely overturn the fyftem of their piedeceffors. Thus, alteiations are continually made in the table of diet, &c. The immediate management of the Poor in the houfe is confided to old people, who appear to be by no means competent to the tafk. Several perfons have remarked, that children, who have been educated in the work-houfe, feldom turn out well.

The houfe is built on a good plan, in an airy fituation ; but is exceedingly dirty.

The following is the ufual weekly fare ; but no regular table of diet is obferved :

	Breakfaft.	Dinner	Suppei
Sunday,	Milk-pottage and bread, or broth	Butchei's meat, and roots, or vegetables	Potatoes, with lard
Monday,	Ditto	Bread and cheefe.	Bioth, oi milk pottage
Tuefday,	Ditto	As Sunday.	As Sunday
Wednefday,	Ditto	As Monday.	As Monday
Thuifday,	Ditto	As Sunday	As Sunday.
Friday,	Ditto.	Suet pudding	Biead and cheefe
Satuiday,	Ditto.	Biead and cheefe, or peafe-foup	Ditto.

[1] The Work-houfe is built on the fcite of Henry the Firft's palace

At

At meat dinners, men receive 6 oz. of meat ; women, 5 oz. ; and boys, 4 oz. without bone; and the fame quantity of bread.

The following particulars are copied, verbatim, from the general ftatement of the laft year's accounts of the Guardians. I infert the whole of it, as it moft evidently proves, that inftitutions of this nature, without unremitting attention being paid by thofe who are entrufted with their management, are continually liable to degenerate into idlenefs and diforder.

"R E C E I P T S.

	£.	s.	d.
Eleven Rates on the united parifhes - -	2547	6	4
On account of the manufactory - - -	716	11	1
Sundries on account of the maintenance of the Poor	160	19	8
For labour and manure - - - -	156	16	7
On account of the militia families - -	234	18	5½
Borrowed, by order of the Guardians, to purchafe hemp	200	0	0

Total receipts - £ 4016 12 1½

P A Y M E N T S.

	£.	s.	d.
Balance paid to the laft Treafurer - - -	58	5	1¼
Relief of the out-poor - - - -	350	17	9
Meat, including pigs and feeding - -	292	17	4½
Flour and wheat - - - -	326	3	6
Malt and hops - - - - -	176	14	0
Grocery, cheefe, oatmeal, and milk - -	338	13	10
Wood and coal - - - - -	95	0	2
Sundries in the houfe - - - -	78	13	0¼
Clothing, exclufive of £ 80. houfe-manufacture -	80	7	3½
Furniture, repairs, and taxes - - -	220	7	8½
Salaries - - - - -	123	0	4
On account of the manufactory - - -	624	11	5
Labour, including horfes, &c. - - -	117	0	10
Militia families and fubftitutes - - -	485	13	3
Intereft and annuities - - - -	334	14	0
Removals and paffes - - - -	10	5	0
Deficiencies and taxes, ftamps, printing and ftationary	46	11	5
Money borrowed to purchafe hemp, with intereft -	203	18	0

Total payments - £ 3963 14 0½

Balance - - £ 52 18 1

State of the Affairs of the House at Midsummer 1794.

	£.	s.	d.
Balance in the Treasurer's hands - - -	52	18	1
Stock of manufactory in the house - -	497	1	0½
Ditto of cloathing - - - -	52	8	8
Ditto of grocery, meat, &c. - - -	64	2	4¾
Debts due to the house for manufacture - -	155	10	4
Ditto for labour and manure - - -	164	14	6
Ditto for militia payments - - -	286	0	0
	£ 1272	15	0¼
Deduct debts due from the house -	410	0	10
Balance in favour of the house - £	862	14	2¼

*** As the balance in favour of the house, at the commencement of the year, was £ 520. 4s. 5d it appears that the house is advantaged this year in the sum of £ 342. 9s. 9¼d ; which is a much greater sum than the amount of the additional tax imposed in the year, notwithstanding the expences incurred by the alterations and repairs.

" The Guardians having now made up their year's accompts, think it incumbent on them, at the same time they submit them to the inspection of their respective parishes, to subjoin the following statement of facts, as well for the satisfaction of the public at large, as for the particular information of those gentlemen who may succeed them in office. And in the first place they must observe, that it was no small mortification to them, on taking a minute survey of the house, to find it in many respects the very reverse of what they conceived a house of industry ought to be. The boundary walls were insufficient to confine the Paupers ; the garden, yard, and offices lay open, and in common with each other ; the windows and doors of the house without proper bars or fastenings ; no regular wards appropriated to the sick, aged, or infirm ; nor nurseries for the children ; the sexes strangely intermixed in their eating and sitting rooms, and also in their shops and exercise grounds : nor any separation between their wards and sleeping rooms. They found too, a considerable manufacture carried on without a superintendant ; the sweeping of the streets without plan or system ; the master's and matron's apartments situated in one cor-

ner

ner of one of the wings of the building, at a diftance from, and out of the fight and hearing of every part of the houfe, where their attention was more particularly demanded. The houfe in general dirty, unfweet, and in a miferable ftate of repair; without a fingle rule or order eftablifhed for the regulation and government of it's numerous family, who were, in general, idle, riotous, and difordeily.

They, therefore, found it neceffary to appoint a committee to take thefe matters into confideration, and on whofe report, and under whofe direction, a fet of general rules and orders have been eftablifhed, for the better government of the houfe.

The mafter's and matron's apartments have been brought into the center of the building, in view of the entrances in front, and at the fame time commanding the yard and offices backward. The fexes have been feparated, as far as the circumftances of the houfe, and the nature of their employment, will at prefent admit of; a fet of wards have been appropriated for the fick, infirm, and aged; and a nurfery and nurfes provided for the children. A regular plan has been laid down for the fweepers, and an active and intelligent fuperintendant of the manufactory appointed, at a very fmall additional expence; and the whole houfe has been whitewafhed, painted, and thoroughly repaired. An interior wall has juft now been finifhed, which will be an additional fecurity to the houfe, and at the fame time detach the Paupers from the garden, bridewell, ftable, pefthoufe, and other out-offices; the want of which had occafioned much injury to the property of the houfe.

Thefe alterations, improvements, and repairs, have been neceffarily attended with a confiderable expence; but which will be amply repaid by the increafed regularity, decency, and good order of the Paupers, as well as by the additional fecurity and fupport of the houfe: and it is with much pleafure the Guardians already obferve a very material alteration for the better in thefe particulars.

The other expences they have reafon to complain of, have arifen from the heavy payments made to the families of the militia, and the ftated weekly payments to the out-poor. The former of thefe, the circumftances of the nation render unavoidable. The latter, which had arifen to the immoderate fum of between £ 6. and £ 7. per week, and which the

Guar-

Guardians found themfelves unable to reduce, or règulate to their fatisfaction, has been necelfarily difcontinued altogether, unlefs in cafes of occafional diftrefs, which is ftrictly conformable to their Act of Parliament.

A very confiderable expence had been incurred by a lofs or wafte in the articles of bread and beer ; but which has been difcovered, and for the prefent put a ftop to ; but no fatisfactory account has yet been given to the Guardians, as to the perfons to whom this lofs or wafte fhould be imputed, or by what means either the bread or the beer was fo deftroyed.

An attempt likewife has been made to promote and encourage virtue and induftry amongft the Paupers, and to difcourage idlenefs and every fpecies of vice, by holding out rewards and premiums to the one, and making the others objects of fhame and correction. In fhort, the Guardians may with truth affert, that they have laboured with zeal and affiduity to make the houfe, what a houfe of induftry ought to be—a comfortable afylum for the aged and infirm, a place of ufeful employment for thofe who are able to work, and a houfe of correction for the idle and profligate."

In the city of Oxford, 1200 houfes pay the window-tax : the number exempted is eftimated at about 600. The number of ale-houfes is 200 ; and of Friendly Societies 7, confifting, on an average, of 101 members each. They have all had their rules confirmed by the magiftrates. The land-tax, in Oxford, varies from 5s. to 6s. in the pound.

The prices of provifions are : beef, $5\frac{1}{2}$d. the lb ; mutton, 5d. the lb. ; veal, from 5d. to 6d. ; bacon, from 9d. to 10d. ; bread, 1s. 8d. the half-peck loaf ; butter, $10\frac{1}{2}$d. the lb. ; milk, 1d. the pint ; eggs, 6 for 4d.

Common labourers are paid from 15d. to 18d. the day, in winter; in hay-harveft, from 18d. to 20d. the day ; in corn-harveft, 10s. the week ; women, corn-weeders, 8d. the day, without victuals.

In St. Clement's, which is not an incorporated parifh, the Poor are generally maintained by an allowance at home : laft year, they were fent into the general work-houfe, for which the parifh paid 2s. 6d. a head, for the weekly maintenance of each perfon. The old method is adopted this year. The land-tax is about 2s. 5d. in the pound. There are 6 ale-houfes in the parifh. The inhabitants are chiefly fmall tradefmen and fhop-keepers.

Table

Table of Poor's Rates, and Parochial Disbursements, in the Parish of ST. CLEMENT.

Years.				Amount of Rates.			Net Disbursements.			Rate in the Pound.	
				£.	s.	d.	£.	s.	d.	s.	d.
1761	-	-	-	82	11	4	88	19	11		
1762	-	-	-	125	9	9	125	4	0		
1775	-	-	-	174	2	8	182	15	2	4	8
1776	-	-	-	124	2	4	125	6	6½	3	4
1777	-	-	-	144	8	0	140	12	1	4	0
1778	-	-	-	134	13	10	144	11	10	3	8
1789	-	-	-	125	6	0	118	3	6¼	3	4
1790	-	-	-	125	6	4	116	17	1	3	4
1791	-	-	-	128	9	0	148	10	11	3	4
1792	-	-	-	140	4	4	138	16	6	3	8
1793	-	-	-	129	5	0	115	4	5	3	4
1794	-	-	-	172	17	4	179	12	0	4	4
1765 Year ending in May				185	13	8	184	9	10	4	8

July, 1795.

RUTLAND.

EMPINGHAM.

THE lordship of Empingham is four miles in length; and in breadth, on an average, two miles and a half. With all it's angles, it is near seven miles in circumference. The town, which is near seven furlongs in length, consists of 122 houses, in which are 705 inhabitants, viz. 208 males, and 217 females, above 14 years of age; and 147 males, and 133 females, under 14 years. The people are chiefly farmers, and agri-

7

cultural

cultural labourers; and fome few mechanics, viz. fmiths, fhoemakers, tailors, ftone-mafons, and carpenters: there are three fmall grocers' fhops in
Empingham. Theie is no eftablifhed manufactory; but two linen-weav-
ers work for hire. The general employ of the induftrious Poor thioughout the county, is knitting ftockings, and fpinning linen and jeifey: in
the latter way, moft of the wives and children of labourers at Emping-
ham are employed, and earn from 3d. to 8d. a day, according to thei ages
and abilities. The jerfey fo fpun is woven into tammies, by poor weaveis
in the fouth of Rutland, and in Leicefterfhire, and Noithamptonfhire.

Except thiee perfons, the whole parifh profefs the eftablifhed religion
of the Church of England: of the three Diffenteis, two aie Baptifts, and
one a Methodift. The Rector and Vicar, in lieu of tithe, ieceive a coin-
rent, which is regulated by a late Act of Parliament[1].

There

---

[1] See 34 G III c 30, (Private Acts,) entitled, "An Act for dividing, allotting, and inclofing certain open and common fields, &c. within the manor, &c of Empingham, in the
county of Rutland "

   As the claufes which regulate the mode of afcertaining, and of paying the corn-rent, are
very clearly drawn up, I fubjoin them for the information of perfons who may be
defirous of introducing a fimilar commutation into other parifhes

   " AND be it further enacted, That in lieu of, and full recompence and fatisfaction for all
tithes, both great and fmall, and compofitions in lieu of tithes, arifing within the faid parifh of Empingham, and due and payable to the faid Sir Gilbert Heathcote, as leffee of the
faid Prebendary, and to the Vicar of the faid vicarage for the time being refpectively, fuch feveral annual rents or fums of money as the faid commiffioners fhall adjudge to be together
equal in value to one-fifth part of all fuch of the arable or tillage lands, and one-ninth part
of all fuch other lands and grounds, within the faid parifh of Empingham, as are fubject
and liable to the payment of fuch tithes, or compofitions in lieu of tithes as aforefaid, fhall
be for ever, feverally and refpectively, iffuing and payable to the leffee or leffees of the faid
Prebendary, and his fucceffors, and to the faid Vicar and his fucceffors, proportioned, and ao-
cording to the value of their refpective rights and interefts in and to the aforefaid great and
fmall tithes, and compofitions in lieu of tithes, forth and out of the faid feveral lands and
grounds fo liable to the payment of tithes, or compofitions in lieu of tithes as aforefaid,
or fuch part or parts thereof, refpectively, as the faid commiffioners, in and by their faid
award, fhall direct and appoint in that behalf; which faid feveral annual rents, or fums of
money, payable to the leffee or leffees of the faid Prebendary and his fucceffors, fhall be payable, and paid to him and them, at the Prebendal Houfe, in Empingham aforefaid; and which
faid feveral annual rents, or fums of money, payable to the faid Vicar and his fucceffors, fhall
be payable, and paid to him and them, at the Vicarial Houfe, in Empingham aforefaid,
feverally and refpectively, by two equal half-yearly payments, on fuch days and times as the
faid commiffioners fhall, in and by their award, direct and appoint: fubject, neverthelefs, to
the variation of a corn-rent, which the faid commiffioners fhall, and they are hereby
directed and required to afcertain, from or by means of the London Gazette, or by fuch
other ways and means as they fhall think moft equitable and proper, by the average price of
a Winchefter bufhel of good marketable wheat in the county of Rutland, during the term
of twenty-one years, next preceding the twenty-fourth day of June, in the prefent year of
our Lord, one thoufand feven hundred and ninety-four: And the faid commiffioners fhall,

in

There are two well regulated ale-houfes in the townfhip; and one
Friendly Society, confifting of 90 members : it is the only one that has
been

in and by their faid award, fet forth fuch average price, and what quantity of wheat, at
that price, the faid fum, fo to be afcertained, would purchafe; the total number of acres upon which it fhall be charged, and the average quantity, and correfpondent fum per acre, diftinctly charged and made payable to the leffee or leffees of the faid Prebendary and his fucceffors, and to the faid Vicar and his fucceffors, refpectively, from and out of each feparate
allotment and parcel of old enclofure fo liable to the payment of tithes, or compofitions in
lieu of tithes, as aforefaid; and that it fhall and may be lawful to and for the leffee and leffees
of the faid Prebendary and his fucceffors, and the faid Vicar and his fucceffors, and alfo to
and for any one or more of the owners or proprietors of lands charged with the payment
of fuch annual rents or fums, which lands fhall be affeffed in the Parochial Rates at the
yearly fum of two hundred pounds or upwards, and to and for every of them refpectively,
at his and their own proper cofts and expence refpectively, to apply to the Juftices, at their
firft quarter-feffions of the peace, to be held in and for the county of Rutland, in the week
fucceeding the clofe of the feaft of Eafter next after the expiration of twenty-one years,
after the execution of the faid award, (having given notice in the London Gazette, and alfo
in fome news-papers ufually circulated in the county of Rutland, fo long as any fuch fhall
be publifhed, on the firft day of publication in the month of January next preceding; and,
in cafe there fhall be no London Gazette or other news-paper publifhed or circulated, then
by fuch other ways or means as the faid Juftices fhall deem proper and fufficient,) to have
two perfons, (not being interefted in the premifes,) named by the faid Juftices then and
there affembled, to be, together with a third perfon to be chofen by fuch two perfons, (and
which faid third perfon, the faid two perfons are hereby required to choofe,) arbitrators, or
referees, for enquiring into, and afcertaining, by the means aforefaid, the average price of
a Winchefter bufhel of good marketable wheat, within the county of Rutland, for the ten
years then laft paft; which faid three arbitrators or referees, or any two of them, fhall, by
their reports, to be made and delivered into the hands of the Juftices at the court of quarter feffions, to be held in the firft week after the tranflation of St. Thomas the martyr, then
next enfuing, fet forth fuch average price; and in cafe it fhall appear, by fuch report, that
the average price of a Winchefter bufhel of fuch wheat is more or lefs than the average
price fet forth in the faid award, by the value of three-pence or upwards, then, and in that
cafe, the faid yearly rents, or fums fo afcertained, fhall be increafed or diminifhed in proportion, and the exact amount of the yearly rents or fums, to which the fame fhall be fo
increafed or diminifhed, fhall be declared by the order of the faid court, and the fame fhall,
from the half-yearly day of payment preceding fuch order, remain in and continue iffuing
and payable out of the faid feveral allotments and old enclofures, charged by the faid
award therewith, until the end of ten years next enfuing, when the fame may, by
fuch application, and in fuch manner as is herein before mentioned, be again varied,
and fo from time to time at the end of every ten years for ever; which faid yearly
rents or fums fo to be afcertained as aforefaid, fhall be fubject and liable to the land-tax
and parifh rates, in like manner as the tithes or compofitions they are in lieu of, and com-
penfation for, would have been liable to, if this act had not been made   Provided always,
that in cafe the lands out of which the faid yearly rents or fums fhall be iffuing and payable,
fhall at any time hereafter, by fale or otherwife, be divided, and become the property of
different perfons, the property of each fuch perfon fhall be fubject and liable, and be charged
and chargeable with no more of the faid yearly rents or fums fo to be afcertained as aforefaid,
than according to the number of acres which fuch property contains, and the average fum
per acre with which the fame refpectively fhall, by the award of the faid commiffioners, be
made fubject and liable to; any thing herein contained to the contrary thereof in any wife
notwithftanding.

And, in order to prevent any difficulty to the leffee or leffees of the faid Prebendary and
his fucceffors, and to the faid Vicar and his fucceffors, by the divifion of any eftate by fale or
otherwife,

been eftablifhed here, and has had its rules confirmed at the quarter-feffions. This Society was eftablifhed in 1791 ; and the great benefits which refult from it, both to the morals, and the comforts of its members, afford the cleareft conviction of the utility of fimilar inftitutions. The rules are much the fame as thofe in other Friendly Societies ; but befides the regulations refpecting the fubfcriptions and allowances, the following additional refolutions, unanimoufly agreed upon at the general annual meeting held on the 3d of June 1794, are now entered in the rules of the Society.

otherwife, and to facilitate the future regulating the faid yearly rents or fums, be it further enacted, That the faid commiffioners fhall, and they are hereby required to make, or caufe to be made, two complete fchedules or defcriptions of each and every allotment and parcel of ancient enclofure charged with the faid yearly rents or fums refpectively, and of the name of the owner thereof, the exact meafure in acres, roods, and perches, the yearly rents or fums of money iffuing out of each refpectively, and the quantity of wheat which is to govern each of the faid future yearly rents or fums of money payable to the leffee or leffees of the faid Prebendary and his fucceffors, and to the faid Vicar and his fucceffors, and the rate by the acre by which the faid yearly rents or fums of money fhall be charged as aforefaid, and fuch other requifites as fhall be judged proper or neceffary by the faid commiffioners to render every matter refpecting the faid yearly rents or fums of money clear and plain in future ; which faid fchedules or defcriptions fhall be figned by the faid commiffioners, and one of them depofited in the epifcopal regiftry at Lincoln, and the other annexed to the award of the faid commiffioners hereinafter directed to be made. And be it further enacted, That the leffee or leffees of the faid Prebendary and his fucceffors, and the faid Vicar and his fucceffors, fhall and may have and exercife fuch and the fame powers and remedies for recovering the faid yearly rents or fums refpectively, (fubject to fuch variations, reftrictions, and divifions as aforefaid,) when and as often as the fame, or any part thereof, fhall be in arrear, as by law are given and provided for the recovery of rent fervice or other rent in arrear ; and that the power of recovering the arrears of the faid yearly rents or fums refpectively, fhall remain extended to the whole lands and eftate originally charged therewith, until a divifion of the faid lands and eftate, and apportionment of the faid yearly rents or fums, fhall be made known to the leffee or leffees of the faid Prebendary or his fucceffors, and the faid Vicar or his fucceffors, refpectively, by a written notice thereof from the parties ; and after fuch notice, their power of diftrefs and recovery of the faid yearly rents or fums, fo apportioned and being in arrear refpectively, fhall be upon each and every divifion fo made, in the like manner as they are in and by this act directed upon the whole of fuch lands and eftate fo divided as aforefaid ; and that upon the death, ceffion, or refignation of the prefent and every future Vicar of Empingham aforefaid, he, his executors, or adminiftrators, fhall be entitled to, and receive fo much and fuch part of the faid yearly rents or fums as fhall be in proportion to the number of days elapfed from the then laft preceding day of payment, to the day of his death, ceffion, or refignation.

And be it further enacted, That the feveral annual rents or fums fo to be iffuing and payable to the leffee or leffees of the faid Prebendary and his fucceffors, and to the faid Vicar and his fucceffors as aforefaid, fhall for ever, after the commencement thereof, be in lieu of all, and all manner of great and fmall tithes, compofitions, or other payments whatfoever, to the leffee or leffees of the faid Prebendary and his fucceffors, and to the faid Vicar and his fucceffors, or any of them refpectively, from and out of, or in refpect of, all and every the meffuages, homefteads, gardens, orchards, clofes, ancient enclofures, commons, common fields, meadows, common paftures, common grounds, woods, fpinneys, and wafte grounds, and all other lands, tenements, and hereditaments whatfoever, in Empingham aforefaid, (modufes, Eafter offerings, furplice fees, and mortuaries only excepted,) and from thenceforth all fuch great and fmall tithes, compofitions, and other payments fhall ceafe, determine, and be for ever extinguifhed."

" That

" That every perfon hereafter to be admitted into this Society, fhall declare that he will pay allegiance to the King, and duty to the laws of his country.

" That no perfon, whofe fentiments fhall be found, and proved, to be unfriendly to the prefent conftitution of this country, fhall be admitted a member of this Society, whofe duty and boaft it is to fear God, and to honour the King; but that every fuch perfon fhall be excluded the Society, and deprived of all farther benefit from it, from the time of exclufion."

At the fame time £1. 13s. 1½d. was collected among the members, who are in general poor, for the fervice of the Duke of York's army on the continent.

There are, of old enclofure and wood land, about 700 acres; the remainder of the lordfhip, comprehending about 3300 acres, was enclofed this year; total about 4000 acres. There are eighteen large farms, of which none are lefs 100, nor more than 300 acres. The remainder of the land is let in fmall quantities to cottagers, who are thus enabled to keep a cow, or to fatten a pig. The articles of cultivation are, wheat, barley, oats, peafe, beans, and turnips; and fince the enclofure, clover feeds after turnips. The average value, or rent of cultivated land, is 12s. an acre. The whole rental of land and houfes amounts to £3622. 14s. The produce of the land-tax could not be afcertained. There is a cow-pafture, but no wafte land in the lordfhip.

The prices of provifions are: beft beef and mutton, from 5d. to 5½d. the lb.; coarfe ditto, from 4d. to 4½d.; veal, 5d.; wheat, fluctuating from £4. 10s. to £5. the quarter; barley, from £2. to £2. 4s.

In the laft harveft, wheat lands were reaped, and the wheat fheafed, at 6s. and 7s. the acre; barley and oats mown at 2s. and 2s. 6d. the acre; and grafs at 1s. 6d. and 2s. 6d. the acre. In the above cafes, labourers found their own meat and drink. The price of daily labour in harveft is, in general, very indeterminate. At other feafons, 14d. and 16d. a day have been ufually paid for common labour; but at the prefent, rather more is allowed on account of the high price of provifions. Labourers employed in threfhing, are paid, for wheat, 2s. 6d. to 3s. the quarter; for barley, 2s; and for oats, 1s. and 1s. 6d. the quarter.

The

The Poor are chiefly farmed in a Houſe of Protection [1], (as it is called,) for £90 a year. The houſe was built on an extenſive plan, by Sir Gilbert Heathcote, Bart. in 1793, and furniſhed by the pariſhioners. The pariſh ſupply two ſuits of cloaths, and changes of linen, to each Pauper on entering the houſe; and the maſter is bound to keep them, and, (if any leave the houſe,) to ſend them out equally well apparelled. Boys are, occaſionally, let out to farmers : when put out apprenticds, the fee is paid by the pariſh.

In caſe of death, the Maſter defrays all funeral expences; however, ſince the erection of the houſe, of eleven Paupers, then received, and of three, who have ſince entered it, not one has died.

The whole houſe is under the regulation of a Committee, who viſit weekly, in turns, and to whom the Maſter, or the Poor, are to appeal for redreſs, when requiſite.

It will be ſeen by the table of diet, that the Poor have good eating. The infirm and ſickly are not required to work : the healthy are made to exert themſelves. Males are let out at a price proportioned to their abilities : females do the work of the houſe, and ſpin, and knit. The profits, ariſing from their work, are paid to the maſter.

	Breakfaſt.	Dinner.	Supper.
Sunday,	Women—tea, and bread and butter : men—milk or broth.	Beef or mutton, with vege- tables.	Milk, or broth.
Monday,	Same as Sunday.	Broth, and cold meat, ſtewed with plenty of vegetables.	Milk.
Tueſday,	Ditto.	Same as Sunday.	Same as Sunday.
Wedneſday,	Ditto.	Cold meat, ſtewed with plenty of vegetables.	Broth.
Thurſday,	Ditto.	Same as Sunday.	Same as Sunday.
Friday,	Ditto.	Same as Wedneſday.	Ditto.
Saturday,	Ditto.	Apple pudding; or oatmeal and milk—that is, milk boiled, and thickened with oatmeal.	Milk, or water-gruel.

[1] The poor-houſe at Empingham is called the *Houſe of Protection*, both to obviate prejudice againſt the name of *Poor* or *Work-houſe*, and becauſe it is *a protection to the aged, ſick, and infirm.*

7

Table

Table of Baptisms, Burials, and Poor's Rates.

	Baptisms.			Burials.											
Years.	Males.	Fem.	Tot	Males.	Fem.	Tot.	Marr.	Poor's Rates.			Expences for the Poor.			Rate in the Pound.	
1680	5	6	11	14	11	25	12	No account.			No account.				
1685	3	9	12	4	8	12	25								
1690	6	6	12	3	6	9	6								
1691	11	7	18	7	7	14	6								
1692	6	10	16	4	2	6	5								
1693	7	7	14	6	3	9	12								
1694	7	12	19	3	3	6	7								
1695	6	8	14	9	10	19	6								
1696	6	5	11	6	5	11	10								
1697	15	15	30	4	8	12	13								
1698	10	9	19	4	7	11	2								
1699	9	10	19	7	6	13	3								
1700	7	11	18	5	12	17	1								
1720	5	6	11	12	14	26	10								
1740	10	9	19	7	4	11	2	£.	s.	d.	£.	s.	d.	s.	d.
1760	10	15	25	7	17	24	7	57	13	7	49	16	8	1	3
1775	8	7	15	3	5	8	3	85	9	2¾	70	0	5	1	10½
1776	8	12	20	4	8	12	4	73	2	1	72	10	10½	1	5
1777	10	12	22	3	7	10	4	121	12	8½	82	12	3½	1	8
1778	7	10	17	9	5	14	5	98	4	9	82	12	4	1	8
1779	13	8	21	6	9	15	4	149	10	4½	104	6	5	3	9½
1780	15	18	33	11	10	21	11	123	12	3	102	0	3	2	6
1781	10	12	22	7	10	17	8	113	12	8	106	3	8	2	3½
1782	11	9	20	7	7	14	7	113	12	8	105	0	7	2	3½
1783	14	9	23	11	11	22	3	124	4	4	133	15	3	2	6
1784	14	15	29	6	5	11	5	128	17	8	119	1	10½	2	6
1785	11	13	24	7	11	18	1	127	4	5	119	1	11	2	6
1786	6	13	19	3	8	11	5	148	5	11¾	127	14	2	3	1½
1787	10	9	19	5	9	14	6	160	16	1	152	3	8	3	4½
1788	18	4	22	8	7	15	7	199	0	5	190	14	8	4	2
1789	16	11	27	9	4	13	10	160	16	1	148	3	10½	3	4½
1790	8	10	18	5	3	8	3	146	18	1½	139	9	6	3	1
1791	14	16	30	4	6	10	5	138	19	2	142	12	4	2	11
1792	9	9	18	5	3	8	2	125	1	2½	129	4	0½	2	7½
1793	15	8	23	8	4	12	6	178	13	4	174	4	3	3	9
1794	15	9	24	8	4	12	5	232	16	10½	282	5	9¾	5	0
1795	8	20	28	7	6	13	9	The accounts for 1795 not complete.							

The

The expences of a labourer's family are, in general, equal to the earnings. Bread made of wheaten and barley flour, mixed, is the principal food. During the laſt ſummer, beef and mutton weie ſold, at a reduced price, throughout the county, to prevent the too great conſumption of bread. The meat was generally made into broth, of which the Poor are becoming more fond than they formerly were : they begin alſo to uſe vegetables very generally, and it is thought that their prejudices in favoui of any particular diet are wearing away very faſt.

Five labouiers in Empingham have received premiums fiom the Society of Induſtry, for bringing up four children, or more, (the youngeſt of which was 14 years of age,) without having ſolicited relief from their pariſh.

Of the inſtitution of this Society, the following account is chiefly tranſcribed from the View of the Agriculture of the County of Rutland, drawn up by Mr. John Crutchley, for the conſideration of the Board of Agriculture:

" At the general quarter ſeſſions of the peace for the county, held on the 14th of July 1785, his Majeſty's juſtices of the peace then aſſembled, having taken into their conſideration the increaſe of the Poor Rates, the want of regard to the employments of the Poor in general, and of the infant Poor in particular; reſolved, that the following rates and orders (purſuant to the ſtatutes made and provided for the relief and maintenance of the Poor) ſhould be obſerved within the ſeveral paiiſhes of the ſaid county.

1, That the overſeers of the Poor, of each pariſh, do immediately provide ſuch raw materials, as wool, woollen yarn, hemp, and flax, as alſo wheels, and other implements for the employment of the Poor of every denomination, as ſhall be neceſſary to enable them to do ſuch work as they are capable of performing, either by ſpinning, knitting, or any other employment which the overſeer may direct ; and that the overſeers do make complaint, before a juſtice of the peace, of thoſe who refuſe to work, or who wilfully ſpoil the raw materials given them ; and that the overſeers ſhall, in the ſeveral reſpects above mentioned, act according to the direction of the neareſt juſtice.

2, That no perſon be allowed any relief, till they have done ſuch work as they are capable of.

3, That from and after the 1ſt day of Januaiy then next, no perſon be
allowed

allowed any relief, on account of any child above [1] fix years of age, who fhall not be able to knit.

4, That no perfon be allowed any relief, on account of any child above nine years of age, who fhall not be able to fpin, either linen, or woollen.

5, That the overfeers of the Poor of each parifh, fhall meet, at the leaft, once every month, in the church of their refpective parifhes, upon the Sunday, after divine feivice ; there to confider of the beft courfe and oider to be taken and made in the employment of the Poor."

That the magiftrates might have the advice and affiftance of the county at laige, in endeavouring to check the progiefs of the evils above mentioned, a meeting of the owners and occupiers of lands and tenements in the county of Rutland, was requefted to be holden at Oakham, in September 1785. At which meeting, it was refolved, to adopt a plan which a few years before had been propofed, and with great fuccefs carried into execution, by the Rev. Mr. Bowyer, in the fouthern diftrict in the parts of Lindfey, and the county of Lincoln ; and the following propofals were agreed upon, and ordered to be made public in the county of Rutland :

1, That every parifh be requefted to fubfciibe a fum, amounting to the proportion of one per cent. upon the Poor Rates of the laft year, and to authorife (at a veftry to be immediately called for that purpofe) the overfeer of the Poor, to pay the faid fubfcription into the hands of the neareft chief conftable, before the 10th day of November.

2, That individuals be folicited to fubfcribe the fum of five fhillings each, annually ; larger fums to be received as benefactions.

3, That a meeting be holden at Oakham, on the 14th day of November next, to choofe a committee for the management of the bufinefs.

4, That piemiums, confifting of cloathing, be given from the faid fubfcription, to fuch children of ceitain ages and defciiption, as in a given time fhall have pioduced the greateft quantity of work, of different kinds, and of the beft quality.

5, That when any young perfon fhall go out to apprenticefhip, or to feivice [2], or fhall be married with the approbation of the committee,

---

[1] Since the eftablifhment of this Society, many children of five, and fome of four years old, have obtained premiums.

[2] The fum of £21. 10s has been given, by the committee, to 13 young perfons in fervice.

fuch

fuch perfons fhall receive not lefs than £5. nor exceeding £10. if he or fhe fhall have received three of the annual premiums given by the committee; not lefs than £2. nor exceeding £3. if he or fhe fhall have received two of the annual premiums; and not lefs than 30s. nor exceeding £2. if he or fhe fhall have received one premium.

6, That premiums, at the direction of the committee, be given to thofe day labourers [1] who bring up four or more children, born in wedlock, to the age of 14 years, without relief from the parifh.

7, That, as the moft effectual means of preventing families becoming chargeable, it be ftrongly recommended to the parifh officers, to furnifh (gratis) wheels to thofe perfons who wifh to employ themfelves, although they fhould not be chargeable to the parifh; and to order the teachers, in the work-houfes, to allow them free admiffion into the fpinning room, and to teach them (gratis,) and that the profits arifing from the work of fuch children be for the benefit of their parents.

And at a general meeting of the county on the 14th day of November 1785, a committee was appointed, confifting of 23 perfons, who undertook the management of the bufinefs for one year.

The committee, having at their next meeting, on the 10th day of December, afcertained the number of fubfcribing parifhes to be 46, proceeded to divide them into five claffes, having regard to neighbourhood, and to the amount of the parifh rates; and each member of the committee undertook to [2] fuperintend one or more parifhes.

It appearing to the committee, at their meeting on the 7th day of February 1786, that the fum of [3] £208. 19s. 4½d. had been received by

---

[1] The fum of £76 13s has been given to 27 day-labourers.

[2] Thofe who undertake to fuperintend the parifhes, are called truftees; and it is the bufinefs of a truftee to acquaint the children of the parifh, which he fuperintends, with the rules and orders of the committee; to take care that the work, required to be done, be punctually performed; to collect the fubfcriptions and benefactions; and prevent any impofition that may be attempted to be made upon the Society: fo that the fuccefs of this undertaking depends very much upon the attention of the truftees.

	£.	s.	d.
[3] Benefactions - - - - - -	112	4	3
Annual fubfcriptions of 5s. - - - - -	67	17	3
Parifh fubfcriptions of 1 per cent. of the Poor's Rates	28	17	10¼
	£208	19	4¼

their

their treafurer, they refolved that [1] £22. 19s. fhould be allowed for that year, to each of the five claffes, to purchafe cloathing for thofe children who fhould be found to be the moft induftrious.

On the 27th day of May 1786, the committee proceeded to the diftribution of the premiums: the number of [2] candidates amounted to 236.

Money allowed by the Committee, in each Year, for purchafing Cloathing.

		£.	s.	d.
In 1786	—	108	9	0
1787	—	104	6	0
1788	—	104	6	0
1789	—	83	5	0
1790	—	83	5	0
1791	—	86	5	0
1792	—	88	10	0
1793	—	92	5	0

The Number of Candidates in the different Years, from the Inftitution of the Society.

1786	Spinners of Jerfey	211	
	Linen	3	
	Knitters	22	
			236
1787	Jerfey	302	
	Linen	9	
	Knitters	37	
			348
1788	Jerfey	257	
	Linen	15	
	Knitters	60	
			332

[1] This fum was divided into 25 premiums, making, in the 5 claffes, 125 premiums.

[2] A certain quantity of work is required to be done, in two months, before any child can be admitted a candidate; and a perfon, well acquainted with fpinning and knitting, is appointed to fee each candidate fpin or knit one hour; which hour's work is produced to the committee, on the day the premiums are difpofed of.

1789

1789	Spinners of	Jerfey	203	
		Linen	8	
		Knitters	29	
				240
1790	- -	Jerfey	232	
		Linen	15	
		Knitters	40	
				287
1791	- -	Jerfey	263	
		Linen	19	
		Knitters	57	
				339
1792	- -	Jerfey	279	
		Linen	15	
		Knitters	69	
				363
1793	- -	Jerfey	261	
		Linen	21	
		Knitters	89	
				371

The following refolutions were unanimoufly agreed upon at a meeting of the committee of induftry for the county, held at the White Horfe inn, in Empingham, on the 9th of February 1795.

1, That Thomas Exton, of Empingham, labourer, be allowed £ 1. 1s. for having brought up two more children to the age of 14 years, without relief from the parifh.—John Scot, of Empingham, labourer, £ 1. 11s. 6d. for three more children.—William Sapcote, of Empingham, labourer, £ 2. 2s. for four children.—Elizabeth Scotney, of Ryal, £ 1. 10s., fhe having obtained the firft premium in the fourth clafs, in the year 1790, and having continued in the fame fervice one year.

2, That the fum of £ 106. be allowed to purchafe premiums for cloathing, for the five claffes into which the affociated parifhes are divided.

3, That the beft fpinner of jerfey be entitled to a premium of the value of £ 1. 10s. ; that the fecond beft fpinner be entitled to a premium of

£ 1. 5s.;

£ 1. 5s. : that the candidates for thefe premiums do not exceed the age of fourteen years, on the firft day of April 1795. That the beft fpinner of the year be entitled to a further premium of 20s ; and that fhe be called the Queen of the Spinners.

4, That four premiums, of the value of 16s. each, be given to the four beft fpinners of jerfey, not exceeding the age of thirteen years.

5, That four premiums, of the value of 10s. each, be given to the four beft fpinners of jerfey, not exceeding eleven years.

6, That four premiums, of the value 8s. each, be given to the four beft fpinners of jerfey, not exceeding nine years.

7, That four premiums, of the value of 7s each, be given to the four beft fpinners of jerfey, not exceeding feven years.

8, That fix premiums, of the value of 6s. each, be given to the fix beft fpinners of jerfey, not exceeding fix years.

9, That two premiums, of the value of 10s. each, be given to the two beft fpinners of jerfey, of different ages, who have not gained higher premiums, provided they have performed the work required for their refpective ages.

10, That one premium, of the value of 20s. be given to the beft fpinner of hemp or flax, not exceeding the age of fourteen years.

11, That one premium, of the value of 15s. be given to the beft fpinner of hemp or flax, not exceeding the age of twelve years.

12, That one premium, of the value of 10s. be given to the beft fpinner of hemp or flax, nor exceeding the age of ten years.

13, That three premiums, of the value of 10s. each, be given to the three beft knitters, not exceeding the age of eight years.

14, That five premiums, of the value of 8s. each, be given to the five beft knitters, not exceeding the age of feven years

15, That five premiums, of the value of 6s. each, be given to the five beft knitters, not exceeding the age of fix years.

16, That all the premiums will be open, not only to the parifh paupers, but to the children of thofe perfons who fubfift by their manual labour, or whofe parents do not rent more than £ 10. per annum, or poffefs more than £ 6. per annum, of their own.

17, That no fpinner of jerfey be admitted a candidate for the firft fet of premiums, who fhall have fpun lefs than 32 dozen of hanks, from Monday the 16th day of March next enfuing, to Saturday the 9th day of May following, inclufively.

18, That no fpinner of jerfey be admitted a candidate for the fecond fet of premiums, who fhall have fpun lefs than 26 dozen of hanks within the fame time.

19, That no fpinner of jerfey be admitted a candidate for the third fet of premiums, who fhall have fpun lefs than 22 dozen within the fame time.

20, That no fpinner of jerfey be admitted a candidate for the fourth fet of premiums, who fhall have fpun lefs than 18 dozen within the fame time.

21, That no fpinner of jerfey be admitted a candidate for the fifth fet of premiums, who fhall have fpun lefs than 14 dozen within the fame time.

22, That no fpinner of jerfey be admitted a candidate for the fixth fet of premiums, who fhall have fpun lefs than 10 dozen within the fame time.

23, That the feveral candidates for the fpinning premiums be directed to carry, every Saturday during the time above-mentioned, the work of that week, to be infpected by the perfons approved of by the truftee of the parifh in which they live, that the jerfey of each fpinfter may be ticketed : and no perfon will be allowed to be a candidate for any of the aforefaid premiums, who fhall refufe to fubmit their work to be fo examined.

24, That the feveral truftees be defired to fend to the chairman, according to the form given below, on or before Saturday the 23d day of May, the names of the candidates for the different premiums in the parifhes under their direction ; with their ages, and the quantity of work performed by each : and the parifhes whofe accounts are not fent to the chairman on or before that day, to be excluded the chance of premiums for this year.

25, That no fpinner of hemp or flax will be admitted a candidate for the firft premium, who fhall not have fpun as much of the faid materials, from Monday the 16th day of March, to Saturday the 9th day of May, inclufive, as fhall have coft, or been worth, the fum of 14s ; nor will any fpinner be admitted a candidate for the fecond premium,

o   who

who fhall not have fpun as much of the faid materials as fhall have coft, or been worth, the fum of 11s.; nor will any fpinner be admitted a candidate for the third premium, who fhall not have fpun as much of the faid materials as fhall have coft, or been worth, the fum of 8s.: and the fpinners are to have their work infpected, and trials of their fkill and difpatch made in like manner as the fpinners of jerfey.

26, That every perfon that is admitted a candidate for a knitting premium, muft have their work infpected, and trials of their fkill and difpatch made in the fame manner as the fpinners.

27, That the ages of the feveral candidates be certified under the hand of their minifter, according to the form here given.

28, That fome perfon or perfons of fkill be appointed to go, after the 23d day of May, to the feveral candidates, who fhall have delivered in their names, and fubmitted to the conditions required as aforefaid, to fee each of them fpin for the fpace of one hour precifely, and to take an exact account of the number of hanks or fkeins, lees, and rounds, the jerfey fpun by each of them within the faid hour fhall reel to; the weight of hemp or flax fpun in the faid hour; and the weight of worfted knitted within the faid hour : which account, properly ticketed, fhall be laid before the committee.

29, That Thomas Coleman be appointed infpector for the fpinning of jerfey; and that the faid Thomas Coleman be directed, previoufly to his attending the committee for the purpofe of determining the premiums, carefully to examine the work of the feveral candidates.

30, That the premiums ordered to be given, at the difcretion of the committee, to thofe day-labourers who bring up four or more children, born in wedlock, to the age of fourteen years, without relief from the parifh, be limited to thofe perfons whofe youngeft child, under whom the premium is claimed, fhall have attained the age of fourteen years fince the 9th day of June 1794.

31, That any perfon difcovering an attempt to obtain any premium by fraudulent or falfe pretences, fhall, upon proving fuch fraud to the fatisfaction of the committee, receive double the value of the premium fo attempted to be gained, if the fuccefs of fuch fraud fhall be prevented by fuch difcovery : and if the fraud be fully proved, but too late for

prevention,

prevention, the difcoverer fhall, neverthelefs, be handfomely rewarded ; and the perfon or perfons guilty of fuch fraud fhall be declared
for ever incapable of receiving any of the premiums, rewards, or encouragement given by this Society.

32, That the committee do adjourn to Saturday the 6th day of June, at
ten o'clock in the forenoon, at the George Inn, in Oakham ; and the
early attendance of the members is requefted, as the chair will be taken
and bufinefs proceeded upon immediately.

33, That thefe refolutions be printed.

34, That the feveral truftees be requefted to obferve, that the form of the
certificates for the ages of the candidates, and the work performed by
each, be attended to.

Names of Spinners of Jerfey	When baptifed	Age	1ft Week d h	2d Week d h	3d Week d h	4th Week d h	5th Week d h	6th Week d h	7th Week d h	8th Week d h	Total. d h.
Adcock, Sarah	Mar. 15, 1776	13	4 2	ʒ 0	4 6	4 8	4 1	4 10	4 6	4 0	35 0
Clarke, Anne	Mar 20, 1777	11	3 6	3 8	3 10	3 6	3	3 7	3 5	3 6	28 10
Winterton, Hannah	Sept. 8, 1779	9	3 4	2 11	3	2 10	3 6	2 6	3 0	4	25 1
Stevens, Mary	June 10, 1781	7	2 4	2 2	2	2 0	2 2	2 0	2 4	2 6	17 10

Spinners of Hemp or Flax

Johnfon, Mary	Sept 20, 1775	13	Hemp or flax, coft	-	-	14s.
Smith, Jane	Oct 10, 1775	9	Hemp or flax, coft	-	-	11s
			Hemp or flax, coft	-	-	8s.

Knitters

Danfon, Thomas	Jan. 5, 1782	7	Knitted 2 pair of men's hofe ; 1 pair of boys' do.
Jones, William	Dec 14, 1782	6	Knitted 2 pair of women's hofe.
Ofborn, Mary	Mar. 17, 1783	7	Knitted 1 pair of women's hofe ; 1 pair of boys' do.

A true Copy of the Regifter of the Parifh of
Teigh (or as it may be) taken May the
8th (or as it may be) by me,
A B. minifter.

THOMAS FOSTER, Chairman.

It appears from the following ftatement of the Rates for the whole
county for 13 years, that they had been fomewhat reduced in the year
1793, from what they were in 1785, the period of the inftitution of
the Society of Induftry; but I think that 8 years are not a period fufficiently
long to enable the public to decide whether the benefits hitherto received,
and hereafter to be expected, from the Society of Induftry, are neceffarily
interwoven with it's principles, or are chiefly afcribable to the laudable zeal
and enthufiafm of the gentlemen who firft planned, and now fupport, the
inftitution.

Table

Table of Poor's Rates[1].

Years.	£.	s.	d.	
1776 —	2664	6	6	Expences for the Poor. See Returns to Par-
1780 —	2886	19	0	Poor's Rates. [liament.
1783 —	3775	5	10	
1784 —	4040	11	2	Ditto, from Returns to Parliament.
1785 —	3750	9	9	
1786 —	3415	16	0	Poor's Rates.
1787 —	3008	15	0	Ditto.
1788 —	3075	14	0	Ditto.
1789 —	3567	0	0	Ditto.
1790 —	3171	19	0	Ditto.
1791 —	3537	3	0	Ditto.
1792 —	3274	19	0	Ditto.
1793 —	3443	6	0	Ditto.

The Poor's Rates, in this county, are faid to be higheft in the un-enclofed parifhes.

December, 1795.

NORTH LUFFENHAM.

THIS parifh, according to an old furvey, contains about 1322 acres of open field, and near 200 acres of old enclofure. Here are 70 houfes, inhabited by 310 perfons; of whom, 149 are males, and 161 females, who, (except 2 linen-weavers, who work for hire, and whofe wives and children fpin jerfey, &c.) are chiefly farmers, and agricultural labourers. They all profefs the eftablifhed religion, except a few, who are Arminian Metho- difts. 23 houfes pay the window-tax; 47 are exempted.

Meat, on an average, is about 5d. the lb; wheat, £4. 10s. the quarter; barley, £2. the quarter: all other articles of provifion are at high prices.

Labourers, in winter, are chiefly employed in threfhing grain by the quarter, by which they earn 8s. or 9s. a week.

There are only 2 ale-houfes in this parifh. A Friendly Society has lately

[1] General View of the Agriculture of the County of Rutland, 25. I do not vouch for the correctnefs of all this Table. The Rates in 1785, are ftated, in the View, &c. at £3537. 5s.; and in the Returns made to Parliament, at £3750. 9s. 9d.

been

been eftablifhed ; and the members intend to have their rules confirmed at the next quarter feffions.

The land-tax is levied on a rental of about £700. per annum, exclufive of the tithe-rent.

The tithes are rented of the Rector, by the tenants or owners of each eftate.

In this parifh, there are 8 farms, of a middling fize, and a few cottages : the principal articles of cultivation are, wheat, barley, beans, white peafe, &c The land is fallowed once in 3 years ; after which, turnips are fown. There is a common pafture, containing about 107 acres, for which rent is paid to the proprietor.

Moft of the Paupers belonging to this parifh are maintained in a houfe of induftry, under the infpection of a perfon, who is paid by the parifh. The overfeers fend in the provifions, as they are wanted ; but the inhabitants find the expences run fo high, that they intend to adopt the fyftem of farming the Poor, as foon as they can meet with a proper contractor No particular rules are obferved refpecting their diet.

A Table of Baptifms, Burials, Marriages, Poor's Rates, and Expences for the Poor, in the Parifh of NORTH LUFFENHAM.

Years	Baptifms.			Burials			Mar	Affeffments			Net Expenditure			Rate in the Pound
	Mal	Fem	Tot	Mal	Fem.	Tot.		£.	s.	d.	£	s.	d.	s. d.
1766	2	1	3	4	2	6	—							
1767	4	8	12	2	3	5	—							
1768	3	1	4	4	1	5	—							
1769	9	5	14	3	0	3	—							
1770	5	7	12	2	3	5	3	31	8	6	29	13	2	0 8
1771	3	8	10	5	3	8	2	33	8	6	29	4	8	0 9
1772	7	5	12	4	3	7	0	42	2	0	36	11	0	0 10¼
1773	4	7	11	3	2	5	3	51	9	7	46	17	11	1 2
1774	5	6	11	1	2	3	3	66	11	8	60	1	1	1 6
1775	5	5	10	2	2	4	4	83	7	9	68	5	6	1 7½
1776	2	5	7	5	6	11	0	54	9	9	50	4	2	1 2
1777	4	5	9	0	5	5	1	62	19	9	57	18	3	1 3¼
1778	0	4	4	2	4	6	1	55	2	0	50	17	5	1 2
1779	4	8	12	1	4	5	5	61	13	6	52	16	5	1 3½
1780	4	3	7	6	7	13	2	75	0	6	69	4	0	1 7
1781	8	5	13	0	1	1	1	102	8	0	89	13	8	2 2
1782	3	1	4	7	3	10	0	70	10	3	66	19	9	1 5
1783	7	4	11	3	3	6	2	77	1	3	70	19	9	1 8½
1784	4	3	7	3	2	5	2	80	2	0	74	14	6	1 9
1785	8	2	10	6	4	10	1	61	4	7	58	10	7	1 1
1786	7	10	17	3	2	5	2	77	0	0	70	13	1	1 7
1787	10	4	14	2	5	7	1	55	13	7	49	19	9	1 2
1788	6	5	11	5	2	7	2	84	8	8	73	11	0	1 8
1789	6	3	9	6	2	8	1	75	1	0	56	3	0	1 4¾
1790	0	6	6	6	2	8	2	93	3	7	81	18	10	1 10¼
1791	9	5	14	1	1	2	0	125	13	6	109	7	11	2 6
1792	5	7	12	2	3	5	1	106	8	7	105	18	11	2 0
1793	4	5	9	4	7	11	4	107	5	0	90	11	10	2 0¼
1794	6	2	8	4	12	16	6	94	11	10	81	14	7	1 11
1795	4	8	12	3	2	5	2							

A fever prevailed in the parifh in 1794.   *December*, 1795.

SHROPSHIRE.

BISHOPS CASTLE.

THE parish of Bishops Castle is divided into two parts, viz. the borough, or township, of Bishops Castle, which contains 1100 inhabitants; and the hamlet, which contains 250: they consist of farmers, shop-keepers, inn-keepers, common mechanics, and labourers; and all profess the religion of the Church of England. 128 houses in the borough, and about 28 in the hamlet, pay the window-tax; it is supposed that 30 or 40 in the former, and near 15 in the latter, are exempted. The prices of provisions are: beef and mutton, from 4d. to 4½d. the pound; pork, 5d.; bacon, 9d. and 10d.; butter, 10d.; potatoes, 2s. 6d. for 10 gallons; wheat, 13s. for ditto; barley, 5s; oats, 3s. 6d.; milk, 1½d. the quart: coals are 25s. the ton. Labourers earn 7s. a week, in winter; and from 8s. to 9s. in summer; without board. About eight years ago, there were 29 ale-houses in the parish: there are now only 16: the magistrates keep down their number as much as they can. Of three Friendly Societies, one consists of 100 members; one of 70 members; and the third of 50 members: they have all had their rules confirmed at the quarter sessions. The rent of land varies from 12s. to £4. an acre; the average value is about 26s. Farms let from £100. to £350. a year; but are principally about £100. a year: every common grain and root is cultivated. Tithes are chiefly taken in kind. The land-tax is collected at 1s. in the pound on the net rent, in the borough; and in the hamlet, at about 11d. on the net rental. There are about 50 acres of common or waste land in the parish. The Poor of the borough have generally been, and are now, farmed in a work-house; the present contractor has £105. a year; for which he agrees to feed and cloath them; and to defray all other expences, except what may arise from appeals: in

consideration

confideration of the high price of provifions, the parifh gave him an additional gratuity of £5. the laft half-year. 14 Paupers, (confifting chiefly of old, infirm, or infane,) are at prefent in the houfe. Thofe, who can work, are employed in fpinning lint, or in other common work, according to their ages and abilities. The contractor has now, upon his lift, 11 or 12 out-penfioners, who receive from 6d. to 1s. a week, each; and a baftard, who cofts 1s. 6d. a week: he alfo pays feveral houfe-rents. His rule is, not to allow more than 1s. a week to each family of out-penfioners; and if that fum does not fatisfy them, he requires them to come into the houfe. It is not fuppofed that he can fupport them at a cheaper rate in the houfe; but a reluctance to enter it, often induces a poor family to acquiefce in a very fmall out-allowance.

It is generally believed, that if the Poor were not farmed, the Rates would be much higher than they at prefent are.

Table of the Diet in the Work-houfe.

	Breakfaft.	Dinner.	Supper.
Sunday,	Broth; or milk, and water-gruel.	Hot meat and vegetables.	Same as breakfaft.
Monday,	Ditto.	Cold meat and vegetables.	Ditto.
Tuefday,	Ditto.	Ditto.	Ditto.
Wednefday,	Ditto.	Same as Sunday.	Ditto.
Thurfday,	Ditto.	Same as Monday.	Ditto.
Friday,	Ditto.	Ditto.	Ditto.
Saturday,	Ditto.	Ditto.	Ditto.

No bread is allowed at dinner; fometimes potatoes and milk are ferved for fupper: the matron always gives each perfon a little bread and cheefe after breakfaft.

The houfe is kept pretty clean; of 10 beds, fix are ftuffed with feathers, and four with chaff: both beds and bed-cloaths are very old.

A committee of 12 gentlemen vifit the work-houfe very regularly.

A Table

Table of Baptisms, Burials, Marriages, Poor's Rates, and Expences for the Poor in the Borough.

Years.	BAPTISMS Males and Femals	BURIALS Males and Females.	Mar.	Years.	Poor's Rates. £ s d	Net Expenditure for the Poor. £ s d	Rate in the £.
1680	36	23	7	1764	160 13 2	161 5 3	
1685	21	45	4	1765	124 13 6	98 12 3	
1690	32	17	2	1766	104 17 0	103 16 9	s. d
1691	23	15	3	1767	124 19 11	106 0 8	1 2
1692	23	21	3	1768	112 1 1	115 5 2	1 0
1693	21	23	4	1769	105 18 5	114 1 10	1 2
1694	25	20	4	1770	108 2 6	117 3 1	1 2
1695	22	15	1	1771	107 0 0	113 4 3	1 2
1696	27	17	2	1772	109 3 2	113 6 9	1 2
1697	26	20	3	1773	115 8 10	110 8 2	1 2
1698	24	20	3	1774	117 11 8	112 1 11	1 2
1699	21	21	6	1775	115 7 0	108 9 6	1 2
1700	28	24	4	1776	114 12 7	124 4 0	1 2
1720	37	20	4	1777	118 9 7	119 0 5	1 2
1740	39	16	6	1778	120 10 0	117 2 3	1 2
1760	41	18	7	1779	121 0 0	117 3 8	1 2
1775	—	30	—	1780	122 5 10	118 3 5	1 2
The Registers are imperfect in 1775, and the seven following years.				1781	130 8 6	116 16 1	1 2
				1782	113 0 0	135 2 11	1 0
1783	33	15	4	1783	112 5 7	143 8 5	1 0
1784	39	26	2	1784	138 14 1	171 14 1	1 2
1785	35	11	6	1785	186 8 0	187 12 8	- -
1786	38	28	7	1786	141 12 0	144 10 7	1 3
1787	42	24	8	1787	159 1 0	152 1 2	1 4½
1788	41	26	6	1788	136 6 6	131 9 0	1 2
1789	41	20	7	1789	136 11 11	162 17 10	1 2
1790	40	22	11	1790	159 2 9	152 19 4	1 4
1791	46	17	6	1791	158 18 6	163 3 4	1 3
1792	36	21	6	1792	171 6 0	170 10 5	1 4
1793	32	18	5	1793	168 0 0	166 15 11	1 4
1794	35	28	7	1794	169 0 0	173 15 6	1 4
1795	—	—	—	1795	161 7 0	148 1 2	1 2

These affessments are as nearly on the full rental as can be afcertained. The land, within the borough, is eftimated at little more than 200 acres: About £10. or £15 a year, are paid out of the Rates, to conftables, for removing vagrants, &c. and £10. a year are paid for the rent of the work-houfe.

VOL. II.   4 K   *Table*

Table of Rates and Disburfemeuts in the Out-Hamlet, or Out-Libesties of the Borough of BISHOPS CASTLE.

Years.	Poor's Rates			Total Expenditure.		
	£.	s.	d.	£.	s.	d.
1769	77	13	9	77	9	4
1770	68	2	11	73	18	9
1771	75	13	0	70	12	1
1772	73	17	0	74	8	9
1773	76	1	0	66	9	7
1774	51	6	8	70	18	11
1775	No account.			81	2	3
1776	93	2	3	84	10	9
1777	66	8	4	69	15	2
1778	79	9	0	85	7	6
1779	85	15	0	86	9	1
1780	86	17	0	75	12	0
1781	85	12	4	87	2	6
1782	66	12	5	70	14	11
1783	107	12	6	113	6	2
1784	104	0	0	104	3	10
1785	108	7	8	112	14	0
1786	94	14	0	106	3	10
1787	94	16	0	107	3	4
1788	90	2	0	83	17	6
1789	96	13	0	97	12	1
1790	96	15	0	99	3	9
1791	122	7	9	146	15	5
1792	146	2	6	147	5	11
1793	123	5	0	120	12	6
1794	110	18	5	117	15	9
1795	126	4	8	128	10	9

The rate in 1795 was 1s. 2d. in the pound.

The affeffments in the hamlet are faid to be at full rental.

The Poor, in the hamlet, are relieved at their own houfes: 20 regular penfioners receive 31s. a week; fome have cafual relief; and feveral have their houfe-rents paid by the hamlet.　　　　　*November*, 1795.

o　　　　　　　　　　　　　　　　　　　　　　　E L-

ELLESMERE.

THE Poor of Ellefmere, and of four other parifhes, lately incorporated by Act of Parliament, are chiefly maintained in a Houfe of Induftry, which was opened for their reception on the 6th of January laft. £8000 the fum which the incorporated parifhes were empowered to borrow, have been already expended in buildings, and furniture ; and it is thought that a frefh application muft be made to Parliament for power to borrow £2000. more, in order to complete the neceffary detached offices. The diftribution of the rooms, the bye-laws relative to the external concerns, and the regulations for the internal government of the houfe, the table of diet, &c. are very fimilar to thofe adopted in the Shrewfbury Houfe of Induftry. The number of inmates, at prefent, is 198 ; of whom, 50 are women, 34 men, and the reft children. Every article of wearing apparel is manufactured in the houfe : flannels alfo are made for fale ; and a hop-bag manufacture has lately been fet on foot. The houfe ftands in an open, healthy fituation, on the banks of an extenfive piece of water, near the town of Ellefmere : the dormitories are extremely clean and neat, and every appearance within doors evinces the unremitting affiduity of the governor to the duties of his fituation. An inftance of feeling attention to misfortune, (which is not often to be met with in Houfes of Induftry,) is here manifefted, in appropriating particular apartments for the reception of perfons who have borne a fair character, and have been undefervedly precipitated, from eafy circumftances, into that fituation, which obliges them to folicit parochial aid. All the family, however, dine together. Notwithftanding the promifed advantages of this inftitution, it is faid that the incorporated parifhes are, in general, now heartily forry that they ever engaged in the erection of an Houfe of Induftry.

The following were the annual average difburfements of the five incorporated parifhes, for 12 years previous to the year 1790 :

			£.	s.	d.
Ellefmere	-	-	- 882	1	9
Middle	-	-	- 127	15	2
Balchutch	-	-	- 269	8	1
Hadnal	-	-	- 59	0	0
Hordley	-	-	- 83	8	3

Total - £ 1421 13   3

The following is a ſtatement of the Expenditure and Receipts on ac‑count of the Houſe, from July 26, 1791—to September 29, 1795 :

Dr	£	s.	d.		Cr	£	s.	d
To money borrowed -	8150	0	0		By Act of Parliament - -	430	13	3¼
To caſh received from the united					Seal and preſs - - -	9	19	6
pariſhes - - -	1320	6	8		Purchaſe of land - - -	570	0	0
To rent of premiſes - -	80	15	6		Conſecration of burial ground by			
Balance in hand - - -	1549	7	2		Biſhop - - -	37	6	8
					Annuities, intereſt - -	612	3	9
					Furniture, fixtures, ſtock, &c. -	1012	13	9
					Stamps and taxes - -	11	8	0
					Inſurance from fire - -	18	3	0
					Buildings - - -	5075	13	6
					Cloathing Poor - -	226	14	0
					Maintenance of Poor, ſalaries,			
					gratuities, &c - -	1537	6	10¼
					Bills unpaid on various accounts	1558	7	0
£ 11100	9	4			£ 11100	9	4	

It is ſaid, that the aſſeſſments are 4s. 6d in the pound, on one third of the rack rent. The expences for the Poor, this year, will, it is expected, amount to £ 3500. The corporation do not allow out-pay to any perſon under 70 years of age ; and to perſons above that age, only 1s. a week. At preſent, 30 families receive £ 1. 10s. a week, on this account ; children at nurſe coſt £ 3. a week ; and militia-men's families about 18s. a week.

A ſmall farm of 45 acres is attached to the houſe : four cows are kept there.

The prices of proviſions, in Elleſmere, at preſent, are : beef, from 3½d. to 4d. the lb. ; mutton, from 4d. to 5d. ; veal, from 4d. to 5d. ; pork, 5d. ; butter, 1s. ; potatoes, 1s. 6d. to 1s. 8d. for 38 quarts or 90lb. : wheat,

12s.

12s. to 14s. ditto; barley, 6s. 5d. ditto; oats, 3s. to 4s. ditto; milk, 1d. the quart; very little is fold.

Common labourers receive from 1s. 2d. to 1s. 4d. the day, in winter; and from 1s. 4d to 1s. 6d. the day, in fummer, without victuals, except a fmall allowance of beer: harveft-men are paid 1s. 6d. a day, with diet. Day wages are fuppofed to have rifen 2d. or 3d. this year The malting and tanning bufinefs are carried on to a confiderable extent here; but wages in both thefe branches of employment are low, and do not exceed 7s or 8s. a week, without board.

The average rent of land in the neighbourhood is £1. 10s. an acre: tithes are partly taken in kind, and partly compounded for. Small farms are going very faft out of ufe in this country: as they drop in, they are let to the large farmer: a practice which, both in this county and in Herefordfhire, is very much complained of, and to which the dearnefs of provifion is, (I think, erroneoufly,) afcribed.

There are 15 ale-houfes in Ellefmere.

The following is a ftatement of the earnings and expences of a labourer's family, confifting of a man, 42 years of age; his wife, 40 years of age; and two daughters, one 11, and the other 13 years of age. The man works in a malt-houfe, and in hedging, ditching, and threfhing, &c.: his wages vary with his different employments; and he fuppofes, that, from lofs of time, from bad weather, want of work, &c. he does not earn above 6s. a week, on an average, through the year.

	£.	s.	d.
He, therefore, receives annually - - -	15	8	0
His wife was formerly a laundry maid; and earns, by wafhing, 3s. a week: a fum that not one woman in 20, here, ever earns; annually - - - -	7	16	0
The children earn nothing - - -	0	0	0
	£23	4	0

EXPENCES.

	£.	s.	d.
The bread ufed by this family is made of wheat and rye, and, at the prefent price, cofts 4s. a week; annually -	10	8	0
Carried over -	£10	8	0

	£.	s.	d.
Brought over -	10	8	0
No cheefe is ufed: 1 lb. of butter, at 1s. is confumed eveiy week ; annually - - - -	2	12	0
Potatoes coft 5d. a week ; annually - - -	1	1	8
Milk cofts 2d a week ; annually - - -	0	8	8
Small beer, ditto - - - -	0	8	8
Of tea and fugar, the weekly expence is 7d. ; annually -	1	10	4
Candles and foap are eftimated at 8d. a week ; annually -	1	14	8
Shoes coft about £1. 10s. a year; fhirts and fhifts, about £1. ; other cloaths, about £1. 5s. - -	3	15	0
The children's education cofts yeaıly - -	0	10	0
Houfe-rent - - - - -	4	4	0
Fuel is eftimated at - - - -	3	3	0
	£29	16	0

This ftatement, like moft others that I have been able to piocure, exhibits a confiderable deficiency. It fhould, however, be 1emaıked, that every article has been chaıged at the prefent piice ; and that the man fometimes works for an employer, who allows him his boaıd. It is owing to this circumftance, that the weekly confumption of bıead, in this family, has been only eftimated at 4s.

November, 1795.

SHREWSBURY.

THE Poor of the fix united parifhes in Shrewfbuıy are maintained in a Houfe of Induftry, which was opened for their reception in the year 1784, and is under the management of a board of directors, appointed according to the provifions of the Act of Parliament by which the parifhes were incorporated [1]. The important points to be regarded in an inftitution
of

See 24 G. 3 Seff. 2 cap 15. The act provides, That the inhabitants of the parifhes, being rated and affeffed, and poffeffed of an eftate or annuity of thirty pounds, or being rated at fifteen pounds per annum, be incorporated as Guardians of the Poor ; that thofe guardians
fhall

of this nature; namely, the granting occasional relief to those whom it is unnecessary to admit into the house; the withholding of it from those, who, upon a careful investigation, may be found not to want it; the providing suitable employment for those, who are either averse to labour, or unable to procure it; and the educating of the infant poor, in habits of industry and virtue; have been attended to, and provided for, with so much caution and foresight, in the bye-laws which the directors were empowered to enact, that, it is presumed, a recital both of their rules respecting the external concerns, and their regulations for the internal government, of the house, may afford much solid information to parishes that may be desirous of forming a similar establishment.

Bye-laws, &c. relative to the General and External Concerns of the House of Industry.

1, That the acting officer of each of the united parishes, or, in case of sickness, or absence on necessary business, another officer in his place and stead, attend each weekly court[1], before the hour of eleven in the forenoon.

shall elect twelve directors; and that, every year, four directors shall go out, and four more be elected in their place; that the directors shall annually elect eight guardians, out of whom the directors shall choose four, to fill up the place of those who quit the direction The directors are empowered to purchase or erect the necessary buildings; to borrow any sum not exceeding £10,000; and to assign the estates they purchase, and the Poor's Rates, as a security for the same; to ascertain the necessary annual assessment for paying the interest of the money borrowed, for discharging any part of the debt, and for maintaining the Poor; to issue their warrants to the church-wardens and overseers, requiring them to pay the same into the hands of their Treasurer, in such proportions, and at such times, as they shall judge necessary The proportion to be paid by each parish, as their quota, is directed to be fixed and ascertained according to the average expenditure of each parish for 12 years prior to the passing of the Act The parish officers are required to assist the directors, and carry their resolutions into execution, under a penalty for each default. The directors are empowered to make bye-laws, &c for effecting the purposes of the Act; to take up vagrants, and other idle and disorderly Poor, and employ them in the house; where they are to be subject to such corporal, or other punishment, for misconduct, as the directors shall judge necessary; or to hire out any of the Poor, for the benefit of the house The Act also provides for a weekly board of the directors, in order to receive the applications of the out-poor, and transact the business of the house

[1] The weekly Court is held by three, or more, of the twelve Directors.

2, That

2, That they make themfelves acquainted with the fituations, circumftances, and characters of perfons applying for relief, and report the
fame to the directois.

3, That they do not defray any lying-in expences, or relieve any pauper
whatfoever, but by order of the weekly couit, except in cafes of fudden
emergency, and then only with the confent of three directois.

4, That they do not order, or engage to defray the expence of, any
coffin, or other funeral charges, without the wiitten confent of three
directois.

5, That they give notice, to the weekly court, of all peifons likely to become chargeable, who may come to refide within their refpective
parifhes, not belonging thereto, nor bringing certificates from their
laft legal places of fettlement, within forty days of their fo coming to
refide therein, agreeably to the directions of the Act.

6, That they ufe their utmoft endeavours to obtain the eailieft information of all fingle women in a ftate of pregnancy, refident within their
refpective parifhes, and give notice thereof to the next weekly court.

7, That they keep regular accounts of their weekly pay, occafional relief,
and other incidental expences, and produce the fame once a fortnight
to the directois at their weekly courts, in order to their being examined and allowed.

8, That they infert in their books, the names, ages, number of family,
ftate of health, and refidence of the Poor relieved by order of the
directors.

9, That they deliver all certificates, paffes, orders of removal, orders of
filiation, letters, and all other papers refpecting the Poor, to the next
weekly court after receiving the fame, in order to their being filed by
the fteward.

10, That the fteward give them copies of fuch orders and directions as
they aie refpectively required to carry into execution.

11, That no weekly pay be allowed to the out-poor, (children at nuife
excepted,) unlefs in cafes of lunacy, ficknefs, or where their admiffion
into the houfe fhall be judged improper by the weekly court.

12, That children fhall not be taken into the houfe before they are two
years old, nor continued at nurfe (except in very particular cafes)
after the age of four.

13, That

13, That where families are too large to maintain themselves by their own labour, the mode of relief shall be by taking one or more of their children into the house, at the discretion of the directors.

14, That no Pauper whatsoever be admitted into the house without an order of the weekly court, or, in cases of emergency, a written order signed by three directors.

15, That no cloathing whatsoever be allowed to the out-poor, except in case of sickness, when the weekly court, or, if immediately necessary, the committee for the distribution of cloathing, may exercise a discretionary power.

16, That, to prevent improper expence or imposition, no sum be allowed towards any funeral, where the Pauper is not buried entirely at the charge of the united parishes, and in the accustomed manner.

17, That Paupers admitted into the house for temporary relief only, shall not be deprived of their houshold goods or other property.

18, That an apothecary be annually appointed, who shall, by himself, or his approved deputy, duly attend, and administer proper medicines to such sick Poor, both within and out of the house, as may be put under his care by the directors; and that he shall make a weekly report, to the court, of their names and cases, in a book provided for that purpose.

19, That the latter part of the 31st rule for the internal government of the house be advertised twice every year, the first week in January, and the first week in July, in the Shrewsbury Chronicle; as also a caution to the keepers of lodging-houses, not to take in and harbour single pregnant women, who do not belong to the united parishes; and offering to any person giving information where such women are harboured and concealed.

Bye-Laws, &c. relative to the Internal Government of the House of Industry.

1, That the steward and matron reside within the house; that they be not on any occasion absent at the same time; and that neither of them be out later than ten o'clock at night, without leave from three or more of the directors.

2, That, in case the steward or matron shall absent him or herself, con-

trary

trary to the meaning of the above rule, the door keeper is required to report the same to the weekly court the following Monday, on pain on being difcharged from his place.

3, That the fteward and matron fhall have a feparate table to themfelves.

4, That the fteward and matron fee that all the fervants, and perfons employed in the houfe, perform their duty in their refpective departments; and that thefe bye-laws, rules, and ordinances, be carried into full effect.

5, That the fteward and matron fhall allot the quantity of provifions for each day's confumption, agreeable to the following bill of fare; fhall fee them weighed, and take care that the cook, with proper affiftance, drefs and diftribute the fame.

Bill of Fare.

	Breakfaft.	Dinner	Supper.
Sunday,	Broth	Butcher's meat and garden ftuff	Broth
Monday,	Milk-porridge.	Hafty pudding, with butter and treacle fauce.	Mafhed potatoes.
Tuefday,	Ditto.	Stewed meat, with potatoes or other garden ftuff.	Peafe foup
Wednefday,	Ditto.	Bread and cheefe.	Broth.
Thurfday,	Broth.	Butcher's meat and garden ftuff.	Broth.
Friday,	Milk-porridge.	Yeaft dumplins.	Mafhed potatoes.
Saturday,	Ditto.	Stewed meat, with potatoes or other garden ftuff.	Broth

6, That the fteward fhall examine the goodnefs and price of provifions; fhall fuperintend the weighing, and compare the quantities thereof, and of all other goods whatfoever, with the tradefmen's bills of parcels.

7, That the fteward and matron fhall take care that the larder, kitchen, back-kitchen, and other offices, together with the utenfils and furniture thereof, be kept fweet, clean, and decent; that the dininghall, tables and feats, be cleaned immediately after each meal, and the feveral wards or dormitories, every morning before, or immediately after breakfaft, when the windows thereof fhall be thrown open, the doors locked, and the keys delivered to them; and that the ftricteft cleanlinefs and decency be obferved in every part of the houfe.

8, That the fteward take care that Grace be faid before and after meat; read, or caufe to be read, prayers every morning before breakfaft, and

every

every evening before fupper; that every perfon in the houfe, not neceffarily engaged elfewhere, be required to attend; and that a lift of
abfentees, if any, be laid before the next weekly court.

9, That the fteward and matron take care that every perfon in the houfe,
nurfes excepted, do go to bed, and the fires and candles be extinguifhed, at nine o'clock from the fiift of May to the firft of September, and at eight from the firft of September to the firft of May.

10, 'I hat, to avoid infectious diftempers, the fteward fhall not place any
peifon in the wards, without being fiift carefully examined and wafhed,
and, if thought neceffary, new cloathed; and in this cafe the fteward
fhall caufe the old cloaths to be well cleaned; and, if there be a probability that fuch perfon will be difcharged from the houfe, his or her
old cloaths fhall be kept, in oider to be re-delivered at the time of
difmiffion, in exchange for the cloaths found by the houfe.

11, That the fteward fhall iegulaily and diftinctly keep the following
accounts, for the conftant infpection of the directors, viz.

A book of affignments.

A general order-book.

Minutes of the proceedings at the weekly courts.

A Ledger, No. 1. containing accounts with the debtors and creditors
of the houfe.

A book of receipts and difburfements.

Ditto, abftracted under various heads.

A weekly abftract of the cafh account.

A ftate of the year's account to the 15th of July in each year.

A lift of the in-poor, with their ages, time of admittance and difcharge, &c. and occafional remaiks.

A Ledger, No. 2, containing accounts refpecting the manufactory.

A men's cloathing book, with an alphabetical lift of the perfons to
whom cloaths are diftributed, columns for the various articles,
the time when given, and the value thereof.

A women's ditto.

An account of each piece of flannel or other goods manufactured,
the number of yaids, prime coft, and value, &c. &c.

12, That the fteward fhall deliver in to each weekly court, a lift of all the
Poor received into, or difcharged fiom the houfe, the preceding week.

13, That no bill above the fum of £5. be difcharged 'till it hath been laid before the weekly court, and an order made by the directors for the payment thereof.

14, That the matron do diftribute fuch milk, pearl-barley, rice, or other neceffaries, to the young children, and the fick, as the phyficians or apothecary fhall direct in a book of diet, to be lodged in the hands of the matron for that purpofe.

15, That the wards or dormitories be fupplied with clean fheets, once a month, or oftener, if neceffary; and the Poor, with clean linen, once a week.

16, That the matron deliver to the laundrefs an inventory of the articles to be wafhed, by which inventory the fame fhall be compared when returned from the wafhing; and if any lofs or deficiency fhall happen, fhe report the fame to the next weekly court.

17, That the matron fhall take care that fuch girls, as are of proper age, be, by rotation, employed and inftructed, as much as may be, in cookery, houfewifery, wafhing, fcouring, and fuch other work as may beft qualify them for fervice.

18, That the matron recommend proper nurfes to the weekly court, by which they are to be appointed.

19, That the nurfes caufe all the children under their care to have their hands and faces wafhed, and their hair combed every morning, by the hour appointed for beginning to work.

20, That the nurfes give immediate information of the death of any per-fon under their care to the fteward, who fhall caufe the corpfe to be conveyed in due time to the place appointed for that purpofe, and fhall provide a coffin and jerfey for the funeral; that they alfo deliver to the fteward all the cloaths, money, or goods, belonging to the perfon deceafed, an inventory whereof he fhall lay before the next weekly court.

21, That the Poor fhall breakfaft, dine, and fup together in the dining-hall, except fuch only as are by age or infirmities rendered unable, or improper objects to attend in that place, of whom proper care muft be taken in feparate apartments.

22, That the Poor be called up by ring of bell, and fet to fuch work as their feveral abilities will permit, from fix o'clock in the morning to

4   fix

fix in the evening, from the firft of March to the middle of October; and from feven in the morning till fuch hour at night as the directors may appoint, from the middle of October to the firft of March; being allowed half an hour at breakfaft, and an hour at dinner. That neverthelefs they fhall not work on Sundays; Saturday afternoons from three o'clock; Good-Friday; Chriftmas-day, and the two following days; and Monday and Tuefday in the Eafter and Whitfun-weeks, and on Shrewfbury Show-day.

23, That, in order to excite the Poor to induftry, they fhall be rewarded, every Saturday, with a gratuity of one fixth part of the value of their week's work, except in cafes of mifconduct.

24, That a ftanding committee of three or more directors be appointed for the management of the manufactory, who fhall report their proceedings to the weekly court every fortnight; and that, without the orders of two members of that committee, no goods, manufactured or unmanufactured, be bought or fold.

25, That a ftanding committee of three directors be likewife appointed for the purpofe of diftributing fuch wearing apparel as any two of them may judge neceffary to be given to the Poor.

26, That the linen, wearing apparel, and bed-cloaths, be mended under the direction of the matron, by fuch of the Poor as are capable of fo doing.

27, That the houfe barber fhall fhave the men-poor, at leaft every week, and cut the children's hair as often as neceffary.

28, That no perfon be admitted to fee any of the Poor within the houfe, but by leave of the fteward, or, in his abfence, of the matron. Nor any of the Poor be allowed to go out, without permiffion of the fteward, who fhall limit the time of their return. The fteward to lay before the weekly court, a lift of thofe who have had leave of abfence during the preceding week.

29, That the porter fhall carefully keep the doors and gates, and fhall not fuffer any perfon to pafs in or out without proper permiffion, nor allow ftrong or fpirituous liquors to be brought in, unlefs prefcribed by the phyficians or apothecary; and that he lock the doors and gates, and deliver up the keys to the fteward, or, in his abfence, to the matron, immediately after the hour of going to bed.

30, That

30, That one or more fchoolmafters and miftreffes be appointed, who fhall
keep the children in good order, and inftruct them in reading and other
ufeful branches; fuch as are not employed in the manufactory or work
of the houfe, to be taught from eight to eleven in the morning, and
from one to four in the afternoon; and fuch as are fo employed, at
thofe hours when they can be beft fpared from their work.

31, That if any officer, nurfe, or fervant of the houfe, receive any fee or
gratuity from any tradefmen, or from the poor, or their friends, they
fhall be immediately difcharged from their employments; and if any
tradefman fhall be known to beftow any fee or gratuity on any officer
or fervant of the houfe, he fhall be deemed incapable of ferving the
faid houfe in future.

32, That an inventory and appraifement of all the fixtures, furniture,
working implements, and goods manufactured and unmanufactured,
be laid before the weekly court upon the laft Monday in July, in
each year, by the fteward; in which fhall be particularly fpecified
fuch new furniture or implements as have been purchafed within the
year: and that a clear ftate of the year's account be then made out
by him.

33, That as the perfonal comfort of the Poor, the inftruction and morals
of the younger part of them, their attention to labour, and the economical management of the houfe, depend much upon a conftant and
vigilant infpection into it's interior concerns, there fhall be always two
or more directors appointed by the weekly court, as a vifiting committee, each to act a fortnight, and then to be fucceeded by others in
rotation; but that no new director may, from want of experience, be
at a lofs how to execute the office of vifitor, at the end of every week
one of them to go out, and another be affociated with the remaining
vifitor appointed the week before, by whom he will be attended the
week enfuing.

34, That the vifiting committee, daily, or as often as poffible, attend the
houfe; fee that the Poor, particularly the fick, be taken care of, and
regularly attended by the apothecary and nurfes; that all infectious
perfons be removed to the apartments appointed for their reception;
that the fchoolmafters and miftreffes do their duty; that the working
ing Poor be diligent in their refpective employments; that the houfe
be

be kept clean, the windows of the dormitories kept open in the day-time, and the doors of thofe rooms be locked:—that they compare the flour fent in with the famples; examine the bread, beer, and other provifions; enquire into the complaints and the offences of the Poor; and enter, in a book kept for that purpofe, whatever obfervations ftrike them as material.

35, That the chaplain of the houfe read prayers and preach a fermon to the Poor every Sunday afternoon, adminifter the Sacrament the firft Sunday in January, and the firft Sunday in July, in each year, cate-chize the children once a month, vifit fuch of the fick as fhall defire it, and perform the other duties of his function.

36, That, for the more effectually maintaining perfect order and good government in the houfe, if any perfon fhall profanely curfe or fwear, or appear to be in liquor, he fhall be immediately confined in the ftocks, by order of the vifiting committee or fteward, for any time not exceeding four hours; or if any perfons having permiffion to go out of the houfe, fhall not return within the time allowed, or fhall return drunk or diforderly, or fhall be otherwife refractory or difobedient to the reafonable orders of the fteward or matron; or if they fhall pretend ficknefs, or make any falfe excufe in order to avoid working; or if they fhall wilfully deftroy or fpoil any materials or implements; or if they fhall be guilty of difhoneft practices, breach of truft, lewd, indecent, immoral or diforderly behaviour, or of any other mifchief or tranfgreffion repugnant to the peace and well-being of the houfe; they fhall be admonifhed, or confined, according to the magnitude of their offences, at the difcretion of the vifiting committee or fteward, and the cafe be reported to the next weekly court, when the offender, upon conviction, fhall be fentenced to fuffer fuch corporal punifhment, confinement, tafk-work, diftinction of drefs, abatement of diet, or lofs of gratuity, as the directors fhall judge proper, agreeably to the powers vefted in them by the Act.

37, That thefe bye-laws, rules and ordinances, be read once a year at the general meeting, the fecond Monday in Auguft, after the election of new directors.

Rules to be hung up in the House.

The Poor in this house are required to obferve the following Rules :

1, THAT they obey the fteward and matron in all their reafonable commands.

2, That they demean themfelves orderly and peaceably, with decency and cleanlinefs.

3, That they never drink to excefs.

4, That they be diligent at their work.

5, That they work from fix o'clock in the morning till fix at night, in fummer ; and from feven in the morning to fuch hours in the evening as the directors fhall appoint, in the winter ; except on Saturday afternoons, from three o'clock ; and on Good-Friday, Chrift-mas-day, and the two days following; and Monday and Tuefday in the Eafter and Whitfun-weeks, and Shrewfbury Show-day, which are to be regarded as holidays.

6, That they do not pretend ficknefs, or other excufes, to avoid their work.

7, That they do no wilful damage, but execute their work to the beft of their abilities ; one fixth part of their earnings to be given them every Saturday, by way of gratuity or reward for their diligence, except in cafes of mifconduct.

8, That they regularly attend divine fervice on Sundays, and prayers before breakfaft and fupper, every day.

9, That they go to breakfaft, to dinner, and to fupper, in the dining-hall, when fummoned by ring of bell.

10, That they be allowed half an hour at breakfaft, and an hour at dinner.

11, That no ftrong or fpirituous liquors be allowed in the houfe, except by order of the phyficians or apothecary.

12, That they do not curfe, nor fwear, nor lie.

13, That they do not fteal, fell their provifions or cloathing, nor be guilty of any other breach of truft.

14, That they never go out during working-hours, nor at any other time, without leave.

15, That when permitted to go out, they do not ftay longer than the hour appointed.

Whoever

Whoever fhall offend againft the above rules, will be punifhed, either by confinement in the ftocks, or in the dungeon, or elfewhere ; or by diftinction of drefs, by abatement of diet, lofs of gratuity, or by fuch corporal or other punifhment as may be determined and adjudged by the weekly court of directors, according to the powers vefted in them by the Act of Parliament.

Rules for the Regulation of the Weekly and Quarterly Courts.

1, That a weekly court be held every Monday, between the hours of ten and two, agreeably to the Act ; and at every court, whether weekly, quarterly, or fpecial, a chairman be elected by the directors prefent, who fhall prefide over, and regulate the proceedings, and who, in cafe of an equal divifion, fhall have a cafting vote.

2, That the orders of the laft court be firft read.

3, That if any matter be propofed by a member, and feconded by another, it fhall be debated, and, if defired, put to a vote, before any other bufinefs be confidered.

4, That after the bufinefs of the day is concluded, the minutes of the proceedings be read over.

5, That a table of the days on which the quarterly courts are required by the Act to be held, fhall be hung up in the court-room.

The Paupers in the houfe are chiefly employed in the woollen manufactory, in which they are inftructed by proper perfons, verfed in fcribbling, carding, and fpinning wool Several weavers are conftantly employed. Paupers, who have been fhoemakers, tailors, carpenters, &c. are fet to work at their different occupations. The boys are inftructed in the different work-fhops, in which thefe trades are carried on ; the girls are employed in fpinning, in making gloves, in the laundry, and other labour that is fuited to their fex, their ages, and abilities. The decent and orderly are in a great meafure feparated from the profligate and debauched, who are kept in diftinct working-rooms and dormitories[1]. The family break-

[1] The Treafurer, Mr Wood, (who is the author of a very able account of the Shrewfbury Houfe of Induftry, from which I have extracted the above bye-laws, and feveral other particulars,) very judicioufly recommends the lodging proftitutes, and other abandoned females, in a detached building: I am ignorant, whether this defirable alteration has yet taken place.

faft, dine, and fup together, in a hall 120 feet by 20. Prayers are read twice a day by a chaplain, who is allowed a regular falary. The apothecary, who attends the houfe, and out-poor, is paid £ 70. a year : at firft there was an annual contract with him ; but this was objected to, as furnifhing him with a ftrong temptation to fupply the Poor with bad drugs. Adjoining to the houfe are two ranges of buildings, one of which contains apartments to which the Poor are fent, upon their admiffion, to be ftripped and wafhed ; women and men, with infectious diforders, are likewife placed there, in feparate rooms, till cured. One room is appropriated to fevers. There is likewife an apartment, to which the dead are conveyed, to remain till interment. The other building is the infirmary, in which the fick and infirm are lodged, in feparate wards, according to their fex, under the care of proper nurfes. In furgical cafes, the patients are, generally, fent to the county infirmary, to which the directors annually fubfcribe.

There is a grazing farm of 50 acres belonging to the houfe, at which 20 cows are kept. The butter, except what little is ufed by the fick, is fold, and produces annually about £ 70. It is very difficult to difcover from the printed accounts of the houfe, whether this farm is a profitable concern, as the amount and value of the articles furnifhed from it, for the ufe of the houfe, are not fet down. I obferve, that in the year ending in July 1794, the receipts for cattle, pigs, and butter, (I fuppofe from the farm,) amounted to £397. 19s. ; and the difburfements for cattle, pigs, fodder, and farming expences, (exclufive of rent, taxes, and repairs,) to £398. 3s. 3½d.

There is an open contract for the flour ufed in the houfe, once a quarter. A baker and brewer are conftantly employed in the houfe.

Prior to the opening of the houfe, the expences of maintaining the Poor were £ 4605. 3s. 1½d, for one year[1]. The Poor's Rates were immediately reduced

---

[1] This fum was paid by the fix parifhes in the following proportions :

					£.	s	d.
St. Alkmond	-	-	-	-	529	8	9
St. Chad	-	-	-	-	2190	4	8
Holy Crofs	-	-	-	-	374	0	7½
St. Julian	-	-	-	-	453	4	6½
St. Mary	-	-	-	-	872	12	9
Meol Brace	-	-	-	-	185	1	9½
					£ 4605	3	1½

reduced to £2992. 12s. at which fum they have continued ever fince. This fum, together with other receipts, arifing from the profits of the farm, compofitions for baftardy, and the fale of manufactured goods, has been hitherto fufficient to defray all the expences of the houfe; but it is expected, that a rife will foon become neceffary. Their amount, during each of the laft nine years, may be feen in the following table[1] :

			£.	s.	d.
1787	-	-	5423	1	1
1788	-	-	5296	8	3
1789	-	-	5855	1	8
1790	-	-	4453	8	2
1791	-	-	4804	11	7
1792	-	-	5119	18	$3\frac{1}{2}$
1793	-	-	4769	18	1
1794	-	-	4822	15	2
1795	-	-	5641	6	3

The Poor's Rate is now 2s. in the pound, on the rack rent.

The following account of receipts and difburfements for one year, is copied from the only one that the Governors have ever publifhed. They mean to print one every eight years.

Stated

[1] The following amount of Expences for the Poor, in 1776, and of Affeffments in 1783 and 1784, were extracted from the Returns made to Parliament:

	Net Expences for the Poor in 1776				Money raifed by Affeff- ment in 1783				Money raifed by Affeff- ment in 1784.		
	£.	s	d		£	s.	d		£	s	d.
St Alkmond	261	8	0	-	495	5	0	-	462	13	0
St Chad	1245	15	6	-	1740	16	6	-	2507	14	10
Holy Crofs	286	0	0	-	320	18	0	-	478	3	9
St Julian	338	3	4	-	Omitted.			-	525	16	6
St Mary	433	18	8	-	625	0	0	-	778	19	3
Meol Brace	75	2	2	-	201	16	0	-	177	2	8
Total -	£2640	7	8		£3583	10	6		£4930	10	0

4 M 2

*Stated Account of the Debts and Credits of the House of Industry, for the
six united Parishes of Shrewsbury, and the Liberties thereof, for one year,
ending 20th July* 1794.

RECEIPTS.

	£.	s.	d.	£.	s.	d.
For cattle, pigs, and butter — —	397	19	0			
Rent of boat — — —	20	0	0			
Sundry articles fold to hired weavers —	16	1	4			
Support of baftard children — —	142	17	6			
Rents and other payments, being the property of Poor relieved — — —	58	7	1½			
Two years' annuity of widow Baugh's bequeft to the Poor — —	16	5	5			
Work done in the houfe, by fhoemakers, tailors, &c. — — —	25	9	2½			
Manufactured goods fold — —	836	19	4			
Tallow fold — — —	14	0	8			
From an Amicable Society of women on fecurity — — —	70	0	0			
From the united parifhes — —	2992	12	0			
Balance due to the Treafurer — —	232	3	7			
				4822	15	2

Due for goods fold, £ 361. 11s. 9d. rent, £4. £365 11 9

STOCK IN THE HOUSE.

	£.	s.	d.	£.	s.	d.
Butcher's meat, fmall beer, oatmeal and peafe	14	10	10			
Salt — — — —	6	5	0			
Soap — — — —	8	4	6			
Pearl and other afhes for wafhing —	5	4	0			
Candles — — —	0	12	0			
Flour — — — —	40	0	0			
Bran — — — —	1	15	0			
Cheefe — — — —	72	0	0			
Coals and oven fuel — —	60	0	0			
Wool, yarn, flannels, cloth and oil —	800	7	10			
Hemp, flax, linen cloth, linen yarn, &c.	108	11	0			
Cloathing, fhoes, &c. made up —	106	8	0			
Cattle, fodder, pigs, and farming ftock —	287	6	0			
Jerfey, brooms, brufhes, &c. — —	3	12	0			
				1880	7	11
				£6703	3	1

PAYMENTS,

	£.	s.	d.
To the Treasurer, a balance due 20th July 1793 — — —	117	4	3
Butcher's meat — — —	525	6	7
Garden-stuff — — —	125	4	6
Flour — — —	798	4	5
Pease — — —	14	8	0
Oatmeal — —	30	17	6
Salt — — —	35	3	3
Malt, fugar, hops, &c. for brewing —	253	4	6
Groceries, candles, and lamp oil —	49	13	2
Soap, afhes, and materials for wafhing —	16	6	5½
Coals, and oven fuel — —	185	6	8
Furniture, brooms, brufhes, &c. —	41	19	9½
Raw materials for cloathing, leather for fhoes, breeches, &c. — —	283	11	9
Wool, oil, and fize — —	370	3	5
Repairs of machines, wheels, and cards	13	14	2½
Stationary, printing and advertifing —	4	3	2
Infurance from fire — —	3	16	2
Cattle, fodder, pigs, and farming expences	398	3	3½
Lewns, taxes, and tithes — —	18	0	4
Repairs and alterations — —	113	17	6
Rent of Kingfland — —	25	0	0
Premiums with children apprentice —	9	0	0
Wages to hired weavers — —	165	8	7
Dyeing, dreffing, and fcouring cloaths and flannels — — —	113	13	10
Funerals, and expences attending fick —	32	16	4
Subfcription to Salop Infirmary —	5	5	0
Nurfes pay, and occafional relief —	298	1	6
Salary to apothecary — —	70	0	0
Chaplain, matron, fecretary, and fteward	105	5	0
Wages to porter, brewer, baker, and barber	37	14	0
Benevolcuces to Paupers difcharged from the houfe, and other rewards — —	10	5	4
Stamps, poftage, &c. — —	2	13	5
Expences of taking vagrants — —	3	13	6
Gratuities to Poor employed as fervants, labourers, nurfes, &c. — —	78	2	0

Carried over - £ 4355 7 5

	£.	s.	d.	£.	s.	d.
Brought over -	4355	7	5			
Ditto, to fhoemakers, tailors, feamftreffes, &c.	27	2	11			
Ditto, to thofe employed in the manufactory	149	14	10			
Diftiibuted to the Poor in part of widow Baugh's annuity and intereft of arrears	13	4	0			
Intereft of money borrowed — —	277	6	0			
				4822	15	2
Balance, being the amount of ftock and book debts — — —				1880	7	11
				£ 6703	3	1

Abftract of the Debts and Credits of the Shrewfbury Houfe of Induftry, from 20th July 1784, *to* 20*th July* 1794.

DR.

	£.	s.	d.
To principal debt, being money borrowed — —	6346	10	0
Four months intereft due thereon to July 20th 1794 —	104	12	0
Due to fundry perfons in account — —	439	2	5
Ditto to Treafurer's balance of his year's account as above	232	3	7
Total balance in favour of the houfe — —	2475	16	3
	£ 9598	4	3

CR.

	£.	s.	d.
By purchafe of houfe and premifes — —	5500	0	0
Solicitor's bill, and expences of Act of Parliament —	391	2	5
Several additional buildings, work-fhops and improvements — — — — —	770	13	11
Prefent value of furniture, fixtures, &c. — —	720	0	0
Ditto, machines, wheels, cards, looms, &c. — —	336	0	0
Ditto, ftock in houfe, and book debts — —	1880	7	11
	£ 9598	4	3

The

The number of Paupers in the houfe at prefent is 389: they confift of perfons of various defcriptions and ages. As the directors do not grant out-penfions, the number of young and ftout is, as might be expected, very confiderable. This circumftance eafily explains the greatnefs of the earnings.

The prefent expence of maintaining the Poor in the houfe, in meat and drink alone, is eftimated at 22d. or 23d. a week, for each perfon. The coft of cloathing for each Pauper, admitted into the houfe, is as follows:

	£.	s.	d.
A man's fuit, confifting of coat, waiftcoat, leather breeches, fhoes, 2 fhirts, and 2 pair of ftockings, cofts - -	1	16	0
A boy's ditto - - - - -	0	18	0
A woman's drefs, confifting of a bed-gown, 2 petticoats, linfey apron, fhoes, 2 fhifts, 2 pair of ftockings, and a handkerchief, cofts - - - -	1	7	0
A girl's ditto - - - - -	0	18	0

The men's and boys' coats and waiftcoats are made of woollen cloth, that is manufactured in the houfe, and is eftimated to coft 1s. 6d. a yard.

The women's cloaths are manufactured in the houfe, at 1s. 6d. a yard; except the flannel petticoats, which coft about 10d. a yard.

The following account of the number admitted into the houfe, during the three firft years of the inftitution, was obligingly communicated by the governor and the treafurer.

From January 1784 to October 1787.

Admitted and born in the Houfe.

Born in the houfe - - -	60
Admitted under 2 years of age - -	52
From 2 to 15 years - -	356
From 15 to 30 - -	116
From 30 to 50 - - -	68
From 50 to 70 - -	226
From 70 to 90 - -	69
From 90 to 100 - -	4
	951

Dif-

Difcharged.

Under 2 years, fent out to nurfe - - -	42
Bound apprentices - - - - -	61
Sent to fervice, or to their refpective parifhes - - -	78
Difcharged, to get their own living, and at their own requeft -	315

Total - 496

Died.

Under 2 years old - -	22
From 2 to 15 - -	16
15 to 30 - - -	15
30 to 50 - -	18
50 to 70 - - -	27
70 to 90 - -	35
90 to 100 - - -	4

Total - 137

In the year 1788, confiderable fubfcriptions were raifed for the necef-fitous Poor, by which 920 families, and 328 fingle perfons, were relieved. Laft year, 1036 families, and 217 perfons, were relieved in a fimilar manner. Three liberal fubfcriptions were likewife opened, laft fpring, for the fuccour of the induftrious Poor, who had fuffered by an extraordinary inundation of the river; and it appears, from an account publifhed in March, by the treafurer, Mr. Wood, that 403 families, and 40 fingle perfons, comprifing 1603 perfons, had been fupplied three feveral times with coal, and with bread gratis, during the flood, to the amount of £121. 1s.; and that £698. worth of bread had, during the months of January and Februaiy, been fold to the Poor at lefs than half the market price, amounting altogether to 1716 eighteen-penny loaves; 6348 twelve-penny loaves; and 1128 fixpenny loaves. The whole of the contributions for this pur-pofe amounted to £483. 16s. 6d.

Since the above period, the high price of provifions has produced another veiy libeial and feafonable contiibution for the rclief of the Poor: which,

which, (it appears from a printed statement of the committee,) was distributed in the following manner:

Parochial committees having made out lists of the Poor, from personal enquiry and inspection, tickets were issued, which entitled them to purchase flour weekly, at 2d. the pound, in quantities proportioned to the number each family consisted of; and as the object of the subscribers was to induce a moderate and frugal use of that prime necessary, the relief was extended also to other articles. The same number of tickets was emitted, allowing them 1d. per pound in the purchase of the like proportions of butcher's meat; and premiums were given for bringing early potatoes to the Shrewsbury market.

By dividing the town into three districts, allotting different days for the sale of flour to each, and adopting other salutary precautions, that loss of time, those tumults, and other inconveniencies, which had formerly been experienced in these general sales, were almost entirely prevented

The number of Poor thus relieved, consisted of 1365 families, and 283 single persons, amounting in the whole to 5503 individuals.

The quantity of corn purchased, ground into flour, and thus disposed of, was 1260 bushels; the average produce of flour from which was 62 pounds per bushel.   10,991 pounds of flour were sold to the Poor each week, together with the like quantity of butcher's meat; so that the Poor of Shrewsbury, at this critical period, were enabled, to purchase, weekly, 21,982 pounds weight of the chief necessaries of life, at a very reduced and reasonable price.   The premiums allowed for bringing potatoes to market[1], had also a most happy effect, by increasing the quantity, and very considerably reducing the price of that most invaluable root.   This relief was continued for seven weeks, from the latter end of July, to about the middle of September, when, the markets falling, the balance in hand was reserved for some future occasion.

---

[1] These premiums were as follows:

If the potatoes were brought 20 miles,	-	9d. per strike.
If brought 15 miles,	- - -	6d. per strike.
If brought 10 miles,	- - -	4¼d. per strike.
If brought 5 miles,	- -	3d. per strike.

ACCOUNT.

RECEIPTS.		£.	s	d.	DISBURSEMENTS.		£	s.	d.
Subfcriptions	- - -	711	4	10	Paid for corn, grinding, and expence				
For flour and bran	- -	687	12	7	of fales - - -		1006	3	5
					Butcher's meat tickets - -		222	12	6
					Premiums for potatoes, ftationary and				
					advertifing - -		33	16	3
					Loft by light gold - -		1	0	0
					By bad filver and copper - -		1	2	0
					Balance refeived -		134	3	3
		£1398	17	5			£1398	17	5

There are 116 inns and ale-houfes in the 6 united parifhes, and 14 Friendly Societies for men, and 8 for women: the number of members in each is from 70 to 150: they have all, except one, had their rules confirmed at the quarter feffions.

. The prices of provifions in Shrewfbury are: beef, from 4d. to 4½d. the lb.; mutton, 4d. to 4½d.; veal, 5d.; pork, 5½d.; bacon, from 8d. to 9d.; butter, from 11d. to 1s.; new milk, ½d. the pint; fkim-milk, ½d. the quart; potatoes, 2s. the bufhel, (about 90 lb.); wheat, 12s. the bufhel; barley, 6s.; oats, 3s. 8d.: coals are 13s. the ton.

The wages of labourers are from 1s. 2d. to 1s. 4d. a day in winter, and from 1s. 4d. to 1s. 6d. in fummer, without diet. In harveft, they receive 1s. 6d. a day, and board; and fometimes 1s. 8d. a day, and board.

The rent of land near the town is from £2. to £4. an acre: at 8 or 10 miles diftance, from £1. to £2. an acre. The average is about £1. 5s. or £1. 8s. in large farms. Tithes are compounded for, at 5s. an acre for meadow; and 3s. in the pound, for grazing ground.

There are, in Shrewfbury, one congregation of Quakers, one of Roman Catholics, one of Prefbyterians, one of Anabaptifts, one of Calvinifts, and two of Methodifts.

The woollen manufacture, here, is rather on the decline.

15 parifhes near Montgomery have lately been incorporated, in order to erect a houfe of induftry, on which £12,000. have already been expended: £5000. more are wanted. The houfe was opened laft March, and contains, at prefent, about 500 Paupers. Their regulations are very

7   fimilar

fimilar to the Shrewfbury bye-laws; but many perfons think the houfe will not fucceed, as it is at a great diftance from any market, and the expence already incurred muft operate as a very heavy burthen on the united parifhes.

Another houfe of induftry, upon a lefs extenfive plan, has lately been opened, about 5 miles from Shrewfbury; but, as yet, no opinion can fairly be formed on the probability of it's fucceeding.

November, 1795.

SOMERSETSHIRE.

FROME.

THE extent of this parifh is eftimated at 6 miles by $3\frac{1}{2}$ miles. From an enumeration taken in 1785, it was found to contain 1684 houfes, and 8105 perfons; it is fuppofed that the number had increafed before the prefent war; above 800 men, from this place, have entered his Majefty's fervice. Among the inhabitants, are 220 weavers; 146 fheermen; 141 fcribblers; 230 labourers; 55 farmers; 47 clothiers; 39 attornies, clergymen, and other gentlemen; and 183 widows. There are, here, 1 Quaker, 1 of Mr. Wefley's, 1 of Lady Huntingdon's, 1 Prefbyterian, and 2 Anabaptift congregations. The prices of provifions are: beef, from 5d. to $5\frac{1}{2}$d. a pound; mutton, ditto; veal, 6d.; bacon, from 9d. to 10d.; butter, 11d.; bread, 13d. the gallon, or quartern loaf; potatoes, 7d. the peck; coals are 1s. the cwt.; cheefe, from 5d. to $7\frac{1}{2}$d. the lb. Sheermen earn from 15s. to 20s. a week; fcribblers, about 12s.; and weavers, about 20s. a week. Women and children are employed in the manufactories, either in picking wool, in burling or dreffing cloth, and attending the machines, &c. Women have 8d. a day at prefent; children of 7 or 8 years of age, earn 2s. 6d. a week, for attending the machines: common labourers receive from 16d. to 18d. the day; but when

work

work is done by the piece, which is ufu ally the cafe heie, they can earn from 2s. to 2s. 6d. a day. The manufactures of this place are, cloths of the following denominations; fuperfine, of Spanifh wool; fuper, and beft fuper, of Englifh wool; and keifeymeres. The prefent war has taken off a number of hands; but has not leffened the demand for cloths, except in the inftance of kerfeymeres, which were chiefly fent to France: that branch of manufacture is now almoft ruined: laft year, theie was a great demand for broad cloths. To the introduction of machines, a few years ago, fome perfons afcribe the great increafe of the Poor's Rates here; by others, it is imputed to the great number of foldiers and militia-men's families, who are chaigeable at piefent. This town is very ancient, and has been the feat of the woollen manufacture for feveral centuries; yet, the external appearance of the town does not indicate that wealth which is ufually attendant on commerce: the houfes are very different fiom the elegant dwellings that are to be found in the Yorkfhire manufacturing towns, or their neighbourhood; the ftreets are narrow, unpaved, and dirty. In this town there are 36 ale-houfes; which, a gentleman of credibility fuppofes, difpofe of about 6700 hogfheads of ftrong beer annually.

Grafs land, near the town, lets for £3. an acre; at a diftance, from 20s. to 40s. the acre: arable farms let from 14s. to 18s. an acre. Tithes are taken by compofition.

The Poor are chiefly maintained at home, where it is thought they can be relieved at a lefs expence to the parifh, than if they were all fent to the work-houfe. 120 perfons, however, confifting, moftly, of old people and children, are now in the work-houfe. The food ufed in the work-houfe is chiefly bread, cheefe, and beer, except on Mondays and Thurf-days, when beef, veal, or pork, and vegetables, are allowed for dinners; breakfaft is generally a compofition of milk, onions, and broth. About £75. a week are paid to militia-men's families and other out-poor, amounting altogether to about 800 families.

The following is a ftatement of the earnings and expences of a cooper's family, confifting of the father and mother, (who are each about 50 years old,) a daughter, 18; a fon, 16; another, 13; a girl, 11; and a boy 7 years old.

EARN-

EARNINGS.

	£.	s.	d.
The father, at his trade of cooper, earns about 2s. a day -	31	4	0
The wife earns nothing: the eldeſt girl dreſſes cloth, and earns 8d. a day - - - -	10	4	0
The oldeſt boy is a cooper, and earns about 9d a day -	11	14	0
The two youngeſt children work a little in the manufactory, and earn about 1s. 6d. a week - - -	3	18	0
The father employs a journeyman, by whom he gains about 2s. 6d. a week: the journeyman does not board with the maſter - - - -	6	14	0

Total earnings - £63 14 0

The boy of 13 years of age earns nothing, being chiefly employed in fetching and carrying tubs, &c. to, and from, cuſtomers.

EXPENCES.

	£.	s.	d.
The cooper ſays, his family expend at preſent 2s. 6d. a day in bread only, which, at the preſent price, would amount annually to - - - - -	45	10	0
Butter, 2 lb. a week, at 11d. a pound; and cheeſe, about 2s. a week - - - -	9	19	4
Butcher's meat, about 3s. a week; tea, 6d. a week; ſugar, 1½ lb. at 10d a week - - -	12	7	0
8 buſhels of malt, at 7s. the buſhel; hops, 6s. - -	3	2	0
Potatoes, 1½ peck a week, at 7d.: milk, about 4d. a week	3	1	4
Houſe-rent - - - - -	7	7	0
Coals coſt him £2. 4s.: he burns a great quantity of chips of wood, which coſt him nothing - -	2	4	0
Soap and candles, about - - -	2	12	0
Cloathing for the family is eſtimated at - -	14	0	0

Total expences - £100 2 8

It

It is evident this man muſt have been much miſtaken in his calculations, as he ſays his expences have, hitherto, not exceeded his income. In the article of bread, he ſays, he is pretty accurate, and rather below than above the mark: with regard to the other particulars, he does not pretend to ſpeak with certainty; but his account clearly proves, that there is a great want of economy in his family. Each perſon conſumes about 1½ pound of bread a day. The man lays by nothing; but as he is not in debt, it is probable his earnings are under-rated.

The ſum of £237. 2s. 6d. were ſubſcribed, during the late ſevere ſeaſon, for the relief of the Poor, and was applied towards enabling them to purchaſe bread at a reduced price.

	£.	s.	d.
The expences for the Poor, in 1776, amounted to	1755	3	11
Money raiſed by aſſeſſment in 1783 - -	2466	16	0
Ditto in 1784 - -	2474	0	10
Ditto in 1785 - -	2444	8	10 [1]

The following information, reſpecting the laſt three years, was readily communicated by the ſtanding Overſeer.

	Total Aſſeſſments	Total Expenditure	Rates uncollected	No of Rates
	£ s. d.	£. s d.	£ s d.	£ s. d
Poor's Rates 1793	1971 13 6	1968 3 5½	44 2 9	72 at 27 7 8¼ each.
1794	2631 14 0	2936 16 11½	56 16 10	96 do do. do.
1795	3125 14 9	3286 18 4	89 5 1	114 do. do. do.

120 Rates have been already granted for this year, and, it is ſuppoſed, will ſerve till next Eaſter. The Rates are collected by a very old aſſeſſ-ment; but it is difficult to aſcertain what they are in the pound on the net rental. A very intelligent perſon conjectures, that each Rate is collected at about ¼d. in the pound on houſes, and ½d. on land, according to the preſent rent.　-

　　　　　　　　　　　　　　　　　　　　　October, 1795.

　　　-　　　　-

[1] From the Returns made to Parliament in 1786

MINE-

MINEHEAD.

THIS parifh is about 3 miles in length, and rather more than 2 miles in breadth: it contains about 1220 inhabitants; all of the eftablifhed chuich, except about a dozen Quakers; and confifting of weavers of coarfe cloth, wool-combeis, tiadefmen, and agricultuiifts; laboureis' wives are moftly employed in fpinning worfted and yarn: 110 houfes pay the window-tax; and about 170 are exempted There aie 11 ale-houfes, and one inn, in Minehead. The prices of provifions are: mutton and beef, 4d. a lb.; pork, 5½d.; and butter, 10d. the pound. Common laboureis ieceive from 6s. to 7s. a week, with two or three pints of ale, or cyder, a day. Heie is one Friendly Society, confifting of about 90 members: they have had their rules confiimed; and have about £300. in the public funds; no member is admitted unlefs he can earn more than 7s. a week.

The rent of land is from £1. to £3. an acre. Farms are moftly fmall; but, of late, farmers in this neighbouihood have been defirous of extending their farms: the principal articles of cultivation are, wheat, barley, and tuinips, a few peafe, beans, and potatoes. Tithes aie partly taken in kind, but moftly compounded for. The land-tax is about 1s. 10d. in the pound. There is a large common in this parifh, on which a great number of fheep are kept: a few acres have been inclofed at different times; and now produce good crops of various forts of grain.

The Poor are maintained in a work-houfe, for which a rent of £6. 5s. is paid by the parifh, who likewife pay one guinea a year for the ufe of a large garden adjoining: a governefs, appointed by the parifhioners, has a falary of 5 guineas a year; a doctor, who attends the Poor, receives 6 guineas a year.

Table of Diet obferved in the Poor-houfe.

	Breakfaft.	Dinner	Supper
Sunday,	Half a pound of bread, and a pint of fmall-beer, to each perfon.	Beef, or mutton.	Bread, and fmall beer.
Monday,	Broth.	Fried greens and potatoes, with bread.	Ditto.
Tuefday,	Ditto.	Oatmeal and water boiled, and meat	Bread and cheefe.
Wednefday,	Ditto.	Same as Monday.	Same as Sunday.
Thurfday,	Ditto.	Same as Sunday.	Ditto.
Friday,	Ditto.	Same as Monday.	Ditto.
Saturday,	Ditto.	Same as Tuefday.	Bread and cheefe.

A Table

A Table of Baptisms, Burials, Marriages, Poor's Rates, Expenditure, and Earnings of the Poor.

Years	Baptisms			Burials			Mar.
	Ma	Fem	Tot.	Ma	Fem	Tot	
1680	41	37	78	29	22	51	11
1685	33	24	57	39	24	63	7
1690	41	26	67	28	11	49	13
1691	36	21	57	40	35	75	6
1692	30	17	47	21	20	41	9
1693	28	28	56	20	24	44	10
1694	18	16	34	22	33	55	3
1695	20	27	47	22	26	48	15
1696	15	35	50	15	10	25	
1697	20	15	35	25	40	65	
1698	23	32	55	16	19	35	
1699	32	26	58	17	20	37	
1700	32	32	64	20	27	47	
1720	20	18	38	19	18	37	
1740	17	24	41	19	20	39	
1760	19	15	34	12	22	34	
1775	18	18	36	25	31	56	
1776	11	11	22	14	18	32	
1777	9	12	21	16	15	31	
1778	13	13	26	8	17	25	
1779	20	18	38	7	16	23	
1780	15	16	31	7	6	13	
1781	14	10	24	13	15	28	
1782	15	13	28	12	15	27	
1783	12	10	22	13	16	29	
1784	14	13	27	15	11	26	
1785	12	15	27	14	10	24	
1786	8	13	21	6	16	22	
1787	15	15	30	5	9	14	
1788	19	15	34	10	11	21	
1789	13	16	29	9	17	16	
1790	24	13	37	10	14	24	
1791	12	16	28	10	16	26	
1792	17	18	35	11	15	26	
1793	23	22	45	7	10	17	
1794	8	9	17	4	6	10	
1795	7	12	19	8	12	20	

Burials of the Poor from Work-house

Years	Ma	Fem	Tot	Mar.
1734	1	1	2	8
1735	1	1	2	11
1736	2	2	4	21
1737	4	3	7	18
1738	2	4	6	16
1739	2	2	4	10
——	4	4	8	14
——	3	6	9	18
——	1	2	3	5
——	3	1	4	8
——	4	1	5	5
——	2	6	8	7
——	2	2	4	10
——	-	-	4	13
——	8	4	12	9
——	3	4	7	7
——	3	1	4	5
——	1	6	7	5
——	2	-	2	6
——	2	2	11	6
——	3	3	6	6
——	6	5	11	6
——	-	-	8	6
——	-	-	3	6
——	-	-	6	6
——	-	-	3	8
——	-	-	-	4

No. of Rates collected for the Poor		Net sums expended on the Poor			Gained by the Labour of the Poor in the Work-house		
Years	Rates	£	s	d	£	s	d
1734	2	115	12	10			
1735	2	109	10	3			
1736	2	118	9	2			
1737	1½	95	8	2			
1738	1½	102	16	3			
1739	1½	108	9	7			
——	2¼	148	8	5			
——	3	178	6	1	16	17	7
——	5	315	0	0	13	19	9
——	4	269	0	0	13	4	0
——	6	330	0	0	14	3	4
——	6	365	0	0	9	10	0
——	5	295	18	0	9	11	11
——	6	285	0	0	8	16	0
——	5	247	0	0	8	8	10
——	7	301	0	0	5	7	10
——	5	323	0	0	8	2	6
——	5	303	0	0	16	7	4
——	5	315	0	0	12	18	11
——	6	314	0	0	12	15	8
——	5	324	0	0	15	0	0
——	6	337	9	0	15	14	8
——	6	320	0	0	9	1	0
——	6	355	10	0	19	19	3
——	6	336	17	0	15	7	0
——	6	348	14	0	20	12	11
——	6	359	6	0	16	5	6
		353	4	0	14	10	2

not finished this year.

No Poor's book could be found prior to 1734, at which period, it appears, the parish rented a poor-house at £6. 5s. a year; but no salary is mentioned for the governor before 1738, when he was allowed £10. a year: nothing occurs in the books relative to the labour of the Poor, anterior to 1760. When the Rate was first made, (60 years ago,) it was laid at 4d. in the pound on houses, and 6d. in the pound on land; and then amounted to £63. 3s.; since which time it has decreased, in consequence fequence of many houfes falling into decay, and the late two fires, which have altogether reduced it to 53. 1s. It is thought that the Rate cannot be now more than 3d. in the pound on the net rental, as lands are very much improved in this county.

In the parifh register of baptifms, burials, and marriages, in Auguft 1698, after the names of many perfons, there follows a declaration, that they were Paupers: this mode was obferved till the end of the year; but was afterwards difcontinued.

There are generally about 30 Paupers in the work-houfe: 20 out-penfioners are partly maintained by their friends, and receive a parifh allowance of from 6d. to 2s a week, each: very few receive 2s. which is the higheft weekly fum allowed to an out-penfioner. A labourer, who works conftantly with a farmer, for 6s a week, is generally allowed wheat for his family, at 1s. a bufhel lower than the market price: and at this time, few farmers charge their labourers more than 6s. or 7s. the bufhel, for which other perfons pay 10s. 6d. or 11s.

Before the year 1760, much live cattle was imported at this place, from Ireland: about that period, the importation was ftopped, by order of Government; and many cattle, which were imported afterwards, were feized, and fold, according to Act of Parliament, for the ufe of the Poor; but as the amount of the money was very confiderable, and the number of the Poor, then wanting relief, very trifling, a furplus remained, with which an eftate, in the parifh of St. Mary Ottery, in the county of Devon, was purchafed, for the ufe of the Poor: it now produces £ 20. a year, which are annually diftributed among the moft neceffitous, under the name of cow-money. *December*, 1795.

WALCOT.

THE Poor of the parifh of Walcot, in the city of Bath, are partly farmed in a work houfe, and partly fupported by the parifh at home: 101 are, at prefent, in the work-houfe. The contractor receives 2s. 6d. a week, for each perfon; befides an annual allowance of £ 40. In confideration of the dearnefs of provifions, the parifh has lately given him an addition of 6 guineas a week. He provides every neceffary wanted in the work-houfe. 294 regular penfioners are, at prefent, paid by the parifh, and coft about £ 121. 18s for four weeks: about 10 or 12 Poor receive cafual relief. Settlements are gained here, principally, by fervice. There are only two farms in this parifh, about £ 100. or £ 150. a year each. The rent of land is from 50s to 60s. an acre. The land tax is faid to be under 1d in the pound. The minifter of this parifh is fupported by voluntary contributions, which, it is faid, amount to about £ 1000. a year. Here is, at leaft, one congregation of every defcription of Diffenters Several Friendly Societies are in this parifh, but no information of their numbers could be obtained; moft of them have had their orders confirmed.

The price of butcher's meat is from 4d to 5d. the pound.

Labourers' wages are from 14d. to 18d. the day.

Four fixpenny Rates, on the net rent, were collected laft year: each Rate amounted to £ 718. 4s 9d; but £ 200. of it remained unexpended; the officer faid, that the expenditure would be more confiderable this year: the Rates for 2 or 3 years back, he faid, had been nearly the fame. A confiderable part of the city of Bath ftands in this parifh; in which moft of the houfes have been built within the laft 50 years.

A Table of Baptifms, Burials, and Marriages, in the Parifh of WALCOT.

Years.	Baptifms.	Burials.	Marriages
1691	2	—	—
1694	1	—	—
1695	1	—	—
1696	1	—	—
1697	1	—	—
1720	13	—	—
1740	71	81	—
1760	85	81	—
1775	264	201	—
1776	268	251	—
1777	279	162	—
1778	287	162	—
1779	294	180	122

Years.

Years.		Baptifms.		Burials.		Marriages
1780	-	267	-	216	-	115
1781	-	281	-	190	-	104
1782	-	328	-	182	-	116
1783	-	295	-	181	-	130
1784	-	314	-	237	-	143
1785	-	326	-	196	-	143
1786	-	304	-	228	-	129
1787	-	348	-	230	-	149
1788	-	371	-	218	-	163
1789	-	411	-	233	-	173
1790	-	446	-	235	-	188
1791	-	522	-	267	-	194
1792	-	549	-	308	-	247
1793	-	572	-	417	-	210
1794	-	601	-	279	-	191

According to the Returns made to Parliament in 1786,

The expences for the Poor	in 1776	were	1033	3	9
The money raifed by affeffment	in 1783	——	1621	19	0
Ditto	in 1784	——	1463	14	1
Ditto	in 1785	——	1661	5	8

October, 1795.

S T A F F O R D S H I R E.

L I T C H F I E L D.

LITCHFIELD contains 3 parifhes, viz. St. Mary's, St. Chad's, and St Michael's: the firft has moft houfes and inhabitants, but no land; the other two have few houfes, but a confiderable quantity of land.

In 1781 the number of houfes in Litchfield was 722, and of inhabi-

tants,

tants, about 3555: it is fuppofed, that, fince that period, the population has confiderably increafed.

In the whole city, 408 houfes pay the window-tax; the number exempted could not be afcertained,

The prices of provifions are: beef and mutton, 5d. the lb.; veal, 4½d.; bacon, 9½d. and 10d. the lb.; milk, ¾ of a quart for 1d.; butter, 11d. the lb.; potatoes, 4s. the bufhel; bread flour, 5s. the ftone; coals, 6d. the cwt.

The wages of labourers are from 9s. to 12s. a week, according to the feafon: women, for weeding, are paid 8d. a day; for hay making, 10d. a day, and victuals. Thofe who fpin lint, earn from 4d. to 6d a day.

There are 46 ale-houfes in this city; and 5 Friendly Societies for men, and 2 for women; from 100 to 200 members belong to each Society.

Land, near the city, lets for £ 3. or £ 4. an acre: the average is about 30s. an acre. Farms are generally fmall: the principal articles of cultivation are, wheat, barley, oats, turnips, and clover. Tithes are, moftly, taken in kind. The total land-tax, for the city, is £ 420. 19s 4d. The Poor are maintained at their own houfes: about 23 penfioners, at prefent, receive £ 2 17s. 6d. a week; fix of thefe are baftards: feveral houfe-rents are paid, and cafual reliefs are given to many of the neceffitous.

The Rates in St. Mary's, are about 3s. in the pound on the nominal rental: in St. Chad's, and St. Michael's, half the rack rents are affeffed. St. Mary's and St. Chad's have each a work-houfe. In St Mary's work-houfe, there are, at prefent, 41 Paupers: they manufacture a little blanketing, for the ufe of the houfe. The bill of fare, till very lately, included puddings, and bread and cheefe dinners, about 3 days a week: at prefent, on account of the fcarcity of bread and flour, the following diet is generally ufed:

	Breakfaft.	Dinner.	Supper.
Sunday,	Milk pottage.	Meat and vegetables.	Bread and cheefe.
Monday,	Ditto.	Broth, and cold meat.	Ditto
Tuefday,	Ditto.	Same as Sunday.	Ditto
Wednefday,	Ditto	Same as Monday.	Ditto.
Thurfday,	Ditto	Same as Sunday	Ditto
Friday,	Ditto.	Same as Monday	Ditto.
Saturday,	Ditto.	Bread and cheefe	Ditto.

A Table

A Table of Baptisms, Burials, Marriages, and Poor's Rates, in the Parish of ST. MICHAEL, *Litchfield.*

Years	Baptisms			Burials			Mar.	Poor's Rates.			Expenditure.			Rate in the Pound.
	Males.	Fem	Tot	Males.	Fem.	Tot.		£.	s.	d.	£	s.	d.	
1774	—	—	—	—	—	—	—	116	13	6½	115	10	9	
1775	14	12	26	29	12	41	14	110	9	3	104	7	1	
1776	21	16	37	33	23	56	1)	157	9	10	130	9	3	
1777	14	13	27	32	33	65	9	142	13	1	137	9	11½	
1778	19	21	40	19	25	44	8	121	16	10	121	14	1	
1779	14	17	31	30	28	58	13	163	0	1	155	17	1	
1780	7	12	19	31	30	61	13	150	15	0	147	1	2¼	
1781	21	18	39	29	23	52	9	156	12	7	142	1	1	
1782	27	13	40	39	45	84	19	191	19	11	191	15	11	
1783	—	—	32	—	—	49	—	129	2	4	114	6	10	
1784	—	—	32	—	—	45	—	181	16	4	182	10	11	
1785	—	—	40	—	—	75	—	169	13	4	169	8	0¼	
1786	—	—	38	—	—	80	—	—	—	—	—	—	—	
1787	—	—	—	—	—	65	—	209	3	1½	186	6	3½	
1788	—	—	26	—	—	39	17	150	14	3	161	9	7	
1789	—	—	29	—	—	38	22	196	13	8	195	19	3	
1790	—	—	26	—	—	46	16	188	3	6	188	2	11	
1791	—	—	29	—	—	35	27	—	—	—	226	16	8½	This is on the nominal rental
1792	—	—	37	—	—	46	20	225	17	7	209	14	2	
1793	—	—	27	—	—	53	33	—	—	—	187	7	7½	
1794	—	—	32	—	—	57	20	—	—	—	270	17	2	s. d.
1795	—	—	—	—	—	—	—	—	—	—	282	4	8	1 8

It is neceſſary to obſerve, that a great part of the other pariſhes bury at St. Michael's, and chriſten at their own churches: it is owing to this cir-cumſtance, that the burials greatly exceed the births. 7 or 8 ſmall ham-lets likewiſe bury and chriſten here. In the Poor's Rates, the compoſitions for baſtardy are included: the Poor's Rates do not include the hamlets. The lowneſs of the Rates is aſcribed to the pariſh having a conſiderable quantity of land. An attempt was made to examine the pariſh of St. Mary's, in this city, the aſſeſſments of which are all raiſed on houſes; but the books were found to be in ſuch a confuſed ſtate, (ſome years ac-counts

counts being loft, and others not fettled,) that very little information could be collected from them. The following ftatement, however, of the receipts and difburfements for a few years, is accurate:

Years.		Receipts.				Total Expenditure.		
		£.	s.	d.		£.	s.	d.
1757	-	307	3	1½	-	301	13	5
1777	-	304	0	7½	-	309	9	7
1784	-	474	2	7	-	—	—	—
1787	-	544	3	9	-	538	17	1½
1792	-	632	4	9	-	626	7	7½
1793	-	459	9	1	-	568	13	8½
1794	-	663	7	7	-	654	12	9
1795	-	504	0	0	-	Not fettled.		

In 1793, and 1795, the net affeffments, £ 504. are faid to have been raifed at 4s. 8d. in the pound; but it fhould be remarked, that fome houfes are not rated at ⅓ of their real rent; fome at more; and fome even below ¼ of their value: this is the cafe in almoft every populous parifh.

In the parifh of Clifton, which is fituated between Litchfield and Afhby de la Zouch, the Rates have, for many years back, been about 8d. in the pound: they are now only 1s. 3d. in the pound. The late rife is afcribed to the dearnefs of provifions, and the confolidation of fmall farms. This parifh belongs to one proprietor. The farms are from £ 20 to £1000. a year.

In 2 or 3 fmall parifhes in this neighbourhood, which confift of large farms, there are very few Poor: the farmers, in order to prevent the introduction of Poor from other parifhes, hire their fervants for 51 weeks only. I conceive, however, that this practice would be confidered, by a court of juftice, as fraudulent, and a mere evafion in the mafter; and that a fervant thus hired, if he remained the 52d week with his mafter, on a frefh contract, would acquire a fettlement in the parifh.

Auguft, 1795.

WOL-

WOLVERHAMPTON.

THE prices of provisions in Wolverhampton are: beef, mutton, and veal, from 4½d. to 5d. the lb.; bacon, 8½d.; butter, 10½d.; bread flour, 5s. the stone; milk, 2d the quart.

The wages in the different manufactures vary from 9s. to £ 2. a week: men, in full employment, earn, on an average, from 15s. to £1. 5s. a week. The manufactures are the heaviest forts of hard ware; such as axes, shovels, &c.; buckles, watch-chains, toys, spectacle-cases, &c.

A few years ago, there were 134 public houses in this town; but the number is supposed to have decreased The population is estimated at near 20,000 fo ls: I should, however, think the number was exaggerated.

The Dissenters, here, consist of Anabaptists, Calvinists, Presbyterians, Roman Catholics, and Methodists: they are supposed, altogether, to amount to one third of the inhabitants.

The average rent of land in the neighbourhood of the town, is about £ 3. an acre: no information could be obtained relative to the land-tax. Tithes are chiefly taken in kind. Wheat is the principal grain cultivated in the parish: much land is in pasture. There are neither commons, nor waste-lands, in the parish.

Friendly Societies are in great repute in Wolverhampton. There are, in all, about 34 Clubs, of which only one has taken the benefit of the late Act of Parliament. They were apprehensive that the provisions of the Act were intended as a prelude to taxation; and that the magistrates would be authorized to controul the disposal of their funds: they likewise thought, that applications to the quarter sessions would be expensive; and, being prepossessed with these various ideas, it is not astonishing that they were not much inclined to apply to the magistrates A few Societies, however, presented their rules to the Justices, for their sanction; but, upon their being informed that they could not be confirmed unless they were made agreeable to the Act of Parliament, these slight difficulties deterred them from proceeding farther. They say: " We cannot see that any advantage would accrue from having our rules confirmed: the
expence

expence would be fo much money thrown away : we will adhere to our old rules, which, by long experience, we have found to be very beneficial " While thele impreffions remain, it is not aftonifhing that it fhould be difficult to obtain any information relative to the circumftances of the Societies : the only refult of various enquiries has been to learn that 12 of the male clubs contain 637 members; and 6 of the female clubs, 351 members. The following are the principal rules of a Society, confifting of 71 tradefmen, who meet once a fortnight. They are fimilar to thofe of feveral other Societies in Wolverhampton.

4, That every perfon muft pay for his entrance 1s. until the money in the box amounts to £ 10.; and then 1s. 6d. till it amounts to £ 20. ; 2s. 6d till it amounts to £ 30. ; 3s. till it amounts to £ 40. ; 5s. for £ 40, and 1s more for every £ 10, till it amounts to £ 100 ; and 12s. for any greater fum : every member fhall be allowed fix months to pay his entrance money in, but if not paid in that time, fhall be excluded. Any perfon that means to enter, fhall be propofed one club night, and entered the next, or rejected, except all the members are in one voice.

5, That no perfon fhall have any benefit from this Society until he hath belonged thereto twelve months ; then, if he be fick, lame, or blind, and not able to work at his trade or occupation, fhall receive the fum of 7s. per week, fo long as he fhall continue fo. And if any member fhall die before he hath been entered one year, his widow, or neareft relation, or whom he belongs to, fhall receive the fum of 30s. for a decent burial ; but he muft be a member fix months before he is entitled to receive it ; and that every member fhall attend the corpfe to the grave, and fhall return to the houfe in the fame order, or forfeit 2s. 6d. to the box, unlefs prevented by any emergent occafion, or being out of town, which fhall be adjudged by the committee ; and that, the third Society night after his burial, every member fhall pay 1s. to the box ; and if any member fhall refufe fo to do, he fhall be then excluded this Society.

6, That when the money in the box amounts to the fum of £ 10. any member that fhall then die after he has been entered one year, his widow or neareft relation fhall be entitled to 10s. ; when £ 20.—

20s. ;

2os.; when £ 30 —30s ; when £ 40.—40s.; when £ 50.—50s.; when £ 60.—£ 5 ; or he may leave it by will as he thinks proper. That if any member fhall die after he has been entered one year, there fhall be 30s. allowed for a decent burial ; when £ 40. in the box, there fhall be 40s allowed for a decent burial : and every member fhall attend the corp fe to the grave, as before-mentioned, and appear decent and clean, or forfeit 2s. 6d to the box. And if any perfon fhall enter, after the money in the box amounts to £ 60 , and being entered one year, there fhall be allowed 40s. for a decent burial, but not the benefit of the £ 5. till he has been a member three years, then at his death he may difpofe of the £ 5. over and above the 40s. allowed for his burial, which money fhall be paid as long as there fhall remain £ 60. in the box. When the money in the box entitles the reprefentative to receive £ 5. they fhall alfo receive 1s per man out of the box, which fhall be returned the third Society night, by the members.

7, That when the money in the box amounts to £ 30. or £ 40 , and by fick or lame members fhould be reduced fo low as £ 20. or under, then every member fhall pay 2d. each Society night over and above his contribution money, which 2d. a piece fhall be paid fo long as fhall be thought needful.

8, That the ftewards fhall vifit the fick, and appoint four members upon the roll to do the fame, one of them every day, or forfeit 6d. to the box for every default.

9, That if any member of this Society fhall go out of town to refide, he fhall give notice thereof to the ftewards ; and if the next place of his abode be not above fixty miles, he fhall have eight weeks time allowed to fend his contribution money ; but if more than fixty miles, fhall have fourteen weeks allowed ; and if fick or lame, and not able to work at his trade, fhall fend a certificate, (poft paid,) figned by the minifter, church-wardens, and overfeers of the parifh where he refides, or the major part of them, certifying how long he hath been ill, and what is his diftemper, inclofed in a letter directed to the Father of the Society, and then he fhall receive the money the fame as if he was in town. No money fhall be paid out of the kingdom of England.

10, That

10, That there fhall be allowed, from this Society, £. 1. 10s. for the burial of a member's wife, after he has been entered one year, but not allowed to have it more than once; and a bachelor fhall be entitled to the fame benefit, when he has been a member three years, to bury any relation or friend, or who they think proper; but they fhall never receive it more than once: if under 61 members, every member fhall pay according to what it amounts to his fhare; if 61, or above, then every member fhall pay 6d. each to the burial, the third meeting night after, or be for ever excluded the faid Society: the overplus to the box. Any member claiming 30s. for the funeral of a wife, friend, or relation, if at a diftance, and not known by the father or ftewards, fhall bring a certificate, figned by the minifter, church-wardens, and overfeers of the parifh where fuch perfon lived, or the major part of them, certifying the veracity of fuch death.

14, That there fhall be a feaft provided at the Society-houfe on the 11th day of July, and another on the 26th day of December: every member fhall pay 1s. towards the feaft, feven days before, or forfeit 1s. to the box; every member fhall alfo pay 1s. for liquor, (if he be in town,) immediately after the cloth is drawn, or forfeit 2s. the next Society night. The old ftewards and the committee fhall choofe two new ones, and whofoever refufes to ftand, being lawfully chofen, fhall forfeit 2s. to the box. The old ftewards fhall give up a juft account to the new ones. And no member of this Society fhall either give or fend any victuals from the feaft to any perfon whatfoever, except to a fick member of the faid Society. It is farther agreed, that, on the market-day, that the father and ftewards buy the meat for the feaft, they fhall be allowed 2s. for ale, to be fet down to the fhot on the feaft-day; and each of them allowed to invite two members to partake of the fteaks, at fix o'clock at night. Every member fhall take up his articles on the feaft day, or forfeit 1s. to the box.

15, That, at every election of new ftewards, a committee fhall be chofe by the old and new ftewards, of eight members, fuch as they fhall think to be of the beft abilities and knowledge in the Society's affairs, which, including the father and two ftewards, will make eleven, and entered as fuch in the Society's book, and fhall have full power vefted in them

to

to fettle and determine all grievances or differences that shall or may happen at any time, by and between any of the members thereof, whose determination shall be final and conclusive.

16, That if the stewards or father do not bring or send their keys by seven o'clock each Society night, they shall forfeit and pay 1s. to the box : and if any member shall call either of the stewards by any other name than Mr. Steward, during Society hours, he shall forfeit and pay 2d. to the box. That one book of accounts may be kept by the father of the Society, and another by the stewards, or one of them.

17, That if any member should be absent from the Society after the space of six weeks, being in town, and doth neither come nor send his contribution money, shall forfeit 2d to the box, and be allowed one night more, and if not made good the fourth Society night, shall be excluded. And whosoever shall propose the breaking of this Society, shall not only be denied the benefit thereof, but be for ever excluded the same.

18, That whosoever shall talk of state affairs, or challenge any one to work at his trade, or be heard, by any two present, to curse or swear, or propose to lay any wagers, shall forfeit and pay, for every one particular crime, 2d. to the box; and if any controversy arise amongst the Society, the same shall be determined by the committee thereof.

19, That every member of the said Society shall pay, every fortnight, in the manner following, viz. 4d. to the box, and 2d for his ale ; and if he forbear a month, then he shall pay 8d. to the box, and 4d. his ale ; and if he forbear six weeks, then he shall pay 1s. to the box, and 6d. his ale : and if any person offer bad money in the Society-room, he shall forfeit 6d. to the box.

24, That, in case any member, through age, or any accident, be blind or lame, so that he is rendered incapable of working at his trade or occupation, and his case be judged incurable, then he shall receive 4s. per week, with liberty of doing any thing for his further subsistence, if he thinks fit; which money shall be paid so long as he lives.

32, That

32, That if any member of this Society shall be preffed into his Majesty's service, either by sea or land, he shall have an equal share of the money in the box, and be no longer a member; but if he enters himself into his Majesty's or merchant's service, for a soldier or sailor, he shall be excluded this Society without any money : or if any member lay violent hands upon himself, he shall not be buried at the Society's expence, nor shall his widow or representative be entitled to any benefit of this Society.

33, That if any member of this Society is allotted a militia-man according to law, a substitute shall be procured, at the Society's expence; but if a member hire himself to serve in the militia, he shall be excluded.

36, That, at any time the committee is summoned, they shall have three days notice, and be allowed 5s. 6d. for expence, out of the Society night's drink ; and any one not attending at the time, shall forfeit 6d. And any member that lays information of another, so as to cause the committee to be summoned, and doth not prove it to the satisfaction of the committee, shall forfeit 2s 6d. and ask the injured member pardon in public Society.

The following is a statement of the earnings and expences of a spectacle-frame maker. He is 40 years of age ; has a wife, and 4 children, viz. a boy, 10; a boy, 7 ; a girl, 2 years old ; and another girl, 6 months old.

EARNINGS.

	£.	s.	d.
The man earns, on an average, 16s. a week, which, (allowing one week for holidays, sickness, &c) amount annually to	40	16	0
He at present employs 2 boys, by whom he gains 2s. a week; annually - - - - - -	5	4	0
He lets part of his house for 1s. 4d. a week; annually -	3	9	4
His wife earns nothing: the eldest boy has worked in the shop, for some months ; but not being very expert in the business, and requiring much attention from his father, his work produces more trouble than profit - -	0	0	0
Total earnings -	£49	9	4

4

EXPENCES.

	£.	s.	d.
This family ufes 7 ftone of flour in a month, (or about 14 lb. a week,) which, at the laft year's price, 2s. 3d. (now 5s.) coft annually - - • - -	10	4	9
12 lb. of meat a week, at 4d. the lb. (now 5d) annually -	10	8	0
Cheefe, 2 lb and butter, 2 lb. a week; annually - -	4	11	0
Milk, about 6d. a week; fmall beer, ditto; ftrong beer, about 1s. a week; annually - • - -	5	4	0
Potatoes, about ½ a bufhel a week, and other vegetables; annually about - - - - -	4	0	0
Tea, fugar, foap and candles, &c. are eftimated annually at	5	0	0
Rent - - - - - -	6	0	0
Taxes, about - - - - -	0	10	0
Shirts, fhoes, and other cloathing; annually about - -	4	10	0
Total expences - -	£50	7	9
Total earnings - -	49	9	4
Deficiency of earnings -	£0	18	5

The man could give no account of his difburfements for fuel, for his wife's lying-in, which occurs about once in two years, and other cafual expences. Notwithftanding the great apparent deficiency, he declares, that he has never received relief from the parifh; that he is fometimes obliged to bend to difficulties, but never permits his expenditure to exceed his income: I believe I may add, with truth, that, in times of profperity, he is equally careful in preventing his income from exceeding his outgoings. The daily meals of this family are: bread and milk for the man and his fon's breakfafts, and tea for the wife and young children; bread and cheefe, or meat and vegetables, for dinner; and generally the fame, for fupper.

Table

Table of Baptisms, Burials, and Poor's Rates in the Parish of WOLVERHAMPTON.

Years.	Baptisms.	Burials.	Net Sum raised by Assessment.			Total Expenditure.			Rate in the Pound on the net Rental.	
			£.	s.	d.	£.	s.	d.		
1603	86	48	1773 and 1774 } 2647	4	1½	2811	14	10		
1700	123	131								
1775	383	447	1194	7	8	1290	14	1		
1776	—	—	1407	13	7	1559	8	3		
1777	—	—	1177	11	6½	1287	18	5¼		
17.8	—	—	1179	11	1	1315	12	7		
1779	—	—	1452	12	0¼	1617	3	5		
1780	—	—	1712	4	11	1945	19	0		
1781	—	—	1474	0	7	1878	12	2		
1782	—	—	1443	3	7½	1863	7	11		
1783	—	—	1691	8	11½	1920	16	3½		
1784	—	—	1697	18	8	1805	4	0½		
1785	388	524	1918	18	2	2018	18	2		
1786	—	—	1914	6	6½	2017	6	5		
1787	425	452	1862	18	3	2036	3	2		
1788	—	—	Accounts of these years not made out.							
1789	432	464								
1790	—	—							s.	d.
1791	—	—	1535	13	9	2175	18	3	1	3
1792	—	—	1557	6	3¾	1813	15	0	1	3
1793	—	—	Accounts not made out.							
1794	454	477	1564	3	7	2323	12	6	1	3
1795	—	—	— — —			— — —			1	8

An

An Account of Money received of the Town of WOLVERHAMPTON, *from Easter* 1790, *to Easter* 1791, *(being 55 weeks,) by the Overseers of the Poor, and how it was applied.*

Drs.   OVERSEERS   Crs.

	£.	s.	d		£.	s.	d.
To cash from the late overseers -	324	7	7½	By 55 weeks out pay to the Poor	665	0	1
To three grants, amounting to -	1535	13	9	Balance of the Birmingham account	24	15	1
To cash collected from the old collecting book - - -	106	18	9	Flour - - -	271	1	4
				Butcher's meat - - -	159	7	10
To cash received for the Poor's labour - - -	72	16	7	Mercery and drapery goods -	107	12	0
To cash, weekly pay for bastardy	40	16	0	Cheese - - - -	51	6	0
To composition of ditto - -	89	13	6	Malt and hops - - -	65	5	1
To cash received from Mr Horton, balance of his accounts 1782	9	12	6	Shoes - - - -	58	2	0
To ditto from different parishes, paid to their out poor - -	23	19	3	Coals - - - -	43	18	10½
				Apprentices' fees - - -	36	2	6
To cash received from Mr James Shaw, errors in his accounts	171	16	0	Coffins and burials - -	24	5	2
				Removals and litigations - -	36	17	7¼
				Expences of days of appeal -	11	15	11
				Store pigs - - - -	13	2	0
				Soap, candles, and grocery -	29	19	6
				Oatmeal - - -	34	9	0
				Governor's monthly bills of sundry articks confumed in the houfe	19	5	3
				Clothes making - - -	4	6	10
				Surgeons and midwives - -	21	5	0
				Juftices' clerks - - -	33	15	9
				Conftables' accounts - -	141	14	11
				County Rates - - -	40	6	2
				Milk - - - - -	16	8	0
				Salt - - - - -	7	9	6
				Expences of the new building -	104	18	7
				Stationary - - -	7	5	2
				Wool and flocks - - -	7	14	1
				Hats and hofe - - -	8	16	2
				Manure - - -	3	15	0
				Potatoes and garden-ftuff -	8	11	6
				Yeaft - - -	4	19	6
				Care of lunatics - - -	6	1	6
				Plumbing and glazing - -	2	7	1
				Bed mats, wheelbarrow, cutlery, trenchers, and feveral other articles	9	15	9
				Ringing the market-bell, and care of the clock, four years -	10	8	0
				Lofs in light gold and bafe filver	1	12	6
				Stephen Godfon's falary - -	40	0	0
				William Bradley's (governor) do.	30	0	0
				Hannah Perry's (governefs) do	10	0	0
				John Robinfon, for fhaving the the people in the houfe - -	2	2	0
					£ 2175	18	3
				Balance to the next overseers -	199	15	8¼
£ 2375	13	11½		£ 2375	13	11½

An

An Account of Money received of the Town of WOLVERHAMPTON, from Easter 1791, to Easter 1792, (being 50 weeks,) by the Overseers of the Poor, and how it was applied.

Dis.	£	s	d		OVERSEERS	Cr.	£	s	d
To balance from the late overseers	199	15	8½		By 50 weeks out-pay	-	640	17	10½
To three giants, amounting to -	1557	6	3½		Balance of the Birmingham account	24	5	0
To cash collected from the old collecting book -	34	15	10¼		Flour -	-	153	16	0
					Butcher's meat -	-	118	19	2
To cash received for the Poor's labour -	52	14	3½		Mercery and drapery goods	-	70	18	5
To cash, weekly pay for bastardy	26	7	0		Cheese	-	41	15	8½
To composition of ditto -	106	11	0		Malt and hops -	-	57	10	0
To cash received from different parishes, paid to their out-poor	47	19	0		Shoes -	-	46	5	9
					Coals -	-	30	14	9½
					Apprentices' fees -	-	38	6	6
					Coffins and burials -	-	25	17	9
					Removals and litigations	-	45	3	8
					Store pigs -	-	9	9	0
					Grocery, candles, and soap	-	23	1	0
					Oatmeal -	-	20	6	5
					Governor's monthly bills of sundry articles consumed in the house	-	10	10	2
					Clothes making -	-	6	3	6
					Surgeons and midwives	-	27	19	0
					Justices' clerks	-	16	19	0
					Constables' accounts	-	177	15	7
					County Rates	-	65	11	8
					Milk -	-	15	2	0
					Salt -	-	6	6	6
					Wool -	-	2	18	8
					Hats and hose	-	5	9	8
					Manure -	-	1	12	0
					Potatoes and garden-stuff	-	5	7	8
					Yeast -	-	4	8	7
					Care of lunatics	-	7	16	4
					Plumbing and glazing -	-	5	15	10½
					Cutlery goods, bed mats, &c.	-	2	0	10¼
					Repairs of the building	-	3	7	9
					Cooper's goods, and repairing ditto	5	16	2
					Braziery ditto, ditto, ditto	-	2	11	1½
					Expences on appeals -	-	2	13	0
					Ditto on auditing the town's accounts -	-	6	6	0
					Loss in light gold and base silver	-	1	14	10
					Messrs. Godson's salary -	-	40	0	0
					William Bradley's (governor) ditto	30	0	0
					Hannah Perry's (governess) ditto	10	0	0
					John Robinson, for shaving the people in the house	-	2	2	0
					Total disbursement -	£1813	15	0
					Balance to the next overseers	-	211	14	2
	£2025	9	2			£2025	9	2

An

An Account of Money received of the Town of WOLVERHAMPTON, from Easter 1793 to Easter 1794, (being 55 Weeks,) by the Overseers of the Poor, and how it was applied.

Drs.   OVERSEERS   Crs

	£.	s	d		£.	s	d.
To balance from last year's account	313	3	2	By 55 weeks out-pay	735	9	8
To three grants, amounting to	1564	3	7	Fifty-five weeks out-pay to militia families	172	10	6
To balance of the Birmingham account	35	16	6	Flour	237	7	3
To cash collected from the old collecting book	16	10	2½	Butcher's meat	150	2	8
				Mercery and drapery goods	63	3	1½
To cash from the treasurer of the county for militia-families	73	18	6	Cheese	47	3	6
				Malt and hops	76	16	9
To cash from different parishes, for militia-families	27	18	0	Shoes	46	4	4
To cash for Poor's labour	74	19	3	Coals	45	19	9¼
To weekly pay for bastardy	27	19	11	Apprentices' fees	31	14	6
To composition of ditto	67	5	6	Coffins and burials	23	8	8½
To cash from different parishes, paid their out-poor	35	9	4	Removals and litigations	36	18	10
				Store pigs	6	13	0
	£2237	3	11½	Soap, candles, and grocery	33	1	4½
To balance due from the town	86	8	7	Oatmeal	30	15	10
				Governor's monthly bills of sundry small articles consumed in the house	9	17	3
				Cloaths making	2	5	0
				Surgeons and midwives	23	14	6
				Attorney's bill, (four years,)	58	8	6
				Justices' clerks	18	9	9
				Constables' accounts	191	1	0
				County rates	81	12	2
				Milk	16	18	0
				Salt	6	6	6
				Wool and flocks	2	17	7
				Hats and hose	4	15	0
				Potatoes and garden stuff	10	13	2
				Yeast	5	9	6
				Repairing the building	7	19	3½
				Braziery, cutlery, and bed mats	4	4	11
				Stationary goods	8	0	4
				Cooper's goods, and repairing do.	4	2	10
				Expences on appeals	14	1	11
				Ditto auditing the town's accounts	6	6	0
				Loss in light gold and base silver	1	17	6
				Henry Roliston, serving overseer,	20	0	0
				Messrs. Godsons, collectors	40	0	0
				William Bradley, governor	30	0	0
				Hannah Perry, governess	10	0	0
				Samuel Robinson, shaving the people in the house	2	2	0
	£2323	12	6¼		£2323	12	6¼

The following is the weekly rotation of diet at prefent obferved in the houfe:

	Breakfaſt.	Dinner.	Supper.
Sunday,	Oatmeal haſty-pudding, and milk	Meat and vegetables.	Bread, cheefe, and beer,
Monday,	Bread and broth.	Broth, and beer.	Ditto.
Tuefday,	Ditto.	Same as Sunday.	Bread and beer.
Wednefday,	Ditto.	Same as Monday.	Same as Sunday.
Thurfday,	Ditto.	Same as Sunday.	Same as Tuefday.
Friday,	Ditto.	Same as Monday.	Same as Sunday.
Saturday,	Ditto.	Same as Monday.	Same as Sunday

On meat-days, the Poor generally endeavour to fave a little meat, to add to their dinner the fucceeding day. At broth and beer meals, no bread is allowed. As the victuals are not weighed, the proportion given to each perfon could not be afcertained.

The following particulars of parochial difburfements and receipts were copied verbatim from printed accounts, the only ones ever publifhed. It is much to be defired, that fimilar ftatements, with a lift of the in and of out-poor, and a table of deaths in the work-houfe, fhould be publifhed annually. I think, too, that the *quantity* of flour and other articles purchafed for the poor-houfe[1], and the *articles manufactured* by the Poor, fhould be particularized[2]. The number of the out-poor, &c. might be ftated on the Dr. fide of the account, without requiring a larger fheet than what has hitherto been ufed, in the following manner:

Lift of the In and Out-Poor, and of the Births and Burials in the Work-houfe, between Eafter 1796 and Eafter 1797.

		No. of Out-Poor	No. of Militia-men's Families.		No. of Poor in the Work houfe	In the Work houfe	
			Wives	Children		Births.	Deaths.
April	1, 1796;	—	—	—	——	—	—
May	1,	—	—	—	——	—	—
June	1,	—	—	—	——	—	—
July	1,	—	—	—	——	—	—
Auguſt	1,	—	—	—	——	—	—
September	1,	—	——	—	——	—	—
October	1,	—	—	—	——	—	—
November	1,	—	—	—	——	—	—
December	1,	—	—	—	——	—	—
January	1, 1797,	—	—	—	——	—	—
February	1,	—	—	—	——	—	—
March	1,	—	—	—	——	—	—
April	1;	—	—	—	——	—	—

[1] See p 185.   [2] See p. 250.

The

The Poor belonging to the parish of Wolverhampton are either relieved
at home, or maintained in a work-house. Of the out-poor, lists have been
published annually by the overseers for some years back. The following
are the earliest and latest lists that could be procured. The last affords
evincing proofs, that the war has added very considerably to the number
of out-poor.

A List of the Poor who receive Out-Pay.

Sept. 11, 1787.

Weekly Allowance.

		s.	d.
Tup ſtreet.—Willington's child — —		0	6
Robert Bate and family — —		1	0
Nock's child, at Smith's — —		0	9
Zachary Bellamy and family —		2	0
Widow Darling, blind — —		1	6
Mary Legg, at Cork's — —		1	0
Widow Taylor — — —		1	0
Mary Fowler's child — —		1	0
Widow Gardiner, junior, blind —		1	0
Barton's child — — —		0	6
Widow Jones — — —		1	0
William Ruſſel — — —		0	6
Widow Mills, in the Chapel-Yard —		1	0
Johnſon's family, at Wadham's-Hill —		3	0
Granger's family — —		3	0
Lancaſter's child — — —		0	9
Hamphlett's children — —		1	6
Edward Wilks — — —		1	0
Horſe-Fair.—Widow Nock — — —		1	0
Widow Davis — — —		0	6
Mary Nightingale — —		0	6
Widow Bickerton — — —		1	6
Widow Wiggin — — —		1	6
Pitt's child — — —		0	9
Fletcher's child, with the grandmother		0	9
Old Church-Yard.—Winifred Nightingale —		0	9
Baker's child — — —		1	0

4 Q 2

			Weekly Allowance.
		s.	d.
Stafford-street.—Widow Sedwick	- -	- 1	3
Ann Swann	- -	- 1	0
Widow Cadman	- -	- 0	6
Widow Reynolds	- -	- 0	6
Fox's child	- -	- 0	9
Groom's child, at Groom's	-	- 0	9
Pratt's child	- -	- 1	0
Widow Perry	- -	- 1	0
Ann Mansel	- - -	- 0	6
Berry-street.—William Lees, blind	-	- 1	6
Parkes's child	- -	- 1	0
Prince's-street.—Turner's children	- -	- 1	6
Widow Unett	- -	- 0	6
Canal-street.—Edward Slater and wife	-	- 1	6
Monday's child	- -	- 1	0
Widow Harper	- -	- 0	6
Thomas Clarke	- - -	- 0	6
Kendrick's family	- -	- 1	0
Beard's family	- -	- 1	0
Lichfield-street.—Widow Lambert	- -	- 1	0
Ann Horton	- ..	- 0	6
Bilston-street.—William Swatman	- -	- 0	9
Widow Duce	- -	- 1	0
Widow Ridley	- -	- 0	6
Widow Bellamy	- -	- 0	9
Sarah Martland, almost blind	-	- 1	0
Walsall-street.—Lawrence's family	- -	- 1	0
Widow Alport	- -	- 1	0
Mary Lees, at Joseph Dean's	- -	- 1	0
Mary Clarke	- -	- 0	9
Widow Garbett	- -	- 1	0
Widow Hamer	- -	- 1	0
Grooby's child	- -	- 0	9
Garbett's children	- -	- 0	6

Wal-

	Weekly Allowance.	
	s.	*d.*
Walfall ſtreet.—Widow Dalton - - -	1	0
Bradford's child - - -	1	0
Dudley ſtrect.—Smith's family - - -	1	0
Widow Davis - - -	0	9
Mary Clewley - - -	1	0
Bell-ſtreet —Lane's family - - -	2	0
Worceſter-ſtreet.—Widow Morris - - - -	1	0
Elizabeth Green - - -	0	9
Widow Nightingale - -	1	0
Widow Bagley, at William Roberts's -	0	6
William Martlin - - -	1	0
Elizabeth Palmer's child - -	1	0
Cork's family - - -	2	0
Widow Lowe - - -	0	6
Snow-hill.—Benton's family - - -	2	0
James Vernon - - -	1	0
Elizabeth Ward - - -	1	6
Widow Hipwood - - -	0	6
Brick-kiln-ſtreet.—Auguſtus Connor, blind - -	1	0
Mary Mitton - - -	0	6
Sharp's family, at Samuel Jones's -	1	6
Mary Horton - - -	0	9
Sarah Wood's child - -	1	6
Meek's child, at Walford, Hallat's-Row -	0	9
Salop-ſtreet.—Gonderton's child - - -	0	9
Widow Lees - - -	0	6
Mary Cockin, at Hazelock's - -	1	0
Widow Poolton - - -	0	9
Thomas Jones - - - -	1	0
Ann Pixley - - - -	0	6
Bloſſom's-Fold.—Richardſon's children, at Atkins's -	2	0
St. John's-ſtreet.—Richard Spittle's family - -	4	0
Sarah Aſtley's child - - -	1	0
Tottey's children - - -	1	0

Floyd's

		Weekly Allowance.
		_s._ _d._
St. John's ſtreet.—Floyd's child, at Floyd's, in Farmer's Yard	-	1 0
Cribby-Iſland.—Widow Gardiner, ſenior	-	1 6
Gardiner's child	-	1 0
Richard Baddeiley	-	1 0
Becket's children	-	1 6
Wiley's child	-	1 0
Ann Wiley	-	0 6
Fletcher's children	-	1 0
Alms-houſes—Widow Williams	-	0 9
Sturmy's child	-	1 0
Thomas Rawlett	-	1 0
Blakemore's family	-	1 0
Joſeph Howe	-	1 6
Widow Wilkes	-	0 9
Daniel Davis's family	-	1 6
Middle-Row, ⎱ —Turner's children, at Stringer's	-	1 6
F our-Aſhes ⎰ Ann Clarke	-	1 0
Town-Well-Fold.—Mace's child	-	0 9

OUT RESIDENTS.

Alice James and three children, at Birmingham	-	2 3
Peter Price and wife, at ditto	-	1 0
Ann Fielding, ditto	-	1 0
Margaret Davis and two children, ditto	-	1 6
William Walker, ditto	-	2 0
Widow Thornſworth, ditto	-	1 0
Jones's children, ditto	-	1 0
James Smith and children, ditto	-	2 6
Widow Poiner, ditto	-	1 0
Thomas Wilkes, ditto	-	1 0
Gueſt's wife, Darlaſton	-	0 6
Maria Moor and three children, Ludlow	-	1 6
Hannah Baylis, Codſal	-	0 6
Widow Medcroft, Derby	-	1 0

Blew's

	Weekly Allowance.	
	s.	d.
Blew's child, Stourbridge - - - -	1	0
Widow Bolas, ditto - - - -	1	0
Price's child, Bilston - - - -	1	0
Westwood's family, ditto - - - -	1	6
Firm's child, ditto - - - -	0	6
Perry's child, ditto - - - -	0	9
Lydia Trueman, Birmingham - - -	1	0
Mary Seabury, ditto - - -	1	0
John Andrews and family, Bilston - -	1	0
John Lowe, Monmore-Green - -	1	0
Bratt's family, ditto - - -	1	0
Thomas Morris's family, ditto - -	1	0
Robert Paine and family, ditto - -	0	10
Ann Cottrell, Tettenhall - - -	1	0
Hobson's child, ditto - -	0	9
Harvey's children, Brewood - -	1	6
Sutton's child, Dudley-Wood - -	0	9
Taft's child, Penn - - -	1	0
Alice Perry's child, ditto - -	1	0
Collins's family, Fordhouses - .	2	0
Whitehouse's family, London - -	3	0
Furnace's family, near Penkridge - -	1	6
Mary Bridgen, Bushbury - - -	0	9
William Bridgen, Wednesfield - -	0	9
Widow Titley, Oxley - - -	1	0
Widow Legg, Broseley - - -	1	0
Francis Simpson, Walsall - - -	1	0
Paul Nightingale, ditto - - -	1	0
Richards's child, Worfield - - -	1	0
William Dunn's family, Worcester, soldier - -	2	0

A List

A Lift of the Poor who receive Out-pay. September 29, 1794.

			Age	Fam	Pay s. d.
Alms-houfes.	Widow Wilks		70		0 6
	Widow Redley		72		1 0
	Thomas Ward		76		1 0
	John Nabbs's family	foldier	2 6 mo.	2 ch.	2 0
	Widow Swatman		80		1 0
	Widow Giles		75		0 6
	Thomas Shinton and wife		71 72		1 0
	John Jordain	lame	55		1 0
	William Taylor's family	foldier	6 4 1	3 ch.	2 0
	Widow Bellamy		77		1 0
Berry-ftreet.	Ann Edwards's child		3	1 ch.	1 0
	Thomas Prefton's family	foldier	2 2 mo	2 ch.	1 6
	Benjamin Hoftick's family	foldier	3	1 ch.	0 9
	Rawlet's children		5 3	2 ch.	1 6
	John Allen's family	foldier	1	1 ch.	0 9
	Ann Smith's child		2	1 ch.	0 9
Brick-ki'n-ftreet.	Samuel Mofley	blind	13		1 0
	Thomas Fellows's family	foldier	5 4 2	3 ch.	2 0
	Michael Bate's family	foldier	1 mo.	1 ch.	0 9
	Widow Huffer's family		6 3 1	3 ch.	2 6
	J Albaften's family	foldier	2	1 ch.	0 9
	Mary Fitcham's child		2	1 ch.	1 0
	John Price		77		1 0
	Jofeph Bate's family	foldier	4 2	2 ch.	1 6
	Widow Nightingale		82		1 0
	J Leatherbarrow's family	foldier	4 2	2 ch.	1 6
	Edward Fellows's family	foldier	6	1 ch.	0 9
	Zack Turley		71		0 9
	James Brittle's family	foldier	6 4 1 m.	3 ch.	2 0
	Cath. Jones's child		5		1 0
Bilfton-ftreet.	Jane Muchell's child		3		1 0
	Ann Hawkins	lame	16		1 0
	Barth. Morgan's family	foldier	6 4 1	3 ch.	2 0
	John Meriden's family	foldier	6	1 ch.	1 0
	Widow Rudge		55		0 9
	Sarah Perry's child		5		1 0
	Ann Smith's child		5		1 0
Canal-ftreet.	Onions's family		4 2	2 ch.	1 0

John

		Age.	Fam	Pay
				s | d.
Canal-ftreet.	John Barton's family	foldier	2	1 ch.	0 9
	William Benfon's family	foldier	4	1 ch	0 9
	Benjamin Taylor's family	foldier	1	1 ch.	0 9
	Shale's child		2		1 0
	Widow Winkler		66		0 6
	Charles Hume	blind	50		1 0
	Widow Jones		74		1 0
	Widow Iddins		70		1 0
	John Gower's family	foldier	6 4	2 ch.	1 0
	Coleburn's child	idiot	8		1 6
	John Huge's family	foldier	4 1	2 ch	1 6
	John Harrifon's family	foldier	4 1	2 ch.	1 6
	Wm. Mullender's family	foldier	6 mo.	1 ch.	0 9
	William Webb		73		1 0
Salop-ftreet.	William Bradley's family		6 4	2 ch.	1 0
	William Afh's family	foldier	3	1 ch.	0 9
	Widow Earp		73		0 6
	Paul Bennet		72		1 0
	Thomas Jones		80		1 6
	John Northwood's family	foldier	4 2	2 ch.	1 6
	John Lane		77		1 0
	Jofeph Shinton	lame	45		1 0
	Widow Jones		72		0 9
	John Griffiths		70		1 0
	John Crefwell's family	foldier	2	1 ch.	0 9
	John Watter's family	foldier	1	1 ch.	0 9
	Hill's child		4		0 9
	Widow Jones's family		6 3	2 ch	1 6
	Widow Green's family		3	1 ch	0 9
	Richard Dovey's family	foldier	4 2	2 ch.	1 6
	Wm. Momford's family	foldier	1	1 ch.	0 9
	John Adams's family	foldier	1	1 ch	0 9
Stafford-ftreet.	Widow Reynolds		68		0 6
	John Walker	lame	50		1 0
	Jofeph Earp's family	foldier	4 2 8 mo	3 ch.	2 0
	Tho. Tunnicliff's family	foldier	5 2	2 ch	1 6
	Benjamin Little		76		1 0
Cribby-Ifland.	Ann Green's child		3 mo.		1 0
	J Perry's fam. (wife fick)	foldier	3 mo.	1 ch.	1 6
	John Baddeley's wife		76		1 0
	Thomas Dyke	lame	26		1 0

			Age.	Fam	Pay s.	d.
Cribby-Island.	Thomas Woodall's family	foldier	6 3	2 ch.	1	0
	Wm. Cartwright's family	foldier	6 3 1	3 ch.	2	0
Four-Afhes.	Ann Swan		6 7		1	0
	Henry Hanfon's family	foldier	2	1 ch.	0	9
	William Mathews's family	foldier	6 mo.	1 ch.	0	9
	Widow Nock		79		1	0
	John Griffith's family	foldier	6 4 1	3 ch.	2	6
	Ann Smith's child		5		1	0
	Stringer's family		6 2	2 ch	1	6
Walfall-ftreet.	Widow Hamer		74		1	0
	R. Wainwright's family	foldier	7 4	2 ch.	1	6
	Gardiner's child		6		0	9
	Ifaac Hadley's family	foldier	1	1 ch.	0	9
	John Horton's family	foldier	3 1	2 ch.	1	6
	Elizabeth Martin's child		4		1	0
	Thomas Birkin's family	foldier	5 2	2 ch.	1	6
Dudley-ftreet.	William Watts's family	foldier	9 6 1	3 ch	2	0
	Hannah Dalton, Red cow-yard		63		1	0
	Francis Butler	lame	60		1	0
Piper's-row.	Widow Simpfon		4 2	2 ch	1	6
	Poulton's family		6 4 3 1	4 ch.	2	6
	Sarah Wood's child		1		1	0
	Elias Lamfdale's family	foldier	3 1	2 ch.	1	6
	George Southall's family	foldier	5 2	2 ch.	1	6
Horfe-Fair.	Davis's child		6		0	6
	Jane Beard's child		1		1	0
	William Maus's family		1	1 ch.	1	0
	Widow Bond		62		0	6
Lichfield-ftreet.	Thomas Baugh's family		6 4 3 1	4 ch.	2	0
	Sarah Cotterell's child		3 mo.		1	0
Wheeler's-fold.	Elizabeth Hurft's child		5		1	0
	John Hayes's family	foldier	6 4 3	3 ch.	2	0
North-ftreet.	Edward Jones's family	foldier	1	1 ch.	0	9
	John Price's family	foldier	6 4 3 1	4 ch.	3	0
	William Willock's family	foldier	2	1 ch.	0	9
	William Jackfon's family	foldier	4	1 ch.	0	9
	Widow Jeavens		76		1	0
	Benjamin Raby's family	foldier	1	1 ch.	0	9
	Coleburn's child		5		0	9
	Slater's child		6		0	9
	A groom's child, Dunftall-lane		6		1	0

Widow

			Age	Fam	Pay s	d
North-street.	Widow Huges		73		0	10
	Robert Bate's family			4 ch.	1	0
	Ann Patrick, at Fowler's				1	0
	Joseph Butcher		5 3 2	3 ch.	1	0
Church-yard.	Perks's children		5 2	2 ch.	1	6
	John Lane's family	soldier	6 1	2 ch.	1	6
	Widow Nightingale		73		0	6
Worcester-street.	Ann Wright, widow		80		1	0
	Widow Webb		2	1 ch.	0	9
	Isaac Perry		74		0	9
	John Roberts's family	soldier	6 mo.	ch.	0	9
	William Wood's family		7 4	2 ch.	1	0
	Widow Lowe		77		1	0
Cock-street.	W Davis's family, Farmer's-yard,	soldier	2 1	2 ch.	1	6
	William Floyd, ditto		80		1	0
	Bouncer's fam. near the Round-about	soldier	4 2 1	3 ch.	1	6
	Fitzallen's family, ditto	soldier	4 2	2 ch.	1	6
St. John's-street.	John Thomas		63		0	9
	Cooper's family		9 4	2 ch.	1	0
	John Formstone's family	soldier	5	1 ch.	0	9
	Thomas Clarke's family	soldier	2 mo.	1 ch.	0	9
	Thomas Atherley's family			4 ch.	1	0
	Thomas Davis's family	soldier	5 2	2 ch.	1	6
	Mary Handley's child		1 mo.		1	0
Snow-hill.	Joseph Coley's family	soldier	1	1 ch.	0	9
Prince's-street.	John Hodgetts		70		1	0
New-street.	Ann Challenwood's child		1 mo.		1	0
Bell-street.	Lea's family		6 4	2 ch.	1	6
	F. Watt's family	soldier	2 mo.	1 ch.	0	9
Dudley-road.	Samuel Batham	filly	17		1	0
	William Fox's family	soldier	4 2	2 ch.	1	6
	F. Whitehouse's family	soldier	4 2	2 ch	1	6
	Widow Smith		81		1	0
Bilston-road.	Hannah Southall		74		0	6
	Ann Sutton's family		5 3 1	3 ch.	2	0
	Richard Allen's family	soldier	3 3 mo.	2 ch.	1	6
	Ann Hill's child		3		1	0
	Widow Baddeley		75		0	10

Out-

Out-pay Refidents at Birmingham.

		Age.	Fam.	Pay. s. d.
Thomas Beckett's family, Snow-hill	foldier	3 1	2 ch.	1 6
Widow Smith, Livery-ftreet		73		0 9
Daniel Davis's family	foldier	6 4 2	3 ch.	2 0
George Bayley's family	foldier	4 2	2 ch.	1 6
Thomas Webb's family, Mill-lane	foldier		1 ch.	0 9
Wainwright's family, Pinfold-ftreet	foldier	4 3 3 m.	3 ch.	2 0
Mary Cank, widow, ditto		71		1 0
Mary Clarke's child, Inge-ftreet		5		0 9
Alice Davis, Snow-hill		61		0 6
Ann Evans, widow, Dale-end		70		1 0
Widow Poiner, Edgbafton-ftreet		80		1 0
Mary Pool, widow, Afton-ftreet		70		1 0
Pitt's children, Water-ftreet		5 3	2 ch.	1 6
Catharine Withey, Edgbafton-ftreet		58		1 0
Truman's family, London-'prentice-ftreet		6 4 3 1	4 ch.	3 0
Sarah Brooker		83		1 0
Widow Anflow, Edgbafton-ftreet		66		1 0
Benfon's child, Stafford-ftreet		5		1 0
Weftwood's family, Suffolk-ftreet	foldier	3 1	2 ch.	1 6
Price's family, Little Charles-ftreet	foldier	3 1	2 ch.	1 6
Devey's family, Stafford-ftreet	foldier	5 3 1	3 ch.	2 6
Randle Lewis, Navigation-ftreet		80		1 0
Efther Grove's family, Steel-houfe-lane		4 2	2 ch.	1 6
John Bickley's family, ditto	foldier	2	1 ch.	0 9
Widow Avery, ditto		70		1 0

Out-Refidents.

		Age.	Fam.	Pay. s. d.
William Bifhop's family, Bewdley,	foldier	6 mo.	1 ch.	0 9
Thomas Baling, near Shrewfbury	lame	42		1 0
Hannah Baylis, near Bridgnorth		77		1 0
William Fofter's family, Penkridge	foldier	5	1 ch.	0 9
Thomas's child, ditto		1		0 6
Widow Uncks, near Worcefter		76		0 6
Afton's child, Wednesfield		6		1 0
Widow Brindley, Tipton		71		0 6
Widow Mitton, ditto		75		0 6
Widow Afton, ditto		70		1 0

Widow

		Age.				Fam.	Pay. s. d.
Widow Charlefworth, Bradley-moor		74					1 0
Ann Williams, Wednesfield		72					1 0
Mary Phillips's child, Willenhall		4					1 0
Spittle's child, Lancafhire		6					1 0
Jofeph Foxley, Albrighton		77					0 9
Sarah Sadler's child, Wombourn		1					1 0
John Edward's family, Willenhall	foldier	5 3 2				3 ch.	2 0
Tonk's child, Cofeley		3					0 6
Sim Hartill's family, Compton	foldier	1				1 ch.	0 9
John Walker's family, Brewood	foldier	6 4 2 1				4 ch.	2 0
James Bird's family, Darlafton	foldier	6 5				2 ch.	1 6
Widow Morgan, Bilfton		61					0 6
Allbut's family, Bufhbury		6 4				2 ch.	1 6
Widow Pool's, Goldthornhill		72					0 6
Pool's child, ditto		4					1 0
Mary Barnefley's child, Chapel-afh		1					1 0
John Whitehoufe and wife, Wyrley		72 73					1 0
William Bigford's family, Cofely	foldier	5 3 2 1				4 ch.	3 0
Widow Green, Penn-road		66					1 0
Jane Beeche's child, Compton		4					1 0
John King's family, Dudley	foldier	3 1 mo.				2 ch.	1 6
Ann Ford's child, near Stafford		2					1 0
Mary Coffin's child, Shropfhire		3					1 0
Widow Mill's family, Wombourn		4 2				2 ch.	1 6
Catharine Sheet's child, Tettenhall		1					1 0
Bryan's child, Brofely		4					1 0
Francis Simpfon and wife, Walfall		72 70					1 6
Harvey's family, Stretton		5 3				2 ch.	1 6
Thomas Daws and wife, Brewood		76 72					1 6
Johnfon's family, Sedgley							1 0
Sarah Arnold's child, ditto		5					1 0
William Adney and wife, Stourbridge		78 79					2 6
Widow Bowlas, ditto		72					1 0
Billingfley's family, Billbrook		6 3				2 ch.	1 6
Shepherd's child, Cannock		3					1 0
Stokes's child, Burton		5					1 0
William Barne's family, Wednefbury	foldier	5 3 2				3 ch.	2 0
Dyk's child, Kemberton		3					1 0
Follows's family, Bifhop's-caftle	foldier	3				1 ch.	0 9

The

The work-houfe is an inconvenient building, with fmall windows, low rooms, and dark ftair-cafes. It is furrounded with a high wall, that gives it the appearance of a prifon, and prevents the free circulation of air. There are 8 or 10 beds in each room : they are chiefly of flocks, and confequently retentive of ill fcents, and very productive of vermin. The paffages are in great want of white-wafhing. No regular account is kept of births and burials ; but I am informed that whenever the fmall-pox, meafles, or malignant fevers make their appearance in the houfe, the mortality is very great.

Of 131 perfons, (the number of Poor at prefent in the houfe,) about 60 are children, and the reft foldiers' wives with families, and others, either infirm, old, or infane. Thofe, who are able to work, are employed in making hop-facks in a work-fhop, which is provided by the parifh, under a manufacturer, who pays 1s. 2d. a head, for every pauper above 8 years old, that can work; for which he is entitled to their earnings, which generally amount to about £80. a year.

In the year ending in 1793, the average number of Poor in the houfe was 69 : the expence of their food was 2s. 4½d. a week, each perfon. In the year ending in 1794, the average number was 101 : and the expence of diet 2s. 3d. a week, each perfon.   *Auguft*, 1795.

S U F F O L K.

B U L C A M P.

THE Poor of 46 incorporated parifhes in the hundred of Blything, are maintained in a houfe of induftry, which is fituated on an eminence in the parifh of Bulcamp. The expence of erection was £12,000. : the houfe was opened, for the reception of the Poor, in October 1766. The whole annual fum, to be paid by the parifhes, (which was fixed at the average of

7 years

7 years expenditure, previous to their incorporation,) was £3084. 12s 8d. ; in 1780, half the debt was paid off, and the rates reduced one eighth, or to £2699. 1s. 1d. : in June 1791, the whole debt was discharged. The Rates have been continued at the reduced sum of £2699. 1s. 1d. In 1793, the corporation found it necessary to apply to Parliament for farther powers, relative to the binding out poor children apprentices, which cost £350. 15s.

The work done in this house is chiefly spinning for the Norwich manufacture : cloaths and bedding, &c. for the house, are also made at home. The following were the last week's earnings : an account of the annual earnings could not be procured ; but it appears, that they have been about £8. a week, or £400. a year, for several weeks past.

			£.	s.	d.
Worsted spinners	-	-	4	3	1¾
Tow spinners	-		1	12	1
Semstresses	-	-	0	7	3
Tailors	-	-	0	9	0
Knitters	-	-	0	8	0
Weavers	-	-	0	7	0
Shoemakers	-	-	0	16	0

Total earnings for one week - £ 8   2   5¾

Number of Paupers in the house in June, in each of the following Years; (the average number in the year must, probably, be more;) and Table of Mortality [1].

Years.	Number of Persons.	Deaths.
1782	- 297	- 87
1783	- 298	- 69
1784	- 265	- 76
1785	- 295	- 82
1786	- 143	- 70

[1] In the year 1781, a putrid fever carried off one third of the inhabitants of the neighbouring town of Bliburgh: 130 persons died in the house.
The number of Paupers admitted between Oct. 13, 1766; and Aug. 8, 1793, was   5207
The number of deaths within the same period   -   -   -   -   1381

RUGGLES, Hist. of the Poor, ii. 266.

Years.	Number of Perfons.	Deaths.
1787	256	67
1788	290	52
1789	207	37
1790	192	18
1791	235	34
1792	243	9
1793	260	23
1794	270	37

Average of 13 years - $50\frac{11}{13}$

The number at prefent in the houfe is 40 men, 60 women, and 255 children : total, 355.

The houfe is very roomy and convenient. The beds are chiefly of feathers : the dormitories and other rooms are kept very clean. More work is done now than formerly ; but, owing to the lownefs of wages, the receipts have decreafed.

The number of deaths is very great; and, I prefume, rather arifes from the number of old perfons admitted into the houfe, than from any inattention towards the fick. In houfes of this defcription, much more depends on the conduct of the governor, than the weekly committees, or the ableft code of regulations the corporation can devife. A governor and matron, who know how to blend firmnefs with humanity, are invaluable fervants, and cannot be too liberally rewarded.

The affeffments, in the incorporated parifhes, vary fiom 10d. to 3s. in the pound.

The following are the moft material of the regulations drawn up in 1767, for the government of the Poor in the houfe :

1, That the governor do admit no poor perfon into this houfe, unlefs fuch perfon fhall produce a certificate in writing, under the hands of the churchwardens and overfeers of fome parifh within the hundred where fuch perfon claimeth a fettlement, certifying that fuch perfon hath a legal fettlement within that parifh, and that they are not able to maintain and fuppoit themfelves ; and if the officers of any parifh aie doubtful concerning the legal fettlement of fuch poor perfon, they are to ceitify their doubts to the next weekly committee, and, if

3   thought

thought neceffaiy by them, the faid chuichwardens and oveifeers aie immediately to caiiy fuch poor peifon befoie one of his Majefty's Juftices of the Peace, acting within the faid hundied, to be examined, and paffed to the place of fettlement, if it be found to be elfewheie.

2, That the governor fhall in no cafe place any peifons in the waids till they be caiefully examined, wafhed, and cleaned, and new cloathed, if it be neceffaiy : and in that cafe he is to caufe the old cloaths to be well cleaned; and if fuch poor peifons be likely to be difchaiged fiom the houfe, theii old cloaths aie to be kept until they be difchaiged, and then deliveied to them to wear, in exchange for the cloaths found by the houfe.

3, That the goveinoi and mation do keep peace and good oidei in the houfe, and peimit none to fight, quarrel, oi give abufive oi iude language, without punifhment.

4, They aie to keep all the able Poor to fuch woik or employment as they aie fit for, and call them to it by ring of bell at the houis following ; from Lady-Day to Michaelmas, from fix in the morning to feven in the evening; from Michaelmas to Lady-Day, fiom feven in the moining to fix in the evening; and they aie to allow them half an hour for breakfaft, and an hour and a half foi dinner and play in the fummei-time, and an hour for thofe purpofes in the winter; to oblige the children to play abroad, if the weather will permit, and to allow them a fufficient time foi learning to read.

5, That they make ieady the provifions in a clean and wholfome manner, and fee that breakfaft be ieady by nine o'clock, dinner at one, and fupper againft the woikers leave work.

13, The goveinor fhall, on the Monday in eveiy week, give an account of all piovifions received and expended in the week preceding, to the committee ; and likewife of all work done at the houfe ; and make his complaint to them of all the peifons mifbehaving undei him, and their feveral offences: and, at all times, in the committee-ioom, a book fhall lie open, with pen and ink near it, that in cafe any guaidian, or othei peifon vifiting the houfe occafionally, fhall perceive any thing amifs, oi can fuggeft any new piopofal foi the bettei conducting this undeitaking, he may wiite his thoughts oi obfeivations theiein, that the weekly committee may confider the fame, and iepoit it to the next quaiterly meeting, if they think piopei

14, The goveinoi is to keep a book, in which he is to entei the admiffion of eveiy poor perfon admitted into this houfe, expieffing theii names, age, place to which they belong, by whom fent and ceitified, and the day when admitted, with blank columns to be filled up with the time and manner of theii being difcharged.

15, That the matron do deliver out the foap and candle, and fee all the linen wafhed and got up, that the beds may be fheeted once a month; and that no l nen be hung to dry in any of the lodging waids.

16, That the nurfes take care to make and mend all the linen and cloaths; and when any peifon dies, to deliver his or hei cloaths, clean and neat, to the governoi, to be laid up in the wardiobe, and alfo eveiy thing elfe they died poffeffed of, belonging to the corporation, for the ufe of the houfe; and he is to deliver an inventoiy theieof to the next weekly boaid.

18, That no penfion be allowed out of the houfe, unlefs in cafes of ex-tieme neceffity, and to ceitified. undei the hand of the parifhioneis at a paiifh-meeting to be called for that purpofe, and allowed of by the weekly committee.

19, That theie be a fchool in the houfe, where all childien above thrze yeais of age fhall be kept till they fhall be five years old, and then fet to fpinning, and fuch other pioper and beneficial woik as they aie able to perform.

21, That fuch girls as are of a pioper age be employed and inftrucéted (as far as the matron and fervants belonging to the houfe aie capable of teaching them) in cookery, houfewifeiy, wafhing, fcouiing, and all other work, to qualify them for feivice.

22, That the governoi provide wormwood from time to time, to fumigate the rooms, which is alfo to be ufed in wafhing linen, and in the beds; and the mation is to care that the nurfes lay it in all the bed-fheets

23, That an exaét account be kept, in a book, of all houfhold goods, cloaths and linen, belonging to the work-houfe, &c.

24, That neither the governor nor goveinefs buy or fell, or fuffer any diftilled liquors to come into the houfe.

25, That the following bill of fare be punétually obferved by the mafter and miftrefs, until any alterations be made by the general court :

	Breakfaft.	Dinner.	Supper
Sunday,	Biead and cheefe, or butter	Boiled beef, dumplin, and roots	Bread and cheefe, oi butter.
Monday,	Meat-broth.	Peafe-pottage, with beef broth and dumplin.	Ditto.
Tuefday,	Milk-broth.	Boiled beef, dumplin and roots.	Ditto.
Wednefday,	Meat-broth.	Rice milk, or milk broth	Ditto.
Thuifday,	Biead and cheefe, or butter.	Boiled beef, dumplin and roots.	Ditto
Fiiday,	Meat-bioth	Baked fuet pudding.	Ditto
Satuiday,	Bread and cheefe, or butter.	Hot cakes.	Ditto

26, That the tradefmen employed in ferving the houfe of induftry do always fend notice of the weight and prices of their goods, which are

to

to be filed by the governor, as foon as he has made proper entries of the faid goods in the books of the houfe ; and if they deliver bad goods, immediate notice to be given of it to the acting directors and guardians.

28, That for the encouragement of thofe who fhall difcharge the bufinefs they are appointed to do, with care and diligence, rewards fhall be given them from time to time, as the board fhall judge of their merit.

30, That the governor and matron do not, upon any pretence whatfoever, fuffer any poor perfon belonging to the houfe to drink tea therein, except on Sundays, and that to be at their own expence.

31, That the governor do, every Monday morning, lay before the weekly committee, an account of all materials fent in for the employment of the Poor, and the work done by them ; and fhall every quarter make out, and lay before the directors and guardians, at their quarterly meeting, a general account of the quantity and price of fuch materials, and of the work manufactured, with the neat profit of the fame ; and that no fuch work be difpofed of without an order from the weekly board.

36, If any perfon fhall purloin, fell, or pawn any of the goods or provifions belonging to the houfe, fuch perfon or perfons fhall be carried before a magiftrate, to be dealt with according to law.

37, That the governor keep a juft account of all the provifions received into the houfe, and duly weigh and keep an account thereof, and how many perfons are provided for.

38, That no director or directors, acting guardian or guardians, or other perfon or perfons, fhall, at any time, without the affent and concurrence of the weekly committee for the time being, give any orders or directions relative to the employment, maintenance, relief, or management of the Poor, which are or fhall be within the Poor's houfe, or to any other matter or thing concerning the faid corporation.

This diftrict extends 12 miles by 8, and contains 46 parifhes ; no account of the population could be obtained. The inhabitants are, univerfally, agriculturifts ; and are chiefly of the eftablifhed church.

The prices of provifions and labour are the fame as in Loes and Wilford hundreds[1]: wages for fpinning worfted are now little more than half what they were before the war

In this hundred there are feveral Friendly Societies : their number could not be obtained ; but it is faid that they have, moftly, complied with the late Act of Parliament.

[1] See p 692.

The

The average rent of land is about 16s. an acre. Farms here let from £50. to £200. a year: the chief articles of cultivation are turnips, barley, wheat, clover, peafe, and beans. Tithes are generally taken by a compofition of 4s 6d. an acre. In this hundred, there are feveral fmall tracts of wafte or common lands; but they bear a fmall proportion to the land in cultivation.

At Oulton houfe of induftry, near Leoftoff, there are 150 Paupers. It has been built about 25 years: the original debt was £6000. Owing to the bad management of the firft governors, the receipts much exceeded the difburfements; and, in 1781, the quota fixed on the incorporated parifhes was advanced ten per cent. However, £2000. of the debt have been paid off: the rates, at prefent, are about 16d. in the pound on the rack rental.

Spinning woollen yarn, and making nets, are the principal manufactures carried on in the houfe. The out-payments are very heavy.

July, 1795.

MELTON.

THE hundreds of Loes and Wilford were incorporated in 1765: their houfe of induftry, which ftands in the parifh of Melton, was finifhed and inhabited in 1768. Their original debt was £9200. none of which has ever been difcharged; it has fince been increafed to near £11,000.

The quotas paid by the incorporated parifhes amounted, in 1765, to £2069. 10s. 1d. a year; at which fum they continued till 1791, when, in confequence of an application to Parliament, they were raifed to £2759. 6s. 1d.; and it is faid, that the corporation, notwithftanding their increafed income, find their expences fo heavy, that they muft again have recourfe to the affiftance of the Legiflature.

The books of former governors have been kept in fo carelefs and confufed a manner, that the average number in the houfe, each year, and the whole number admitted each year, could not be afcertained. The prefent governor, however, has been able to make out the average number of Poor in the houfe, for a few years.

In

In 1781 there were - 170
　　1782　　-　-　220
　　1783　　-　-　226
　　1793　　-　-　212
　　1794　　-　-　230
At prefent, there are - 289, principally children.

The principal work, done in the houfe, is fpinning of wool, or worfted : a few men are employed, out of doors, on a farm of about 30 acres; three acres of hemp are cultivated for the ufe of the houfe : fix cows and two horfes are kept on the farm. The boys are employed as tailors, fhoe-makers, and in other handicrafts.

The earnings of the 4 laft years, (exclufive of work done for the houfe,) were as follows :

		£.	s.	d.
1792 By wool-fpinning	- -	91	5	0
Out-labour	- -	10	0	0
		—— 101	5	0
From June 1794, to June 1795, wool-fpinning	64	2	9	
Out-labour	- -	48	11	2
		—— 112	13	0

An account of the earnings of the other years could not be obtained.

Table of Diet ufed in the Houfe of Induftry at MELTON.

	Breakfaft.	Dinner.	Supper.
Sunday,	Bread and milk gruel.	Beef, 5 oz.—dumplins, 14 oz.—and 6 oz. of vegetables for each perfon.	8 oz. of bread, and 2 oz of cheefe to each perfon.
Monday,	Bread and broth.	12 oz of feed-cakes to each.	Ditto, ditto.
Tuefday,	As Sunday	As Sunday.	Ditto, ditto.
Wednefday,	As Monday	Dumplins and fweet fauce.	Ditto, ditto.
Thurfday,	As Sunday	As Sunday.	Ditto, ditto.
Friday,	As Monday.	Suet puddings, 14 oz. each.	Ditto, ditto.
Saturday,	As Sunday.	Bread and cheefe.	Ditto, ditto.

Beer is allowed at every meal, when neither broth nor gruel are ufed. Children receive as much victuals as they can eat.

The affeffments, in the different incorporated parifhes, vary from 1s. to 2s. in the pound on the net rental.

The prefent governor of this houfe has made feveral very nice calculations,

on

on the expence of diet for any number of Poor : the following is the weekly quantity, which, he finds, is required, for 280 peifons; of flour, 140 ftone; beef, 25 ditto; cheefe, 9 ditto; butter, 3 ftone 7 lb. ; falt, 3 ftone; oatmeal, 3 pecks ; beer, 6 barrels ; foap, 1¼ ftone ; candles, 10 lb.; coals for one year, 90 chaldron ; groceries, £1. a week ; draperies, yearly, £320. ; leather for one year, 880 lb.

Table of Mortality in the House of Industry at MELTON

Years.	Deaths.	Years.	Deaths.
1768	10	1781	35
1769	69	1782	67
1770	22	1783	42
1771	31	1784	55
1772	28	1785	29
1773	39	1786	41
1774	45	1787	9
1775	28	1788	19
1776	16	1789	18
1777	15	1790	25
1778	23	1791	21
1779	14	1792	15[1]
1780	52		

$$13) 392$$

$$12) 376$$

Aver. of 13 years $30\frac{2}{13}$ Average of 12 years $31\frac{1}{3}$

The earnings in this houfe are chiefly by children ; yet although more work is done now than formerly, the amount of earnings are lefs ; as fome work that produced 10d. previous to the war, is now paid only 6d. The prefent governor procures as much work from the neighbouring farmers as he can, becaufe by that means his earnings are increafed. He fays, no diforders prevail much in the houfe, that are not common in the neighbourhood; and that the great number of deaths is occafioned by old people being brought thither in their laft ficknefs : feveral of the paupers are

[1] The governor could not give any accurate account of the years 1793 and 1794, but fuppofes the number of deaths was about 30 each year.

now

now infected with the fmall-pox; they are lodged, during their illnefs, in a fort of hofpital, which is fituated 3 or 400 yards from the houfe. The greateft neatnefs prevails in the hall, and dormitories: the beds are of feathers; and are each provided with 2 fheets, 2 blankets, and a coverlet: they are placed at a proper diftance from each other: fome apartments, however, contain 16 or 18 beds: half the number would be better. The married people have feparate rooms. The boys and girls are divided into claffes of about 20 or 30; and are employed, under the fuperintendance of a fchool-mafter or miftrefs, in feparate work-rooms. The houfe is pleafantly fituated on a dry foil.

$£.$

The governor, (who is alfo committee clerk,) and his wife have			50	a year.
The furgeon, who refides in the houfe	-	-	70	ditto.
Out-doctor	-	-	15	ditto.
Chaplain	-	-	35	ditto.

$£\ 170$

The prefent very high price of provifions, and the lownefs of wages given in the woollen manufacture, fufficiently account for the late rife of the Rates: but the reafons generally affigned for this houfe never having paid off any of it's original debts, are the bad management of former governors, and the inattention of former committees.

I have fubjoined a few of the Rules for the government of Poor in thefe hundreds, as they differ, in feveral refpects, from thofe already noticed under accounts of fimilar eftablifhments.

2, That, in all cafes, (excepting thofe of urgent neceffity,) the following Table of Allowances be obferved:—

A fingle man, or fingle woman, ill; 1s. per week refpectively.

A man and his wife, both ill; 2s per week.

A man and his wife, with one or more children, (the man being ill); 2s. per week, with an addition of 6d. per head for children under 10 years of age, if neceffary.

A man and his wife with more than two children, (the woman being ill); 1s. per week.

A fingle woman with a baftard child; not an object of relief.

A widow woman in health, having only one child; not an object of relief.

A man

A man in health, having only three children; not generally to be considered as an object of relief.

That no allowance shall be made for a midwife exceeding five shillings, and that no such allowance be granted, except in extraordinary cases, such as a man having more than two children, or not being in health.

5, That when any parish officer is called upon to apply for relief for the burial of any pauper, he shall take an account of the effects (if any) of the deceased, and state the circumstances of the case to such director or acting guardian as resides in or nearest to the parish where such pauper died, that such director or acting guardian may order, under his hand, such sum as he shall think necessary for the funeral of such pauper, and direct the parish officer to deliver such order, to the next weekly committee, provided that no more than twenty shillings be (in any case) allowed. And to prevent improper and unnecessary expences to the family or friends of the deceased, as well as imposition upon the corporation, it is directed that no sum be allowed towards any funeral, where the whole expences of it shall exceed twenty shillings

8, That all paupers who now are, or shall hereafter be, received into the house, as well as those receiving quarterly allowances, be badged with the letters   P
                                    L   W.

OVERSEERS.

1, That as it is the duty of every overseer of the Poor to be well acquainted with the situation, circumstances, and characters of all persons who apply to them for relief, so is it when they apply for relief for for any pauper, to report the same in writing, to the weekly committee.

3, That, when any pauper, by accident, or sudden illness, wants any pecuniary relief between one weekly committee and another, no overseer shall grant such relief, without first applying to, and having an order in writing from, a director, specifying the sum to be allowed, such allowance being in conformity to the general rules before laid down; which order the overseer is expected to produce to the next weekly committee, and then report in writing the case of the pauper.— That this order, as far as it respects relief to be given, cannot extend to orders made by Justices of the Peace, but that all orders of Justices of the Peace be brought to the next weekly committee.

4, That overseers of the Poor, when they remove any pauper or paupers to the House of Industry, are expected to make strict inquiry, whether such pauper or paupers have any annual or weekly allowance, (not

arising

arifing from any Friendly Society,) and report the fame in writing to the next weekly committee, that proper fteps may be taken to have fuch allowance paid to the corporation, in aid of the maintenance of fuch pauper or paupers.

5, That overfeers of the poor, when they bring any children (who are paupers) to the houfe of induftry, they are expected to obtain a certificate of the age of fuch children, and bring or fend the fame as foon as they conveniently can, to the governor of the houfe of induftry.

6, That all paupers fent, by orders of removal, to any parifh within the incorporated hundreds, fhall be as foon as poffible conveyed to the houfe of induftry, but if fuch paupers cannot be removed the fame day, that fix-pence a day only be allowed for each pauper, unlefs fuch paupers be ill, in which cafe, application fhall be made to the neareft director for fuch further relief, or directions, as may be thought neceffary.

7, That, in the removal of paupers, 20 miles fhall be confidered as a day's journey;—two-pence be allowed for a fingle horfe;—three-pence for a double horfe, or a cart with one horfe, and fo in proportion per mile, all expences included: But if the diftance exceeds 20 miles, or the overfeer be obliged to be out all night, in fuch cafe two fhillings fhall be allowed for himfelf,—one fhilling for his horfe,—and fix-pence for each pauper.

11, That overfeers be required to give notice that no allowance will be granted to any perfon who keeps a dog, unlefs fuch perfon be a fhepherd, or a warrener.

GOVERNOR and CLERK.

1, That the governor be directed to deliver in at every weekly committee a ftate of the paupers in the houfe, the quantities of provifions in hand, received, left, and expended, together with the amount of the work done in the preceding week, according to a plan in a book ruled for that purpofe, which, if approved, is to be figned and allowed by fuch weekly committee

2, That the governor fhall enter into a book, an exact account of all provifions, and fuel, fent into the houfe, examine their goodnefs, weight, and quantity, and make his report thereof to the weekly committee.

3, That the governor fhall enter into a book, an exact account of all houfhold goods, cloaths, linen, fhoes, and other things fent into the houfe, examine their goodnefs, weight, quantity, and quality, and make his report thereof to the weekly committee. That he shall also deliver in a general inventory of the houshold goods and furniture, &c. of and belonging to the house, &c. annually, at the Michael-mas quarterly meeting.

4, That the governor shall receive no provision, coals, wood, or goods of any kind, without a bill of the same, to be delivered with them, signed by the respective tradesmen and merchants; and that he shall keep the same upon a file.

5, That stamped weights and scales, and measures, be provided for the governor.

6, That the governor shall keep a general register of all paupers that now are, or hereafter may be admitted into the house, after the manner laid down in a book ruled for that purpose; and that he shall report to every weekly committee, or at any time when required, such as are well, and fit to be discharged.

7, That he shall also keep a proper register of all apprentices.

10, That the governor shall see the provisions cut out, and properly delivered to the matron, that there be no waste; that no bread be cut under one day old; and that no more fires be kept in the house than are absolutely necessary.

MATRON.

1, That the matron shall employ proper nurses from among the Poor, to attend the sick, and also the infant children;—that she shall diligently inspect their conduct and behaviour with respect to the Poor under their care;—that she shall see that all the beds, furniture, wards, rooms, and sick wards, and every part of the house, are swept daily and kept clean, and that all the rooms be washed once a week in winter and twice in summer,—the bed cloaths turned down, the windows opened, and the doors locked 'till ten o'clock every morning.

2, That she takes care that the women and girls wash and comb themselves every morning and evening; and that the children have their hair cut close, and their heads kept clean.

3, That she delivers out the soap, starch, and blue, by weight, for washing the linen; and give an account, the first Monday in every month, to the weekly committee, of the quantity used.

4, That she sees that the washerwomen and laundresses employed do their business well, and enter into a book an account of the linen delivered, and the like account when it is clean and got up; and that every poor person have a clean shirt or shift once a week:—that the beds have clean sheets once a month; and that no linen be dried in any of the wards, but as much abroad as may be.

5, That

That the mation diftributes to the nurfes, for the fick poor, and the young children, fuch a quantity of milk, pearl barley, rice, and other neceffaries, as the furgeon fhall advife, and that the common diet be ftopped until they are well.

6, That fhe attends all meals with the governor, and fee that the provifions are fairly and duly delivered.

7, That the mation fhall receive from the governor, cloth neceffary for fhirts, fhifts, and fheets, and fhall cut them out, taking care that they are well made, no wafte committed, and, when finifhed, be placed in the ftore-room, and an account thereof given once a month to the weekly committee.

8, That the old linen fhall be repaired and mended every week.

9, That fhe keeps an account of the number of women and girls employed as fempftreffes, or in other work for the ufe of the houfe, and of what they earn by fuch work, and report the fame once a month to the weekly committee.

CERTIFICATES.

1, That no certificate be granted, unlefs the perfon applying for fuch certificate fhall produce an examination taken before one of his Majefty's Juftices of the Peace, fhewing that he belongs to one of the parifhes within the incorporated hundreds.

2, That no certificate fhall be granted to labourers or hufbandmen out of the hundreds, except to perfons belonging to the parifh of *Kenton*, and in fuch cafe not to exceed the diftance of 3 miles.

3, That no certificate fhall be granted to any tradefman, artificer, or manufacturer, exceeding the diftance of 20 miles from the parifh to which he belongs.

4, That no certificate fhall be granted to any perfon into any corporation town.

APPRENTICES.

In apportioning Apprentices, the following Table and Rules are agreed upon, as moft agreeable to the Rules of Law, and the Principles of Equity.

	£.		No.	Order of Apprenticing:					
Every perfon occupying per ann	300	who fhould have	6	1ft	3d	6th	10th	15th	21ft
And every perfon occupying	250	Ditto	5	2d	5th	9th	14th	20th	
Ditto - - -	200	Ditto	4	4th	8th	13th	19th		
Ditto - - -	150	Ditto	3	7th	12th	18th			
Ditto - - -	100	Ditto	2	11th	17th				
Ditto - - -	50	Ditto	1	16th					

That

That every perfon occupying under £50. and above *ten*, or any fum between £50. and £100. fhall have one each, beginning with the higheft.

That every tradefman (if judged capable) fhall take one each, a male or female being appointed, as beft fuited to the trade.

That in all cafes where more than one child is to be apprenticed to any parifh, the eldeft child fhall be firft appointed, and fo on to the youngeft.

That care be taken (if poffible) that two girls be not apprenticed to the fame perfon, immediately following each other.

That no child fhall be apprenticed, who has not had the fmall-pox.

The extent of the hundreds of Loes and Wilford is about 14 miles by 5½ : the inhabitants are agriculturifts, and are chiefly of the eftablifhed church. The prices of provifions are : beef, from 5d. to 6d. the lb. ; mutton, 6d. ; veal, 5d. ; lamb, 5½d. and 6d. ; pickled pork, 8d. to 9d. the lb ; butter, 10d. to 1s. for 20 oz. ; milk, 1½ pint for 1d. ; wheat, £4 the quarter ; barley, from 36s. to 40s. ditto. Common labourers are paid from 1s. 2d. to 1s. 6d. the day, with beer ; women weeding corn, hoeing, &c. 8d. to 1s. a day ; women and children who are employed in fetting wheat, fpinning wool, &c. earn from 3d. to 6d. a day. The average rent of land in this diftrict is eftimated at 16s. an acre. Farms are from £50. to £200. a year. All the common forts of grain are cultivated. Tithes are principally taken by compofition, which varies from 4s. to 6s. an acre. The farmer generally makes an agreement with the minifter for 3, 7, or 14 years, and fometimes for the life of the clergyman. There is not much wafte land in thefe diftricts.

At Tatingftone, 6 miles from Ipfwich, there is a Houfe of Induftry, which was incorporated in 1765 : one-fourth of their original debt has been paid off ; but the corporation is now under the neceffity of applying to Parliament for authority to increafe the Rates. The 25 parifhes incorporated, are almoft unanimous in wifhing to have the corporation diffolved ; as they think they can maintain their Poor at lefs expence, and with more comfort, at home ; but this meafure is ftrenuoufly oppofed by a neighbouring gentleman.

July, 1795.

S U R-